European Economic Integration

We work with leading authors to develop the strongest
educational materials in economics, bringing cutting-edge
thinking and best learning practice to a global market.

Under a range of well-known imprints, including
Financial Times Prentice Hall, we craft high quality print
and electronic publications which help readers to understand
and apply their content, whether studying or at work.

To find out more about the complete range of our
publishing, please visit us on the World Wide Web at:
www.pearsoned.co.uk

Fourth Edition

European Economic Integration

Edited by

Frank McDonald
Stephen Dearden

FT Prentice Hall
FINANCIAL TIMES

An imprint of Pearson Education
Harlow, England • London • New York • Boston • San Francisco • Toronto • Sydney • Singapore • Hong Kong
Tokyo • Seoul • Taipei • New Delhi • Cape Town • Madrid • Mexico City • Amsterdam • Munich • Paris • Milan

Pearson Education Limited

Edinburgh Gate
Harlow
Essex CM20 2JE
England

and Associated Companies throughout the world

Visit us on the World Wide Web at:
www.pearsoned.co.uk

First published 1992
Second edition 1994
Third edition 1999
Fourth edition published 2005

First edition © Longman Group UK Limited 1992
Second edition © Longman Group Limited 1994
Third edition © Addison Wesley Longman Limited 1999
Fourth edition © Pearson Education Limited 2005

ISBN 0 273 67908 2

British Library Cataloguing-in-Publication Data
A catalogue record for this book is available from the British Library

Library of Congress Cataloging-in-Publication Data
European economic integration / [edited by] Frank McDonald, Stephen Dearden.—4th ed.
    p. cm.
    Includes bibliographical references and index.
    ISBN 0-273-67908-2 (alk. paper)
    1. Europe—Economic integration. 2. European Union countries—Economic policy. I.
McDonald, Frank, 1951– II. Dearden, Stephen, 1950–

    HC241.E7853 2005
    337.1′42—dc22

                                                                2004051222

10 9 8 7 6 5 4 3 2 1
08 07 06 05

Typeset in 10/12.5pt Sabon by 35
Printed and bound by Bell & Bain, Glasgow

The publisher's policy is to use paper manufactured from sustainable forests.

Brief contents

Detailed contents

Chapter 2
Macroeconomic policy coordination   75

Nigel Healey

Chapter 3
Economic and monetary union   99

Nigel Healey

Chapter 4
The budget of the European Union   125

Clara Mira Salama

Contributors

Stephen Dearden, Senior Lecturer in Economics, Department of Economics, Manchester Metropolitan University – Introduction, Chapters 7, 9, 10 and 14.

John Hassan, Senior Lecturer in Economic History, Department of History, Manchester Metropolitan University – Chapter 9.

Nigel Healey, Professor of Economics and Pro-Vice-Chancellor, College of Business and Economics, University of Canterbury, New Zealand – Chapters 2 and 3.

John Kemp, Senior Lecturer in Economics, Department of Economics, Manchester Metropolitan University – Chapter 5.

Andrei Kuznetsov, Reader in International Business, International Business Unit, Manchester Metropolitan University – Chapter 13.

Olga Kuznetsova, Research Fellow, International Business Unit, Manchester Metropolitan University – Chapter 12.

Frank McDonald, Professor of International Business at Hull University Business School – Introduction, Chapters 1, 6 and 15.

Reiner Martin, Head of Section, Convergence and Structural Analysis, European Central Bank – Chapter 8.

Clara Mira Salama, Senior Economist, International Relations and International Economy, Banco de España – Chapter 4.

Tidings P. Ndhlovu, Senior Lecturer in Economics, Manchester Metropolitan University – Chapter 11.

Margaret Potton, formerly a Senior Research Fellow at Manchester Metropolitan University and a Research Assistant for Cambridge University – Chapter 6.

The views expressed by the contributors are in an individual capacity and do not necessarily reflect those of their respective institutions.

Preface to the fourth edition

Much has changed in the European Union since publication of the third edition. The euro has successfully been launched and ten new member states have acceded. However, the pace of change varies across different policy areas of the Community and a textbook such as this can only offer a snapshot. At the time of writing the new Constitutional Treaty has yet to be agreed and this leaves the future role and institutional shape of the Community uncertain, while the negotiations for the post-2007 budget are only just beginning. Although the structure of the book is little changed, the opportunity has been taken to comprehensively revise many chapters, as well as introduce new contributors. It remains orientated towards students of economic geography and European and business studies, as well as economics.

To understand the European Community it is essential to place it in its economic and historic context. This remains a prime purpose of this book. But for the most recent material the reader is directed to the EU's website (**www.europa.int**). This comprehensive, if not always comprehensible, website offers an excellent source, whether for the undergraduate student or the specialist researcher.

Although this textbook focuses principally upon the economic dimension of the EU it cannot be divorced from the political debates. It must not be forgotten that the European Union's origins lay in the political imperatives of the post-war years. These political imperatives still underlie expansion of the Community into Central and Eastern Europe. The dramatic expansion of the membership of the Community from its original six members has placed, and will place, considerable strains upon the Commission administration and the political decision-making process. Serious weaknesses have already resulted in the wholesale resignation of a Commission and the attempt to impose a reform agenda. The Constitutional Convention was faced with the onerous task of reconciling the existing interests of current member states with the aspirations and expectations of the new members. The failure of the subsequent inter-governmental conference raises the serious prospect of the European Union becoming 'the elephant with 25 legs' that some commentators fear. It remains to be seen whether, by the time of publication, these fears are being realised.

Acknowledgements

The editors would like to thank the contributors for their willingness to conform to the demands placed upon them by the editors. We would also wish to acknowledge the research support provided by Carolyn Waknine in the preparation of some of the chapters.

We are grateful to the following for permission to reproduce copyright material:

The Office of Official Publications of the European Communities for permission to reproduce extracts from *European Commission Strategy Paper* 9 October 2002; Tables 1.1 and 1.2, adapted version of Table 10.2 (p. 216) and adaption of Bullet points 1–4 (p. 228) into a table from 'The Economics of 1992' by Emerson, M. *et al.* (1989). By permission of Oxford University Press; Table 1.3 from 'Internal Market Scoreboard (2002) – 10 years without frontiers', with permission from the European Community, Office of Official Publications of the European Communities; Table 1.4 from 'Internal Market Scoreboard (2002) – 10 years without frontiers', with permission from the European Community, Office of Official Publications of the European Communities; Table 4.2 from 'European Commission press release 27 May 2003', with permission from the European Community, Office of Official Publications of the European Communities; Table 4.3 from 'European Commission (2000)' with permission from the European Community, Office of Official Publications of the European Communities; Table 4.4 from 'European Parliament (2003) Decision 2113/429/EC' with permission from the European Community, Office of Official Publications of the European Communities; Figures 5.1 a&b 'Annual Report European Competition Policy 1996, 1998 and 2002' with permission from the European Community, Office of Official Publications of the European Communities; Figures 5.2 a&b 'Annual Report Competition Policy 1998 and 2002' with permission from the European Community, Office of Official Publications of the European Communities; Table 6.1 from www.europa.eu.int/comm/enterprise/enterprise_policy/sme_definition/index_en.htm with permission from the European Community, OPOCE; Figure 7.1 from 'Employment in Europe (2000)', with permission from the European Community, Office of Official Publications of the European Communities; Figure 7.2 'Employment in Europe' (1998), with permission from the European Community, Office of Official Publications of the European Communities; Figure 7.3 from 'Employment in Europe (2000)', Eurostat Information Office, with permission from the European Community, Office of the Official Publications of the European Communities; Figure 7.4 from 'Employment in Europe (1996)', with permission from the European Community, Office of the Official Publications of the European Communities; Figure 8.2 from *Statistics in Focus, 1997,* Eurostat Information Office, with permission from the European

Community, Office of the Official Publications of the European Communities; Figure 8.4 from *Statistics in Focus, 1997,* Eurostat Information Office, with permission from the European Community, Office of the Official Publications of the European Communities; Table 8.2 from 'First report on Economic and social Cohesion, Table 28, p. 14' with permission from the European Community, Office of Official Publications of the European Communities; Table 10.1 from 'EU Energy and Transport in Figures 2001' with permission from the European Community, Office of the Official Publications of the European Communities; Table 10.2 from 'Second Survey on State Aids, 1992' with permission from the European Community, Office of the Official Publications of the European Communities; Table 10.4 from 'EU Energy and Transport in Figures 2001' with permission from the European Community, Office of the Official Publications of the European Communities; Exhibit 11.2 diagram from *European Economic Integration,* Addison Wesley Longman, MacDonald, F., and Dearden, S., 1999 reprinted with permission of Pearson Education Limited; Table 12.1 from '*2004 External and Intra-European Union Trade – Monthly Statistics*', with permission from the European Community, Office of the Official Publications of the European Communities; Table 12.2 from '*EU trades sectors 2004*', with permission from the European Community, Office of the Official Publications of the European Communities; Table 13.1 from World Economic Outlook, December 2001, International Monetary Fund, reprinted with permission; and from 'Eurostat, August 2002', Directorate General, EU Commissions, with permission from the European Community, Office of the Official Publications of the European Communities; Table 14.1 from Direction of Trade Statistics Yearbook, 1999, International Monetary Fund, reproduced with permission; Table 14.7 from 'Aid Review, 1992–93 and 1994–95' with permission from the European Community, Office of the Official Publications of the European Communities; Table 14.8 from '*Volume of aid for the first five years of Lomé IV in comparison with Lomé III*', with permission from the European Community, Office of the Official Publications of the European Communities; Table 14.9 from 'The Courier, No. 155', European Commission, January 1996, with permission of the European Community, Office of the Official Publications of the European Communities; Table 14.10 from 'The Courier, No. 153', with permission of the European Community, Office of the Official Publications of the European Communities; Table 14.11 from *World Investment Report,* 1994, Pp. 409–12, UNCTAD, reprinted with permission

In some instances we have been unable to trace the owners of copyright material, and we would appreciate any information that would enable us to do so.

Abbreviations

A	Austria
ACP	African, Caribbean and Pacific countries
AFTA	ASEAN Free Trade Agreement
ASEAN	Association of South East Asian Nations
ASEM	Asia-Europe Meeting
B	Belgium
BL	Economic union of Belgium and Luxembourg
BRIDGE	Biotechnology Research for Innovation and Development in Europe
BRITE	Basic Research in Industrial Technologies in Europe
CAP	Common Agricultural Policy
CEDEFOP	European Centre for the Development of Vocational Training
CEECs	Central and Eastern European countries
CEFTA	Central European Free Trade Agreement
CEN	Comité Européen de Normalisation (European Standards Body)
CENELEC	Comité Européen de Normalisation Electronique (European Standards Body for Electrical Equipment)
CET	Common External Tariff
CF	Cohesion Fund
CFC	Chlorofluorocarbon
CI	Community Initiatives
CM	Common Market
COMECON	Council for Mutual Economic Assistance (also known as CMEA)
COMETT	Community Action Programme for Education and Training for Technology
COREPER	Committee of Permanent Representatives
COST	European Co-operation in the Field of Scientific and Technical Research
CSF	Community Support Framework
CSS	Country Support Strategy
CTP	Common Transport Policy
CU	Customs Union
D	Germany
DELTA	Developing Learning through Technological Advance
DG	Directorate General
DK	Denmark
E	Spain
EAGGF	European Agricultural Guidance and Guarantee Fund

EAP	Environmental Action Programme
EBRD	European Bank of Reconstruction and Development
EC	European Community
ECB	European Central Bank
ECCP	European Climate Change Programme
ECJ	European Court of Justice
ECSC	European Coal and Steel Community
ECU	European Currency Unit
EDF	European Development Fund
EEA	European Environment Agency (also European Economic Area)
EEIG	European Economic Interest Group
EFTA	European Free Trade Association
EIA	Environmental Impact Assessment
EIB	European Investment Bank
EMI	European Monetary Institute
EMP	Euro-Mediterranean Partnership
EMS	European Monetary System
EMU	Economic and Monetary Union
EP	European Parliament
EPA	Economic Partnership Agreements
ERDF	European Regional Development Fund
ERM	Exchange Rate Mechanism
ESCB	European System of Central Banks
ESF	European Social Fund
ESPRIT	European Strategic Programme for Research and Development in Information Technology
ETUC	European Trade Union Confederation
EU	European Union
EURATOM	European Atomic Energy Community
EUR6	Six original members of the EU (B, F, D, I, L and the NL)
EUR12	EUR6 plus DK, E, GR, Irl, P and the UK
EUR15	EUR12 plus A, Fin and Sw
EUREKA	European Research Cooperation Agency
EUROFER	European Confederation of Iron and Steel Industries
EWC	European Works Council
FDI	Foreign Direct Investment
Fin	Finland
FTC	Fair Trade Commission (Japan)
G8	Group of seven largest Western industrial countries plus Russia
GATT	General Agreement on Tariffs and Trade
GDP	Gross Domestic Product
GNP	Gross National Product
GR	Greece
GSP	General System of Preferences
I	Italy
ILO	International Labour Organisation
IMF	International Monetary Fund

IMP	Integrated Mediterranean Programme
Irl	Ireland
ISPA	Structural Instrument for Accession
IT	Information technology
JRC	Joint Research Centre
L	Luxembourg
LDC	Less developed countries
M	Imports
Marpol	International Convention for the Prevention of Pollution from Ships
MCA	Monetary Compensation Amount
MEP	Member of the European Parliament
MERCOSUR	Agency seeking to create a common market for Argentina, Brazil, Paraguay, Uruguay and Free Trade area with Bolivia and Chile
MES	Minimum Efficiency Scale
MFA	Multi Fibre Arrangement
MFN	Most favoured nation
MITI	Ministry of International Trade and Industry (Japan)
MNC	Multinational company
MPC	Mediterranean Partner Countries
MRA	Mutual Recognition Agreements
MTIP	Multi-annual Transport Infrastructure Programme
NAFTA	North American Free Trade Area
NATO	North Atlantic Treaty Organisation
NIC	Newly Industrialised Country
NIP	National Indicative Programme
NL	Netherlands
NTA	New Transatlantic Agenda
NUTS	Nomenclature of Territorial Units
OAD	Official Development Assistance
OECD	Organisation for Economic Cooperation and Development
OEED	Organisation for European Economic Development
OP	Operational Programmes
P	Portugal
PHARE	Pologne-Hongrie: Actions pour la reconversion économique (Programme for the Reconstruction of Poland and Hungary)
PPS	Purchasing Power Standard
PSO	Public Service Obligation grant
QMV	Qualified majority voting
RACE	Research and Development Programme in Advanced Communications Technologies for Europe
R&D	Research and Development
RECHAR	Fund for the Reconversion of Coal Mining Areas
RENAVAL	Fund for the Reconversion of Shipbuilding Areas
RESIDER	Fund for the Reconversion of Steel Areas
RETEX	Fund for the Reconversion of Textile Areas

ROW	Rest of the World
RPK	Revenue passenger kilometres
RTD	Research and Technological Development
SAS	Structural Adjustment Support
SEA	Single European Act
SEM	Single European Market
SF	Structural Funds
SGP	Stability and Growth Pact
SME	Small and medium-sized enterprise
SPRINT	Strategic Programme for the Transnational Promotion of Innovation and Technology Transfer
STABEX	Fund for the Stabilisation of Primary Product Prices
STC	Specific Transport Instrument
STRIDE	Science and Technology for Regional Innovation and Development in Europe
Sw	Sweden
SYSMIN	Fund for the stabilisation of mineral prices
TACIS	Programme for Technical Assistance to the Commonwealth of Independent States
TBR	Trade Barriers Regulation
TBT	Technical barriers to trade
TEMPUS	Trans-European Mobility Scheme for University Studies
TEU	Treaty on European Union (Maastricht Treaty)
TGV	Train à Grande Vitesse
TIC	Transport Infrastructure Committee
UIC	Union Internationale des Chemins de Fer
UK	United Kingdom
UNCTAD	United Nations Conference on Trade and Development
UNICE	Union of Industrial and Employers' Confederations of Europe
VAT	Value Added Tax
VER	Voluntary Export Restraint
VSTFF	Very Short Term Financing Facility
WTO	World Trade Organisation
X	Exports

The origins and development of the European Union

Frank McDonald and Stephen Dearden

Introduction

The completion of the Single European Market (SEM) and the progress towards Economic and Monetary Union (EMU) focused attention on the European Union (EU) as the key actor in the process of European integration. The EU has also become involved in a host of policies that affect many aspects of the economic and social activities of the member states. Agricultural matters, especially the Common Agricultural Policy (CAP), were once the only significant policy of the EU. However, the increasing integration of the member states brought competition, social, regional, and environmental policies to the forefront of the activities of the EU.

A number of other factors have contributed to a growing focus on the EU. The Community experienced several enlargements that increased its membership from the original six states to fifteen members, with a further ten scheduled to join in 2004. The end of the Cold War, the demise of communism in Central and Eastern Europe, the reunification of Germany and the collapse of the Soviet Union led to the EU becoming the unchallenged centre of economic and business activity in Europe. These developments presented a series of new problems for European integration. One of the main issues is the future development of the Community's relations with Central and Eastern European Countries (CEECs) and the republics of the former Soviet Union. The importance of the EU in world trade has also led to a growing role for the Community in the World Trade Organisation (WTO). Moreover, the Community's links to many less developed countries through special arrangements, for example, with the African, Caribbean and Pacific countries (ACP), has increased the importance of the EU in development issues. Strong trade links with the USA, Japan and the newly industrialised countries (NICs) have further contributed to the importance of the EU in the important forums of world politics and trade. Therefore, in global forums that discuss problems in areas such as trade, global pollution, organised crime and security matters, the EU has become an important player.

What is the European Union?

The term European Union (EU) came into common usage in 1993 after the Council of Ministers renamed itself the Council of the European Union. This name stems from the Maastricht Treaty (more correctly called the Treaty on European Union) which created the term to encompass the variety of cooperation and integration work that was carried out by the member states. However, the EU did not replace the European Community (EC). The EC is itself a composite term for the European Coal and Steel Community (ECSC) (founded by the Treaty of Paris in 1951), the European Economic Community (EEC) and the European Atomic Energy Community (EURATOM) (founded by the Treaty of Rome in 1957). These three entities were merged in 1965 when a common institutional structure to govern the work of these agencies was established. This body was called the European Community (EC) or, more accurately, the European Communities. The Maastricht Treaty created three pillars – the EC, justice and home affairs, and foreign and security policy – and called the umbrella structure for these three pillars the EU. The EC is governed by the institutions of that agency (e.g. the European Commission, the European Parliament and the European Court of Justice), while the two other pillars are not subject to these institutions but are governed by the Council of the European Union (ministers from the national governments of the member states). The Amsterdam Treaty transferred immigration and asylum policy to the institutions of the EC, but the complex distinctions and interconnections between the ECSC, EEC, EURATOM and the two other pillars still remain. A new Constitutional Treaty to replace the complex treaty basis of the EU and to enable new institutional frameworks to be developed to cope with the demands of planned 2004 enlargement has been proposed (for details see **www.europa.eu.int/futurum/constitution/index_en.htm**).

The term EU has come to be used as the generic term for all of the agencies of the member states. This has led to mistakes in terminology. For example, reference is made to EU law, but there is no such concept because the EU does not have a legal personality. Furthermore, prior to 1993 the EU did not have any kind of existence. However, reference to the EU as a term for the EC or even the EEC is widespread in newspapers and even in academic journals and books. Indeed, the Commission often uses the term EU when referring to policies or programmes that are related to EC matters. This confusion is understandable given the difficulty of clearly identifying the time period and changing role and names of the various agencies that compose the EU. The use of the EU as a generic term is well established and it is unlikely that greater precision in its use will emerge except by pedants and in areas where distinguishing between the component parts of the EU is important (e.g. in legal matters and when examining the role and functions of the institutions of the different parts of the EU).

This book uses the term EU or Community, except in historical contexts when the terms ECSC, EEC and EC are used. However, as the book is mainly concerned with economic matters, most of the references to the EU should perhaps be to the EC or to the EEC. However, the editors believe that the use of the generic terms EU and Community does not lead to any grave errors and avoids unnecessarily complicated explanations in the text.

The European Unity movement

The origins of what developed into the EU can be traced to the European Unity movement. A full description and analysis of the historical development of the European Unity movement can be found in Nugent (2003), and a review of the main elements in this process is provided in Swann (1998) and European Commission (1990). The origins of the move to achieve European unity stemmed from a desire to avoid the periodic wars between the nation states of Europe. There was also some consideration of the advantages of creating a larger market in Europe to allow benefits from economies of scale to be reaped. However, although there were economic factors in the background, it was the political factors that predominated in the early attempts to achieve European unity. When the first steps towards creating the EU were made, specific economic objectives were the main methods advocated to achieve European unity; they were, however, generally regarded as means to an end, and the end was the establishment of some kind of political union.

In the aftermath of the Second World War the countries of Europe were faced with several difficult issues. Much of the continent of Europe was severely war damaged and a large reconstruction process was necessary. The Cold War was developing, dividing Europe into two opposing camps, with a divided Germany as a potential flashpoint for renewed conflict in Europe. Any such conflict would have been between the two new superpowers, the USA and the Soviet Union, and could have involved the use of nuclear weapons. In such circumstances it was not surprising that the Europeans should have looked for some methods to ensure that they had a voice in shaping the dramatic events that were taking place in Europe. The main obstacles to this were that Europe could not speak with one voice because it was composed of a number of sovereign nation states and these states did not have a common view on the solutions to the problems of post-war Europe.

The main powers in Europe were the USA and the Soviet Union. The UK, the strongest European power, was not particularly interested in becoming involved in attempts to achieve European unity. Rather, the UK was interested in promoting stability in Europe that would allow the UK to concentrate on creating zones of influence in the British Commonwealth and developing a 'special relationship' with the USA. Although the UK was not opposed to European unity, it favoured loose inter-governmental arrangements between the countries of Europe where each country retained sovereignty (the right to make decisions independently of other governments or agencies) in the important areas of policy-making. Consequently, the UK was not prepared to become involved in attempts to create any supranational European agencies which would have powers that would erode the sovereignty of the member countries. Most of the Scandinavian countries were concerned with maintaining their neutrality, faced with the growth of the Cold War, and wished to retain sovereignty in key economic and political areas. They were, therefore, unwilling to become involved in the creation of supranational European agencies. The countries of Southern Europe were scarcely connected to these events. Spain and Portugal were dictatorships and were not considered to be eligible to join the democratic countries of Europe in creating new arrangements to forge European unity. Greece was in a state of political flux, with the possibility that it could go communist and forge links with the Soviet Union. Indeed, the main focus of attention on the countries of Southern Europe was to ensure that they were not recruited to the communist side and to enrol them in the defence coalition opposing the Soviet Union.

In the immediate post-war period Europe was divided not only into East and West, but also into those countries that favoured the creation of some kind of supranational European agencies and others who looked for some loose forms of inter-governmental cooperation. There was also division between the democratic countries of Western Europe and the dictatorships of Southern Europe.

By the 1980s the geographically based divisions began to crumble and the division with Southern Europe vanished. The USA no longer dominated Europe economically and the ending of the Cold War reduced its political and military influence in Europe, but there was no consensus on the future role of the USA in European economic, political and military matters. Although Europe largely ceased to be divided into different camps on the basis of ideology, there were still considerable disputes over the characteristics that the European Unity should have. These disputes stem from differences of opinion about the approach that should be adopted to creating European unity.

The European Unity movement split into a variety of approaches on how best to achieve viable integration (Nugent, 2003). Three main approaches emerged:

1 *Federalists* – This group favours the creation of a political community founded on strong constitutional and institutional frameworks. The resulting Federation would have supranational powers that would take precedence over the powers of the member states. Achieving European unity, therefore, is seen as requiring the creation of new federal structures.

2 *Functionalists* – This group advocates integration based on the 'functional' activities of governments. It regards security, defence and foreign policy as being very 'political' and considers that national governments are reluctant to surrender sovereignty in these areas. However, in less 'political' areas, such as policies towards particular sectors and detailed economic areas such as trade rules, it is easier to obtain agreement to integrate government policies. Neo-Functionalists argue that, as functional areas of governments are integrated, the political and bureaucratic elite that handle these policies will increasingly switch their loyalties, expectations and goals from the national government arena to the overall aims of the integration agencies. In this scenario a Functionalist approach would gradually move the elite towards the goals of European political integration.

3 *Nationalists* – This group regards the nation state as the prime focus for all government activity, in areas such as trade rules and sectorial policies as well as in the 'big' policy areas such as security and defence. In this view European integration should be based on inter-governmental cooperation in cases where all parties can expect to benefit from such cooperation. Agencies with supranational powers should only be created if the benefits available from such agencies are very large and cannot be captured by some kind of inter-governmental body.

Federalists and Functionalists have a common goal – an integrated Europe based on the creation of new supranational structures. Their only substantial difference is over the means to this end. The Federalists favour a 'big bang' approach based on dramatic constitutional and institutional change. In contrast, the Functionalists work towards a gradual drift into European unity as the elite become more and more entangled in the functional work of the integration agencies. Nationalists have a very different agenda. They regard integration as primarily a process of inter-governmental cooperation to achieve mutually beneficial outcomes. In their view the integration process is not seen as a method of building European political union, but as a method of collaborating to find solutions to common problems. However, European political union could emerge from the Nationalists' approach if there were overwhelming benefits from such a union.

The Nationalists versus the Federalists and Functionalists battle has had a powerful influence on the development of the EU. The continuing dispute between Federalists and Functionalists has been about the speed and type of change, whereas the Nationalists have fought against the direction of integration when it has led towards the growth of supranational governmental structures. These disputes have contributed to the rather strange governmental structures that have been developed in the Community. The Community institutions are a mixture of supranational and inter-governmental structures, reflecting the lack of consensus on how best to promote the well-being of European countries.

In spite of these disputes there is a consensus that, in economic matters, the EU is the key to the development of Europe. In political and even security matters, the EU, or at least institutions with strong connections to it, is seen as the way forward to allow adjustment to the new conditions that prevail in Europe. The European Economic Community (EEC) and its precursor the European Coal and Steel Community (ECSC) always had economic objectives to the fore, and this remains true even though the EU is beginning to expand into more overtly political objectives. Indeed, many of the pressures to move into political areas stemmed from the need to create the necessary conditions under which economic objectives such as establishing the Single European Market (SEM) and Economic and Monetary Union (EMU) could be achieved. There are also pressures to modify the political structures to aid in the growing role that the EU plays in the world economy. The process of European economic integration is therefore at the heart of the current changes in Europe, and the EU is the key agent in this process.

The origins of the European Union

The origins of the EU stem from the failure of the main countries of Europe in the early post-war period to reach agreement on how to proceed towards European unity. France and West Germany formed an alliance to promote European integration to rebuild their shattered economic systems and to foster the conditions that would prevent war between Western European countries. The Franco-German alliance favoured the creation of limited supranational agencies in order to curb potential nationalistic tendencies that could have led to poor relations between

European countries. However, in major issues it was considered important to retain power at national government level. This approach gave the Franco-German alliance a major role in defining and developing the European Unity movement. Italy, Belgium, Holland and Luxembourg supported the Franco-German approach and these six countries started the process that ultimately led to the EU. In the UK and the Scandinavian countries the predominant view was that an inter-governmental approach should be taken to rebuild Europe and to secure stability in the region.

These early developments in the European Unity movement have had long-lasting effects. The Franco-German alliance came to dominate the process of European integration. The Franco-German view has tended to regard European unity as primarily a political issue and that economic considerations are a means to a political end. This end was seen as being primarily the creation of security and prosperity by integration, and that economic efficiency considerations were second-ary to the goal of achieving unity. The importance of this view can perhaps be best observed in the creation of such policies as the Common Agricultural Policy (CAP), which is very strong on stability, security and the prosperity of farmers, but has little connection with any concept of economic efficiency. The British and Scandinavian views of European integration were based on a more economic and pragmatic view of the need for integration programmes. Therefore, the driving force for integration programmes was very different among the countries of Western Europe.

The EU has developed largely in accordance with the vision of the Franco-German alliance. The alliance has tended to guide the development of the Community, but this has led to resistance by Italy and the smaller member states. They have sought to curb the power of the alliance by increasing the supranational aspects of the Community. The scepticism of the UK and the Scandinavians towards plans for greater political integration and the extension of supranationalism stems in part from their different perception of the purpose of the EU. However, they have not been able to steer the Community away from the powerful influence of the Franco-German alliance.

These differences can be seen in attitudes to European monetary union. The Franco-German alliance regard monetary union largely as a political imperative to weld the countries of the Community together while allowing the alliance to continue to drive developments in the EU. Italy and the smaller member states regard it as a means to lessen the power of Germany in monetary matters. The British and the Scandinavians tend to regard the project in a more pragmatic light and consider it to be a potentially beneficial move for some, but not necessarily all, of the member states. However, they also regard monetary union as raising very serious questions about the sovereignty of the member states.

In the 1950s matters relating to foreign relations and military arrangements were heavily influenced by the development of the Cold War. The dominance of the USA and the Soviet Union in security and military matters resulted in the setting up of opposing alliances in Europe based on the Warsaw Pact alliance in Eastern Europe, and the North Atlantic Treaty Organisation (NATO) in Western Europe. The former institution was dominated by the Soviet Union and the latter by the USA. The early attempts to establish economic and non-military political arrangements in Western Europe were centred on the Organisation for European Economic Cooperation (OEEC) and the Council of Europe. The OEEC failed to develop because of disputes about the need for some kind of supranational decision-making powers. It eventually expanded its membership and became the Organisation for Economic Cooperation and Development (OECD). The Council of Europe was not granted any supranational powers and still exists as a forum for inter-governmental discussion on issues of interest to Europe. Its main advantage is that its membership includes most European countries. It has not played a significant role in the integration of Europe.

By the early 1950s a series of inter-governmental agencies existed in Western Europe – the Council of Europe, the OEEC and NATO. For those countries that favoured more supranational powers for European agencies these institutions did not seem to be capable of integrating Europe. In 1948, Belgium, Luxembourg and the Netherlands had agreed to form a Customs Union (CU). This example of the use of specific economic means of achieving European unity was to come to the fore in the development of the Community. The main political and military issues in Western Europe were heavily influenced by NATO and the Americans, and were firmly based on inter-governmentalism. The European Federalists and Functionalists were therefore unable to expand their ideas into these areas. The involvement of West Germany in any attempt to form a type of supranational agency with responsibility for political and defence issues was restricted by the opposition of the Soviet Union to any German involvement in these matters. In the immediate post-war period there was popular opposition within Western Europe to allowing Germany any such role in these areas. Consequently, the Federalists and the Functionalists were restricted to economic matters in proposals for any supranational agency.

In those countries where Federalist and Functionalist views were strong (France, Germany, Italy, Holland, Belgium and Luxembourg: the original six), there was a desire to establish agencies with some supranational powers and this led them to establish the ECSC in 1951. One of the motives for this was to integrate the coal and steel industries of Germany, the heart of its war machine, into an interdependent European industrial structure, thereby making war between Western European countries impossible. The ECSC had a High Authority that had some supranational powers in the areas of coal and steel, but the main decision-making powers rested with the Council of Ministers. This Council was composed of the Ministers of the member states and was therefore inter-governmental in character. Nevertheless, the ECSC was an agency that had some supranational powers and was a kind of cross between an inter-governmental and a supranational agency. This strange mixture was also to characterise the EEC and EURATOM, the agencies that followed the ECSC and from which the EU arose. Consequently, the origins of the EU led to an institutional structure that was focused on economic matters and was neither a pure inter-governmental nor a supranational agency, but rather a mixture of these forms.

The setting up of the EEC and EURATOM resulted from the Spaak Committee, first convened in 1955. The UK joined with the original six countries represented on this committee, but withdrew when it became clear that they wanted new institutional forms based on the ECSC model and were also seeking wide-ranging economic integration. Therefore the UK did not join the original six when they established the EEC and EURATOM by the Treaty of Rome, signed in 1957. Instead, the UK formed the European Free Trade Association (EFTA) in 1960 with Austria, Switzerland, Norway, Sweden, Denmark and Portugal. The arrangements within EFTA were considerably less ambitious than in the EEC. The EEC had elements of supranationality in decision-making and was committed to the establishment of a Customs Union and a Common Market, and had vaguely defined objectives to create EMU, while EFTA was purely inter-governmental and was aiming to achieve a free-trade area.

By the early 1960s Europe appeared to have created a new political order based on the division of Europe into East and West, with the Soviet Union and the USA largely directing events in this area, and an economic order based on the EEC, EFTA and the Council for Mutual Economic Assistance (COMECON). However, the EEC was soon to emerge as the dominant economic agency in Europe.

The development of the European Union

The EU developed in a series of phases beginning with the enlargement of the original six members to nine and then to twelve, fifteen and, in 2004, twenty-five. During the 1970s and early 1980s the integration process did not progress until the deadlock was broken by the agreement on the Single European Act (SEA). This led to the Maastricht Treaty and the preparation for EMU. After the Maastricht Treaty the EU struggled to cope with the problem of high unemployment, the inability to tackle the issue of institutional reform and the efforts to integrate the CEECs into the Community.

The enlargement of the original six

The original six experienced high growth rates in the 1960s which were often attributed to the ambitious programme of economic integration on which the EEC had embarked. It may, however, have had more to do with the rapid growth of West Germany as it experienced an 'economic miracle' in the post-war reconstruction process. In this period Germany became the leading industrial power in Europe and the other members of the EEC benefited from their growing economic links with this dynamic economy. Whatever the reason for the relative success of the member states of the EEC, certain groups in the UK eventually came to regard the Community as the key to the future economic prosperity of Britain. It had become clear to key decision-makers in the UK that the Commonwealth was not a viable economic bloc and that EFTA was not large enough to provide the necessary market size to allow for the reaping of benefits of economies of scale. The EEC, with the new economic power of Germany at the centre, was deemed to be the appropriate vehicle to allow the UK to halt and then reverse its relative economic decline. It was therefore mainly economic reasons that drew the UK towards applying for membership of the EEC. The accession of the UK to the EEC was a long and difficult process because the CAP and the commitment of the EEC to a degree of supranational decision-making ran counter to long-held traditions in the UK. However, after a series of long and complex negotiations (see Swann, 1998 for a survey), the UK, along with Ireland and Denmark, joined the EEC in 1973. This had a profound influence on the development of the EU. The EEC now included the four largest economies in Western Europe – Germany, France, Italy and the UK. There was also an increase in the conflicts within the EEC as the UK had an economic and political structure that did not sit easily with that of the EEC. This became obvious with disputes about the CAP and the connected budgetary problems. The regional problems of the EEC were also brought more sharply into focus as the membership of both the UK and Ireland greatly increased the number of relatively deprived regions in the Community.

The expansion of EEC membership in 1973 was not followed by fast progress in implementing the integration programme of the Community. Indeed, the 1970s was a period of considerable stagnation in the Community. The problems in adjusting to the issues raised by the enlargement were one factor in the lack of progress in developing the necessary policies and programmes to allow greater integration to take place. There were also problems raised by the OPEC oil price increases and the ending of the Bretton Woods arrangement of fixed exchange rates, leading to instability of the international monetary system. These problems led to poor growth rates in the member states. The EEC did not manage to adopt a united approach to these issues and generally there was a pronounced lack of momentum in the Community. By the 1970s the Community had accomplished the creation of the Customs Union (although a large number of non-tariff barriers remained in place), but was not making much progress to create a Common Market. The CAP was the only significant common policy of the EEC and was causing considerable problems both within the Community and with the rest of the world. In the movements towards EMU practically no progress was being made. However, this state of affairs was to change dramatically in the 1980s.

A new momentum began to arise with the second enlargement of the EEC when Greece joined in 1981, and Spain and Portugal in 1986, creating a potential market of 320 million consumers. Incorporating these countries into the Community resulted in few problems, in spite of the large differences in their levels of economic development compared with the rest of the EEC. There were also movements to alter the Treaty of Rome to remove some of the constraints imposed by the cumbersome nature of the decision-making process of the Community. This led to the SEA and the start of the SEM programme. The launching of the European Monetary System (EMS) in 1979, and the implications of the creation of the SEM for monetary and other macro-economic policies, increased pressures for monetary integration in the Community.

The Maastricht Treaty

By the early 1990s the Community had made considerable progress in establishing the SEM. It had also developed detailed plans for the creation of monetary union and there was a growing momentum to increase Community competencies in the social, environmental and regional areas. Furthermore, issues connected with foreign and security policies and other types of political policies increased in importance. The reunification of Germany and the collapse of communism in the CEECs swept away the post-war economic and political order of Europe. These factors led to pressures to increase the integration programmes of the Community. Germany and France, in particular, sought to deepen the integration of the Community. To investigate the means to achieve these aims the Community established two Inter-Governmental Conferences (IGCs): one on Economic and Monetary Union and the other on Political Union. The IGCs sought to build upon the changes that the SEA had brought about and to develop the ideas that had been advocated in the Delors report on Economic and Monetary Union (European Commission, 1989).

The IGCs led to the negotiations on the Maastricht Treaty, also known as the Treaty on European Union (TEU). The debates and arguments that emerged in the drafting of this treaty clearly indicated that there was little consensus among the member states about how 'federal' the Community should become. The UK made it clear that the concept of a federal Community was not acceptable. France and Germany were also opposed to granting significant new powers to the European Parliament (EP) and the European Commission, although many of the smaller member states were in favour. The negotiations consequently proved to be very difficult. Agreement was reached to establish monetary union but the UK and Denmark secured the right to 'opt out' of the process. The Maastricht Treaty also contained a Social Chapter as a basis for expanding EU competencies in the social policy area. However, the UK obtained an 'opt-out' from implementing any legislation that might emerge from the Social Chapter. In the areas of foreign and security policy, and justice and home affairs, the TEU created new structures that were separate from the existing institutions of the Community. In these fields any cooperation or coordination was to be achieved by inter-governmental procedures (Duff et al., 1994).

The difficulties that were encountered in ratifying the TEU further exposed the lack of consensus on the future development of the Community. A referendum on ratification, held in Denmark in 1992, produced a 'no' verdict. This was followed by a narrow 'yes' vote in a referendum in France. In the UK the government faced considerable difficulties in processing the ratification bill through Parliament, and the Conservative Party experienced a deep and damaging split over its European policy. A second referendum in Denmark, in 1993, secured a small majority for ratification. The final obstacle was a referral to the constitutional court in Germany. This followed from a claim, by a former German Commissioner, that the German government could not ratify the TEU because it did not have the right to transfer sovereignty to non-German institutional structures. The court ruled that the TEU could be ratified. The final irony of the ratification process was that Germany, one of the strongest supporters of the Maastricht Treaty, was the last country to ratify the treaty.

In 1992, speculative pressures began to undermine the Exchange Rate Mechanism (ERM) and by the end of 1993 the ERM had effectively ceased to operate as an effective mechanism for managing the exchange rate policies of the member states. By early 1993 both the UK and Italy had withdrawn from the ERM, and Spain, Ireland and Portugal had experienced substantial devaluation of their currencies within the EMS. By the end of 1993 the ERM bands had been widened to ±15 per cent (except for the deutschmark/guilder rate).

The Community also experienced considerable difficulties in reforming the CAP in order to satisfy the conditions for reaching agreement on the Uruguay Round of the General Agreement on Tariffs and Trades (GATT). France caused some concern by refusing to agree to the reform of the CAP that had been agreed between the Community and the USA. Agreement over CAP reform was necessary if the Uruguay Round was to be successfully completed. France also objected to the liberalisation of trade in television programmes and films in the GATT round. Eventually, this area had to be removed from the GATT round in order to allow agreement to be reached. However, the French stance on these issues caused considerable concern in the EU, especially in the UK, Germany and the Netherlands.

Problems such as these led to growing confusion among both governments and citizens as to the future role of the Community. Despite these difficulties the Community reached agreement, in 1993, to establish the European Economic Area (EEA). The EEA was an area composed of the twelve member states and most of the countries of EFTA. In the EEA free movement of goods, services, capital and labour was to be established, and most of the laws relating to the SEM were also accepted by the EFTA members of the EEA. The EFTA members of the EEA also agreed to contribute towards the costs of helping the poorer regions of the Community. However, in March 1994 agreement on conditions for Community membership was reached with Austria, Finland, Norway and Sweden. This agreement led to full membership for Austria, Finland and Sweden in 1995. Norway decided not to proceed to membership. Switzerland rejected membership of the EEA after a referendum in 1993 and also removed its application for full membership of the EU.

In the early 1990s progress was made to increase the help that was given to the poorer regions of the Community. The structural adjustment funds were considerably expanded and proposals on how to make best use of the 'Cohesion Fund' and the structural funds were put forward in a package of proposals commonly called Delors II. The 'Cohesion Fund' (founded on the basis of Article 130d of the Maastricht Treaty) is intended to help in the areas of the environment and trans-European networks in transport infrastructures. Delors II (European Commission, 1992) recommended that the funds should be concentrated in Objective 1 areas: regions with a per capita GDP less than 75 per cent of the EU average, namely Ireland, Northern Ireland, Portugal, Greece, Southern Italy, most of Spain, Corsica and the French Overseas Departments. However, Germany and the UK, the two largest net contributors to the budget of the Community, expressed concern over the cost of the structural funds and the Cohesion Fund. The prospect of some of the countries of Central and Eastern Europe joining the Community caused even more concern about the cost to the richer member states of transferring large amounts of funds to the poorer members. These concerns led to calls for the Community to concentrate on creating an effective SEM as the best method of increasing the living standards of the citizens of the Community. However, the Southern European member states and Ireland regarded the transfer of funds as a crucial component in the attempt to boost the living standards of all of the citizens of the Community. Once again dispute emerged as to the future direction of the Community.

The EU experienced a remarkable change in its fortunes in the early 1990s. It moved from being an agency making seemingly unstoppable progress towards some kind of 'federal' system to an agency that was unclear as to which direction it should take. The Community was very much a child of the Cold War, and consequently a Western European club. The Community found it difficult to develop its role in a Europe that was no longer divided into hostile blocs.

Recession and the third enlargement

In the mid-1990s the EU experienced a series of problems that led to searching examinations of the role and purpose of the Community (see Henning et al., 1994 for a review of these issues). The problems arose from economic conditions in continental Europe, the difficulties of making the institutional structures work effectively, and the issues raised by the desire of many of the CEECs to become full members of the EU.

In the mid and late 1990s continental European economies suffered a prolonged and deep recession. This was related to the aftermath of German reunification and the need to curb government budget deficits in the run-up to European monetary union. The recession added to the problems with high unemployment that had afflicted Europe since the early 1990s. The high levels of unemployment in some of the member states made it difficult for governments to persuade their electorates that European monetary union was beneficial and also to allow them to press ahead with plans to liberalise their national markets in areas such as telecommunication services, energy and airlines.

The enlargement of the EU in 1995 exposed the inadequacies of the institutional structure of the Community. The basic structure of the institutions has not substantially altered since the formation of the EEC in 1957. The only major changes (agreed in the SEA and the TEU) were to grant some increases in the power of the Commission and the EP to influence legislation and to reduce the power of veto by national governments in some areas of law making. However, the EU had developed from six members to fifteen and had enlarged its policies and legislation from trade and agricultural matters to nearly all aspects of economic life and a substantial part of civic and social life. In these circumstances the institutions of the Community found it difficult to govern effectively the wide range of policies and programmes that had emerged from the integration process.

The desire of many of the CEECs to become full members further increased concerns about the institutional structure of the EU. If the EU found it difficult to govern fifteen member states effectively, the prospects of a Community with twenty-five member states might prove to be too much for the existing institutional structure. The problems of transforming the CEECs into modern market-based economies were clearly revealed to be a major challenge by the experiences of German reunification. The German economy encountered considerable problems in integrating the former East Germany. These problems arose despite large budgetary transfers from the West to the East. The former East Germany was also one of the most developed of the CEECs, but the problems of modernising such systems were clearly considerable. This experience indicated that the EU would face significant difficulties if the CEECs were to be granted full membership of the Community. Such an enlargement would also put pressure on the financial arrangements of the agricultural and regional policies of the EU.

Widening versus deepening and flexibility

A vigorous debate about the future direction of the EU arose in the light of these problems. The debate focused on the widening versus deepening controversy. Some argued that the EU should concentrate on widening by integrating the economies of the CEECs into the Community and that less emphasis should be placed on developing new agendas such as EMU and Political Union. Others argued that the Community should deepen by developing EMU and Political Union and placing less emphasis on enlargement. A third route was envisaged that involved both widening and deepening simultaneously. This route was usually thought to require a multi-tiered or two-speed approach to integration that would allow member states to opt out of some parts of the integration process (Duff, 1997). The concept of opt-out or two-speed integration had been given a boost by the provisions of the TEU that had allowed for countries to opt out of parts of the integration programme or to join in at a later stage. This type of approach permits a complex and flexible set of linkages to be established and also allows those member states who wish to make faster progress to proceed. The Schengen Agreement is another example of this type of agreement and allows member states to remove all frontier controls on the movement of people within the Schengen area. However, this flexible approach may lead to damaging splits in the EU (e.g. in the case of EMU) and it could allow member states to gain competitive advantage (e.g. the UK opt-out from the Social Chapter of the TEU).

The confusion about how best to proceed was revealed in the negotiations on the Amsterdam Treaty. This treaty does not contain any major changes to the institutional structure of the Community, nor did it resolve the issues connected to widening versus deepening. However, it eliminated one opt-out (the UK opt-out from the Social Chapter of the TEU) and created another (the opt-out by Denmark, Ireland and the UK from the Schengen Agreement). The Amsterdam Treaty contains provisions on the use of 'flexibility' that might allow for a two- or multi-speed Community to develop. However, the provisions do not provide a firm foundation for the widespread use of the concept of flexibility (Duff, 1997). The Amsterdam Treaty required that these unresolved issues on institutional structure be referred to yet another IGC. The Amsterdam Treaty left a large number of unresolved issues and achieved only minor changes to the institutional structure of the Community. The problems that the member states encountered in the negotiations for the Amsterdam Treaty clearly indicate that a Federalist solution to the problems of integration does not have widespread support across the member states. Equally, the approach of the Functionalists can be seen to have many problems – in particular, frequent recourse to compromise solutions that permit the continuance of ineffective structures that hamper the development of the integration process.

Notwithstanding these problems, the EU continued to press on with its ambitious integration programmes. The process of European monetary union commenced in 1999 and included initially eleven of the member states. Greece adopted the euro in 2001 after it had succeeded in meeting the convergence criteria bringing the total to twelve. Three member states have not adopted the euro: Denmark, Sweden and the UK. Sweden rejected the euro in a referendum in September 2003, while the UK could delay holding a long promised referendum until late 2005 or even 2006. However, most European Union citizens have been using the euro since 2002. Meanwhile the future of economic and social cohesion was one of the major issues discussed in the European Commission (1997) Agenda 2000 communication (presented in July 1997), largely because of their financial implications. The structural and cohesion funds had been the Community's second largest budget item over the years 1994 to 1999 (around 35 per cent of the budget). In anticipation of the accession of countries with national incomes well below the Community average, the Community structural policy was reformed in 1999 and its budgetary allocation increased from €208 bn to €213 bn for 2000–06.

Although the EU had experienced a period of pronounced political and economic difficulties in the 1990s it still managed to enlarge the Community from twelve to fifteen members, to prepare the way for European monetary union and for the accession of some of the CEECs into full membership. These 'successes' say much for the ability of the EU to press on with its integration programmes in the face of complex and uncertain political and economic conditions.

The fourth eastern enlargement

Preparations for the next enlargement of the Community began in 1993 at the Copenhagen European Council where it was decided that 'the associated countries in eastern and central Europe that so desire shall become members of the EU'. However three criteria had to be met – democracy, human rights and rule-of-law; a functioning market economy; the ability to adopt Community policies (the Community *acquis*), including economic and monetary union. Association Agreements had already been established with these countries, with the aim of creating a free-trade area in industrial products with the EU by 2002. In 1989, to assist in the economic and institutional adjustment required, the PHARE programme had been created. For the period 2000–06 PHARE will total €10.5 bn, concentrating upon 'institution building' and investment support (70 per cent). A further €3.5 bn is provided for agricultural development (SAPARD) and €7 bn for infrastructural investment (ISPA). Given the importance of adapting their legislation to EU requirements a technical assistance office was specifically created (TAIEX) to meet this need.

Negotiations for accession began in 1997 with six countries – the Czech Republic, Estonia, Hungary, Poland, Slovenia and Cyprus – joined in 2000 by Romania, Slovakia, Latvia, Lithuania, Bulgaria and Malta. Each of these countries was subject to annual assessments by the Commission as to their progress towards satisfying the three 'Copenhagen Criteria'. In October 2002 the Commission was able to recommend to the European Council that all the applicant countries, except for

Bulgaria, Romania and Turkey, had met the requirements for accession and should join the EU in May 2004. Bulgaria and Romania are expected to join the Union in 2007, but Turkey's position remains problematic. As the occupier of Northern Cyprus a Greek veto on entry would be inevitable. Indeed the negotiations for the entry of Southern Cyprus had been complicated by the failure of UN efforts to arrive at a settlement to the islands division. However, the Turkish application also raises more fundamental questions as to the nature of the European Union and its geographical limits. An under-developed country, geographically part of Asia Minor, with a Muslim population, if with a secular tradition, Turkey appears to many to be too distinct from mainstream Europe to be easily accommodated. At the practical level the entry of Turkey would open up Europe to unregulated Turkish migration, a particular concern to Germany with its already substantial Turkish population.

The expansion of the EU eastwards has presented the EU with a number of significant problems. The new members have an average income of less than 40 per cent of the current EU average and substantial agricultural sectors. They will inevitably place considerable demands upon the structural and agricultural support funds of the Community. Negotiations as to their future entitlements proved highly controversial, as existing members defended their own 'share of the cake'. The problem of accommodating their demands upon the structural and cohesion funds will have to be finally settled by 2007 when the EU's new financial programme commences. Similarly, CAP support is to be phased in but a final settlement has yet to be agreed and will doubtless be caught up in the general ongoing debate about CAP reform. Beyond financial questions the expansion eastwards created a greater sense of urgency in addressing the weaknesses in the EU's current organisation. To consider these problems in 2001 a Constitutional Convention was called to prepare reform proposals for presentation to an Inter-Governmental Conference. The results of these deliberations are discussed below.

The institutional structure of the European Union

The institutional structure of the EU is determined by the various treaties that have been agreed by the member states. The Treaties of Paris (1951) and Rome (1957), as amended by the SEA (1986) and the TEU (1992), form the current basis of the EU. The Amsterdam Treaty did not alter the fundamental basis of the institutional structure of the EU.

The five main institutions of the EU are:

1 The Council of the European Union

2 The European Commission

3 The European Parliament (EP)

4 The European Court of Justice (ECJ)

5 The European Monetary Institute (EMI), replaced by the European Central Bank (ECB) in 1999

The Council of the European Union

The Council of the European Union (commonly called the Council of Ministers) is composed of the relevant government ministers of the member states; for example, proposals concerned with agricultural matters are considered by the ministers of agriculture from the member states. The Presidency of the Council of the European Union rotates around the member states every six months. The government of the member state that holds the Presidency has the task of seeking to make progress with proposals that have been held up by disagreements among the member states and to further the objectives that have been agreed by the Council. The Council of Ministers has a standing committee of civil servants, composed of the permanent representatives of the national governments. This committee is called COREPER and it does most of the groundwork on any proposed legislation. The ministers generally become involved at the end stage to settle unresolved problems, or to agree to disagree. In the latter case a proposal can be returned to the European Commission and the European Parliament for further consideration, or it can be left on the table until some sort of compromise can be reached. This means that the governments of the member states have considerable powers to prevent, delay or modify any proposal for new Community laws. Voting in the Council of Ministers can be by unanimity (on matters connected to industry, taxation, culture, R&D programmes and regional and social funds) or by qualified majority (on issues related to agriculture, fisheries, the internal market, the environment and transport). It is therefore possible for EU legislation to become Community law against the wishes of a member state. Hence the power that the governments of the member states have to control the legislative programme of the Community depends on how far they are in agreement with each other, and on the extent of qualified majority voting.

The Council of the European Union holds regular meetings of the heads of government of the member states – the European Council. Although the European Council had no treaty basis until the role of this body was recognised in the SEA, since 1974 it has held regular summit meetings. The summits are chaired by the member state holding the Presidency of the Council and include, in addition to the heads of government, the President of the Commission and the President of the European Parliament, who gives a presentation of the views of the Parliament at the start of each summit. European Council meetings are generally strongly influenced by whoever holds the Presidency. The Council is an inter-governmental institution, and often reflects the interests of the country that holds the Presidency. In spite of this some of the most significant steps in the integration process have been initiated by the European Council, such as the SEA and the moves towards EMU. Indeed, no major developments in the integration process would be possible without the approval of the European Council. The European Council therefore plays a key role in the development of the EU and is very clearly under the control of the governments of the member states. This does not mean that the EU has no significant supranational characteristics. Once the European Council decides to establish elements of supranational decision-making into Community policies or programmes, member states effectively lose sovereignty in that area.

The European Commission

The European Commission is a cross between a civil service and an executive body. The Commission has a college of 20 members. The President, the two Vice-Presidents and the 17 other members of the Commission are chosen for their general competence, and all present guarantees of independence. They have all held political positions in their countries of origin, often at ministerial level. Commissioners are appointed by their member states, but are not responsible to them. The Commission is reappointed every five years, within six months of the elections to the European Parliament. This interval gives the new Parliament time to approve the Commission President proposed by the member states, before the President-designate constitutes his future team, in collaboration with the governments of the member states. Parliament then gives its opinion as to the entire proposed college through an approval process. Once accepted by the Parliament, the new Commission can officially start work the following January.

In its role as an administrative body it is split into a number of Directorates General (DGs), which have specific areas of responsibility (see Box I.1 and **www.europa.eu.int/comm/dgs_en.htm** for details). The Commission is the guardian of the Treaties and is responsible for monitoring and policing EU law. It does not implement these laws, but depends on the governments of the member states to carry out this function. The Commission has the power to investigate suspected breaches of EU law by governments, companies and individuals, and can impose fines if it considers that the law has been broken. It also has powers to compel changes in the policies of national governments if it considers that they are contrary to Community law. The governments of the member states are obliged to ensure that the decisions of the Commission in these matters are implemented unless they dispute the ruling of the Commission. When this occurs the case is sent to the European Court of Justice (ECJ). The Commission therefore has supranational powers in certain areas. The day-to-day operation of EU policies and programmes, and the administering of the Structural Funds, are also under the control of the Commission. All proposals for new Community legislation must be initiated by the

---

Box I.1 The Directorates

The Commission of the EU is split into Directorates General (DGs), which have responsibilities for both the day-to-day administration of Community operations and the framing of proposals for new laws. The current DGs are:

Agriculture	Regional Policy	Environment
Economic and Financial Affairs	Taxation and Customs Union	Health and Consumer Protection
Employment and Social Affairs	Development	Internal Market
Enterprise	External Relations	Joint Research Centre
Fisheries	Competition	Research
Information Society	Education and Culture	Enlargement
Justice and Home Affairs	Energy and Transport	Trade

Commission on the basis of the Treaties or the decisions of the European Council. The Commission also provides help and information on Community matters to companies and organisations of various types.

The European Commission acts for the European Union on the international stage, in particular when it comes to negotiating international agreements on the external aspect of EU policies. The Commission also maintains a worldwide network of Delegations. At the moment these concentrate upon trade and aid relations with their host countries and provide limited consular protection to European Union citizens.

The European Parliament

The European Parliament (EP) has three essential functions:

1 It shares with the Council of the European Union the power to legislate, i.e. to adopt European laws (Directives, Regulations, Decisions) in many, but not all areas (see **www.europa.eu.int/institutions/decision-making/index_en.htm** for details). Its involvement in the legislative process helps to guarantee the democratic legitimacy of the texts adopted.

2 It shares budgetary authority with the Council and can therefore influence EU spending. At the end of the procedure, it adopts the budget in its entirety.

3 It exercises democratic supervision over the Commission. It approves the nomination of Commissioners and has the right to censure the Commission. It also exercises political supervision over all the institutions.

The EP is not responsible to, nor appointed by, the governments of the member states. Since 1979 the citizens of the Community have directly elected the EP. Although there are loose arrangements between the political parties in the EP they do not form a coherent political party system. The number of Members of the European Parliament (MEPs) which a country elects depends upon population size, the larger countries having more seats than the smaller. The powers of the EP are limited, but have been growing since the SEA. In principle, the EP can dismiss the Commissioners and can refuse to approve the budget of the EU. These powers are, however, too great to be used, as they would effectively make the government of the Community impossible. The SEA granted the EP more influence in the process of making EU law in many areas and the TEU extended this by introducing the concept of co-decision-making between the Council and the EP. The Amsterdam Treaty simplified and extended the principle of co-decision-making (see Box I.2). With the Amsterdam Treaty most of the proposals for new EU law in economic matters will be subject to the co-decision process. The EP also investigates the activities of the Commission by means of a series of committees that examine the working of the various policies of the Community. It has influence on the appointment of the Commission and has the right to refuse to accept the nominations for the President of the Commission. However, the Council of Ministers is not accountable to the EP.

Box I.2 The legislative process of the Community

The legislative process of the Community is complex. What follows is a simplified outline of this process (for a fuller treatment see Nugent, 2003).

Box I.2 *(continued)*

The Community has four main methods of making law and for issuing rules. These are:

1 regulations: these are binding and have direct effect in the member states;

2 directives: these must be incorporated into the law of the member states in accordance with their national legislative practices;

3 decisions: these are binding rulings by the Commission on specific issues and are directly applied to governments, companies and individuals;

4 recommendations and opinions: these have no legal standing.

In practice most Community law-making consists of issuing directives. The use of regulations and decisions is mainly to govern or amend policies that have already been agreed. The method of issuing directives involves a series of protracted discussions and negotiations between the Commission, the EP and the Council of Ministers. Since the Maastricht Treaty this is primarily done by the co-decision procedure.

The European Court of Justice

The European Court of Justice (ECJ) is composed of 15 judges who are appointed by the member states. As the judicial institution of the Union, it ensures that Community law is interpreted and applied consistently across all member states. If EU law and national law conflict, then Community law must take precedence. The ECJ is the final court to which disputes on EU law can be brought, and national courts must accept and implement the judgements of the Court. In some respects the ECJ is the most supranational institution in the EU as it is not accountable to any national government, and its decisions are influential in the development of national law. The decisions of the ECJ are also important in the operation of Competition Policy as the Court has established many important principles by its judgements in particular cases. Furthermore, decisions of the ECJ are important in establishing principles in the area of employment law and equal opportunities.

The European Central Bank

The Maastricht Treaty called for the creation of two further institutions – the European Monetary Institute (EMI) and the European Central Bank. The EMI, which began operation in 1994, developed the procedures for strengthening cooperation between the central banks of the member states and monitoring the convergence of the economic and monetary conditions that were necessary to achieve monetary union. Monetary Union has brought with it a new currency, the euro, and a new central bank, the European Central Bank (ECB), which replaced the EMI in 1998. The ECB and the central banks of the countries that have adopted the euro are part of a new entity known as the 'Eurosystem'. As certain member states of the European Union have not yet adopted the euro, it is important to make a distinction between the Eurosystem of 12 countries and the European System of Central Banks (ESCB), which comprises 15 countries. The ECB is the pivot of the Eurosystem; it ensures that the tasks delegated to it are performed either by itself or by the participating national central banks. The Executive Board of the ECB comprises the President, Vice-President and four other members, all appointed by the common accord of the heads of state or government of the member states in the eurozone. The ECB frames and implements European monetary policy, conducts foreign exchange operations and ensures the smooth operation of payment systems.

The technical details of monetary and exchange rate policy *are* determined by the ECB and will be independent of national governments and other EU institutions. The prime objective of the ECB, according to the Maastricht Treaty, is the pursuit of price stability.

Other institutions

There are four other major institutions in the Community: the Economic and Social Committee, the European Investment Bank, the Court of Auditors and the Committee of the Regions.

The Economic and Social Committee is a forum for interest groups and sectoral interest (e.g. farmers, trade unionists and representatives of employers) to express opinions on proposed legislation. Through its opinions, the Committee contributes to the formulation and implementation of the European Union's policies. However, it does not have any powers other than being able to express its views on proposed legislation.

The European Investment Bank provides loans to finance capital projects that help to develop the process of European integration and which aid in achieving the aims of the EU.

The Court of Auditors ensures that all the Union's revenue has been received and its expenditure incurred in a lawful and regular manner and that financial management of the EU budget has been sound. As these activities are often carried out by national governments, this gives it rights to investigate the practices of the governments of member states. One of its key functions in the institutional system is to assist the budgetary authority (the European Parliament and the Council) by presenting them with an annual report covering the previous financial year. The Court of Auditors is generally concerned with the proper use of funds and countering fraud, rather than value-for-money evaluations. In 1999, following the Treaty of Amsterdam, its auditing and investigation powers were extended so as to combat fraud against the Community budget more effectively.

A Committee of the Regions, composed of representatives from regional and local authorities, was established in 1994 in accordance with Article 198a of the Maastricht Treaty. This Committee is appointed by the Council on the recommendations of the national governments of the member states. It is at the discretion of the Council and Commission whether it is consulted on matters that affect the regions. In this respect the Committee would appear to have less power than the Economic and Social Committee. It may, however, issue an Opinion on its own initiative.

The institutional structure of the EU is complex, with many different bodies responsible for decision-making and for the implementation, monitoring and policing of Community laws. Most of the members of these institutions are appointed by national governments. Furthermore, in the case of directives, the governments of the member states must transpose the objectives specified in the directives into national law. The differences in national institutional structures and cultures further complicate the influence that national governments and cultures have on Community laws (see Box I.3).

Box I.3 Interrelationships between Community laws and national systems

Directives must be transposed into national laws and regulations by national governments. Moreover, national governments and courts are responsible for the monitoring and enforcing of these national laws and regulations to ensure that directives are properly implemented. National institutional frameworks and cultural characteristics influence the way in which directives affect companies, organisations and individuals. For example, some member states have a strong commitment to equal opportunities and have special agencies within their institutional frameworks that seek to promote equal opportunities; other member states have less emphasis on such matters. The Commission has the responsibility to assess if directives have been properly implemented and cases can be referred to the ECJ, which makes final judgements on matters related to Community law. These rather complicated procedures mean that a range of bodies affect the manner in which Community laws affect companies, organisations and individuals in the member states. Given the differences in national institutional frameworks and cultural characteristics, it is possible that directives do not have equal effect across the member states. The figure below provides a schematic outline of these factors.

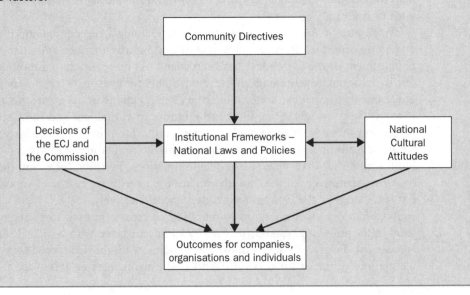

The main challenges facing the European Union

A number of major political issues face the EU and underlie the debate that took place at the IGC to discuss the future Constitutional Treaty, which would determine the character of the Union for many decades to come. Although the Constitutional Treaty has been driven by the need to accommodate the accession of ten new members in 2004 it will also embody important institutional changes that attempt to address a number of recurring difficulties and challenges that have emerged since the inception of the Community. These challenges include the pace of future progress towards political union, the division of responsibility between national governments and the Community (i.e. subsidiarity) and the powers of the European Parliament relative to those of the Council of Ministers. But first we will examine the most pressing economic challenge facing the Community, the persistence of relatively high levels of unemployment.

Unemployment

Throughout the 1990s unemployment had clearly been a more serious problem for the EU than for the USA and Japan. Both the Americans and the Japanese seemed better able to deal with the problems of unemployment that had emerged in the developed economies. The USA was able to generate more jobs from growth than were the Europeans, while the Japanese seemed to be more able to retain employment levels in the face of pressures on jobs resulting from recession and structural change. However, in the late 1990s unemployment rose in Japan, although the unemployment rate did not reach the levels experienced in the EU.

Concern over unemployment led to a reappraisal of policies to counter unemployment. At the Edinburgh meeting of the European Council in 1992, an initiative was put forward to coordinate macroeconomic policies to help boost non-inflationary growth in the EU. The prime objective of this initiative was to lower unemployment. However, the initiative envisaged only a small boost to the economy of the EU and was largely based on an aggregation of existing public expenditure plans by the member states.

The debate on the appropriateness of using the Social Chapter of the Maastricht Treaty to improve working conditions was also brought into question. The UK government consistently argued that to use EU legislation to improve working conditions would result in higher non-wage costs (and possible wage costs) of hiring labour and that this would inevitably lead to higher unemployment. The implications of increasing the non-wage costs (and/or wage costs) of hiring labour are that either such increases are compensated for by higher productivity or EU-based producers become less competitive. In the latter case the EU would have to protect its industries and/or seek to use depreciation of the currencies of the member states (relative to its main trading partners) in order to defend the competitive position of EU-based companies. Outcomes such as these are not attractive because of the problems that would be caused to trading relations, in particular with the USA, Japan and the NICs. Such actions could also harm the allocation of resources within the EU by encouraging production and consumption from high-cost European sources when lower-cost supplies are available from outside the EU. The long-term position of the EU could also be harmed by such policies because they could encourage European producers to maintain production in areas where they do not have comparative advantage.

In 1993 the Commission published a White Paper on Growth, Competitiveness and Employment (European Commission, 1993). The White Paper set a target of 15 million new jobs in the EU by the year 2000. To achieve this objective the member states were encouraged to pursue policies that would deliver non-inflationary growth, create more jobs from growth and improve the global competitiveness of EU-based companies.

In order to ensure that the growth is non-inflationary, the White Paper argued that the member states should not expand their public sector deficits; the Commission maintained rather that it is important for macroeconomic stability that the current high levels of these deficits should be reduced. This objective was also connected to the plan for the convergence of the economies of the member states in preparation for monetary union. The White Paper therefore did not favour Keynesian type aggregate demand management measures to boost growth rates in order to reduce unemployment.

To encourage the creation of more jobs from growth, the White Paper recommended that the structural problems that have led to unemployment should be addressed. Thus the Commission advocated encouragement of new fast-growing industries such as information technology, telecommunications services and equipment, and biotechnology. This would seem to indicate an increased role for Industrial Policy in the EU.

The problems caused by high non-wage costs were also considered to be a significant obstacle to the creation of jobs, and the White Paper recommended that labour market regulations should be compatible with labour market flexibility. Nevertheless, the Commission made it clear that it did not wish to see a deterioration in working conditions and in the rights of employees. In particular, the White Paper recommended that steps should be taken to avoid the creation of large numbers of low-paid and low-skilled jobs. However, the White Paper advocated that part-time working should be encouraged and that work-sharing might also contribute to the solution of finding ways to lower the unemployment rate. The Commission also recommended the use of government help to lower the costs to companies of hiring the long-term unemployed and young people (these groups constitute the majority of the unemployed in most member states).

The White Paper regarded the creation and maintenance of an open economy for the EU as a crucial requirement for promoting an efficient and dynamic economy. The use of protectionist policies was therefore not advocated as a solution to the high levels of unemployment in Europe. The Commission also maintained that large fluctuations in exchange rates were not conducive to stable and growing world trade. Thus, the White Paper did not advocate the use of depreciation of currencies as a viable solution to the unemployment problem. However, it recommended that the EU adopt a more robust commercial defence in WTO procedures.

The White Paper provided a clear statement that unemployment was the major economic problem facing the EU. On the other hand, it did not provide any significantly new proposals as to how to solve this problem.

For those who favour an EU based on an open trading system with the rest of the world, these proposals were welcome. However, some of the recommendations of the White Paper were less welcome, for example the indications of a need for a more interventionist Industrial Policy and the possibility of a stronger use of the Common Commercial Policy to protect EU industries that faced 'unfair competition'. The indications that the Commission was still committed to using the Social Chapter to improve working conditions by use of laws that may increase the non-wage costs of hiring labour were also not welcomed by free-traders. The free-traders regard the creation of an open and competitive economy as the best method to boost productivity and thereby to tackle the unemployment problem. According to this view, the role of the EU in helping to find solutions to the problem of unemployment is mainly associated with the creation of an effective SEM and the development of an open economy with the rest of the world. Employment should also be generated by the adoption of monetary union with the elimination of the barriers to free trade (within the EU) caused by exchange rate fluctuations and the transaction costs that result from the existence of different currencies. In the long run it is also possible that monetary union could lead to further benefits arising from higher rates of non-inflationary growth and from a more efficient allocation of capital.

The EU faces considerable difficulties in reconciling the opposing views as to the best methods of reducing unemployment in Europe. The free-traders advocate liberalisation of markets, in particular labour markets, and an opening up of Community markets to foreign trade and investments. The free-traders are also reluctant to commit significant funds to Industrial Policy initiatives that seek to identify new and expanding industries; on the whole they would favour the use of market forces to promote the creation of new jobs. The interventionists are keen to promote active government involvement in the encouragement of new industries and to use the law to improve living and working conditions. Indeed, the debate is not unlike the debates that take place within any modern advanced economy between right-wing (or pro-market forces) groups and left-wing (or interventionist) groups.

At a number of meetings between 1993 and 1995 (Edinburgh, Essen and Madrid) the European Council constructed a strategy to combat unemployment. The main elements of the strategy were:

- to complete the Single European Market (SEM) and promote a competitive and dynamic economic environment;
- to encourage small and medium enterprises (SMEs) to develop and adopt new technologies;
- to establish EMU to enhance the ability of the economy to grow and thereby create jobs;
- to take action to reduce the non-wage costs of employing labour;
- to improve education and training to improve the skills of the unemployed;
- to target specific groups to help them to obtain work;
- to concentrate the structural funds on job-creating activities and investments.

The strategy proposed very few concrete plans for reducing unemployment that were not associated with the existing programmes of the EU, for example completing the SEM and EMU. The tone of the strategy was in line with the view that competitive and flexible markets were important for job creation. This reflected a move away from the development of interventionist legislation in the areas of employment and working conditions. The SEA and the Social Chapter led to a large number of new laws in this area in the early and mid 1990s. However, this type of approach appears to have fallen out of favour and there was a greater focus on avoiding imposing undue costs on employers. In areas where positive policies were advocated, for example education and training and targeting particular groups of the unemployed, the EU had very little influence on the development of policies that may help to reduce unemployment. The strategy adopted an approach that saw the role of government as being primarily to create a low inflation and stable macroeconomic environment, together with the fostering of a climate that permitted companies to improve productivity. The latter requirement was seen as demanding the need for flexible labour markets and laws and policies that did not burden companies unnecessarily.

The Amsterdam Treaty required the Council to monitor employment conditions in the member states and, in the light of the information gathered on employment, to make proposals that would help to reduce unemployment. The Treaty did not envisage that large-scale legislation or new EU policies would be generated by this procedure, rather that information on what is happening in the member states would be shared to help national governments to craft their own responses to their unemployment problems (Duff, 1997).

At the Luxemburg summit discussions in 1997 employment issues were still a central theme, and at the European Council of Lisbon (2000) a new emphasis was given to a coherent approach towards economic development, social cohesion and employment, giving social issues a European dimension never before acknowledged. Member states committed themselves to the principal social policy objectives of:

- Achieving full employment
- Improving the quality of work and productivity
- Making labour markets more accessible
- Placing greater emphasis upon education and training
- Increasing employment in services
- Promoting equal opportunities and guaranteeing efficient social policies.

To achieve these objectives the EU has adopted Broad Economic Policy Guidelines (BEPG), which make both general and country-specific recommendations. They identify the key economic policy areas which will contribute to economic stability and structural reforms. From 2003 the BEPGs have been published simultaneously with the employment guidelines and recommendations.

These BEPGs complement the Stability and Growth Pact (SGP), to which members of the eurozone are required to subscribe. The SGP is intended to provide the national fiscal discipline necessary to underpin EMU. It involves the submission of member states' stability and convergence programmes to the Council for collective assessment and a commitment to the medium-term objective of balanced government budgets, while allowing some flexibility during the economic cycles as long as the deficit does not exceed 3 per cent of GDP. Should any country breach this limit there is a formal 'excessive deficit procedure'. If the deficit is a result of 'exceptional circumstances' beyond the control of the member state or a result of a severe economic recession (defined as a 2 per cent fall in annual GDP) then no further action will be taken. Otherwise the member state has four months to take correct-ive action or face the possibility of sanctions being imposed by the Council. Such sanctions take the form of non-interest bearing deposits with the Commission equal to 0.2 per cent of GDP plus an element linked to the size of the deficit up to a total maximum of 0.5 per cent of GDP. If after two years the excessive deficit has not been corrected then the deposit becomes a permanent fine distributed to the other member states. This quite draconian sanction is, however, subject to a Council decision and the mechanism failed its first real test in 2003, when both Germany and France were exceeding the deficit limit. The decision not to impose any sanctions has raised serious questions as to the credibility of the SGP.

The principle of subsidiarity

The inclusion of the concept of subsidiarity in the Maastricht Treaty was an attempt by the EU to tackle the problems of assigning governmental competencies within the Community. Article 3b of the Maastricht Treaty states:

> The Community shall take action, in accordance with the principle of subsidiarity, only if and in so far as the objectives of the proposed action cannot be sufficiently achieved by the Member States and can therefore, by reason of the scale or effects of the proposed action, be better achieved by the Community.

The concept of subsidiarity is therefore concerned with discovering the appropriate tier structure of government. The key is to give to that level of government those functions that would be best performed at that level. The Padoa–Schioppa report (1987) recommended that the EU should be governed at the local, regional, national or Community level depending on which tier of government could carry out the task most efficiently. This principle is analogous to the recommendations that arise from fiscal federalism (Oates, 1972).

The principle of subsidiarity requires that the EU undertake only those policies that it would be most efficient in administering. The main issue, if this principle is to be related to efficiency considerations, is to identify those national policies that have significant spill-over effects into other countries.

If the market fails to deliver an optimal allocation of resources, because of externalities or monopoly power, there is a clear case for government action to seek to improve the allocation of resources. Therefore, a case can be made for government policies in areas such as R&D expenditures, education and training, environmental standards and public health. The case for such intervention depends on the existence of the external effects of these activities (i.e. the benefits and/or costs of these activities affect other agents as well as the producers and/or con-sumers of such activities). Similarly, the case for government action to create and maintain a competitive environment is a clear requirement for an efficient alloca-tion of resources in a market-based economy.

However, the existence of a rationale for government policies within a country does not necessarily mean that there are good reasons for supranational policies in these areas. Only if national policies have significant spill-overs to other countries do sound reasons exist for supranational policies in these areas. This can be analysed by means of a pay-off matrix (see Box I.4).

Taking account of the policy decision of other countries makes sense only if countries are interdependent with respect to the outcomes of policy actions, i.e. they must experience spill-overs. However, the existence of such spill-overs does not mean that common policies are sensible. In some cases coordination of policies to take account of spill-over effects is all that is required. Furthermore, the existence of spill-overs is not a sufficient reason for coordination. If the costs of

---

Box I.4 Subsidiarity and R&D expenditures

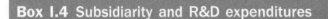

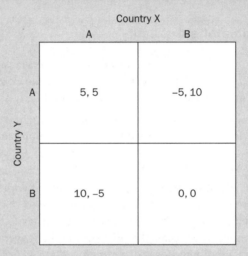

The matrix illustrates the pay-off for two countries from the various options that are available for a particular policy, for example help with R&D expenditures.

In case A the country provides help to its companies to cover the external benefits of R&D payments, while in case B the country does not provide help in the R&D area. If both countries adopt policy A, they reap benefits of pay-offs of 5 each, shown by the outcome in the top left-hand corner of the matrix. If they both adopt policy B, they end up at the bottom right-hand corner with pay-offs of zero. However, if country X adopts policy A and country Y opts for policy B, the pay-offs will be 10 for country Y and –5 for country X, shown in the bottom left-hand corner. In this situation country X meets the cost of helping with R&D expenditures, while country Y benefits from these expenditures without incurring any expenditures. In other words, country Y benefits from the spill-over effects of the R&D policy of country X. The outcomes of country X adopting B and country Y choosing A are shown in the top right-hand corner of the matrix. In this situation the outcome for each country depends on the choices made by the other country. The two countries are interdependent because of the spill-overs that arise from their policies. If both countries are averse to risk with regard to the costs of policy mistakes, they will both choose policy B (leading to the outcome illustrated in the bottom right-hand corner). This outcome is preferable to policy A because it avoids the risk of a negative outcome. However, if the countries coordinate their policies, to ensure that both countries adopt policy A, they reap the pay-offs shown in the top left-hand corner of the matrix. This is a more desirable outcome than the non-cooperative outcome shown in the bottom right-hand corner of the matrix.

coordination are greater than the benefits of taking into account spill-over effects, it is not efficient to coordinate policies. Thus in the example in Box I.4, if the costs of reaching agreement on coordination exceeded 5, the countries would be better off not seeking to reach agreement to coordinate policies. In these circumstances it would be better to find methods of internalising the spill-over effects. This could be achieved by taking action to prevent spill-over from occurring, i.e. retaining all the benefits of the policy within the country. If this proves too costly to achieve, the countries could form one government agency to deal with the policy that is creating the spill-over effects, i.e. adopt a common policy. This analysis suggests that good reasons for common policies in the EU may arise when the costs of reaching coordinated agreements, or preventing spill-overs, are high. In other areas it may be better to seek to coordinate policies and, where there are no (or insignificant) spill-overs, countries should adopt policies independently from other countries.

However, the allocation of government competencies using such criteria requires considerable knowledge (and agreement among affected parties) about the extent and size of spill-overs and about the cost of coordinated or common policy solutions. And the EU is not necessarily the appropriate agency to be used for coordinated or common policies. In cases where spill-overs extend beyond the frontiers of the EU, or where the spill-overs affect only parts of the EU, it may be more efficient to have other governmental agencies to determine policies. In these circumstances an agency appointed to find the most efficient solution may be useful. The EU could provide the institutional framework to determine such solutions for the member states, whether there should be coordinated policies, common policies for all the Community, common policies that are operative for part of the Community or policies (coordinated or common) that extend beyond its frontiers.

In such a scenario the EU would assess the costs and benefits of assigning governmental competencies and would seek to find the best solution. However, this would require a federal-type constitution for the EU with clear rules on the powers of the federal government relative to those of the member states. This analysis suggests that the principle of subsidiarity can work efficiently only if the EU develops a federal system of government with a constitution backed by an independent court. In other words, the EU would need to become a federal state not dissimilar to the USA or Germany. Attempts to implement the subsidiarity principle in the present governmental system of the EU are likely (at best) to lead to a good deal of confusion or (at worst) to an inefficient and problematical system for determining governmental competencies.

Democratic deficit

There have been concerns about the 'democratic deficit' in the EU. Only the EP is directly elected and therefore subject to the choice of citizens of the Community. However, the Council of Ministers and the Commission take decisions that impinge on many of the activities of the citizens of the Community. Furthermore, the establishment of monetary union has led to the creation of another powerful Community institution – the ECB. The ECB could develop into the most important economic agency in the EU, but its accountability to the citizens of the Community is very indirect. These issues have led to pressures to expand the powers of the EP, to reduce the size of the Commission and to develop governmental structures that would be more accountable. The member states of the EU were committed by the Maastricht Treaty to examining these issues. This led to the establishment of an IGC to consider plans to reform the institutional structures of the EU. The IGC led to the negotiations on the Amsterdam Treaty. However, the member states could only agree on a limited number of changes to the institutional structures, leaving these issues to be resolved at the 2003/4 IGC negotiating the Constitutional Treaty.

The voting procedures of the Council of Ministers has also caused some problems. The Council could take decisions by unanimity, simple majority vote or qualified majority vote (QMV). The QMV system allowed the smaller member states, in principle, to exercise some power in the decision-making systems of the EU. The four large member states could not, in cases that require QMV, obtain a winning coalition only among themselves, that is, they needed the support of some of the smaller member states in order to secure a majority. Furthermore, a coalition of most of the smaller member states could result in a blocking vote, i.e. a voting bloc that is sufficiently large to prevent the fulfillment of the criteria for QMV – 62 votes. A blocking coalition could also be constructed by an alliance between some of the larger member states and a group of smaller states. This ability to use blocking coalitions gave the smaller member states leverage in the decision-making frameworks of the EU. This leverage arose from the process of 'log-rolling'. 'Log-rolling' involves bargaining between the parties to use strategic voting to further their objectives (Buchanan, 1978). Thus a group of smaller member states could agree to vote with some of the larger member states on issues in which they have no particular interest, in return for the support of the larger member states on issues in which they do have a strong interest. Such log-rolling behaviour has both advantages and disadvantages. It allows the smaller member states to exercise some degree of power in the EU and, therefore, helps to overcome some of the problems that may arise from the power of the larger member states. However, log-rolling can allow rejection of proposals that have net benefits for the EU. Outcomes such as this can arise when the benefits of implementing proposals are skewed towards certain member states, but these member states cannot secure a winning coalition because of strategic voting by disinterested parties who are engaged in log-rolling exercises (Buchanan et al., 1990).

The extension of the areas of decision-making that are subject to qualified majority voting increased the problems that the EU experienced with the voting procedures of the Council and the accession of a large number of smaller member states in 2004 expanded the opportunities for log-rolling behaviour in the EU.

Political union

The EU has had a long-standing commitment to European Political Cooperation (EPC). This was restricted to a series of meetings of member states' foreign ministers to discuss and, where possible, to reach common positions on issues relating to foreign relations and security matters. This was necessary in areas connected with trade as the EU has sole competence in most areas of the external economic relations of the member states. There have also been attempts to arrive at common positions on matters concerned with the prevention of terrorism, relations with the former Soviet Union and Eastern Europe, and on the security of Europe in the light of the ending of the Cold War.

The Community sought to reach a common position on the two Gulf Wars and to act collectively in response to the civil war in the former Yugoslavia. These attempts to act collectively were not successful. During these crises the Community could do little more than reflect the differences in the interests of the member states. Attempts by the Community to act in the civil war in the former Yugoslavia were hampered by the reluctance to become involved militarily by providing a peace-keeping force and by the failure of member states to reach agreement on anything other than a minimum intervention by imposing trade embargoes and providing the means for the various parties to negotiate cease-fires with a view to arranging a lasting peace. The disappointment caused by this failure to reach effective common positions resulted in increased calls for a radical restructuring of the political integration programme of the EU.

The SEA contained rather vague statements on the need for closer cooperation on foreign and security matters. There was considerable pressure to move beyond such statements towards a clearer policy on political union. The Maastricht Treaty envisaged a Community with a single currency and with a commitment to establishing a stronger political union. In particular, the member states agreed to use inter-governmental procedures based on general guidelines from the European Council, with the Council of Ministers taking policy decisions. Joint actions (or positions) may be adopted by unanimous decision of the Council of Ministers, and in some cases qualified majority voting could be used. These procedures cover two of the three 'pillars' of the EU (the other 'pillar' being the economic arrangements of the EC). The two new 'pillars' were foreign and security issues; and justice, home affairs and immigration. The Amsterdam Treaty made some minor modifications to the three-pillar system; in particular asylum and immigration matters were transferred from the third pillar to the EC pillar, and QMV can be used in some areas of foreign policy (Duff, 1997).

The political and institutional nature of the Community is becoming more supranational. This prospect has caused alarm among some politicians and decision-makers, particularly in Denmark, Sweden and the UK. The possible emergence of what would be some sort of federal Europe brings with it the prospect of national governments being little more than regional assemblies, with their legislative programmes constrained by the growing integration of markets that will lead to common or harmonised policies in many areas. The establishment of a common monetary policy in the eurozone has also constrained the taxation and expenditure plans of national governments through their commitments to the Stability and Growth Pact. If many aspects of foreign policy and security, and justice and home affairs, were determined by QMV at the Council of Ministers, national governments would indeed begin to resemble regional or local government.

In spite of such reservations there are strong forces at work to enhance the political integration of the EU. In international trade matters the Community is already more important than the member states in negotiations with other countries and with the WTO. The establishment of monetary union also requires a Community voice in organisations such as the IMF and the G8 group of countries. Many issues of foreign policy and security matters are related to international trade flows. Therefore, growing economic integration of the EU will increasingly require a measure of consistency by the member states in these areas.

The loss of sovereignty (the ability of a state to determine its own policies independently of other governments) is already undermined by the dominance of the USA in matters related to global political and security issues. The major question is whether the Community is in a position to achieve a degree of political integration sufficient to allow a more independent line to be pursued. This would perhaps require a common and effective European foreign policy and security arrangements, and a European defence force. In these circumstances Europeans could exercise a significant counterbalancing force if US policies were considered to be against European interests. Such an outcome would involve a radical revision of the foreign and security policies of the member states, and may not be feasible unless all the major member states come to regard this as a viable and desirable goal. The recent Iraq conflict, with the differing views of 'old' and 'new' Europe, clearly demonstrates the difficulties of arriving at such a consensus.

In political matters more directly related to the economic integration programme the need for some change to the policies and political arrangements of the Community is widely accepted. The granting of new powers for the EU to act in the social area may be necessary to overcome fears that the more competitive conditions induced by the SEM will result in a downward spiral in social and working conditions. There are also growing pressures to grant new competencies to Community institutions in industrial and research and development policies to help in the restructuring of the economy of the EU induced by the creation of the SEM and EMU.

The new European Constitution

In order to prepare for the accession of ten new member states and to consolidate the existing Treaties, a European Convention was proposed at the Laeken European Council in December 2001 to prepare a draft Constitutional Treaty for submission to an Inter-Governmental Conference (ICG). The Convention was charged with examining four main issues – division of competencies, institutional reform, simplification of the treaties and democratisation. The Convention consisted of representatives of the governments and parliaments of the EU member states and the candidate countries, members of the European Parliament and representatives of the European Commission. The Convention for the Future of Europe began its work in February 2002 and submitted its draft Constitutional Treaty in July 2003, achieving a broad consensus.

The draft Constitutional Treaty was presented in four parts. Part One sets out the objectives, powers and institutions of the Union. Part Two incorporates the existing Charter of Fundamental Rights, which was agreed in Nice in 2000.

However, its specific inclusion should give greater legal weight to its provisions. Part Three incorporates the provisions of the existing Treaties, defining the areas of activity and the requirements for financial management. Part Four outlines the procedures for implementing and amending the Treaty.

In its preamble the draft Constitutional Treaty avoids references to 'ever closer union' and use of the term 'federal'. More significantly it defines the principles of 'conferral, subsidiarity and proportionality'. Member states confer powers on the EU and not the other way round, while the EU will only act collectively where the objectives cannot be achieved by the member states acting individually ('subsidiarity') and only to the minimum extent essential ('proportionality'). The separate 'legal personality' of the Union is asserted and its instruments for action are classified under three headings: European Laws (previously Regulations), European Framework Laws (previously Directives) and the non-legislative European Regulations (previously Opinions, Recommendations and Decisions).

Changes are proposed in various aspects of the organisation of all the institutions of the Community. With the European Council of heads of government, the Presidency will no longer rotate every six months: instead a President will be elected, by QMV, for a period of two and half years. This change is intended to give greater continuity and coherence to policy making. For the individual Councils of Ministers, covering the different areas of EU policy, the President (Chairperson) will serve annually by rotation; except in the case of Foreign Affairs, where the new EU Foreign Minister will preside. To ensure that there is no decision-making paralysis the national veto would be abolished in twenty additional areas. It would remain, however, for defence, foreign policy, taxation and social security matters, and unanimity would still be required for an area of responsibility to move to QMV. From 2009 the current system of QMV, weighted by economic importance, would be replaced by one based upon population. Thus for legislation to be accepted 60 per cent of the EU's population, as represented by their governments, would need to support it. Where action is blocked by a national veto it would still be possible for the some EU member states to pursue 'enhanced cooperation', provided at least one-third of member states supported this action.

To provide similar focus for the EU's external policy the creation of an EU 'Foreign Minister', with a supporting European External Action Service, is also proposed. Again elected by the Council under QMV, the Foreign Minister will combine the roles of the External Relations Commissioner and the High Representative covering the EU's Common Foreign and Security Policy (CFSP). For the former he will be a Vice-President of the European Commission, while for the CFSP, which remains inter-governmental, he will be directly responsible to member states.

In terms of the Commission, in order to accommodate the increase in the number of member states, it was agreed at Nice that each will have one Commissioner until 2009. After that date the Convention proposes that a two-tier College of Commission would be created, with the President, Foreign Minister and thirteen other 'European Commissioners' having full voting rights, while the remaining ten 'Commissioners' would assist in drafting and implementation. All twenty-five member states would be treated equally, holding the senior Commissioners every ten out of fifteen years. The Commission President would be nominated by the Council of Ministers, again under QMV, having taken account of the results of the European elections. The candidate will have to be approved by the European Parliament. He in turn would select his Commissioners from three nominations each provided by the member states. Again, this list will be approved by the European Parliament.

The Parliament itself would see a significant extension of its powers. Currently it is involved in the approval of legislation in 34 policy areas; under the new proposals this would increase to 70, including issues such as regional and social policy. Its control over the budget would also increase and would include, for the first time, agriculture expenditure. To accommodate the accession of the new member states the composition of the Parliament will change, with a reduction in the number of seats for all existing members, except for Germany and Luxembourg. After the 2005 elections Parliament will have 732 seats, a significant increase from the present 626.

For the first time a role is also given to the national parliaments. The Commission would be required to submit its proposals to them, outlining their implications and cost. If a national parliament is concerned it may ask the Commission to reconsider. If this occurred with one-third of the parliaments it must be reviewed, although it could be re-tabled. National parliaments would still have recourse to the European Court of Justice if their objections remained.

In addition the draft proposes the abolition of the 'third pillar' with police and judicial issues brought within the EU's normal structures. This would allow the extension of EU legislation to cover cross-border and serious crime (e.g. terrorism), setting the penalties, and offer the possibility of creating an EU justice department, with its own Public Prosecutor.

The IGC to discuss the Convention's proposals began in October 2003 but failed to reach any agreement. No further progress is expected until 2005. Although the draft Constitution represented a high degree of consensus among the Convention members a number of issues were of crucial importance to different member states. A number of states, including the UK, the Netherlands and Denmark, had made it clear that they would resist any extension of QMV to taxation matters, reflecting a resistance to moves towards further tax harmonisation. The UK also opposed the harmonisation of the criminal law and the appointment of a European Public Prosecutor, preferring the mutual recognition of judgements, and sought assurances that the Charter of Fundamental Rights did not compromise existing national law. Further the UK also objected to a mechanism for the future extension of QMV, even though this required unanimity, as this was seen as making constitutional reform a continuous process. Germany objected to the extension of the Commission's role in energy policy while France, by contrast, sought additional powers for the eurozone members. However, it was the rejection of the proposed changes in weighting of votes for QMV by Spain and Poland that proved the final sticking point. Poland and Spain had been awarded 27 votes at the Nice summit in 2000, only two less than France, Italy, Germany and the UK. Under the proposed double majority rule – 50 per cent of countries and 60 per cent of the EU's population – their influence in the European Council would have been reduced.

Conclusion

The EU has achieved a remarkable degree of integration among its member states in the post-war period. It has extended its membership to include the largest economies in Europe and has become one of the most important economic blocs in the world. In the mid to late 1980s it experienced a surge in implementing its integration programmes, particularly with the SEM programme and the moves towards monetary union. However, in the 1990s the EU has experienced a series of problems that cast doubt on its future development. The end of the Cold War and the collapse of communism did not provide an easy opportunity for the EU to expand its membership, while it was also deepening its integration programmes. The problems encountered in ratifying the Maastricht Treaty illustrated the difficulties of convincing the EU citizens that further integration was in their interests. The crises in EMS and the return to floating exchange rates by some member states were also a disappointment for those who looked to a deepening of the integration programmes of the EU.

Despite these problems the EU succeeded in expanding its membership to include 15 member states, set in motion the process of admitting most of the CEECs into full membership and established the eurozone. However, high levels of unemployment continue to persist in many member states and the constraints of the Stability and Growth Pact continue to present problems.

Politically, the failure of the IGC to agree a new Constitutional Treaty has raised the spectre of policy paralysis and revived the question of a 'two-speed', or perhaps a 'multi-speed' Europe, This approach, particularly favoured by France and Germany, has already been followed in the adoption of the euro and the Schengen system of a common external border. The failure of the IGC has also left a legacy of hostility between Germany and Poland, with the implicit threat by Germany, the EU's largest net contributor, of reductions in Poland's financial receipts under the next EU budget settlement from 2007. Indeed, reaching agreement on the budget is likely to be the next major challenge for the EU. Already France, Germany, Austria, the Netherlands, Sweden and the UK have indicated that they expect the EU budget to be limited to 1 per cent of the Community's GNP, but CAP reform remains problematic and the current beneficiaries of Structural Funds will have to accept their diversion to the new members from Central and Eastern Europe.

Nonetheless, the EU remains at the heart of the process of constructing economic and political frameworks in Europe. In world terms the EU plays a major part in global economic arrangements and it may increase its role on the political stage in the coming decades.

References

Buchanan J (1978) *The Economics of Politics*, Institute of Economic Affairs, London.

Buchanan J, Pöhl K, Curzon-Price V and Vibert F (1990) *Europe's Constitutional Future*, Institute of Economic Affairs, London.

Duff A (1997) *The Treaty of Amsterdam*, Sweet & Maxwell/Federal Trust, London.

Duff A, Pinder J and Pryce R (1994) *Maastricht and Beyond: Building the EU*, Routledge, London.

European Commission (1989) *Report on Economic and Monetary Union in the European Community*, Office for Official Publications of the European Communities, Luxembourg.

European Commission (1990) *European Unification: The Origins and Growth of the European Community*, Office for Official Publications of the European Communities, Luxembourg.

European Commission (1992) *From the Single Act to Maastricht and Beyond: The Means to Match our Ambitions*, COM(92)2000, Brussels.

European Commission (1993) *White Paper on Growth, Competitiveness and Employment*, COM(93)700 Final, Brussels.

European Commission (1997) *Agenda 2000: For a Stronger and Wider Union*, Communication from the Commission to the Council and the EP, COM(97)2000, Brussels.

Henning C, Hochreiter E and Hufbauer C (1994) *Reviving the European Union*, Institute for International Economics, Washington DC.

Nugent N (2003) *The Government and Politics of the European Community*, Palgrave, Basingstoke.

Oates W E (1972) *Fiscal Federalism*, Harcourt Brace, New York.

Padoa–Schioppa T (1987) *Efficiency, Equity and Stability*, Cambridge University Press, Cambridge.

Swann D (1998) *The Economics of the Common Market*, Penguin, London.

Further reading

Baimbridge M (2003) *Economic and Monetary Union in Europe*, Edward Elgar, Cheltenham.

De Grauwe P (2003) *Economics of Monetary Union*, Oxford University Press, Oxford.

Hansen J D (2001) *European Integration: An Economic Perspective*, Oxford University Press, Oxford.

Ingham I and Ingham M (2003) *EU Expansion to the East*, Edward Elgar, Cheltenham

Richardson J (2001) *European Union: Power and Policy-making*, Routledge, London

Many journals have relevant articles on issues related to European Economic Integration, e.g.

European Business Journal
European Economy
Economic Policy: A European Forum
Journal of Common Market Studies
Journal of European Integration
Journal of European Public Policy

For the most recent developments on the institutional structures, policies and other EU matters see the Europa website: **www.europa.eu.int**

Good websites on issues connected to EMU are available at **www.euro.co.uk** and **www.ecu-activities.be**

Part 1

THE FOUNDATIONS OF THE
EUROPEAN UNION

Chapter 1

Market integration in the European Union

Frank McDonald

Introduction

The Treaty of Rome (1957) commits the member states to creating a Customs Union (CU) and a Common Market (CM). This requires free movement of goods, services, capital and labour to exist among the member states. To achieve this outcome, legal barriers that prohibit or restrict free trade between the members of the Community must be removed. Legal and governmental systems may also need to be modified to allow free movement to exist. Therefore, regional economic integration requires negative policies (the removal of barriers to trade) and it may also need some positive policies (the creation of legal and governmental systems that ensure that effective free movement is possible).

Tariffs, quotas and non-tariff barriers (NTBs) must be removed to establish free movement. However, commercial, competition, environmental and social policies and some sectoral policies (for example, agriculture and transport) may require modification to enable effective free movement to be established. To achieve the latter objective requires a deeper level of integration than simply the removal of barriers to trade. Furthermore, macroeconomic policies may distort free movement because of the effects of national monetary and fiscal policies on interest and exchange rates. Therefore, the establishment of an effective CU and CM may require a fairly high degree of economic and possibly political integration.

Defining economic integration

The foundation of the analysis of various types of regional economic integration was established by economists who investigated the early attempts by Western European countries to engineer regional economic integration (Viner, 1950; Tinbergen, 1954; Balassa, 1961). Five major types of economic integration can be identified:

1 A Free Trade Area – a group of countries where all barriers to trade in goods are removed.

2 A Customs Union – a free trade area with a common external tariff.

3 A Common Market – a CU plus free movement of capital and labour.

4 An Economic Union – a CM with harmonisation of economic and social policies to ensure effective free movement and harmonisation of macroeconomic policies to ensure trade flows are not distorted.

5 Economic and Monetary Union (EMU) – an Economic Union plus a common monetary policy.

It is possible to regard the above definitions as tracing out a path that ultimately leads to a complete economic integration – that is, EMU. The EU may be regarded as seeking to follow this path, starting with a CU and going progressively towards deeper economic integration. The EU has also developed a clear commitment to progress towards Political Union – the harmonisation or integration of political policies and institutional frameworks. Thus the EU can be viewed as moving towards ever greater economic and possibly political integration.

However, these concepts of integration do not describe a process of self-contained and inevitable steps to EMU or Political Union. A movement towards Economic or even Political Union can start early in the process of creating free movement. The Treaty of Rome established the European Court of Justice (ECJ) to clarify the meaning of Community laws, and the European Commission to pro-pose, implement, monitor and enforce laws and policies to ensure that free movement within the Community was effectively implemented and developed. These institutions have significant implications for the development of legal and governmental systems in the member states (Nugent, 2003). Furthermore, common policies for commercial relationships with third parties, for competition rules and for agriculture and transport were thought to be essential to allow effective free movement to be established. Therefore, the Community began the process of creating a CU and a CM with institutions that had significant leverage over national legal and governmental systems.

The Community was founded on the basis that some type of Economic Union and possibly Political Union was required to enable it to fulfil its objectives. The Treaty of Rome has been significantly amended to allow for an increase in the number of common policies, for example environmental, regional and social policies. Monetary integration has also become one of the central concerns of the EU. These amendments to the Treaty of Rome have often been based on arguments that they are necessary to ensure that the conditions for free movement are fully and effectively implemented.

It is not clear, however, if free movement requires the type of institutional structures with the accompanying political dynamics that were laid down in the Treaty of Rome. No other regional economic agency has approached the creation of a CU or a CM in the same manner as the European Community. Regional economic agencies such as NAFTA or Mercosur do not have elaborate institutional frameworks, and none has a court such as the ECJ. The appropriate institutional frameworks to enable the creation of a single market may be illustrated by analysing existing single markets where the conditions for effective free movement have been established.

Types of single markets

Most nation states are single markets in the sense that frameworks have been created and developed to allow effective free movement to take place. Nation states provide three main frameworks that affect the operations of markets:

- Legal frameworks create, develop and maintain the legal conditions that permit free movement to exist.
- Regulatory frameworks govern taxation, public procurement and economic and social policies.
- Macroeconomic policy frameworks seek to secure a stable economic environment.

Legal- and government-created barriers to free movement exist in some nation states that would be regarded as single markets. For example, different laws govern the production and sale of goods and services in the states of the USA (Pelkmans and Vanheukelen, 1988). As state laws on technical regulations and environmental standards vary considerably between the states, companies that wish to trade across state frontiers have to conform to the laws in the different states. Taxation systems also vary among the states of the USA. The goods and services that are subject to sales taxes and the level of these taxes differ from state to state. State income tax and taxes that relate to income from savings are also different. Federal laws in the USA are concerned with ensuring that there are no prohibitions or limitations applied to non-state suppliers simply because the companies are not based in the state. Federal laws also ensure that markets (for inter-state trade) are not distorted by anti-competitive practices by companies. However, there are no federal laws on public procurement contracts issued by state agencies. Therefore, states are free to limit their public procurement contracts to state-based companies. Furthermore, there are no federal laws that restrict the use of government aid by states who wish to subsidise the operations of companies located within their area of jurisdiction.

The EU has advocated a very different approach towards removing barriers to free movement that are thought to arise from such factors as different taxation systems, technical regulations, public procurement and state aid policies. Differences in taxation treatment on the sale of goods and services and on income from savings are considered to be a serious distortion of free movement. Consequently, many plans have been put forward to harmonise the differences in taxation on the sale of goods, services and savings. The Cassis de Dijon case (see p. 49) heralded a new approach to removing barriers associated with technical regulations by requiring member states to accept the technical regulations of other member states by using mutual recognition. Attempts have also been made to harmonise the taxation of companies (Aisbettt, 2002) and taxes on savings and financial assets. An overview of the EU's taxation policy is given in European Commission (2000a) and up-to-date information on all aspects of taxation policy can be found on **www.europa.eu.int/pol/tax**.

Laws governing public procurement and government aid are also very different in the EU compared with the USA. The Community has been involved in a long legislative process that seeks to ensure that public procurement contracts are open to Community-wide competition. In the area of state aids the EU has strong treaty-based powers to monitor state aids and the Commission can prevent state aids being used to favour nationally based companies. Full details on EU policies towards public procurement and state aids can be found on **www.europa.eu.int/comm/competition/state_aid** and **www.europa.eu.int/scadplus/leg/en/s11000.htm.**

The differences between the USA and the EU become more evident when regulatory frameworks concerned with the allocation of resources are considered. Some countries adopt an approach that tends more to the market-based approach while others are more geared towards a social market approach (Harris and McDonald, 2004).

The market-based approach is based on minimum interference by the state in the working of the market process. This approach has a strong emphasis on anti-trust policies to limit the ability of companies to acquire monopoly power and use anti-competitive practices. Efficiency considerations are regarded as a separate issue from equity or even considered to conflict with equity concerns. Therefore, the best method of attaining high living standards is seen to stem from concentrating on efficiency issues. The social market approach regards the promotion of competitive markets as important, but also links equity issues to efficiency concerns. Thus policies to promote social cohesion and to help disadvantaged groups are seen as an important function of governments to help the economy to deliver high living standards.

The USA tends to adopt a more market-based approach to regulating the market process than, for example, Germany or France. The UK could be regarded as occupying a position between that of most continental European countries and the USA. The enlargement of the EU to include 10 new members will add more diversity to the type of market-based systems that will compose the Single European Market. These examples demonstrate that the importance of the regulation of the market process relating to efficiency and equity issues varies considerably among existing single markets.

A remarkably standard condition in most single markets is that they are also economic and monetary unions. The only exceptions to this are those regional economic agencies, such as the EU, that are attempting to create single markets. Macroeconomic policies affect the operation of markets because monetary, fiscal and exchange rate policies determine the inflation and growth environment in which companies operate. All existing single markets other than the EU have common monetary and exchange rate policies. Members of the EU that have joined the European Monetary Union are subject to common monetary and exchange rate policies but those that are not members of the eurozone retain their national policies in these areas. Fiscal policies within monetary unions are normally harmonised such that the central or federal governments have a strong influence on fiscal policy. However, the federal government of the USA has no power over the taxation, expenditure and borrowing decisions of the states. In contrast, the EU has imposed control over the fiscal policies (particularly government borrowing) of those member states that have joined the European Monetary Union (see Chapter 3).

The existence of a single market does not mean that some markets within the area are not fragmented into specific geographic areas. Fragmentation of markets in single markets arises from economic and social barriers to labour mobility or consumer preferences that require different products and or marketing approaches for the various cultural groupings within the single market. Many of these cultural groupings are geographically concentrated, therefore fragmentation of markets can have a distinctive spatial character.

Transaction costs and single markets

Single markets are influenced by the transaction costs that companies incur in complying with the cultural, economic and legal conditions that prevail in the environment in which they operate. Transaction costs arise when companies organise the production, marketing and sale of goods and services. These costs include establishing contracts with suppliers, buyers, labour and other inputs necessary for the company to engage in business activities. Transaction costs also arise from the need to conform to laws and social conventions that govern economic and social interaction (Williamson, 1975). For single market areas three main factors influence the type and significance of the transaction costs that companies face:

1 The characteristics of legal and regulatory frameworks.

2 Macroeconomic policy frameworks.

3 The extent of the fragmentation markets within the single market area.

Fulfilling legal and regulatory conditions can impose transaction costs on companies because they must alter products or marketing policies to conform to different regulations in the states that compose the single market area. Transaction costs may also arise from the obligations to obey the requirements of economic and social policies, for example legislation that affects employment rights. Macroeconomic policies can lead to transactions costs if the single market area does not have a single currency. In such single markets companies will be faced with exchange rate risk and currency conversion costs. Moreover, in single markets where macroeconomic policies are not harmonised, costs may arise because inflation and growth rates may vary considerably between the members of the single market area, thereby requiring companies to alter their pricing and sales policies in different parts of that area. Fragmented markets impose costs by requiring companies to adjust their product and marketing policies to accommodate the conditions that prevail in the various parts of the fragmented market. The impact of transaction costs in single market areas is illustrated in Exhibit 1.1.

The process of creating the SEM can be viewed as one of reducing the size of the transaction cost box. However, many European companies may already be well within the existing cost box of the EU. A company that faces few transaction costs from fragmented markets, low compliance with laws and has low costs associated with the lack of monetary integration may be comfortably within the cost box.

Exhibit 1.1 Transaction costs and single markets

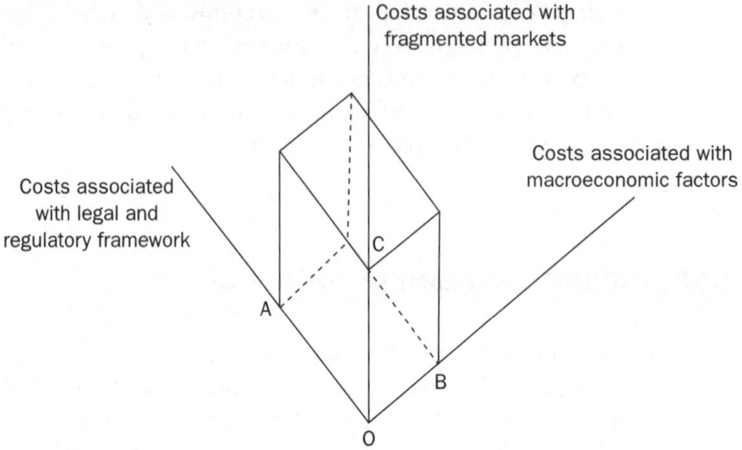

Costs associated with
fragmented markets

Costs associated with
macroeconomic factors

Costs associated
with legal and
regulatory framework

C

A

B

O

At point O the transaction costs relating to legal, regulatory and macroeconomic frameworks and those associated with fragmented markets are zero. If the maximum costs related to legal and regulatory frameworks are given by OA, macroeconomic factors by OB and fragmented market costs by OC, the box area within the diagram indicates the maximum possible transaction costs that companies operating in the single market area would face. The position in which companies would find themselves within this cost box would depend upon three factors. Firstly, the level of fragmentation of the market in which the company operates. Secondly, the extent to which companies are subject to costs from the legal and regulatory frameworks that prevail in the single market area. Thirdly, the importance of exchange rate risk and other costs associated with the macroeconomic policies to the operations of the company. A single market area that had a single currency, a low level of market fragmentation and few economic and social policies that affected the costs of companies would have a smaller cost box than a single market area that did not have these characteristics. Increasing the integration of markets and reducing the transaction costs related to legal and macroeconomic factors would reduce the size of the transaction cost box. The process of creating the SEM can be regarded as attempts to reduce the size of the transaction cost box.

Efforts to further integrate the SEM will, therefore, bring little benefit to such companies. However, moves to further integrate the SEM could impose costs on such companies because of the need to comply with new laws or to adjust to a new currency (McDonald, 1997).

The enlargement of the EU to include some of the former communist countries and Cyprus and Malta will further increase the diversity of the dimensions of the national transaction cost boxes that compose the transaction cost box of the EU because the legal and regulatory frameworks, and macroeconomic frameworks vary considerably among the 10 applicant countries (see **www.europa.eu.int/comm/ enlargement** for details on conditions in these countries). Moreover, the extent of market fragmentation will increase with enlargement. Enlargement to embrace countries such as Romania, Bulgaria and Turkey would further enhance these differences. Cleary, enlargement holds the prospect of several years of what might be painful adjustment for the new members as they come to terms with the demands of the SEM (Brenton et al., 2001; Carlin et al., 2000). Until this process is complete the transaction costs of operating in the different parts of the SEM will vary significantly. In terms of harmonisation of macroeconomic frameworks the time period could be very long as the new member states join, and adjust to the conditions of, the European Monetary Union.

The evolution of the SEM programme has resulted in a variety of what are often complex and confusing rules (Mayes, 1997). The impact of these rules on the transaction costs of companies has become important because of the growth of legislation associated with the SEM programme, some of which requires companies to adopt new and costly procedures. The impact of these costs, particularly on SMEs, has led to (the beginnings of) attempts to seek to reduce the transaction costs to companies of complying with EU legislation. The transaction costs of complying with EU legislation may not be uniform throughout the Community because of the way that EU legislation is transposed into national laws (McDonald, 2000a). It is possible that EU legislation can be over-implemented by national governments (gold plating of directives) or under-implemented (when the conditions specified in directives are not fully implemented by national governments). The latter is contrary to EU law, but it is probably quite widespread. A large number of complaints have been registered with the Commission on issues connected to recognition of technical regulations. (see European Commission, 2000b and 2003). The transaction costs to companies of complying with EU legislation are shown in Exhibit 1.2.

It is possible that a single market area such as the USA has lower transaction costs than the EU because the USA has a single currency, fewer cultural and institutional differences (and, therefore, less fragmented markets) and fewer economic and social policies that impact on the transaction costs of companies. However, in some areas the EU may have lower transaction costs than the USA, for example the use of mutual recognition may reduce the costs associated with conforming to technical regulations. Nevertheless, the characteristics of existing single markets suggest that the USA is likely to have lower transaction costs than the EU. There is also some evidence that the single market environment in the USA has delivered an environment that is more conducive to the development of competitiveness by companies (Commission, 1997). However, the cultural differences between the US and the EU are held to require different types of single market environments that will allow European companies to create and maintain competitiveness in a global market (Jacquemin and Pench, 1996). This argument accords with the views of those who regard institutional frameworks as important to the effective working of economies.

The characteristics of single markets depend to a large extent on the nature of the institutional frameworks of societies. Institutional frameworks are formed by legal and governmental systems and cultural norms that determine the rules of human interaction. Effective institutional frameworks reduce uncertainty and transaction costs in economic and social exchange. Successful single markets, therefore, have succeeded in creating effective institutional frameworks. Different societies, however, have different institutional frameworks as a result of their history and their cultural characteristics. They are, therefore, path determined (they emerge from the history of societies) and cannot be quickly altered into very different systems (North, 1990). Hence, institutional frameworks that provide the necessary

Exhibit 1.2 Transaction costs and legislation

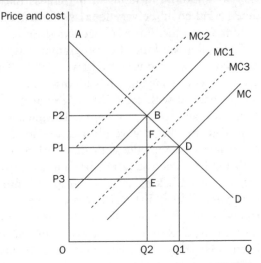

D = demand   MC = sum of the marginal costs of companies in the industry

MC1 = marginal cost including the transaction costs of legislation (equal to BE)

P1 : Q1 = price and quantity before the imposition of legislation

P2 : Q2 = price and quantity after the imposition of legislation

P3 = price received by companies after imposition of legislation (i.e. market price P2 minus transaction costs of legislation BE)

Effects of legislation

Consumer surplus before legislation = P1AD

Consumer surplus after legislation = P2AB

The legislation reduces consumer surplus. The burden of the costs is shared between producers and consumers. Consumers pay an area equal to P1P2BF, while producers pay P3P1FE. The more elastic are demand and supply, the more the transaction cost burden will fall on companies. This analysis suggests that legislation should be carefully framed to minimise the transaction costs burden that will fall on companies and consumers.

If legislation is over-implemented, the marginal cost curve may shift further to the left (e.g. MC2). This will increase the cost burden of the legislation. However, if the legislation is under-implemented (e.g. MC3), companies located in countries that implement properly or over-implement the legislation will suffer a loss of competitiveness relative to those companies based in countries that under-implement the legislation.

conditions for effective free movement in one society may not be appropriate for another society that has a different history and cultural composition.

The EU is attempting to create an institutional framework that can provide a low transaction cost single market. However, this process requires the integration of the institutional frameworks of the member states. The member states have a variety of institutional frameworks because their histories are different. If such path determinacy is important, the EU faces considerable problems in its attempt to establish institutional frameworks that can deliver a low uncertainty and transaction cost real single market. Moreover, the enlargement of the EU will add to these problems.

Customs union

A CU is an area where tariffs and quotas on goods are removed for all intra-Union trade, and where there is a common tariff and quota system for all extra-Union trade. In 1948 the Netherlands, Belgium and Luxembourg formed Benelux, a CU in industrial goods. The Treaty of Paris that established the European Coal and Steel Community (ECSC) required the original six members (Benelux, France, Germany and Italy) to create a CU in coal and steel. The Treaty of Rome extended the CU of the original six to all industrial goods. Article 3 of the Treaty of Rome called for 'the elimination, as between Member States, of customs duties and quantitative restrictions on the import and export of goods, and of all other measures having equivalent effect'. This article requires the removal of NTBs – measures having equivalent effect – as well as tariffs (customs duties) and quotas (quantitative restrictions).

A CU should act as a greater stimulus to intra-Union trade than a free-trade area because the introduction of a common external tariff (CET) should ensure that the same tariff is imposed on imports regardless of the country importing the product. Therefore, the CET ensures that all imports into the CU are treated in the same manner. The CET avoids problems with rules of origin. This problem arises when imports from outside the free-trade area are used as intermediate products in the production of goods that are subsequently exported to another country in the free-trade area. In these cases it is necessary to assess the value of the imported intermediate good in the final good that is exported. This value is required to work out how much of the exported good should be free from customs duties. In the case of products that have large inputs from countries outside the free-trade area the proportion of the final exported goods that was tariff free could be quite small. The Community did not eliminate all rules of origin problems with the introduction of the CET. In the 1980s a series of rules of origin problems arose over the non-Community inputs in the final outputs from Japanese plants that produced output in a member state (see Chapter 15). Nevertheless, on the whole the CU of the EEC did not suffer the same degree of difficulties that free-trade areas such as EFTA encountered with rules of origin problems (Herin, 1986).

The importance of tariffs as a barrier to trade in the EU is influenced by Article 18 of the Treaty of Rome. This article commits the Community to seek to reduce the barriers to trade on the basis of 'reciprocity and mutual advantage to reduce customs duties below the general level of which they could avail themselves as a result of the establishment of a customs union'. This article required the Community to seek to reduce tariffs and quotas against non-member states in the context of world trade negotiations. Membership of the General Agreement on Tariffs and Trade (GATT) also required this undertaking because a CU is against the spirit of the GATT as it does not confer most favoured nation treatment to non-members. Thus the CU was tolerated by the GATT on the grounds that it would pursue a coherent and sustained attempt to achieve a general reduction in barriers to trade by negotiations.

The Single European Market

The move to establish the Single European Market (SEM) was simply a programme to enable the EU to complete the creation of a CM. The EU has been committed to establishing a CM since the Treaty of Rome was signed in 1957. Before agreement was reached to establish the SEM by the end of 1992, there had been very little progress towards establishing the CM. The main problem was the difficulty of reaching agreement about eliminating the many NTBs that hindered free movement. A range of NTBs based on diverse national rules, regulations, taxation and subsidies governed the movement of goods, services, capital and labour. Consequently, frontier controls were necessary to ensure that cross-frontier trade in goods adhered to the various national requirements. Cross-frontier trade in some service sectors was rendered impossible by different national rules and regulations. Capital movements were restricted by capital and exchange controls imposed by some member states. Labour mobility was hampered by differences in professional qualifications, and by labour and social security laws and regulations. Before the agreement on the Single European Act (SEA), the EU had attempted to eliminate these NTBs by creating a set of European laws and regulations to govern all aspects of economic activity. This resulted in attempts to determine European standards for a large range of products. Member states could, however, veto any proposal that they thought was detrimental to their economies, so there was very little progress to harmonise common European standards or eliminate the barriers to the free movement of services, capital and labour. Hence the EU did not take any significant steps towards establishing the CM, although the Treaty of Rome clearly committed the member states to achieving this objective.

In the 1980s a process was begun which greatly accelerated the progress towards creating a Common Market. In this period the member states were experiencing lower growth rates and higher unemployment than the USA and Japan. The Japanese were successfully entering many of the most sensitive markets in the EU (e.g. cars, consumer electronic equipment, computing equipment), and the NICs were becoming an increasing threat to many of the industries of the member states. The leading high technology companies tended to be American or Japanese, and many European companies were unable to maintain a presence in these markets. Within the EU continuing conflict over the CAP and associated budgetary problems (see Chapter 11) had diverted the EU from making progress on establishing the Common Market. A view emerged that the EU was stuck in a rut, and was losing its vision and direction.

In spite of these problems there were signs of the EU making some progress. The European Monetary System (EMS), founded in 1979, had not collapsed as had been predicted in many quarters; rather it had achieved some success in stabilising exchange rate fluctuations and in helping to promote convergence of inflation rates. Greece joined the EU in 1981, and Spain and Portugal in 1986, creating a potential market of 320 million consumers. An ECJ ruling in 1978 in the Cassis de Dijon case established the principle of mutual recognition. In this case the ECJ ruled that Germany could not ban the importing of Cassis de Dijon (a French alcoholic drink) on the grounds that it did not conform to German rules and regulations governing the sale of alcoholic drinks. The ECJ established that goods that adhered to the national rules and regulations in the member state in which they were produced should be able to be sold in any member state without need to adhere to the rules and regulations governing the production and sale of the goods in the importing member state. The principle outlined in the Cassis de Dijon case provided an escape route from the long process of establishing common European rules and regulations for all goods. This process could be replaced by the mutual recognition of each other's rules and regulations. The use of mutual recognition was accepted by the EU when the 'New approach to technical harmonisation' was adopted in 1985. The acceptance of the concept of mutual recognition was a major step in the process of removing NTBs caused by differences in rules and regulations. Harmonisation could be limited to essential requirements in order for health and public safety considerations to be accounted for, and to ensure technical compatibility of products. The combination of these factors contributed to the idea that the EU still had potential to be a dynamic body in Europe and the world.

In 1983, at the Stuttgart summit, there was an acknowledgement of the need to take new initiatives to restore some dynamism into the activities of the EU. This took the form of a Solemn Declaration of European Union. There was a growing feeling that the failure to establish the CM (now called the Internal Market) within the EU resulted in major handicaps for EU companies. There was a strong opinion that EU firms faced considerable disadvantages compared with US and Japanese firms. It was noted that US firms had a domestic market of over 200 million consumers, and Japanese firms had a market of 100 million. If the EU were to become a single market it would have a domestic market of 320 million consumers, making it the largest market in the world.

In 1984 the European Parliament issued a draft treaty on European Union. This called for political and economic change, in particular the creation of an internal market and the reform of decision-making procedures of the EU to make them more democratic, or at least more accountable to the European Parliament. At the Fontainebleau summit of 1984, two committees (the Adonnino and the Dooge committees) were set up to consider how the Community might develop. Both of these committees called for institutional change, and the Dooge called for the creation of an Internal Market. In 1985 a White Paper, 'Completing the Internal Market', was published (European Commission, 1985). The White Paper called for a programme of legislation to be implemented to create an Internal Market by the end of 1992. At the Milan summit of 1985 all these moves came to a head, and an Inter-Governmental Conference was set up to discuss European Union. This resulted in agreement on the SEA that was approved by all member states in 1986 and implemented in 1987.

The SEA was a compromise between countries such as France and Germany that wanted a new Treaty on European Union, and the UK and Denmark that did not, but wanted simply the implementation of the White Paper to create an SEM. The

SEA allowed for a limited set of changes to the Treaty of Rome that included majority voting in the Council of Ministers in areas related to establishing the Internal Market. The main thrust of the SEA was to establish the SEM by 31 December 1992. When the SEA was approved it was considered to be a poor substitute for a new Treaty on European Union, but given the opposition of the UK and Denmark it was the best that could be achieved. However, the SEA resulted in a dramatic increase in the activities of the EU, and led to a chain of events that focused attention on the EU as being one of the most successful and dynamic economic agencies in the world. At the heart of the 1992 programme was Article 13 of the SEA: 'The internal market shall comprise an area without internal frontiers in which the free movement of goods, persons, services and capital is ensured according to the provisions of this Treaty.'

This was simply a reformulation of the original commitment, in the Treaty of Rome, to establish a CM. The major difference now was that there was the political will, and a detailed programme with a practical method of implementation, to achieve this objective. The EU had finally adopted a comprehensive programme to establish a CM. This programme involved the removal of all legal barriers to the free movement of goods, services, capital and labour.

The economic effects of establishing free movement

The early attempts to assess the economic implications of the formation of the CU (Viner, 1950; Meade, 1955; Lipsey, 1970) continue to influence the type of economic analysis that is used to assess the effects of regional economic agencies. The economic effects of regional economic integration can be classified as arising from either static or dynamic effects of establishing free movement. Static effects are concerned with the allocation of resources when factors of production and technology are fixed, and where the characteristics of the competitive environment are also constant. Dynamic effects arise when regional economic integration induces changes in the quantity and quality of factors of production, improvements in technology and changes to the competitive environment.

Static effects

Viner (1950) showed that the formation of a CU was not necessarily advantageous to all members of a regional economic agency or indeed to the world as a whole. In his analysis he developed the concepts of 'trade creation' and 'trade diversion'. Trade creation arises when a CU leads to the movement of trade from a high-cost to a low-cost producer, whereas trade diversion occurs when the reverse arises. The analysis of trade creation and diversion focuses on the removal of tariffs; however, the basic method of analysis can be extended to cover other barriers to trade, for example quotas and NTBs. Trade creation and diversion effects can arise in any regional economic agency that reduces barriers to trade that are not extended to non-members.

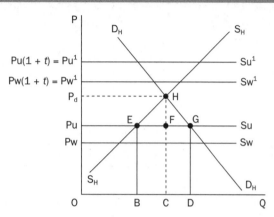

Exhibit 1.3 Trade creation

D_H and S_H represent the home demand and supply curves for the good. PuSu and PwSw are the CU and rest-of-the-world supply curves. Before membership of the union, both external producers are excluded from the home market by the imposition of a tariff which results in the import supply curves being above the equilibrium price in the domestic economy. The home country is self-sufficient at an equilibrium price of OP_d and quantity of OC. After membership of the CU, the CET does not apply to the union partner, but it applies to the rest of the world. The union partner's supply curve now becomes PuSu, and imports of BD are supplied to the home country. Domestic supply falls from OC to OB, but domestic demand rises from OC to OD. The resource cost of producing BC of the good has fallen from BCHE to BCFE, a saving of EFH. This is beneficial in terms of both CU and world welfare. The home country has gained, for although producers' surplus has fallen by PuEHPd, consumers' surplus has risen by PuGHPd, leading to a net gain of HEG. The gain would have been larger had the home economy adopted a policy of free trade rather than membership of a discriminatory trading regime. However, in terms of welfare gain, participation in the union is obviously a step in the right direction, because there is a gain from free trade. Nevertheless, free trade with all trading partners would lead to greater welfare gains.

The formation of a CU leads to the elimination of tariffs between members and to the establishment of the CET against all non-members. The removal of tariffs against members will increase imports from the lowest-cost member of the CU to members who have higher-cost producers. If the exporting CU member is also the lowest-cost producer in the world a process of trade creation will arise because imports will come from the least-cost producer in the world. However, if the country with the lowest-cost producers is not in the CU and, if the imposition of the CET results in an import price into the CU that is higher than the price that will be charged by the lowest-cost producer in the CU, trade diversion will result, because imports could be obtained at a lower cost if tariffs had been eliminated against all countries rather than just for the members of the CU. The concepts of trade creation and diversion are illustrated in Exhibits 1.3 and 1.4.

Trade creation allows resources to be allocated according to comparative advantage. However, even in the case of trade diversion, gains can be reaped by shifting resources to allow specialisation to lower-cost producers within the regional economic agency. This effect is illustrated in Exhibit 1.5.

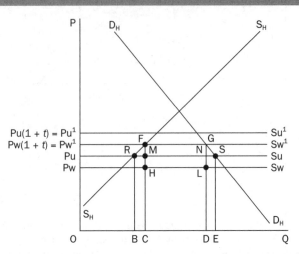

Exhibit 1.4 Trade diversion

Before participation in a CU and with a tariff level t on potential partner and rest-of-world supplies, the lowest priced source of import supply is the rest of the world Pw^1Sw^1. Domestic production is OC and imports are CD. Tariff proceeds FGLH go to the government of the home economy. The home country joins a CU whose external tariff is identical to that of the home country prior to participation. Domestic production falls to OB but domestic consumption rises to OE; BE imports now come from the union partner at a tariff-free price of OPu. Trade diversion has arisen. The cost of the original quantity of imports CD has risen by HLNM. There is a loss of tariff revenue to the domestic government of FGLH. Moreover, producers' surplus falls by $PuPw^1RF$ and consumers' surplus rises by $PuPw^1GS$. The gain in consumers' surplus minus the loss in producers' surplus is RFGS. Part of this – FGNM – is part of the lost tariff revenue, and consequently this reduces the gain of RFGS to the areas RFM and SGN. The other part HLNM (the amount of trade diversion) may be compared with the two triangles RFM and SGN. Clearly, here, there is a net trade diversionary loss. The extent of this loss will be the greater, the larger the gap between world prices and union prices.

A fuller account of trade creation and diversion can be found in Hansen and Neilsen, 1997.

In static terms, a CU is beneficial if trade creation is greater than trade diversion. This outcome is more likely to occur if the CU includes countries that have large numbers of low-cost producers and if the CET is set at a low level. However, in global terms, trade diversion can be avoided if tariff reductions are offered on a most favoured nation basis, i.e. the highest level of tariff reductions offered to any nation is made available to all nations. Therefore, the justification for a CU rests on arguments that tariff reductions can be more substantial between a group of countries than if they are granted to all countries.

The case for and against regional economic agencies tends to focus on the overall welfare gains from establishing free movement. However, there are distribution effects from the static effects of establishing free movement. The overall effect of reaping comparative advantage is to increase welfare by relocating production to those countries (within the CU) that are relatively most efficient at providing output. In those markets where exports rise, however, the price in the domestic market

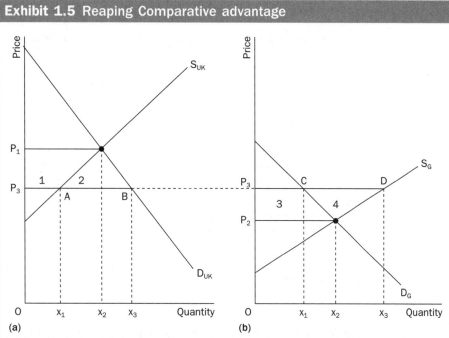

Exhibit 1.5 Reaping Comparative advantage

In **(a)** the demand and supply conditions for a good in the UK are shown; **(b)** shows market conditions in Germany. The lower equilibrium price in Germany shows that it has a comparative advantage in producing this good. If trade is prevented by the imposition of an NTB, such as rules and regulations after the removal of these barriers, the UK would import the good from Germany. This would result in the price increasing in Germany and falling in the UK. When the price reached the level where imports into the UK were equal to exports from Germany, a new equilibrium price would have been established, i.e. at P_3 where UK imports (AB) equal German exports (CD). This results in a rise in consumer surplus in the UK equal to areas 1+2. Area 1 is a transfer of producer surplus to consumers; it is not a net welfare gain as it is transferred from producers in the UK to consumers in the UK. The remaining consumer surplus gain of area 2 represents the net welfare gain to the UK. Areas 3+4 represent the gain in producer surplus in Germany. Area 3 is a transfer of consumer surplus to German producers from German consumers. The net gain in Germany is therefore represented by area 4. Therefore, the net gain to both countries is equivalent to areas 2+4.

increases and induces a decline in quantity bought in the domestic market. Thus, consumers in the exporting country suffer a loss of real income because after the rise in exports they must transfer a larger amount of (nominal) income to receive the same output. Consumers in the importing country face the opposite effects because the supply of the product increases, thereby reducing the price. Producers are also differentially affected by the change in prices induced by the establishment of free movement. In the exporting country they experience higher prices and therefore increased revenues, whereas producers in the importing country face the opposite effect as prices fall in their economies. Furthermore, producers must adjust to the new allocation based on comparative advantage. This may involve temporary unemployment of resources as labour and capital move into those areas in which the country has a comparative advantage.

Dynamic effects

Three major dynamic effects of regional economic integration can be identified:

- Reducing monopoly power.
- Reducing levels of x-inefficiency – overmanning, excessive holdings of stocks and other types of slack management practices.
- Reaping benefits of economies of scale and learning effects.

The removal of barriers to trade can reduce monopoly power by increasing the possible sources of supply from other countries within the regional economic agency. Reductions in monopoly power will lower prices and increase output, thereby leading to net gains for consumers (see Exhibit 1.6). Increasing the competitive environment may encourage producers to improve non-price competition factors such as the qualities of their products. This may also lead to benefits by increasing the demand for higher quality products (see Exhibit 1.7).

The removal of trade barriers should lead to the integration of fragmented markets and thereby create a larger market for products. If transport costs are low,

Exhibit 1.6 Reduction in monopoly power

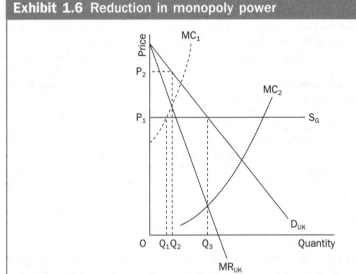

If the UK had a domestic monopolist totally protected by an NTB, then price would be P_2 and output Q_2 if the monopolist faced the marginal cost curve shown by MC_1. Assuming a perfectly elastic supply of this good from Germany, the ruling market price in the absence of the NTB would be P_1 and the total demand in the UK would be Q_3. If the NTB were removed, the price in the UK would fall to P_1, and the monopolist would be constrained to this price. The monopolist would have to adjust output to Q_1, and the gap in satisfying market demand in the UK at this price would be met by imports from Germany of Q_1–Q_3. There would be benefits in the UK from a lower price and higher output provided that the domestic monopolist's marginal cost curve lay above MC_2. A paper by Jacquemin (1982) shows that this disciplinary effect from foreign competition can also work in oligopolistic markets.

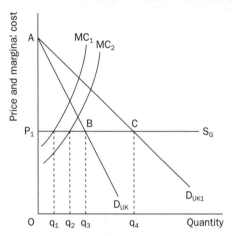

Exhibit 1.7 X-inefficiency and the SEM

This situation is similar to Exhibit 1.6, i.e. a UK monopolist constrained to the price P_1 because of imports from Germany. If this increase in competition is also accompanied by R&D and innovation to improve the non-price characteristics of this good, the demand curve shifts to D_{UK1}. Consumer surplus is increased from P_1AB before the improvements in non-price factors, and to P_1AC after the improvements. Initially, the increase in demand in the UK is met by increased imports from Germany, i.e. imports rise from q_1–q_3 to q_1–q_4. If, however, the UK firm responds by reducing X-inefficiency, this could shift the marginal cost to MC_2 and allow the UK firm to increase its share of the market from q_1 to q_2. If the UK firm reduced X-inefficiency without any increase in the non-price characteristics of the good, the result would be that the UK firm would increase market share and its producer surplus. There would be no benefit in terms of increased consumer surplus. This implies that reductions in X-inefficiency do not necessarily lead to net welfare improvements for consumers. Only if the lowering of production costs results in lower prices will there be any benefits to consumers.

it may be possible to serve the integrated market from existing or new plant and thereby allow companies to reap the benefits of internal economies of scale, the size of which depend upon the nature of the technical relationship between cost and output, in particular the rate at which costs fall as output is increased and the level of output at which costs are minimised, i.e. minimum efficiency scale (MES). Therefore, the magnitude of the benefits is determined by the degree of integration of fragmented markets, the significance of transport costs and the technical relationship between cost and output. If the new larger markets are competitive, prices should be reduced as production costs fall (see Exhibit 1.8).

If production in national markets is characterised by large economies of scale, the competitive environment may be strongly oligopolistic if the market is only large enough to sustain a few plants. In these circumstances the creation of a larger market by establishing a CU or a CM may allow an expansion of suppliers to the new larger market and thereby lead to a reduction in price (Krugman, 1989). Thus the establishment of free movement can lead to benefits by increasing the number of suppliers to the market. The emergence of these benefits depends on the existence of a competition policy able to stop companies from

Exhibit 1.8 Economies of scale

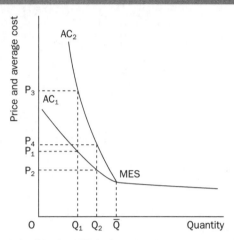

The level of output constrained by the NTB is Q_1, and this results in a price of P_1. If the NTB is removed, the firm could increase exports and thereby expand output to Q_2, which would reduce the price to P_2. This outcome is dependent on the level of competition being sufficient to ensure that firms are constrained to making normal profits, and that they are therefore forced to reduce price when costs are lowered. It is also necessary for the firm to be operating at above minimum efficiency scale (MES), the low point of the average cost curve. If the firm is operating at MES, the opportunity to expand output will not result in lower costs. If the AC curve was given by AC1 (i.e. a steeper AC curve) the reduction in price of the expansion of output from 0Q1 to 0Q2 would be greater. This demonstrates the importance of the technical relationship between cost and output for the magnitude of the cost (and hence possible price reduction) of any increase in output that might arise from economic integration.

acquiring control over plants and thereby preventing an increase in the competitive environment.

The integration of fragmented markets may also lead to external economies of scale (Krugman and Obstfeld, 1993). External economies of scale can arise when companies cluster in a specific geographical area and form networks that result in reduced transaction costs in conducting their business. These external economies of scale arise from such factors as the development of a pool of skilled labour, the creation of a network of suppliers and support services, etc. Silicon Valley in California is the best known example of a cluster. However, other examples exist – the City of London for foreign exchange dealing, Milan for high fashion and networks of SMEs that have formed clusters in northern Italy (Porter, 1990). The establishment of free movement may allow the market to become large enough to allow for the development of existing clusters or for the emergence of new clusters (Vertova and McDonald, 2001; Harris and McDonald, 2004).

The benefits of internal and external economies of scale may also help to further reduce production costs as learning takes place because, as output increases, companies learn how to produce products more cheaply. Learning can also arise from the development of clusters as companies learn how to utilise effectively the networks of business relationships that are at the heart of clusters.

Other effects of establishing free movement

The creation of a CM requires free movement of labour and capital as well as of goods and services. The removal of barriers to movement of factors of production will lead to net benefits and distribution effects that are similar to those that arise from the reaping of comparative advantage (see Exhibits 1.9 and 1.10).

The increase in the competitive environment that should follow from the establishment of free movement may reduce levels of x-inefficiency and thereby boost the effectiveness of the use of capital and labour in production processes. This will enhance growth because better use will be made of existing production processes. A further expansion of the growth potential will result from the incentive to increase investment to meet the demands of the new larger markets. As income

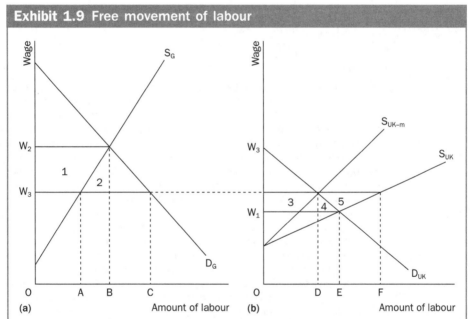

Exhibit 1.9 Free movement of labour

Before the establishment of free movement of labour in the UK, wage would be W_1 with employment at E, and in Germany the wage would be W_2 and employment at B. When the barriers to labour mobility are removed, a new equilibrium wage will emerge – W_3. At this wage the number of migrant workers from the UK is equal to the inflow to Germany. Employment in the UK would fall to D, with DF of migrant workers. This reduces the supply of labour in the UK to S_{UK-m}, the supply of labour in the UK minus migrants. Employment of German workers would fall to A, with AC of migrant workers from the UK. This leads to gains and losses of economic rent (area above the supply curve of labour, and below the wage line) for labour. Workers in Germany lose an amount equal to area 1, while workers who remain in the UK gain higher wages, leading to economic rent equal to area 3. Migrant workers from the UK would gain areas 4+5. Employers also make gains and losses (areas below the demand for labour and above the wage line). In Germany employers gain area 2 from the employment of migrant workers, while in the UK employers lose an amount equivalent to areas 3+4. Areas 1+3+4 are transfers, area 1 from German workers to German employers, and areas 3+4 from UK employers to UK workers. This leaves areas 2 and 5 as net welfare gains of allowing free movement of labour.

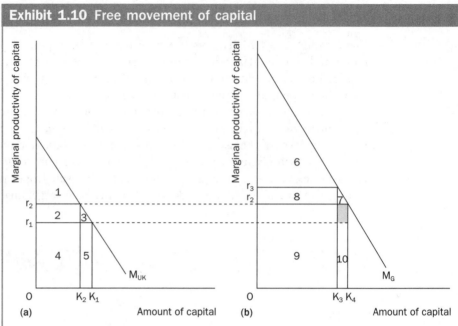

Exhibit 1.10 Free movement of capital

The stock of capital in the UK is given by K_1 and in Germany by K_3. The marginal productivity of capital is shown by M_{UK} and M_G. The marginal productivity of capital in Germany is higher than in the UK, therefore the rate of return to capital in Germany (r_3) is higher than in the UK (r_1). In the UK, capital receives a total reward equal to areas 4+5, while labour receives 1+2+3. In Germany the total return to capital is shown by areas 8+9, and area 6 is the payment to labour. If barriers to capital mobility are removed, capital will flow from the UK to obtain the higher rate of return available in Germany. This will continue until the rate of return is equal in both countries, i.e. at r_2. This results in an export of capital from the UK of K_1–K_2, corresponding to the capital stock increase in Germany of K_3–K_4. This reduces total product in the UK to an amount equal to areas 1+2+4. However, the exported capital results in a transfer of profits to the UK from Germany, equal to area 10. In Germany national product is increased by areas 7+10, leading to a net welfare gain to Germany equivalent to area 7. The shaded part of area 10 is equal to the higher return to UK capital from being invested in Germany. In **(b)** this area is twice the size of area 3. Hence the net loss of areas 3+5 to the UK is more than compensated for by the remittance of profits from Germany, as area 10 is greater than areas 3+5. So the net welfare gains of allowing free movement of capital are equal to area 7 plus half the shaded area. There are, however, distribution effects to labour resulting from capital mobility. Labour's share in the UK falls by areas 2+3, while in Germany it rises by areas 7+8.

grows, savings will rise, providing the resources for extra investment (Baldwin, 1989). Therefore, the establishment of free movement should have two beneficial effects on growth, arising from the increase in efficiency and from the incentive to invest to benefit from larger markets (see Exhibit 1.11).

The adjustment costs of free movement

Economic analysis of free movement implies that the removal of trade barriers offers the potential to reap net benefits. But these net gains cannot be acquired

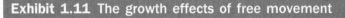

Exhibit 1.11 The growth effects of free movement

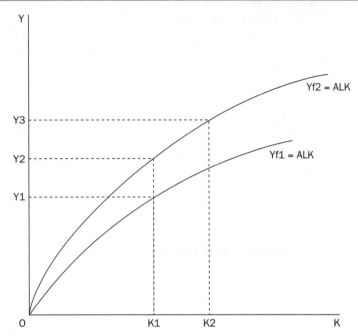

Y = output/income   A = efficiency factor in the use of capital and labour

L = labour   K = capital

Yf = A,L,K (production function, that is Y, is determined by a fixed amount of labour (L) and variable amounts of capital (K) and the efficiency factor (A))

Creating free movement will improve the efficiency of the use of capital and labour (A) because the increase in competition that follows from free movement will reduce the level of X-inefficiency in the use of capital and labour. This is shown by a shift from Yf1 to Yf2. Therefore, at every level of capital a higher level of output will result. This is the static growth effect.

However, there is another possible growth effect from the establishment of free movement. The boost to the size of the market that follows from the establishment of free movement will stimulate incentives to increase investment, thereby boosting the amount of capital that is employed in the economy. The increase in income from the improvement in the efficiency of the use of capital and labour also leads to an increase in savings, which can provide the resources to boost investment (providing that individuals are prepared to sacrifice consumption now for consumption in the future). This is the dynamic growth effect.

If the optimal level of capital is given by K1, the static effect would be to increase Y to Y2. The dynamic effect would result in an increase in the amount of capital employed to, say, K2 leading to an income level of Y3. See Baldwin (1989) for a fuller explanation.

without changing the distribution of income and they also lead to adjustment costs as companies and individuals respond to changes induced by the establishment of free movement. Adjustment costs are likely to be temporary because in the long run factors of production will relocate, geographically and across sectors, in response to the new market environment. Nevertheless, these costs may be significant and persistent if labour and capital mobility are limited. The changes in the distribution of income are, in principle, capable of compensation from the net benefits that arise from the establishment of free movement.

These factors are likely to lead to powerful political pressures to redistribute income, geographically, across sectors and among different groups of workers to compensate those who feel harmed by the integration process. Legislation can be used to limit the scale of changes and to direct the changes in ways that are considered to be less onerous than those that emerge from the unconstrained market process. Furthermore, action to slow down and reduce the impact of trade liberalisation programmes may be adopted by members of regional economic agencies in efforts to mitigate against the cost of adjustment. These responses have certainly been evident in the EU and have led to a significant amount of redistribution and to slow progress in [effectively] implementing the programmes to remove barriers to trade.

Problems with empirical studies

Empirical studies on the effects of regional economic integration have taken two main forms:

1 Estimating the changes to the size and pattern of trade flows before and after trade liberalisation. This is done by creating a model of what trade would have been if a country had not removed or reduced trade barriers, and comparing that outcome with that which occurred after a country liberalised its trade.

2 Estimating the costs and benefits of the programme as indicated by economic theory. This approach requires clear predictions to be derived from theoretical models, and access to reliable data that can be used to test the predictions.

Both of these approaches have major conceptual problems and considerable caution has to be exercised in interpreting the results of empirical studies on the effects of regional economic integration.

Most studies of the effect of the CU have sought to ascertain the effects of tariff reductions by comparing what the situation would have been if a country had not been a member of a regional economic integration agency (the anti-monde position) with the actual outcome of that country after its participation in such an agency (Mayes, 1978; Winters, 1987). An anti-monde model of the determinants of trade flows is constructed and predictions are made on what trade flows there would be in this world. These predictions are then compared with actual outcomes to estimate the effects of the regional economic agency.

The main problem with this approach is that it is very difficult to ascribe any observable differences from the anti-monde position to the effects of the elimination of trade barriers. A multitude of factors determines trade flows (e.g. growth in income levels among trading partners, reductions in barriers to trade not related to the regional economic agency, changes in the technological and the competitive environment). If these factors are not accurately captured by the model, the comparison with actual outcomes may reflect the factors that are not fully specified in the model as well as the effects of the regional economic agency. This problem arises in studies of both the static and dynamic effects of regional economic integration.

Predictive models have also been used to estimate the effects of regional economic integration. The Cecchini Report was an attempt to estimate the net benefits of the creation of the SEM (see Emerson et al., 1988, for a summary of the report). The Cecchini Report was largely based on a statistical estimation of the net benefits of trade liberalisation as indicated by economic theory. The theories used were more sophisticated versions of those outlined above, including a general equilibrium approach based on an imperfectly competitive model of interaction between firms (Smith and Venables, 1988). The Cecchini Report used a variety of economic models to examine particular aspects of the creation of the SEM – economies of scale (Pratten, 1988; Schwalbach, 1988) and innovation (Geroski, 1988). Surveys and studies by management consultants were also used to assess the potential effects of the creation of the SEM for particular sectors and to obtain data for the statistical estimation of the net benefits – foodstuffs (Group MAC, 1988), road haulage (Ernst & Whinney, 1988), telecommunication services (Muller, 1988) and financial services (Price Waterhouse, 1988).

The main problem with the approach used in the Cecchini Report was that other models may have led to different indications of the likely costs and benefits of trade liberalisation. For example, a model based on external economies of scale and trade (e.g. Krugman, 1989) may have focused more on the geographical impact of economic integration such as the incentive to develop clusters of industries in response to the potential to reap external economies of scale. This type of geographical impact was largely missing from the Cecchini Report.

It is very difficult to know which model, or models, captures the major factors that are likely to arise from a wide-ranging economic integration programme such as the SEM. It is possible, therefore, that empirical studies based on such an approach will miss major and fundamental effects of large-scale integration programmes. Moreover, obtaining data to estimate the costs and benefits indicated by the theoretical work and the surveys is not an easy task. Consequently, empirical estimates of the impact of economic integration by agencies like the EU are likely to be subject to wide margins of error.

Some studies seek to assess the costs and benefits to individual member states by including all of the trade effects of regional economic integration by using a rough and ready anti-monde model and the budgetary costs of being a member. These types of studies are heroic attempts to discover the meta effects of membership. A good example of this type of approach is the study on the impact of British withdrawal from the EU (Hindley and Howe, 1996).

The problems of using anti-monde models and Cecchini types of approach mean that it is very difficult to obtain reliable and accurate information on the effects of regional economic integration on major economic variables such as trade flows, growth and employment. Empirical evidence on the effects of regional economic integration can therefore only provide an indication of the economic gains and losses associated with regional economic integration.

Empirical studies

Numerous studies have attempted to estimate the effects of membership on a country joining the EU. Some studies have concentrated on the CU aspect of membership (Kreinin, 1969, 1972; Resnick and Truman, 1971; Williamson and Bottrill, 1971; Balassa, 1987). Other studies have cast a wider net to embrace other elements in the balance of payments (Featherstone, Moore and Rhodes, 1979; Mayes, 1978; Winters, 1987). These studies find little evidence of strong trade diversion effects. However, they do not indicate that the static effects of economic integration are large. Therefore, the main economic benefits of economic integration were thought to arise from the dynamic effects of establishing free movement. The first major study that investigated these dynamic effects was the Cecchini Report (Cecchini, 1988; Emerson et al., 1988).

The Cecchini Report

The Cecchini Report established the main barriers that were to be removed by implementing Article 13 of the SEA. These barriers were identified by reference to those outlined in the 1985 White Paper, 'Completing the Internal Market', and by a series of surveys of businesses in the EU. The White Paper listed three main types of barriers that were to be eliminated.

1 *Physical barriers* – frontier controls and customs formalities.

2 *Technical barriers* – restriction on economic activities resulting from national rules and regulations. These include technical specifications which limit or prevent trade in goods; rules and regulations governing services which hinder non-domestic companies from trading across frontiers; discriminatory public procurement rules which limit tendering for government contracts to domestic companies; and legal obstacles faced by foreign companies seeking to set up subsidiaries in other member states.

3 *Fiscal barriers* – the need to adjust VAT and excise duties as goods cross EU frontiers. This is necessary as member states operate different coverage and levy different rates of VAT and excise duties.

The Cecchini Report reclassified these barriers to estimate the benefits of removing these NTBs. Five main barriers were identified – tariffs, quotas, cost-increasing barriers, market-entry restrictions and market-distorting activities practised by governments. Tariffs and quotas had largely been eliminated by the CU, but some remained, in particular Voluntary Export Restraints (VERs), relating to cars and electronic equipment, and quotas on textiles associated with the Multi Fibre Arrangement (MFA). These were national quotas and were removed or harmonised to allow frontier controls to be eliminated. The majority of the benefits were thought to arise from eliminating the remaining barriers. Cost-increasing barriers include customs formalities such as VAT and excise duty assessments, verification of technical regulations and costs incurred by companies in adhering to different

Table 1.1 Estimates of the benefits of removing barriers to create the SEM

	ECU (bn)		GDP of the EC %	
	(a)	(b)	(a)	(b)
Stage I Barriers affecting trade (frontier controls)	8	9	0.2	0.3
Stage II Barriers affecting production (technical and regulatory rules)	57	71	2.0	2.4
Stage III Barriers preventing the reaping of benefits of economies of scale	60	61	2.0	2.1
Stage IV Barriers which allow X-inefficiency and monopoly rents to exist	46	46	1.6	1.6
Total benefits	171	187	5.8	6.4

Notes:
(1) (a) Low estimates (b) High estimates
(2) For the EU6 plus the UK
(3) At 1985 prices
Source: Based on the Cecchini Report, Emerson et al., 1988

technical regulations, such as modifications to products, changes to packaging, etc. Market-entry restrictions include prohibiting or restricting access by foreign companies to the services sector, and rules and regulations that prevent foreign firms from bidding for public procurement contracts. Market-distorting activities arise from state aids such as subsidies, tax concessions and other financial help given to domestic companies.

Using this taxonomy of barriers, estimates of the benefits of removing them were made. This was carried out for the EU as a whole; no attempts were made to estimate the redistribution effects of removing these trade barriers. The estimates were based on a four-stage assessment of the effects of creating free movement. Stage I is connected with the benefits from removing barriers affecting trade, i.e. frontier controls. Stage II benefits arise from the removal of technical and regulatory rules that increase companies' costs. Economies of scale provide the benefits in Stage III. Finally, Stage IV estimates gains from increased competition leading to reductions in X-inefficiency and monopoly rents. The magnitude of these gains is outlined in Table 1.1.

There is some dispute whether the Cecchini Report attempted to quantify the impact of increased competition on levels of X-inefficiency. In Emerson et al. (1988) the tables indicate that estimates of gains from reductions in X-inefficiency were included in the Cecchini study; however, Smith (in Dyker, 1992) maintains that the Cecchini estimates do not include any effects that arise from reductions in X-inefficiency.

These benefits were deemed to stem from three separate but connected effects of removing the barriers to free movement. These were the effects of: (a) reducing frontier controls; (b) reducing market entry barriers; (c) reducing cost-increasing barriers. Effect (a) results from the reduction in the cost of frontier formalities, that is delays at frontiers and administration costs of dealing with customs forms. The removal of these would have a small but direct effect by increasing trade between EU countries and would lead to secondary effects of lower prices and incentives to increase investment. Effect (b) arises when barriers are of such a high level as to prevent any entry into the market. Such barriers are common in public procurement where standards and rules and regulations can prevent entry by non-national firms. They are also obstacles to the free movement of labour and capital. The removal of such barriers would increase market entry leading directly to an increase in competition and reductions in X-inefficiency and monopoly pricing practices. There would also be stimulation of investment to benefit from economies of scale, and to rationalise production and distribution systems. Effect (c) brings benefits by reducing costs incurred by different technical standards for goods and by removing the barriers caused by the variety of rules and regulations governing key business and consumer services such as financial, legal, accounting and transport services. The removal of these barriers would lead to a direct lowering of costs by reducing the price of imported goods and services. There would also be secondary effects that would increase the degree of competition and the level of investment.

The bulk of the benefits are seen to derive from the effects of increased competition and lower costs that lead to lower prices and stimulate investment. New market opportunities allow for increased economies of scale and the rationalisation of artificially segmented markets. The increase in competition allows for considerable improvements in the effective use of inputs, and reductions in the anti-competitive practices of companies. This process is aided further by reductions in the costs of business and consumer services made possible by the liberalisation of the service sector. The creation of the SEM is seen by Cecchini as a programme that boosts the effectiveness of the supply side of the economy. This improvement in the supply side leads to an increase in aggregate demand by increasing real purchasing power, increasing investment and improving the competitiveness of the EU relative to the rest of the world. These changes to the supply side also lead to improvements in public sector budgetary positions, because of reductions in the costs of public procurement and the growth of GDP that increases taxation revenues. This could allow for the consideration of a policy of expansion of the economy led by government expenditure. Such an expansion could help with temporary unemployment problems associated with the reconstruction of the economy, which is induced by the creation of the SEM. These supply-side changes improve the productive potential of the economy and enhance the ability to reach higher levels of non-inflationary growth. Such government-led expansion of aggregate demand would need to be coordinated to avoid problems of inconsistent growth levels. The Cecchini Report does not have much to say on this issue, but the implication of such a policy is that monetary policies would need to be coordinated to prevent the growth of monetary instability. Cecchini estimated these accompanying macroeconomic policies to have very significant effects on the overall benefits of creating the SEM (see Table 1.2).

The Cecchini Report was subject to considerable criticism because of its rather rosy view of the benefits and its underplaying of the costs of economic integration (see Cutler et al., 1989; Davies et al., 1989; Grahl and Teague, 1990). However, the report was a brave attempt to estimate systematically the economic effects of establishing the SEM.

Table 1.2 Macroeconomic benefits of creating the SEM

	GDP (%)	Prices (%)	Employment (millions)	External balance (%) of GDP
Without accompanying measures	4.5	−6.1	1.8	1.0
With accompanying measures				
Public finance	7.5	−4.3	5.7	−0.5
External position	6.5	−4.9	4.4	0.0
Disinflation	7.0	−4.5	5.0	−0.2

Notes:
(1) Estimates for EU12
(2) Time scale 6+ years from full implementation of programme (assumed to be 1 January 1993)
(3) Estimates subject to a margin of error of ±30%
(4) Accompanying measures:

- Public finance – this allows for an expansion of public investment and/or reductions in taxation; if the full room for manoeuvre is used it results in the benefits shown above.
- External position – the benefits here assume that the Community seeks to maintain a balance of payments equilibrium. This reduces the potential for government-led expansion of the economy. This result is very dependent on the state of the world economy and, in the model used to make these predictions, on the exchange rate of the dollar.
- Disinflation – this assumes that there would be a utilisation of 30 per cent of the room for expansion of the economy which would be brought by the fall in prices and the improvements in public finances which follow from the creation of the SEM. This option would protect the external balance and would allow for a significant disinflationary effect on the level of prices, and also create more employment than the previous option.

Source: Cecchini Report, Emerson et al., 1988

The 1996 Review of the Single European Market programme

A large scale review of the SEM was conducted in 1996 (*European Economy*, 1996; Monti, 1996). This Review included a survey of 20,000 enterprises, a number of specific industry studies, an investigation of particular issues (e.g. public procurement, capital market liberalisation, price convergence, market concentration) and studies on the growth and regional development effects of the SEM programme. The Review concentrated on three main economic effects of the SEM programme.

1 Allocation effects – improvements in efficiency in the use of resources.

2 Accumulation effects – growth effects.

3 Locational effects – geographical implications.

Allocation effects

The allocation effects of the SEM programme arise from the static effects (trade creation and diversion) and dynamic effects (economies of scale and the increase in competition) that were thought to be available from the establishment of the SEM. The Review covered the period 1987 to 1994. This is a relatively short time in which to estimate the effects of the SEM, especially as much of the necessary legislation to establish free movement was not implemented until the early 1990s.

Moreover, there were very significant changes that affected the EU economy in this period, for example German reunification, the transformation of Central and Eastern Europe and recession in continental Europe in the early 1990s. In these conditions, estimates of the effects of the SEM programme are somewhat suspect and should be 'viewed as a highly tentative exercise' (*European Economy*, 1996, p. 2).

The effects of establishing the SEM were examined by considering the implications of:

- the removal of frontier controls;
- the reductions in costs associated with different technical regulations and standards;
- public procurement liberalisation;
- changes to the level and composition of trade flows;
- developments in the nature of the competitive environment and in price differentials.

The Review discovered that the allocation of resources had improved, measured by increase in intra-EU trade, reduction in price differentials and improved competition. However, the Review identified a number of problem areas such as inadequate implementation and enforcement of SEM legislation, and problems of liberalisation of markets in areas such as financial and business services, public procurement and utilities. Differences in taxation systems were also identified as an obstacle to greater free movement and therefore to the expected gains in terms of increased competition and reduced price differentials (see **www.europa.eu.int/ comm/internal_market/en/update/impact** for details and *European Economy*, 1996).

Accumulation effects

The short period that has elapsed since the beginning of the SEM programme made it difficult for the Review to estimate any growth effects. Moreover, significant shocks to the economic systems of the member states have occurred in this period – German reunification, the end of communism in Central and Eastern Europe, and the move towards EMU. Nevertheless, the Review estimated that an additional boost to growth of between 1.1 and 1.5 per cent of GDP of the EU had occurred due to the SEM programme. This was thought to have generated some 300,000 to 900,000 extra jobs. Furthermore, the SEM programme is credited with reducing inflationary pressures associated with growth because of the supply-side improvements that have resulted from the establishment of free movement (European Commission, 1996). These estimates are subject to a considerable degree of possible error because of the problems outlined above. However, they are significantly lower than the estimates given by the Cecchini Report (see Table 1.2).

The low level of extra growth that can be attributed to the SEM programme may arise from deficiencies in the legislative programme that have limited the establishment of effective free movement. The special circumstances that were experienced in the early 1990s in Europe may also have contributed to the relatively poor growth performance of the EU. It is also likely that the Cecchini Report overestimated the likely growth potential from the establishment of the SEM. Nevertheless, it has been argued by some economists (see Exhibit 1.11) that the Cecchini Report may have underestimated the possible growth effects.

Location effects

The growth of intra-industry trade has encouraged the development of geographically based specialisation in the EU. This has also been confirmed by independent studies (Amiti, 1998; Brülhart, 1998). The Review indicated that the member states had experienced a measure of convergence in levels of economic development that was at least partly attributable to the SEM programme (*European Economy*, 1996). Ireland and Portugal had made the most progress, but Greece and Southern Italy had not made significant progress towards closing the development gap. Their heavy reliance on inter-industry trade, based on low labour costs, was held to be mainly responsible for the failure to improve the relative position of these economies (Monti, 1996).

Reliance on inter-industry trade of itself is not a sufficient reason for the development gap. Denmark, for example, has a heavy reliance on inter-industry trade, but could hardly be regarded as a less developed economy. Ireland also had a strong reliance on inter-industry trade, although intra-industry trade grew rapidly in the 1990s. However, Ireland has been one of the success stories of development in the EU. In the 1990s, the Irish economy experienced a sustained and high level of growth that led to Ireland closing the gap with the richer economies of the EU. Ireland's experience cannot be fully explained by the benefits of the growth of intra-industry and/or inter-industry trade because of the development of the SEM or the large-scale transfer of EU funds to Ireland (Barry, 1999; Bradley et al., 2001). Clearly, factors other than patterns of trade, free movement of capital and labour, and even access to the structural funds of the EU are important to the development process of the poorer member states. Modern theories of growth suggest that factors such as geography (Krugman, 1991, 1995), institutional structures (North, 1990), the quality of factors of production (Romer, 1986), and the evolution of technology (Nelson and Winter, 1982) are crucial for the successful development of economies. In view of these considerations the Review indicates that the integration process per se is not harmful to the growth processes of the poorer member states, and it may contribute to successful development for those countries that have the appropriate conditions for sustained growth.

The tendency for integration to lead to specialisation based on intra-industry trade that is based on differences in price and quality factors may lead to concentration and locking into lower value-added activities. However, these forces may be at work in any system of international trade. Therefore, regional economic integration agencies such as the EU may only reinforce existing trends. The key to the development of high income economies appears to rest on the historical, geographical, institutional and technology conditions that prevail in the countries concerned.

Evaluation of the Review

The Review, like most Commission-backed studies on the SEM, tends to paint a rosy picture of the effects of the integration process. Nevertheless, the Review was unable to confirm the estimates that were made by the Cecchini Report. In nearly every case the Review could not identify benefits of the magnitude that were suggested by the Cecchini Report. The difficulties of isolating those changes that are due to the SEM programme may account for some of the discrepancies in the size of the benefits. Those who considered that the Cecchini Report was an overoptimistic assessment of the effects of the creation of free movement can find some evidence for their view in the fairly low estimates of the benefits of the SEM programme that were found by the Review. However, the Review did find evidence that substantial changes had occurred with industrial structures, trading patterns and market conditions from the SEM programme. The Review does not indicate that the SEM programme has had no significant effects; rather it suggests that they have been fewer in number than were expected by the Cecchini Report.

Evidence on the effects of the SEM since the 1996 Review

The Commission has established a number of studies and systems to monitor the impact of the SEM. A summary of the first 10 years of the SEM was published in 2002 – The Internal Market: 10 Years Without Frontiers (available on **www.europa.eu.int/comm/internal_market/10years**). This report confirmed that the slow progress towards achieving the expected benefits from the SEM identified in the 1996 Review had continued. However, many of the same problems, also identified in the 1996 Review, remained especially with implementation and enforcement of SEM legislation and failure to achieve effective free movement in several sectors such as financial and business services and public procurement. Problems with access to networks had also hindered the development of integrated utilities provision for gas, electricity and telecommunications. The 10-Year Review confirmed many of the findings of an earlier study arising from the Cardiff summit in 1999 (**www.europa.eu.int/comm/update/economicreform/cardiff99en.pdf**).

An annual scoreboard system has also been put in place to provide regular assessments of the impact of the SEM (**www.europa.eu.int/comm/internal_market/en/update/scoreboard**). The scoreboard system provides evidence of the delays in transposing SEM legislation, problems with implementation of legislation (non-conformity to directives and/or bad application), detailed surveys on the problems faced by consumers and firms when operating in the SEM, and reports on the progress towards European standardisation. A special issue of the scoreboard system appeared in 2002 to assess the first 10 years of the SEM – Internal Market Scoreboard 10 Years Without Frontiers. This provided evidence that intra-EU trade in goods relative to GDP had slightly improved since 1992 for most countries and for the EU as a whole with the smaller member states experiencing the largest gains (see Table 1.3). This evidence suggests that the SEM has not had a dramatic impact on intra-EU trade. However, the data does not include trade in services and utilities.

Table 1.3 The importance of intra-EU trade in goods relative to GDP (1992–97)

	1992 %	1993 %	1994 %	1995 %	1996 %	1997 %	1992–97* %
Belgium-Luxembourg	85.0	80.9	82.0	86.0	89.7	93.8	86.5
Denmark	36.5	33.7	35.7	38.7	37.8	40.0	37.2
Germany	26.7	22.2	23.0	24.2	24.5	25.6	24.4
Greece	22.9	20.4	20.2	21.6	18.5	17.9	20.1
Spain	18.7	19.2	22.7	25.8	27.0	27.3	23.6
France	25.7	21.7	23.6	25.2	25.3	26.8	24.8
Ireland	72.7	72.6	77.5	83.5	81.1	79.8	78.4
Italy	18.7	18.8	20.9	23.8	22.0	22.4	21.1
Netherlands	66.5	60.7	64.6	70.3	70.9	74.1	68.2
Austria	36.4	32.8	34.1	38.1	38.6	40.8	37.0
Portugal	41.3	37.0	40.3	42.1	45.0	45.4	42.0
Finland	26.4	28.1	30.2	33.7	34.1	35.1	31.7
Sweden	26.7	30.2	33.3	40.0	37.5	39.5	34.7
United Kingdom	22.3	22.9	24.0	26.4	26.6	24.6	24.5
Large Member States**	**23.4**	**21.3**	**22.9**	**24.9**	**24.8**	**25.2**	**23.8**
Small Member States***	**49.1**	**47.7**	**50.1**	**54.4**	**54.3**	**56.3**	**52.2**
EU 15	**28.4**	**26.5**	**28.3**	**30.9**	**30.8**	**31.5**	**29.5**

Notes:
* As of 1993 a revised methodology has been used for the collection of EU trade data, which explains the discontinuity in the time series between 1992 and 1993
** Germany, France, Italy, UK and Spain (ranked according to GDP average 1992–97)
*** All other member states

Source: Internal Market Scoreboard: 10 Years Without Frontiers, 2002

Table 1.4 Developments over time in EU price dispersion (coefficient of variation)

	1985 %	1993 %	1996 %
Private final consumption	21.9	15.9	15.9
Government final consumption	25.4	25.9	27.2
Gross fixed capital formation	12.8	14.5	13.5
Construction	19.2	23.6	22.0
Machinery and equipment	9.1	6.7	7.7
Gross Domestic Product	20.1	16.2	16.3

Source: Internal Market Scoreboard: 10 Years Without Frontiers, 2002

However, the 1996 Review and subsequent studies reveal that these sectors are proving to be resistant to large-scale liberalisation despite 10 years of legislative and policy action by the EU. It seems that more work is required before the full benefits of SEM can be secured.

The evidence on price differentials also confirms that more work remains to be done to achieve the desired benefits from the SEM. Although there is some evidence of a decline in price dispersion in some areas these have deteriorated since 1985 and also between 1993 and 1996 (see Table 1.4).

Plans to improve the effectiveness of the SEM

In the light of the failure of the SEM to provide benefits of the extent predicted by studies such as the Cecchini Report and because of the evidence provided by the 1996 Review, the 10-Year Review and the data uncovered by the scoreboard system, the EU agreed at the Amsterdam summit in 1997 to endorse an action plan for the single market (**www.europa.eu.int/comm/internal_market/en/update/action**). This action plan has been developed and a strategy to improve the effectiveness of the SEM in 2003–06 has been approved (European Commission, 2003). The Commission has also issued an implementation report to improve the working of the SEM based on the 10-Year Review (**www.europa.eu.int/comm/internal_market/en/update/strategy/sec-2003-43_en.pdf**).

The thrust of the SEM strategy is to continue to facilitate free movement and to promote an integrated services market by improving cooperation between national governments and the institutions of the EU in matters connected to the governance of the SEM and to develop legislation and policies that will promote a more effective SEM. This involves a number of key areas for improvement in the governance of the SEM and in the area of EU policy-making:

- Simplifying the regulatory environment;
- Improving the monitoring and enforcement of SEM regulations;
- Expanding public procurement opportunities;
- Further liberalisation of the utilities sector;
- Improving access to networks for the distribution of utilities;
- Reducing the impact of taxation obstacles to free movement;
- Promoting greater use of European standards;
- Improving the legal and institutional environment to aid pan-EU operations by firms;
- Promoting improved consumer protection policies to increase customer confidence when making cross-frontier transactions.

The main thrust of the strategy is not new. The Sutherland Report (European Commission, 1992) contained many ideas that are similar to the main themes of the current strategy to improve the effectiveness of the SEM. There are new elements and increased focus on certain issues in the current strategy. Improving access to networks is an important new element in the strategy. Emphasis on this has been seen to be necessary because of the failure to promote significant integration of utilities markets despite a large legislative programme to liberalise them. The importance of developing consumer protection policies has also become a focal part of the strategy (McDonald, 2000b). The 10-year struggle to implement effective governance of the SEM and to overcome vested interests in member states highlights the fact that creating a single market capable of delivering high benefits is a long and complex task. Clearly, enlargement of the EU will add to these problems as decision-making systems have to cope with more national governments and as EU institutions adapt to these new challenges. Furthermore, the accession countries will have to adjust to a new economic and business environment and existing member states will also be faced with new challenges arising from enlargement and more competitive markets in areas such as services, utilities and public procurement. It seems that completing the SEM is likely to require considerably more effort in terms of economic adjustment and improvements in governance systems.

Conclusion

Attempts by the EU to integrate the markets of member states have come a long way from the tentative beginnings of the ECSC. The formation of a CU and the SEM programme led to significant changes that have moved the EU towards greater free movement. However, the EU is not an effective free movement area in the sense that the USA or Germany are single markets. The establishment of EMU may help in the move towards the creation of such a free movement area, though the legal, institutional and economic conditions for it are not yet fully in place. Moreover, the EU is unsure of the type of free movement area that it wishes to create and enlargement, which will include many Central and Eastern European countries, is likely to complicate the process still further. The long haul towards creating a free movement area, started by the Treaty of Paris in 1951, still has a long way to go before the task can be finally completed.

References

Aisbett S (2002) 'Tax and Accounting Rules: Some Recent Developments', *European Business Review*, Vol. 14, pp. 92–7.

Amiti M (1998) 'New Trade Theories and Industrial Location in the EU: A Survey of the Evidence', *Oxford Review of Economic Policy*, Vol. 14, pp. 45–53.

Balassa B (1961) *The Theory of Economic Integration*, Allen and Unwin, London.

Balassa B (1987) 'Trade Creation and Diversion in the European Common Market', *The Manchester School*, Vol. XLII, No. 2, pp. 93–125.

Baldwin R (1989) 'On the growth effects of 1992', *Economic Policy*, Vol. 2, pp. 247–81.

Barry F (1999) *Understanding Ireland's Growth*, Macmillan, Basingstoke.

Bradley J, Barry F and Hannan A (2001) 'The Single Market, the Structural Funds and Ireland's Recent Growth', *Journal of Common Market Studies*, Vol. 39, pp. 537–52.

Brenton P, Sheehy J and Vancauteren M (2001) 'Technical Barriers to Trade in the European Union: Data, Trends and Implications for Accession Countries', *Journal of Common Market Studies*, Vol. 39, pp. 265–84.

Brülhart M (1998) 'Trading Places: Industrial Specialisation in the European Union', *Journal of Common Market Studies*, Vol. 36, pp. 319–46.

Carlin W, Estrin S and Schaffer M (2000) 'Measuring Progress in Transition and Towards EU Accession: A Comparison of Manufacturing Firms in Poland, Romania and Spain', *Journal of Common Market Studies*, Vol. 39, pp. 265–84.

Cecchini P (1988) *The European Challenge: 1992 The Benefits of a Single Market*, Wildwood House, Aldershot.

Cutler T, Halsem C, Williams J and Williams K (1989) *1992: The Struggle for Europe*, BERG, Oxford.

Davies E, Kay J and Smales C (1989) *1992: Myths and Realities*, London Business School, London.

Dyker D (ed.) (1992) *The European Economy*, Longman, London.

Emerson M, Aujean M, Catinat M, Goybet P and Jacquemin A (1988) *The Economics of 1992*, Oxford University Press, Oxford.

Ernst & Whinney (1988) *The Costs of Non-Europe: An Illustration in the Road Haulage Sector*, Research on the Costs of Non-Europe, Basic Findings, Vol. 4, Office for Official Publications of the European Communities, Luxembourg.

European Commission (1985) *Completing the Internal Market: The White Paper*, Office for Official Publications of the European Communities, Luxembourg.

European Commission (1992) *The Internal Market After 1992*, Office for Official Publications of the European Communities, Luxembourg.

European Commission (1996) *The Single Market Review, 38 Reports*, European Commission/ Kogan Page, London.

European Commission (1997) *The Competitiveness of European Industry*, Office for Official Publications of the European Communities, Luxembourg.

European Commission (2000a) *Tax Policy in the European Union*, Office for Official Publications of the European Communities, Luxembourg.

European Commission (2000b) *Internal Market Scoreboard: 10 Years Internal Market without Frontiers*, Office for Official Publications of the European Communities, Luxembourg.

European Commission (2003) *Internal Market Strategy: Priorities 2003–2006*, Com(2003) final, Brussels.

European Economy (1996) *Economic Evaluation of the Internal Market*, Reports and Studies No. 4, Office for Official Publications of the European Communities, Luxembourg.

Featherstone M, Moore B and Rhodes J (1979) 'EEC Membership and UK Trade in Manufactures', *Cambridge Journal of Economics*, Vol. 3, pp. 399–407.

Geroski P (1988) *Competition and Innovation*, Research on the Costs of Non-Europe, Basic Findings, Vol. 2, Office for Official Publications of the European Communities, Luxembourg.

Grahl J and Teague P (1990) *1992: The Big Market*, Lawrence and Wishart, London.

Group MAC (1988) *The Costs of Non-Europe in the Foodstuffs Industry*, Research on the Costs of Non-Europe, Basic Findings, Vol. 12, Office for Official Publications of the European Communities, Luxembourg.

Harris P and McDonald F (2004) *European Business and Marketing*, Sage, London.

Herin J (1986) *Rules of Origin and Differences Between Tariff Levels in EFTA and the EEC*, EFTA Occasional Paper No. 13, EFTA, Stockholm.

Hindley B and Howe M (1996) *Better Off Out: The Benefits and Costs of EU Membership*, Institute of Economic Affairs, London.

Jacquemin A (1982) 'Imperfect Market Structure and International Trade: Some Recent Research', *Kyklos*, Vol. 35, pp. 75–93.

Jacquemin A and Pench L (1996) *Europe Competing in the Global Economy*, Edward Elgar, Cheltenham.

Kreinin M E (1969) 'Trade Creation and Diversion by the EEC and EFTA', *Economia Internazionale*, Vol. 22, pp. 1–43.

Kreinin M E (1972) 'Effects of the EEC on Imports of Manufactures', *Economic Journal*, Vol. 82, pp. 897–920.

Krugman P (1979) 'Increasing Returns, Monopolistic Competition and International Trade', *Journal of International Economics*, Vol. 9, pp. 469–79.

Krugman P (1989) 'Economic Integration: Conceptual Issues', in A Jacquemin and A Sapir (eds), *The European Internal Market*, Oxford University Press, Oxford.

Krugman P (1991) *Geography and Trade*, MIT Press, Cambridge, Mass.

Krugman P (1995) *Development, Geography and Economic Theory*, MIT Press, Cambridge, Mass.

Krugman P and Obstfeld M (1993) *International Economics: Theory and Policy*, HarperCollins, New York.

Lipsey R G (1970) *The Theory of Customs Unions: General Equilibrium Analysis*, Weidenfeld & Nicolson, London.

McDonald F (1997) 'European Monetary Union: Some Implications for Companies', *Journal of General Management*, Vol. 23, pp. 47–64.

McDonald F (2000a) 'The European Union and Employment Relationships', *European Business Review*, Vol. 12, pp. 208–15.

McDonald F (2000b) 'Consumer Protection Policy in the European Union', *European Business Journal*, Vol. 12, pp. 39–46.

Mayes D (1978) 'The Effects of Economic Integration on Trade', *Journal of Common Market Studies*, Vol. 17, pp. 1–25.

Mayes D (1997) *The Evolution of the Single European Market*, Edward Elgar, Cheltenham.

Meade J E (1955) *The Theory of Customs Unions*, North Holland, Amsterdam.

Monti M (1996) *The Single Market and Tomorrow's Europe*, European Commission/Kogan Page, London.

Muller J (1988) *The Benefits of Completing the Internal Market for Telecommunications Services*, Research on the Costs of Non-Europe, Basic Findings, Vol. 10, Office for Official Publications of the European Communities, Luxembourg.

Nelson R and Winter S (1982) *An Evolutionary Theory of Economic Change*, Harvard University Press, Cambridge, Mass.

North D (1990) *Institutions, Institutional Change and Economic Performance*, Cambridge University Press, Cambridge.

Nugent N (2003) *The Government and Politics of the European Community*, Palgrave, Basingstoke.

Pelkmans J and Vanheukelen M (1988) *The Internal Markets of North America, Fragmentation and Integration in the US and Canada*, Research on the Costs of Non-Europe, Basic Findings, Vol. 16, Office for Official Publications of the European Communities, Luxembourg.

Porter M (1990) *The Competitive Advantage of Nations*, Macmillan, London.

Pratten C (1988) *A Survey of the Economies of Scale*, Research on the Costs of Non-Europe, Basic Findings, Vol. 2, Office for Official Publications of the European Communities, Luxembourg.

Price Waterhouse (1988) *The Costs of Non-Europe in Financial Services*, Research on the Costs of Non-Europe, Basic Findings, Vol. 9, Office for Official Publications of the European Communities, Luxembourg.

Resnick S A and Truman E M (1971) 'An Empirical Examination of Bilateral Trade in Western Europe', *Journal of International Economics*, Vol. 3, pp. 305–35.

Romer P (1986) 'Capital Accumulation in the Theory of Long Run Growth', in R Barro (ed.), *Modern Business Cycle Theory*, Basil Blackwell, Oxford.

Schwalbach J (1988) *Economies of Scale and Intra-Community Trade*, Research on the Costs of Non-Europe, Basic Findings, Vol. 2, Office for Official Publications of the European Communities, Luxembourg.

Smith A and Venables A (1988) *The Costs of Non-Europe: An Assessment Based on a Formal Model of Imperfect Competition and Economies of Scale*, Research on the Costs of Non-Europe, Basic Findings, Vol. 2, Office for Official Publications of the European Communities, Luxembourg.

Tinbergen J (1954) *International Economic Integration*, Elsevier, London.

Vertova G and McDonald F (2001) 'Geographical Concentration and Competitiveness in the European Union', *European Business Review*, Vol. 13, pp. 157–65.

Viner J (1950) *The Customs Union Issue*, Carnegie Endowment for International Peace, New York.

Williamson J and Bottrill A (1971) 'The Impact of Customs Unions on Trade in Manufactures', *Oxford Economic Papers*, No. 23, pp. 323–51.

Williamson O (1975) *Markets and Hierarchies: Analysis and Antitrust Implications: A Study in the Economics of Internal Organisation*, The Free Press, New York.

Winters L A (1987) 'Britain in Europe: A Survey of Quantitative Trade Studies', *Journal of Common Market Studies*, Vol. 25, pp. 315–35.

Chapter 2

Macroeconomic policy coordination

Nigel Healey

Introduction

Growing economic integration increases the policy interdependence between countries. Only truly autarkic states are insulated from economic developments elsewhere. For countries linked by trade and finance, changes in demand and interest rates are quickly transmitted from one economy to another. The external debt crises experienced by many developing countries following the 1980–82 recession in North America and Western Europe, which cut the developed world's demand for basic commodities, remain among the most dramatic examples of this interdependence. More recently, the 'Asian crisis' in the summer of 1997, which quickly spread to developing countries in Latin America and Eastern Europe, bears testament to the speed with which developments in one financial market can be transmitted to the rest of the globe's financial centres.

Within the EU, decades of economic integration have deepened and strengthened the economic linkages between the member states. As Table 2.1 shows, for the major member states such as Britain and Germany, intra-EU15 trade typically accounts for 55–60 per cent of total imports and exports; for the smaller EU states like Belgium and Denmark, the proportion of intra-EU15 trade is closer to 70 per cent. Cross-border investment, including mergers and acquisitions as well as transnational movement of labour, have been systematically promoted through, *inter alia*, the single market programme, the European Economic Area and the EU enlargements of 1973, 1981, 1986, 1995 and 2004. While the need for greater policy coordination has increased in line with closer economic ties, member states were, until the mid-1980s, reluctant to act cooperatively in setting macroeconomic policy. The pursuit of national self-interest led to countries pursuing divergent fiscal and monetary policies, which interacted across the EU to produce economic and financial instability.

The establishment of the European Monetary System (EMS) in 1979 offered member states that participated in its exchange rate mechanism (ERM) an opportunity to coordinate their macroeconomic policies more effectively. After a spate of early realignments, the ERM successfully provided a framework for policy coordination between 1983 and 1992. Inherent weaknesses in the system, brutally exposed by the exchange rate chaos of 1992–93, led the EU to adopt an alternative arrangement in the form of economic and monetary union (EMU) (see Chapter 3). This chapter examines the need for macroeconomic policy coordination within the EU and assesses the EU's record over the period 1979–2004.

Table 2.1 Intra- and extra-EU15 trade, selected countries, 2002

	Intra-EU15 (€m)	Extra-EU15 (€m)	Intra-EU15 (% total)	Extra-EU15 (% total)
Belgium				
Exports	166577	62031	72.9	27.1
Imports	148730	61591	70.7	29.3
Denmark				
Exports	40074	20729	65.9	34.1
Imports	37504	15711	70.5	29.5
Germany				
Exports	354804	294367	54.7	45.3
Imports	286416	232072	55.2	44.8
France				
Exports	215411	135392	61.4	38.6
Imports	229680	118217	66.0	34.0
Italy				
Exports	144890	124170	53.9	46.1
Imports	150464	110762	57.6	42.4
UK				
Exports	174297	122018	58.8	41.2
Imports	192556	173684	52.6	47.4

Source: Adapted from Eurostat

Policy interdependence between member states

The countries of the EU are primarily linked via the balance of payments (Cooper, 1968). Any change in macroeconomic policy within one country changes aggregate demand (and so its demand for other countries' exports) and its interest rate; and with flexible exchange rates, changes in interest rates mean a change in relative exchange rates vis-à-vis other member states, with further knock-on effects for aggregate demand in all countries. The induced effects and the path back to equilibrium depend upon the nature of the initial change in macroeconomic policy. Exhibits 2.1 and 2.2 show that changes in fiscal and monetary policy affect trading partners in different ways: with flexible exchange rates, an expansionary fiscal policy tends to 'spill over' and stimulate activity in other states; an expansionary monetary policy, on the other hand, has the opposite effect, increasing demand in the originating state (which benefits from an exchange rate depreciation), but reducing activity in the other countries (which suffer an exchange rate appreciation).

The speed and scale of the external effects of macroeconomic policy also depend upon the degree of economic and financial integration (Buiter and Marston, 1985; Hodgman and Wood, 1989). The greater the integration of goods markets (i.e. the openness of economies), the greater the extent to which changes in demand in one country will spill over to its trading partners. And the more integrated the financial markets, the greater the extent to which international capital will move across the foreign exchanges, changing exchange rates and driving together interest rates. The

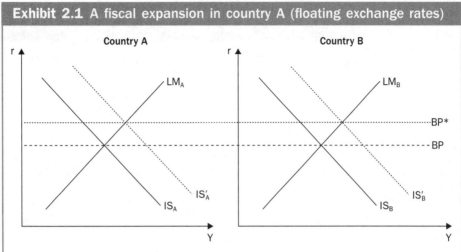

Exhibit 2.1 A fiscal expansion in country A (floating exchange rates)

This exhibit shows the standard IS–LM model for a two-country world. The interest rate is on the vertical axis, with output on the horizontal axis. IS_A, LM_A represent goods market and money market equilibria in country A, and IS_B, LM_B represent goods and money market equilibria in country B. There is perfect capital mobility, which means that interest rates must be harmonised, here along the BP schedule.

Suppose that in country A the government increases government spending, shifting IS_A to the right to IS_A'. This fiscal expansion puts upward pressure on interest rates in country A and causes a capital inflow, leading to an appreciation of the exchange rate vis-à-vis country B. Part of the fiscal expansion is 'crowded out', limiting the rightward shift in IS_A. In country B, the fiscal stimulus on country A, taken together with the *depreciation* of its exchange rate vis-à-vis country A, leads to an induced shift to the right of its IS_B curve to IS_B' and upward pressure on interest rates in country B. Equilibrium is finally restored when interest rates have risen in both countries, shifting the BP function to BP*.

The final result of the fiscal expansion in country A is to increase output and interest rates in both country A and country B and cause the exchange rate of country A to appreciate vis-à-vis country B. As a consequence, the structure of demand in countries A and B is altered. In country A, government spending and imports are higher and (interest sensitive) investment is lower. In country B, government spending is unchanged, investment is lower, but exports are higher.

EU is highly integrated in both senses. The single market programme completed the elimination of non-tariff barriers to trade in goods and services, while also dismantling the remaining exchange controls that had previously allowed partial isolation of national money markets.

The discussion outlined in Exhibits 2.1 and 2.2 highlights the externalities involved in macroeconomic policymaking for interdependent countries. Under flexible exchange rates and with perfect capital mobility, part of the benefits of a fiscal expansion spills over to other trading partners, while a monetary expansion benefits the originating country at the expense of its partners. The terms of the 'share-out' in each case, however, depend upon the relative size of the countries involved. In the figures above, countries A and B are assumed to be of approximately equal size. Both share equally in the benefits of country A's fiscal expansion, while the proportionate boost to output in country A following its monetary expansion is broadly equal to the proportionate contraction suffered by B. If the

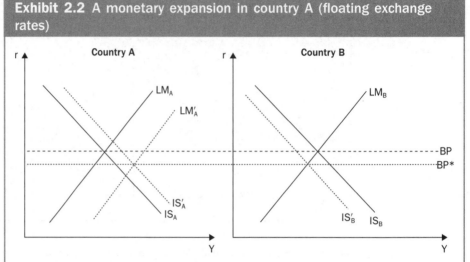

Exhibit 2.2 A monetary expansion in country A (floating exchange rates)

This exhibit shows the effect of a monetary expansion in country A, shifting LM_A to the right to LM_A'. This has the effect of increasing demand in country A and putting downward pressure on interest rates, inducing a capital outflow and a depreciation of the exchange rate vis-à-vis country B. This has the knock-on effect of shifting IS_A to the right to IS_A'. In country B, the increase in demand in country A for its exports is more than offset by the appreciation of the exchange rate, shifting IS_B to the left to IS_B' and putting downward pressure on interest rates in country B. In equilibrium, output increases in country A and falls in country B, with interest rates falling. This effect is often known as 'exporting unemployment' by engineering a competitive depreciation. The pattern of demand is altered in country A (with consumption, investment and exports higher) and country B (with consumption lower and investment and imports higher).

countries are of unequal size, the share-out tips in favour of the larger country. For example, a large country will internalise most of the benefit of a fiscal expansion, while a small country will suffer most of the benefit spilling over to its larger neighbour. This issue of differing sizes is very important in Northern Europe, where the German economy is very large relative to the smaller states (e.g. Denmark, the Netherlands, Belgium/Luxembourg) with which it is most closely integrated. This question is re-examined in the discussion of so-called 'German policy leadership' during the ERM era later in this chapter.

The case for policy coordination

The existence of significant policy spill-over effects raises the risk that, unless countries cooperate in setting policy, there may be significant inefficiencies (Cooper, 1968, 1985). Consider first the case of fiscal policy under floating exchange rates. It has already been shown that, with perfect capital mobility, if a country pursues an expansionary fiscal policy, part of the expansionary effect will spill over to its trading partners. If all countries are seeking to reduce unemployment, smaller countries may be tempted to 'free-ride' on the expansionary policies of larger countries.

Table 2.2 Effects of expansionary fiscal policy (floating exchange rates)

	Initiating country	Free-rider countries
Government budget balance	Worsen	Improve
Current account	Worsen	Improve
Output/Employment	Increase	Increase

Table 2.2 summarises the impact of an expansionary fiscal policy on the initiating country, together with the induced effects on trading partners (free-riders). Significantly, both the initiator and the free-rider enjoy benefits in terms of increased output and employment. But the cost, in terms of a deterioration in the government's budget deficit and the current account, is borne by the initiating country, while the free-riders enjoy improvements in both sectoral balances (this is because for the free-riders the induced growth is 'export-led').

Table 2.2 suggests that countries have a strong incentive to free-ride on the expansionary fiscal policies of their larger trading partners. This tendency was classically in evidence during the mid-1980s (Ishii, McKibbin and Sachs, 1985). After the election of President Reagan in 1981, the US administration embarked on a series of deep tax cuts designed to stimulate the economy. Output and employment did begin to recover, but at the cost of a large budget deficit and, as the US dollar appreciated due to the high US interest rates, an unprecedented current account deficit. As the value of the dollar peaked in 1985, the US administration accused the EU and Japan of free-riding on its expansion, enjoying the benefits of recovery while leaving the United States to pay the cost in terms of its budget and current account deficits. Under the 'Plaza Accord', the United States managed to coerce the leaders of the other two G3 countries, Japan and Germany, to adopt more expansionary fiscal stances and the imbalances gradually eased thereafter.

The external effects of monetary policy under floating exchange rates give rise to a different problem when macroeconomic policy is not coordinated. Recall that the country initiating the monetary expansion effectively 'exports' its unemployment to its trading partners, by using a competitive depreciation of its exchange rate to increase output by boosting net exports (since this is symmetrical, a country could equally export its inflation, by using a monetary contraction and an exchange rate appreciation). In this case, the risk is not of free-riding, but rather of retaliation by countries adversely affected by the negative spill-over effects (see Table 2.3).

Table 2.3 Effects of expansionary monetary policy (floating exchange rates)

	Initiating country	Free-rider countries
Government budget balance	Improve	Worsen
Current account	Improve	Worsen
Output/Employment	Increase	Reduce

Uncoordinated monetary policy and the prisoner's dilemma

It is clear that, under floating exchange rates, it is the uncoordinated use of monetary, rather than fiscal, policy which poses the greater problem (Canzoneri and Minford, 1989). If other countries retaliate against a competitive depreciation by switching to more expansionary monetary policies, then not only will this cancel out the original depreciation, but all countries will be forced to adopt more inflationary monetary policies for no gain in terms of higher output and employment or an improved current account. In this sense, monetary policy is subject to the 'prisoner's dilemma' problem, in which rational decision-making by individual states leads to a collective outcome that is sub-optimal for all participants (in this case, inflation).

Under floating exchange rates, countries concerned to increase their competitiveness and employment face a choice between engineering a depreciation (by adopting a more expansionary monetary policy) or pursuing an unchanged monetary stance. The decision is complicated by the fact that their trading partners face the same choice. The pay-off to country A is positive if it depreciates and its trading partner, country B, does not, but negative (due to higher inflation, with unchanged competitiveness) if both attempt to depreciate at the same time.

Table 2.4 illustrates the matrix of pay-offs that face each country. The first figure in each cell represents the change in economic welfare for country A, and the second for country B, of each set of outcomes. Clearly, their collective welfare is maximised if neither country attempts to depreciate its currency. However, for each country, the decision to depreciate is 'dominant'. For country A, depreciation is welfare-increasing if country B does not depreciate and the least welfare-reducing if country B does depreciate. Because the exchange rate policy 'game' is symmetrical, country B will similarly always choose depreciation. The net result is that both countries depreciate, cancelling out each other's attempt to gain a competitive advantage and causing only inflation (the worst possible collective result).

Because lack of coordination in the area of monetary policy provides the greater risk of a sub-optimal outcome, most examples of international policy coordination have tended to focus on monetary, rather than fiscal, policy (Foreman-Peck, 1991). Examples include the Gold Standard (*circa* 1821–1913), the interwar Gold Exchange Standard (1925–31), the Bretton Woods system (1944–73), the EU's currency 'snake' (1972–79) and the EMS (1979–99) and the G3's 'Louvre Accord' (1987). These all represent attempts to coordinate monetary policy through a system of managed (or fixed) exchange rates. In the absence of capital controls or other obstacles to the free movement of international capital, pegging the exchange rate to that of another country provides a mechanism for automatically bringing about convergence in

Table 2.4 Uncoordinated monetary policy as an example of the 'Prisoner's Dilemma'

		Country A	
		Depreciate	Do not depreciate
Country B	Depreciate	−5, −5	−10, +10
	Do not depreciate	+10, −10	0, 0

monetary policies. It is to a consideration of managed exchange rates as a solution to the prisoner's dilemma that the next section turns.

Monetary policy coordination through managed exchange rates

While managed exchange rates provide a framework for coordinating monetary policies across participating countries, such arrangements do not completely eliminate the problem of uncooperative policymaking. This is known as the 'N-1 problem'. Within a managed exchange rate system, the monetary policies of the members must converge on some 'average' policy. The crucial issue is how that average is determined. For a very small country, managed exchange rates provide a discipline which forces its monetary policy into line with that of the exchange rate bloc as a whole. However, for large countries, their monetary stance both contributes to, and is determined by, the average monetary stance of the bloc.

The monetary effects of the balance of payments

Before turning to these more complex issues, consider the basic principle underlying exchange rate management. The starting point is the money supply identity:

$$M = D + F \tag{2.1}$$

The money supply, M, comprises the sum of domestic credit, D (i.e. bank credit to the government and private sector) and foreign exchange reserves, F. In terms of first differences (i.e. changes):

$$\Delta M = DCE + \Delta F \tag{2.2}$$

and

$$\Delta F = BP$$

so that,

$$\Delta M = DCE + BP \tag{2.3}$$

where ΔM is the growth in the money supply, DCE is domestic credit expansion (net bank lending to the government and private sector), and the change in foreign exchange reserves, ΔF, is equal to the balance of payments (on current and capital account) financed by foreign exchange intervention, BP. If the exchange rate is floating, there is no foreign exchange rate intervention by definition and BP = 0. For example, if there is a balance of payments deficit, this implies that the private sector's demand for foreign currency (to buy imports and foreign assets) exceeds the supply (from sales of exports, etc.). To maintain the target exchange rate, the central bank must satisfy the excess demand for foreign currency by selling from its official reserves, thereby reducing the domestic money supply.

These monetary side-effects must continue as long as the balance of payments is in deficit. Herein lies the automatic adjustment mechanism of a fixed exchange rate system: payments imbalances automatically lead to changes in the money supply which work to eliminate the cause of the imbalance. For example, a country may have a balance of payments deficit either because aggregate demand is too high or because it is uncompetitive (i.e. at the target nominal exchange rate, domestic wages and prices are higher than those abroad). The monetary contraction caused by the balance of payments deficit will deflate aggregate demand and put downward pressure on prices and nominal wages, improving its competitiveness, until the deficit is eliminated.

Exhibit 2.3 illustrates the monetary linkages between member states in an exchange rate bloc. It shows that monetary policy becomes partly endogenous through

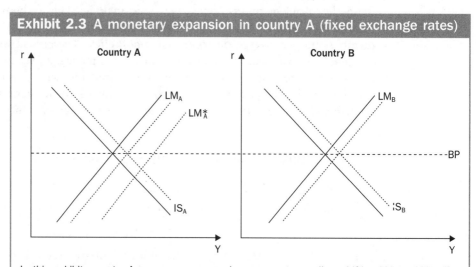

Exhibit 2.3 A monetary expansion in country A (fixed exchange rates)

In this exhibit, country A pursues an expansionary monetary policy, shifting LM_A to LM_A^*. The result is a balance of payments deficit, which country A can accommodate in the short run by buying its own currency and running down its foreign exchange reserves. This foreign exchange rate intervention leads to a steady reduction in the money supply, gradually reversing the original shift in the LM curve. If country A is very small relative to the rest of the exchange rate bloc, then in time the monetary expansion will be completely reversed and the LM schedule will return to LM_A. Only the composition of the money supply will be altered (the domestic credit component will be higher and the foreign reserve element smaller).

The situation is altered if country A is large enough for the monetary spill-over effects to have an impact on monetary policy in other countries. In the exhibit above, the initial monetary expansion causes a rightward shift from LM_A to LM_A^* in country A, with a resulting balance of payments deficit. In country B, the increase in demand for its exports by country A leads to a rightwards shift in IS_B and a corresponding balance of payments surplus. For country A, the sales of foreign exchange reserves necessary to finance the balance of payments deficit gradually shift LM_A^* back to the left. But in country B, the purchases of foreign exchange reserves required to 'cap' its exchange rate in the face of a balance of payments surplus shift LM_B to the right. The resultant increase in output in country B feeds back to country A as higher demand for country A's exports, shifting IS_A to the right. Crucially, equilibrium is finally restored with output and the money supply higher in both countries. Country A has exported part of its monetary expansion to country B.

The significance of the relative size of the countries involved in an exchange rate system is clear. When one country adopts a more expansionary monetary policy, it increases the money supply of the exchange rate bloc as a whole. Because the countries are interlinked through the balance of payments, the money supply increase is gradually shared across all countries. For a small country, almost all the increase is 'exported', making monetary policy ineffective. For large countries, however, part of the increase is retained, giving them a residual power to use monetary policy for domestic purposes.

the foreign exchange reserves component of the money supply, but that it retains an exogenous component through domestic credit. For small countries, almost all monetary discretion is lost in an exchange rate system because most of any exogenous increase in the money supply will be 'exported'. Large countries, however, can continue to exercise some monetary sovereignty. For example, consider two members of an exchange rate system. For country X, its money supply is equal to 5 per cent of the money supply of the bloc as a whole, while country Y has a share equal to 50 per cent. This implies that, if country X were to increase its money supply by 10 per cent, 9.5 per cent of the increase would be 'exported' to the rest of the bloc. Across the exchange rate system as a whole, including in country X, the money supply would increase by only 0.5 per cent. For country X, its ability to pursue monetary policy would be effectively eliminated by its membership of the exchange rate system. For country Y, conversely, only half of an initial 10 per cent increase in its money supply would be 'exported'; that is, the money supply of the bloc as a whole, including country Y, would increase by 5 per cent, delivering a significant expansionary boost. For country Y, therefore, its domination of the exchange rate system allows it considerable residual monetary discretion.

The deflationary bias of managed exchange rates

Before considering the alternative ways in which the N-1 problem can be resolved, it is important to recognise a significant asymmetry in the monetary side-effects of exchange rate intervention. In the preceding discussion, it is implicitly assumed that all countries in the system, whether those with deficits or those with the offsetting surpluses, intervene to support or cap their exchange rates respectively and, crucially, that they allow the monetary consequences of this intervention to work its way through their economies. Consider, however, the situation faced by the two groups of countries. The deficit country will lose foreign exchange reserves for as long as the balance of payments deficit persists. The knowledge that, if its reserves run out before the deficit is eliminated, the country will have to either devalue or leave the foreign exchange system, means that countries with a deficit often take policy action to reinforce the automatic adjustment mechanism (e.g. by reducing the domestic component of the money supply, tightening fiscal policy).

The surplus country, however, faces a different prospect. There is no limit to its capacity to accumulate foreign exchange reserves, while automatic adjustment implies allowing a monetary expansion to feed through to aggregate demand and increase prices and wages. There is a strong incentive for surplus countries, fearing the inflationary consequences of adjustment, to inhibit rather than supplement automatic adjustment. By selling, say, extra government bonds to its non-bank private sector, thereby reducing the domestic component of the money supply, a surplus country can 'sterilise' (i.e. neutralise) the monetary side-effects of its capping intervention in the foreign exchange market. That is:

$$\Delta M = DCE + BP \qquad (2.4)$$

$$-ve \quad -ve \quad +ve$$

In this way, a balance of payments surplus can be made consistent with an unchanged monetary stance, with the structure of the money supply shifting from domestic credit in favour of foreign exchange reserves. Clearly, if surplus countries sterilise their foreign exchange intervention, then the whole burden of adjustment to equilibrium must fall on deficit countries, which must adjust or leave the system.

This asymmetry is enormously important and gives surplus countries a powerful influence over the exchange rate bloc as a whole. In the absence of sterilisation, a country that increases its money supply 'exports' part of the increase to the rest of the bloc; conversely, a country that cuts its money supply can 'export' part of the reduction to the rest of the bloc. Sterilisation breaks the first of these links, but not the second. It prevents monetary expansions being exported and forces countries initiating monetary expansions to claw back the increase. But it still allows countries pursuing tight monetary policies to 'export' cuts in their money supply.

There are three possible solutions to the N-1 problem:

- Cooperative monetary policies, in which the members of the exchange rate system agree a common monetary stance, which is in the best interests of the bloc as a whole.

- Non-cooperative monetary policies, in which each country makes domestic monetary policy in its own self-interest, attempting to 'export' inflationary or deflationary monetary shocks. Given the deflationary bias due to sterilisation, the result will be that the low inflation members can pursue tight monetary policies, while the more inflationary members will repeatedly be forced to devalue or leave the system.

- Hegemony, in which the largest, low inflation member of the bloc dominates the rest, setting a tight monetary stance to which the others adjust.

This set of alternatives provides a useful way of categorising EU monetary policy since 1979. The architects of the EMS set out to design a system built around monetary policy cooperation, in which symmetry was ensured and participating member states would agree a common monetary policy. Its early operation, however, was marred by non-cooperation, especially in the period 1979–83 and again in the period 1992–93. For the period in between, the EMS operated on a hegemonic basis, under so-called 'German policy leadership'. Between 1993 and 1999, as the EU built the new framework for EMU, monetary policy cooperation was re-established, ultimately leading to the creation of the European Central Bank (ECB) setting interest rates for the eurozone bloc (see Chapter 3). It is to a consideration of these issues that the next sections turn.

EU macroeconomic policy coordination since 1979

Over the last quarter of a century, the 'core' EU members – for none of the macroeconomic policy initiatives has ever enjoyed the full support of all member states – have moved from a managed, and at times chaotic, exchange rate system to full EMU. This transition has involved the adoption of a single currency, with interest rates set by the ECB, and constraints on the pursuit of fiscal policy. The following sections examine the history of macroeconomic policy coordination in the EU since 1979.

The European Monetary System

EMS began operation on 13 March 1979, with its membership comprising those countries that were then members of the EU. The core of the system, however, consisted of those member countries that participated in the exchange rate mechanism (ERM). The provisions of the EMS were basically fourfold and were designed to solve the N-1 problem through monetary policy cooperation rather than hegemony:

1 a set of provisions regarding exchange rates;
2 a supporting set of provisions regarding access to credit facilities;
3 a common currency of denomination, the European Currency Unit (ECU);
4 a framework for agreeing a common monetary stance.

The ERM was a system of fixed, but adjustable, exchange rates. Its central feature was the parity grid, which showed the central rates between each pair of member countries. The central parities could be realigned, but only with the agreement of all other ERM members. Each member was required to maintain its currency's bilateral exchange rate against every other currency within a maximum permitted band of fluctuation around these declared central parities. The size of this band was ±2.25 per cent of central parity between 1979 and 1993. Exceptionally, countries could enter with wider transitional bands of ±6 per cent, which Italy, Spain, Portugal and the United Kingdom used before 1993. The standard band was increased to ±15 per cent in August 1993 following severe speculative pressures on some of the weaker currencies, although the Netherlands and Germany retained the previous narrow band for the guilder and the deutschmark and Belgium/Luxembourg and Austria informally respected the previous ±2.25 per cent band against the deutschmark.

Intervention to maintain currencies within the bands was intended to be a collaborative effort, with the monetary authorities of both the weak and strong currencies taking reinforcing action. In the absence of sterilisation, such foreign exchange intervention leads to a monetary contraction in the weak currency country and a monetary expansion in the strong currency country.

As intervention in the foreign exchange markets was obligatory to prevent a currency from breaking through its bands, the ERM involved credit provisions under which the issuer of the strong currency was required to lend (without limit) to the issuer of the weak currency for purposes of intervention at the margin. The most important component of the credit mechanism was the so-called Very Short Term Financing Facility (VSTFF). Repayment was normally required within 75 days (45 days from 1979 to 1987), although revolving credits were possible. Finally, central banks also pooled 20 per cent of their gold and foreign exchange reserves in exchange for ECU in a central fund, the European Monetary Cooperation Fund (EMCF), which was superseded in January 1994 by the Frankfurt-based European Monetary Institute, the forerunner of the ECB.

The ECU and the 'divergence indicator'

The identity of the EMS was enhanced by the provision for a common currency, the ECU, which was the forerunner of the present-day euro. The ECU was a composite currency, consisting of a fixed quantity of French francs (FFr1.33200), German deutschmarks (DM0.62420) and so on. The composition was chosen so that the respective currency weights in the ECU broadly reflected an average of their shares in the EU's GDP and trade. The ECU was used as the currency of denomination for EU transactions (e.g. for the EU Budget, farm support prices, etc.) and the central exchange rates of the ERM currencies were also expressed in ECU.

Part of the rationale of the ECU was to prevent larger members of the ERM exporting inflation or deflation. The parity grid and credit arrangements *per se* would, by enforcing symmetry of adjustments, allow larger countries to influence the monetary stance of the ERM bloc as a whole. Given the scope for sterilisation, this meant in practice that the ERM faced the serious risk that the largest, low inflation country, namely Germany, would give the system a significant deflationary bias.

The architects of the ERM hoped that, by adding parities against the ECU to the parity grid and specifically limiting each currency's fluctuations against the ECU to less than the maximum permissible against other individual currencies, the system could prevent domination by large members. To illustrate the logic of this approach, consider a unilateral tightening of monetary policy by the German Bundesbank, which leads to the deutschmark appreciating x per cent against other member currencies. Because of the symmetrical nature of foreign exchange rate intervention, German open-market sales of deutschmarks (which, in any event, may be sterilised to prevent an increase in the German money supply) would be paralleled by open-market purchases of their own currencies by the N-1 other central banks, thereby allowing part of the German monetary contraction to be exported to the rest of the ERM bloc.

Against the ECU, however, the deutschmark will have appreciated by $(1-wG)x$ per cent, where wG is the weight of the deutschmark in the composition of the ECU (approximately 35 per cent), while each of the other, smaller currencies, which have depreciated against the deutschmark but not against each other, will have depreciated by $(wG)x$ per cent against the ECU. To illustrate this with some simple arithmetic, if the deutschmark appreciates 10 per cent against all other currencies, it will appreciate by 6.5 per cent against the ECU, while all other currencies will depreciate by only 3.5 per cent against the ECU. The ECU exchange rate therefore serves to identify currencies which are 'diverging', not simply from some other individual currency, but from all the others together.

The 'divergence indicator' was intended to impose a requirement for unilateral adjustment whenever a currency diverged from its central ECU rate by more than $0.75(1-wi)y$ per cent, where wi is the weight of country i in the ECU and y per cent is the maximum permitted deviation from central parities against other currencies (i.e. 2.25 per cent pre-1993, 15 per cent thereafter). The key point is that this threshold would be reached first by a currency moving out of line with the average, thereby forcing adjustment on countries pursuing a monetary policy at variance with its ERM partners. This concept of singling out a particular currency and forcing the presumption of adjustment upon it, whatever the direction of its deviation (i.e. weak or strong), was greeted as a radical innovation at the time of the inception of the system, promising a correction of the bias against weak currency (i.e. deficit) countries that tends to be endemic in fixed exchange rate systems. More directly, it was an attempt to free the EMS from German policy dominance, which had given a strong deflationary bias to earlier EU attempts at policy coordination.

Non-cooperative monetary policy-making, 1979–83

While the architects of the EMS sought to solve the N-1 problem by cooperative making of monetary policy, bolstered by mechanisms to ensure symmetry of adjustment and to prevent individual countries 'exporting' inflationary or deflationary monetary policies, the early years of the EMS were characterised by policy conflict. The failure to prevent sterilisation by the surplus countries, a reluctance to use the divergence indicator as intended, and initially divergent views of the goals of monetary policy almost completely undermined the vision of cooperative policy-making coordinated through the ERM. In the years that followed, non-cooperative policy-making and the resulting exchange rate instability gave way to German hegemony.

The early years of the EMS can best be described as a period of non-cooperative monetary policy-making and featured a number of realignments of central parities. Table 2.5 shows the dates and sizes involved of all the realignments undertaken

Table 2.5 Realignments within the Exchange Rate Mechanism

	B/L	DK	D	EL	E	F	IRL	I	NL	A	P	FIN	S	UK
24/09/79		−2.9	+2.0											
30/11/79		−4.8												
23/03/81							−6.0							
05/10/81			+5.5			−3.0		+3.0	+5.5					
22/02/82	−8.5	−3.0												
14/06/82			+4.25			−5.75		−2.75	+4.25					
21/03/83	+1.5	+2.5	+5.5			−2.5	−3.5	−2.5	+3.5					
22/07/85	+2.0	+2.0	+2.0			+2.0	+2.0	−6.0	+2.0					
07/04/86	+1.0	+1.0	+3.0			−3.0			+3.0					
04/08/86							−8.0							
12/01/87	+2.0		+3.0						+3.0					
08/01/90								−3.7						
08/09/92												Float		
13/09/92								−7.0						
16/09/92														Float
17/09/92					−5.0			Float						
19/11/92													Float	
22/11/92					−6.0						−6.0			
01/02/93							−10.0							
13/03/93					−8.0						−6.5			
02/08/93						Target bands widened to ±15%								
06/03/95					−7.0						−3.5			

Notes: B/L = Belgium/Luxembourg; DK = Denmark; D = Germany; EL = Greece; E = Spain; F = France; IRL = Ireland; I = Italy; NL = Netherlands; A = Austria; P = Portugal; FIN = Finland; S = Sweden

Source: Adapted from Eurostat, European Commission

between 1979 and the move to wider (15 per cent) bands in August 1993 (see Ozkan, 2003 for a detailed analysis of ERM realignments). It shows the frequent, generalised realignments that took place in the first four years of the EMS. The frequency with which realignments occurred provoked the description of the early EMS as a 'crawling peg' (e.g. Gros and Thygesen, 1992). This was a reference to the concept devised by Williamson in the 1960s (Williamson, 1983) of an exchange rate system in which real rates of exchange (i.e. nominal exchange rates adjusted for differential national inflation rates) are kept constant by periodically changing nominal rates in line with inflation differentials. Such a system allows countries to pursue quasi-independent monetary policies, while protecting their competitiveness (i.e. their real exchange rates). Between 1979 and 1983, inflation differentials were indeed high and member countries found it easy to resort to realignments to ape a 'crawling peg' arrangement.

This phase of the EMS proved temporary as countries began to adopt a more determined counter-inflationary policy stance. The pace at which countries adopted this new determination varied. For the system as a whole, the switch was gradual, but many commentators pick out the decision by the French government in early 1983 to adopt severe counter-inflationary measures as marking the end of the 'crawling peg' era (see Sachs and Wyplosz, 1986). This convergence in policy objectives on the tough, anti-inflationary stance of the German Bundesbank made formerly expansion-minded countries like France and Italy more prepared to accept German hegemony. Thereafter, they increasingly allowed Germany to 'export' deflation and chose to follow the German policy lead, rather than seeking the soft option of devaluation. Paradoxically, the threat of German hegemony that had so preoccupied the architects of the EMS gradually came to be seen by its members as a positive strength in the mid-1980s, rather than a weakness (Wyplosz, 1989).

German policy leadership, 1983–92

The end of the 'crawling peg' period gave way to a period of German hegemony. Realignments became less frequent, as member countries consciously used their membership of the ERM as a means of disciplining inflationary expectations and achieving low inflation. The increased willingness of the other ERM members to accept German hegemony stemmed, in turn, from changing attitudes across the EU to the trade-off between inflation and unemployment. By the early 1980s, it was becoming increasingly accepted among EU governments that inflation is a 'monetary phenomenon' in the long run, so that higher inflation rates could not deliver sustainably lower levels of unemployment. It was the earlier belief in a stable trade-off between unemployment and inflation, and national differences over the point at which to strike a balance between these two social 'evils', that had resulted in the divergent national monetary policies of the 1970s. The gradual official conversion to the concept of a vertical long-run Phillips Curve (Friedman, 1968) persuaded many EU governments that price stability was the only sensible objective of monetary policy. In this new intellectual climate, the prospect of the ERM bloc being dominated by a low-inflation Germany no longer caused the concern it had when the EMS had first been mooted.

Moreover, advances in economic theory suggested that, not only was German hegemony unlikely to impose long-run economic costs on other member states (in terms of permanently higher unemployment), but the ERM might actually reduce the transitional costs of achieving low inflation. The theory of 'reputational policy' (Barro and Gordon, 1983; Backus and Driffill, 1985) suggests that a country's ability to reduce its inflation rate and the cost in terms of higher unemployment of doing so depend on its 'reputation'. A government that is credible (i.e. has a good reputation) is able to make announcements about its counter-inflationary intentions which are believed and, because they are believed, inflationary expectations are reduced and the unemployment cost of getting inflation down is reduced.

The problem for the historically high inflation countries of the EU is establishing a reputation for pursuing low inflation, thereby reconditioning inflationary expectations in a way which makes disinflation less costly. ERM membership appeared to provide a solution: by maintaining an exchange rate fixed to low-inflation Germany, member governments were able to make a public commitment to price stability that was visible and easy for people to monitor and understand. For this reason, it became increasingly accepted during the mid-1980s that governments which participated in the ERM were able to 'import' the Bundesbank's anti-inflation reputation (De Grauwe, 1990; Weber, 1991). Shifts in governments' attitudes to the inflation/unemployment trade-off and widespread belief in the importance of reputation combined to make German hegemony not just acceptable, but positively desirable. Such was the transformation in government thinking over the 1980s that, by the time Britain joined in 1990, membership was publicly discussed almost exclusively in terms of the disinflationary benefits for Britain and hardly at all in terms of greater exchange rate stability on intra-EU trade.

During the period 1983–92, the evidence supports the thesis that German hegemony became established. For example, although all the formal provisions of the EMS are symmetrical, Germany sterilised the effect of foreign exchange intervention to a much greater extent than other countries, thus pursuing its own independent monetary policy. Foreign exchange intervention was almost always conducted 'intra-marginally' (i.e. before the exchange rate hit the band) and by countries other than Germany. Germany never devalued against any other currency in any realignment, and the divergence indicator fell into disuse (Mastropasqua, Micossi and Rinaldi, 1988; Haldane, 1991). It is easy to see that, when the name of the policy game is the reduction of inflation, the divergence indicator would become useless (it would be inconsistent to ask Germany to raise its inflation rate towards the average in the name of symmetry when the overriding purpose of policy was to cut inflation).

The return of non-cooperative monetary policymaking, 1992–93

The phenomenon of high inflation countries choosing to follow Germany's anti-inflationary example, rather than devaluing against the deutschmark (or leaving the ERM altogether), was entirely unintended, but by the early 1990s had come to be regarded as the system's greatest attraction. Germany provided a strong, anti-inflationary anchor for Europe. By setting domestic interest rates at whatever level was necessary to maintain their exchange rates within their target bands against the deutschmark, other ERM states could effectively be guaranteed that their inflation rates would come down to low German levels. For countries (like the UK) that had unsuccessfully experimented with monetary targets and were left with no clear guide for monetary policy, ERM membership offered the prospect of both greater exchange rate stability and low and stable inflation rates.

However, while being one of its most attractive features, the German anti-inflation anchor also created a 'fault-line' in the system. The Bundesbank's hostility to unlimited intervention in support of weak currencies meant that currencies which fell to their trading floors were vulnerable to speculative attack. In other words, the ERM parities (and, indeed, the system as a whole) were simply not credible (Eichengreen and Wyplosz, 1993). During the 1980s, German policy leadership became steadily established, but the significance of the fault line was not fully realised for two reasons. First, until 1990 almost all the ERM members maintained some form of capital controls, which placed legislative restrictions on capital movements and artificially limited the scale of a speculative attack on a weak currency. Secondly, the business cycles of the EU economies were broadly synchronised during the 1980s, so that the policy adjustments necessary for other countries to follow the German lead and keep comfortably within their target bands against the deutschmark were relatively painless.

Tensions began to emerge almost immediately after German reunification in 1990. In order to control mounting inflationary pressures, the Bundesbank was forced to adopt a much tighter monetary stance, at a time when deflationary pressures were already intensifying in other EU states (notably the United Kingdom, France and Italy). The protection that capital controls had given to weak currencies was thus removed just as the costs (in terms of higher unemployment and lost output) of following the German policy lead were temporarily increased. Those countries which could not, or would not, continue to match German monetary policy accordingly became increasingly vulnerable to speculative attack, as high German interest rates forced their currencies towards their trading floors. For the United Kingdom in particular, international investors watched as growing political pressure to address the recession forced the Government into a series of interest rate cuts between October 1990 and September 1992, despite the fact that German rates were rising over the same period.

In the immediate run-up to sterling's withdrawal from the EMS clear signals given by the Bundesbank (to the effect that it regarded sterling as over-valued at DM2.95 due to a premature relaxation of British monetary policy) contributed to a massive speculative attack on sterling which (despite a 5 per cent interest rate rise on 16 September 1992) drove the pound below its floor and culminated in its formal suspension from the ERM. The Italian lira was forced out at the same time, and a series of devaluations by the remaining weaker currencies failed to settle the financial markets. Table 2.5 shows the spate of devaluations in the weeks following so-called 'Black Wednesday' on 16 September 1992. Eventually, with pressure refusing to abate, the EU was forced to introduce ultra-wide ±15 per cent bands in August 1993 to head off a politically embarrassing devaluation of the French franc. As De Grauwe (1997) notes, 'although in a legal sense the EMS remained in existence, for all practical purposes the system ceased to exist'.

Towards economic and monetary union, 1993–99

The events of 1992–93 highlighted the inherent weaknesses that had been allowed to develop within the ERM. As originally designed in 1979, the system was secure against speculative attack. Provided that symmetry was maintained in foreign exchange intervention, the central banks of both the weak and strong currencies involved in a speculative attack must come to its assistance. While the capacity of the 'weak' central bank (which must use the strong currency to buy its own in the market) to support its currency is limited to its foreign exchange reserves and the amount it can borrow through the VSTFF, there were no such restrictions on the 'strong' central bank. The latter could sell its own currency in unlimited amounts to buy the weak currency and, in this sense, could always defeat any speculative pressure to force it into a revaluation of its currency.

German policy leadership and the deflationary bias of the ERM, however, turned on the Bundesbank's unwillingness to provide unlimited support to weak currencies, for fear of the inflationary consequences that the resulting monetary expansion would have caused in Germany. The growing commitment to low inflation across the EU and the broad synchronisation of business cycles during the 1980s allowed the fault line in the ERM to remain hidden, until it was brutally exposed by German reunification after 1990.

The travails of the ERM in 1992–93 have been interpreted in different ways. One school of thought maintains that the speculative pressures of this period prove that the EU is unsuited to fixed exchange rates. If even a relatively modest arrangement like the ERM cannot work, in which there is a considerable margin for exchange rate fluctuations and scope to realign central parities periodically, then there is little point in further monetary integration. Within the core EU member states, however, a different lesson has been learned. The disintegration of the ERM proves not that the original design was misconceived, but rather that German policy leadership was allowed to develop contrary to the intentions of its architects. Supporters of greater monetary integration point out that, had the system of monetary policy cooperation operated as intended, then the ERM could have provided a framework for low inflation without exposing the system to speculative attack. The German Bundesbank would have been able to support weaker currencies at times of speculative pressure, without having to worry that its long-run objectives of low inflation would be undermined by other states.

The EU's vision of EMU, which was launched on 1 January 1999 with the locking of exchange rates against the ECU/euro, is its preferred way of reconstructing the EMS. Within a monetary union, exchange rates are irrevocably locked: this implies that foreign exchange intervention to defend the central parities must be symmetrical and unlimited. After 1 January 2002, when the monetary union was transformed into a currency union and the euro replaced national currencies, the monetary adjustments required to maintain the union became automatic and invisible. Interest rates are now set for the eurozone as a whole by the ECB. The economics of EMU are explored in detail in Chapter 3. However, before concluding, it is instructive to examine some ongoing issues of macroeconomic policy coordination which endure, and which continue to preoccupy policymakers, after EMU.

Macroeconomic policy coordination, 1999–2004

At first sight, EMU appears to represent the ultimate form of monetary policy coordination. With a single currency and a single monetary authority setting interest rates, however, potential monetary policy conflicts between member states still exist. So long as macroeconomic conditions vary from one country to another, the 'one size fits all' monetary policy stance of the EMU will not be equally appropriate to the needs of each member state. Political economy suggests that the decision-making board of the monetary authority will be plagued by divisions between the national representatives of each state, despite the best efforts of the system's architects to design institutional structures that are politically independent of national governments and other sectional interests.

Table 2.6 illustrates the dilemma for the ECB. It shows that since 1999 the ECB has almost, but not quite, managed to keep eurozone inflation at or below its 2 per cent target ceiling – its overriding policy objective. However, the inflation performances of member states have been rather variable around the eurozone's weighted average. In Greece, Ireland and even the Netherlands, inflation has been running at almost twice the targeted maximum, while in Germany inflation had slowed to only 1 per cent pa by 2003. Clearly, the common monetary stance over this period was too loose for the higher inflation states and too restrictive for countries like Germany.

Table 2.6 Growth and inflation* in selected Eurozone countries

	1996–2000	2001	2002	2003
France				
GDP % change pa	2.8	2.1	1.2	0.2
HCIP % pa	1.3	1.8	1.9	2.2
Germany				
GDP % change pa	1.8	0.8	0.2	−0.1
HCIP % pa	1.1	1.9	1.3	1.0
Greece				
GDP % change pa	3.4	4	3.8	4.7
HCIP % pa	4.6	3.7	3.9	3.4
Ireland				
GDP % change pa	9.8	6.2	6.9	–
HCIP % pa	2.6	4.0	4.7	4.0
Netherlands				
GDP % change pa	3.7	1.2	0.2	−0.8
HCIP % pa	1.9	5.1	3.9	2.2
Spain				
GDP % change pa	3.8	2.8	2.0	2.4
HCIP % pa	2.6	2.8	3.6	3.1
Eurozone				
GDP % change pa	**2.6**	**1.6**	**0.9**	**0.4**
HCIP % pa	**1.6**	**2.3**	**2.3**	**2.1**

* Harmonised Index of Consumer Prices

Source: Adapted from European Central Bank

The policy conflict is even more stark when the focus is switched to real economic performance. The table shows that the two major economies, France and Germany, experienced a very sharp slowdown after 2000, with growth virtually zero or negative by 2003; the Netherlands, with particularly close links to the German economy, followed suit – average growth rates in the period 1996–2000 of 3.7 per cent pa have faded into stagnation over the period 2000–03. In contrast, Ireland and Greece have both been booming, with average growth rates over the period 2000–03 of 6.5 per cent and 4.2 per cent pa respectively; Spain also appears immune from the slowdown in the eurozone economy as a whole. Clearly, the relaxation in monetary policy necessary to reflate the German and French economies would further overheat the fast-growing economies of Greece and Ireland.

Much has been written on the political economy of policymaking by the ECB (e.g. Roel, Beetsma and Bovenberg, 2000; Bibow, 2002; Cecchetti and O'Sullivan, 2003; Heisenberg, 2003; Maier, 2003). Some critics have suggested that, rather than replacing the German hegemony of the ERM with a genuinely cooperative monetary regime, the ECB will be 'captured' by the Franco-German axis and policy will be made in the interests of the two major states rather than the eurozone as a whole. On the basis of the data in Table 2.6, it is striking that the ECB appears to have been less successful in achieving an inflation target of 2 per cent in the period 2000–03 than member states were in the preceding period 1996–2000; one interpretation may be that the ECB was reluctant to bear down too strongly on inflation when the German and French economies were so fragile.

A second major issue of policy coordination that has come to the fore since the start of EMU is fiscal policy. In an era of pooled monetary sovereignty, fiscal policy offers governments an alternative way of stabilising their national economies through more activist demand management – and as Table 2.6 shows, macroeconomic conditions across eurozone states continue to vary significantly. Moreover, economic theory suggests that fiscal policy may be more powerful in an EMU than with floating exchange rates (see Exhibit 2.4). This is because government borrowing tends to raise interest rates and, with flexible exchange rates, the exchange rate will appreciate, crowding out net exports and dissipating the expansionary effects of the original fiscal stimulus.

In the EMU, however, a national government will be able to borrow on a unified capital market, meaning that the deficit financing associated with stabilising demand within one country will have only a small impact on the EU interest rate (and no impact on intra-EU exchange rates). Critically, this 'small impact' on the common interest rate will be insufficient to offset the fiscal stimulus in the initiating country, but will adversely impact all other member states. The net effect is that one government can internalise almost all the benefits of a fiscal expansion, while allowing the crowding out (through a higher interest rate and an appreciation of the euro against other currencies) to be borne by the eurozone as a whole.

This analysis can be interpreted in two ways. One is that, post-EMU, national fiscal policy offers an alternative, enhanced policy tool to replace the monetary sovereignty which has been pooled – i.e. to the extent that business cycles are not closely harmonised across member states, more activist fiscal policy can provide an essential shock absorbing function for individual member states. The less

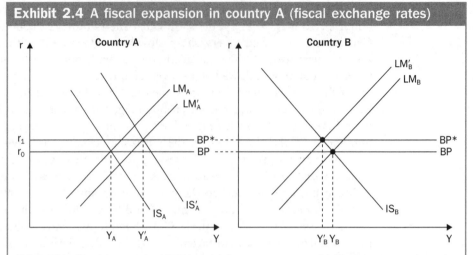

Exhibit 2.4 A fiscal expansion in country A (fiscal exchange rates)

This exhibit shows the standard IS-LM model for a two-country world. The interest rate is on the vertical axis, with output on the horizontal axis. IS_A, LM_A represent goods market and money market equilibria in country A, and IS_B, LM_B represent goods and money market equilibria in country B. There is perfect capital mobility, which means that interest rates must be harmonised, here along the BP schedule.

Suppose that in country A the government increases government spending, shifting IS_A to the right to IS_A'. This fiscal expansion puts upward pressure on interest rates in country A and causes a capital inflow. This leads to an increase in the demand for currency A, which requires open-market operations (sales of currency A by the central banks of both countries). These open-market operations in the foreign exchange markets increase the money supply in county A (causing a rightwards shift in LM_A) and a corresponding decrease in the money supply in country B (and so a leftwards shift in LM_B). Equilibrium is finally restored when interest rates have risen in both countries, shifting the BP function to BP*. Hence, under fixed exchange rates, interest rates are higher in both countries and output is higher in country A (the initiator of the fiscal expansion) and lower in country B. This amounts to country A effectively being able to 'export its unemployment', by increasing output at the cost of its neighbour.

Note that for a monetary union, as opposed to a fixed exchange rate regime, the analysis is broadly the same. The difference is that, instead of the money supplies being driven by open-market operations in the foreign exchange market, in a monetary union there is a single capital market. If there is upward pressure on interest rates in one country, capital will simply move into that country's banking system from other parts of the monetary union, increasing the local money supply and reducing it elsewhere. In this way, increased demand for money in the country initiating the fiscal stimulus leads to higher interest rates throughout the union, but the initiating country benefits from the fiscal stimulus (only partly offset by higher interest rates) while all other members suffer only the effects of higher interest rates.

optimistic interpretation is that fiscal policy in an EMU has strong 'prisoner's dilemma' characteristics. Because countries initiating a fiscal expansion benefit economically by externalising most of the crowding-out effects, and those countries that pursue strict fiscal policies cannot prevent their economies suffering from the fiscal laxity of other member states, there is a potential bias in favour of systemic fiscal excess. Critics of this latter view point out that, while there is conceptually a single EMU-wide interest rate, the actual rate that each national government pays to lenders will depend on, *inter alia*, its own international credit ranking and that governments with high deficit and debt ratios will be penalised – and so deterred from excessive borrowing – by having to pay higher risk premia.

The controversy over whether the EMU would lead to more activist or more irresponsible fiscal policy-making proved very intense during the 1990s, with the architects of the Maastricht Treaty coming down firmly on the side of caution. German policy makers, in particular, were fearful of the fiscal histories of some of the Mediterranean states, notably Italy and Greece, and their concerns inspired both the Maastricht convergence criteria (which required entrants to EMU to have budget deficits of no more than 3 per cent of GDP and public debt : GDP ratios of no more than 60 per cent) and the Growth and Stability Pact, which proscribed budget deficits in excess of 3 per cent of GDP after entry (although larger deficits are permitted to combat severe downturns, defined as four successive quarters in which the economy contracts at an annualised 2 per cent per year).

In practice, and rather ironically, macroeconomic performance since 1999 has been weakest in some member states historically most closely associated with fiscal rectitude – and which were the fiercest proponents of the Growth and Stability Pact. Table 2.7 sets out the real macroeconomic indicators and the budget figures for France and Germany. It shows that, as economic growth has slowed and unemployment has increased, a combination of automatic fiscal stabilisers and structural policy changes in taxation and government spending has pushed budget deficits and government debt in both countries above the Maastricht convergence criteria thresholds – and violated the budget deficit limits in the Growth and Stability Pact. The early years of EMU have demonstrated the limitations of a mechanistic budget deficit ceiling and the potential dangers of forcing member states in recession to offset the operation of automatic stabilisers with deflationary spending cuts and tax increases. On the other hand, the 'prisoner's dilemma' aspects of fiscal policy in EMU remain and rebuilding a sustainable framework for fiscal policy coordination in the eurozone is now a key challenge for the twelve participating member states (Calmfors and Corsetti, 2002; Buiter and Grafe, 2003; Buti et al., 2003).

Table 2.7 The real economy and fiscal policy in France and Germany

	1996–2000	2001	2002	2003
France				
GDP (% change per annum)	2.8	2.1	1.2	0.2
Unemployment (% of labour force)	11.0	8.5	8.8	9.4
Budget deficit (% GDP)	–	–1.5	–3.2	–4.1
Government Debt (% GDP)	–	56.8	58.6	63.0
Germany				
GDP (% change per annum)	1.8	0.8	0.2	–0.1
Unemployment (% of labour force)	8.7	7.8	8.6	9.3
Budget deficit (% GDP)	–	–2.8	–3.5	–3.9
Government Debt (% GDP)	–	59.4	60.8	64.2

Source: Adapted from European Central Bank

Conclusion

Increasing trade and financial integration has steadily increased the economic interlinkages between the member states of the EU. As a result, fiscal and monetary policies pursued by one member state spill over and affect exchange rates, interest rates and economic activity across the rest of the EU. In the absence of formal mechanisms for coordination, fiscal and monetary policies have different external effects. With floating exchange rates, the external effects of fiscal policy tend to be positive: a fiscal stimulus in one country tends to boost output and employment in others. Monetary policy leads to more destructive 'beggar-thy-neighbour' effects: a monetary expansion 'exports' unemployment to other countries. Monetary policy is therefore plagued by 'prisoner's dilemma' considerations, with non-cooperation likely to lead to sub-optimal outcomes for all countries.

Managed exchange rate systems provide the most common solution to this problem. However, such systems can be dominated by their larger members. Moreover, given the inherently asymmetric nature of managed exchange rate systems and the scope for sterilisation of monetary inflows by low inflation countries, there is a danger of a deflationary bias. The architects of the ERM tried to prevent this bias by building in mechanisms to ensure symmetry and promote cooperative monetary policy making. In practice, however, the ERM was overtaken by a shift in government attitudes to inflation, which encouraged other member states to submit willingly to German policy leadership, making the original design redundant.

The system as it evolved was flawed by a fundamental weakness. German hegemony was inconsistent with guaranteeing unlimited support to weak currencies. The price of the anti-inflation anchor was a 'one-way bet' for speculators, whose activities effectively destroyed the system in 1992–93. The EU's reconstruction of a monetary policy framework has been around EMU, in which the ECB sets interest rates and pursues a clear policy of price stability. Paradoxically, however, EMU reopens the debate on fiscal policy coordination, which now provides an alternative, greatly enhanced policy tool for stabilising national aggregate demand, while externalising most of the crowding-out effects. A flexible framework for coordinating fiscal policy is now the outstanding challenge for the EU.

References

Artis M J (2002) 'The Stability and Growth Pact: Fiscal Policy in the EMU', in F Breuss, G Fink and S Griller (eds), *Institutional, Legal and Economic Aspects of the EMU*, Vienna-New York, Springer.

Backus D and Driffill J (1985) 'Inflation and Reputation', *American Economic Review*, Vol. 75, pp. 530–38.

Barro R J and Gordon D B (1983) 'Rules, Discretion and Reputation in a Model of Monetary Policy, *Journal of Monetary Economics*, Vol. 12, pp. 101–22.

Bibow J (2002) 'The Monetary Policies of the European Central Bank and the Euro's (Mal-)Performance: A Stability-oriented Assessment', *International Review of Applied Economics*, Vol. 16, pp. 31–50.

Buiter W and Grafe C (2003) 'Reforming EMU's Fiscal Policy Rules: Some Suggestions for Enhancing Fiscal Sustainability and Macroeconomic Stability in an Enlarged European Union', in M Buti (ed.) *Monetary and Fiscal Policies in EMU: Interactions and Co-ordination*, Cambridge University Press, Cambridge.

Buiter W and Marston R C (eds) (1985) *International Economic Policy Co-ordination*, Cambridge University Press, Cambridge.

Buti M, Eijffinger S and Franco D (2003) 'Revisiting EMU's Stability Pact: A Pragmatic Way Forward', *Oxford Review of Economic Policy*, Vol. 19, pp. 100–111.

Calmfors L and Corsetti G (2002) 'How to Reform Europe's Fiscal Policy Framework', *World Economics*, Vol. 4, pp. 109–16.

Canzoneri M and Minford P (1989) 'Policy Interdependence: Does Strategic Behaviour pay?', in D Hodgman and G E Wood (eds), *Macroeconomic Policy and Economic Interdependence*, Macmillan, London.

Cecchetti S and O'Sullivan R (2003) 'The European Central Bank and the Federal Reserve', *Oxford Review of Economic Policy*, Vol. 19.

Cooper R (1968) *The Economics of Interdependence*, McGraw-Hill, London.

Cooper R (1985) 'Economic Interdependence and the Co-ordination of Economic Policies', in R Jones and P Kenen (eds), *Handbook of International Economics* Vol. 2, North Holland, London.

De Grauwe P (1990) 'The Cost of Disinflation and the European Monetary System', *Open Economies Review*, Vol. 1, pp. 147–73.

De Grauwe P (1997) *The Economics of Monetary Integration*, 3rd edn, Oxford University Press, Oxford.

Eichengreen B and Wyplosz C (1993) 'The Unstable EMS', *Brookings Papers on Economic Activity*, No. 1, Washington DC.

Foreman-Peck J (1991) 'Historical Reflections', in J Driffill and M Beber (eds), *A Currency for Europe: The Currency as an Element of Division or a Union of Europe*, Lothian Foundation Press, London.

Friedman M (1968) 'The Role of Monetary Policy', *American Economic Review*, Vol. 58, pp. 1–17.

Gros D and Thygesen N (1992) *European Monetary Integration: From the European Monetary System to European Monetary Union*, Longman, London.

Haldane A (1991) 'The Exchange Rate Mechanism of the European Monetary System: A Review of the Literature', *Bank of England Quarterly Bulletin*, February, pp. 73–82.

Heisenberg D (2003) 'Cutting the Bank Down to Size: Efficient and Legitimate Decision-making in the European Central Bank after Enlargement', *Journal of Common Market Studies*, Vol. 41, pp. 397–420.

Hodgman D and Wood G E (eds) (1989) *Macroeconomic Policy and Economic Interdependence*, Macmillan, London.

Ishii N, McKibbin W and Sachs J (1985) 'The Economic Policy Mix, Policy Co-operation and Protectionism: Some Aspects of Macroeconomic Interdependence among the United States, Japan and other OECD Countries', *Journal of Policy Modelling*, Vol. 7, pp. 533–72.

Maier P (2003) *Political Pressure, Rhetoric and Monetary Policy*, Edward Elgar Publishing, Cheltenham.

Mastropasqua C, Micossi S and Rinaldi R (1988) 'Interventions, Sterilization and Monetary Policy in European Monetary System Countries 1979–87', in F Giavazzi, S Micossi and M Miller (eds), *European Monetary System*, Cambridge University Press, Cambridge.

Ozkan F (2003) 'Explaining ERM Realignments: Insights from Optimising Models of Currency Crises', *Journal of Macroeconomics*, Vol. 25, pp. 491–507.

Roel M, Beetsma A and Bovenberg L (2000) 'Designing Fiscal and Monetary Institutions for a European Monetary Union', *Public Choice*, Vol. 102, pp. 247–69.

Sachs J and Wyplosz C (1986) 'The Economic Consequences of President Mitterand', *Economic Policy*, Vol. 2, pp. 261–322.

Weber A (1991) 'Reputation and Credibility in the European Monetary System', *Economic Policy*, Vol. 12, pp. 57–102.

Williamson J (1983) *The Exchange Rate System*, Institute of International Economics, Washington DC.

Wyplosz C (1989) 'Asymmetry in the EMS: Intentional or Systemic', *European Economic Review*, Vol. 33, pp. 310–20.

Chapter 3

Economic and monetary union

Nigel Healey

Introduction

On 1 January 2002, the new European single currency, the euro, was introduced to 300 m citizens across twelve EU member states. Within two months, the franc, the deutschmark and peseta had ceased to be legal tender and were withdrawn from circulation. For the first time since the Roman empire, most continental Europeans shared a common currency. While the euro was technically born on 1 January 1999, when the participating member states locked the values of their currencies against the euro, it was a 'virtual' currency for its first three years, existing only as a unit of account for paper transactions. Its establishment as a physical currency in 2002 and the removal of so-called 'legacy' currencies from circulation was a massive psychological change and, for most EU citizens, made the euro 'real' for the first time.

Economists spent the 1990s debating the theoretical costs and benefits for individual member states of participating in economic and monetary union (EMU). Proponents argued that EMU would eliminate exchange rate uncertainty and make prices more transparent, promoting cross-border trade and investment within the eurozone. Critics feared that these benefits would be outweighed by greater macroeconomic instability in participating member states, as national governments found themselves denied the usual tools of monetary policy, notably interest rate adjustments, to deal with fluctuations in aggregate supply and demand. This chapter opens with a brief account of the process by which the EU achieved the goal of EMU and then reviews the theoretical benefits and costs of belonging to an EMU. Although it is too early in the great euro experiment to draw definitive conclusions – and the net balance of benefits and costs will, in any case, vary from country to country and change over time – the chapter concludes by exploring the lessons of the first five years of monetary union.

What is EMU?

EMU, as the term suggests, involves the integration of both the real (economic) and monetary sectors of participating countries. For the EU, economic union has always been a central goal. During the 1960s and 1970s, member states dismantled quotas and tariff barriers to trade between each other and set up central policy-making institutions to manage 'problem' industries such as coal, steel and agriculture. In the 1980s, following the 1985 White Paper (European Commission, 1985) and the 1986 Single European Act, the EU set about dismantling the remaining non-tariff barriers to the free movement of goods, labour and capital and economic union was largely achieved by the target date of 1992.

With economic union in sight, the EU set about adding the missing component of EMU, namely monetary union. As Mundell (2003) notes, 'a common market without common money is at best an imperfect market'. In technical terms, a 'monetary union' consists of an arrangement between participating countries in which:

1 bilateral exchange rates (i.e. the exchange rates between one member state and another) are permanently fixed, with no margins for permissible fluctuations; and

2 there are no institutional barriers (e.g. legal controls) to the free movement of capital across national frontiers.

In addition to irrevocably fixed exchange rates and the abolition of all capital controls, the form of monetary union (i.e. a 'currency union') always favoured by the EU entails replacing national currencies with a common currency. Although monetary union technically requires no more than permanently fixed bilateral exchange rates, a currency union has the advantages of eliminating the transaction costs of switching between national currencies and making the prices of products across the EU more transparent. The adoption of a single currency is also generally felt to promote confidence in the permanency of the monetary union, by increasing the costs to participating states of withdrawing from the arrangement.

The Maastricht Treaty and the road to EMU

While the origins of a single European currency date back to the Roman empire, the plan to create a single currency within the EU has an altogether more recent history. Following the ill-fated 'Werner Plan' for monetary integration, conceived in 1969 during the heyday of the Bretton Woods fixed exchange rate regime and brought down by its subsequent demise in 1973, the European Council (of heads of state or government) was sufficiently emboldened by the apparent success of the European Monetary System and the single market initiative during the late 1980s to reconsider a single currency.

In June 1988, the European Council appointed a committee, chaired by Jacques Delors, then president of the European Commission, to examine the issue of EMU and propose concrete stages by which this could be achieved within the EU. The committee was made up of the governors of the (then twelve) national central banks of member states and the Bank for International Settlements and advised by, *inter alia*, Professor Niels Thygesen, a well-known monetary economist. The resulting 'Delors Report' proposed a three-stage process to EMU (Delors, 1988).

Stage One (July 1990–December 1993)

The European Council endorsed the basic principles of the Delors Report in June 1989, setting 1 July 1990 as the date for the start of the first stage of EMU (coincidentally later chosen as the date for German economic, social and monetary union, ahead of full political reunification in October 1990). The primary objective was that all restrictions on the movement of capital between member states should be abolished. The significance of this first step was that, prior to this date, several member states still had controls on the convertibility of their national currencies, which distorted the operation of foreign exchange markets and prevented financial integration.

At the same time, the 'Committee of Governors of the Central Banks of Member States', which had been set up to promote cooperation in monetary policy in 1964, took on a new and more important role. This committee, which was to evolve into the European Monetary Institute and later the European Central Bank, was charged with coordinating national monetary policies much more actively, with the aim of eliminating the need for exchange rate realignments within the exchange rate mechanism (ERM) and promoting price stability. The Committee of Governors also began to set up an organisational infrastructure of sub-committees and working groups to begin practical preparations for the move to Stage Two in 1994 and Stage Three in 1999.

It was clear at the outset that the realisation of EMU would require significant revisions to the 1957 Treaty of Rome in order to create the appropriate institutional structures. An Inter-Governmental Conference (IGC) on EMU was convened in 1991 and worked in parallel with the IGC on political union. The negotiations jointly culminated in the Treaty on European Union (TEU) (often known as the 'Maastricht Treaty' after the Dutch city in which it was signed), which was agreed in December 1991 and signed in February 1992. The TEU included provisions for the establishment, in Stage Two, of the European Monetary Institute to coordinate the monetary policies of member states and, in Stage Three, the independent European Central Bank (ECB) with a mandate to pursue price stability. The ECB's design reflected the growing theoretical consensus that central banks should be independent of national governments and was closely modelled on the Bundesbank (see Berger et al., 2000 for a recent review of the relevant theoretical literature). So close does this modelling appear to have been, the ECB has been dubbed the Bundesbank's 'Twin Sister' in the economic literature on central banking (e.g. Debrun, 2001).

The Maastricht Treaty set out five 'convergence criteria' that member states are required to satisfy before they can accede to EMU. These convergence criteria fall into two categories:

1 inflation criteria, which are designed to ensure that the transitional costs of joining are tolerable to the member state – with 'inflation' being measured using current inflation rates, market forecasts of future inflation rates as reflected in long-term interest rates and recent inflation rates relative to other EU members as reflected in past exchange rate movements; and

2 fiscal criteria, which are intended to guarantee that the ECB will not find its commitment to price stability undermined by excessive government deficit

---

Box 3.1 Maastricht convergence criteria

1 Successful candidates must have inflation rates no more than 1.5 per cent above the average of the three EU countries with the lowest inflation rates.

2 Long-term interest rates should be no more than 2 per cent above the average of the three countries with the lowest rates.

3 National currencies must not have been devalued and must have remained within the normal (15 per cent) bands of the EMS for the previous two years.

4 National budget deficits must be less than 3 per cent of GDP.

5 The national debt must be less than 60 per cent of GDP (or satisfactorily falling towards this level).

---

spending – measured by current budget deficit : GDP and public debt : GDP ratios. The convergence criteria are outlined in Box 3.1.

Stage Two (January 1994–December 1998)

Stage Two began on 1 January 1994, only months after the ERM had been all but destroyed by waves of speculative attacks on the weaker currencies. This period undoubtedly represented a low point in the process of monetary integration, with currency instability and recession threatening to derail the whole project. The main feature of Stage Two was the transformation of the Committee of Governors into the European Monetary Institute (EMI), which was a fledgling ECB designed to strengthen central bank cooperation and monetary policy coordination and to prepare for the establishment of the 'Eurosystem' (i.e. European System of Central Banks – see Box 3.2), the conduct of the single eurozone monetary policy and the creation of a single currency in Stage Three.

In December 1995, the European Council convened to decide a name for the new single European currency. Despite the attractiveness of one popular candidate, 'monnet', which would have reflected the pivotal role Jean Monnet played in the early years of European integration and coincidentally sounded like 'money' in English and 'la monnaie' in French, the European Council opted for the more pedestrian 'euro'. At the same meeting, the European Council decided that Stage Three of EMU would start on 1 January 1999, rather than the earlier optional date of 1 January 1997 incorporated in the TEU. A timetable for the changeover to the euro was agreed, based on detailed proposals worked out by the EMI, and the EMI was charged with carrying out preparatory work on the future monetary and exchange rate relationships between the eurozone and other EU countries.

Reflecting German concerns about the risk of some of the southern states reverting to type after the start of Stage Three and running lax, and potentially inflationary, budgetary polices, the European Council agreed to adopt the Growth and Stability Pact in June 1997. Under this pact, there are strict limits on the ability of a member government to run a budget deficit in excess of 3 per cent of gross domestic product and, after the start of Stage Three, all member governments (including non-eurozone

Box 3.2 The Eurosystem

Under the terms of the Maastricht Treaty, monetary policy-making from Stage Three onwards passed to the so-called 'Eurosystem', although Eurosystem and ECB are often used as interchangeable terms. The 'Eurosystem' comprises the ECB and the twelve national central banks of the eurozone. The overriding objective of the Eurosystem is to maintain price stability. Its secondary objective is to support the general economic policies of eurozone members (i.e. promoting growth and employment), but only provided this does not prejudice the primary goal of price stability. Monetary policy is made and formulated by two key bodies:

1 the Executive Board, comprising the President (currently Mr Jean-Claude Trichet), the Vice-President and four other members appointed by the European Council in consultation with the European Parliament and the Governing Council of the ECB; and

2 the General Council comprising the Executive Board of the ECB and the governors of the participating national central banks.

The role of the Executive Board is to work directly with the national central banks, which act as agents of the ECB, to implement the monetary policy guidelines and decisions of the Governing Council, while the Governing Council formulates monetary policy for the eurozone, taking into account the economic conditions across the participating member states, and making decisions relating to intermediate monetary objectives and interest rates (see Bertaut, 2002 for a summary of the structures).

members) are required to submit a report to the European Commission outlining their budgetary policies (European Commission, 1997).

On 2 May 1998, the European Council met to consider which of the member states had met the five convergence criteria required for admission to EMU (see Box 3.1). It decided unanimously that eleven member states (Belgium, Germany, Spain, France, Ireland, Italy, Luxembourg, the Netherlands, Austria, Portugal and Finland) had fulfilled the necessary conditions for the adoption of the single currency on 1 January 1999; it agreed that Greece, provided it made further progress in achieving macroeconomic stability, could be considered for entry some time after January 1999. Later the same month, the European Council appointed the President, the Vice-President and the four other members of the Executive Board of the ECB. Their appointments took effect on 1 June 1998, at which time the EMI was dissolved and the ECB was established to take over final preparations for the start of Stage Three (see Box 3.2).

Stage Three (January 1999–February 2002)

Stage Three was the most dramatic and visible, starting with the irrevocable locking of the currencies of the eleven member states (see Table 3.1) and the transfer of monetary policy-making from national central banks to the ECB on 1 January 1999 and culminating in the complete replacement of national currencies by the euro by the end of February 2002. In between these two milestones, the European Council reconvened in June 2000 to assess Greece's position and determined that it

Table 3.1 Euro conversion rates and the legal tender deadlines

	1 euro =	Legal tender deadline
Austria	13.7603 schillings	28 February 2002
Belgium	40.3399 francs	28 February 2002
Germany	1.95583 marks	28 February 2002
Finland	5.94573 markka	28 February 2002
France	6.55957 francs	17 February 2002
Greece	340.750 drachmae	28 February 2002
Ireland	0.787564 punts	9 February 2002
Italy	1936.27 lire	28 February 2002
Luxembourg	40.3399 francs	28 February 2002
Netherlands	2.20371 guilders	28 January 2002
Portugal	200.482 escudos	28 February 2002
Spain	166.386 pesetas	28 February 2002

Source: Adapted from HSBC

had fulfilled the convergence criteria. Greece duly joined the eleven members of EMU on 1 January 2001, when the drachma's exchange rate was locked against the euro.

1 January 2002 symbolised the endpoint in the process of monetary unification, when physical euro banknotes and coins were introduced across the eurozone. The short 'changeover' period during which both national and euro notes and coin circulated alongside each other as legal tender ended on 28 February 2002 (earlier in some countries). Bank automated teller machines (ATMs) machines began dispensing euro notes on 1 January and retailers, who had been given advance stocks of the new currency, accepted national (now known as 'legacy') currencies and gave change in euros during the changeover period. Commercial banks accepted legacy currencies for deposit (into accounts denominated in euros) or exchanged them into euro banknotes. The ECB estimates that about 70 per cent of euros entered circulation via withdrawals from ATMs, with the remainder coming through exchange at banks, change from retailers and cash payments from employers and social welfare.

By the end of February 2002, the full transition to euro was complete: the twelve national currencies' notes and coins ceased to be legal tender, leaving just euros in circulation. While making and receiving payments electronically in euros had been possible from January 1999, and indeed many companies had switched to invoicing in euros at this time, from 1 January 2002, all non-cash transactions within the eurozone were legally required to be in euros. The conversion to euro banknotes and coins, which involved the production and distribution of 14 billion banknotes and 50 billion coins, was a massive logistical challenge, unprecedented in economic history (see Table 3.2).

In the first half of 2002, there were widespread reports of a surge in prices of real estate and expensive consumer goods in member states plagued by large informal economies, although these were not verified by official statistics measuring consumer prices. Changing legacy currency amassed through illegal or unofficial activity into euros through the banking system exposes the holder to official scrutiny and possible investigation and the alternative was to spend the hoarded currency

Table 3.2 New currency in circulation, 1 January 2002

	Euro banknotes		Euro coins Volume (bn)	Eurozone GDP, 2002 (€bn)
	Volume (bn)	Value (€bn)		
Total	14.26	633.7	50.66	7073.3

Source: Adapted from European Central Bank

before it ceased to be legal tender. Although there are many anecdotal accounts of Italian grandmothers using shoeboxes full of lire to buy designer shoes and fur coats over Christmas 2001, organisations engaging in illicit business on a serious scale have always had to find ways to 'launder' money and the advent of the euro simply meant they had to find a way to change 'black' francs into legitimate euros, rather than legitimate francs. Interestingly, national guidelines on changing legacy currency to euros, and the period for which exchange can continue to take place after the legal tender deadline, varies considerably from country to country, reflecting different national circumstances (see Table 3.3).

Curiously, some countries outside the EU have effectively slipped into the eurozone as backdoor members. In 1997, both Bulgaria and Bosnia-Herzegovina locked their exchange rates at Lev 1 = DM 1 and BAM 1 = DM 1 respectively. This was achieved by a device known as a 'currency board', under which the central bank agrees to fully back the issue of local currency by official reserves of a foreign currency (in these cases, deutschmarks) and stands ready to exchange, on demand, local currency for deutschmarks (or vice versa) at the fixed rate. Under this arrangement, deutschmarks and the local currency were interchangeable. Since January 1999, the Bulgarian lev and the Bosnian mark have been locked against the euro at the same parity as the deutschmark (1.95583/€) and local interest rates have been set by the ECB. In the run-up to 1 January 2002, both central banks converted their foreign reserves from deutschmarks to euros. Although the lev and the (Bosnian) mark are still legal tender, they now circulate alongside the euro and it would be only a technicality to withdraw the former from circulation. In Montenegro and Kosovo, where monetary arrangements are less formalised, euros are also now widely used as a medium of exchange.

The theoretical benefits and costs of EMU

Economics textbooks typically characterise exchange rate systems as 'fixed' or 'floating' and, on this basis, monetary union can be seen as the 'hardest' form of fixed exchange rate regime (i.e. an arrangement in which the value of national currencies can neither fluctuate within bands nor be periodically realigned). To a large extent, therefore, the economic arguments for and against EMU are an extension of the long-running 'fixed versus floating rates' debate, which turns on whether the economic benefits of stabilising the exchange rate (reduced exchange rate uncertainty) outweigh the costs of giving up exchange rate flexibility (sacrificing

Table 3.3 Arrangements for the exchange of legacy currencies to euros

	Free-of-charge exchange by banks	Exchange at banks after legal tender deadline	Exchange at National Central Bank after legal tender deadline	Approach to dual pricing
Austria	Recommended Sch50,000	Decided individually by banks after 28/02/02	Notes and coins: indefinitely	Compulsory 01/10/01– 28/02/02
Belgium	No limit until 28/02/02; exchange via bank account until 31/12/02	31/12/02	Notes: indefinitely Coins: end 2004	Voluntary agreement
Finland	No limit	To be decided individually by banks	Notes and coins until 29/02/12	Voluntary agreement
France	No limit	30/06/02	Notes: 17/02/12 Coins: 17/02/05	Voluntary agreement
Germany	Subject to each bank's decision	At least until 28/02/02	Notes and coins indefinitely	Voluntary agreement
Greece	No limit	Period still to be defined	Notes: 01/03/12 Coins: 01/03/04	Compulsory 01/01/01– 28/02/02
Ireland	Recommended I£500	Period still to be defined	Notes and coins indefinitely	Voluntary agreement
Italy	Recommended €500	Banks take decision by 28/02/02	Notes and coins until: 01/03/12	No decision
Luxembourg	Free for clients	30/06/02	Notes: indefinitely Coins: 31/12/04	Voluntary agreement
Netherlands	No limit until 01/04/02: exchange via bank account	31/12/02 (banks may charge thereafter)	Notes: 01/01/32 Coins: 01/01/07	Voluntary agreement 01/07/01–28/01/02
Portugal	Free for bank customers	30/06/02	Notes: 30/12/22 Coins: 30/12/02	Compulsory 01/10/01– 28/02/02
Spain	No limit until 30/06/02	30/06/02	Notes and coins: indefinitely	Voluntary agreement

Source: Adapted from European Central Bank

'monetary sovereignty'). These costs, in turn, depend critically upon the characteristics of the national economies (e.g. degree of wage flexibility) and the linkages between the economies whose exchange rates are pegged.

The additional dimension of EMU is the transition to a single currency managed by an independent central bank, which promises extra benefits over and above reduced exchange rate uncertainty. As noted above, a single currency makes prices more transparent and underscores the permanence of the monetary union. Moreover, the ECB, which has a mandate to pursue price stability, may be able to deliver lower inflation and lower interest rates within the eurozone than some member states could achieve independently. The following sections briefly review the theoretical benefits and costs of EMU.

The economic benefits of EMU

The benefits of EMU are reasonably uncontentious. For supporters of EMU, the euro promised an end to exchange rate uncertainty on intra-EU trade, elimination of transactions costs on cross-border trade, greater price stability and a guarantee of future monetary stability through the commitment of the ECB to price stability. Importantly, some of the economic benefits of monetary union, such as the elimination of exchange rate uncertainty, increase with the size of the euro area (i.e. they are subject to 'network externalities').

Reduced exchange rate uncertainty

EMU ended the uncertainty that exchange rate fluctuations previously brought to intra-EU trade and investment. While financial markets offer 'insurance' against exchange rate uncertainty in the form of 'hedging' facilities, the cost of such facilities reflects the savings to the eurozone of adopting the single currency. Moreover, for longer time horizons, so-called 'forward' facilities are not universally available. Such considerations have a special importance for members of the EU, the *raison d'être* of which is to facilitate cross-border movements of goods, services, labour and capital. Advocates of EMU have long argued that the potential gains from membership of the EU cannot be realised in the long term unless countries are able to fully exploit their own, unique comparative advantages (e.g. Jenkins, 1979). To achieve this, economic resources (land, labour, capital and enterprise) must be transferred from relatively less to relatively more efficient sectors and the commercial decisions which make such reallocations possible depend critically upon expectations of the future. To the extent that past uncertainty about the course of intra-EU exchange rates inhibited the restructuring of production, EMU should accelerate economic integration within the EU (Emerson, 1992; Rose, 2000, 2001).

Critics of EMU point out that, while a single currency will eliminate exchange rate risk from intra-eurozone trade, the euro itself is still prone to fluctuations against other major trading and investment currencies, notably the US dollar and the Japanese yen. Whether EMU succeeds in reducing exchange rate risk overall will depend on the stability of the euro vis-à-vis the dollar and the yen, and the way in which the ECB manages its cooperation with, *inter alia*, the US Federal Reserve Bank and the Bank of Japan.

Transactions costs

The transaction costs involved in changing currencies are levied by banks to reflect their deployment of resources (e.g. personnel and equipment), as well as the opportunity costs of holding stocks of foreign exchange (i.e. the interest forgone). For tourists dealing in small retail amounts, these charges can easily amount to 10 per cent of the value of the currency changed. For large, multinational businesses, however, the transaction costs of switching between currencies are much smaller (typically less than 1 per cent). Small- and medium-sized companies (SMEs) that lack sophisticated treasury departments are likely to benefit more from the euro than larger multinational companies. Early estimates suggested that, for the EU as a whole, eliminating transaction costs by the adoption of a single currency would yield savings of 2–3 per cent of total EU gross domestic product (e.g. Artis, 1989), but a more recent estimate puts the savings at less than 1 per cent of GDP (Mendizabal, 2002).

Price transparency

Since the start of 2002, the circulation of the single currency throughout the eurozone has allowed consumers and corporate buyers to compare prices across different national markets in the same currency, thereby enabling them to more easily identify unjustified price differences and switch to more competitive suppliers. Parallel markets in large consumer goods like cars have emerged over the last decade to exploit the potential gains from international arbitrage – that is, buying goods in low-priced markets and reselling them in high-priced markets. The fact that these parallel markets have been particularly strong in the UK, with British resellers sourcing cars in Belgium and Germany and motorcycles in Japan, suggests that EMU is not a precondition for such trade to take place. However, price transparency makes it easier for buyers to spot price differentials and, at a time when the Internet is making access to both information and foreign suppliers easier and cheaper, EMU should help make many consumer and industrial markets across the eurozone more competitive.

Low and stable inflation

The ECB was designed by the architects of the Maastricht Treaty to be a guarantor of low, stable inflation across the eurozone. While the northern EU states, notably Germany and those countries whose exchange rates were most closely pegged to the deutschmark in the 1980s and 1990s, had relatively good inflation records, the same was not true of the southern states. Countries like Italy, Spain, Portugal and Greece historically suffered high, unstable inflation and participation in EMU offers a way to break with their inflationary pasts.

High inflation rates impose costs on economies in several ways. Inflation means higher nominal interest rates to compensate lenders for expected inflation in the future (the 'Fisher effect'). High nominal interest rates distort the way that companies repay loans, by bringing forward capital repayment and shortening the acceptable lifetime of a loan. This may inhibit investment, even though the real interest rate is not affected. But high inflation also tends to be more volatile and this can lead to a risk premium being added to interest rates to compensate for erratic changes in nominal rates – that is, high and volatile inflation rates can lead to higher *real* rates of interest. If the ECB delivers low and stable inflation, the real interest rate may decline in those member states that previously suffered high, unstable inflation rates (Emerson, 1992).

The economic costs of EMU

The costs of monetary union have proved much more controversial. EMU entails the 'pooling' of monetary sovereignty – that is, transferring the power to change interest rates and the exchange rate from national governments (where it can be used with exclusive reference to national economic conditions) to the ECB (where it is used to set policy for the eurozone as a whole). Experience suggests that the monetary stance appropriate to a single member state may not coincide perfectly with the stance appropriate to the eurozone countries as a group. It is important at the outset to draw a distinction between stabilisation policy and growth (or supply-side) policy. It is now widely accepted by economists that inflation is a monetary phenomenon in the long run. Monetary policy can be used to stabilise output and unemployment about their trend paths in the short run, but the trend paths them-selves are determined by supply-side factors (e.g. the rate of capital formation, investment in human capital through training and education, technological progress, size of the labour force, etc.) (see Exhibit 3.1). Monetary policy cannot, in the long run, alter real economic variables.

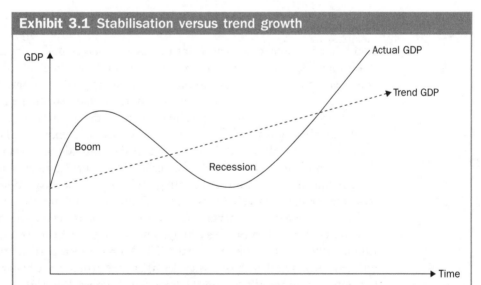

Exhibit 3.1 Stabilisation versus trend growth

The broken line shows the trend rate of growth of GDP over time, while the solid line shows the cyclical fluctuations in actual output about the underlying trend. Periods during which actual output exceeds GDP are typically termed 'booms', with 'recessions' characterised by episodes when actual GDP is below trend. Turning points in the economic cycle are signalled by the rate of growth of GDP rising above trend (the start of a recovery from recession) or falling below the trend rate of growth (the end of a boom and the onset of recession). The role of supply-side policy is to increase the underlying trend rate of growth of GDP. The purpose of stabilisation policy is to minimise fluctuations around trend GDP.

The costs of pooling monetary sovereignty

The costs of EMU stem from member states giving up the ability to use monetary policy to stabilise their national economies around trend growth paths. The obvious danger is that the monetary stance (and the implied common inflation rate) chosen by the ECB may be inappropriate for certain member states. A useful starting point is to identify the conditions under which EMU would *not* result in greater variability of national output and employment about its trend path. Pooling monetary sovereignty will be costless if the following four conditions hold:

1 The business cycles of member states are synchronised and the effects of the common monetary policy made by the ECB are the same on each state.

2 Fiscal policy can be used to adjust demand differentially in member states.

3 Wages within member states are perfectly flexible.

4 Labour markets are perfectly integrated across the eurozone.

If condition 1 is fulfilled, it makes no difference whether monetary policy is pursued centrally by the ECB or independently by national governments. If condition 1 is not fulfilled, then EMU may still be costless provided that at least one of the alternative adjustment mechanisms set out in conditions 2–4 is available; that is, either demand can be stabilised by fiscal, as opposed to monetary, policy or asymmetric shocks to demand in member states can be absorbed through changes in wages or movements of labour from areas of high to low unemployment.

'One monetary policy fits all'

Condition 1 is sometimes known as the 'one monetary policy fits all' requirement. If it is fulfilled, then the monetary policy stance taken by the ECB will be identical to, and as effective as, the policy response that each national government would choose in isolation. For example, in response to an inflationary shock the ECB would raise the interest rate and reduce aggregate demand. If the inflationary shock is common to all member states and the interest-sensitivity of demand is the same in each country, then it makes no difference whether the optimal policy response is taken by the ECB (on behalf of all member states) or by member governments individually.

Economic theory suggests that, with growing economic integration and a common monetary policy stance, business cycles should become more broadly harmonised and, prior to the massive asymmetric shock of German reunification in 1991, there is some evidence that this was happening within the ERM countries (Artis and Zhang, 1995). While the early years of EMU have seen participating countries at different points in their business cycles, there are grounds for believing that greater harmonisation should occur in the long run (Kempa, 2002; Artis et al., 2004).

A major threat hanging over EMU, however, is that, even if business cycles do become harmonised over time, 'asymmetric' economic shocks (i.e. supply-side or demand-side shocks which disproportionately affect one country more than the rest) may lead to sharp divergences in the future. The economic structures of member states are not identical and further economic integration may actually increase national specialisation in production, making such structures more *unalike*. In the United States, which is widely taken as a model for the EU, individual states are much more specialised than is currently the case in Europe. The danger of asymmetric shocks causing business cycles to become desynchronised may actually increase, rather than fall, in future (Minford and Rastogi, 1990; Bayoumi and Eichengreen, 1992).

For EMU to be costless, national economies must also behave in broadly the same way in response to a change of monetary policy. Critics of EMU point out, for example, that the interest-sensitivity of demand in Britain is typically higher than elsewhere in the EU, because a higher proportion of the population has borrowed money at variable interest rates to buy homes (e.g. Britton and Whitely, 1997). There are clearly historical, cultural and social differences between spending and borrowing patterns in different countries which will mean that the interest rate chosen by the ECB is not optimal for every state, even if each were at the same point in the business cycle (Huchet, 2003; Rodriguez-Fuentes and Dow, 2003). On the other hand, increasing integration in the financial sector may, in the longer term, lead to convergence in borrowing and saving behaviour over time.

On balance, it seems clear that condition 1 is not satisfied. Although business cycles are likely to become more harmonised, there is a real danger that asymmetric shocks will periodically cause a schism in the economic conditions of different groups of member states, making it impossible for the ECB to find a 'monetary policy that fits all'. For these reasons, it is important that at least one of the alternative shock absorbers set out in conditions 2–4 can help to stabilise national output and employment.

Fiscal policy

In the short run, fiscal policy provides an alternative instrument to monetary policy for stabilising demand. In just the same way that individuals smooth their consumption over their lives, by borrowing in their earlier years to finance house purchases and saving in their middle years to provide income in retirement, so governments can borrow against future tax revenue to stimulate aggregate demand during a recession and repay past borrowing to depress aggregate demand during a boom. Moreover, as Chapter 2 explains, economic theory suggests that national fiscal policy may be more powerful with EMU than when the exchange rate is flexible. This is because government borrowing tends to raise interest rates: with flexible exchange rates, the exchange rate will appreciate, crowding out net exports and dissipating the expansionary effects of the original fiscal stimulus; with EMU, governments will be able to borrow on a unified EU capital market, so that their borrowing has a more muted impact on the union-wide interest rate and, of course, cannot disturb intra-Union exchange rates.

While this analysis implies that fiscal policy might offer an enhanced policy tool to stabilise demand post-EMU, the architects of the Maastricht treaty were fearful that the increased ease of borrowing to finance budget deficits might lead some governments to pursue unsustainable fiscal policies. The Growth and Stability Pact imposes a limit of 3 per cent of GDP on the size of the budget deficit, although larger deficits are permitted to combat severe downturns (European Commission, 1997). If the Growth and Stability Pact were respected in the way its creators intended, the scope for more activist fiscal policymaking to compensate for the loss of monetary sovereignty would be significantly reduced for most member states (Buiter et al., 1993; Buiter, 2003).

On balance, with the Growth and Stability Pact restrictions on national fiscal policy, EMU may result in greater instability of aggregate demand within member states. The greater the differences between a member state and the *average* EU state in terms of economic structure (and risk of asymmetric shocks) and responsiveness to changes in interest rates, the greater the instability. In the absence of the stabilisation provided by monetary and fiscal policy, adjustment will fall on either wages (condition 3) or labour migration (condition 4).

Wage flexibility

The need for active stabilisation policy stems, ultimately, from the inflexibility of labour markets. Clearly, if nominal (and real) wages were highly flexible, economic shocks (whether demand-side or supply-side) could be absorbed by changes in wages (and so prices), rather than changes in employment and output (see Exhibit 3.2). In the absence of either exchange rate flexibility or adjustments in fiscal policy, the time it takes for equilibrium to be restored depends critically upon nominal wage flexibility. The available evidence suggests that, while labour market institutions vary across the EU, in general European labour markets remain much less flexible

Exhibit 3.2 Adjusting to shocks by use of wage flexibility

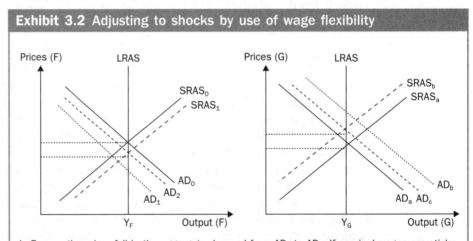

In France, there is a fall in the aggregate demand from AD_0 to AD_1. If nominal wages are sticky, the economy moves down the short-run aggregate supply schedule, $SRAS_0$, and output falls below its trend or natural rate, Y_F. Prices fall, but with nominal wages sticky, real wages must increase and unemployment rises. Conversely, in Germany, aggregate demand increases from AD_a to AD_b and, again if wages are sticky, the economy moves up $SRAS_a$. In Germany, output increases above Y_G, prices rise and real wages fall, so that unemployment falls below its natural rate. For adjustment to long-run equilibrium, unemployment in France must push down nominal wages, shifting the short-run aggregate supply schedule down from $SRAS_0$ to $SRAS_1$. In Germany, the upward pressure on wages forces the short-run aggregate supply schedule upwards from $SRAS_a$ to $SRAS_b$. Falling French wage costs and rising German wage costs alter the relative price of French and German goods, leading to an offsetting shift in demand which increases aggregate demand in France from AD_1 to AD_2 and reduces demand in Germany from AD_b to AD_c. In final equilibrium, aggregate demand, prices and wages fall in France and rise in Germany, with both economies eventually returning to full employment.

than, say, the United States (e.g. Heylen and Van Poeck, 1995; Van Poeck and Borghijs, 2001). The responsiveness of nominal wages to shocks is not, moreover, a simple linear function of the degree of trade union monopolisation, as many politicians suppose. As Calmfors and Driffill (1988) show, when wage setting is very decentralised (in the limit to company level), workers and employers can observe the effects of their wage bargains on their own competitiveness, so that wages tend to adjust more quickly to external shocks. The same is true for highly centralised corporatist systems, in which national employers' federations negotiate directly with national unions. In this case too, unions and employers can take full account of the implications of their wage-setting behaviour for competitiveness and employment. It is in countries where there is partial centralisation that wages tend to be most unresponsive. Where trade unions represent only a proportion of workers in an industry and negotiate with only a proportion of the employers, it is difficult for wage bargainers to gauge the impact of their settlements on the employment prospects of the workers affected. The result is a classic 'prisoner's dilemma', with unions fighting for wage increases and resisting wage cuts, in the knowledge that their rivals are doing the same. Unfortunately, most EU member states fall into this intermediate category, suggesting that wage inflexibility is likely to severely inhibit 'natural' economic adjustment to asymmetric shocks.

Labour mobility and optimum currency areas

In the absence of monetary or fiscal stabilisation, labour mobility provides an alternative to wage flexibility as a way of absorbing asymmetric shocks (Mundell, 1961; McKinnon, 1963; Gros, 1996). However, in contrast to the United States, where large-scale movements of labour have taken place in response to the changing economic fortunes of different regions, labour mobility in Europe is more limited (De Grauwe and Vanhaverbeke, 1991). Although the EU's 1992 programme to complete the single market abolished many legislative obstacles to the free movement of labour, different national languages and social and cultural traditions restrict the ability of workers to move to jobs. Moreover, it is highly doubtful if the EU has the political will to increase inter-country labour mobility sufficiently to act as an effective buffer. The prospect of large numbers of unemployed and unskilled southern and eastern European workers moving to the richer northern states is not appealing to most EU politicians – as evidenced by widespread concern about potential mass migration from Eastern Europe in the run-up to the 2004 EU enlargement. For such reasons, the EU has traditionally preferred to use regional policy initiatives to 'take work to the (unemployed) workers', rather than the reverse, fearing the social consequences of unfettered labour migration.

The performance of the euro since 1999

On balance, the analysis above suggests that the benefits of EMU are reasonably predictable and fairly modest, while the economic costs of EMU are more controversial: although there may be pressures leading to greater convergence of business cycles, the eurozone could be plagued by asymmetric shocks to different member states; pooling monetary sovereignty necessarily means that the less integrated countries may be disadvantaged by a 'one monetary policy fits all' rule after EMU and fiscal policy will be unable adequately to take over a stabilising role; adjustment will thus be thrown more heavily on wage flexibility and, to a much lesser extent, labour mobility, neither of which are suited to this new role.

Happily for economists, the start of Stage Three in 1999 brought to an end an exhausting decade of theorising about the likely economic benefits and costs of EMU. Already, a number of provisional studies have been published (e.g. Allsopp and Artis, 2003; Ehrmann et al., 2003; De Grauwe, 2002). It is clearly too early to draw definitive conclusions about the impact of EMU on the ultimate policy objectives of trade, investment and GDP growth, but some preliminary insights can be drawn in number of areas:

1 Has the euro reduced or increased overall exchange rate stability for eurozone members?

2 Has the ECB delivered more stable, lower inflation and lower nominal and real interest rates?

3 Has the loss of monetary sovereignty led to greater divergence in real macroeconomic performance within different member states of the eurozone?

Exchange rate stability

Figure 3.1 illustrates the euro's performance against the world's two major trading and investment currencies, the US dollar and the Japanese yen, as well as against the most important EU currency outside the eurozone, the UK pound. The figure shows that, against the US dollar, the euro declined almost continuously for the first 18 months after its creation, falling from \$1.16/€ in January 1999 to a nadir of \$0.85 by June 2001, a decline of 27 per cent. From February 2002 it began a sharp recovery, reaching \$1.16/€ in October 2003 and continuing to appreciate into 2004. Against the Japanese yen, the early slump in value was even more extreme, with the euro depreciating 30 per cent between January 1999 and October 2000, before staging a bumpy but otherwise continuous recovery. Against the UK pound, the volatility was less extreme, but the euro shows a similar pattern, falling 17 per cent over the same early period before making a recovery and, over the period under consideration, fluctuating around £0.65/€ ±7.5 per cent.

There are a number of reasons for this very considerable volatility vis-à-vis the other major currencies. The start of 1999 saw the eurozone growing at a sluggish 2 per cent pa, while the United States, which had been in an unbroken expansion since the early 1990s, defied widespread market expectations of an imminent slowdown and continued to boom with growth averaging 4 per cent throughout 1999 and 2000. With corporate profits high in the United States and the markets anticipating an upward trend in US interest rates as the Federal Reserve Bank acted to reduce inflationary pressures, short-term capital flooded out of the euro and into the dollar, driving the value of the euro down. At the same time, the Japanese economy rebounded much faster than expected from the recessionary impact of the

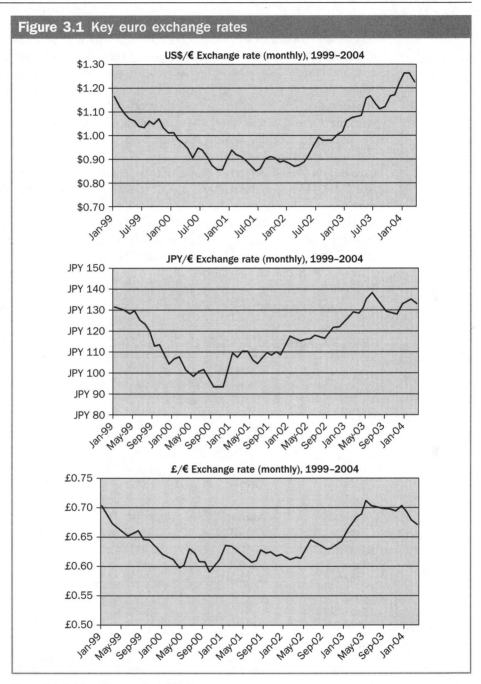

Figure 3.1 Key euro exchange rates

Source: Adapted from European Central Bank

1997 Asian financial crisis, achieving positive growth figures throughout 1999 and 2000. The subsequent reassessment of the medium-term outlook for Japan and the South-East Asian economies led to an unwinding of the capital flight triggered by the 1997 crisis and a switch out of euros into yen.

More sober reflection by market analysts also led to a downgrading of the likely impact of a switch of official reserves from dollars into euros. Between 1990 and 1998, the share of the dollar in official reserves rose from approximately 30 per cent to 45 per cent, almost exclusively at the expense of eurozone currencies, whose share fell from 30 per cent to 15 per cent. While the launch of the euro may encourage central banks to readjust their official reserves in favour of the euro, it is working against a significantly adverse medium-term trend.

The factors working against the euro began to ease in 2001, as the US economy began a rapid slowdown and the recovery in Japan faltered. In the period since, the euro has recovered strongly against all three currencies, reaching pre-1999 levels by late 2003. However, the real message of the last 4–5 years is that the early years of the euro clearly illustrate the limitations of EMU as a means of reducing trade-weighted exchange rate uncertainty. Table 3.4 gives some impression of the problem. While the smaller states like Belgium and Denmark are closely integrated with the rest of the EU15, carrying out approximately twice as much trade with other EU15 states as with the rest of the world, the same is not true of the large EU states. Extra-EU15 trade for Germany, Italy and the UK accounts for around 45 per cent of average exports/imports. With some 22 per cent of average eurozone (EU12)

Table 3.4 Intra- and Extra-EU15 Trade, 2002

	Intra-EU15 (€m)	Extra-EU15 (€m)	Intra-EU15 (% total)	Extra-EU15 (% total)
Belgium				
Exports	166577	62031	72.9	27.1
Imports	148730	61591	70.7	29.3
Denmark				
Exports	40074	20729	65.9	34.1
Imports	37504	15711	70.5	29.5
Germany				
Exports	354804	294367	54.7	45.3
Imports	286416	232072	55.2	44.8
Spain				
Exports	94846	38072	71.4	28.6
Imports	117478	57126	67.3	32.7
France				
Exports	215411	135392	61.4	38.6
Imports	229680	118217	66.0	34.0
Italy				
Exports	144890	124170	53.9	46.1
Imports	150464	110762	57.6	42.4
Netherlands				
Exports	199833	58717	77.3	22.7
Imports	122618	109261	52.9	47.1
UK				
Exports	174297	122018	58.8	41.2
Imports	192556	173684	52.6	47.4

Source: Adapted from Eurostat

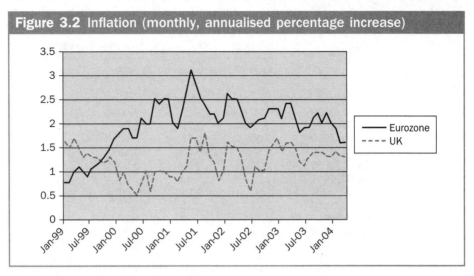

Figure 3.2 Inflation (monthly, annualised percentage increase)

Source: Adapted from European Central Bank

trade being undertaken with the other three EU15 states, this suggests that, for countries like Germany and Italy (and even France), the *majority* of trade is taking place across fluctuating exchange rates – and in the period 1999–2004, the volatility of the euro has been unusually extreme.

Inflation and interest rates

Figure 3.2 shows the record of the ECB on consumer price inflation over the period 1999–2004 compared with the performance of the Bank of England. The comparison is interesting, because the Bank of England's operating procedures were altered by the incoming Labour Government in 1997 to make it independent of political control, in order to allow it to focus on achieving price stability. By a different route, the Bank of England acquired a degree of political independence similar to that of the ECB.

It is notable that, apart from the first half of 1999, when both the eurozone and the UK were experiencing inflation rates some way below the target ceilings of 2 per cent, the Bank of England has performed rather better than the ECB, achieving an average monthly rate of annualised inflation of 1.22 per cent over the whole period as against 1.96 per cent; indeed, in 30 of the 63 months under consideration (January 1999 to March 2004), the monthly rate of annualised inflation in the eurozone was above the 2 per cent ceiling.

As with the reasons for the volatility of the euro over its first five years, the explanations for the apparently weaker performance of the eurozone than the UK on inflation are complex and do not imply, per se, either design faults in the EMU institutional infrastructure or policy mismanagement. It does suggest, however, that EMU under the control of a strong, anti-inflationary monetary authority is not the only route to low and stable inflation and that the same end can, in principle, be achieved by central bank reform at home.

Table 3.5 Key European Central Bank interest rates

Date changed	Deposit rate		Refinancing operations		Marginal lending rate	
	Level %	Change %	Level %	Change %	Level %	Change %
01/01/1999	2.00	–	3.00	–	4.50	–
04/01/1999	2.75	0.75	3.00	–	3.25	–0.25
22/01/1999	2.00	–0.75	3.00	–	4.50	1.25
09/04/1999	1.50	–0.50	2.50	–0.50	3.50	–1.00
05/11/1999	2.00	0.50	3.00	0.50	4.00	0.50
04/02/2000	2.25	0.25	3.25	0.25	4.25	0.25
17/03/2000	2.50	0.25	3.50	0.25	4.50	0.25
28/04/2000	2.75	0.25	3.75	0.25	4.75	0.25
09/06/2000	3.25	0.50	4.25	0.50	5.25	0.50
28/06/2000	3.25	–	4.25	–	5.25	–
01/09/2000	3.50	0.25	4.50	0.25	5.50	0.25
06/10/2000	3.75	0.25	4.75	0.25	5.75	0.25
11/05/2001	3.50	–0.25	4.50	–0.25	5.50	–0.25
31/08/2001	3.25	–0.25	4.25	–0.25	5.25	–0.25
18/09/2001	2.75	–0.50	3.75	–0.50	4.75	–0.50
09/11/2001	2.25	–0.50	3.25	–0.50	4.25	–0.50
06/12/2002	1.75	–0.50	2.75	–0.50	3.75	–0.50
07/03/2003	1.50	–0.25	2.50	–0.25	3.50	–0.25
06/06/2003	1.00	–0.50	2.00	–0.50	3.00	–0.50

Source: Adapted from European Central Bank

Since taking over monetary policy for the eurozone, the ECB has pursued an activist stance, as shown in Table 3.5, making eighteen adjustments in its key interest rates in the first five years. Like the Bank of England, the ECB targets the forecast rate of inflation two-to-three years into the future, using a range of leading indicators, including the growth of the broad money supply, to inform its decision-making (Svensson, 1997; Jansen, 2004). A key issue for the ECB is that, while its main policy objective is to keep forecast eurozone inflation rates below a 2 per cent ceiling, the 'one size fits all' policy stance may not be appropriate for all member states – even in terms of controlling inflation as opposed to stabilising growth. As Table 3.6 shows, there has been a significant variation in national inflation rates around the eurozone average, with countries like Greece, Ireland, Italy, Portugal and Spain – the very group of historically high-inflation countries predicted to benefit most from EMU membership – continuing to experience inflation rates well above the ECB's target ceiling of 2 per cent. Significantly, the Netherlands, which had one of the best pre-EMU anti-inflation records, has experienced inflation rates in excess of 2 per cent over the last three-to-four years.

Real macroeconomic performance

If arguably there are questions over the extent to which EMU has delivered the promised benefits of greater exchange rate stability and lower inflation and interest rates in its first five years, an equally important 'acid test' is whether

Table 3.6 Inflation (harmonised index of consumer prices) annual percentage changes

	1996–2000 %	2001 %	2002 %	2003 %
Austria	1.2	2.3	1.7	1.3
Belgium	1.6	2.4	1.6	1.5
Finland	1.6	2.7	2.0	1.3
France	1.3	1.8	1.9	2.2
Germany	1.1	1.9	1.3	1.0
Greece	4.6	3.7	3.9	3.4
Ireland	2.6	4.0	4.7	4.0
Italy	2.4	2.3	2.6	2.8
Luxembourg	1.7	2.4	2.1	2.5
Netherlands	1.9	5.1	3.9	2.2
Portugal	2.4	4.4	3.7	3.3
Spain	2.6	2.8	3.6	3.1
Eurozone	**1.6**	**2.3**	**2.3**	**2.1**
Britain	1.6	1.2	1.3	1.4
Denmark	2.0	2.3	2.4	2.0
Sweden	1.1	2.7	2.0	2.3
EU 15	**1.7**	**2.2**	**2.1**	**2.0**

Source: Adapted from European Central Bank

membership has imposed greater costs in terms of the increased real macro-economic instability its opponents predicted. In this area, reaching definitive judgements are particularly difficult, given the problems of distinguishing between deep-rooted structural imbalances and cyclical departures from trend output and employment.

Figure 3.3 shows the performance of the eurozone over the last six years, using the UK as a benchmark. Surprisingly, it shows a relatively high degree of synchronisation in the period immediately before and after EMU in 1999, but with growth slowing much more sharply after the end of 2001. Given the complexity of the issues involved, it is dangerous to reach any firm conclusions from this relatively short snapshot of macroeconomic performance, but it does raise questions over the ability of the ECB to steer the eurozone's economy, made up of twelve heterogeneous national sub-economies, using the single policy pool of interest rates.

Of perhaps more significance, however, is the differential performance of the twelve national eurozone economies themselves. Table 3.7 shows that the average growth rates of the eurozone, which have slowed from 1.6 per cent pa in 2001 to 0.4 per cent in 2003, disguise a considerable degree of variability. Ireland and Greece, for example, have continued to return high rates of economic growth, while the three major economies – Germany, France and Italy – have experienced a dramatic slowdown. The Netherlands, which suffered uncharacteristically high rates of inflation during the early years of the euro, has also slumped from average growth rates of 3.7 per cent pa in the period 1996–2000 to average growth of only 0.2 per cent pa in the period 2001–03. This differential pattern of economic expansion in some parts of the eurozone economy, coexisting with slowdown and recession in others, begs the important question of whether the Growth and Stability Pact is

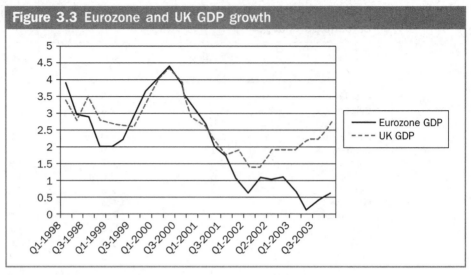

Figure 3.3 Eurozone and UK GDP growth

Source: Adapted from European Central Bank

Table 3.7 Growth rates (percentage change in real GDP pa)

	1996–2000 %	2001 %	2002 %	2003 %
Austria	2.7	0.8	1.4	0.7
Belgium	2.7	0.6	0.7	1.1
Finland	4.7	1.1	2.3	1.9
France	2.8	2.1	1.2	0.2
Germany	1.8	0.8	0.2	−0.1
Greece	3.4	4.0	3.8	4.7
Ireland	9.8	6.2	6.9	–
Italy	1.9	1.8	0.4	0.3
Luxembourg	7.1	1.2	1.3	–
Netherlands	3.7	1.2	0.2	−0.8
Portugal	3.9	1.8	0.5	−1.3
Spain	3.8	2.8	2.0	2.4
Eurozone	**2.6**	**1.6**	**0.9**	**0.4**
Britain	3.1	2.1	1.6	2.2
Denmark	2.7	1.6	1.0	0.0
Sweden	3.3	1.2	1.8	–
EU 15	**2.7**	**1.6**	**1.0**	**0.7**

Source: Adapted from European Central Bank

constraining the ability of national governments to use fiscal policy as an alternative macroeconomic stabiliser.

Figure 3.4 shows the patterns of budget deficits for three selected member states over the period 1999–2003. It shows, for example, that in response to a booming economy and above-target inflation rates, Ireland allowed its budget surplus to reach almost 5 per cent in 2000 in an attempt to deflate the economy. In contrast, France and Germany have both used growing budget deficits to try to stimulate

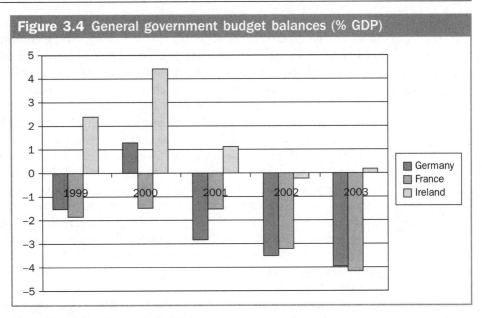

Figure 3.4 General government budget balances (% GDP)

Source: Adapted from European Central Bank

their weakened economies, such that by 2002 their deficits exceeded the 3 per cent limit embedded in the Growth and Stability Pact. While the Pact allows for temporary increases in deficits to counter recession, many commentators predicted that institutionalised limits on fiscal activitism risked making EMU inherently deflationary, not least because of the asymmetry – that is, high-growth countries could increase their budget surpluses without limit, while low-growth countries are subject to penalties. The apparent willingness of the European Commission to tolerate the apparent flouting of the Pact by Germany and France has been seen by some commentators as welcome pragmatism and by others as a breakdown in fiscal discipline within the eurozone (e.g. Artis, 2002; Buti et al., 2003; Fatas and Mihov, 2003; Amtenbrink and de Hann, 2003).

Conclusion

Every since the Delors Report was published, launching the EU on the road to a single currency, economists and politicians have argued about the costs and benefits of EMU. Indeed, in non-eurozone member states such as the UK the debate is as fierce as ever. The debate was characterised by widespread agreement that EMU would benefit intra-member state trade and investment by eliminating exchange rate uncertainty and transaction costs and question marks over whether it would reduce overall trade-weighted exchange volatility for individual member states. It was generally agreed that price transparency would strengthen competition within the internal market, while modern macroeconomic theory, stressing the importance of central bank independence for the maintenance of low, stable inflation, suggested that the design of the ECB should deliver price stability and lower real interest rates. The real area of controversy was always whether these benefits would be bought at an unacceptably high price, in terms of the reduced ability of member states to stabilise their economies in the face of asymmetric shocks.

Now that the great euro experiment is under way, there is a growing body of evidence against which the various claims and counterclaims for EMU can be empirically validated. The early evidence is mixed. The data analysed in the sections above suggest that, for some eurozone members, the elimination of exchange rate risk on intra-eurozone trade and investment may have been offset, at least in the early years of the euro, by greater trade-weighted exchange rate variation, due to the considerable fluctuations of the euro against, *inter alia*, the US dollar and the Japanese yen. While the ECB has been broadly successful in containing eurozone inflation, there is some evidence of considerable variability in both inflation and growth performance between member states. Perhaps most significant has been the apparent inability of the major economies, France and Germany, to stabilise their national economies, despite breaching the Growth and Stability Pact limits on budget deficits.

It is still very early in the life of the euro. Almost all major changes of policy regime take time to settle down. The monetary conversion which introduced physical euro notes and coins, the biggest in history, was achieved smoothly on schedule and stands as a testament to the determination of eurozone members to make EMU work. It is also worth reiterating the conclusion of this chapter in the 1998 3rd edition:

> Despite the economic caveats, EMU is about much more than a simple calculation of economic costs and benefits. For the EU, economic integration has always been a means to political unification, rather than an end in itself. The commitment of the key member states to the ideal of political union means that EMU must be seen as part of a wider commitment to a unified, peaceful Europe rather than a limited exercise in trading off economic costs for economic benefits.

This conclusion remains as valid today as it did in 1998.

References

Allsopp C and Artis M (2003) 'The Assessment: EMU, Four Years On', *Oxford Review of Economic Policy*, Vol. 19, pp. 1–29.

Amtenbrink F and de Haan J (2003) 'Economic Governance in the European Union: Fiscal Policy Discipline versus Flexibility', *Common Market Law Review*, Vol. 40, pp. 1075–1106.

Artis M (1989) *The Call of a Common Currency*, The Social Market Foundation, Paper No. 3, London.

Artis M (2002) 'The Stability and Growth Pact: Fiscal Policy in the EMU', in F Breuss, G Fink, and S Griller (eds) *Institutional, Legal and Economic Aspects of the EMU*, Springer, Vienna-New York.

Artis M, Krolzig H and Toro J (2004) 'The European Business Cycle', *Oxford Economic Papers*, Vol. 56, pp. 1–44.

Artis M and Zhang W (1995) *International Business Cycles and the ERM: Is There a European Business Cycle?*, CEPR Discussion Paper No. 1191, Centre for Economic Policy Research, London.

Bayoumi T and Eichengreen B (1992) *Shocking Aspects of European Monetary Unification*, CEPR Discussion Paper No. 643, Centre for Economic Policy Research, London.

Berger H, de Haan J and Eijffinger S (2000) *Central Bank Independence: An Update of Theory and Evidence*, CEPR Discussion Paper No. 2353, Centre for Economic Policy Research, London.

Bertaut C (2002) 'The European Central Bank and the Eurosystem', *New England Economic Review*, Second Quarter, pp. 25–9.

Britton E and Whitely J (1997) 'Comparing the Monetary Transmission Mechanism in France, Germany and the United Kingdom: Some Issues and Results', *Bank of England Quarterly Bulletin*, Vol. 37, pp. 63–84.

Buiter W (2003) 'Ten Commandments for a Fiscal Rule in the EMU', Oxford Review of Economic Policy, Vol. 19, pp. 84–99.

Buiter W, Corsetti G and Roubini N (1993) 'Sense and Nonsense in the Treaty of Maastricht', *Economic Policy*, Vol. 16, pp. 57–100.

Buti M, Eijffinger S and Franco D (2003) 'Revisiting EMU's Stability Pact: A Pragmatic Way Forward', *Oxford Review of Economic Policy*, Vol. 19, pp. 112–131.

Calmfors L and Driffill J (1988) 'Bargaining Structure, Corporatism and Macroeconomic Performance', *Economic Policy*, Vol. 6, pp. 13–61.

Debrun X (2001) 'Bargaining over EMU vs. EMS: Why Might the ECB be the Twin Sister of the Bundesbank?', *The Economic Journal*, Vol. 111, pp. 566–91.

De Grauwe P (2002) 'Challenges for Monetary Policy in Euroland', *Journal of Common Market Studies*, Vol. 40, pp. 693–718.

De Grauwe P and Vanhaverbeke W (1991) *Is Europe an Optimum Currency area?: Evidence from Regional Data*, CEPR Discussion Paper No. 555, Centre for Economic Policy Research, London.

Delors J (1988) *Report on Economic and Monetary Union in the European Community*, Committee for the Study of Economic and Monetary Union, European Commission, Brussels.

Emerson M (1992) *One Market, One Money: An Evaluation of the Potential Benefits and Costs of Forming an Economic and Monetary Union*, Oxford University Press, Oxford; summarised in European Commission (1990) 'One Market, One Money', *European Economy*, No. 44.

Ehrmann M, Gambacorta L, Martinez-Pages J, Sevestre P and Worms A (2003) 'The Effects of Monetary Policy in the Euro Area', *Oxford Review of Economic Policy*, Vol. 19, pp. 58–72.

European Commission (1985) *Completing the Internal Market: The White Paper*, Office for Official Publications of the European Communities, Luxembourg.

European Commission (1997) *Broad Economic Policy Guidelines: The Outcome of the Amsterdam European Council on Stability, Growth and Employment*, European Economy, No. 64.

Fatas A and Mihov I (2003) 'On Constraining Fiscal Policy Discretion in EMU', *Oxford Review of Economic Policy*, Vol. 19, pp. 112–131.

Gros D (1996) *A Reconsideration of the Optimum Currency Approach: The Role of External Shocks and Labour Mobility*, Centre for European Policy Studies, Brussels.

Heylen F and Van Poeck A (1995) 'National Labour Market Institutions and the European Economic and Monetary Integration Process', *Journal of Common Market Studies*, Vol. 33, pp. 573–95.

Huchet M (2003) 'Does Single Monetary Policy Have Asymmetric Real Effects in EMU?', *Journal of Policy Modeling*, Vol. 25, pp. 151–178.

Kempa B (2002) 'Is Europe Converging to Optimality?: On Dynamic Aspects of Optimum Currency Areas', *Journal of Economic Studies*, Vol. 29, pp. 151–178.

Jansen E (2004) *Modelling Inflation in the Euro Area*, ECB Working Paper No. 322, Frankfurt.

Jenkins R (1979) 'European Monetary Union', *Lloyds Bank Review*, No. 127, pp. 1–14.

McKinnon R (1963) 'Optimum Currency Areas', *American Economic Review*, Vol. 53, pp. 717–25.

Mendizabal H (2002) 'Monetary Union and the Transaction Cost Savings of a Single Currency', *Review of International Economics*, Vol. 10, pp. 263–77.

Minford P and Rastogi A (1990) 'The Price of EMU', in R Dornbusch and R Layard (eds), *Britain and EMU*, Centre for Economic Performance, London.

Mundell R (1961) 'A Theory of Optimum Currency Areas', *American Economic Review*, Vol. 51, pp. 657–64.

Mundell R (2003) 'The Significance of the Euro in the International Monetary System', *American Economist*, Vol. 47, pp. 27–39.

Rodriguez-Fuentes C and Dow S (2003) 'EMU and the Regional Impact of Monetary Policy', *Regional Studies*, Vol. 37, pp. 969–980.

Rose A (2000) 'One Money, One Market: Estimating the Effect of Common Currencies on Trade', *Economic Policy*, Vol. 30, pp. 7–46.

Rose A (2001) 'Currency Union and Trade: The Effect is Large', *Economic Policy*, Vol. 31, pp. 433–62.

Svensson L (1997) 'Inflation Forecast Targeting: Implementing and Monitoring Inflation Targets', *European Economic Review*, Vol. 41, pp. 1111–46.

Van Poeck, A and Borghijs, A (2001) 'EMU and Labour Market Reform: Needs, Incentives and Realisations', *The World Economy*, Vol. 24, pp. 1327–1352.

Chapter 4

The budget of the European Union

Clara Mira Salama

Introduction

Since the early years of the creation of the European Coal and Steel Community (ECSC) in April 1951, the European Economic Community (EEC) and the European Atomic Energy Community (EURATOM) by six Member States in 1957 with the Treaty of Rome, the European Union (EU) has experienced significant change: its tasks and competences have increased (deepening) and its membership has expanded (widening), its structure having been fundamentally changed as a result of subsequent treaties amending the original Treaty of Rome. This explains the increase in the size of the budget of the Union and the changes in the rules governing budgetary procedures.

Initially each of the three original Communities (the ECSC, the EEC and Euratom) had their own specific budgets. The resources to finance these budgets came from the member states' contributions, with the Council having a prominent role in the whole budgetary procedure. As a result of further integration this situation evolved over time in a number of ways:

Unification of budgetary instruments

The 1965 Merger Treaty left only two budgets, one for the ECSC and the general budget for the rest of the Communities activities. This was the case until the expiry of the ECSC Treaty in July 2002;[1] after that date, coal and steel were placed under the ordinary general regime, so that there is now only one EU budget. However, one budgetary instrument is not included in the general budget: the European Development Fund (EDF) which finances development cooperation policies towards the African, Caribbean and Pacific (ACP) countries (in the framework of the Lomé/Cotonou Conventions). The EDF is funded directly by member states' contributions.[2]

Progressive achievement of institutional balance

Initially the Council was the sole budgetary authority, retaining all budgetary powers. Over the years the European Parliament (EP) became more involved in the procedure and gained many competences in all fields of activity, including budgetary procedure, although this was not without difficulties. In 1975 the European Parliament was granted the power to reject the draft budget, and increase non-compulsory expenditure[3] within a maximum limit.[4] A long evolution has been necessary to reach the current situation where, as we will see, both the EP and the Council are considered budgetary authorities and this may be subject to further change along the same lines in the near future.

Implementation of the own resources system

Initially, the budget was financed by member states' contributions, but in 1970 an *own resources* system was introduced.[5] The Treaty of Rome had stated in its Article 210 (now Art. 269 under the Amsterdam Treaty) that 'the budget shall be financed wholly from own resources', meaning that the Community should be financially autonomous and that its resources should belong to the Community itself.

Between 1975 and 1988 there was a period of budgetary crisis. Tensions between the institutions, and between the member states, distorted and obstructed the normal functioning of the procedures, creating delays in the adoption of the budget. Actions were brought before the European Court of Justice and the EP even rejected the budget. The origins of the crisis lay not only in the EP's desire to play a more important role, but also in the growing gap between revenues and expenditures and the need to find new sources to finance the new commitments that the EU was entering into. To try to overcome these difficulties, and following the accession of Spain and Portugal and the coming into force of a new treaty (the Single European Act), the Commission presented a reform proposal, known as the 'Delors Package'. This package was crystallised in the adoption of the 1988 Brussels Inter-institutional Agreement, where financial projections of resources and expenditures ('perspectives') for the years 1988–92 were established. The main changes that the Delors Package introduced can be seen in Box 4.1. They are important as many of them are still in force.

At the Edinburgh European Council (December 1992), new financial perspectives for the period 1993–99 were adopted, based on the so-called 'Delors II package', that took into consideration the policies that the Maastricht Treaty had introduced. As a result the *own resources* ceiling was raised to 1.27 per cent of Community GNP in 1999 and the rate applied to the VAT base was scheduled to fall progressively to 1 per cent in 1999. The financial perspectives for the period 2000–06, known as 'Agenda 2000', are the ones currently in force, although with some modifications, and they will be explained in detail below.

In this chapter we will analyse the structure and functions of the budget; the main sources of finance of the EU; its revenues; how the budget is created and the role of each institution. The budgetary consequences of enlargement and the future 'financial constitution' will also be discussed, bearing in mind that we are living a moment of significant change, with the new Constitutional Treaty recently agreed upon and in the process of being signed. But the final text will have to be ratified by member states, so it may take some time for the new rules to come into force.

Box 4.1 The Delors reform (or 'Delors Package')

- Introduction of a system of multiannual financial framework. Since then there have been three financial perspectives: 1988–92, 1993–99, 2000–06, preceded by three inter-institutional agreements.

- Creation of a new category of resources based on the GNP of member states, matching the ability to pay of each country.

- Establishment of a total ceiling for own resources, as a percentage of the EU GNP (1.2 per cent of GNP by 1992).

- Establishment of an agricultural guideline–ceiling to control agriculture expenditure (74 per cent of the Community's GNP growth).

- Introduction of a maximum rate of increase of non-compulsory expenditure subject to the decision of the EP.

- Correction of the VAT resource: the base to which the rate is applied was capped at 55 per cent of GNP.

Source: Adopted from European Commission (SCADPLUS)

The budget: main concepts, structure and principles

Main concepts

The budget of the EU is an instrument that determines the amount of expenditure to be allocated to each policy area in which the EU is involved, and the revenue it expects to collect to finance these activities during the year in question. According to the 2002 Financial Regulation, it can be defined as 'the instrument which, for each financial year, forecasts and authorizes all revenue and expenditure considered necessary for the European Community . . .' (Article 4).[6]

If we consider a state, it is clear that each country needs a budget in which revenues and expenditures for a given period of time, usually a year, are established. But the budget of the EU cannot be compared to a national budget; it has peculiarities that make it different. For example, in its decision-making and functioning the EU has to respect rules and reach compromises between very different member states. If we consider regional or agricultural policy we find very clear examples of the EU members defending very different, sometimes opposed, national interests. But at the same time the EU is not similar to a traditional international organisation, financed by member states' contributions, since it is not a mere organisation for cooperation but intended to foster increasing integration. Since we cannot rely on national or international organisations' budgetary rules, the EU needs peculiar budgetary rules and procedures concerning how it is to be financed and managed.

The rules concerning the budgetary procedure, resources and expenditure are currently contained mainly in Articles 268 to 280 of the EC Treaty. The Financial

Regulation – known sometimes as the 'financial bible' – provides more specific details concerning the budgetary procedure and implementation. There is also an important body of other dispositions – known as soft law, since some are Recommendations or Joint Resolutions, which are not legally binding – around the subject, that have been consolidated by the Inter-institutional Agreement of 6 May 1999.

The size of the EU budget is not great; in 2003, for example, the budget of the EU amounted to €99.68 bn, which represents 1.02 per cent of the EU GNP. If we compare this amount with any national budget we can see that it is quite small. For example in 2002 the EU budget (€95 bn) amounted to less than 20 per cent of the UK's central public budget (Schreyer, 2002).

To ensure the smooth functioning of the budgetary procedures and prevent the frequent budgetary crises of the 80s, the system is now based on medium-term programming of expenditure through the 'financial framework'. The Commission, the EP and the Council together establish the detailed ceilings of expenditure for each of the main categories for a period that usually covers six years. This framework is meant to reflect the political priorities of the institutions for the period and, once adopted, is binding upon the three institutions. The main categories of expenditure correspond to the following headings:

1 Common Agricultural Policy (CAP)

2 Structural operations

3 Internal policies

4 External action

5 Administration

6 Reserves

7 Pre-accession aid

The financial framework is then translated into annual budgets, which, to make implementation and control easier, are also structured into the same seven categories. This system has advantages, as mentioned, but it also introduces rigidity into each year's budget.

As well as directing money to finance European activities (Schreyer, 2002), the EU budget also has an important redistributive function, transferring funds from richer to poorer regions to achieve convergence (structural policy) in keeping with the principle of solidarity and convergence upon which the EU is based.[7]

Budgetary structure

If we examine any year's budget,[8] the first entry we find is a general statement on revenue (A. 'Total revenue') where the *own resources* are itemised, followed by the main part of the budget, structured into Sections for each institution. The 2003 budget, for example, had eight Sections: Parliament (Section I), Council (Section II), Commission (Section III), Court of Justice (Section IV), Court of Auditors (Section V), Economic and Social Committee (Section VI), Committee of the Regions (Section VII) and European Ombudsman and European Data-protection Supervisor

(Section VIII). Each Section is subdivided into statements of Revenue and Expenditure. On the Revenue side are the receipts derived from the functioning of the institution and its staff (deductions from staff remuneration, from property and miscellaneous taxes, revenues accruing from the administrative operation of the institutions, interests on late payments and fines). The Expenditure element covers the institutions' administrative costs, except for that of the Commission which has two parts, one for administrative expenditure (Part A) and the other devoted to operating appropriations (Part B). It is Part B of the Commission's Section where policy expenditure (Agricultural, Regional, etc.) is specified; this part in itself accounts for approximately 95 per cent of the general budget, which explains why, when discussing the structure of the budget, the other Sections are often ignored. The structure of this budget's section has just been modified as a result of the introduction of the Activity-Based Budgeting (ABB) system, under which all of the Commission's expenditures are classified under the heading of an activity or policy, with 30 policy areas identified. This new system, used for the first time in the 2004 budget, allows a clearer identification of the amounts devoted to each activity and makes the process more political and transparent.

Budgetary principles

The budget has to comply with several rules established by the Treaty, which can be considered budgetary principles because of their importance. The main rules are the following:

- *Unity*: all revenues and expenditures should be presented together, in a single document; the EU has only one budget (Article 268, Treaty). This principle does not prevent European agencies from having their own budgets, and there is also a specific budget – the European Development Fund – to finance the development of the ACP countries. In principle, the Common Foreign and Security Policy (CFSP) and Justice and Home Affairs (JHA) operations are also financed from the general EU budget, but a distinction has to be made here between administrative expenditure – which is always charged to the general budget – and operating expenditure, which may not be charged to it if the Council unanimously decides otherwise, and, in the particular case of the CFSP, if the expenditure arises from operations having military or defence implications (Articles 28 and 41, Treaty on the European Union).[9]

- *Universality*: all of the revenue of the budget is used to finance all of the expenditure. This principle in fact entails two rules: the rule of non-assignment (it is not possible to assign a specific source of revenue to a specific expenditure – (hypothecation)) and the gross budget principle (all revenue and expenditure items have to be included individually within the budget without the possibility of prior offsetting of revenue items against particular expenditures).

- *Equilibrium*: revenue should equal expenditure, i.e. there should be a balanced budget (Article 269 Treaty establishing the European Community, TEC). Despite this rule, sometimes there is a surplus at the end of the year or, less often, a deficit. When this happens the surplus is entered as an additional revenue item in the budget for the following financial year. The economic effects of this rule are clear; the budget of the EU cannot be used as a tool for fiscal fine-tuning: the EU cannot borrow or lend and therefore it cannot be used to steer the economy as Keynesian policy might suggest.

■ *Annuality*: the period of time covered by the budget is a calendar year (Article 272.1).

The rules of unity, universality and annuality ensure the transparency of the budget and make control easier; there cannot be individual and specific budgets for projects or policies that might not be controlled by the institutions.

The revenue side: where the money comes from

As already mentioned, in the first years of the European Communities the budget was financed by direct contributions from member states, as with other international organisations. Since the 1970 Decision on *own resources*, the EU has always had its own sources of financing: something fundamental to ensure the independence and self-identity of the EU as distinct from its member states. Thus the Community's *own resources* may be defined as 'tax revenue allocated irrevocably to the Community to finance its budget and accruing to it automatically without the need for any subsequent decision by the national authorities' (European Commission, 2001).

Since the *own resources* system was established in 1970, and following the reform of 1988 (the Delors package), with some adaptations, the main sources of finance of the EU are the following:

Traditional own resources, established in 1970:

1 Duties deriving from the Common Agricultural Policy and sugar and isoglucose levies.

2 Customs Duties charged by the Common Custom Tariff and collected at the Community's external borders.

'New' or 'non-traditional' *own resources*:

3 A proportion of the VAT collected by the member states. A uniform rate, which in 1975 amounted to 1 per cent, is applied to a common VAT base.[10] The rate increased in 1985 to 1.4 per cent in order to fund the growing expenditure of the Community and to address the reduction of the VAT base. Nonetheless the Berlin European Council of March 1999 established that the rate should fall to 0.75 per cent in 2002 and to 0.50 per cent from 2004 onwards. The aim of this reduction is to make the system more equitable. Since studies show that, generally, consumption represents a higher proportion of GNP in the less prosperous countries, and VAT is based upon consumption, the increase in this resource fell more heavily upon these poorer states (i.e. VAT had a regressive effect) (European Commission, 1998).

4 A percentage of each member state's GNP. Introduced in 1988, this uniform rate is intended to balance the Community's budget. The introduction of such a

resource was necessary as the other resources were proving insufficient to finance the budget. During recessions VAT revenues diminished and, as a result of World Trade Organisation tariff reduction agreements, custom levies were also falling significantly. Furthermore, this resource introduced a welcome degree of equity and progressivity in the system, given the previous reliance on regressive VAT contributions. This resource, based upon GNP, matches contributions more closely to the ability to pay. Nonetheless, this principle does not take into consideration aggregate GNP in per capita terms. This is the reason why a proposal was tabled by Spain in July 1998, supported by Portugal and Greece, suggesting that 'national modulation coefficients' be applied so that the contributions would reflect per capita income and not just GNP.

These resources are collected by member states' authorities and transferred to the Community at the adoption of the budget, with a 25 per cent retention allowance for collection costs. The *own resources* collected each year by the Community have a ceiling established to prevent the budget from becoming too large. This limit was set at 1.2 per cent of the EU GNP in 1988, increasing by stages to 1.27 per cent by 1999.[11]

Traditional own resources were fundamental in the early years of the Community, but currently, as can be seen in Table 4.1, agricultural duties, sugar levies and customs duties are far less significant; the main source that has gained in importance over the years is the fourth resource – percentage of GNP.

As for the contribution of the different member states, we can see in Table 4.2 that Germany, France, Italy and the UK together finance nearly 70 per cent of the EU budget, which is consistent with their size and GNP. The contribution of the UK is peculiar, since from 1984 it has received a budgetary rebate, which will be discussed below.

The principles against which the effectiveness of a good *own resources* system can be assessed, according to the Commission, are those of financial autonomy, equity in gross contributions (equal distribution of the burden between member states), cost-effectiveness, transparency, simplicity and resource adequacy (the resources must match the financing needs and their changes). The Commission considered in 1998 that the Community's financial system complied with the principles of adequacy and equity, but not completely with those of financial autonomy,

Table 4.1 Contribution from types of revenue to the EU budget, 1971–2003 (%)

	Traditional own resources	VAT-based %	GNP-based own resources
1971	55.6	–	–
1980	48.1	44.2	–
1990	26.1	59.1	0.2
2000	15.3	38.1	42.3
2001	15.1	35.6	48.5
2002	12.2	23.6	48.7
2003	12.5	24.7	60.9

Sources: Caesar 2002, European Commission 2003

Table 4.2 Member states' contribution to the EU budget, 2003

Member state	% financing of 2003 budget
Germany	22.96
France	17.87
Italy	14.15
UK	12.90
Spain	8.63
The Netherlands	5.78
Belgium	3.97
Sweden	2.77
Austria	2.32
Denmark	2.15
Greece	1.80
Finland	1.58
Portugal	1.55
Ireland	1.33
Luxembourg	0.23
Total	100

Source: European Commission, Press Release 27 May 2003

cost-effectiveness and transparency/simplicity (European Commission, 1998). The problems arise from the delegation of tax collection to the national authorities together with the limited budgetary powers of the EC authorities. At the same time citizens cannot distinguish which part of their taxes goes to the national government and which to the EU. Thus, to improve the situation, several proposals to modify the system have been made, including the creation of a truly European *own resource*, such as a European tax,[12] or a new fifth resource. Among these proposals we find ideas such as a new CO_2 energy tax, excise taxes on tobacco, alcohol and mineral oil; corporate income tax; communications taxes, personal income tax and ECB seignorage.[13] Other initiatives suggest the system as a whole should be modified and the GNP instrument be given greater emphasise, which would introduce a more important element of progressivity in the system. The Commission has just put forward new proposals in this sense, suggesting a modification of the system, to centre it upon a tax rate on energy consumption, the national VAT rate or a corporate income tax.[14]

The expenditure side: how the money is spent

The funds are used to finance the whole range of EU policies, which are allocated in the financial perspective and in each year's budget to the seven headings already mentioned: 1. Common Agricultural Policy; 2. Structural Operations; 3. Internal Policies; 4. External Action; 5. Administration; 6. Reserves; 7. Pre-accession Aid. Under the heading 'Internal Policies' we find the broad range of areas in which the EU is involved, for example, research and technological development, education and vocational training, culture, information and communication, consumer policy, the internal market, the area of freedom, security and justice.

The allocation of resources to these policies corresponds to the changing political priorities of the EU. Thus agriculture expenditure, in particular the Guarantee Section of the European Agricultural Guidance and Guarantee Fund (EAGGF), represented a very important part of the budget in the early years (86.9 per cent in 1970). This figure declined to 68.4 per cent in 1985 and to 50 per cent in 1996.[15] By contrast Structural Policy (which includes structural and cohesion funds) has gained in importance; in 1970 it only represented 2.7 per cent of the budget, while in 2001 it already accounted for 33.2 per cent. Agriculture and Structural Policy together account for the majority of the budget; for the 2002 budget they represented nearly 80 per cent of the total.[16] This evolution can be seen in Table 4.3.

The current financial framework covers the period 2000–2006, and was established in May 1999 by an Inter-institutional Agreement. Nonetheless the ceilings established then had to be modified with a view to enlargement in 2003 (Table 4.4).

The budget for the year 2003 amounts to €99,686 m in commitments and €97,503 m in payments (in current prices), amounts that are below those fixed in

Table 4.3 Community expenditure from 1970 to 2000 (in % of the general budget, outturn in payments)

	1970	1975	1980	1985	1990	1995	2000
CAP – EAGGF Guarantee Section	86.9	70.9	68.6	68.4	56.1	50.4	45.0
Structural Funds	2.7	6.2	11.0	12.8	21.0	28.1	34.6
Research	1.8	1.9	2.2	2.4	3.9	3.6	3.9
External Action	0.0	4.1	3.7	3.3	3.1	5.0	6.0
Administration	3.2	6.0	5.0	4.5	5.1	5.7	5.1
Others	0.0	6.3	5.8	5.2	7.3	4.5	2.3

Source: Adapted from European Commission, 2000

Table 4.4 Financial perspectives 2000–2006 (at 2004 prices, million €)

	2000	2001	2002	2003	2004	2005	2006
1. Agriculture	41738	44530	46587	47378	49305	50431	50575
2. Structural & Cohesion Funds	32678	32720	33638	33968	41035	41685	42932
3. Internal Policies	6031	6272	6558	6796	8722	8967	9093
4. External Action	4627	4735	4873	4972	5082	5093	5014
5. Administration	4638	4776	5012	5211	5983	6154	6325
6. Reserves	906	916	676	434	442	442	442
7. Pre-accession Aid	3174	3240	3328	3386	3445	3445	3445
8. Compensation	–	–	–	–	1410	1299	1041
Total appropriations for commitments	93792	97189	100672	102145	115434	117526	118967
Total appropriations for payments	91322	94730	100078	102767	111380	112260	114740
Ceiling, appropriations for payments as % GNI (ESA 95)	1.07%	1.08%	1.11%	1.09%	1.08%	1.06%	1.06%
Margin unforeseen expenditure	0.17%	0.16%	0.13%	0.15%	0.16%	0.18%	0.18%
Own Resources Ceiling (% GNP)	1.24%	1.24%	1.24%	1.24%	1.24%	1.24%	1.24%

Source: Decision of the European Parliament and the Council on the *Adjustment of the Financial Perspective for Enlargement*, 19 May 2003, (2003/429/EC), OJ 14.6.2003

the financial perspective for that year because of the 'very tight grip on budget growth' (European Commission, 2003). The budget for 2004, adopted on 18 December 2003, had to be modified by an amended budget in March 2004 to adapt it to the accession of the ten new countries on 1 May 2004, and it is peculiar in that it applies to a Union of 15 members from January to May and 25 members from May onwards. For the second part of the period, with EU-25, the budget amounts to €111,300 m in appropriations for commitments and €99,724 m in appropriations for payments.

It is important to understand the distinction between payments and commitments. Commitments are legal obligations entered into for operations that may last more than one financial year, whilst payments are the real transfer of money in each particular period. The budget therefore establishes ceilings in terms of appropriations for both commitments and payments. The commitments' ceiling is established in each financial perspective as a total figure (currently 1.335 per cent of the Community GNP) and for each category, to ensure the smooth functioning of the system.

As we can see in Table 4.4 the margin between the total appropriations for payments and the ceiling on *own resources* – the margin for unforeseen expenditure – is considerable, ranging from 0.13 per cent in 2002 to 0.18 per cent in 2006. This margin introduces a significant degree of flexibility in the system, allowing the EU to respond to new situations, and also acts as a safety net to ensure that expenditure will never exceed revenue.

Budgetary imbalances: the UK rebate

Budgetary balances can be defined as the difference between a member state's payment to the EU budget and the expenditure of the Community in that territory. This is a very straightforward and formalistic mechanism for calculating the net financial benefits that a member state obtains from belonging to the EU. It does not consider many of the other important advantages that may be derived from EU membership, such as the economic benefits of the internal market (economies of scale, greater competition, etc.), enhanced external relations, development aid and the area of freedom, security and justice and many others. At the same time, we have to take into consideration the redistributive function of the budget, which is also inspired, as is the EU as a whole, by the principle of solidarity.

When the UK joined the EU, it was in a peculiar situation: it could not take significant advantage of EU expenditure while it had to make a major contribution to its financing. This situation arose because of two factors, as stated by the Commission:

- In relation to EU expenditure, the British agricultural sector was small, while imports from outside the Community were significant. As a consequence the UK could not profit significantly from CAP funds, which accounted for nearly 80 per cent of the EU budget.

- On the financing side, the UK's contribution to the EC budget from the VAT resource was substantial since consumption expenditure was relatively high as a proportion of GNP.

As a result of these characteristics the UK's payments to the budget were significantly greater than its receipts. This became a cause of considerable political concern in the UK, with the UK Prime Minister, Mrs Thatcher, threatening to veto any further expenditure increase until the UK situation had been resolved. Several alternatives were suggested, with the one finally chosen, the 'Fontainebleau mechanism' (European Council, June 1984), offering a 66 per cent reduction in the UK's net balance. The preferred means to achieve this reduction was the application of a lower rate for the VAT resource ('tax-relief' for the UK).

The details of the calculation and financing of the rebate are very complex and offer neither transparency nor accountability, as the Commission itself observed in its 1998 Report 'Financing the European Union'. The amount of the rebate varies from year to year; in 2001, it was worth about £2.8bn. This mechanism has been reviewed several times (in 1988, 1992 and 1999) and it is included in every Council decision on the system of *own resources*.

The reduction in the UK's contribution is financed by the rest of the member states initially through their shares of VAT payments, while from 1988 it was funded on the same basis as the 'fourth resource' – GNP – based contributions. With the 2000 *own resources* decision there were further changes in the way the rebate is financed: the part of the rebate financed by Germany, the Netherlands, Austria and Sweden was reduced to 25 per cent of their normal share. Such a reduction was justified with the argument that these countries suffer from budgetary imbalances as large as those of the UK. In Figure 4.1 we can see that, even after the UK rebate, the UK is a net contributor in relation to its GNP, but the imbalance is even greater for countries such as the Netherlands, Sweden, Luxembourg and Germany.

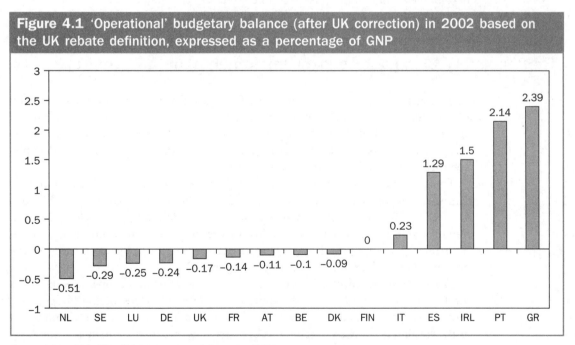

Figure 4.1 'Operational' budgetary balance (after UK correction) in 2002 based on the UK rebate definition, expressed as a percentage of GNP

Source: Adapted from Commission Services, 18 September 2003

As for the redistributive effects of the EU budget, those member states that have a greater budgetary surplus – the 'cohesion' countries, Greece, Portugal and Spain – are also those with a GNP per capita below the EU average (with the exception of Ireland). Similarly those member states with negative budgetary balance usually have above average GDP per capita, although the rankings are not exact. If this were to accurately reflect GNP per capita then the greatest contributor would be Luxembourg, followed by Denmark, Ireland, Sweden, the UK and the Netherlands.[17]

The future of the rebate continues to be debated, especially recently. Even if it is true that, in general terms, the mechanism is considered to have achieved its objective and reduced the net contribution of the UK, circumstances have perhaps changed significantly. The CAP does not account for as significant a proportion of the budget as it used to when the rebate was adopted. Further, enlargement has altered significantly the former 15 member states' budgetary positions, since the new member states have a standard of living well below the EU average. At the same time other member states now face a similar financial situation to that of the UK. This point was raised by some countries at the Nice European Council (December 2000) and the French President, Mr Chirac, argued that the situation needed to be reviewed so that the costs of enlargement would be borne equally by all member states. Despite the tensions that this declaration caused, the rebate issue was not raised during discussions on how to finance the enlargement, since this item was 'not in the agenda', according to the Chairman Mr Rasmussen, the Danish Prime Minister. Nonetheless, the issue has been raised again following enlargement, and the Commission has just proposed to the Council the revision of the system to generalise the UK correction to any member state with an excessive net budgetary burden, defined as exceeding 35 per cent of a country's GNP,[18] so developments in this field remain to be seen.

The budgetary procedure: budget implementation and control

The budgetary procedure is no more than a legislative process with the three main EU institutions – Commission, EP and Council – involved. The Council and the EP are the two arms of the budgetary authority, taking the main decisions, while the Commission plays its role in preparing and submitting a draft budget, and implementing it. The budget is drawn up in euros.

The procedure is long and complex, involving several phases, each with a precise timing to ensure that the new budget is adopted before 1 January. If the EU fails to meet this deadline then a system of 'twelfths' would apply (Article 273): each month a sum equivalent to one-twelfth of the previous year's budget appropriations may be used, but only to finance current expenditure. The main steps of the budgetary procedure are summarised in Figure 4.2.

There are several mechanisms that ensure coordination and cooperation between the Community's institutions throughout the different stages of the budget procedure: the Council and the EP in 'conciliation' meetings, and with the Commission in the 'trialogue'.[19] These discussions are necessary because the budget is the crystallisation of a political agenda and sets the EU's priorities. The frequent meetings

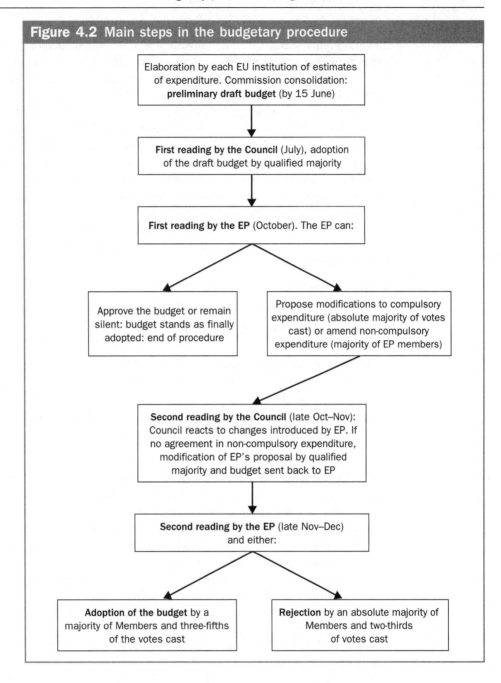

Figure 4.2 Main steps in the budgetary procedure

Elaboration by each EU institution of estimates of expenditure. Commission consolidation: **preliminary draft budget** (by 15 June)

First reading by the Council (July), adoption of the draft budget by qualified majority

First reading by the EP (October). The EP can:

Approve the budget or remain silent: budget stands as finally adopted: end of procedure

Propose modifications to compulsory expenditure (absolute majority of votes cast) or amend non-compulsory expenditure (majority of EP members)

Second reading by the Council (late Oct–Nov): Council reacts to changes introduced by EP. If no agreement in non-compulsory expenditure, modification of EP's proposal by qualified majority and budget sent back to EP

Second reading by the EP (late Nov–Dec) and either:

Adoption of the budget by a majority of Members and three-fifths of the votes cast

Rejection by an absolute majority of Members and two-thirds of votes cast

under such a system allow the three institutions to work along similar lines and to reconcile any differences that might appear. The Constitutional Treaty proposes to reinforce this coordination and cooperation, suggesting regular meetings between the Presidents of the Commission, the EP and the Council. These would be organised on the initiative of the Commission, not only during the preparation of the budget, but also during its implementation.

The current procedure has evolved with the EP progressively increasing its powers. Nonetheless, these EP powers are still limited in regard to compulsory expenditure (which represents around 45 per cent of the budget (European Communities, 2000), and includes, for example, agriculture). Steps have been taken to try to alleviate this deficiency by two Joint Declarations,[20] in which the distinction between compulsory and non-compulsory expenditure is further clarified and a procedure – conciliation – established to give the EP an opportunity to express its views with regard to Community legislation that might have 'appreciable financial implications' and therefore give rise to compulsory expenditure. This weakness would be solved if the Constitutional Treaty is ratified as it now stands since it proposes the elimination of the distinction between compulsory and non-compulsory expenditure. Indeed the Constitutional Treaty includes a number of significant proposals which would simplify the budgetary procedure. If this Constitution is ratified and comes into force, the major changes in the procedure would be as follows:

■ The Commission would produce a draft budget, and it would transmit it to the Council and the EP at the same time.

■ The Council would adopt a position on the draft budget as a whole, with no distinction between compulsory and non-compulsory expenditure.

■ When transmitting the draft budget to the EP, the Council should inform the EP of the reasons which led it to adopt its position.

■ If the Council does not agree with the amendments introduced by the EP, a Conciliation Committee meeting would be scheduled in which the EP and the Council would meet and try to reach agreement.

The rules concerning the *implementation of the budget* are contained in Article 274, with the more specific details in the Financial Regulation, the implementing rules and the *own resources* decision. The responsibility for implementing the budget lies with the Commission, in cooperation with the member states, guided by the principles of sound financial management, economy, cost-effectiveness and cooperation with member states (Article 274 and Article 2 Financial Regulation). The Commission has to present an Annual Financial Statement to the EP and the Court of Auditors, as well as quarterly and monthly reports to these institutions and the Council – the Budgetary Implementation Report. The Constitutional Treaty also proposes that the Commission should be required to present an Evaluation Report based on the results achieved to the EP and Council. The Commission is accountable for the management of the budget until the EP grants it the discharge, which ends the procedure.

As for budget management, there are different *levels of control*. The first level takes place within each institution, in the so-called internal control. A system has also been designed to control revenue and expenditure when they are administered by member states, in an effort to combat fraud and manage the resources efficiently. Above that level we have the external control, which is undertaken in the first place by the European Court of Auditors, an independent body that monitors the legality and regularity of the implementation of the budget, and also the economy, efficiency and effectiveness of the financial management. Despite the name, the

Court of Auditors is not a Court in the legal sense, since it has no powers of sanction. Secondly, the European Parliament, which, on the basis of a Council Recommendation and taking into consideration the report produced by the Court of Auditors, grants the discharge to the Commission (Article 276), ending the budgetary cycle. This discharge is part of the external control, but is in fact more 'political' than the role of the Court of Auditors and the political consequences that can follow when it is not granted can be very serious. The EP has only twice refused to discharge the budget, in 1984 (the 1982 budget) and in 1998 (the 1996 budget). In the latter case allegations of fraud, nepotism and mismanagement led the EP to establish a Committee of Independent Experts; following their report,[21] the whole Commission resigned, something unique in the history of the European Community.

The budget and enlargement

The Eastern enlargement of the EU that has just taken place in May 2004 has been very different from the previous ones; for the first time ten countries have joined at the same time, which in itself has created a much greater degree of heterogeneity in the Union, as these newcomers are significantly different from the current EU members from a socio-economic and structural perspective. If we consider GDP after enlargement, according to Commission estimates, there would be a doubling of the income gaps between countries and regions.[22] From a structural point of view, the agricultural sector is very important in the new member states. Institutional reform and the means to finance this accession therefore have been topics of heated discussion in recent years.

The preparation and readjustment of the financial perspectives

As early as 1995, the Madrid European Council mandated the Commission to start working on future reforms of the financial system of the Community with a view to accommodating enlargement. As a result, the Communication 'Agenda 2000' (European Commission, 2000) was presented, followed by further proposals, communications and reports in March and October 1998.[23] Negotiations to reach agreement on Agenda 2000 lasted two years, and it was finally adopted at the Berlin European Council in March 1999. The aim of Agenda 2000 was to strengthen the Union and prepare it for enlargement, with modernisation of some of its most important policies such as the CAP and regional policy (structural funds). In drawing up the Agenda and its proposals, the Commission made an effort to strike a balance between the interests of current and new member states.

Agenda 2000 established the new Financial Framework for the period 2000–06, assuming the accession of six new States in 2002 and calculating the perspectives for 21 member states from 2002 to 2006. Since this scenario was not realised – ten new member states joined on 1 May 2004[24] – expenditure categories needed to be readjusted. The European Council established the maximum figures for additional budgetary expenditure for the new members from 2004 to 2006[25] that would need to be accommodated. Altogether this figure represents €40.8 bn in commitments, but since the new member states may not be able to make use of all the money allocated to them, and their contributions are expected to represent around €15 bn, the net budgetary cost for this period could be considered to be approximately €10 bn (Kok, 2003). The readjustment process nonetheless proved controversial; the Commission presented the proposal in February 2003 (European Commission, 2003b), but the Council and the EP only reached agreement in April 2003, after a very important inter-institutional quarrel that nearly blocked the signature of the Accession Treaty by the EP.

The budgetary implications of enlargement

Despite the increasing expenditure resulting from enlargement, the budget will have to accommodate it without increasing the *own resources* ceiling of 1.27 per cent of the combined EU GNP. Even if it would have been reasonable to raise the ceiling, the weak macroeconomic conditions in the EU in this period, the need for fiscal tightening and the discomfort of some member states with their existing position (Sapir et al., 2003), created an unfavourable atmosphere for such an increase. Thus, in its February 2004 Communication, the Commission suggested how the new priorities could be achieved within the current budgetary ceiling, through a combination of 'shifts in the balance between different spending priorities, careful costing, and only limited increases in the current size of the budget'.

As for the contributions of the ten new member states, they are expected to total €15 bn over the period. With regard to payments, agriculture support will be phased in, reaching the usual EU level by 2013.[26] As for regional policy, an overall figure has been set at €23 bn. Temporary budgetary compensation has been accepted for any of the new members that experience a negative cash flow between 2004 and 2006 to ensure that their financial situation will be no worse than in 2003; it has been accepted that none of the new member states will be net contributors to the budget during these initial years. These kinds of transitional arrangements were also granted to new members in previous enlargements. Bearing all this in mind, the net budgetary cost for this period could amount to €10 bn (Kok, 2003).

In terms of the costs of enlargement after 2006, it will all depend on the decisions that are subsequently made, mainly regarding CAP reform and the structural funds. A study that compares the different possible scenarios, according to decisions that could be made after 2006, suggests that the costs of enlargement will mainly depend upon whether the current member states are compensated for the fall in structural funds received by their regions (Karlsson, 2002). Even in the worst-case scenario (with no reform of the CAP and the current rules applying to regional policy) the ceiling of *own resources* would not be threatened; total payments to the budget would still amount to 1.12 per cent of EU GNP in 2007.

In the debate as to how to finance enlargement, there has been agreement that burden-sharing is fundamental: member states should contribute fairly in meeting the cost of enlargement. In the years to come this may result in significant changes in the current institutional arrangements such as the rebates system.

Conclusion

We are witnessing a fundamental moment in the process of the construction of the EU: the recent enlargement in May 2004 increased the number of EU member states from 15 to 25, increasing the diversity of the EU. An agreement has just been reached for a new Constitutional Treaty for Europe (Brussels European Council, 17–18 June 2004), which should be signed in Rome on 29 October 2004, and the Nice Treaty entered into force in February 2003. The budget, inextricably linked to the functioning of the EU, will undoubtedly be affected by all of these developments. It will face the challenge of accommodating the entry of the new members and financing their economic convergence, without creating too great a burden for the existing member states. At the same time, the budget has to provide the necessary means to finance the EU's continued expansion in its responsibilities. How this will be achieved remains to be seen. The challenge is immense.

Concerning future steps in financial programming, the Commission presented a communication on the broad guidelines for the next financial perspective in February 2004, in which it describes broadly what the new priorities of the EU should be, and how they could be financed. The three suggested priorities are achieving sustainable development through the completion of the Internal Market, giving full content to European citizenship through the completion of an area of freedom, justice, security and access to basic goods and the role of the EU as a global partner. Some of the initiatives hinted in this communication were further outlined in a new package of proposals presented in July 2004. As already mentioned, the novelty for the financing system is the Commission's proposal to modify the *own resources* system, to base it on a tax on energy consumption, the national VAT rate or a corporate income tax. It is also in this context where the new proposals for the generalisation of the UK correction mechanisms have been raised.

Even if these initiatives are only the starting point for a long and difficult debate, and therefore changes in the short run should not be expected, we see many new initiatives being developed in this field, in an effort to increase budget transparency and efficiency, and thus make it more understandable to EU citizens.

The new financial framework, to cover the period from 2007, should be adopted by the new Commission, EP and Council by the end of 2005. The Commission has suggested that, exceptionally, the duration of the new Financial Perspectives should be seven years, since agricultural ceilings have been set until 2013, so they would cover the period 2007–2013, but that after that they should cover a five-year term in line with the mandate of the institutions.

As we have seen, the current budgetary procedure is the result of a difficult evolution. The role of the institutions and the identification of new resources to finance a growing expenditure, have been two of the major issues of debate. The search for effectiveness and fairness in the system has also been a recurring consideration. The weight of the most regressive elements of the budget, mainly the VAT resource, has also been reduced to make the system more equitable. Thus, we could conclude that the current arrangements have so far succeeded in creating a smoothly functioning system.

Nonetheless, it is also true that the budgetary procedure is obscure and complicated, with many provisions that are neither completely reasonable nor transparent. Therefore further reform is clearly needed. The Constitution has proposed important changes, the Commission is exploring new roads, and suggestions have also been tabled by a report prepared by a Group of Independent Experts commissioned by the President of the Commission. This Group has recommended 'a radical restructuring of the EU budget to support the growth agenda . . . in line with the Lisbon objectives' (Sapir et al., 2003).

Thus, if the Constitutional Treaty is ratified as proposed and progress continues along these lines, the budgetary provisions and procedure would be clarified and simplified, making a significant contribution to the functioning of the Union at a crucial moment in its history.

References

Barberán Ortí R (2002) *La Hacienda Pública de la Unión Europea*, in *Economía de la Unión Europea*, Jordán Galduf, J M (ed.), 4th edition, Civitas.

Buchholz-Will W, Dahlström G, Huffschmid J, Karrass A, Mathes M and Schratzenstaller M (2002) *Progressive Fiscal Policy in Europe*, in Euromemorandum, Chapter 1.

Caesar R (2002) Haushalts- und Steuerpolitik in der EU, *Jahrbuecher fuer Nationaloekonomie und Statistik*, Vol. 221, pp. 132–50.

European Commission (1998) *Financing the European Union*, Commission Report on the Operation of the Own Resources System, October.

European Commission (2000) *Agenda 2000: for a stronger and wider Union*, Bulletin EU, Supplement 5/97 COM (97).

European Commission (2001) *Adaptation of the ceiling of own resources and of the ceiling for appropriations for commitments following the entry into force of Decision 2000/ 597/EC, Euratom*, communication to the Council and the European Parliament, 28 December.

European Commission (2002a) *European Union Public Finance*, DG Budget.

European Commission (2002b) *For the European Union: Peace, Freedom, Solidarity. Communication of the Commission to the Institutional Architecture*, COM (2002) 728, 12 December.

European Commission (2003a) *General Budget of the European Union for the financial year 2003: The figures*, January.

European Commission (2003b) *Proposal to adapt the financial framework for enlargement*, COM (2003) 70, 11 February.

European Commission (2004) *Building our common Future. Policy changes and Budgetary means of the Enlarged Union 2007–2013*, communication to the Council and the European Council, COM (2004) 101 final, 10 February.

European Communities (2000) *The Community budget: the facts and the figures*, Office for Official Publications of the European Communities, Luxembourg.

European Council (2000) *Decision on the system of the European Communities' own resources*, 29 September.

European Parliament (2003) *EP resolution containing the European Parliament's recommendations to the Council on the introduction in the draft Accession Treaty of a financial framework*, 27 March.

Inter-institutional Agreement of 6 May 1999 between the European Parliament, the Council and the Commission on budgetary discipline and improvement of the budgetary procedure, OJC 172, 18.6.1999, p. 1.

Karlsson B (2002) *What price enlargement? Implications of an Expanded EU*, report to the Expert Group on Public Finance, Ministry of Finance, Stockholm, September.

Kok W (2003) *Enlarging the EU. Achievements and Challenges*, report to the European Commission, Robert Schuman Center for Advanced Studies, European University Institute, Florence, 26 March.

Sapir A, Aghion P, Bertola G, Hellwig M, Pisani-Ferry J, Rosati D, Vinals J and Wallace H (2003) *An agenda for a growing Europe. Making the EU Economic System Deliver*, report of the Independent High-Level Study Group established on the initiative of the President of the European Commission, July.

Schreyer M (2002) *The Reunification of Europe*, Public Service Review, Accession States, Winter, Public Service Communication Agency.

Schreyer M (2003) [Speech] *The New Financial Framework: Challenging EU Road for the Future*, Finnish Ministry of Finance, Helsinki, 27 February.

Further reading

European Commission (2002) *European Union Public Finance* DG Budget, European Union website: **europa.eu.int/comm/budget/infos/publications_en.htm**

Kabatusuila F (1999) *Budgetary Issues in the European Union*, Discussion–working paper from the European Trade Union Institute, DWP 99.01.01.(E), February.

Mayhew A (2003) *The Financial and Budgetary Impact of Enlargement and Accession*, Sussex European Institute, Working Paper No. 65, May.

End notes

1 The ECSC Treaty was concluded for a period of 50 years. Having entered into force on 23 July 1952 it was due to expire on 23 July 2002, and it was decided that it was wise to let it expire as scheduled.

2 Nonetheless, this might change if a recent Commission proposal is endorsed, in which it is suggested that the EDF be incorporated into the general budget, in an effort to improve transparency, accountability and efficiency (European Commission communication, 8 October 2003).

3 The distinction between compulsory and non-compulsory expenditure will be addressed below.

4 Up to one-half of a rate made by the arithmetic mean of: the trend of GNP of EU members; the average rise in the budget of members; and the trend in the cost of living.

5 Decision of 21 April 1970, renewed in 1988, 1994 and 2000.

6 Council Regulation (EC, Euratom) No. 1605/2002, 25 June 2002, on the Financial Regulation applicable to the general budget of the European Communities.

7 To promote solidarity is considered one of the main tasks of the European Community in Article 2 TEC, and of the EU (Article 1 Treaty on the European Union).

8 They are available on the web: for the 2003 budget, see: **europa.eu.int/eur-lex/budget/www/index-en.htm**

9 In this case there are particular provisions; in most cases expenditure would be charged to member states in accordance with the GNP scale, unless the Council unanimously

decides otherwise or, in the context of the CFSP, the member state has made a formal declaration.

10 To calculate this amount, firstly a uniform VAT base is determined, in accordance with EC rules. This base was capped at a maximum of 55 per cent GNP for all member states and at 50 per cent GNP for the least prosperous states (Greece, Spain, Ireland and Portugal), but this was gradually harmonised and now the maximum base is 50 per cent for all member states.

11 This 1.27 per cent equals 1.24 per cent under the new ESA 95 accounting system, according to the European Commission Communication of 28 December 2001.

12 This point has been made again by French Minister Mr Villepin in his contribution to the 'Reform of the Treaty's financial provisions' part of the European Convention. According to him, the European tax should substitute and not be added to current taxes.

13 Annex 2: 'A review of possible own resources for the European Union', European Commission, 1998.

14 Rapid Press Release 'Forging the link between citizens and the EU budget' IP/04/906, 14 July 2004.

15 Decision 88/377 of 24 June 1988, and Inter–institutional Agreement of 6 May 1999.

16 45.2 per cent for Agriculture and 34.5 per cent for Structural Policy.

17 According to the data provided by Eurostat, in 'Statistiques en bref, Comptes Nationaux', the ranking of EU Member States in terms of GDP per capita would be: 1) Luxembourg 2) Denmark 3) Ireland 4) Sweden 5) UK 6) The Netherlands 7) Finland 8) Austria 9) Germany 10) Belgium 11) France 12) Italy 13) Spain 14) Greece and 15) Portugal (2002 data).

18 Rapid Press Release 'Preventing excessive budgetary imbalances in the EU', IP/04/908, 14 July 2004.

19 The trialogue is composed of the Commissioner in charge of the Budget, the President of the Budget Committee of the EP and the President of the Council of the Budget.

20 Joint Declaration of 4 March 1975, and Joint Declaration of 30 June 1982.

21 Committee of Independent Experts, 'First Report on Allegations Regarding Fraud, Mismanagement and Nepotism in the European Commission', Brussels, 15 March 1999.

22 For example, Poland has an income level of 18 per cent of the EU15 average (Karlsson, 2002).

23 Such as the following: European Commission documents: *Communication on the establishment of a new financial perspective for the period 2000–06* COM(98)164, 18 March 1998: *Report on the implementation of the interinstitutional agreement of 29 October 1993 on budgetary discipline and improvement of the budgetary procedure, Proposals for renewal*, COM(98)165 18 March 1998 and: *Commission working document. Draft interinstitutional agreement on budgetary discipline and improvement of the budgetary procedure*, SEC(1998) 698, 29 April 1998.

24 These countries are Cyprus, the Czech Republic, Estonia, Hungary, Latvia, Lithuania, Malta, Poland, the Slovak Republic and Slovenia.

25 Copenhagen European Council, December 2002.

26 The path will be as follows: 25 per cent in 2004, 30 per cent in 2005, 35 per cent in 2006, 40 per cent in 2007 and then further annual 10 per cent increases until reaching 100 per cent in 2013.

27 The views expressed in this paper are those of the author and do not necessarily represent those of the Banco de España.

Part 2

THE INTERNAL POLICIES OF THE EUROPEAN UNION

Chapter 5

Competition policy in the European Union

John Kemp

Introduction

This chapter surveys the status and workings of EU competition policy and explores the implications arising from the creation of the Single European Market (SEM). Initially, an economic rationale is presented for intervention in private industry, whether this is seen primarily as a policy to promote competition or as a corrective action for monopoly abuse. The next section provides a brief discussion of the alternative policy approaches. This is followed by a section outlining current EU policy. The concluding section discusses the process of harmonisation with respect to EU and UK policies, along with an assessment of the effectiveness of current policy and, with the creation of the SEM, the important implications arising from the Treaty of Rome.

An economic rationale for intervention

Democratic nations, whether they have governments of the right or the left, usually have well articulated policies towards intervention in private industry. Such policies are designed to promote the efficient allocation of resources through the encouragement of competition, which is seen as the active progenitor of economic efficiency and welfare. They are, likewise, employed to limit the losses in efficiency that can arise from the presence of elements of monopoly. There is a clear underpinning economic rationale for competition policy and consequently the broad thrust of policy is rarely ideologically contentious. Thus, where disagreement does arise it is usually of degree rather than of substance and is more likely to concern the detailed application of policy as opposed to general principles. It is currently fashionable to talk of 'competition policy' where one formerly talked of 'monopoly' or 'anti-monopoly policy'. The fact that this is partly a semantic change reflects the existence of an underlying consensus.

The relative efficiency of competition and monopoly

The results of this section depend upon a number of underlying assumptions. If any one of these does not hold, then the results cannot be upheld. First, it is assumed that consumers are utility maximisers and that producers are profit maximisers. It is assumed that the prices paid and received represent the value of the marginal unit traded both to the buyer and to the seller. Further, it is assumed that units of consumers' and producers' surplus can be added and subtracted, that is, a unit of surplus represents the same quantity of benefit irrespective of whether it accrues to the buyer or the seller.

If the objective of policy is to maximise economic welfare this implies that total surplus (i.e. consumer and producer surplus) should be maximised. Thus, in comparing alternative economic structures, the most efficient is defined as the one that generates the greatest total surplus. This concentration on efficiency ignores altogether the important question of income distribution. As far as economic efficiency is concerned it is irrelevant whether surplus accrues to consumers or to producers. If a situation is deemed to be inequitable, then it is in principle possible to redistribute income according to some appropriate canon of equity. In other words, if we 'bake the biggest cake' it should be possible to provide greater shares for all. This is not to deny that questions of income distribution are important, but they do not concern us here.

A comparison of the relative efficiency of perfect competition and pure monopoly demonstrates the inherent inefficiency of monopoly. The heart of the case against monopoly is that it reduces output, increases price and reduces welfare compared with perfect competition. This is a very powerful result. It means that it can be stated categorically that the effect of monopolisation per se is to reduce economic welfare. This result is illustrated in Exhibit 5.1.

However, this result depends critically on the caveat that 'other things are equal'. In particular, subsequent monopolisation costs are unlikely to remain unchanged. Indeed, the argument is often advanced that mergers bring benefits through reducing costs of production because of the attainment of economies of scale. It is undeniable that large-scale production can be technically more efficient. Following an analysis detailed by Williamson (1968) it is possible to consider how the previous result is affected if, after monopolisation, production takes place with lower costs. This analysis suggests that, if economies of scale are significant, it is possible that monopolisation will result in net benefits in terms of the relative welfare gains to losses. The conditions under which such an outcome is possible are shown in Exhibit 5.2.

Empirical evidence on economies of scale across a large number of British industries suggests considerable diversity in their extent (e.g. Pratten, 1971; Silberston, 1972; HMSO, 1978). Thus, on the basis of empirical evidence about the nature of costs it is not possible to make a definitive statement of the effects of monopoly. It should, however, be noted that, while the analysis cautions against outright condemnation of monopoly and merger, the case against restrictive practices and collusive agreements is not weakened. This is because after agreements, unlike mergers, individual firms maintain their separate existence. It is, therefore, difficult to envisage how, under these circumstances, offsetting economies of scale could be attained without any rationalisation of productive units.

The analysis suggests that there is no theoretical justification for condemning monopoly and/or merger outright, since the ill-effects of output restriction could be more than offset by reductions in costs. Under such circumstances monopolisation would result in an increase in total surplus. Therefore, the policy implication that arises from theory is that in seeking to determine the effects of monopolisation it is

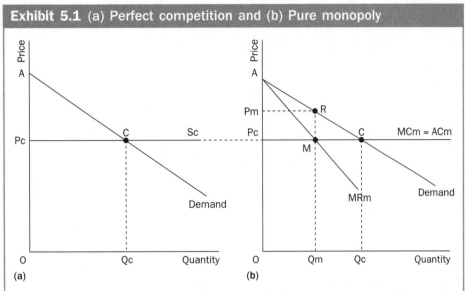

Exhibit 5.1 (a) Perfect competition and (b) Pure monopoly

Purely for reasons of diagrammatic simplicity we assume that the perfectly competitive industry supply curve (Sc) is infinitely elastic and can be drawn as a horizontal straight line as in **(a)**. This simplification does not in any way affect the qualitative nature of the results. Price (Pc) and output (Qc) are determined by the intersection of the supply and demand curves at C. There is no producer surplus and total surplus is composed entirely of consumer surplus which is given by the area ACPc.

Suppose the industry is now monopolised with (unrealistically) no change in costs, i.e. all productive units are merged into a single firm without any change in their numbers or their costs of production and, further, this newly created firm acts solely as a costless decision-making and coordinating mechanism for the activities of what were formerly the independent units. It follows that the supply curve (Sc) of **(a)** becomes identical to the marginal cost curve (MCm) of the monopoly firm. As such, it can be read horizontally across to **(b)**. A consequence of the assumption of constant costs is that the monopolist's marginal costs are equal to average costs (ACm) as shown. There is no reason for consumers' tastes to have changed, and so the demand curve is unaffected. In **(b)** we can observe the changes due to monopolisation. Faced with the downward sloping market demand curve, the monopoly producer will maximise profits by producing where marginal cost is equal to marginal revenue at M, output will be cut back to Qm and price will be raised to Pm. Consumer surplus is now reduced to area ARPm. Surplus of PmRMPc has been transferred from consumers to producers and total surplus has fallen to ARMPc. There is, therefore, a net loss of surplus of RCM. Thus, economic welfare has unambiguously been reduced. With the important proviso 'other things being equal', monopoly inevitably distorts resource allocation and is inefficient *vis-à-vis* perfect competition.

necessary to weigh carefully the costs against the benefits, to examine the trade-off of one against the other. In these circumstances it is of crucial importance to have some means of measuring welfare changes. Clearly, this might not be a task that can be undertaken with any great degree of precision.

Some qualifications to the theoretical results

Economic theory suggests that monopoly leads to an inefficient allocation of resources in the sense that the level of output is restricted. There are a number of qualifications to this prediction, apart from the possibility of economies of scale. These are particularly important when considering the likely effects in the real world.

Exhibit 5.2 Pure economies of scale

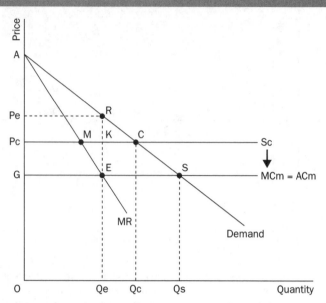

In this Exhibit price and output under perfect competition are, as before, at Pc and Qc. Suppose that, under monopoly, costs are lower, which is shown as supply curve of competition (Sc) shifts downwards to form the monopolist's marginal cost curve (MCm). The monopoly equilibrium now occurs where the MR curve intersects this lower MC curve at E (as opposed to M). Thus monopoly price and output become Pe and Qe. Output has fallen and price risen, but not by as much as in the case depicted in Exhibit 5.1(b).

Total surplus is now equal to AREG, of which ARPe is consumer surplus and PeREG is producer surplus. Compared with the competitive surplus of ACPc this change has been brought about by a loss of RCK, due to output restriction (i.e. monopolisation) and a creation of additional producer surplus of PcKEG, due to the ability of the enlarged monopolised firm to achieve lower costs. Area PeRKPc is simply a transfer from consumers to producers and can therefore be ignored. Thus, whether or not total surplus under monopoly (AREG) is greater or lesser than (ACPc) under perfect competition depends on whether the gain (PcKEG) is greater than the loss (RCK). There is no *a priori* justification for stating which will be the dominant effect. The net effect will vary according to the cost conditions within the particular industry under consideration, and within the real world we might expect considerable variation from one industry to another.

First, the analysis is entirely static, ignoring changes that may take place over time. Thus, any demonstrated effects on surpluses may be exacerbated or ameliorated as the industry progresses, and welfare losses which occur over time may cancel out immediate gains or vice versa. Further, this static analysis is cast in terms of certainty. Real firms have to make decisions within a climate of uncertainty, and market outcomes will differ according to their attitudes to risk.

Secondly, the competition of economic theory is cast solely in terms of price competition and narrowly defined profit maximisation. The foregoing analysis neglects the effects of firms' other competitive variables such as product quality, product range and product differentiation. Furthermore, if firms pursue objectives other than profit maximisation then the picture becomes even less clear-cut (Sawyer, 1979). For example, the theory of sales revenue maximisation (Baumol, 1959) assumes that managers pursue the objective of maximising revenue rather than profits. As a consequence, higher levels of output are predicted than under profit maximisation. The implication of this is that any policy proposal for a particular industry can be made only after an investigation of not only the structure of the industry, but also the objectives and conduct of the firms within it.

Thirdly, in economic theory it is presumed that any level of output is always produced at the lowest technically feasible cost. For the economist, inefficiency arises because the wrong level of output is produced. However, in the real world there is an additional concept of efficiency, which takes cognisance of the fact that real firms are never as technically efficient as the theorists' firm. This type of inefficiency arises because workers and management are often ill-equipped or lacking in motivation and so do not perform to the best of their abilities. Inefficiency of this sort, which involves a given level of output being produced at a cost higher than the theoretical minimum, is termed 'X-inefficiency'. It is what the average person understands by 'inefficiency'. Clearly, such inefficiency is incompatible with perfect competition where the competitive threat would be sufficient to remove any less efficient firm. However, in monopoly markets X-inefficiency could arise because of the absence of competitive discipline. This would seem to strengthen the case against monopoly, for now there is reason to believe that a movement towards monopoly could lead to higher costs through the creation of X-inefficiency. This would offset, to some extent, any cost reductions due to economies of scale. The net effect on costs is therefore unclear, for the picture is now becoming highly complex. It is, however, evident that it would be necessary to weigh carefully all the costs and benefits before any categoric policy recommendation could be made (Rowley, 1973).

Fourthly, the theoretical proscription of monopoly has been arrived at by comparing the two theoretical extremes of perfect competition and pure monopoly. In the real world there is never a movement from one to the other, and it is correspondingly less clear what the implications for both allocative and X-efficiency are. For example, if a merger takes place between two firms in an industry of ten firms, so moving the industry apparently closer to monopoly, it is not at all apparent, *a priori* (even in the absence of any economies of scale), what the effects on either type of efficiency will be. Again, it would seem that this matter could only be resolved after a detailed investigation of the particular industry in question.

Fifthly, even if there are undisputed economies of scale so that there is a net increase in surplus, it can still be argued that there is a social opportunity loss. Surplus could be increased further if the monopoly firm were required to produce where its marginal cost was equal to price. Thus in Exhibit 5.2 an administered move from equilibrium at E to S would lead to an output of QS and price of G, with a further increase in total surplus to ASG.

Sixthly, and most importantly, the theoretical analysis normally used is entirely partial. That is, in considering the effects on one industry in isolation repercussions throughout industry as a whole have been ignored. Thus, an individual merger might be seen to be totally innocuous, but, if it is just one more merger among a spate, then the overall trend towards the monopolisation of industry in general may be worrying. This is rather like the problem of litter louts: one dropped piece of paper is harmless in itself, but the problem involves the total volume of litter!

Seventhly, Baumol *et al.* (1982) have argued that resources will be allocated efficiently (in the sense that prices will be equal to marginal costs) in industries which are perfectly contestable, and that this result holds irrespective of the number of firms in the industry (Button, 1985). A perfectly contestable industry is one that, in addition to free entry, is characterised by completely free exit. Thus, in the absence of any costs of leaving the industry, even modest profits will always be an incentive to enter. Subsequently firms can leave quickly without cost, once those profits have been competed away. The only protection against this potential threat of competition is afforded by firms charging prices equal to marginal costs and earning only normal profit. The implication is that large numbers of firms are not necessary to achieve economic efficiency and so it is equally possible for oligopolies to attain an efficient allocation of resources. Thus, in this view, attention should be focused on the freeing of conditions of exit, rather than solely on encouraging actual competition from increasing numbers of firms.

Finally, the Austrian school of economics puts a different interpretation on the existence of profit. Competition is seen as a process, with profit representing both the spur and the reward of enterprise. Thus profit is a symbol of success, encouraging innovation and progressiveness, rather than being symptomatic of resource mis-allocation. Accordingly, this requires recognition of the dynamics of industrial change, which are often obscured by reference solely to comparative theoretical equilibria as in the neoclassical tradition. Consequently, subscribers to the Austrian tradition would be somewhat less inclined to an actively pro-interventionist stance.

Ideally, all the above qualifications would need to be taken into account in any attempt to prescribe policy. The predictions of economic theory are not sufficiently clear-cut to permit us to proscribe monopoly outright. Theory does point to a clear suspicion that a lack of competition can, most certainly, lead to inefficiencies, but it also identifies possible benefits from the attainment of lower-cost production. An unambiguous policy recommendation would require evaluation of all these costs and benefits. Yet, given the qualifications noted above, this is clearly a daunting task. There have been attempts to establish empirically whether any general conclusions can be drawn on the extent of welfare losses throughout the economy due to the presence of monopoly. If these could be found to be overwhelmingly large or small then the results could be of use in the framing of policy. However, no general consensus has emerged and the conclusions are no less disparate than those of theory (see Clarke, 1985; Hay and Morris, 1991).

Empirical evidence of monopoly welfare losses

A number of studies have reported estimates of the magnitude of the losses due to the presence of monopoly in the economy as a whole. An early attempt was undertaken by Harberger (1954), who calculated that, for US manufacturing industry, the resultant welfare losses were only of the order of 0.1 per cent of GNP. This is clearly very small and, if it were generally representative, it would call into question the necessity for constructing any elaborate and costly policy to oversee monopoly since the benefits gained would be unlikely to justify the costs of implementation. The way in which these estimates were obtained can be seen by reference to Exhibit 5.3.

Exhibit 5.3 Welfare loss due to monopoly

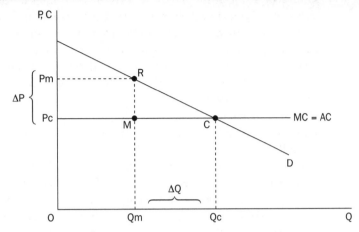

In this Exhibit the welfare loss is equivalent to the triangular area RCM. Thus, the size of this is given by:

$$D = 1/2\Delta P\Delta Q \tag{5.1}$$

where ΔP is the difference between Pc and Pm, and ΔQ is the difference between Qc and Qm. The distortion of the monopoly price from the competitive price or the price cost margin (M) is defined as:

$$M = (Pm - Mc)/Pm \tag{5.2}$$

but, since under perfect competition P = MC, Equation [5.2] can be written as:

$$M = (Pm - Pc)/Pm = \Delta P/Pm \tag{5.2*}$$

The elasticity of demand at R is defined as:

$$E = (\Delta Q/Qm)/(\Delta P/Pm) \tag{5.3}$$

which on rearrangement gives:

$$\Delta Q = (E/Pm)\Delta PQm \tag{5.3*}$$

On substitution of Equation [5.3*] into Equation [5.1] and multiplication of the right-hand side by Pm/Pm (i.e. by unity)

$$D = 1/2(\Delta P/Pm)^2PmQmE \tag{5.4}$$

or

$$D = 1/2M^2SE \tag{5.4*}$$

which is negative (a loss), since with a downward sloping demand curve the elasticity of demand (E) is negative. Thus, the welfare losses are now computable in terms of (i) the level of sales revenue, S (i.e. PmQm); (ii) the rate of return M (i.e. $\Delta P/Pm$), which is the monopoly mark-up expressed as a ratio of the monopoly price; (iii) the elasticity of demand E. In principle, it is possible to make estimates of these magnitudes. The level of sales revenue is readily obtainable. Given constant average costs (for which there is considerable supportive evidence in manufacturing), it follows that marginal and average costs are equal. Hence, ΔP is the difference between price and average costs, since under perfect competition Pc = MC. Thus, industry rates of return can be estimated. The direct measurement of the elasticity of demand is not easy, and so an appropriate assumption has to be made concerning its magnitude.

Harberger made two assumptions in order to calculate the welfare losses for a sample of 2,046 firms. First, he took the average rate of return in manufacturing industry as typical of the rate of return that would have been earned in competitive industry, and then took deviations from this as indicative of the size of the price-cost margin. Secondly, he assumed that the elasticity of demand was unity. Both these assumptions have been challenged on the grounds that they create downwardly biased estimates and thereby the true losses would be understated. However, subsequent studies by Schwartzman (1960) and Worcester (1973) also showed low estimates of welfare losses and, despite a study by Kamerschen (1966) showing somewhat higher losses, the general consensus view was that monopoly losses were typically not very high for the US economy.

Later, as a result of further studies of both the US and the UK economies, this consensus was challenged. Posner (1975) has suggested that, in situations that are not perfectly competitive, firms engage in promotional activities and in attempts to create barriers to entry. To the extent that these activities raise firms' costs, it can be argued that they are wasteful and thus should be included as further elements of losses due to monopoly. If this is done then, clearly, much higher estimates of losses are obtained than those of Harberger. A difficulty is now apparent in that there are no clear criterion available for deciding everything that should or should not be included as elements of welfare loss. Inevitably, decisions on what to include and what to leave out are based on the value judgements of the researcher, and on practical considerations involving the limitations of available data. Consequently, it should not be surprising to find disparate estimates. Cowling and Mueller (1978) have produced estimates based on UK as well as US data which suggest that welfare losses amount to as much as one-half of monopoly profits – around 10 per cent of manufacturing output for the UK and 4 per cent for the USA.

Cowling and Mueller's methodology has been criticised by Littlechild (1981), and their estimates may, arguably, be biased upwards. However, their results along with Posner's have helped to dispel the previously held consensus view that monopoly losses were generally relatively small. This lack of any general conclusion from both theory and empiricism gives support to the piecemeal or cost–benefit approach to monopoly policy, whereby individual industries are evaluated on their merits. However, even this has not been a view acceptable to all, as is discussed in the following section.

Alternative policy approaches

In the light of this ambiguity in the theoretical predictions, allied with a lack of any clear empirical consensus on the extent of these losses and benefits, the question arises as to what form a pro-competition or anti-monopoly policy should take. The clear implication would appear to be that an individual cost–benefit approach is appropriate, with each monopoly situation being judged on its own merits only after a careful weighing of the gains and losses. Such an approach comes closest to the spirit of the pragmatic investigatory stance currently taken within the EU and also in the UK, where the Competition Commission pronounces on individual cases. However, this *ad hoc* procedure has not been without its critics, largely because of doubts about whether it is possible to perform the exercise with sufficient precision to arrive at a clear-cut evaluation (see Crew and Rowley, 1970, 1971; Howe, 1971, 1972).

During the 1970s there was a vigorous debate surrounding the alternative approaches to UK policy. The issues raised are no less relevant to the formation of an appropriate EU policy, and so they are reviewed here. The main discussion and disagreements have centred around the appropriate policy for dealing with mergers. In the case of restrictive practices there is less contention. They are generally seen as anti-competitive and necessitating legislation to proscribe them, since they almost invariably create the detrimental effects of monopoly without engendering the benefits. In the case of single or dominant firm monopolies, while it is accepted that these may behave detrimentally to the public interest at large, few democratic governments have had, or are likely to have, the political will to intervene directly in their operation, particularly where their market positions have been legitimately attained and their activities are not overtly illegal. Usually the most that governments have been prepared to do has been to publicise their activities and/or to seek voluntary undertakings. Whether or not governments should take greater powers to break up already existing monopolies is an issue as much political as economic, for it involves issues of the freedom of the individual and the state. However, where attempts have been made to build up a monopoly by merger there has been a heightened awareness of the inherent dangers, and governments have been more willing to take direct action to prohibit them.

Those who strongly doubt whether the cost–benefit exercise can be adequately performed are more inclined to a rules-based or structural approach. The major proponents of a rules-based approach in the UK have been Crew and Rowley (1970, 1971). They argue that it is simply not possible to quantify all the costs and benefits involved, so any judgement must inevitably be inadequately based. In support of this they indicate that there have been worries about the ability of the former Monopolies Commission to maintain consistency across its investigations. Thus, they claim that a climate of uncertainty is created that militates against the decision-taking ability of firms. On the other hand, they are not prepared to countenance the complete free rein of market forces since the dangers of monopoly are well known. Consequently, they propose a policy more akin to that of the USA based on rules that would automatically forbid mergers above a given size. This would remove the uncertainty and leave firms free to operate unconstrained within the legally created framework. They recognise that such arbitrary rules would result in some beneficial mergers being stopped, but argue that this sacrifice would be offset by the improvements in X-efficiency. In support of this approach they claim (contentiously) that economies of scale are, in general, only moderate and also (on the basis of scant evidence) that the association between monopoly and X-efficiency is strong. Thus they contend that losses resulting from the automatic prohibition of mergers above a certain size are unlikely to be substantial and are more than likely to be offset by the benefits arising from the creation of a climate of greater certainty and competition.

A *laissez-faire* approach of non-intervention has had few adherents in the past, since most economists have accepted that theory and evidence suggest that matters cannot be left entirely to the market. However, Beacham and Jones (1971) came close to taking this line on the grounds that it is not possible to perform the cost–benefit exercise well enough to obtain a soundly based conclusion. On the other hand, they could see little merit in a policy based on a rules approach, since rules are inevitably arbitrary and lacking in any underlying economic logic. As a result they have considerable doubts about the validity of the case for the control of mergers. More recently George (1989) has re-examined this approach, pointed out its drawbacks and concluded that the balance of theory and evidence does suggest that there is a need for a mergers policy. In contrast, economists of the Austrian tradition (e.g. Littlechild 1981, 1989) have come closer to the *laissez-faire* view, partly as a consequence of their different interpretation of profit. It is possible that they had some influence on the UK government during the 1980s, which was markedly less disposed to intervene directly in industry than its predecessors. However, most economists (and possibly politicians) accept that some form of control is required and that this has to be exercised within one of the alternative frameworks.

It is the lack of clear and unambiguous predictions from both theory and evidence that is the source of the dispute over the nature of the approach to monopoly policy. However, on balance a majority of UK economists have appeared to favour the discretionary cost–benefit approach, or have thought the rules approach too dogmatic (see Sutherland, 1970; Howe, 1972; Utton, 1975; Fleming and Swann, 1989; George, 1989), and have tended to argue for a continuation of the present investigatory policy with some considerable strengthening of procedures. To some extent this has been attained in the UK through the Competition and Enterprise Acts (1998 and 2002). These Acts have resulted in a reorientation of UK policy so that it is now much closer in spirit and in practice to that of the EU. In its overall approach to competition, EU policy corresponds more closely to that of discretionary intervention than it is to any of the other alternatives discussed above. This recent convergence between UK and EU policies is to be welcomed on the grounds that it is clearly desirable that national and EU policies should be broadly similar, if only because this is less confusing to the business community.

European Union competition policy

The EU has sought to develop a policy designed to secure the benefits that arise from a competitive market, since as national barriers to inter-state competition are removed there is a danger that these can be replaced by privately erected barriers. The competition policy of the EU stems from the Treaty of Rome and is mainly embodied in Articles 81 and 82. (NB Prior to the Treaty of Amsterdam 1999 the Articles were numbered 85 and 86 respectively. To avoid confusion we use the new numbering throughout this chapter, even when dealing with matters prior to 1999.) These Articles were designed to ensure free competition within the EU, with the Commission being charged with the responsibility for applying the legislation. In the process of doing this the Commission has to work closely with national governments, and it is therefore clearly desirable that domestic and EU law should be mutually consistent. Individual states still retain the right to develop their own distinct policies on competition where trade is contained within their national boundaries. Therefore, even after the completion of the SEM the UK, for example, maintains its own competition policy towards internal trade, though as noted above procedures are now very similar to those of the EU. In respect of trade between member states, however, national legislation becomes subordinate to EU legislation.

Article 81 – Restrictive or concerted practices

Article 81 is concerned with the operation of restrictive practices, where they affect trade between member states. Thus, Article 81(1) prohibits agreements '... which may affect trade between Member States and which have as their object or effect the prevention, restriction or distortion of competition within the common market ...', and continues by listing specific types of agreement that are prohibited. The types of agreements that the legislation is designed to catch are precisely the same as those at which UK legislation is aimed, namely price fixing, market sharing, restrictions on supply, etc. Article 81(3) grants exemptions in the case of beneficial agreements '... which contribute to improving the production or distribution of goods or to promoting technical or economic progress, while allowing consumers a fair share of the resulting benefit ...', provided that such agreements do not impose any indispensable restrictions or provide the possibility of eliminating competition.

These exemptions may be granted either as block exemptions for certain categories of agreement (e.g. cooperative research and development, exclusive distribution, exclusive purchasing) or on a case-by-case basis. In Article 81, the emphasis is on the *effects* of a restriction, rather than the *form* of it. Thus, within EU law it is the object or effect of an agreement that determines whether or not it is subject to the law. For example, in the *Dyestuffs* case, the manufacturers did not admit to having formed an agreement but it was still possible to find them guilty of operating a concerted practice. On a number of occasions dyestuff producers had been observed to make simultaneous and similar price revisions. The producers did not admit that they were engaged in a concerted practice, but argued that the parallel price changes were simply a natural consequence of oligopolistic competition. Irrespective of this, their behaviour in making parallel price changes was found to have the *effect* of limiting competition and consequently enabled the EU to find them guilty of operating a concerted practice for which they were substantially fined (Jacquemin and de Jong, 1977; Swann, 1983, 1988). Such an effects-based approach is seen as being more effective than a form-based one, as was embodied in UK restrictive practices legislation prior to the 1998 Competition Act. This is because it is envisaged that an effects-based policy will capture for investigation a greater number of anti-competitive agreements and fewer of those that are innocuous.

Agreements that fall within the ambit of Article 81 are investigated by the Commission on the receipt of a complaint and/or request for exemption. The appropriate body within a member state (e.g. DTI, OFT and/or Competition Commission within the UK) is then consulted and assists in an advisory capacity, following which the Commission delivers judgement. The Commission has considerable powers of enforcement and can fine firms up to 10 per cent of their turnover for operating an anti-competitive practice. Firms then have the right of appeal to the European Court of First Instance, and ultimately to the European Court of Justice (ECJ). The Commission's record on attacking cartels and concerted practices is impressive, as it has vigorously pursued and successfully secured the termination of a substantial number and variety of concerted practices. In particular, it has taken a strong line against price fixing (e.g. dyestuffs, glass containers) and market sharing or quantity agreements (e.g. cement) to the extent that such practices are now unlikely ever to be granted exemptions. However, the existence of legislation in itself is not sufficient to preclude firms from engaging in concerted practices. The Commission has to be vigilant and has uncovered cases involving the highest levels of management (e.g. Belgian breweries).

In the *Glass Containers* case of 1974, producers within five European countries were found to subscribe to an agreement to notify each other immediately of price changes, and also to align export prices with the domestic prices of the price leader within the importing country. The anti-competitive features of this practice are obvious and the Commission accordingly declared the system illegal (Swann, 1988).

The practice of exclusive dealing has also been the subject of investigation. If manufacturers appoint exclusive dealerships, then this could facilitate the division of the European market into sub-markets with restricted competition between and within them. In 1964 the *Grundig Consten* case highlighted this problem. The German manufacturer gave exclusive distribution rights to Consten for the sales of Grundig products within France, and forbade its non-French distributors from exporting into France. The effect of this policy was that prices in France were 20 to 50 per cent above those in West Germany. The Commission accordingly found this an infringement of Article 81.

In the 2001 *Belgian Breweries* case, surprise investigations at Interbrew's premises led to the Commission uncovering the operation of a cartel by Belgian brewers. This involved agreements on market sharing, price fixing and information exchange. A striking feature was that the Chief Executive Officers and other top management of the companies regularly met to initiate and monitor these arrangements. As a consequence, Interbrew and four other Belgian brewers were fined a total €91 m.

Article 82 – Abuse of dominant market power

Article 82 is concerned with the behaviour of dominant firm or near-monopoly situations and bans the abuse of a dominant position where it affects trade between member states through the imposition of 'unfair' trading conditions. A non-exclusive list of examples of such abuses is included in Article 82:

- Directly or indirectly imposing unfair purchase or selling prices or other unfair trading conditions;
- Limiting production, markets or technical development to the prejudice of consumers;
- Applying dissimilar conditions to equivalent transactions with other trading parties, thereby placing them at a competitive disadvantage;

- Making the conclusion of contracts subject to acceptance by the other parties of supplementary obligations that, by their nature or according to commercial usage, have no connection with the subject of such contracts.

For Article 82 to be invoked there has to be an effect on trade, as it is not dominance itself that is contrary to Article 82, but the abuse of that dominance. Within the Article there is no definition of what comprises dominance in terms either of market share or of other criteria. To some extent, this lack of guidance enables flexibility on the part of the authorities, who are not constrained by a requirement to satisfy some precisely defined criterion of dominance as a precondition for investigation. Consequently, the conditions of dominance can vary from case to case. If an abuse is found to exist then, almost by definition, there must be some element of dominance, otherwise there would be no basis for that abuse. Indeed, it has been argued (Fairburn *et al.*, 1986) that the authorities, having found an abuse, have then adopted the device of contriving to define the market in such a way that the discovered behaviour of the firm becomes an abuse of a dominant position. Thus, dominance can be seen to arise where a firm has the power to behave independently of its competitors and customers, and this may result from a combination of a number of factors, none of which separately would necessarily imply dominance. This was the situation in the *United Brands* case (see Box 5.1).

The procedure for investigation and possible sanctions follows the same pattern as outlined earlier for matters dealt with under Article 81. Under Article 82, the Commission has dealt successfully with a number of abuses such as the granting of loyalty rebates (e.g. Hoffman-la Roche), refusals to supply (e.g. Commercial Solvents), price discrimination (United Brands) and the tying of dealers to suppliers (Michelin) among others. Some of these cases are outlined below.

In the case of *Hoffman-la Roche* the Commission found that the practice of offering major buyers loyalty rebates in return for taking all their requirements from Hoffman-la Roche was an abuse of a dominant position, and thus incompatible with Article 82. The practice had the effect of restricting the buyers' freedom to take up alternative supplies and also acted as an entry barrier by making it difficult for new products to secure outlets.

The Commission held that refusal to supply, in order to eliminate competition, was contrary to Article 82 in the decision on *Commercial Solvents*. ZOJA, a major

Box 5.1 The *United Brands* Case

The company was found to have abused its dominant position in the market for bananas within the Community in four ways: (i) distributors and ripeners were prohibited from reselling green bananas; (ii) it refused supplies to distributors or ripeners who had participated in advertising campaigns for rival brands; (iii) different prices were charged according to the buyer's country, although there was no ostensible reason for this; (iv) unfair prices were charged in Germany, Denmark and the Benelux countries. The Commission fined the company and ordered it to cease the practices. The first three of these are clearly anti-competitive. However, it is not as easy to be objective about what are or are not 'unfair' prices, and on appeal to the European Court of Justice this charge was overturned for lack of proof.

manufacturer of drugs for treating tuberculosis, had been the subject of a failed takeover bid. In response to this, the United States Solvents Corporation and its Italian subsidiary, Istituto Chimoterapico Italiano, decided to refuse ZOJA supplies of essential intermediate products for which they held a world monopoly. Additional steps were then taken to ensure that ZOJA could not obtain supplies anywhere else on the world market. In the face of this attempt to eliminate it from the market, ZOJA complained. The Commission imposed fines and ordered the companies to resume supplies.

The Commission found that between 1990 and 1998 *Michelin* had abused its domination in the French markets for replacement and retread tyres for heavy vehicles. Michelin had introduced a complex system of bonuses, rebates and agreements. This had the effect of tying dealers to Michelin and as a consequence Michelin's competitors were effectively barred from entering these markets. A heavy fine of €19.76 m was imposed to reflect the seriousness and duration of the infringement along with the fact that Michelin had previously committed a similar infringement.

The levels of cases falling under Articles 81 and 82 are depicted in Figures 5.1(a) and 5.1(b) for the period 1992–2002. It can be seen that, despite a continuous rise in the proportion of cases arising as a result of complaints or opened on the Commission's initiative (Figure 5.1(a)), the vast majority of cases are able to be settled informally and without necessitating a formal prohibition or fine (Figure 5.1(b)).

Despite this, where serious abuse has been uncovered, the Commission has not shrunk from imposing substantial penalties as, for example, evidenced in the case of *Michelin* above and of *Irish Sugar* (see Box 5.2).

Box 5.2 The *Irish Sugar* Case

In May 1997, under Article 82 of the EC Treaty, the Commission found that Irish Sugar had infringed and abused its dominant position. It therefore imposed a fine of ECU 8.8 m on the company. Irish Sugar plc (a subsidiary of the Greencore Group) was the sole processor of sugar in Ireland with 95 per cent of the market, and had abused its dominant position since 1985 by seeking to restrict competition from imports and from small Irish sugar packers. It had done this by offering selectively low prices to the customers of an importer of French sugar and also by offering selective rebates to customers who were geographically close to suppliers based in Northern Ireland. Rebates were also granted on purchases of bulk sugar by industrial customers who exported part of their final output to other member states. These rebates varied between customers without any systematic relationship to sales volumes or currency changes, and were seen as discriminating against customers who supplied only the Irish market. Irish Sugar had also sought to restrict competition from small sugar packers within Ireland by discriminating against them in the prices that it charged for bulk sugar, thereby placing them at a competitive disadvantage. Further, Irish Sugar had offered rebates to certain wholesalers and food retailers, making it difficult for smaller competitors to gain entry to the market. Through these diverse arrangements Irish Sugar had been able to maintain a significantly higher price level for packaged retail sugar in Ireland and for bulk sugar for 'domestic' Irish consumption compared with that in the other member states. This was to the detriment of both industrial and final consumers in Ireland. In setting the level of the fine the Commission took into account the fact that the infringements represented a serious breach of Community law, that they had been recognised as abuses of a dominant position by the decision of the ECJ, and that they had taken place over a long period of time.

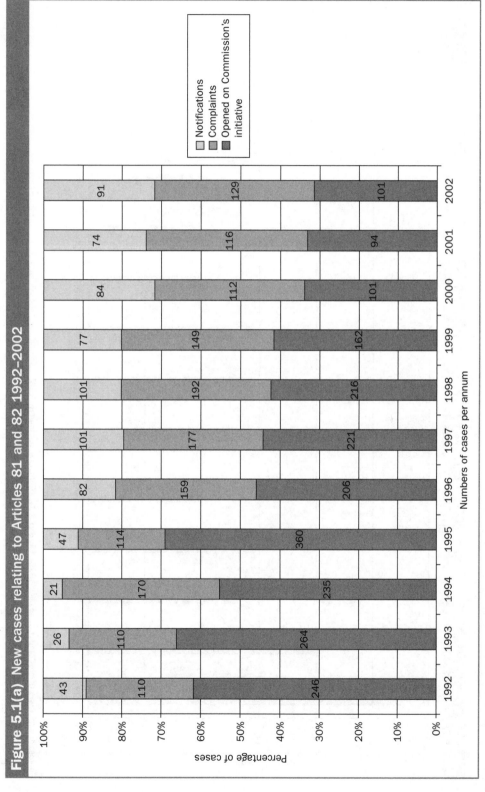

Figure 5.1(a) New cases relating to Articles 81 and 82 1992–2002

Source: Annual Reports on Competition Policy 1996, 1998 & 2002, European Community DGIV

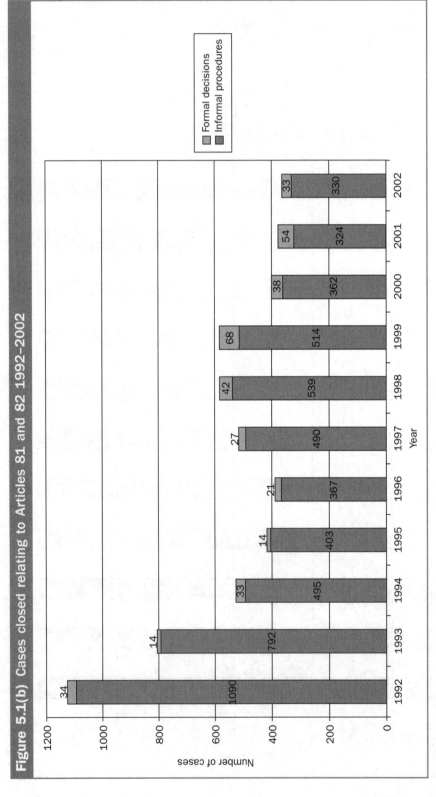

Figure 5.1(b) Cases closed relating to Articles 81 and 82 1992–2002

Source: Annual Reports on Competition Policy 1996, 1998 & 2002, European Community DGIV

It is important to emphasise again that it is not dominance in itself which is contrary to Article 82, but the abuse of that dominance. This, combined with the greater flexibility in defining dominance, leads to a European approach based more on the *effects* of, rather than on the formal *structure* of monopoly, as distinct from the situation in the UK prior to the 1998 Competition Act when structural criteria had to be satisfied before investigation could proceed.

Mergers

Until 1990 there was no specific European legislation to deal with mergers. The only avenue for EU control was through the application of Article 81 and/or Article 82, which was only open to those cases involving the operation of restrictive practices and/or the abuse of a dominant position. Thus, if a merger was to lead to the creation of a dominant position and a consequent restriction of competition, this could arguably be classed as an abuse under Article 82. This procedural approach was successfully established by the Commission in the *Continental Can* case, where the merger further enhanced existing dominance, following the take-over of Dutch and German metal container firms by a Belgian subsidiary of Continental Can. This challenge was subsequently overturned by the ECJ in 1973, because the Commission had not demonstrated that competition had been sufficiently restricted.

However, the important general principle that Article 82 could be applied to mergers that restricted competition was accepted, although this power was weakened by the fact that the Article could only be applied to mergers *ex post*, that is, to mergers already completed. Later, in the *Philip Morris* case of 1987 it was demonstrated that Article 81 had a relevance for merger control and could be applied where a firm acquired an influential shareholding in a competitor. However, given the growth of international competition and the emergence of the multinational enterprise, control of mergers through Articles 81 and 82 came to be widely recognised as too weak, particularly as leading up to 1992 the numbers of all types of mergers including cross-border mergers were increasing, although cross-border mergers did not appear to represent a rising proportion of the total (Geroski and Vlassopoulos, 1993). Thus, 'at best the existing rules were limited and technically inadequate for a proper merger control policy' (Brittan, 1992).

After a long period of drafting and redrafting, a European Merger Control Regulation (Council Regulation 4064/89) finally came into force on 21 September 1990. This now enables the Commission to investigate and control those 'concentrations' (i.e. mergers and takeovers) that have an 'EU dimension', while those mergers not having an EU dimension remain subject to domestic policies. Details of the Merger Regulation are given in Box 5.3. A critical evaluation of the Merger Control Regulation is given in Bishop (1993). A defence of the Regulation has been provided by a leading Commissioner (Brittan, 1992).

Table 5.1 displays detailed statistics on the operation of the Merger Control Regulation for the period from its inception. By the end of 2002 the Commission had examined some 2120 merger proposals. Of these, a majority of 2013 were found to raise 'no serious doubts' and were cleared at phase I. Of these, 54 fell

Box 5.3 The Merger Control Regulation

Mergers with an EU dimension are defined as those where the parties have an aggregate turnover in excess of EUR 5 bn, and where at least two of those parties have an EU turnover greater than EUR 250 m. If, however, each of the enterprises achieves more than two-thirds of its turnover within the same single member state, then the merger does not come under the Regulation. Special criteria apply for mergers between financial institutions. Mergers that are found to possess an EU dimension must be notified to the European Commission, which then carries out an investigation to determine whether they are 'compatible with the common market'. In phase I the Commission will decide, within a period of one month, whether there are any 'serious doubts' as to the merger creating or strengthening a dominant position to the likely detriment of effective competition. In the absence of such doubts the merger is permitted to proceed. If such doubts exist, then a phase II investigation is carried out over a maximum of four months to determine whether the merger should be prohibited or not.

outside the Regulation, 1816 were found compatible with the common market, 127 were found compatible with undertakings and 22 were referred to member states for their consideration. However, in 107 notifications 'serious doubts' were raised and these were referred for detailed investigation in phase II. After investigation, 22 were allowed to proceed without conditions and 62 were allowed to proceed with conditions imposed. In only 18 cases was the merger prohibited and in a further 4 cases effective competition was required to be restored.

Figure 5.2(a) portrays the growth in merger decisions, and Figure 5.2(b) shows the breakdown by type of operation. However, only a very small proportion of mergers referred to the Commission was found incompatible with the common market and resulted in prohibition and/or the requirement to restore effective competition (see Neven *et al.*, 1993 for an early discussion).

The proposed acquisition of *Alfa-Laval* by *Tetrapak* is an example of a notification where initial 'serious doubts' were expressed, but which was then approved following the subsequent detailed investigation. Alfa-Laval was a major manufacturer of milk and juice processing machines, whereas Tetrapak had a dominant position in liquid packaging machinery. First indications were that the merger could create or enhance a dominant position. However, in the subsequent enquiry the markets for packaging and processing machines were found to be distinct, and so there would be no extension of dominance. Accordingly, the takeover was allowed to proceed unconditionally.

In the case of *Aerospatiale/MBB*, the proposed merger was seen to lead to a high market share in civilian helicopters. However, because of competition on the international market from manufacturers in the USA, such as Sikorsky and Bell, the Commission did not feel that the merged firm would attain a dominant position. No serious doubt was raised, and no further investigation was required.

However, this was not so in the disallowed merger of *Aerospatiale/Alenia/DeHaviland*. ATR was the leading manufacturer of turbo-prop aircraft on the world market, and was jointly owned by Aerospatiale and Alenia. DeHaviland was

Table 5.1 Number and type of final decisions, European Merger Control, 1990–2002

Article, kind of decision	1990	1991	1992	1993	1994	1995	1996	1997	1998	1999	2000	2001	2002	Total
Phase 1														
6.1 (a) Out of scope of the Control	2	5	9	4	5	9	6	4	6	1	1	1	1	**54**
6.1 (b) Compatible with common market	5	47	43	49	78	90	109	118	207	236	293	299	242	**1816**
6.1 (b) Compatible with commitments		3	4		2	3		2	12	19	28	13	10	**96**
9.3 Partial referral to member states phase 1			1		1			6	3	1	4	6	9	**31**
9.3 Full referral to member states				1			3	1	1	3	2	1	4	**16**
Total decisions in Phase I	7	55	57	54	86	102	118	131	229	260	328	320	266	**2013**
Phase 2														
9.3 Partial referral to member states phase 2										1				**1**
8.2 Compatible with common market		1	1	1	2	2	1	1	3		3	5	2	**22**
8.2 Compatible with commitments		3	3	2	2	3	3	7	4	8	12	10	5	**62**
8.3 Prohibition		1			1	2	3	1	2	1	2	5		**18**
8.4 Required to restore effective competition								2					2	**4**
Total decisions in Phase II		5	4	3	5	7	7	11	9	10	17	20	9	**107**
Total final decisions	**7**	**60**	**61**	**57**	**91**	**109**	**125**	**142**	**238**	**270**	**345**	**340**	**275**	**2120**

Source: Adapted from European Commission (2003) **www.europa.eu.int/comm/competition**

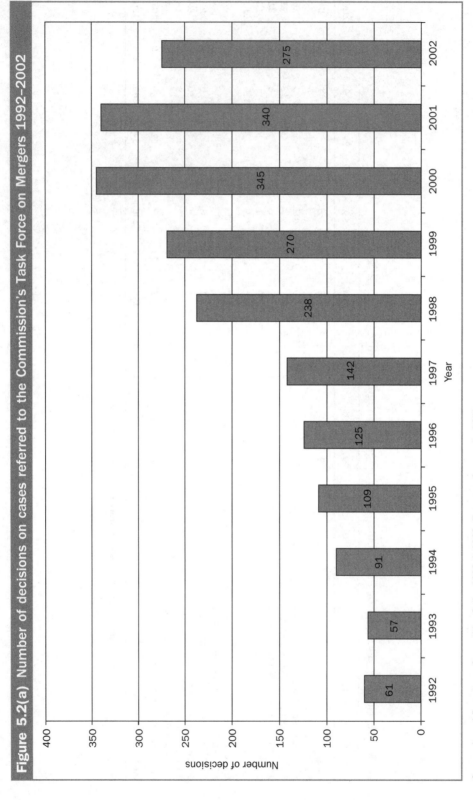

Figure 5.2(a) Number of decisions on cases referred to the Commission's Task Force on Mergers 1992–2002

Source: Annual Reports on Competition Policy 1998 & 2002, European Community DGIV

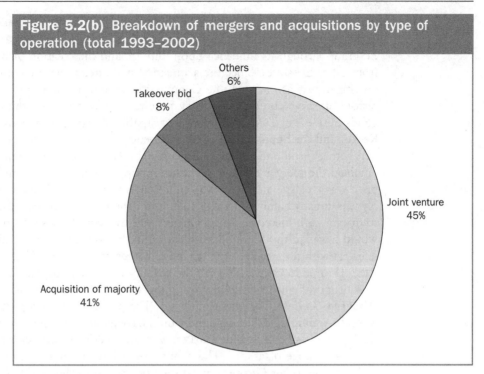

Figure 5.2(b) Breakdown of mergers and acquisitions by type of operation (total 1993–2002)

Source: Annual Report on Competition Policy 2002, European Community DGIV

the second major producer of turbo-prop aircraft, and Aerospatiale and Alenia were seeking to purchase it. Such an acquisition would have led to the creation of a firm with more than 50 per cent of the world market in turbo props, and in some sub-market categories considerably more than this. On examination, the Commission found that there was unlikely to be sufficient competition from other small-scale suppliers of turbo props and that exit from the market was more likely than any new entry. Therefore the Commission decided to prohibit this merger.

In a number of instances where original merger proposals have been unacceptable, firms have had the choice of abandoning them or negotiating conditions for acceptance with the Commission. Typically, this has involved some divestment of existing activities. Thus, in *Accor/Wagons-Lits*, the Commission found that the combined firms would account for 89 per cent of motorway catering and 69 per cent of light meals. Also, the merged firm would have been some 18 times larger than its nearest rival in light meals, and any new entrants would face very high entry barriers. The market would have been clearly dominated by a single firm, and so approval was given only on condition that Accor divest itself completely of Wagons-Lits operations in France. This section will conclude with a look at some of the prohibited mergers, four of which are examined below.

If requested by a national authority, the Commission can investigate a merger even though it falls below the normal EC turnover thresholds. This was so in the *Kesko/Tuko* acquisition. In May 1996 Kesko acquired Tuko and attained a 55 per cent market share in retailing in Finland. In November 1996 the Commission declared the operation to be incompatible with the common market on the grounds that it had led to a dominant position and had significantly impeded competition in the Finnish retail and cash-and-carry markets. Additionally, it had affected intra-EU trade through its influence upon imports and the creation of barriers to entry from other EU states. Since the acquisition had already been completed before the investigation was initiated, the Commission set out measures in February 1997 to restore effective competition. They required Kesko to divest the daily consumer goods business of Tuko to a purchaser capable of acting as an active competitor to Kesko, and the appointment of an independent trustee to ensure compliance.

Another prohibited merger was that of *Gencor/Lonrho*, which would have involved the merger of their platinum mining operations. Demand was growing, price was inelastic and there was an absence of countervailing buying power. Supply was already highly concentrated in four suppliers, with Russian supplies expected to dry up, and there were high barriers to entry with high sunk costs. The merger would have led to a duopolistic position in the worldwide platinum and rhodium markets with no incentive for any post-merger competition. Thus, the merger was deemed to be incompatible with the sustaining of a competitive market.

A proposed joint venture involving the silicon carbide interests of *Saint-Gobain/Wacker-Chemie/NOM* was prohibited. The parties to the proposed joint venture were the technological leaders and would have gained a 60 per cent market share in the European silicon carbide market, with no other producers capable of providing the whole range of grades. The result would have been a lack of potential competition from other European producers or the rest of the world. The joint venture was accordingly declared incompatible.

The proposed acquisition *General Electric/Honeywell* was prohibited in July 2001. General Electric already held a dominant position in the market for jet engines for large commercial aircraft and proposed to take over Honeywell. Honeywell was the leading supplier of engines for corporate jets and also of avionic and non-avionic products. The Commission ruled that a merger would also have created dominant positions in the markets for avionics, non-avionics and corporate jet engines, while further strengthening General Electric's dominance in commercial jet engines. This would have had the effect of foreclosing competitors and eliminating competition with consequent adverse effects upon quality, service and prices. General Electric offered undertakings but these were insufficient to offset the Commission's perceived detriments and the merger was duly prohibited.

The foregoing examples illustrate the breadth of the powers available to the Commission to deal with concentrations, and also the importance the Commission attaches to actual or potential competition as mechanisms for delivering the public interest.

Further European developments

Currently there have been two new developments in European policy. In 1997 a revision of the Merger Control Regulation was finally adopted which addresses issues detailed in a Green Paper (European Commission, 1996). Secondly, in 1997 the Commission published a consultative Green Paper setting out options for the treatment of vertical restraints (European Commission, 1997).

Following the merger review it had become clear that many mergers with cross-border effects were not notified to the Commission since they did not meet the EU turnover criteria. However, many of these were being notified to multiple national competition bodies, thus creating unnecessary burdens on both businesses and regulators. Consequently, for mergers involving activity in at least three member states, the turnover thresholds have been reduced. This should have the benefit of capturing smaller mergers that have important cross-border effects. It will also simplify the process and extend the 'one stop' principle by avoiding the unnecessary duplication that occurs with referrals to multiple national authorities.

The review of vertical restraints addressed a number of issues. Vertical restraints have been considered on a case-by-case basis in accordance with the strict application of Article 81(1), but with block exemptions for exclusive dealing, exclusive purchasing and franchising under Article 81(3). However, the economic effects of vertical restraints are less clear-cut than is the case with horizontal restraints. As with horizontal restraints, vertical restraints may be used deliberately to restrict competition. For example, Volkswagen was fined €30.96 m for instructing its German dealers in 1996 and 1997 not to sell the new VW Passat at prices below the recommended retail price (see also *Grundig/Consten* and *Michelin* above).

However, the single market has provided opportunities for firms to enter new markets, and that process can be facilitated by the development of efficient distributive systems. Thus, vertical restraints between producers and distributors can be pro-competitive where they enhance such market penetration, and in these circumstances could be justifiable *for a limited period*. This may be facilitated in a number of ways. For example, by the attainment of standardisation and quality by distributing through specialist outlets; by the exploitation of economies of scale by concentrating sales through a limited number of outlets; by the encouragement of dealer investment to help establish the brand.

Therefore, given that (i) the single market legislation was largely in place, (ii) the exemptions governing vertical restraints were shortly to expire, (iii) there had been major changes in distribution methods, and (iv) the economic effects can be pro-competitive, the Commission sought consultations with a view to formulating a more coherent and consistent policy towards vertical restraints. Following the review the Commission came to recognise that, with a changed economic situation and current distribution practices, the existing approach was too rigid. Accordingly, in 1999, scope was given to grant exemptions to vertical restraints subject to stringent vetting. Thus, for example, the Commission may now exempt a restraint

(i) between two or more firms relating to the purchase, sale or resale of goods or services;

(ii) between two firms that impose restrictions on purchases or on the use of intellectual property rights or know how

provided that:

(i) the full details of a restraint are given prior publicity;

(ii) the restraint applies for a limited period only.

This liberalisation in the treatment of vertical restraints brings European policy closer to the attitude in the UK, where it is concluded that 'on balance, we believe that there are potentially significant benefits in excluding vertical restraints, so long as they are not price-fixing restraints, from the scope of the prohibition of anti-competitive restraints' (DTI, 1997, p. 1).

The relationship between EU and UK competition policy

In recent years there has been a number of wide-ranging official reviews of most aspects of UK competition policy, alongside widespread consultations with academia, business and other interested parties. This consultative process culminated initially in the passing of the Competition Act of 1998. While still maintaining an independent domestic policy towards competition within the UK, this Act had the effect of bringing that policy into close alignment with the approach under EU policy. The Restrictive Practices Court was abolished and the Monopolies and Mergers Commission replaced by a new Competition Commission. In the case of restrictive practices, there has been a major shift towards a European-type approach closely modelled on Article 81. Policy towards dominant firm monopoly and anti-competitive practices has also involved a shift to an approach much closer to that of Article 82. In mergers, changes were largely procedural with no significant reorientation of policy, despite specific concerns. For many years there have been worries over the increasing monopolisation of British industry through structural change, as evidenced by increased levels of both aggregate and market concentration. There is little doubt that merger activity has, at times, been a major causal factor (e.g. HMSO, 1978; Hughes, 1993), However, in the case of mergers the Competition Act introduced no major changes in the orientation of policy.

The effect of the Competition Act has been to create a more relevant and effective policy, not only by creating greater harmonisation with EU restrictive practices policy, but also by strengthening domestic policy through the adoption of an approach designed to combat any practice which has the *effect* of restricting competition, as opposed to one that emphasised the *form* of an agreement, sometimes to the neglect of that effect.

In 2002 the Enterprise Act was passed, which has the effect of removing yet further distinctions between UK and European policy. As in the EU, mergers will now be judged against their effect upon competition rather than a wider criterion of being against the public interest. If there is a 'substantial lessening of competition' a merger can either be prohibited or have pre-conditions imposed. Within the UK it will no longer remain the prerogative of a politically accountable minister to decide, acting on the advice of the bureaucracy, whether to permit or to forbid a particular merger. It is envisaged that most decisions will be taken by the OFT and the Competition Commission independently of political control. Similarly, within EU policy there is limited political discretion, since the decision to permit or to forbid an investigated merger is a matter for the administration. Whether political or administrative accountability is the more desirable depends on one's view about the relationships that should exist between state and society, but it is more likely that where decisions are made by political appointees there would be greater uncertainty, for such decisions would embody both a political and an economic dimension. For this reason merger policy in the EU, and now in the UK, *ought* to display less arbitrariness than under the previous UK legislation. However, following the first EU takeover to be disallowed (Aerospatiale/Alenia/DeHaviland), some doubts were expressed over the abilities of Commissioners to submerge their national interests and remain free from political pressures. The potential for such conflict arises from the differing perspectives of industrial and competition policy. Some see the SEM as providing the opportunity for the restructuring of industry and the attainment of international competitiveness, while others see it as providing the opportunity to achieve efficiency by the creation of competitive conditions throughout the EU.

Conclusion

Throughout the debate and proposals on all sides it is the persistent emphasis on competition that has provided the continuing hallmark of policy. The most recent changes in UK policy represent one further stage in the piecemeal development of legislation, with a move yet closer to the *effects*-based approach of the EU and away from the previous *form*-based or structural approach. If, as has been argued in this chapter, there are benefits from the harmonisation of policy approaches, these recent changes are clearly sensible in moving to an approach similar to that embodied in Articles 81 and 82 of the EU.

This slow and piecemeal convergence of EU and UK competition policy is to be welcomed. With greater harmonisation of policies industry and business will be able to operate more efficiently through being able to plan within an environment of greater certainty, and will be more secure in the knowledge that its domestic and international operations are likely to receive compatible treatment from the respective authorities.

However, on the basis of past and continuing experience both in the EU and elsewhere, the existence and growth of legislation designed to prohibit and punish anti-competitive behaviour can never be sufficient to eradicate it. Left to itself business seems always, in the words of Jonas Chuzzlewit, predisposed to 'Do other men for they would do you. That's the true business precept' (Dickens, 1844, Ch. 11). Sufficient examples have been unearthed to demonstrate that this sentiment is not purely fanciful. There remains, therefore, a strong case for the Commission to be vigilant and proactive in its pursuance of policy.

References

Baumol W J (1959) *Business Behaviour Value and Growth*, Macmillan, New York.

Baumol W J, Panzar J C and Willig R D (1982) *Contestable Markets and the Theory of Industry Structure*, Harcourt Brace Jovanovich, New York.

Beacham A and Jones J C H (1971) 'Merger Criteria and Policy in Great Britain and Canada', *Journal of Industrial Economics*, Vol. 19, pp. 97–117.

Bishop M (1993) 'European or National?: The Community's New Merger Regulation', in M Bishop and J A Kay (eds), *European Mergers and Merger Policy*, Oxford University Press, Oxford.

Bishop M and Kay J A (eds) (1993) *European Mergers and Merger Policy*, Oxford University Press, Oxford.

Brittan L (1992) *European Competitive Policy*, Brassey's, London.

Button K J (1985) 'New Approaches to the Regulation of Industry, *Royal Bank of Scotland Review*, No. 148, December, pp. 18–34.

Clarke R (1985) *Industrial Economics*, Blackwell, Oxford.

Cowling K and Mueller D C (1978) 'The Social Costs of Monopoly Power', *Economic Journal*, No. 88, pp. 77–87.

Crew M A and Rowley C K (1970) 'Anti-trust Policy: Economics versus Management Science', *Moorgate and Wall Street Journal*, Autumn, pp. 19–34.

Crew M A and Rowley C K (1971) 'Anti-trust Policy: The Application of Rules', *Moorgate and Wall Street Journal*, Autumn, pp. 37–50.

Dickens C (1844) *Martin Chuzzlewit*, Penguin, London.

DTI (1997) *A Prohibition Approach to Anti-competitive Agreements and Abuse of Dominant Position: Draft Bill*, DTI, London.

European Commission (1996) *Green Paper on the Review of the Merger Regulation*, European Commission, DGIV, Luxembourg.

European Commission (1997) *Green Paper on Vertical Restraints in EC Competition Policy*, European Commission, DGIV, Luxembourg.

European Commission (2003) *European Community Competition Policy*, Annual Reports on Competition Policy, European Commission, DGIV, Luxembourg.

Fairburn J A, Kay J A and Sharpe T A E (1986) 'The economics of Article 86', in G Hall (ed.), *European Industrial Policy*, Croom Helm, London.

Fleming M and Swann D (1989) 'Competition Policy: The Pace Quickens and 1992 Approaches, *Royal Bank of Scotland Review*, No. 162, June, pp. 47–61.

George K (1989) 'Do We Need a Merger Policy?', in J A Fairburn and J Kay (eds), *Mergers and Merger Policy*, Oxford University Press, Oxford.

Geroski P and Vlassopoulos A (1993) 'Recent Patterns of European Merger Activity', in M Bishop and J A Kay (eds), *European Mergers and Merger Policy*, Oxford University Press, Oxford.

Harberger A C (1954) 'Monopoly and Resource Allocation', *American Economic Review*, No. 44, pp. 77–87.

Hay D and Morris D (1991) *Industrial Economics and Organization Theory and Evidence*, Oxford University Press, Oxford.

HMSO (1978) *A Review of Monopoly and Mergers Policy*, Green Paper Cmnd 7198, HMSO, London.

Howe M (1971) 'Anti-trust Policy: Rules or Discretionary Intervention?' *Moorgate and Wall Street Journal*, Spring, pp. 59–68.

Howe M (1972) 'British Merger Policy Proposals and American Experience', *Scottish Journal of Political Economy*, February.

Hughes A (1993) 'Mergers and Economic Performance in the UK: A Survey of the Empirical Evidence 1950–1990', in M Bishop and J A Kay (eds), *European Mergers and Merger Policy*, Oxford University Press, Oxford.

Jacquemin A P and de Jong H W (1977) *European Industrial Organization*, Macmillan, London.

Kamerschen D R (1966) 'An Estimation of the Welfare Losses from Monopoly in the American Economy', *Western Economic Journal*, No. 4, pp. 221–36.

Littlechild S C (1981) 'Misleading Calculations of the Social Costs of Monopoly', *Economic Journal*, Vol. 91, pp. 348–63.

Littlechild S (1989) 'Myths and Merger Policy', in J A Fairburn and J Kay (eds), *Mergers and Merger Policy*, Oxford University Press, Oxford.

Neven D, Nuttall R and Seabright P (1993) *Merger in Daylight: The Economics and Politics of European Merger Control*, Centre for Economic Policy Research, London.

Posner M E (1975) 'The Social Costs of Monopoly and Regulation', *Journal of Political Economy*, Vol. 83, pp. 807–27.

Pratten C F (1971) *Economies of Scale in Manufacturing Industry*, Cambridge University Press, Cambridge.

Rowley C (1973) *Anti-Trust and Economic Efficiency*, Macmillan, London.

Sawyer M C (1979) *Theories of the Firm*, Weidenfeld and Nicolson, London.

Schwartzman D (1960) 'The Burden of Monopoly', *Journal of Political Economy*, Vol. 68, pp. 627–30.

Silberston A (1972) 'Economies of Scale in Theory and Practice', *Economic Journal*, supplement, No. 82, pp. 369–91.

Sutherland A (1970) 'The Management of Mergers Policy', in A K Cairncross (ed.), *The Managed Economy*, Blackwell, Oxford, pp. 106–34.

Swann D (1983) *Competition and Industrial Policy in the European Community*, Methuen, London.

Swann D (1988) *The Economics of the Common Market*, 6th edn, Penguin, London.

Utton M A (1975) 'British Merger Policy', in K D George and C Joll (eds), *Competition Policy in the UK and EEC*, Cambridge University Press, Cambridge.

Williamson O E (1968) 'Economies as an Anti-trust Defence: The Welfare Trade-offs, *American Economic Review*, Vol. 58, pp. 18–36.

Worcester D A (1973) New Estimates of the Welfare Loss to Monopoly, United States: 1956–69', *Southern Economic Journal*, 40, pp. 234–45.

Chapter 6

Industrial policy in the European Union

Frank McDonald and Margaret Potton

Introduction

The 21st Report on Competition Policy of the EC defines industrial policy thus:

> Industrial Policy concerns the effective and coherent implementation of all those policies which impinge on the structural adjustment of industry with a view to promoting competitiveness. The provision of a horizontal framework in which industry can develop and prosper by remedying structural deficiencies and addressing areas where the market mechanism alone fails to provide the conditions necessary for success is the principal means by which the Community applies its industrial policy (Commission, 1991).

This definition appears to include competition policy (to maintain a competitive environment), deregulation policies (to remove legal impediments that prohibit or limit competitive markets) and a wide range of social, regional and R&D programmes (to correct market failures). The EU has been active in all these areas. However, it is not clear if these policies and programmes constitute an effective and/or coherent approach to EU industrial policy. Further, in some areas it is not clear that the EU is the appropriate agency to take the lead in industrial policy. The EU is hampered in devising a coherent industrial policy because of the very diverse approaches that the member states have adopted towards their national industrial policies (Foreman-Peck and Federico, 1999). Nevertheless, the EU has developed a series of programmes that impact on a wide range of industries. Therefore, in a sense, the EU does have an industrial policy. This policy has been developed to cover a wide range of areas and sectors, but especially to help small and medium-sized enterprises (SMEs) to develop, to enhance competitiveness in European firms and to promote innovation and R&D among European firms (see **www.europa.eu.int/comm/enterprise/policy** for details).

Rationale for industrial policy

Three main approaches to industrial policy can be identified:

1 market-based or negative industrial policy;
2 interventionist or positive industrial policy;
3 selective intervention or strategic industrial policy.

Market-based industrial policy is founded on the view that market mechanisms are on the whole effective in generating an efficient and vibrant industrial structure. This approach requires intervention only where there are significant cases of market failure. Thus, if externalities lead to under-provision of R&D expenditures or training for labour there may be a case for government intervention to correct these market failures (see Exhibit 6.1). However, many of the advocates of market-based industrial policies have reservations about the ability of governments to correct market failures successfully, and some argue that government intervention to correct for market failure often leads to a worse outcome than that which arises from the 'imperfect market process'. In other words, government intervention leads to greater inefficiencies than does market failure (see Buchanan, 1978). Therefore, in the market-based approach industrial policy is mainly negative, i.e. the prevention of abuse of market power and the removal of legal impediments to free trade.

Exhibit 6.1 Externalities and industrial policy

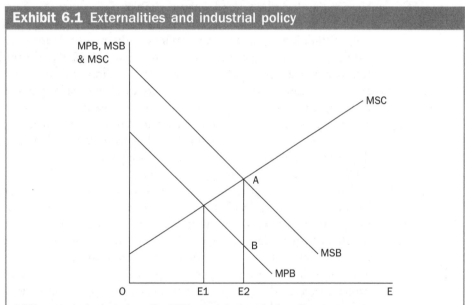

MPB = marginal private benefit   MSB = marginal social benefit

MSC = marginal social cost   E = Expenditure on R&D

Maximisation of net benefits is where MSB = MSC (i.e. the marginal cost to society of R&D expenditures is equal to the marginal benefits to society). The optimal level of R&D expenditures is therefore E2. However, if the spill-over effects of R&D expenditures (i.e. the difference between MPB and MSB) are not taken into account, R&D expenditures will be sub-optimal (i.e. at E1 where MPB = MSC). In order to reach an optimal level of R&D expenditures, a subsidy of AB would be required to compensate the company engaging in R&D expenditures for the spill-over effects.

   If governments do not estimate the size of the required subsidy correctly there would be either too little or too much R&D expenditure. This is 'government failure'. Another solution to the problem of sub-optimal R&D expenditures is to define intellectual property rights clearly such that the spill-over effects are captured by the company which engages in R&D expenditures. This would require the beneficiaries of R&D expenditures to pay the company for the benefits that are conferred on the rest of society from these expenditures, by for example the sale of patent rights. However, many of these expenditures are not amenable to such a property rights solution because of the difficulties of accurately defining intellectual property rights.

Hence, competition policy, the removal of state aids to promote competitive markets and deregulation programmes are regarded as the cornerstones of industrial policy.

Interventionist industrial policy is based on the view that market failure in areas such as R&D and labour training are important obstacles to the development of a dynamic industrial base. Social and regional considerations are also considered to be important factors in devising a 'good' industrial policy. Such social and regional factors are often considered to have important economic effects due to loss of productive potential and high public expenditures that arise from unemployment. Industrial policy that successfully improves the productive capacity of poorer regions or sectors of economies can increase employment levels and income (see Exhibit 6.2). Positive action and financial support by governments to ensure adequate R&D and training expenditures and to provide aid to poorer groups and regions are considered to be an essential part of industrial policy. This approach tends to see a need for intervention in a wide range of industries and sectors covering both declining and emerging industries.

The selective interventionist approach to industrial policy takes a more strategic view of industrial policy. In this approach the main role for industrial policy is to aid the growth of emerging industries to replace those that are in decline. The need for such a strategic approach arises from the imperfect nature of the competitive environment, in particular in cases where there exist strong economies of scale and learning effects. In these cases selective help by use of state aids can give competitive advantages to companies. State aids can also be used to help companies to 'catch up' on foreign competitors that are established in the market (see Exhibit 6.3). The theoretical benefits of this approach have been put forward by Krugman and Obstfeld (1991). However, Krugman is somewhat reluctant to advocate such an approach to industrial policy because of the risks of retaliation from competitors, and also because it is very difficult for governments to gather and assess the appropriate information that would allow them to choose potential 'winners'. However, the benefits of such strategic approaches seem to have been accepted by some American economists (Tyson, 1992). Moreover, European economists have also advocated a strategic interventionist approach (Bianchi, 1998). The economic rationale for projects such as the European Airbus rests on strategic interventionist arguments.

In addition to these economic arguments a political–economic case can be put for industrial policy. Governments affect industry by their public procurement policies, subsidies, competition and regulatory frameworks, taxation systems and other laws and policies that impact on companies. All governments exercise important influences on companies. As such, all governments have industrial policies or, more correctly, policies that have a significant impact on industry (Dormer and Kuyper, 2000; Worthington, 2003). Therefore, governments have no option but to have some kind of an industrial policy (Bangemann, 1993). However, an assessment of the economic arguments on the impact of government policy that affects industry may provide useful insights as to how wisely governments gear their policies with respect to the impact on industry. The general objectives of governments become important in what is regarded as good or bad industrial policy. Therefore, if the creation and maintenance of competitiveness of companies is a high priority, the current orthodox view is that a market-based industrial policy should be followed. However, the legacy of history is important. Decisions taken in the past to subsidise

Exhibit 6.2 Industrial policy as a means of boosting employment

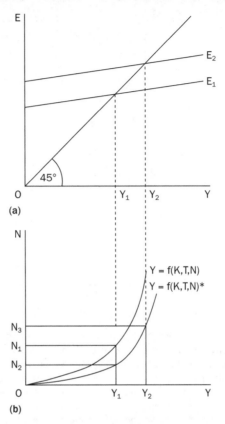

(a)

(b)

In **(a)** the level of national income (Y) is determined by national expenditure (E) at Y1. This will correspond to an employment level (with a given relationship between employment and income shown by the production function in **(b)**) of N1 on production function Y = f(K,L,T), where K = amount of capital, L = amount of labour and T = state of technology (the techniques that link capital and labour together in production processes). This production function is based on a fixed amount of capital and a given state of technology. If parts of the economy have poor levels of technology because of structural deficiencies such as low skill levels in parts of the labour force, it may be possible to improve technology in these areas by use of industrial policy (e.g. help with labour training). This will shift the production function to, say, Y = f(K,L,T)*. In these circumstances, to produce an income level of Y1 would require employment of N2 (that is less than N1). Consequently, the first effect of this policy would be to reduce employment. However, the improvement in technology should lead to lower costs and therefore to lower prices for products. This will lower prices and therefore lead to higher expenditure. Expenditure would shift to, say, E2, leading to a higher income – Y2. This would require a higher employment level – N3. In this scenario a virtuous circle is created of improvements in technology leading to higher expenditures and thereby to higher employment levels.

The size of these effects depends on the scale of the shifts in the production function and the resultant effect on expenditure. The creation of the virtuous circle depends on the government accurately identifying the causes of the low technology in particular regions and sectors, and being able to rectify this at a cost that is less than, or equal to, the value of the benefits of any increase in employment. The potential for government failure in this area may be quite high. Moreover, the causes of the poor performance in the specified regions or sectors must be amenable to correction by government policies.

Exhibit 6.3 The strategic case for industrial policy

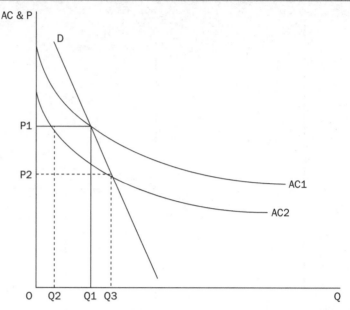

P = price   AC = average cost   Q = quantity

If a company establishes a plant in country A with average cost given by AC1, and it was the first company to produce the product, it would have a first mover advantage. The company will operate at P1 : Q1 (assuming that the company sets price equal to average cost). Therefore, although the company in country B has lower costs than the company in country A (i.e. AC2 rather than AC1) it will not be able to enter the market because the company in country A has a first mover advantage. At the price P1 the company in country B cannot sell output at less than, or equal to, its average cost unless it enters the market with an output level of 0Q2 or above. To be able to realise such an outcome the company in country B would have to take market share from the first mover and it would make losses until it reached an output level of 0Q2. Moreover, as the company in country B entered the market it would put downward pressure on the market price and would therefore worsen its position with regard to the difference between price and its average cost.

However, the government in country B could help the company to enter the market by strategic industrial policy. Thus, subsidies could be given or other types of help to allow company B to offset the first mover advantage of the company in country A. If such help was given the company in country B would eventually replace the company in country A with price and output given by P2 : Q3. This policy would be beneficial because it would allow the most efficient producer to supply the market and it would lower price and increase output (see Krugman and Obstfeld, 1991).

The problem with this approach is that it assumes that government can select companies that would fall into this category and it also assumes that the government of country A would not retaliate in response to the loss of market share by its companies caused by the industrial policies of other countries.

or favour particular industries often result in the creation of strong vested interests that can make it very difficult to alter existing policies. Member states have very different histories in their approach to industrial policy (Foreman-Peck and Federico, 1999) and this makes it very difficult to alter the direction of industrial policy.

Types of industrial policy

Industrial policy can be based on three different approaches.

1 *Horizontal industrial policy*. This involves the creation and maintenance of a competitive and regulatory framework for all industry that is compatible with the objectives of the government, for example the promotion of competitiveness. Horizontal industrial policy can also include help to industry to achieve the objectives of governments, such as education and training policies geared to the needs of industry. These, however, are aimed at all industry, not at selected parts of the economy.

2 *Vertical industrial policy*. Vertical policy selects particular industries for special treatment. This type of policy is often related to help for declining industries and for those industries that are considered to be strategically important in terms of such factors as global competition or avoiding dependency on foreign technologies and products.

3 *Mixed industrial policy*. If governments select key industries for special attention in terms of creating and maintaining the conditions for good performance by modifying competitive and regulatory frameworks and also by help in such areas as R&D, then a type of mixed industrial policy can be said to be in operation. This kind of approach is often observed in the IT and biotechnology industries.

Most countries take an eclectic view of industrial policy. Although the USA, Germany and the UK tend towards a market-based and horizontal approach, and France and Italy towards a more interventionist and vertical approach, these countries have a mixture of these types in their industrial policies (Foreman-Peck and Federico, 1999; Lawton, 1999). In a sense, the majority of countries adopt a mixed approach. However, in many countries there has been a pronounced shift towards a more market-based and horizontal approach to industrial policy (Bianchi, 1998; Johnson, 2003). This movement can be seen in the deregulation programmes in areas such as transport services, telecommunications services and airlines. The growth of privatisation programmes also bears witness to the move towards market-based industrial policies. Nevertheless, the large-scale protection of declining industries and the widespread used of state aids by many countries provide evidence that interventionist industrial policies are still a potent force in many economies.

Industrial policy in the treaties

The first treaty provision for industrial policy was in the Treaty of Paris. The High Authority may 'facilitate the carrying out of investment programmes by granting loans to undertakings or by guaranteeing other loans'. It may also 'assist the financing of works and installations which contribute directly and primarily to increasing production' (Article 54). It can also ban loans if they are contrary to the Treaty. Article 55 says that the 'High Authority shall promote technical and economic research into the production and increased use of coal and steel'. The High Authority may 'initiate and facilitate such research'.

The High Authority also had the power to affect production (Article 58) if the Community 'is confronted with a period of manifest crisis'. It can establish a system of production quotas subject to Article 74. Article 46 established that the High Authority shall 'periodically lay down general objectives for modernisation, long-term planning of manufacture and expansion of productive capacity'. Thus the Treaty of Paris is quite dirigiste. The Treaty establishing the European Coal and Steel Community was concluded in 1952 for a timespan of 50 years. Since 2002 industrial policy towards the steel and coal industries has been governed by the TEU.

The Treaty of Rome scarcely mentions industrial policy. However, State Aids granted by member states are mentioned in Articles 92 and 93. Article 92 states that 'aid to promote the economic development of areas where the standard of living is abnormally low or where there is serious unemployment' is compatible with the Common Market, as is 'aid to promote the execution of an important project of common European interest or to remedy a serious disturbance in the economy of a member state' and 'other categories of aid as may be specified by decision of the Council acting by a qualified majority on a proposal from the Commission.' Article 93 is on the organisation of state aid. Section 1 says that 'the Commission shall, in cooperation with member states, keep under constant review all systems of aid existing in those states. It shall propose to the latter any appropriate measures required by the progressive development or by the functioning of the common market.'

At the time of the signing of the Treaty of Rome the industrial policies of France and Germany, which were then the two dominant member countries, were very difficult to align as they were very different. The French government believed in a dirigiste policy. There was a need in France for the government to have a strong influence on industrial development, if not to plan it centrally as in the then Eastern bloc. In Germany, on the other hand, there was, and still is, a reliance on a more laissez-faire regime wedded to market forces. In 1957 intervention in industry was not really an issue. The main aim was to set up a common market based on competition, and a healthy industrial structure was expected to follow.

Thus, up to the SEA, there was not much specifically laid down in the Treaties concerning industrial policy apart from the above-mentioned provisions in the Treaty of Paris regarding coal and steel. Article 23 of the SEA, however, modified the Treaty of Rome by adding Title V on economic and social cohesion which includes Article 130c on the ERDF, which 'is intended to help redress the principal regional imbalances in the Community through participating in the development and structural adjustment of regions whose development is lagging behind and *in the conversion of declining industrial regions*' [chapter authors' italics]. Title VI, which was also added to the Treaty of Rome by Article 24 of the SEA, is about research and technological development. Article 130f stipulates that the 'Community's aim shall be to strengthen the scientific and technological basis of European industry and to encourage it to become more competitive at international level'.

Thus research and technological development (RTD) programmes were to be implemented by promoting cooperation with undertakings, research centres and universities. Member states were to coordinate their R&D policies and programmes, and the Commission could take any useful initiative to promote such coordination (Article 130h). The Community was to adopt a multi-annual framework programme setting out all its activities. Thus guidelines for policy in research and technological development, which were to become very important in later years, were laid down in 1986 in the SEA.

The TEU amended the Treaty of Rome to include a section on industry, Title XIII, Article 130. This article provided a foundation for the development of a treaty-based industrial policy based on creating the conditions that will encourage companies to pursue competitiveness. A significant step was, therefore, taken in the SEA and the TEU to establish a firm basis for an industrial policy that is strongly focused on programmes for RTD. Therefore, by 1992 a clear, but limited, treaty foundation for an EU Industrial Policy had been established.

The Amsterdam and Nice Treaties made some minor changes and a Consolidated Version of the Treaty Establishing the European Community was produced that clarified the treaty basis of the EU (**www.europa.eu.int/eur-lex/en/treaties/dat/ C_2002325EN.003301.htm**). Article 157 of the Consolidated Treaty specifies the encouragement of competitiveness as the key focus of EU Industrial Policy. The article highlights four major objectives for Industrial Policy:

1 Speeding up the adjustment of industry to structural changes.

2 Encouraging an environment favourable to initiative and to the development of undertakings throughout the Community, particularly small and medium-sized undertakings.

3 Encouraging an environment favourable to cooperation between undertakings.

4 Fostering better exploitation of the industrial potential of policies of innovation, research and technological development.

This article cannot be used to introduce measures that would distort competition, or that require tax provisions or that relate to employment rights. EU measures in these areas are governed by the treaty provisions for taxation and employment matters. Articles 163 to 173 relate to research and technological development. These articles are mainly about the formulation of framework programmes to encourage cooperation in R&D.

Rationale for EU industrial policy

The term Enterprise Policy is used to cover most of what is understood to be the industrial policy of the EU (**www.europa.eu.int/comm/enterprise/enterprise_policy/ index.htm**). The EU began with a significant interventionist approach in the areas of coal and steel with the Treaty of Paris, which founded the ECSC. However, the EEC was more concerned with establishing free movement of goods, services, capital and labour and the development of a strong competition policy. As the EU has developed, more interventionist and strategic approaches to industrial policy have arisen, for example the growth of R&D programmes and policies to aid declining industries and poorer regions. Nevertheless, the EU has also engaged in significant deregulation programmes. For instance, a large part of the SEM programme was predominantly concerned with deregulation, and the Union has embarked on significant deregulation programmes in the telecommunication services and airline industries. The Commission is also encouraging the privatisation programmes that are taking place in many of the member states.

The debate over the characteristics of EU industrial policy has become an important issue due to the growth of Union policies and programmes that affect industry and because of the concept of subsidiarity. Four possible reasons for an EU industrial policy can be put forward – spill-over effects related to externalities, creating the conditions for 'free movement', promoting 'economic and social cohesion', and promoting the goal of political integration.

In order for externality arguments to be a valid rationale for a common industrial policy for the EU, the member states of the Union would have to encompass most of the spill-over effects of R&D and training programmes. Given the lack of labour mobility in the EU, it is difficult to see a pronounced externality effect in labour training that would spill over to other member states. The position with regard to R&D programmes is less clear. However, given the increasing globalisation of business activities and the importance of regional and local adaptation to these pressures, it is not obvious that the EU should be the major agency to provide a coherent and effective R&D policy (Lawton, 1999; Dormer and Kuyper, 2000; Johnson, 2003). The case for a European Industrial Policy on the basis of the spill-over effect is not very strong. However, if there were a case it would require a positive or strategic industrial policy.

The EU has a role to play in providing the conditions for free movement. The various industrial policies in member states create the potential for the establishment of barriers to free movement and distortions to trade flows because of the use of state aids. The EU has played a significant role in reducing these barriers to free movement, but this involves primarily negative industrial policy. Indeed, the main requirements are related to competition policy, the control of state aids and the creation and maintenance of legal frameworks that permit free movement.

The attractiveness of the EU as an effective agency for the provision of industrial policies to promote 'economic and social cohesion' would depend on the acceptance of this as an important goal for the Union and also on whether this goal could be better met by promoting free movement in a predominantly market-based system. Nevertheless, this reason for industrial policy, if it were taken seriously, could involve a significant increase in EU programmes, many of which would be primarily connected to positive or strategic industrial policy. There is much debate as to whether such positive industrial policies complement the objective of boosting competitiveness by making the market-based system more effective by creating appropriate institutional frameworks, or if they are more concerned with redistribution and equity objectives that may undermine the development of competitiveness (Bianchi, 1998).

The use of positive industrial policies to promote a fusion of interests among groups within member states and thereby develop institutional changes that further political integration objectives, is a strong feature of the work of many political scientists that research in this area (see the papers in the *Journal of Common Market Studies* for examples of this approach). This approach to understanding industrial policy and other EU policies evaluates the effectiveness of policies primarily by their contribution to enhancing the development of institutional structures that facilitate greater political integration, either between the national governments of the member states by intergovernmentalism, or by creating and developing supranational governmental structures. In most of these studies an assumption is often made that coordination or harmonisation (normally requiring interventionist policies) is desirable. However, in the case of industrial policy the desirability of coordination or harmonisation is debatable. Some of the literature by political scientists in this area seems to assume that further political integration (especially of a supranational kind) is the desired objective.

Competitiveness and EU industrial policy

Increasingly, the EU has become concerned with promoting competitiveness and innovation among European firms and the conditions under which SMEs can flourish. This has led to the development of a rationale for EU strategic industrial policies for three main reasons (Navarro, 2003):

1 Intervention to help overcome externalities especially connected to network externalities such as access to networks for the distribution of utilities and information and knowledge, especially by the Internet and other electronic means of communication.

2 Policies to help European firms to adjust (or to evolve) in the light of pressures arising from globalisation, technical, social and economic change and the demands raised by the perceived need to protect the physical environment by developing sustainable development policies.

3 The perceived need for government policies to foster the development of clusters (geographically concentrated networks of firms and supporting agencies) that help firms to attain and develop competitiveness.

The advocacy of policies to promote clusters is based on the success of well-known and successful clusters such as Silicon Valley and Route 128 in the USA (Saxenian, 1994), high-tech clusters in various parts of the world (Swann et al., 1998), and Italian Industrial Districts (Pyke et al., 1990). The work of Porter in his studies on the determinants of competitiveness has also stimulated great interest in policies to promote clusters (Porter, 1990, 1998 and 2000). The theoretical basis for the benefits of clusters stems from proximity to other firms and supporting agencies that allow external economies of scale to be reaped and permit the creation and development of cooperation, that stimulates flexibility in the use of resources and promotes innovation and learning (see McNaughton and Brown, 2002 for a review of these benefits). The EU has become a strong advocate of policies to promote clusters (European Commission, 2002). However, many of the national governments in the member states are also strongly involved in promoting clusters (e.g. DTI, 2003) and international agencies are also promoting policies to develop clusters (Roelandt and den Hertog, 1999).

Many national governments are also promoting policies to overcome externalities and to help firms to evolve in the light of economic, social and technical change (e.g. DTI, 1998; Porter and Ketels, 2003). The argument for EU industrial policies in these three areas, as opposed to national or OECD policies rests on a perceived failure by such policy makers to capture externalities by use of national government policies and/or failure to create and implement effective international policies by international agencies. Deregulation and legislation to overcome network externalities and other hindrances to free movement that hampers effective national and/or international industrial policies provide a rationale for EU policies. However, such policies are primarily connected to completing an effective Single European Market that implies a mainly negative industrial policy for the EU.

Negative policies at an international level are also implied by a global approach to deregulation to overcome these problems. Positive or strategic policies at international level are more difficult to justify using a strict economic approach. However, it would be beneficial to seek to develop cooperation with international agencies and national governments outside Europe to overcome the harmful effects on competition by use of positive and strategic industrial policies. This provides a link between industrial policy and the external commercial policy of the EU. Examination of this issue is provided in Chapter 15. There may also be an argument for EU policies to prevent harmful distortions of the market process by competing interventionist and strategic policies in member states. Policies on state aids and attempts to prevent unfair competitive conditions by use of discriminatory taxation systems by member states, suggest that these issues are important considerations in EU policy. But they tend to be internal market policies rather than industrial policies.

These arguments imply that EU industrial policy should be primarily connected to internal market and external economic relations policies. EU industrial policies that replaced or are dominant over the policies of member states or international agencies should only exist in cases where externalities were largely EU-wide, thereby rendering national government policies ineffective. In cases where the externalities spread beyond the frontiers of the EU, international cooperation is required. This may require EU action as the Union often represents member states in negotiations with international agencies on economic matters. This, however, is an external economic relation policy not primarily an industrial policy issue.

If such externalities are not widespread, the rationale for positive EU industrial policies rests on economic and social cohesion arguments, or on attempts to promote political integration by developing the basis for institutional developments to advance the objective of moves towards political union. The first argument presupposes a great deal of agreement on the economic and social goals of the members of the EU and a coherent and effective political framework to create, develop, implement and enforce such industrial policies. It is not evident that such a consensus exists or that the institutional frameworks of the EU can deliver such an outcome. The second argument presupposes a large degree of consensus about the desirability of further political integration by developing more interventionist policies. The enlargement process is likely to reduce the power of both of these drivers of the development of positive industrial policies because the diversity of views and opinions on what is desirable is likely to increase. These two arguments

Figure 6.1 Drivers for EU industrial policy to promote competitiveness

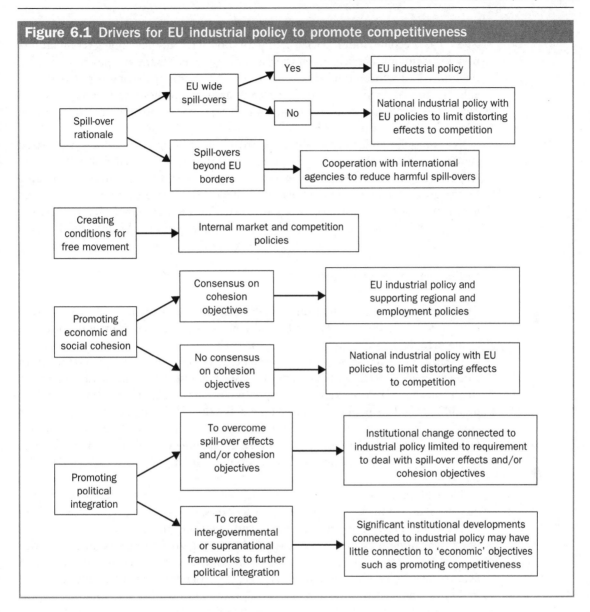

for EU industrial policy seem to be only marginally connected to competitiveness. Indeed, when the focus is on competitiveness, policies normally become more related to negative policies connected to the internal market programme (see Reports of the Competitiveness Council **ue.eu.int/en/summ.htm**).

An outline of the various drivers of EU Industrial Policy to promote competitiveness is shown in Figure 6.1.

There has been a slow but marked change in industrial policy from an interventionist stance towards a more strategic approach. There has also been a move towards horizontal policy with less emphasis on specific industries. However, R&D policies have been heavily geared towards favoured industries such as information and communications technologies (ICT) and biotechnology. The Council of Ministers has become more concerned with obstacles to developing competitiveness by removing barriers to enterprise and by reducing the bureaucratic burden on firms. Notwithstanding this support for a horizontal EU industrial policy to enhance the competitiveness of European-based companies, the Council has also advocated a role for strategic industrial policy geared to promoting certain industries. This issue is discussed below.

EU industrial policy has evolved towards a more horizontal and negative-based stance. However, the strategic rationale for positive industrial policy has been strongly advocated, especially by the Commission. Even EU institutions dominated by the governments of the member states have also promoted strategic objectives based on positive industrial policies for SMEs and for favoured sectors. The encouragement of cooperation in R&D is also a major feature of EU Industrial Policy.

Policies to promote SMEs

The EU adopted a new definition of SMEs in 2003. Three main categories of SMEs have been created – medium-sized, small and micro. The definitions are shown in Table 6.1.

A European Charter for small enterprises was endorsed at the Feira European Council in June 2000 with the aim 'To create the best possible environment for small business and entrepreneurship' (**www.europa.eu.int/scadplus/leg/en/lvb/ n26002.htm**). This policy was based on a belief that SMEs are the driving force for employment growth and innovation. The policy is based on the contemporary fashion to regard entrepreneurship and the development of SMEs as a crucial way to promote a more dynamic and innovative economy (Danson, 1996; Deakin, 2003).

The Charter identifies the commonly agreed obstacles to SME development (e.g. education and training of managers and workers, access to finance, access to help to stimulate innovation and regulatory and taxation burdens). The main method of implementing the objectives of the Charter is to gather evidence on best practice in member states and to encourage national governments to adopt best practice in areas connected to education for enterprise, tax and financial matters and to reduce 'red tape' involved in start-ups and in the running of SMEs. To monitor the progress made to remove these obstacles and to create an environment conducive to increase start-ups of SMEs and to help them to develop, an Annual Implementation Report on the European Charter for Small Enterprises is produced. An annual

Table 6.1 Definitions of SMEs

Enterprise category	Headcount	Turnover	or	Balance sheet total
Medium-sized	< 250	≤ €50 m		≤ €43 m
Small	< 50	≤ €10 m		≤ €10 m
Micro	< 10	≤ €2 m		≤ €2 m

Source: **www.europa.eu.int/comm/enterprise/enterprise_policy/sme_definition/index_en.htm**

report is also prepared on implementation of the Charter in the accession countries (**www.europa.eu.int/scadplus/leg/en/lvb/n26002.htm**).

The entrepreneurial drive of SME owners/managers was also identified as an important factor for regional development and promoting the evolution of new industries. Therefore, programmes to promote conditions conducive to entrepreneurial active have been developed. These programmes are normally linked to information sharing and help to network with other entrepreneurs, especially in other member states. Others are specific programmes to promote particular objectives such as 'helping small and medium-sized enterprises to "go digital"' (**www.europa.eu.int/scadplus/leg/en/lvb/n26003.htm**).

The main method that the EU uses to achieve the objective of promoting a vibrant SME sector has been to set up a host of initiatives and a multiannual programme (**www.europa.eu.int/comm/enterprise/enterprise_policy/mult_entr_programme/ programme_2001_2005.htm**). These initiatives and programmes are mainly geared to sharing information and to preaching the virtues of enterprise. However, on the whole SMEs are not exempt from the flood of EU regulations that impact on the operations of firms. Often the desire to promote an enterprising culture in which SMEs can flourish, plays a secondary role to economic and social cohesion and political integration arguments for interventionist policy developments. Consequently, policy towards SMEs is caught up in the debate on the best methods of achieving industrial policy goals. The official policy towards SMEs is focused on the externality and free movement drivers with a thrust towards lowering bureaucratic and other obstacles to start-ups and the evolution of SMEs. However, other policies, notably in employment, health and safety, corporate social responsibility and environmental areas, which normally impact on SMEs, take a more interventionist stance often based on cohesion and political integration arguments for policy development.

The EU provides regular and detailed reports on matters connected to SMEs. This is done by the Observatory of European SMEs (**www.europa.eu.int/comm/ enterprise/enterprise_policy/analysis/observatory.htm**) and a European Innovation Scoreboard (**trendchart.cordis.lu/Scoreboard2002/index.html**).

The Observatory is composed of decision-makers, academics and SME representatives. Reports and the results of surveys of SMEs in Europe are issued by the Observatory. The reports investigate issues such as the characteristics of SME entrepreneurs, industry and competitiveness indicators and problems associated with bureaucracy, finance and innovation. Reports have also been published on the role of developing clusters to promote innovation and competitiveness. The main policy advocated to achieve this objective is to encourage cooperation by helping to build networks between firms and supporting agencies such as universities, chambers of commerce and local government agencies. The linking of clusters to other similar clusters elsewhere in the EU is also advocated.

A European Innovation Scoreboard has been created with 17 main indicators to indicate performance of the drivers and outputs of innovations. The indicators are divided into four groups: human resources for innovation; creation of new knowledge; transmission and application of knowledge; and innovation finance, outputs and markets. Reports from the Scoreboard suggest that although there has been some progress in improving the conditions under which innovation can flourish in

European SMEs on the whole the environment in the USA is regarded as more conducive to start-ups and innovations.

The Observatory and the Scoreboard, together with other EU reports and programmes, indicate that European SMEs face the same obstacles and challenges as SMEs in all developed economies. Although the various reports suggest that progress is being made to make the business environment more friendly to SMEs they also acknowledge that, compared with the USA, the situation in Europe is less favourable for the development of a dynamic and innovative SME sector. As these reports and programmes originate in the Commission there is little or no mention of the problems caused to SMEs from the large EU legislative programme in areas such as employment, corporate social responsibility and health and safety. Indeed, EU legislation is itself one of the main instigators of new regulations that add to the difficulties of start-ups and evolution of SMEs. An industrial policy that was driven by externality and free movement drivers would place the current EU rhetoric on SMEs into a largely negative-based policy stance that sought to release SMEs from the largely EU-driven regulatory burden. However, cohesion and political integration arguments and a vigorous debate on the nature of the desired capitalist system that the EU should develop, has led to an industrial policy towards SMEs largely based on gathering and disseminating information and preaching the virtues of good practices.

Policies to promote favoured sectors

Notwithstanding the rather weak role of current EU industrial policy as evidenced by policies towards SMEs, European governments do engage in strongly interventionist policies; in some industries such policies are supported or even promoted by the EU. The most notable industry to be subject to such interventionist polices is agriculture (see Chapter 11). However, other industries are also subject to extensive government intervention and support. These industries include defence, aircraft manufacture and many utilities such as gas, electricity and telecommunications. Attempts under the auspices of the internal market programme are being made to liberalise the utilities markets, but many national governments are proving to be very resistant to the opening of theses markets (see Chapter 1). Most defence industries remain outside EU legislation and policy and the EU has actively supported the European Airbus project. The latter is a good example of the promotion of a European champion to provide competition with US producers. Indeed, the success of this project has encouraged a move towards the promotion of European champions in many high-tech industries that are considered to have strategic importance in the challenge of maintaining Europe as a base for high value-added operations that bring growth and high incomes. Defence industries are another area where such European champions are regarded as crucial. Biotechnology, pharmaceutical and (before the Internet-based companies crash in the late 1990s) information communication technologies (ICT) have all received close attention from the Commission, with strong calls to support the development of these industries in Europe.

The Council of Ministers also recommends support for certain industries that it regards as having a key strategic role in the struggle to develop competitiveness among EU-based companies. The wisdom of this approach was to some extent supported in the Report issued in 2003, 'Some key issues of Europe's competitiveness: towards an integrated approach' (**europa.eu.int/comm/enterprise/enterprise_policy/ industry/competitiveness.htm**). The report supports the horizontal approach to EU industrial policy that has developed in the 1990s, but calls for policies in specific areas to aid in the process of adjusting to technical change because of the tendency for relocation of particular manufacturing industries to lower-cost countries outside the EU. The report mentions pharmaceuticals, aerospace, shipbuilding and the automobile industry as areas where policies to help develop or maintain competitiveness is deemed to be important.

This may be the beginning of a move away from a horizontal policy framework to one based on the idea of developing European champions. This has similarities to the old national champions approach that was practised by many European countries in the 1960s and 1970s (Foreman-Peck and Federico, 1999). The main difference is that the objective is to build European champions rather than French or German or British champions. However, the report calls for a continuing effort to reduce the regulatory burden on companies and for progress on legislation that will encourage competitiveness, such as Community Patents Directive, protection of intellectual property rights and a resolution to the European takeover Directive. The need to make progress on removing the remaining barriers to free movement by faster implementation of legislation and policies to complete the internal market (see Chapter 1) is also advocated. Thus, the emphasis is still on horizontal and largely negative EU Industrial Policy. Nevertheless, a tendency towards strategic policies to promote European champions is evident in the report. Measures such as the takeover Directive and the legislation that would ease the development of pan-EU companies are strongly advocated in the report, and would aid in the construction and evolution of European companies that could become champions and in the vanguard of developing competitiveness in the EU.

The industrial policy of the EU has begun to move in the direction of seeking to help the development of European champions, or at least the development of major industries that have a strong European base. This does not preclude operations by multinational corporations, but the desire of many policy makers seems to be to ensure that these multinational corporations have a strong European presence. This policy development has implications for relations with other countries, notably the USA. This issue is taken up in Chapter 15.

Policies to promote innovation

The industrial policy of the EU stresses the importance of promoting innovation among European companies as one of the key objectives of policy (**www.europa.eu.int/scadplus/leg/en/s23000.htm**). This has led to the development of framework policies to promote pan-EU cooperation in R&D and other areas of technological development (**www.europa.eu.int/scadplus/leg/en/lvb/i23012.htm**).

The development of a knowledge-based economy lies at the heart of these framework policies (**www.europa.eu.int/scadplus/leg/en/lvb/n26009.htm**).

The 6th Framework Programme (2003–06) is composed of two parts – a thematic research agenda and structuring the European research area (**www.europa.eu.int/scadplus/leg/en/lvb/i23012.htm**). The total budget for the Programme is €15.95 bn. The thematic section is split into eight areas:

1 Life Sciences, Genomic and Biotechnologies for health (15% of budget).

2 Information Society Technologies (23% of budget).

3 Nanotechnologies, Knowledge-based Multifunctional Materials, New Production Processes (8% of budget).

4 Aeronautics and Space (6% of budget).

5 Food Safety and Risks to Health (4% of budget).

6 Sustainable Development (13% of budget).

7 Citizenship and Governance in a Knowledge-based Society (12% of budget).

8 Other areas (13% of budget).

The structuring of the European research area part of the programme is seeking to build a European research base and accounts for approximately 16 per cent of the budget. The framework programmes are basically attempts to build pan-EU competence in major areas of research and technological developments and to promote a European ethos for such a research base. The framework programmes have elements of seeking to build European champions in the area of research and technological competence. The rationale for this would seem to be closely allied to the political integration driver of policy, as it is not clear that a European research and technological development base is preferable to a global or even a US-orientated base. Clearly, the USA is the technological leader in most of the thematic areas in the 6th Framework, hence linking to US research bases may be a more effective policy. If the objective is to develop European political institutions that foster research and technological development then the framework programmes make sense. However, thus far the EU has not developed audit systems that test for the effectiveness, in terms of output relative to the US research base, of the framework programmes. Moreover, member states' governments maintain their own research and technological development programmes often only marginally linked to the framework programmes.

Conclusion

The EU has developed a treaty basis for industrial policies. The major thrust of the industrial policy since the late 1980s has been on negative policies linked to the creation of the SEM and the development of a common competition policy. The role of the EU in positive industrial policies has been significantly less influential. Industrial policy in the EU has moved away, in most sectors, from the type of interventionist policies that used to dominate in many of the member states in the

1960s and 1970s. However, the desire of some member states to protect some of their industries, and the favoured status of what are regarded as key industries, mean that state aid and/or EU help continues to play an important role in many industries.

Moreover, the increased focus on developing competitiveness has led to the emergence of a new European champions movement. Policies to help companies in specific sectors such as ICT and biotechnology also enhance the vertical dimension of the EU's industrial policy. Nevertheless, there is still a strong focus on horizontal policies that are useful in promoting competitiveness. There are also areas, such as the policy towards SMEs, that are largely based on gathering and disseminating information and preaching good practice. Industrial policy in the EU, like many other EU policies, reflects a multitude of interests and is driven by a complex set of economic and political factors. As such it is not easily understood by a purely economic assessment of its rationale or its performance. Nevertheless, a movement towards a negative and internal market-driven policy framework that emerged in the 1990s seems to be evolving into a more strategically driven policy area connected to a desire to promote competitiveness among European companies. This policy appears to be developing elements of a European champions model and to have as an objective the creation of an institutional system of research and technological development that fosters greater European integration in this area.

References

Bangemann M (1993) *Meeting the Global Challenge*, Kogan Page, London.

Bianchi P (1998) *Industrial Policies and Economic Integration: Learning from European Experience*, Routledge, London.

Buchanan J M (1978) *The Economics of Politics*, Institute of Economic Affairs, London.

Danson M (1996) *Small Firm Foundations and Regional Economic Development*, Routledge, London.

Deakin D (2003) *Entrepreneurship and Small Firms*, McGraw-Hill, London.

Dormer M and Kuyper L (2000) *Industry and the European Union: Analyzing Policies for Business*, Edward Elgar, Cheltenham.

DTI (1998) *Our Competitive Future: Building the Knowledge-driven Economy*, DTI, London.

DTI (2003) *Taking Clusters Forward: The Regional Development Agency (RDA) Clusters Workshop*, DTI, London.

European Commission (1991) *The 21st Report on Competition Policy of the EC*, Brussels.

European Commission (2002) *Final Report of the Expert Group on Enterprise Clusters and Networks*, Enterprise Directorate General, Brussels.

Foreman-Peck J and Federico G (1999) *European Industrial Policy: The Twentieth-Century Experience*, Oxford University Press, Oxford.

Johnson P (2003) *Industries in Europe: Competition Trends and Policy Issues*, Edward Elgar, Cheltenham.

Krugman P and Obstfeld M (1991) *International Economics, Theory and Policy*, HarperCollins, New York.

Lawton T (1999) *European Industrial Policy: Concepts and Instruments*, Macmillan, Basingstoke.

McNaughton R and Brown P (2002) 'Review of Literature on Clusters and Competitiveness' in R McNaughton and M Green (eds) *Global Competition and Local Networks*, Ashgate, Aldershot.

Navarro L (2003) *Industrial Policy in the Economic Literature: Recent Theoretical Developments and Implications for EU Policy*, Enterprise Papers No. 12, Enterprise Directorate-General, Office for the Official Publications of the European Communities, Luxembourg.

North D (1990) *Institutions, Institutional Change and Economic Performance*, Cambridge University Press, Cambridge.

Porter M (1990) *The Competitive Advantage of Nations*, Macmillan, London.

Porter M (1998) 'Clusters and the New Economics of Competition', *Harvard Business Review*, Vol. 76, pp. 77–90.

Porter M (2000) 'Location, Competition and Economic Development', *Economic Development Quarterly*, Vol. 14, pp. 23–32.

Porter M and Ketels C (2003) *UK Competitiveness: Moving to the Next Stage*, DTI, London.

Pyke G, Becattini G and Senbenberger W (1990) *Industrial Districts and Inter-firm Co-operation in Italy*, International Institute for Labour Studies, Geneva.

Roelandt T and den Hertog P (1999) *Boosting Innovation: The Cluster Approach*, OECD, Paris.

Saxenian A (1994) *Regional Advantage: Culture and Competition in Silicon Valley and Route 128*, Harvard University Press, Cambridge, Mass.

Swann P, Prevezer M and Stout D (1998) *The Dynamics of Industrial Clustering: International Comparisons in Computing and Biotechnology*, Oxford University Press, Oxford.

Tyson L (1992) *Who's Bashing Whom?: Trade Conflict in High-technology Industries*, Longman, London.

Worthington I (2003) *The Business Environment*, Financial Times/Prentice-Hall, Harlow.

Chapter 7

Social policy

Stephen Dearden

Introduction

This chapter outlines the evolution of the Community's social policy beginning with the social Articles of the Treaty of Rome, which included the establishment of the European Social Fund. Although a number of Directives were adopted in the 1970s on various aspects of employees' rights, it was the passage of the Single European Act that gave new impetus to the evolution of EU social policies, which continued with the Social Charter and the Maastricht Treaty on European Union.

Central to these developments, however, has been the debate on whether action should extend beyond the immediate needs of the establishment of an internal market. Concern had been voiced that an unregulated internal labour market would undermine the competitive position of those member states who have relatively high wages and social security, and that the additional stresses of the structural transformation required by the Single European Market (SEM), both for individual employees and for industries, required an explicit commitment to policies necessary to maintain 'social cohesion'. The dramatic increase in unemployment across Europe that began in the late 1970s, and that has persisted ever since, has sharpened the polarisation between those who advocate the primacy of market forces and the need for flexible labour markets and those who support an interventionist or corporatist approach to economic and social policy.

The chapter covers six main issues. It begins with a brief review of the major trends in the European labour market and then traces the development of EU social policy up to the Single European Act. It then examines the problem of social dumping and wage flexibility, and reviews those policies intended to foster 'social cohesion'. Having considered the development of the European dimension of industrial relations, embodied in the 'social dialogue', it finally turns to a review of the major elements of the EU's current social policy.

The European labour market

In 2002, of the 375 million population of the EU15 some 170 million were economically active, either employed or unemployed. The overall labour force activity rate of 69 per cent has remained constant for twenty years and is lower than that of either the USA or Japan at 77 per cent. However trends in the activity rates of men and women have differed significantly. While male activity rates have fallen steadily from 89 per cent in 1975 to 78 per cent in 2002, female activity rates have risen over the same period from 46 per cent to 61 per cent. The increased activity rates of adult women, combined with population growth, has led to the number of women in the EU labour force increasing by 6 million between 1991 and 2000, while the number of men remained unchanged. Activity rates have fallen for both sexes for those younger than 25 years old, accompanied by higher rates of participation in education and training. By 2000, 51 per cent of 18–24 year olds were still in education, of whom 16 per cent worked part-time.

Over the period 1980–93 the number of jobs generated in the EU had increased by less than 0.5 per cent pa compared with an increase in employment of 1.5 per cent pa in the USA and 1 per cent pa in Japan. In the recession of the early 1990s 5 million jobs were lost and it was not until 1995 that employment in the EU increased for the first time since 1991. By 1995 the employment rate (total employment as a percentage of the population aged 15–64) was 60 per cent, compared with 65 per cent in 1973, and in contrast to the 73 per cent employment rate in the USA and 74 per cent in Japan. Over the next five years it increased by only another 3 per cent with the creation of 10 million new jobs. Over the period 1995–2000 employment creation was strongest for women, with a net additional 6.2 million jobs, but this was dominated by part-time employment. By 2002 part-time employment represented 18 per cent of total employment, and one-third of all employment for women. In common with other mature economies, most jobs in the EU in recent decades have been created in the service sector. Between 1995 and 2000 40 per cent of new jobs were created in health care, education and social work, 25 per cent in general business services and 10 per cent in IT. By 2002 71 per cent of employment was in the service sectors. By contrast employment in agriculture had declined to only 4.1 per cent, in comparison with 23 per cent in 1960. Even industry has seen a significant reduction in its importance, from 40 per cent of all employment in 1960 to only 25 per cent in 2002.

The rate of population growth, migration, changes in participation or activity rates and the rate of net job creation will all have contributed to the observed unemployment trend. It is the persistence of high unemployment rates across Europe that has now become a major challenge to all EU governments. In 1970 EC12 unemployment was only 2.4 per cent, by 1994 it had peaked at 11.3 per cent in the EU15, and has only slowly recovered to 7.7 per cent (8.9 per cent EU25) in 2003, a rate twice as high as in the USA (see Figure 7.1). Recovery from the recession of the early 1990s has not been fully reflected in employment growth. Unemployment is particularly concentrated among the young. While the difference between youth (15–24 years old) and adult unemployment rates narrowed in the 1980s it widened again in the 1990s recession and is still double that of adults at 16 per cent (see Figure 7.2). In terms of the long-term unemployed, half of those unemployed for more than a year were still unemployed a year later – a similar percentage to that of ten years earlier. Unemployment also varies considerably from state to state; ranging from 2.1 per cent in Luxembourg in 2003, to 11.3 per cent in Spain (EU25: 20 per cent, Poland; 19 per cent, Slovakia; 18 per cent, Bulgaria) (see Figure 7.3). But in recent years those states with the highest unemployment rates (e.g.

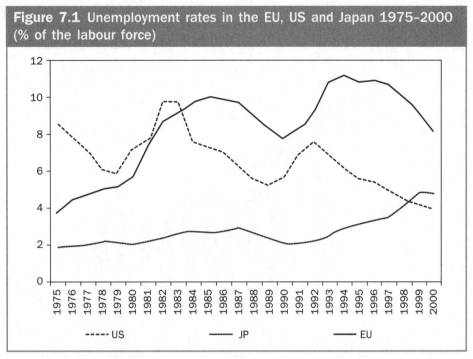

Figure 7.1 Unemployment rates in the EU, US and Japan 1975–2000 (% of the labour force)

Source: Employment in Europe, 2000

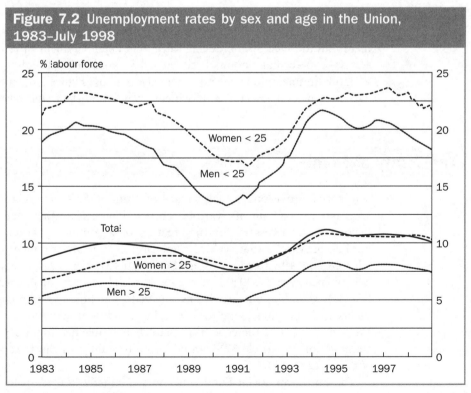

Figure 7.2 Unemployment rates by sex and age in the Union, 1983–July 1998

Source: Employment in Europe, 1998

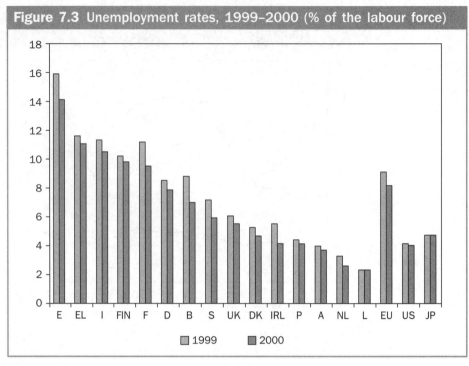

Figure 7.3 Unemployment rates, 1999–2000 (% of the labour force)

Source: Employment in Europe, 2000

Spain, France, Belgium and Ireland) have also experienced the most rapid improvement. But the success in reducing the gap in unemployment rates between member states – 5 percentage points between 1995 and 2000 – disguises the considerable variation in unemployment rates between regions (Figure 7.4), which reflects their variation in service sector employment growth and their skill base.

The Treaty of Rome

The social provisions of the Treaty of Rome (1957) are relatively limited and scattered throughout its various parts. Nonetheless, they extend to concerns beyond those necessary for the creation of a common market. The Treaty has binding provisions that seek to establish freedom of movement of workers (Articles 48 and 49), freedom of establishment (Articles 52–58), equal pay for men and women (Article 119) and rights to social security of migrant workers (Article 51). Non-binding provisions covered paid holidays (Article 120), commitments to improving living and working conditions (Articles 117 and 118) and the laying down of the general principles for implementing a common vocational training policy (Article 128). In addition it established the European Social Fund (Articles 123–128).

The European Social Fund (ESF) was originally limited to localised retraining and resettlement, to providing financial support to the temporarily unemployed

Figure 7.4 Unemployment rates by region, 1996

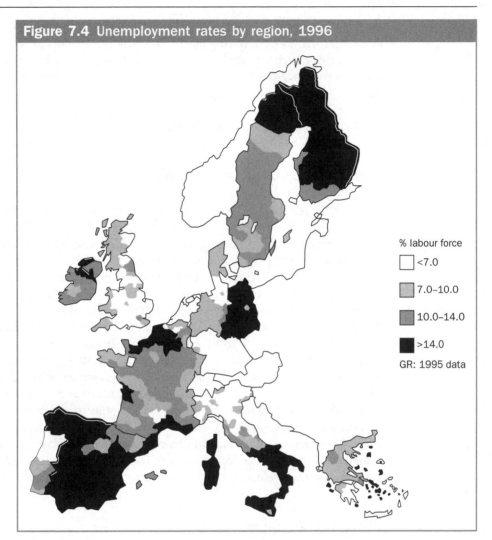

% labour force
<7.0
7.0–10.0
10.0–14.0
>14.0
GR: 1995 data

Source: *Employment in Europe* (European Commission, 1996b)

and to issues associated with migrant workers. However, in 1971 the role and operation of the Fund underwent significant reform. Its financing was switched from levies on member states to the Community's own resources, and it was set two broad objectives: first, to address the employment problems arising from the implementation of Community policies and, secondly, to help overcome the structural problems experienced by certain regions or target groups, i.e. migrant workers, young job seekers, women and the handicapped. To achieve these objectives 90 per cent of the Fund's resources were allocated to vocational training.

In response to the increase in unemployment in Europe in the 1970s the ESF was quadrupled. The increase in unemployment and the lack of a clear set of objectives led, in 1983, to a simplification and concentration of ESF activities. The measures to alleviate youth unemployment received 75 per cent of the ESF budget, and 40 per cent of the remaining general fund was allocated to the depressed regions of the Community (e.g. Greece, Northern Ireland, Eire, Mezzogiorno). Other employment measures adopted during the 1970s included attempts to coordinate national employment policies, with the exchange of information and research, and Resolutions on training schemes for the young, information technology and vocational training. In 1975 the European Centre for the Development of Vocational Training (CEDEFOP) was created to disseminate information on training, and to promote good practice throughout the Community.

Harmonisation of working conditions

Although the remit of the Treaty of Rome was relatively narrow in this area a number of directives were adopted covering: collective redundancies (1975); employee rights in the event of company takeovers (1977) or insolvency (1980); equal pay (1975); equal access to employment and vocational training (1976) and social security (1986). In 1974 an Advisory Committee on Safety, Hygiene and Health Protection at Work was established, leading to a series of Safety at Work Directives, and in 1975 the European Foundation for the Improvement of Living and Working Conditions was created to provide information on employment conditions. As with CEDEFOP it is administered by a quadripartite Board composed of representatives of the Commission, employers, workers and member governments. Non-binding recommendations for the introduction of a 40-hour week and a minimum four weeks' paid holiday (1975) were also adopted, together with a call for the examination of the potential for reorganising working time through early retirement and reduction in overtime working. However, the generally deteriorating economic situation, the widening of internal differences following the second enlargement of the Community and changes in government (especially in the UK) led to a period of inactivity in the development of a Community social policy during the early 1980s.

The Single European Act

With the passage of the Single European Act (SEA) in 1987 much broader social issues were addressed, with a commitment to the harmonisation of national provisions in regard to health, safety, environmental and consumer protection (Articles 100a and 118a), and to policies fostering 'the economic and social cohesion of the Community' (Articles 130a–130e). Although Article 100a introduced Qualified Majority Voting (QMV) to overcome the blocking power of individual member states, this is confined to those measures essential for the establishment of the SEM, i.e. health and safety legislation. Thus proposals relating to the free movement of people and employees' rights remained subject to member state veto. Article 118a also restricted proposed legislation in that it required it to take into account existing national conditions and regulations, and to ensure that they do not impose administrative and financial burdens on enterprises. Article 118b also committed the Community to the encouragement of a 'social dialogue' between management and labour, i.e. the creation of a European dimension to industrial relations. This non-binding provision yielded little success and underlined the difficulties of achieving progress in those social areas that went beyond those minimum conditions essential to the completion of the SEM.

The Single European Market

With the commitment to the completion of the SEM by 1992, and the passage of the SEA, interest was rekindled in the social implications of EU policies.

The movement towards the SEM was recognised as having implications for employment throughout the Community. Changes in costs and relative prices, and stimulation of new technology and economic growth, were all factors which would determine the employment consequences of the Single Market. Econometric studies, although based upon some heroic assumptions, suggested a positive impact upon most EU economies. However, the consequences for employment remained the most ambiguous. Nonetheless a study by DG II did identify those industries and regions most likely to be affected by the completion of the SEM (European Commission, 1985). The industries were usually characterised by state ownership or were dependent upon the state as principal customer. They included telecommunication equipment, computers and office equipment, shipbuilding, railway equipment, iron and steel and pharmaceuticals. In the tertiary sector financial services were likely to be particularly affected by the development of a single financial market.

The SEM was also expected to have a differential regional impact (see Chapter 8). The expected enhancement of economic growth would not benefit all regions equally. Even before the structural changes arising from enhanced economic integration, regional disparities within Europe had increased. This had resulted from the general deterioration in employment conditions since the mid-1970s and from the second enlargement. A region's competitiveness is likely to be influenced by a number of factors: first, the qualifications and skill mix of the labour force, which might be undermined by outward migration, and, secondly, the infrastructure, estimated to be 40–60 per cent below the EU average standard in some regions. Finally, labour costs – differences in labour productivity are often greater than differences in wage levels and the further harmonisation of wage levels with economic integration would continue to undermine the competitive position of some regions. Two types of area were therefore identified as being particularly vulnerable to structural problems – the underdeveloped mainly rural areas and the regions where declining heavy industries were concentrated.

However, concern has also been expressed that particular social problems would emerge from the completion of the SEM across all of the EU. These arguments have focused upon two issues – illicit work (moonlighting) and social dumping.

Illicit work

Illicit work concerns work outside formal labour markets and tax and social security systems and is most frequent among those who are already employed. It is thought to be concentrated in the professions, domestic services, agricultural work and vehicle repairs, and among skilled manual workers in construction. It is also estimated to be twice as prevalent in the southern states of the Community, reflecting differences in the structure of the local economies, levels of taxation, cultural attitudes and the effectiveness of official controls. Studies suggest that 25 per cent of Spain's labour force works in its informal or 'black' economy, 30 per cent in Greece, 18–28 per cent in Portugal and 25 per cent in France. This is of concern within the single market since it distorts the operation of the labour market and competitiveness. Those firms within the Community that employ labour illicitly will reduce their labour costs and gain a competitive advantage, allowing them to displace those firms that finance the social security systems and adhere to established employment and safety regulations. Therefore the Commission has taken a number of actions to attempt to minimise the occurrence of illicit employment. It has sought effective compliance in public contracts to national and EU standards, close attention to sub-contracting arrangements and the monitoring of cross-frontier activities. The Commission has also pursued the adoption of common administrative 'standards' for taxation and social security contributions across both regions and forms of employment (e.g. part-time, temporary workers).

Social dumping

Social dumping expresses the concern that employment will be lost in those states whose higher social standards are reflected in higher average labour costs. Faced with loss of market shares and firm relocation, there will be downward pressure upon social conditions (i.e. wages, social security, minimum labour standards, etc.). There is some evidence that during the 1990s Austria, Belgium, Denmark, France, West Germany and the Netherlands, all countries with above average social security expenditure, moved closer to the international trend line (Alber and Standing, 2000). This fear has led to demands for minimum wage levels, social security provisions and minimum health and safety guarantees to avoid competitive pressure reducing employment standards to unacceptably low levels. However, it has been argued that concern about social dumping is misplaced. It is pointed out that it is not a new phenomena but predates the completion of the SEM. Wage costs are not the only determinant of competitiveness but must be considered within the context of relative productivity, with human and physical capital allowing high wage sectors to maintain their competitive advantage.

It can also be shown that, theoretically, high levels of social security contributions, by either employer or employee, need have no effect upon competitiveness as long as wages are completely flexible (see Exhibits 7.1 and 7.2).

Wage flexibility

The only problem arises in a situation where wages are not downwardly flexible. Studies (Coe and Gagliardi, 1985; Bean, 1994; Dearden, 1995b) have suggested that European labour markets tend to be characterised by a relatively high degree of real wage rigidity and that this inflexibility increased in the 1980s, despite increasing

Exhibit 7.1 Social security financed by employees

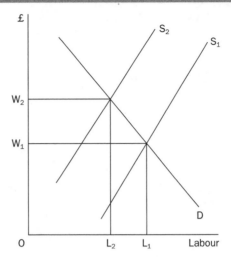

Here all of the social security benefits are financed by payroll contributions by the employee. With employment at L_1 and wages at W_1, the imposition of a payroll contribution on employees is equivalent to a reduction in the net wage offered. However, this fall in the net wage also shifts the supply curve of labour from S_1 to S_2. The equilibrium wage paid by employers now increases to W_2 and employment falls to L_2. But if workers regard the social security benefits that they now receive as part of their total wage package, and it is fully taken into account in their labour supply decision, then the supply curve will shift back to S_1, with wages and employment returning to their original level. Of course, not all social security benefits may be regarded as part of the remuneration package (e.g. maternity benefits to a single man), in which case the labour supply curve will shift only part of the way back to its original position. Nevertheless, the more inelastic the initial labour supply curve, the less impact this disregard of social security benefits will have on employment and wages.

levels of unemployment. However, the Commission expected increasing economic integration, induced by the SEM, to enhance wage flexibility as more competitive product markets increased the elasticity of firms' demand for labour. However, economic integration and monetary union may also increase workers' awareness of comparative rates of pay and conditions of employment across the Community. There is already some evidence that workers' expectations are rising in Spain, Greece and Ireland (European Commission, 1991), while Portugal's 1991 'social pact' linked wage increases to the ECU value of the Escudo and to the relative performance of productivity.

Real wage flexibility can also be achieved by increases in national price levels, while money wages remain constant; but this will undermine international competitiveness unless it is possible to devalue the currency. As the Community moved towards a full monetary union such adjustments became impossible; employment may shift to the low cost regions of the Community, creating a competitive downward pressure upon all wages in the Community. This argument has been challenged on a number of grounds. It has been argued that it is relative unit labour costs, which also reflect variations in the productivity of labour, which are more significant.

Exhibit 7.2 Social security financed by employers

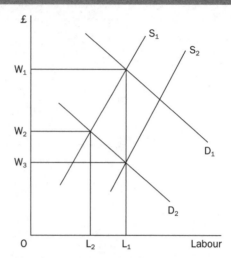

In a social security system financed solely by employers we again begin with an equilibrium wage at W_1 and employment at L_1. Social security contributions are now imposed upon the employer equal to the vertical distance D_1D_2, reducing labour demand to D_2. With labour supply at S_1 the equilibrium wage falls to W_2 and employment to L_2. But again, if employees regard the social security entitlements as part of their total wages, they will respond by raising their total supply of labour in response to the increased value of their remuneration package, i.e. labour supply increases from S_1 to S_2. This returns employment to its previous level at L_1, and lowers the firm's wage rate to W_3. The difference between the original wage rate W_1 and the new lower wage W_3 is equal to the cost to the employer of the social security contribution. Thus the social security tax has been shifted on to the employee, and therefore the firm experiences no loss of profit, nor increase in total labour costs, and no change in its relative competitive position.

Wage costs alone are unlikely to be the major factor in location decisions, except in the case of labour intensive industries. It has also been pointed out that it is this very process of relocation to low wage areas that is the market adjustment mechanism for spreading the benefits of economic growth throughout the Community.

Nevertheless, critics of the 'market forces' approach have also warned of the possibility of cumulative economic divergence as the poorer regions, especially in the southern and eastern member states, find themselves specialising in labour intensive, low wage, low productivity industries where they already face intense competition from the newly industrialising Asian economies.

The differences in labour costs faced by firms operating across the EU arises not only from differences in member states' social security systems, but also from the variation in other elements of the fixed labour costs that firms face. These non-wage costs include the extent of paid holidays, paid sick leave, benefits in kind (e.g. subsidised mortgages, canteens, sports facilities, cars) and redundancy pay. These emerge from collective bargaining and express employees' preferences, reflecting the influence of such factors as the adequacy of state schemes, the structure of the national tax system and countries' cultural characteristics.

In 1992 non-wage labour costs in industry were approximately 30 per cent of total labour costs in France, Italy and Belgium, 25 per cent in Portugal, Spain and the Netherlands, but only 13 per cent in the United Kingdom and 4 per cent in Denmark (European Commission, 1995). High fixed labour costs create competitive pressures to substitute part-time workers when some of these fixed costs can be avoided. This has already been observed in the northern member states of the EU. By 2000 44 per cent of the women who were employed in the UK were working part-time and 70 per cent in the Netherlands. However, female part-time working remains only 17 per cent in Spain, 16 per cent in Italy and 8 per cent in Greece. Overall in the Community 33 per cent of women are employed part-time, in contrast to 6 per cent of men (European Commission, 2001). To eliminate these 'distortions to competition' and casualisation of part of the labour force, the Commission has prepared a number of 'atypical workers' Directives, extending to employees on short-term and part-time contracts the same entitlements to holiday pay, redundancy pay, etc., as full-time workers.

Social cohesion

The negotiations leading to the adoption of the European Community Charter on the Fundamental Social Rights for Workers (the Social Charter) at the Strasbourg summit in December 1989 brought into sharp focus the fundamental divisions between those advocating an interventionist regulatory role for the Community in the social area and those who argue for the primacy of market forces and a laissez-faire approach (see Addison and Siebert, 1993; Rhodes, 1992). The latter were most clearly represented by the UK government, who failed to support the adoption of the Social Charter, and two years later demanded an opt-out from the Social Protocol of the Treaty on European Union (TEU). However, the Union of Industrial and Employers' Confederation of Europe (UNICE) has also resisted the extension of labour market regulation beyond that necessary to ensure fair competition under the SEM.

Proponents of unregulated labour markets, with freely negotiated labour contracts, regard them as providing both economic efficiency in allocating labour and a wide variety of pay and conditions to meet individual workers' preferences. Attempts to impose uniform conditions, such as minimum wages, holiday entitlements, redundancy protection, etc., will impose additional costs upon firms. In response, companies will substitute capital, part-time workers or more skilled workers for their low productivity unskilled employees whose employment costs have now risen, and for whom such regulation was principally intended to benefit.

An alternative view is that such attempts at regulation will encourage the emergence of dual labour markets, a regulated high wage high productivity sector, and an unregulated low wage unskilled sector offering unstable employment. This 'insider-outsider' problem is already found in many member states. In Spain and Greece high levels of youth unemployment and the increase in the amount of part-time employment are blamed upon the existence of tightly regulated procedures for the recruitment and dismissal of full-time workers. A recent study by Morton and Siebert (1997) of personnel policies in five multinational companies, with plants across the EU, found evidence that the plants in the more deregulated UK labour market employed workers with less prior experience, shorter tenure and more age variation. Although this suggested that in the UK employment was more open to 'outsiders' there was also evidence that employees in UK plants worked more over-time, had less generous holiday entitlements and had a higher turnover. Regulation in the EU might thus only benefit existing workers at the expense of those wishing to enter the labour market.

The emergence of dual labour markets could become a major problem for ensur-ing fair competition across the Community. Already member states vary in their ability and willingness to enforce Community, and even national, regulations, the enhanced competitive environment of the 1980s having encouraged a shift to deregulation. The simple 'social dumping' argument of differential social security provisions leading firms to relocate to the lower cost regions of the Community can also be seen as a variant of the 'insider-outsider' phenomenon, as both employers and employees in the high cost member states, such as Germany, attempt to defend their existing conditions from competition. However, it has already been observed that increasing economic integration, far from encouraging such relocation to un-derdeveloped low cost regions, may actually reinforce the advantages of the high productivity areas. Under these conditions of 'cumulative divergence' an interven-tionist social policy is more easily justified. It might be argued that such intervention should confine itself to the supply-side policy of enhancing vocational training, but the general conditions of employment that an employee faces are likely to influence the decision as to whether to invest in human capital. Improving conditions through EU regulation may raise employee morale and therefore productivity, and may also reduce staff turnover. High turnover imposes substantial recruitment and training costs upon firms and they will be unwilling to incur any additional costs, by further investment in their employees, unless there is an expectation of a long-term com-mitment by their labour force. Thus, imposing improved employment conditions may complement, rather than inhibit, the transformation of the low productivity industries and regions of the Community.

Certainly the Commission views the creation of social cohesion as essential to realising the benefits of an integrated European economy. The Social Charter represented a broad statement of the principles that were to achieve this objective.

The Social Charter

Building upon the objective of improving the living and working conditions embodied in the Treaty of Rome, and consolidated in the SEA, both the Eco-nomic and Social Committee and the European Parliament called for an explicit political commitment to fundamental social rights. Existing international agree-ments, such as the ILO Convention, have not been fully ratified by all member states and are regarded as inadequate in providing for the needs of the success-ful creation of the SEM. Thus the Social Charter (see Box 7.1) addressed both the conditions necessary for the completion of the SEM, and attempted to create

Box 7.1 The Social Charter

The Social Charter includes the following commitments:

1 Improvements in Living and Working Conditions

'The development of a single European Labour market must result in an improvement in the living and working conditions of workers within the EC.' To avoid downward pressure upon these conditions a number of issues must be addressed including the form of employment contracts (e.g. temporary, seasonal, part-time) and the organisation of working hours. There is a specific call for the establishment of a maximum working week. In addition procedures relating to collective redundancies and bankruptcies should be addressed.

2 The Right to Freedom of Movement

The establishment of the right to equal treatment with any other EC national in regard to the practice of any trade or occupation, access to training, rights to social security and residence.

3 Employment and Remuneration

All employment must be fairly remunerated, established either through law or collective agreement, with particular attention to those workers not subject to the 'normal' employment contract of indefinite duration. Wages may not be withheld, except in conformity with national regulations, but 'in no case may an employed person be deprived of the means necessary for subsistence'.

4 The Right to Social Protection

'Subject to the arrangements proper to each Member State, any citizen of the EC is entitled to adequate social protection', i.e. social security or a minimum wage.

5 The Right to Freedom of Association and Collective Bargaining

'Every employer and every worker has the right to belong freely to the professional and trade union organisation of their choice.' For a worker, this entails the right to choose whether or not to belong to a trade union and the right to strike. Procedures for conciliation and mediation between the two sides of industry should be encouraged, and contractual relations established at the European level if it is deemed desirable.

6 The Right to Vocational Training

'Every worker has the right to continue their vocational training throughout their working life.' Both public and private bodies should establish continuing and permanent training schemes and provide leave for training purposes.

7 The Right of Men and Women to Equal Treatment

8 The Right to Information, Consultation and Worker Participation

To be developed 'along appropriate lines and in such a way as to take into account the legal provisions, contractual agreements and practices in force in the Member States.'

9 The Right to Health Protection and Safety at Work

10 The Protection of Children and Adolescents

The minimum working age must be set at 16 years, and those over this age shall receive fair remuneration, and for a period of two years shall be entitled to vocational training in working hours.

11 Elderly Persons

Shall receive an income that guarantees a decent standard of living.

12 Disabled Persons

To ensure their fullest possible integration in working life measures must be taken in respect of training, integration and rehabilitation, complemented by action to improve accessibility, mobility, transport and housing.

the social guarantees that the Commission regarded as essential to maintain broad political support for these developments. It should be noted that the Social Charter has no legal status, and many of the rights are qualified so as to accommodate existing national practices. Nonetheless, the Social Charter remains important in that it provided the underpinning for the implementation of a 47-point Social Action Programme (SAP)(COM(89)568). But of these 47 proposals only 28 involved binding Directives or Regulations – ten covering occupational health and safety, three improvements in living and working conditions and two equal opportunities.

Many of the measures in the Social Action Programme were merely a continuation of existing developments aimed at fostering worker mobility within the Community, enhancing training provision and establishing common health and safety requirements. However, some proposals were more controversial and faced strong opposition from the UK government and the European employers. These included three 'atypical worker' Directives, extending to part-time and fixed-term workers the same entitlements as those enjoyed by full-time workers; a Directive establishing minimum employment conditions for young people; three Directives on collective redundancies, written contracts of employment and restrictions on working hours; and a Directive establishing minimum paid maternity leave.

In the case of the most controversial aspects of the Social Charter the Commission has proposed only non-binding Opinions and recommendations. Thus, under the SAP the rights to freedom of association, collective bargaining and to strike have been compromised by being made subject to national 'traditions' (EIRR, 1990). Similarly the discussion about the introduction of an EU-wide minimum wage has been replaced by reference to a Commission Opinion as to 'fair wages', i.e. wages sufficient to maintain a satisfactory standard of living.

However, the Commission has made progress with the working hours, maternity and young workers Directives by a broad interpretation of the Health and Safety Articles of the SEA (Art. 118a), allowing qualified majority voting to overcome UK opposition. After an unsuccessful challenge before the ECJ the Working Time Directive (93/104/EC) has been extended to the UK and now sets minimum daily and weekly rest periods, an entitlement to three weeks' annual paid holidays and 48-hour maximum working week (except by voluntary agreement) across the Community.

Of the three 'atypical' workers Directives the least controversial – extending health and safety protection to temporary staff – was accepted for implementation by the end of 1992 (91/383/EEC). The two remaining proposed Directives would have established equal treatment and set minimum standards for 'atypical workers' employed for more than eight hours per week in regard to access to vocational training, statutory social security and occupational benefits, but they were initially blocked at the Council of Ministers.

Since 85 per cent of all part-time jobs across the EU are held by women, the employment conditions of 'atypical' workers and issues of sex discrimination have become intertwined. Thus a succession of ECJ decisions has established equal treatment for part-time workers in access to and benefits from occupational pension schemes, severance pay or sick leave schemes.

The Agreement on Social Policy

An alternative route for the development of social policy in the Community became available with the adoption of the Social Protocol, part of the TEU agreed at Maastricht in 1991. Within this Protocol is an Agreement on Social Policy, which allowed only eleven of the member states (excluding the UK) to adopt new procedures in the formulation and application of the EU's social policy. It extended qualified majority voting (QMV) to measures covering health and safety, working conditions, information and consultation of workers, equality and the integration of the unemployed. Unanimity is still required for those measures affecting social security and social protection, redundancy, employee representation, immigrant workers and the financing of job creation. The Agreement also provides for a central role for employers' and workers' organisations in the formulation of proposals for legislation (Article 4).

So far the Agreement procedure has been used to adopt three pieces of legislation – the European Works Council, 'atypical work' contracts and Parental Leave Directives. The latter emerged from negotiations between UNICE, CEEP (European Centre for Enterprises with Public Participation) and the ETUC (European Trade Union Confederation) and offers unpaid leave, for both men and women, for a period of up to three months.

The social dialogue

The Social Action Programme associated with the Social Charter had sought the 'continuation and development of dialogue with the social partners' and consideration of the need for collective agreements at the European level. Nevertheless, there is debate about the need to establish a European framework for industrial relations.

As before, there is a conflict between the 'corporatists', who see it as an important dimension in the creation of 'social cohesion' at the European level, and the neo-liberals, who see it as a threat to the economic efficiency of free labour markets. For the latter, efficiency demands flexibility for management in the determination of pay, employment contracts and hiring and firing, i.e. 'the right to manage'. The Union of Industrial and Employers' Confederations of Europe (UNICE) had sought to defend this flexibility by opposing any EU measure that encouraged the emergence of a European dimension to collective bargaining. In addition they had emphasised the significant obstacles that the EU faced in this area, given the substantial variation in collective bargaining traditions across the member states. In particular, the frameworks of industrial relations in each state vary in their emphasis upon rights embodied in legislation or acquired through collective bargaining. Thus in the UK the existing legal framework is limited to immunities, not specific rights. With the loss of trade union membership and consequent weakening of collective bargaining, a highly 'flexible' labour market had been created. By contrast German industrial relations have remained 'corporatist' and in Italy large firms continue to face substantial legal constraints upon their hiring and firing activities.

However, both sides of industry have been involved in the development of Community social policy from its inception. Thus the Economic and Social Committee was established under the Treaty of Rome. But its influence to date has been limited as it covers too broad an area. Since 1972 the 189-member Committee has had the right to draw up opinions on all questions relating to Community economic and social policy, but it remains advisory. Nonetheless it is able to call upon independent experts and is often a source of technical expertise, and has occasionally, as in the Beretta Report on the social aspects of the SEM, made a significant contribution. Two further groups of Committees brought together employers and employees. The Advisory Committees commented on Commission proposals in the areas of vocational training, freedom of movement of workers, social security for workers, safety, hygiene and health protection. The second group were Sectoral Joint Committees, covering industries such as railways, sea fishing, road and maritime transport. However, in 1996 the Commission (1996a) was highly critical of the effectiveness of this group of Committees, finding the sectoral bodies rarely consulted and 'often unable to give their opinions until after the Commission has adopted the text in question'. Thus in 1998 it decided to replace these Joint Committees and informal groups with twenty-five Sectoral Social Dialogue Committees, with extended powers, and to create liason forums. The Sectoral Committees have produced a large number of joint 'texts' (declarations, resolutions, recommendations), but there are far fewer binding agreements and most 'texts' are targeted at the Community rather than being reciprocal undertakings.

The European Trade Union Confederation (ETUC) had begun to press for the need for the development of an active social policy in the late 1960s and in response the first Quadripartite Conference, involving representatives of the Commission, Ministries of Labour, employers and employees, was held in Luxembourg in 1970. This lead in turn to the creation of the Standing Committee on Employment, composed of representatives of the Commission, Council, employers and trade unions. The ETUC and the employers associations have recently proposed widening its role to examine the Community's overall economic and social policy.

From 1974 to 1978 conferences were held annually, but at the 1978 meeting the ETUC expressed its concern at the lack of evidence of any positive results from the meetings. Although the Commission drew up proposals, adopted by the Council in June 1980, no conferences have been held since. Instead a more informal system of meetings between the social partners and the 'troika' of Heads of Government, with the Employment and Social Affairs Council and the ECB, has recently been adopted. Following the Cologne European Council in 1999 a 'macroeconomic dialogue' was set up to improve the coordination between wage trends and monetary, budget and tax policies.

However, a formal Standing Committee on Employment continues to survive. Its deliberations precede decisions by the competent institutions, and it provides a forum for consultation and discussion between the Council, Commission and the two sides of industry ('tripartite concertation'). Until 1974 it focused upon reform of the ESF, but its agenda was widened to include unemployment, reorganisation of working time and youth unemployment. Since 1980 it has also considered new technology and long-run unemployment and now provides a forum for discussion of the Community's broader economic and employment policies. The Committee, however, remains purely consultative.

By the early 1980s the ETUC was expressing increasing dissatisfaction at the lack of progress, and the relationship between the employers and trade unions reached their lowest ebb when employers' opposition ensured the freezing by the Council of the 'Vredeling Directive' on worker consultation in 1986. This proposed Directive had already been substantially revised in response to the comments of the European Parliament and the Economic and Social Committee, and had begun its fruitless journey six years before.

An attempt was made to overcome this impasse by Jacques Delors, who presented an action plan, including the commitment to the completion of the SEM, at the 1984 Fontainebleau Summit. To revive the 'social dialogue' a meeting was held in November 1985 at Val Duchesse, which led to the creation of the Social Dialogue Committee and three working groups, examining macroeconomics, the labour market and training.

More recently some dissent emerged among the national associations within UNICE as to its uniformly hostile approach to EU attempts at fostering a 'social dialogue'. Belgium, Dutch and Italian employers argued that an active involvement in European social policy-making would be more productive than outright hostility, especially when faced with the threat of Directives being imposed. As a result UNICE shifted its policy stance and in November 1991 it reached agreement with the ETUC that they should participate in the Social Agreement consultation procedure of the Maastricht Treaty (Articles 137 and 138). Under these Articles the Commission is required to consult both sides of industry before submitting proposals in the social field. A member state could also entrust implementation of an EU Directive to management and labour if both 'social partners' requested it. But more importantly, if the EU decides to legislate in an area, then UNICE, CEEP and the ETUC have a nine-month period in which to negotiate either a collective agreement on the matter or formulate a draft Directive for approval by the Council of Ministers. Further, the 'social partners' may themselves initiate negotiations on Community-wide contracts, which, if they fall within ten policy categories defined in the Social Agreement, may be implemented by a Council decision on a proposal from the Commission. Subsequently three Framework Agreements have resulted from this process, covering parental leave (1995), part-time employment (1997) and fixed-term contracts (1999). However, agreement proved impossible in regard to temporary employment and the Commission recovered the right of initiative and brought forward its own draft Directive.

The Social Action Programme

Towards the end of the Social Action Programme (SAP) associated with the Social Charter, the Commission began a consultation process which culminated in the 1994 White Paper on Social Policy (COM(94)333). It did not propose a great deal of new legislation but emphasised the importance of implementing existing Community law effectively in the member states and of adopting the outstanding proposed legislation. It also raised questions of whether the Commission's powers to address discrimination issues should be enhanced and whether a Charter of social right for non-workers should be adopted to complement that of the existing Social Charter. Subsequently, in March 1996, the periodically convened Social Policy Forum submitted to the Inter-Governmental Conference (IGC) the proposal that they should incorporate a Bill of Rights into the TEU, with right of appeal to an EU court composed of judges from member states' supreme or constitutional courts.

By 1997, and the end of the medium-term SAP, the legislative framework of minimum labour contract standards and conditions for labour mobility had been established, and employment policy had become the clear priority for the Community. The 1998–2000 Social Action Programme (COM(98)259) continued the emphasis upon coordination, implementation and dialogue. It focused on three broad areas: jobs, skills and mobility; the changing world of work; and social inclusion (Box 7.2). Much of the rest of this chapter examines these Community policies in greater detail.

Box 7.2 The 1998–2000 Social Action Programme

1 Jobs, skills and mobility
- Implementation of the employment strategy, including a monitoring framework.
- Foster adoption of best practice in member states' labour markets.
- Address the problem of 'undeclared work'.
- Examine the issue of modernisation of member states' employment services.
- Utilise the Structural Funds to promote employment.
- Encourage member states and the social partners to focus upon enhanced investment in human capital.
- Place a greater emphasis upon equality of opportunity and increasing opportunities for the disabled.

2 The World of Work
- Better organisation of work to be negotiated through the social dialogue.
- Measures to maximise the contribution of the 'information society' to the social objectives.
- Encouragement of information provision and consultation with workers.
- Effective implementation and updating of the existing health and safety legislation.

3 Social Inclusion
- Making social insurance more employment friendly and portable.
- Addressing the pension consequences of an ageing population.
- Preparation of a Recommendation on minimum income.
- Develop statistical indicators of poverty and social exclusion.
- Incorporate equality objectives into relevant Community policies.
- Pursue the strategy on equal opportunities for the disabled.

Community policy

The Community's policy in the social area may be seen as seeking to fulfil three broad roles. First, harmonisation of national policies, especially in areas where it offers obvious advantages, for example labour mobility. Secondly, encouraging convergence, both through its own discussions and encouragement of inter-state cooperation. This approach is likely to be most appropriate where states are faced by similar problems, for example the impact of demographic changes upon social security systems. Finally, the Commission can act as a focal point for the spreading of innovatory experience throughout the Community.

Community policy can be pursued through a variety of instruments, from Opinions, Recommendations and the 'open method of dialogue' to Directives and Regulations. The balance now appears to be shifting to the former and away from legislation, but at the same time the scope of the EU's social policy has been extended to address the central issue of unemployment. Social policy is now regarded as another dimension of the general economic policy of the Community, reflecting the increasing emphasis upon labour market reform as a contributor to enhanced economic growth.

Employment

The dramatic increase in unemployment across Europe during the 1980s and its persistence into the 1990s had moved this problem to centre stage. The recovery which had begun in 1994 lost momentum in 1995. Employment in 1995, at 148 million, was 4 million fewer than four years earlier. Unemployment averaged 10.7 per cent in 1996, only slightly below its peak of 11.3 per cent in April 1994, and the long-term unemployed now composed half of the total. Most of the new jobs created in the 1990s have been part-time, with 71 per cent of additional male employment being part-time in 1995 and 85 per cent of that for women. Similarly almost all of the increase in employment for men was on temporary contracts, and just under half of that for women (European Commission, 1996b).

The persistence of high unemployment levels had placed the conflict between the Euro-corporatist 'continental' tradition and that of the 'Anglo-Saxon' neo-Liberals in a new context. The arguments for deregulation of the European labour market to increase its flexibility and generate employment, especially among the unskilled and semi-skilled, had been supported by the adverse comparisons that are made between US and EU experiences. Attempts to prevent 'social dumping' by an interventionist social policy are seen as contributing to the persistence of unemployment, and the policy debate among member states began to shift its ground.

In 1994, at the Essen Summit, unemployment had reached the top of the agenda. Five priorities had been identified – promoting investment in vocational training; increasing the employment-intensiveness of growth; reducing non-wage labour costs; improving the effectiveness of labour market policies; and helping disadvantaged groups. The Commission was to examine the impact of social security contributions upon employment, and during 1995 specifically addressed employment creation in its Recommendations on economic policy for the Community (COM(95)228). But despite a succession of reports and opinions emanating from the EU institutions there was no real evidence of policy convergence among national employment policies.

But the Essen Summit's employment objectives may influence the movement towards fiscal harmonisation. A Commission paper (SEC(96)487) had observed that between 1980 and 1994 the implicit tax rate on employed labour had grown by 14 per cent, while that on other factors of production had fallen by 20 per cent. Clearly this is incompatible with the desired objective of increasing employment through reducing indirect labour costs.

Meanwhile, during the preparations for the 1997 Amsterdam Summit, the Commission's President, Jacques Santer, proposed a Confidence Pact on Employment. It focused on a number of areas – the adoption of coordinated macro economic policies favourable to employment creation; policies to encourage job creation in small and medium-sized enterprises; realising the potential of the internal market; and redirection of the Structural Funds towards employment objectives. After discussions with the ETUC, UNICE, CEEP and representatives of the member states, the European Council adopted the proposal in June 1996.

The question of the importance that should be placed upon employment creation in future EU economic policy formation was one of the central issues discussed at Amsterdam. A 'Reflection Group' had argued that unemployment was now a central issue and that employment creation should be seen as one of the duties and tasks of the EU, not merely a side-effect of other policies such as the creation of the SEM and EMU. As a result the Amsterdam Treaty includes an Employment Title, laying the foundations for a European Employment Strategy. This established an Employment Committee, 'mainstreamed' consideration of the employment aspects of all EU policies and adopted QMV. No new money was allocated to this policy, however, although a £700 m programme of job-creating investment was to be funded by the European Investment Bank. Its remit was also to be extended from financing only commercial projects to include 'socially useful employment' projects.

The continuing shift of emphasis to 'supply-side' policies was apparent at the special employment summit held in Luxembourg in November 1997. Member states resolved to create more flexible labour markets, lighten the burden of taxation and promote business and training. The major innovation was the initiation of the 'Luxembourg Process': the establishment of employment guidelines by the Council, the formulation of annual national employment action plans (NEAP) embodying these guidelines, their assessment by the Council and Commission and the publication of a Joint Employment Report, with the subsequent further revisions of the employment guidelines. The 'Luxembourg Process' does not bind member states but is intended to encourage convergence in the pursuit of agreed objectives. The objectives have also been tightened and where possible expressed as quantifiable targets. Such objectives included offering work or training to all under-25 year olds within six months of their becoming unemployed, and within a year for those older.

At the Lisbon European Council in 2000 there was an opportunity to carry out a mid-term review of the European Employment Strategy. It was felt that greater

Box 7.3 Review of the European Employment Strategy

The Commission review (European Commission, 2002a) included the following topics:

- Tax reforms and benefits
- Lifelong learning
- Social inclusion
- Administrative simplification and self-employment
- The creation of employment in services
- Modernising work organisations
- Equal opportunities

It identified four main areas for the reform of the EES:

- The need to set clear objectives
- The need to simplify policy guidelines without undermining their effectiveness
- The need to improve governance and partnership in the execution of the strategy
- The need to ensure greater consistency and complementarity with respect to other EU policies

emphasis needed to be placed upon longer-term challenges including the need to raise employment rates, especially among women and older workers, to sustain growth and fund pensions. There was also a desire to focus on retraining and mobility in order to address the emerging skills gaps in some regional labour markets. At the Barcelona Council there was a further call to strengthen the EES. Subsequently the Commission issued a series of Communications (European Commission, 2002a, 2003) outlining a redesign of the EES (Box 7.3) and intended to provide more concrete targets and foster the greater involvement of the European Parliament and the social partners. It also recommended streamlining the Luxembourg Process (European Commission, 2002b). Thus in April 2003 the Commission presented its *Guidelines Package*, which included the employment and broad economic policy guide lines and recommendations to the member states, which, together with the internal market strategy, is intended to cover the period up to 2006 without further revision.

Labour mobility

Although the Treaty of Rome had laid down the fundamental freedom of movement of workers (Articles 48–51) and the right of establishment in any economic activity across all member states, a succession of secondary legislation has been required to give concrete form to these principles. Any EU national may now reside in any member state to seek or take up employment, accompanied by their family (Directive 68/360/EEC), establish firms or provide services (73/148/EEC) and remain in that territory after having been employed in that State (70/1251/EEC, 72/194/EEC). In addition, any worker and his family should receive equal treatment in respect of social security (Regulations 71/1408/EEC and 72/574/EEC), housing, access to education and training, etc., as any domestic national.

Nevertheless, some problems remained unresolved or unaddressed. Frontier workers, commuting from a country of residence to employment in another state, have a number of established rights, for example social security benefits, but specific difficulties remained, particularly in regard to taxation. EU nationals seeking public sector employment in other member states have faced restrictions. Although discrimination in employment is allowed on grounds of 'public policy, security or health, and exercise of public authority' this has been narrowly interpreted by the ECJ. The Commission therefore decided to take action to eliminate employment restrictions in the public utilities, health services, teaching and non-military research.

The rights so far described are focused specifically upon the needs of workers and their dependents. Those who are not economically active continued to face residence restrictions, usually a test of 'adequate means' for intending migrants. To facilitate labour adjustment the Commission had proposed the transferability of unemployment benefit while workers seek employment in other member states. Although a proposed Directive granting a general 'right of residence' throughout the Community for students and retired and other non-employed people faced substantial opposition from several member states, the Maastricht Treaty (TEU) created citizenship of the Union, with the right to freedom of movement and residence. However, the necessary measures for its realisation still required unanimous agreement and progress was slow. The Commission has also pursued a number of general policies aimed at enhancing worker mobility. In particular it established comparability of vocational qualifications, beginning with hotel and catering, motor vehicle repairs, construction, electrical, agricultural and textile trades. Minimum skill requirements are being defined for training qualifications, with the assistance of CEDEFOP. The Commission has also been given responsibility for developing a broad Community-recognised vocational training pass, but this will have to be built upon current activity in this area.

The Treaty of Rome had sought to enable professionally qualified people to practise anywhere within the Community (Article 57(1)) and the Commission had first addressed this problem of recognition by negotiations on a profession by profession basis. This proved a very slow process. It took until 1975 to achieve Community-wide recognition of doctors, followed by nurses (1977), dental practitioners (1978), veterinary surgeons (1978), pharmacists (1986) and architects (1985). Dissatisfaction with this approach led to the inclusion of a proposal to establish general mutual recognition as part of the programme to complete the internal market. By 1989 the Council had adopted the Diplomas Directive (89/48/EEC), which established mutual recognition of all the regulated professions' qualifications where study is of at least three years' duration. Safeguards remained in the provision of a period of supervised practice, aptitude and language tests. Its impact, however, appears to have been limited. In the UK only 1046 applications were made for recognition of professional qualifications in 1992, 46 per cent of which were from teachers and 40 per cent from Eire (DTI, 1995). There has been criticism that the Directive is imprecise and, as the professional Institutes act as the competent authorities in assessing applicants, they are able to continue to discriminate against non-nationals.

The Community had also established Sedoc (Regulation, 68/1612), a European system of employment information exchange, but this remains inadequate and little used, with only 1,000 job applications processed annually. This is complemented by EURES, a labour market network of 450 employment specialists across the EEA which provides information on recruitment, placements and working conditions.

Despite this legislative programme labour mobility remains low in the EU. In 2000 only 225,000 people moved their residence between member states. With its new responsibilities in fostering employment and economic growth the Commission returned to the issue of labour mobility with the appointment of a group of experts in 1996. Their report (European Commission, 2001b) recommended better language training, higher IT skills, simpler transfer arrangements for pensions and social security and an overhaul of the recognition of qualifications. In 2002 a 25-point action plan implementing these recommendations was adopted by the Council, aiming to establish an 'open European labour market' by 2005. The legislative proposals will aim to minimise the administrative difficulties of obtaining residence documents, extend the right to family reunification and improve mutual recognition of qualifications. EURES will be strengthened and the advisory committees on social security and free movement merged.

Training

Ensuring the provision of adequate training of the labour force was seen as essential to achieve the structural adjustment necessary for the successful completion of the SEM. The process of creating the SEM required both new types of training, for example corporate planning for small and medium-sized firms, and the general expansion of education and training to create a European pool of skilled labour. The Commission sought to develop a strategy building upon discussions with both sides of industry, and focusing upon its three roles. First, the training of young people, building upon a Council Decision (December 1987) calling for the setting up of a system giving all young people the right to up to two years' basic training. Secondly, the Commission sought to improve comparability between national training systems. Finally, the Commission has fostered recognition of the importance of continuing and further training of the labour force by both industry and the State. These general principles have been given expression in the further development of a vocational policy required by Article 128 of the Treaty of Rome. The White Paper on the completion of the internal market (European Commission, 1985) built upon this, calling for comparability of qualifications (Council Resolution, July 1985), a general system of recognition of higher education diplomas and the introduction of a vocational training pass. Two programmes, Erasmus (1987) and Yes (1988) encouraged increased student mobility and youth exchanges respectively, while the Lingua (1989) programme aimed to foster students' knowledge of Community languages.

Following from the White Paper, *Growth, Competition and Employment* (COM(93)700), the Commission presented another White Paper, *Teaching and Learning: Towards the Learning Society* (COM(95)590). This attempted to identify the response that is necessary to meet the challenges presented by globalisation and technological change. It argued for the central role of education and training, and called for recognition of the benefits of broad-based knowledge and training that is relevant to employment. Specifically, it recommended the establishment of a network of EU research centres to identify skill shortages and vocational training centres to meet this need. A Community accreditation scheme was suggested, with the development of personal 'skill cards'.

For higher education it sought to enhance mobility through ensuring the portability between member states of education grants and the mutual recognition of course credits through a European Course Credit Transfer Scheme. For schools the emphasis was upon multilingualism, with a 'School of Europe' quality label. To address the problem of 'school failures', concentrated in the Community's decaying urban centres, the Commission proposed redeploying funds to support national 'second chance' schemes that have been targeted at these groups. Finally the Commission called for the equal treatment of investment in physical and human capital in taxation and accounting terms.

As a contribution to realising the economic and employment objectives agreed at the Lisbon Council in March 2000, the Commission was asked to prepare a strategy to enable any citizen access to continuing education and training. In 2000 only 8 per cent of the EU's adult population (25–64) was participating in education or training. The resulting 'Lifelong Learning Strategy' (COM(2001)678) is based upon six key elements: development of partnerships; a detailed analysis of learning requirements; an increase in public and private investment in learning; access to learning opportunities; valuing learning; and introducing quality control. It proposes the preparation of an EU-wide modular system for accumulating qualifications, the creation of a common system for presenting qualifications and the provision of improved information on learning opportunities at the European level. The Commission is also encouraging the EIB to give greater support to investment in human capital, in particular through the provision of risk capital for the provision of local training centres. Again the Commission emphasises the EU's central role in providing a forum for representatives of member states and the social partners to exchange information and to coordinate their policies, supported by the creation of an EU database of best practice.

The Commission's Action Plan for Skills and Mobility (COM(2002)72) provides a further outline of the specific measures that it intends to adopt up to 2005. Targets for improvements in educational attainment are to be agreed with member states and monitored. In particular it is intended that the number of 18–24 year olds with only secondary education should be halved by 2010. The retraining of older workers is also being emphasised in order to achieve the targeted increase in their 50 per cent employment participation rate. To improve links with business the Commission intends to establish a network of industry/education advisory committees and there is a particular emphasis upon the development of IT skills. The Commission intends to promote EU-wide standards for the accreditation of IT training and of informal learning by the European Forum on the Transparency of Qualifications. Finally, the Commission will be advocating that priority be given to investment in human capital in the mid-term review of the ESF in 2003.

Structural Funds

In defining the role of the Structural Funds in facilitating the changes required by the accelerated economic integration of the SEM, the Commission had followed two broad principles. Restructuring must coincide with the broader Community objectives, and Community funds must be matched by national funds. The structural funds – ESF, ERDF and EAGGF – had been supplemented by sectoral programmes aimed at restructuring the shipbuilding and steel industries. However, these ad hoc measures had created unnecessary complexity. In response the Commission proposed reform of the Structural Funds in a draft regulation (COM(87)376) adopted in February 1988 (see Box 7.4). At the same time the appropriation was doubled, in real terms, from €7 bn per annum in 1987 to €14 bn per annum in 1993. The Structural Funds now accounted for one-quarter of the Community budget, with €156 m allocated for the period 1994–99 under the financial arrangements of the TEU.

The ERDF now focuses upon support for productive investment, modernisation of infrastructure, and studies of the potential for physical planning at the Community level (see Chapter 8).

The ESF was subject to another review in 1997 when, under the Amsterdam Treaty, employment was placed at the centre of the Community's policy agenda. The ESF was now to become the main financial instrument for the European Employment Strategy (EES) and would provide the complementary funding supporting the National Employment Action Plans (NEAP) that are central to the EES. €195 bn has been allocated to the Structural Funds for the years 2000–06, with 70 per cent for the poorest regions (Objective 1), 11.5 per cent for areas facing structural adjustment (Objective 2) and 12.5 per cent for other regions (Objective 3). In its policy priorities (see Box 7.5) the ESF focuses mainly upon assistance to people, with an emphasis upon training, but it can also provide financial support to the improvement of systems, for example employment services, links between work and business. A new element has been the allocation of funds to support small grants to local partnerships and NGOs.

Box 7.4 Structural Funds Reform

To be based upon four principles:

1 Concentration upon five objectives:

   a. Promoting the development and structural adjustment of the less developed regions.

   b. Converting the areas seriously affected by industrial decline.

   c. Combating long-term unemployment.

   d. Facilitating the occupational integration of young people.

   e. Promoting the development of rural areas.

2 Precise definition of the tasks of the structural funds in relation to these objectives.

3 An increase in resources.

4 Rationalisation of both assistance and management methods.

Box 7.5 The European Social Fund's Priorities

- Developing active polices to combat unemployment, preventing long-term unemployment and providing support for those re-entering the job market.
- Promoting social inclusion and equal opportunities.
- Developing education and training as part of a policy of lifelong learning.
- Fostering innovation in work organisation, supporting entrepreneurship and job creation and increasing the potential in science and technology.
- Improving the participation of women in the labour market.

European works councils

A central feature of the proposals for a European company law has been the desire to encourage worker participation, since the Commission believes this to be an important factor in firms' economic success. A number of proposals addressing this issue have been considered including the 'Fifth Directive' concerning company structures and the powers and duties of governing bodies. There has also been a proposed Regulation on the status of the European Limited Liability Company, first drafted in 1970, and the 'Vredeling Directive' (1980). This latter proposal specifically set out to be a piece of social legislation, being concerned with information provision and consultation with the workforce in large, especially multinational, companies. This Directive was 'frozen' in the face of opposition from employers.

In June 1988 the Commission returned to this issue and submitted a new memorandum on the creation of a European Company statute. It proposed a simpler statute abandoning many aspects of the previous draft, and it would be optional. Firms could choose to operate under the new statute or retain their existing national corporate existence. In terms of worker participation three alternative options were available to a European Company: a German model with workers represented on the management bodies; the Franco-Italian system of a works council separate from the management board; and the Swedish model, under which individual firms establish an agreement on participation with the workers. However, various safeguards were proposed. Prior agreement with the workforce on representation would be required before a European Company could be incorporated, with a 'fallback' national standard model specified should there be a failure to reach an agreement. Any member state could also restrict the choice of model available. All three options would require quarterly reports on the company to the employees and prior consultation with the workforce on decisions relevant to them. Despite its increased flexibility these proposals continued to face the implacable opposition of the European employers (UNICE) as part of their general hostility to the emergence of any European level of collective bargaining.

The Commission finally succeeded in establishing European Works Councils through decoupling them from the issue of a European Company Statute. It overcame the political opposition through the use of the Maastricht Social Agreement. A European Works Council Directive was finally adopted in 1994 (94/95 EC) and implemented in September 1996 (see Box 7.6). By 2000, more than 600 agreements

Box 7.6 The European Works Council Directive

1 Applies to undertakings with a minimum of 1,000 employees and at least 150 employees in two or more member states (Article 2).

2 A special negotiating body can be set up by management or at the request of at least 100 employees in at least two undertakings in two or more countries (Article 5).

3 The Directive outlines coverage, composition and how the EWC will operate (Article 6).

4 A default model is provided in the Directive if no agreement is reached between employees and management within three years (Article 8).

5 By agreement alternative arrangements may be made to the establishment of an EWC (Article 6).

6 The Directive does not apply where there are pre-existing agreements in force (Article 13).

had been signed under this Directive and there are proposals to extend its obligations to companies with only 50 or more employees.

Having achieved agreement on the EWC Directive the Commission returned to the stalled negotiations to establish a European Company Statute. It was to take until the Nice summit (2000) for a political agreement and in 2002 the final stages were being reached for the adoption of the complementary Directive establishing a general framework for the consultation of employees. This Directive is intended to extend workers' rights beyond those covered by the EWC for multinational enterprises, or which apply in the specific circumstances of collective redundancies and the transfer of undertakings. The Directive covers firms with more than fifty workers and requires consultation in regard to decisions resulting in major changes in the organisation, especially where redundancies may result. The detailed implementation of the Directive has been delegated to member states with a three-year transition period.

Health and safety

Across the EU five hundred million working days are lost each year as a result of illness and injury, costing up to 4 per cent of GDP. In 1999, 5,350 people were killed at work and there were 12.2 million industrial accidents. As well as having to address this human and economic cost it was recognised that there was a need to establish minimum European standards for health and safety in order to ensure fair competition within the SEM.

EU legislation in this area falls into three groups: measures taken under the framework Directive (89/391/EEC), which covers basic provisions for health and safety at work and on which Directives covering particular groups of workers have been based; Directive 80/1107/EEC which provides the framework for action covering the risks of exposure to particular chemical, physical and biological hazards; and measures targeted at particularly vulnerable groups. As important as the legislation has been the problem of implementation and enforcement. In 1996 only 74 per cent of Directives had been implemented in national laws but by 2000 this had risen to 98 per cent.

The current Commission Action Programme covers the period up to 2006. It employs a mixture of legislation, where standards are required, financial support from the ESF for training, benchmarking of industry and national performance, and the exchange of information. The European Agency for Safety and Health at Work (OSHA) has been created. Based in Bilbao it is tasked with creating a health and safety database and of promulgating best practice. It is working closely with the European Foundation for the Improvement of Living and Working Conditions based in Dublin.

Particular emphasis is also being placed upon the role of employers and trade unions through 'social dialogue' in addressing health and safety issues. As well as their crucial role in implementation they have an important influence upon the framing of the legislation. A good example of the approach being taken is that of the Machines Directive, which covers over half of the total production of the European mechanical engineering industry. This Directive, based upon a Council resolution of May 1985, was innovative in that it only defined basic requirements, leaving detailed specifications to the individual standardisation bodies. The Commission invited representatives from industry, trade unions, European standardisation bodies (CEN and CENELEC) and member governments to be involved from the beginning. A tripartite structure of employers, trade unions and the Commission was created to oversee its implementation.

Social security

Social security remains primarily a matter for each member state. However, the EU has concerned itself with ensuring that incompatible national social security systems do not inhibit labour mobility. Regulations 71/1408/EEC and 72/574/EEC established the principle of equal treatment of domestic and EU nationals, of aggregation of all periods of insurance completed in any member state, and the application of only one set of social legislation at any one time. It also ensures that benefits can be exported throughout the Community. The problem of the portability of private supplementary pension schemes has also begun to be addressed. Directive 98/49/EC attempts to ensure the preservation of acquired rights and cross-border payments, while further discussion continues on the transferability of pension rights and the length of qualifying periods. In 1998 the Commission adopted simpler rules for coordinating national social security schemes. These are revised annually and are increasingly viewed in the context of the rights of European citizens rather than merely the requirements of the SEM.

However, the implications for national social security schemes of the ageing European population have been of greater current concern. Social security accounts for 26 per cent of the EU's GDP and 63 per cent of that funds pensions and health care. Pensions alone account for 10.4 per cent of GDP and this is expected to increase to 13.6 per cent by 2050. In 1997 the Economic Policy Committee (EPC), an advisory body to the Ecofin Council, had begun to examine the problem of pensions funding. It advocated a greater role for funded schemes, delayed retirement, stronger links between individual contributions and benefits and an attention to the fiscal implications of these liabilities (EPC 2000). Although prime responsibility for

Box 7.7 The open method of coordination

This approach of structured cooperation offers an alternative to legislation.

All member states establish common objectives in a given policy area, prepare national action plans, review each other's performance in terms of the Commission's guidelines and accordingly adapt their national policies.

any discussion of social security reform would have been expected to lie with the Social Protection Committee, the equivalent advisory committee to the Employment and Social Council, it is the EPC that has made the running with its emphasis upon fiscal sustainablity. This is seen explicitly in the decision to integrate any reform proposals into the Broad Economic Policy Guidelines. The EPC's latest report (EPC 2001) suggests that further cuts may be necessary in public funding of pensions schemes, implying that individuals will have to continue work for longer or increase their savings through private pensions. They also emphasise that fiscal stability would require avoiding excessive deficits, keeping debt levels below 60 per cent of GDP and ensuring that age-related public expenditure does not squeeze other areas of public funding.

In this controversial area of EU competence a further step was taken at the Lisbon summit in March 2000 when the decision was made to adopt the 'open method of coordination' (Box 7.7). Within the context of four agreed objectives (Box 7.8) member states presented their pension reform proposals for discussion and evaluation by the Commission in 2002. At the same time the Barcelona summit set a target that all member states should aim, by 2010, to increase by five years the age at which workers leave the labour market. To achieve this, early retirement schemes will be discouraged and efforts will be made to increase the opportunities for older workers to remain in the labour market, for example through more flexible pension arrangements.

Box 7.8 Reforming social security systems

The modernisation strategy adopted in 2000 (COM(1999)347) is based upon four broad objectives:

■ reforming the tax and benefit system to encourage employment.

■ ensuring pensions are secure and sustainable.

■ promoting social inclusion.

■ ensuring a high-quality and sustainable health care system.

Equal opportunities

The employment or activity rate for women (55 per cent) remains below that for men (73 per cent), with the largest differences in Greece, Spain and Italy. In these three countries the unemployment rate for women is also significantly higher than for men, while it is 2.8 per cent higher across the whole Community. In 1998 women in the EU continued to earn only 84 per cent of the wages of men (average gross hourly earnings), ranging from 76 per cent in the UK to 94 per cent in Portugal. They are also concentrated in part-time employment and constitute 77 per cent of the lowest paid workers.

Initially the only legal basis for equal rights lay in the Single European Act's commitment to equal pay (Article 141). However, the ECJ placed a broad interpretation on this Article and extended the principle of equal treatment to the prohibition of all forms of sex discrimination in the workplace. Subsequently the Community has adopted a number of Directives covering entitlement to parental leave (96/34/EC), the tightening of the burden of proof in cases of sex discrimination in the workplace (97/80/EC), the removal of discrimination in employment conditions for part-time workers (97/81/EC) and in occupational social security schemes (96/97/EC).

In 1999 the Amsterdam Treaty explicitly introduced the promotion of equality as a task of the Community (Article 2) and required consideration of the equality dimension across its policies (Article 3). The original Article 141 has also been strengthened to allow the Community to adopt measures to ensure equal treatment in employment, including equal pay for work of equal value, to authorise measures of 'positive discrimination' and to tackle discrimination in areas other than employment (e.g. financial services, education.).

The mainstreaming of equality issues can be seen in the Regulations for the Structural Funds covering the period 2000–06. Promotion of equality is enshrined in Article 1, while each Fund has a particular focus. The ESF will concentrate upon getting women into the labour market, the ERDF upon enterprise creation activities and the EAGGF upon women's rural development projects. Member states are also now explicitly required to take into account gender issues in the formulation of their National Employment Action Plans. Salary differences between men and women are now included in the structural employment indicators as part of the EU's monitoring of its economic and social strategies. Increasing female activity rates from 55 per cent to 60 per cent by 2010 is an important part of the EU's employment strategy.

In 2000 the EU adopted a more comprehensive Directive (2000/78/EC) covering all forms of discrimination (gender, disability, religion and age) and intended to provide a general framework for equal treatment in employment. It improves legal protection, adjusts the burden of proof and provides protection against harassment. Racial discrimination is covered by Directive 2000/43/EC. This is complemented by a €98.4 m Community Action Programme to combat discrimination (2001–06) and a €50 m programme (2001–05) focused on gender equality.

Conclusion

The persistence of relatively high levels of unemployment across much of the EU has come to dominate the social policy agenda. Unemployment and the challenge of 'globalisation' has shifted the balance of the argument towards those advocating neo-liberal labour market flexibility (see Addison and Siebert, 1994, 1997) and away from the preservation of the European neo-corporatist tradition, with its emphasis upon 'social cohesion' and workers' rights. While wage flexibility is essential if the economies of member states are to maintain their competitive positions after the abolition of internal exchange rates under EMU, what composes labour market flexibility is open to a variety of interpretations. From a neo-liberal perspective flexibility will be reflected both in variable wages and the right of managers to hire and fire easily. Policies should encourage geographical mobility and there should be an emphasis upon training and educational investment. However, the latter is common ground in the policy debate, with the increasing importance of flexible production underlining the need for employees who are multi-skilled and self-directed. This central role for investment in human capital requires the development of long-term relationships between employees and employers if the returns to such investments are to be realised (Dearden, 1995a). Such stable employment relationships, however, which may be reinforced by the Community's emphasis upon policies of 'social cohesion' and 'social dialogue', are regarded as an anathema by those advocating the primacy of market forces.

But the terms of the social policy debate have clearly been set. At the Lisbon summit the Community's governments identified their primary objective – to turn the EU into 'the most competitive and dynamic knowledge-based economy in the world, capable of sustained economic growth' within the next decade. To achieve this objective, social policy was to be considered in the context of its relationship and contribution to economic and employment policies – social policy was to be a 'productive factor'. Modernising the European social model 'is required to underpin economic dynamism and pursue employment-generating reforms' (European Commission, 2001). Thus the social policy agenda is committed to raising the employment rate to 70 per cent by 2010, 'adapting working conditions and contractual relations to . . . foster a renewed balance between flexibility and security', ensuring the de facto free movement of workers, the development of a 'knowledge-based economy' and the adaptation of social protection systems to 'make work pay'. At the same time the emphasis has shifted from legislative programmes to the more informal 'open' method of coordination.

Although the experience of the UK, which has pursued the US neo-liberal labour market model for two decades, suggests that it can be effective at reducing overall levels of unemployment, its long-term impact upon the rate of economic growth remains far from certain. The US is not Europe, either culturally or economically. The extent of labour mobility, both geographical and occupational, that characterises the US is unlikely to be matched by that of the European labour market. The impact upon the distribution of income of such 'free market' policies may also face greater political resistance this side of the Atlantic.

At the same time the EU faces its own major adjustment problems. The adoption of the single currency may yet create significant economic strains as the full weight of adjustment falls upon regional wage flexibility. The record of regional policy within a national context suggests that it alone can make only a very limited contribution to structural adjustment in the face of economic change. In an EU context the impact is likely to be even more limited, especially given the increasing strains upon the EU's budget. The EU will also be facing the substantial challenge of Community enlargement. Although much of the debate has focused upon the budgetary impact and the recurring problems of the CAP, the impact of EU expansion into Central and Eastern Europe will enhance the competitive position of new low wage member states, and release onto the European labour market substantial numbers of mobile, educated potential employees.

Social policy has clearly moved towards the centre stage in the EU's political debates, but predominantly within the context of its contribution to employment creation. Whether this focus will prove, in the longer run, to be a distortion remains to be seen.

References

Addison J and Siebert W S (1993) 'The EC Social Charter: The Nature of the Beast', *The National Westminster Bank Quarterly Review*, February.

Addison J and Siebert W S (1994) 'Recent Developments in Social Policy in the New European Union', *Industrial and Labor Relations Review*, Vol. 48 No. 1, October, pp. 5–27.

Addison J and Siebert W S (1997) *Labour Markets in Europe: Issues of Harmonisation and Regulation*, Dryden Press, London.

Alber J and Standing G (2000) 'Social Dumping: Catch-up or Convergence?: Europe in a Comparative Global Context, *Journal of European Social Policy*, Vol. 10, No. 2, pp. 99–119.

Bean C (1994) 'European Unemployment: A Survey', *Journal of Economic Literature*, Vol. 32, June.

Coe D and Gagliardi F (1985) *Nominal Wage Determination in Ten OECD Countries*, OECD Economics and Statistics Working Paper No. 19.

Dearden S (1995a) 'European Social Policy and Flexible Production', *International Journal of Manpower*, Vol. 16, No. 10, pp. 3–13.

Dearden S (1995b) 'Minimum Wages and Wage Flexibility in the European Union', *Journal of European Social Policy*, Vol. 5, No. 1, pp. 29–42.

DTI (1995) *Directive 89/48/EEC Article 11 Report: Report of the United Kingdom*, DTI, London.

Economic Policy Committee (2000) *Progress Report to the Ecofin Council on the Impact of an Ageing Population on Public Pension Systems*, EPC/ECFIN/581/00.

Economic Policy Committee (2001) *Budgetary challenges posed by ageing populations*, EPC/ECFIN/630/01.

European Commission (1985) *Completing the Internal Market: The White Paper*, Office for Official Publications of the European Communities, Luxembourg

European Commission (1988) *Social Europe, The Social Dimension of the Internal Market*, Brussels.

European Commission (1991) 'Developments in the Labour Market in the Community: Results of a Survey Covering Employers and Employees', *European Economy*, No. 47, March.

European Commission (1995) *Employment Observatory Trends*, Bulletin of the European System of Documentation on Employment (SYSDEM), No. 21.

European Commission (1996a) *Commission Communication Concerning the Development of the Social Dialogue at Community Level*, COM(96)448.

European Commission (1996b) *Employment in Europe*, Brussels.

European Commission (2001) *Employment in Europe*, Brussels.

European Commission (2001b) *High Level Task Force on Skills and Mobility*, Brussels.

European Commission (2002a) *Taking Stock of Five Years of the European Employment Strategy*, COM(2002)416.

European Commission (2002b) *Streamlining the Annual Economic and Employment Policy Coordination Cycles*, COM(2002)487.

European Commission (2003) *The Future of the European Employment Strategy*, COM(2003)6.

European Industrial Relations Review (1990) Social Charter: Action Programme Released, *European Industrial Relations Review*, No. 192.

Morton J and Siebert S (1997) *Social Dumping and Insider-Outsider Distinctions in the European Union: Company Case Studies*, University of Birmingham, Mimeo.

Rhodes, M (1992) 'The Future of the Social Dimension: Labour Market Regulation in Post-1992 Europe', *Journal of Common Market Studies*, Vol. 30, March, pp. 23–51.

Further reading

Adnett N (1996) *European Labour Markets*, Longman, London.

European Commission (1993) *White Paper on Growth, Competitiveness and Employment*, Brussels.

European Commission (1994) *White Paper on European Social Policy: A Way Forward for the European Union*, Brussels.

European Commission (1994) *An Industrial Competitiveness Policy for the European Union*, COM(94)319, Brussels.

European Industrial Relations Review (1997) 'Commission Sets Out the Options for the Future of the Social Dialogue', No. 256, pp. 24–29.

European Industrial Relations Review (1997) 'The New Social Action Programme', No. 257, pp. 12–19.

Falkner G (1996) 'The Maastricht Protocol on Social Policy: Theory and Practice', *Journal of European Social Policy*, Vol. 6 (1), pp. 1–16.

Majone G (1993) 'The European Community between Social Policy and Social Regulation', *Journal of Common Market Studies*, Vol. 31, No. 2, June, pp. 153–170.

Molle W and Mourik A V (1988) 'International Movements under Conditions of Economic Integration: The Case of Western Europe', *Journal of Common Market Studies*, Vol. 26, March, pp. 317–42.

Read R (1991) 'The Single European Market: Does European Mobility Matter?', *International Journal of Manpower*, Vol. 12, No. 2.

Chapter 8

Regional policy

Reiner Martin

Introduction

During the early years of what is now the European Union (EU), regional policy was not an important policy field. The founding members of the EU were a fairly homogeneous group of countries and the only area encountering major regional problems, such as low per capita income and high unemployment, was the southern part of Italy.

The 1973 enlargement, when Denmark, the Republic of Ireland and the UK joined the Community, increased regional disparities. Some of the UK regions, especially the North of England and Northern Ireland, were experiencing major unemployment problems and had a low level of per capita income compared with the rest of the EU. Moreover, the Republic of Ireland was significantly poorer than the original member states. Its per capita income level in 1973 was just about half the EU6 average (measured in purchasing power standards (PPS) in order to account for differences in relative purchasing power). The accession of Greece in 1981, and Spain and Portugal in 1986, all of whom had per capita income levels significantly below the EU6 average, finally established regional policy as an important item on the European agenda. The sheer size of the new 'poor' regions added by the 'southern' enlargement dwarfed the pre-1981 situation.

The German re-unification in 1990 added another 17 million people to the EU whose average per capita income in PPS at the time was only 35 per cent of the EU average. The 1995 'northern' enlargement, however, which brought Finland, Sweden and Austria into the EU, was comparatively unproblematic, although large parts of Sweden and Finland have also become eligible for European regional support.

The 'eastern' enlargement of the EU in 2004 has increased the economic disparities within the EU. This latest enlargement round brought ten new member states with around 75 million inhabitants into the EU. Most of these countries have a very low level of per capita income. In 2000 the average per capita income for all ten new member states was only 43.7 per cent of the average for EU15.

Over the years, the various enlargements have thus transformed the EU into a more and more heterogeneous group of countries with significant regional economic imbalances. In the next section these income and unemployment disparities are presented in greater detail.

Regional economic disparities within the EU

In principle, the term 'region' can define any geographic entity, irrespective of whether this entity corresponds with national or sub-national boundaries or a group of countries. For regional policy purposes, however, regions refer to national or sub-national administrative areas. The system used to classify regions in the EU is known as 'nomenclature des unités territoriales statistiques (NUTS)' and is explained in Box 8.1.

Box 8.1 Defining regions

Eurostat, the statistical office of the European Commission, has defined various levels of regional disaggregation which are applicable in all EU member states. The so-called 'nomenclature des unités territoriales statistiques (NUTS)' has four main levels (NUTS 0–III), with NUTS 0 being the member states. In the UK, NUTS III is equivalent to counties and local authority regions, NUTS II to county/local authority groupings and NUTS I to standard regions.

Most analyses of regional disparities are based on the NUTS II level of regional disaggregation. Since NUTS II regions differ significantly in terms of size and population, a higher level of disaggregation would be desirable. However, data availability for regions below the NUTS II level is still relatively restricted.

Regional income disparities

Per capita income levels are the most commonly used indicator for differences in economic development. On a national, as well as a regional level, such income disparities are considerable within the EU. Figure 8.1 shows the 1990 and 2000 per capita income of the EU member states relative to the EU15 average (100). Per capita income data for the ten countries that joined the EU in 2004 refers to 1995 and 2000 rather than 1990 and 2000 due to data limitations.

As far as the EU15 member states are concerned, the figure indicates a narrowing of national income disparities during the 1990s. Ireland's performance in particular is remarkable. In terms of PPS, the country is now above the EU average per capita income level. Portugal, Spain and Greece have also made some progress, whereas Germany and France have experienced some relative income decline. In Germany's case, this is mainly due to the impact of reunification. Luxembourg managed to increase its lead vis-à-vis the EU average. All of the ten new member states are well below the EU15 average and, except for Cyprus, the Czech Republic, Malta and Slovenia, per capita GDP relative to the EU15 average is below 50 per cent. Comparing the situation in 1995 with that in 2000, per capita income in most new member states appears to be slowly converging with the EU average.

Income disparities are considerably wider at the NUTS II level of regions. The ratio between Luxembourg, the richest member state, and Greece (Latvia), the poorest EU15 (EU25) member state, was 2.9 to 1 in 2000 (6.3 : EU25). The ratio

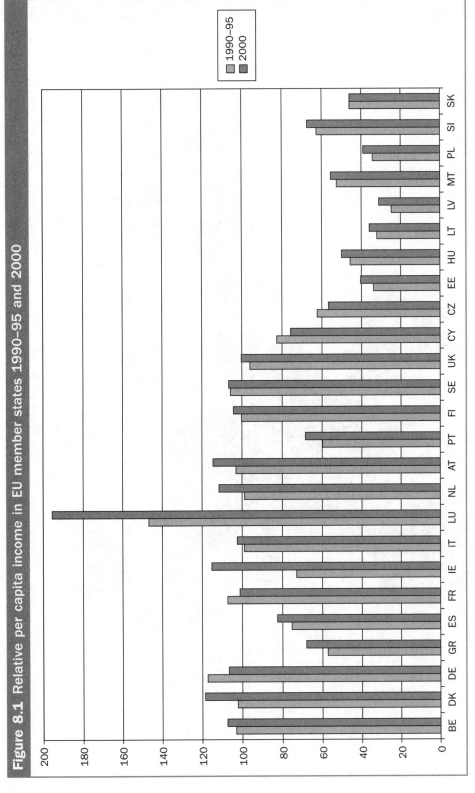

Figure 8.1 Relative per capita income in EU member states 1990–95 and 2000

Source: Adapted from European Commission

Figure 8.2 Gross domestic product (GDP) in NUTS II regions, 2000

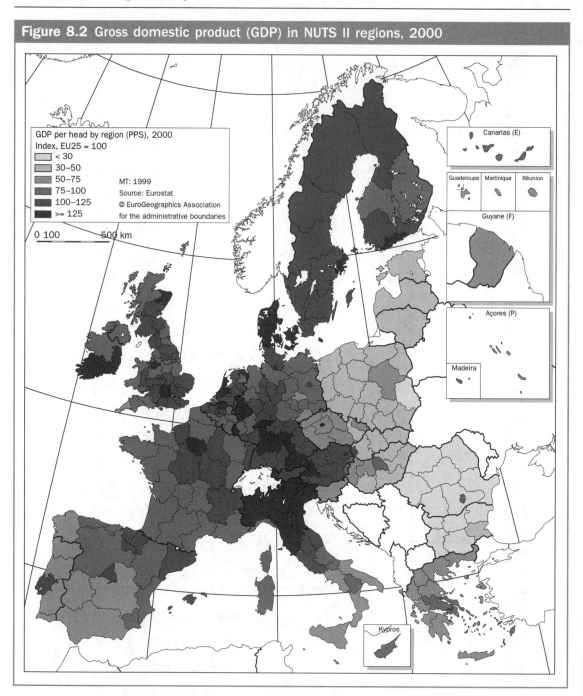

Source: Eurostat © EuroGeographics Association for the administrative boundaries

between inner London, the richest NUTS II region, and the poorest EU15 region, Ipeiros (Greece) (Lubelskie (Poland) : EU25), however, was more than 5.1 to 1 in 2000 (9.1 : EU25). Figure 8.2 provides an overview of PPS per capita in 2000.

Figure 8.2 illustrates the substantial income differences between the geographic core of the EU on the one hand and most of the more peripheral southern and eastern regions on the other hand. This difference is particularly pronounced with regard to the former communist countries of Central and Eastern Europe. Figure 8.2 also shows that many capital regions have a significantly higher level of per capita income than other parts of member states. This applies also to many of the new Central and East European member states. Finally, significant differences in intra-national disparities emerge in some countries, notably Italy, Spain and Germany.

Unlike national income disparities, regional income disparities have tended to widen during the last decade. In 1990, the ten poorest NUTS II regions in EU15 had an average per capita income measured in PPS of 51 relative to the EU15 average of 100. By 2000, this relative income value had increased by 2 percentage points to 53 (21 for the ten poorest regions in the new member states). Relative income in the ten best-off EU15 NUTS II regions, however, has increased between 1990 and 2000 by 26 percentage points, namely from 148 to 174 (71 for the ten richest regions in the new member states). The standard deviation of income disparities at EU15 NUTS II level has also increased from 26.3 in 1990, to 27.8 in 2000 (32.0 including the NUTS II regions located in the new member states).

Regional labour market disparities

Unemployment is another important indicator for the assessment of regional socio-economic disparities. Figure 8.3 shows relative national unemployment rates for the EU member states in 1990 and 2001. Unemployment data for the ten new member states refer to 1998 and 2001 rather than 1990 and 2001 due to data limitations.

Looking at the EU15, particularly striking developments have taken place in Ireland and the Netherlands, which managed to reduce their *relative* level of unemployment very significantly, and in Finland and Sweden, where the opposite development has taken place. The relative position of the relatively 'poor' EU15 member states is mixed. Whereas unemployment seems to be an increasing problem for Greece, the relative unemployment rate for Spain has declined although it remains well above the EU15 average. The relative unemployment rate in Portugal remains low and stable. As far as the new member states are concerned, the differences in relative unemployment are considerable. However, comparing the situations in 1998 and 2001, relative unemployment has strongly increased in most new member states except for Hungary and Slovenia.

The regional incidence of unemployment in 2001 is illustrated in Figure 8.4.

At the NUTS II level, unemployment differences are more pronounced than at member state level. In 1990, the Finnish region of Åland had the lowest unemployment rate (0.8 per cent), a position that was taken over by the Dutch region of

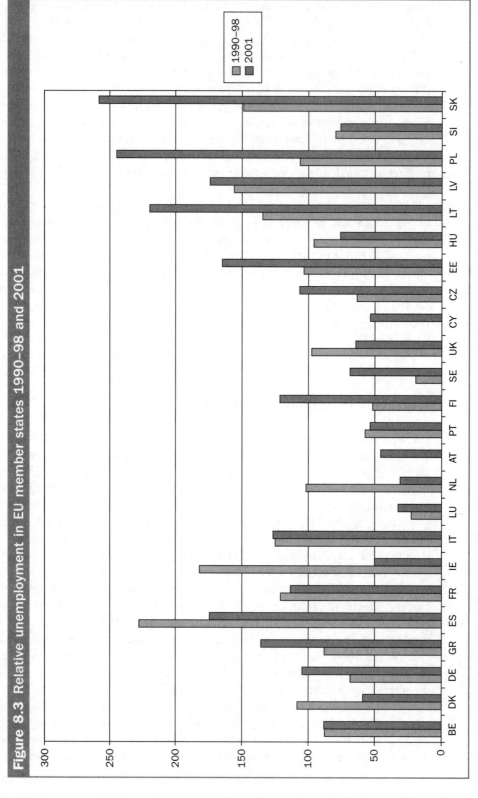

Figure 8.3 Relative unemployment in EU member states 1990–98 and 2001

Source: Adapted from European Commission

Figure 8.4 Total unemployment rates in NUTS II regions, 2001

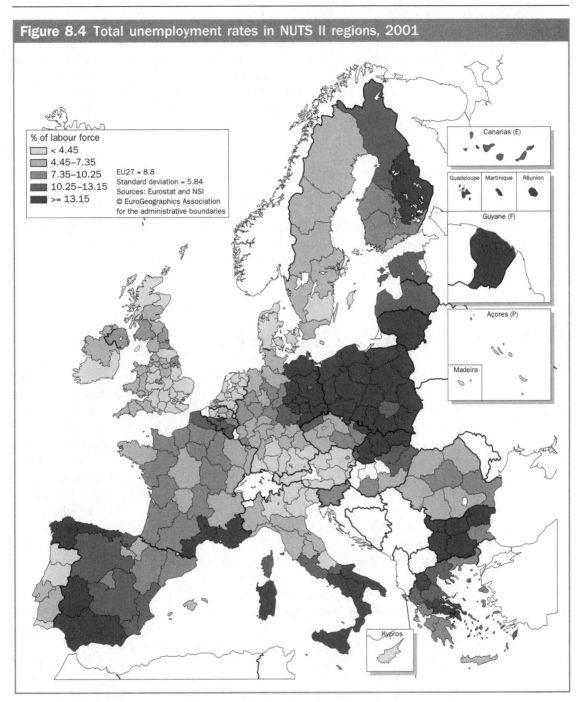

% of labour force
- < 4.45
- 4.45–7.35
- 7.35–10.25
- 10.25–13.15
- >= 13.15

EU27 = 8.8
Standard deviation = 5.84
Sources: Eurostat and NSI
© EuroGeographics Association
for the administrative boundaries

Canarias (E)

Guadeloupe   Martinique   Réunion

Guyane (F)

Açores (P)

Madeira

Kypros

Sources: Eurostat and NSI © EuroGeographics Association for the administrative boundaries

Utrecht in 2001 (1.2 per cent). At the other end of the spectrum the unemployment rate in the Spanish region of Ceuta y Melilla stood at 29.7 per cent in 1990. In 2001 the French region of Réunion had the highest regional unemployment rate of 33.3 per cent. The highest unemployment rate of a 'continental' EU15 NUTS II region was registered in Calabria (Italy) with 24.8 per cent. Regional unemployment disparities also tended to widen over time, with the standard deviation of all EU15 NUTS II regions increasing from 4.9 in 1990 to 6.7 in 2001 (6.0 for all EU25 NUTS II regions).

The regional income and unemployment data demonstrate clearly the existence of significant socio-economic disparities within the EU. Moreover, in many 'poor' EU regions, low income coincides with high unemployment. Not only does Figure 8.2 look in large parts like a mirror image of Figure 8.4 but statistical analysis also shows a high correlation between relative regional income and relative regional unemployment. While these regional disparities are at the heart of EU regional policy, it is an important question for policy makers whether they are likely to be temporary or permanent.

Economic theories of regional disparities

The so-called 'convergence theory' predicts that factor incomes (i.e. wages and returns on capital) in all regions of an integrated economic area like the EU will eventually converge, provided that there are sufficiently strong adjustment mechanisms in the form of goods and factor movements within the integration area. This prediction is based on the argument that all regions have an optimal capital intensity (i.e. an optimal mix between capital and labour), which in turn is determined by the production technology that prevails in the regions concerned. According to the strongest form of 'convergence theory', integration will lead to identical production technologies in all regions and thus identical payments to labour and capital. 'Conditional convergence theory' relaxes this assumption and allows for differences in regional production technologies. Both forms of convergence theory argue that regional output and factor incomes will be below the utility-maximising level as long as the actual capital intensity in a particular region is different from the technologically determined optimal capital intensity. According to neo-classical theory a sub-optimal capital intensity can be altered by movement of goods and services and/or factors of production between regions, or by changes in the savings and investment rates relative to the growth rate of the population. Thus, neo-classical convergence theory predicts that, in competitive markets without impediments to the free movement of goods, services, capital and labour, regional disparities cannot persist. Convergence theorists therefore argue that there is no need for regional policy. Competition policy and the liberalisation of barriers to the free movement of goods, factors of production and technologies are the only necessary measures in order to eliminate regional disparities.

'Divergence theory', however, leads to radically different conclusions. This strand of economic theory stresses the importance of lasting technological differences, transport costs, differences in regional economic structures and the importance of agglomeration effects and economic clusters. Generally speaking, divergence theory predicts the development of a heterogeneous economic landscape within the integration area with significant differences in the factor returns in central and peripheral areas. This in turn leads to substantial out-migration of mobile factors from poor to rich regions, which, in turn, widens the disparities even further. Supporters of divergence theory argue that action by governments is required to bring about regional convergence. A useful overview of both strands of theory is provided in, for example, Barro and Sala-i-Martin (1995). On divergence theory see also Fujita, Krugman and Venables (1999).

Empirical observations provide partial support for both theories. The Commission (European Commission, 2000, 2001) finds clear evidence in favour of income convergence among EU member states but less so at the regional level, partly because income gaps have increased between regions within member states. The convergence process has been fastest during periods of high growth although it has never been fast enough to allow for a significant reduction of regional disparities in less than a couple of decades. Furthermore, it is not clear to what extent income convergence is 'natural' or induced by policy.

Empirical investigations of locational decisions by firms, however, point towards the importance of external and agglomeration effects as well as transport and transaction costs, which supports the divergence point of view (European Commission, 1993). Furthermore, economists have stressed the importance of historical events and first-mover advantages like the location of important inventions as the key determinants of regional disparities (North, 1994). On balance, there is no clear-cut answer to the question of whether convergence or divergence theory provides a more accurate explanation regarding the persistence of regional imbalances. This uncertainty, in turn, helps to understand why regional policy is widely used at the national as well as the EU level.

Possible rationales for regional policy

The literature on the rationale for regional policy usually provides a blend of arguments, mixing social, political and economic reasoning (see e.g. Temple, 1994). The most frequently stated arguments for regional policy are:

1 the flattening of 'unjust' spatial income distributions (equity or fairness argument);

2 the easing of adjustment problems in economies undergoing major transformations or shocks;

3 the employment of unemployed resources by optimising the spatial allocation of production.

A clear separation of the different rationales is often impossible. Literature on the growth effect of income distributions (1) links equity and efficiency arguments by saying that there is a negative link between economic growth and inequality (see e.g. Alesina and Rodrik, 1994). However, improving equity by inter-personal income redistribution may also lead to an inferior allocation of resources and thus a reduction of overall economic welfare. In any case this argument is more suitable to provide support for social rather than regional policy because it relates to the effects of inter-personal rather than inter-regional distributions.

The adjustment problem argument (2) is essentially of a socio-political nature and can have considerable importance in the context of the EU, where adjustment problems can become an obstacle for further integration. A member state that expects major adjustment problems such as a rise in unemployment due to deeper integration may, for example, fail to support further integration although it may increase the welfare of the EU as a whole. In the light of this danger it can become economically meaningful for other member states to compensate the country in question for its (expected) adjustment problems.

The last rationale for regional policy is more clearly of an economic nature. The 'employment of unused resources' rationale (3) argues that certain factors of production, notably labour, are unemployed or under-employed in areas where economic activity is insufficient. Regional policy may help to reintegrate these factors of production into the economic process, thereby increasing aggregate welfare. However, this argument requires two conditions to hold. First, the surplus factors of production have to be too immobile to move to other parts of the integration area. Secondly, the costs to activate them have to be lower than the welfare gains obtainable from their activation.

The first condition is to some extent fulfilled in the EU. Labour mobility in particular is still very low and the Single Market for goods and services is not yet complete. That said, further policy measures to complete the Single Market and to encourage labour mobility may reduce the need for regional policy measures.

The second condition is more difficult to assess. Starting with the costs and benefits of agglomeration, the existence of negative agglomeration effects such as traffic congestion and environmental pollution is generally acknowledged. However, given that they have to be balanced against agglomeration effects such as a shared pool of labour and close customer–client relationships, it is not clear whether they provide a case for regional policy. More generally, regional policy measures to reduce negative external agglomeration effects are normally a second-best solution. It is preferable to internalise external effects such as environmental pollution and traffic congestion by, for example, road use charges for private transport (see Chapter 10).

In those cases where regional policy interventions are chosen, their welfare costs should be weighed against the welfare gains. Most regional policy interventions cause direct costs, opportunity costs and efficiency costs, with the latter arising due to the distortions of the market mechanism caused by the intervention. An attempt to improve the productivity of a lagging region by means of infrastructure investments, for example, is costly (direct costs), the money is no longer available for similar action in other regions (opportunity costs) and price signals in the economy are being distorted (efficiency costs).

Except for the first category, the measurement of these costs is rather difficult. However, in order to identify the preferable instrument, two general rules can be taken into account. First, measures that are trying to increase the underlying competitiveness of regions, such as investment in human capital and infrastructure, are normally superior to measures that are directed at the firm level. Secondly, regional policy should aim at increasing the endogenous potential of lagging regions rather than diverting existing activities from one location to another.

To sum up, there are few convincing economic rationales in favour of regional policy. Lammers (1992), for example, argues that the marginal utility of factors of production in peripheral areas is by definition almost insufficient to generate a positive net welfare effect. Nevertheless, it remains an important policy at the national as well as the EU level, which suggests that equity arguments for regional policy are more powerful than efficiency arguments.

Why national *and* European regional policy?

Given the existence of national regional policy in most EU member states, the need for an additional EU-wide regional policy largely rests on equity arguments and its role as a facilitator for the integration process.

Four main reasons may be advanced to justify regional policy at the EU level:

1 The 'financial targeting' argument, suggesting that the relatively poor member states are unable to target their regional problems themselves due to insufficient resources.

2 The 'vested interest' argument, based on the belief that the solution of regional problems in one member state will be beneficial for other member states.

3 The 'effects of integration' argument, based on the assumption that the benefits of integration are not evenly spread across the EU and require redistribution.

4 The 'effects of other EU policies' argument, stating that the benefits of other EU policies, such as the Common Agricultural Policy (CAP), are not spread evenly across member states so compensation is required.

The 'financial targeting' argument (1) is relatively undisputed although empirical investigations of peripheral countries' expenditure patterns yield some surprising results. During the 1980s and much of the 1990s Greece spent a larger percentage of its GDP on state aids than the EU as a whole. At the same time Ireland and Greece used a smaller share of their national income for infrastructure investments and all four cohesion countries invested a smaller share of their GDP in R&D than the EU average (Martin, 1999). Given the relative lack of infrastructure and R&D in these countries, such low relative expenditure levels for growth enhancing types of investments are difficult to justify.

The 'vested interest' argument (2) needs to be seen in conjunction with the adjustment problems argument mentioned above, stating that further EU integration would be impossible without compensations for those countries that obtain less than their 'fair' share of the aggregate welfare gains (3).

The 'effects of other EU policies' argument (4), finally, is frequently mentioned in defence of EU regional transfers. Some EU policies, such as the CAP, disproportionately favour more prosperous EU (rural) regions although a number of successive reforms have reduced this bias (European Commission, 2001). Other difficult policy areas from a distribution point of view are EU Transport Policy, especially the Trans-European Transport Networks (TETNs) and EU R&D policy. While the

TETNs are likely to be beneficial for convergence at member state level, they also imply that some peripheral EU regions would face a relative decline in accessibility. EU R&D Policy mainly focuses on centres of R&D excellence, which, by definition, tend to be located in the core regions of the EU. Both policies thus imply a potential worsening of peripheral regions' catching-up prospects (Martin, 1999).

Why are there limits to EU regional policy transfers?

EU regional policy operates mainly on the basis of transfers from the EU budget to be used for specific purposes and only in specific, designated regions within member states. It is useful to look at the various arguments that are advanced in favour of the current EU regional transfers system, which from the point of view of the recipient member states is rather restrictive:

1 The 'conditions of the donor' argument. The net contributors to EU regional policy want to make sure that the money is spent in order to improve the growth potential of those regions that are in greatest need of support.

2 The 'insufficiency of regional authorities' argument. This assumes that regional authorities in most member states are unable to make sure that the 'right' measures to achieve regional convergence are pursued.

3 The 'coordination' argument. Regional policy measures in one member state have international spill-over effects that are not sufficiently taken into account if regional policy is conducted at the national level.

4 Purely national regional policy might lead to a wasteful subsidy race between different locations.

The first argument is the main reason for the current system of EU regional policy, namely the reluctance of the better-off member states to fund a fiscal transfer system without strings attached. The main purpose of EU regional policy is to provide temporary support for those EU regions whose present level of competitiveness is insufficient. The net contributors to the EU budget would not have accepted the substantial increase in regional policy funding since the mid-1980s without having a substantial degree of central control over the use of structural fund resources for what they perceive as the 'right' measures for increasing regional competitiveness (CEPR, 1993).

The second argument is essentially a rationalisation of the first argument. However, while the quality of some EU regional authorities may leave something to be desired, it is obviously doubtful whether a central European institution such as the European Commission is in a better position to design 'suitable' measures to increase regional competitiveness.

An economic rather than a political argument for centralised regional policy is provided by the 'coordination' argument (Weise, 1995). Some regional policy measures, for example infrastructure investments, are indeed likely to have cross-border repercussions. However, this holds only for some of the supported measures.

The fear of a subsidy race between different locations is not a very strong argument because efficient state aid control could prevent this outcome.

From the point of view of economic theory it is easier to find arguments against the current regional policy system than arguments in favour of it. Among the most important reasons why direct transfers would be more efficient than the current system is the fact that, within the current system, distributional aims are pursued by means of allocational policy. Although EU regional policy is not officially designed as a redistribution policy, it has significant redistributive effects (European Commission, 1996, 2001). This mix of aims and policies, however, is likely to lead to efficiency losses. Finally, the subsidiarity principle suggests that a strong EU level influence is only compatible with some types of regional policy interventions, notably major infrastructure projects with international spill-overs. Other EU regional policy activities, however, might as well be designed and implemented only by member states. The existing influence of the EU regarding the latter type of activities can therefore only be understood against the background of the 'conditions of the donor' argument.

The development of European regional policy

The oldest elements of today's European regional policy are the European Social Fund (ESF), aimed at 'rendering the employment of workers easier and of increasing their geographical and occupational mobility within the Community' (Article 146, EEC) and the Guidance Section of the European Agricultural Guidance and Guarantee Fund (EAGGF) (Article 34, EEC). However, in financial terms both instruments were very small and there was no clear strategy for promoting regional development (Kenner, 1994).

The 1973 oil shock and the first enlargement of the EEC eventually led to a strengthening of the Community's regional policy activities. Regulation 724/75, EEC ((OJ) L 73/8 1975) established the European Regional Development Fund (ERDF) which was later incorporated into primary Community law:

> The European Regional Development Fund is intended to help to redress the main regional imbalances in the Community through participation in the development and structural adjustment of regions whose development is lagging behind and in the conversion of declining industrial regions (Article 160, EEC).

ERDF resources were originally allocated to member states on the basis of fixed quotas. Member states had to co-finance ERDF-supported projects with national public funding – the principle of additionality. Up to 85 per cent of ERDF-funded projects during the 1970s and early 1980s were connected with infrastructure improvements. The design of EU regional policy during this first phase led to a number of serious problems. First, in order to make sure that the quota allocated to them was used up, member states frequently compromised the economic efficiency of ERDF-supported projects. Secondly, Community funding did not normally lead to additional projects but member states used it in order to reduce national expenditures for projects that would have gone ahead anyway (Tsoukalis, 1997).

The European Commission made several attempts to reform this system with the aim of creating a more encompassing regional policy and to have an increased role vis-à-vis the national authorities, but member states left the quota system more or less intact.

Probably the most important reason for the eventual overhaul of the original system was the southern enlargement of the EU in 1981 and 1986. This not only increased regional disparities, but also led to demands by Greece, France and Italy to be compensated for their willingness to accept southern enlargement. The so-called Integrated Mediterranean Programs (IMPs) for Italy, France and Greece were designed in order to satisfy these demands. The IMPs, launched in 1985, moved beyond the previous project-based approach and towards a more encompassing programme-type policy. They thus became 'pioneer' programmes for the large-scale 1988 EU regional policy reform (Bianchi, 1993).

The main reason for the 1988 reform was the Single European Market (SEM) project, launched in 1986. In light of the uncertainty surrounding the country- and region-specific economic effects of the SEM, the poorer member states requested financial assistance from the EU in order to be able to increase their economic competitiveness. The richer northern member states were willing to satisfy these demands in order to make sure that the economic integration process would further proceed. However, they wanted to make sure that this additional money was spent in a more effective way than previous ERDF funds. As a consequence, the majority of member states were willing to increase the influence of the Commission significantly and to abandon the fixed quotas. However, as discussed above, member states were not willing to establish a system of unbounded fiscal transfers.

The increased EU-level competence for economic and social measures was also manifested by the insertion of the Title 'Economic and Social Cohesion' (Articles 158–162, EEC Treaty) into primary European law.

> In order to promote its overall harmonious development, the Community shall develop and pursue its actions leading to the strengthening of its economic and social cohesion. In particular, the Community shall aim at reducing disparities between the levels of development of the various regions and the backwardness of the least favoured regions, including rural areas (Article 158, EC Treaty).

On the basis of these treaty changes the European Commission drew up a policy approach that was a clear departure from the previous system of EU regional support. The reform affected not only the role and operations of the ERDF but also the other Structural Funds (SFs), namely the ESF and the EAGGF. The most important elements of the reform were arranged around four guiding principles, namely: programming, concentration, additionality and partnership. These principles will be discussed below.

Economic and social cohesion gained even more importance after the treaty revisions at Maastricht. Article 2 of the Treaty on European Union (TEU), listing the objectives of the EU, explicitly refers to the strengthening of economic and social cohesion.

The TEU also led to a number of changes in the instruments of European regional policy. Two further cohesion instruments were created, namely the Cohesion Fund (CF) and the European Investment Fund (EIF), a special credit facility organically linked with the European Investment Bank (EIB). The CF is based on Article 161(2) of the Treaty and provides additional funding for infrastructure and environmental projects in member states with a per capita GDP of less than 90 per cent of the EU average. The EIF is designed to ease the financing of projects in peripheral parts of the EU that involve a higher credit risk than the standard operations of the EIB. The sectoral instruments related to the fishing industry have been reorganised in the form of the Financial Instrument for Guidance in the Fisheries Sector (FIFG) which has become an integral part of the SF operations.

A final change was the establishment of the Committee of the Regions (Articles 263–265). This Committee has advisory status, comparable to the Economic and Social Committee, and is serviced by the same secretariat. However, regardless of its limited power, the existence of a committee consisting of representatives of regional and local bodies reflects the growing importance of sub-national levels of administration within the EU (Kenner, 1994).

Principles of European regional policy

Concentration

One of the guiding principles of the 1988 reform was the concentration of regional policy on those parts of the EU that are in greatest need of support. Prior to the reform, areas eligible for national regional support qualified automatically for support from the European structural funds.

Since the 1988 reform, however, EU-wide regional policy objectives have been developed. The first set of objectives remained valid for 1989–93 and, after some modifications, for 1994–99. A somewhat more substantial reform of the list of objectives was undertaken for the 2000–06 programming period (see Box 8.2).

The objectives can be divided into regional and horizontal objectives. During the 2000–06 period, Objectives 1 and 2 are 'regional', i.e. they refer to certain eligible areas. Under Objective 3, however, it is possible to fund activities throughout the entire EU with the exception of regions covered under Objective 1.

A set of quantitative criteria have been developed in order to make the designation process for region-specific objectives more transparent. In order to qualify for Objective 1 status the regional per capita income, expressed in PPS, must have been less than 75 per cent of the EU average for the last three-year period for which data is available at the start of the programming period. Furthermore, the outermost EU regions (French overseas departments, Azores, Madeira and the Canary Islands) plus the sparsely populated Nordic regions are currently eligible for Objective 1 status. In view of the principle of concentration Objective 1 status is normally given only to NUTS II regions but not to smaller areas.

The designation process for Objective 2 status is somewhat more complex than for Objective 1 regions. This is due to the fact that the overall coverage for Objective 2 was limited prior to the 2000–06 programming period to 18 per cent of the EU population. This aggregate ceiling was further broken down into sub-ceilings for the different types of 'problem' regions covered under Objective 2 (industrial and service areas 10 per cent, rural areas 5 per cent, urban areas 2 per cent, areas

Box 8.2 European regional policy objectives

1994-99

1 Development and structural adjustment of lagging regions.

2 Conversion of regions or parts of regions seriously affected by industrial decline.

3 Combating long-term unemployment and the occupational integration of young people.

4 Facilitating structural change.

5a Speeding up the adjustment of agricultural and fisheries structures.

5b Aimed at the development and structural adjustment of rural areas.

6 Support for areas with very low population density (Nordic regions).

2000-06

1 Combines Objectives 1, 5a and 6 of the 1994–99 period.

2 Combines Objectives 2 and 5b of the 1994–99 period and extends them by including economically 'problematic' urban areas, areas depending on fisheries and highly service-sector dependent areas undergoing conversion.

3 Supporting the adaptation and modernisation of education, training and employment policies and systems (combines Objectives 3 and 4 of the 1994–99 period).

Source: Adapted from European Commission (1999)

dependent on the fishing industry 1 per cent). The Commission starts the designation process by using a set of economic, social and demographic criteria for each of the different types of regions in order to establish ceilings for Objective 2 population coverage in each member state. Member states subsequently submit lists of regions, which they propose for Objective 2 status. These national lists are compiled by the Commission, which, in cooperation with the member states, establishes the final list of eligible regions.

Although it was an explicit aim of the 1988 reform to limit the geographical availability of EU regional assistance, Objectives 1 and 2 regions together still cover around 40 per cent of the EU population. Ever since the EU regional policy reform in 1988 independent commentators have thus argued that the level of spatial concentration should be increased in order to have a higher impact on the recipient economies (Bachtler and Michie, 1993; Martin, 1999). This has also been recognised by the Commission, which has consistently argued in favour of a reduction of the territorial coverage and a clear focus on those regions which are in greatest need of financial assistance. Following a substantial increase in the population coverage from the 1989–93 to the 1994–99 period, the 2000–06 coverage ratio for territorial objectives has declined again and is now slightly below the coverage during the 1989–93 programming period (Objectives 1, 2, 5a, 5b and 6) (see Table 8.1). However, the figures for the 2000–06 period are somewhat too optimistic because those regions that were eligible for support during the 1994–99 period, but not during the 2000–06 period, receive (decreasing levels of) transitional support, mostly until the end of 2006.

Table 8.1 Population covered by European regional policy objectives (%)

Objective	1 and 6 1994	2 1994	5b 1994	1 2000	2 2000	Total 1994	Total 2000
Austria	4	8	29	3	25	41	28
Belgium	13	14	5		12	32	12
Denmark		9	7		10	16	10
Finland	17	16	22	21	31	55	52
Germany	21	9	10	17	13	40	30
Greece	100			99		100	99
Spain	60	20	4	58	22	84	80
Sweden	5	12	9	5	14	26	19
France	4	25	17	3	31	46	34
Ireland	100			25		100	25
Italy	37	11	8	33	13	56	46
Luxembourg		35	8		28	43	28
Netherlands	2	17	5		15	24	15
Portugal	100			65		100	65
UK	6	31	5	8	24	42	32
EU 15	27	16	9	22	18	52	40

Source: Adapted from European Commission

Besides the issue of territorial coverage there is a second aspect to the principle of concentration, namely the allocation of the available funding across the different objectives. During all three programming periods more than two-thirds of the available resources have been allocated to Objectives 1 and 6 regions, arguably those parts of the EU that are in greatest need of structural support. A further 11.5 per cent of the funding is allocated to Objective 2 regions (compared with around 16 per cent for Objectives 2 and 5b during the 1994–99 period) and 12.3 per cent have been allocated to the (non-territorial) Objective 3. This compares with around 11 per cent for Objectives 3 and 4 during the previous programming period. Furthermore, some of the EU funding available for regional policy is used for the so-called Community Initiatives (CIs) (see Box 8.3). All in all little has changed over time regarding the aspect of concentration.

Programming

Prior to the 1988 reforms, aid from the structural funds was granted predominantly on a project basis. This was subsequently changed into the so-called 'programming approach', allowing the integration of different forms of regional support for a particular area into an all-encompassing development plan. The idea behind this change was to improve the coherence between the individual measures, the

---

Box 8.3 Community Initiatives

Some of the EU funding available for regional policy is used for the so-called Community Initiatives (CIs). CIs are designed to support different types of regions suffering, for example, from their location along national borders at the extreme periphery of the EU. The CIs are initiated by the Commission and implemented mainly by the regions. Although some of them have been received rather well, especially INTERREG, which aims to promote cross-border cooperation, the overall assessment of the CIs has tended to be rather negative. In particular, the large number of CIs during the 1989–93 and 1994–99 periods, the resulting lack of concentration and the administrative efforts they require have been criticised.

In response to these criticisms the number of CIs during the 2000–06 period was limited to four, covering the following themes:

1 Trans-national cross-border and inter-regional cooperation (INTERREG).

2 Economic and social conversion of urban areas (URBAN).

3 Rural development through initiatives by local action groups (LEADER+).

4 Transnational cooperation to fight all types of labour market discrimination and inequality (EQUAL).

The funding earmarked for the CIs during the 2000–06 period has been limited to 5.35 per cent of the total Structural Funds budget. This is a considerable reduction compared with the 9 per cent dedicated to the CIs during the period 1994–99. However, given the reduced number of initiatives, it ensures that the available average funding per CI increases markedly.

Source: European Commission, 1999

evaluation of the policy and the coordination between the different institutions involved at EU, member state and regional level.

During the 2000–06 programming period the main steps of the programming are as follows:

First, the Commission adopts guidelines on the common priorities for all three Objectives. These priorities, which should be reflected in all programmes, are relatively general, including, for example, a high degree of competitiveness, high levels of employment and the promotion of equal opportunities for men and women.

Secondly, national regional development plans are drawn up by the national and/or regional authorities. There tend to be substantial variations between these plans. First and most important, plans differ according to objectives. Plans for Objective 1 regions, for example, are obviously rather different from plans for Objective 2 regions. Second, there are also major national and regional differences between areas covered by the same objective. The problems of Puglia in Italy, for example, are only to some extent comparable with those of the western parts of the Republic of Ireland. Furthermore, there are different national preferences for specific regional policy instruments. Some member states or regions put more emphasis on basic infrastructure or education; others prefer to strengthen business-related infrastructures or productive investments.

On the basis of these national or regional plans, the Commission develops, together with the national or regional authorities, the Community Support Frameworks (CSFs). The CSF provide more concrete information on the type and magnitude of the planned expenditures. For the Objective 1 regions in particular, the lion's share of CSF expenditures falls under the categories Productive Investment Support, Human Capital Formation and Infrastructure. The first category includes support measures for industry and services, rural development, fisheries, tourism and agricultural structures. Human Capital Formation covers education, training and R&D, and Infrastructure refers to areas such as transport, communication and energy, but also includes water, environment and health. Table 8.2 provides comparative data on the functional distribution of 1994–99 Structural Funds in the Republic of Ireland, Greece, Portugal and Spain.

The third step in the implementation process is the preparation of more detailed Operational Programmes (OPs). The implementation of the OPs is mainly the task of the national and regional authorities within member states. Intense consultations between national and European authorities take place during the planning and implementation process of the plans, and monitoring committees, made up of national experts as well as Commission officials, are set up for all CSFs and OPs.

Table 8.2 Structural distribution of Objective 1 Structural Fund expenditure in Ireland, Greece, Portugal and Spain, 1994–99

Type of expenditure	Ireland %	Portugal %	Greece %	Spain %
Productive environment	36.2	35.7	27.8	30.5
Human resources	43.9	29.4	24.6	28.4
Infrastructure	19.7	29.7	45.9	40.4

Source: European Commission (1996)

This complex multi-stage programming arrangement has significantly increased the influence of the Commission in regional policy design compared with the pre-1989 period. In fact, it was sometimes argued that it has become too strong (Bachtler and Michie, 1993) and that the process has become too cumbersome. The procedural changes for the 1994–99 and 2000–06 programming periods tried to accommodate this critique by simplifying the process and decentralising the actual management of the programmes. However, given the number of stakeholders involved in the process and the need to ensure sufficient financial control a certain complexity of the process appears unavoidable.

Additionality

The additionality principle dates back to the pre-1989 period and aims to ensure that EU funding actually increases total (national and European) expenditure for structural purposes. More specifically,

> the principle of additionality implies that, throughout the territory concerned, each Member State must maintain its public structural or comparable expenditure for each Objective at least at the same level as in the previous programming period, taking into account, however, the macroeconomic circumstances in which the funding takes place, as well as a number of specific economic circumstances, namely privatisation, an unusual level of public structural expenditure undertaken in the previous programming period and business cycles in the national economy (European Commission, 1999).

Monitoring the additionality principle is a highly complex task, at times resulting in legal disputes between the Commission and member states. A well-documented test case for the additionality debate was the struggle between the Commission and the UK government concerning EU funds under the RECHAR Community Initiative in the early 1990s (McAleavey, 1993). The UK government tried to deduct RECHAR funding allocated to twelve coalmining areas in the UK from the global local authority spending ceilings for these areas. Since this was at odds with the additionality principle, the Commission withheld money earmarked for the UK under RECHAR until the UK government partly accommodated the Commission's objections.

The revised 'coordination regulations' for the 1994–99 and 2000–06 period require member states to provide increasingly detailed financial information to ensure the appropriate implementation of the additionality principle. Nevertheless, it remains doubtful whether more subtle attempts to evade the additionality principle than that practised by the UK government in the RECHAR dispute will be detected.

Partnership

The designers of the 1988 reforms realised that the successful implementation of EU structural policy depends on close partnership and cooperation between European, national and sub-national authorities in order to overcome the formidable information problems created by the involvement of various layers of administration, as well as various sections within these layers.

First, coordination has to take place between the different Structural Funds and between the SFs and related financial instruments of the EU like the EIF. By and large this aspect of partnership does not seem to be a cause of major concern.

The second – somewhat more problematic – aspect of partnership is the link between EU structural policies and non-spatial European and national policies. As argued above, EU expenditures in the context of the CAP, for example, tend to favour the northern European member states more than the cohesion countries. Furthermore, EU rules relating to the use of national state aids are still not fully in line with EU priorities in the field of regional policy. As a result the more prosperous member states still spend more on national state aids than the cohesion countries, thus to some extent offsetting the effects of the latter (Martin, 1999).

The third and probably most prominent aspect of partnership concerns the links between the Commission and the national authorities and bodies. An overall judgement on whether the partnership principle has been successfully put into practice is of course difficult to make. The complex programming system described above certainly creates a large potential for conflicts between the Commission and member states. Especially during the first few years after the 1988 reform such conflicts were regularly mentioned as a major problem of EU regional policy. The absorption of EU commitments by member states, for instance, was in some cases rather low, particularly in Italy. This has been blamed partly on the lack of efficiency of the national administrations and member states' unwillingness to provide the necessary co-finance to match European commitments (Tsoukalis, 1997).

An additional effect of the partnership approach in EU regional policy was the strengthening of the regions vis-à-vis member states. The influence of regional authorities in the Structural Funds' implementation is often greater than in national regional policy schemes. This has been welcomed by a number of commentators as it brings more local knowledge into the regional policy process (Roberts, 1993).

The spatial and functional allocation of Structural Funds support

The development of the financial allocations for European regional policy shows the increased importance of structural action within the overall framework of the EU. Following the 1988 reforms, the available resources for the structural funds have grown from €8 bn pa in 1989 to €32 bn pa in 1999 (at 1999 prices). In relation to the EU budget this represents an increase from around 20 per cent in 1987 to above 35 per cent by 1999.

The financial resources for the 2000–06 period were decided at the 1999 European Summit in Berlin. It was agreed that the resources available for commitment from the Structural Funds and the Cohesion Fund shall be €195 bn over seven years at 1999 prices. In comparison with the 1994–99 period this represents a slight decline of the available resources.

During the 2000–06 period nearly 70 per cent of the SF funding goes to Objective 1 regions, including regions that were de-designated as Objective 1 at the end

Table 8.3 EU resources committed to structural action, 2000–06: breakdown according to member state and objective

	Obj. 1 €m	Obj. 1 (trans.) €m	Obj. 2 €m	Obj. 2+5b (trans.) €m	Obj. 3 €m	CF €m	CIs €m	Fisheries support €m	Total €m
Belgium		625	368	65	737		209	34	2038
Denmark			156	27	365		83	197	828
Germany	19229	729	2984	526	4581		1608	107	29764
Greece	20961					3060	862		24883
Spain	37744	352	2553	98	2140	11160	1958	200	56205
France	3254	551	5437	613	4540		1046	225	15666
Ireland	1315	1773				720	166		3974
Italy	21935	187	2145	377	3744		1172	96	29656
Luxembourg			34	6	38		13		91
Netherlands		123	676	119	1686		651	31	3286
Austria	261		578	102	528		358	4	1831
Portugal	16124	2905				3300	671		23000
Finland	913		459	30	403		245	3	2053
Sweden	722		354	52	720		278	60	2186
UK	5085	1166	3989	706	4568		961	121	16596
EU 15	127543	8411	19733	2721	24050	18240	10281	1078	212057

Note: 1999 prices

Source: Adapted from European Commission

of the 1994–99 period but receive 'transitional' support. The remaining third is divided in roughly even parts between Objectives 2 and 3.

Since 1993, the four cohesion countries – Ireland, Spain, Portugal and Greece – can also benefit from the Cohesion Fund (CF) for the financing of large transport infrastructure and environmental projects. This has become a very significant part of the total assistance that the cohesion countries receive from the EU. As a proportion of total funding – SFs and the CF taken together – the Cohesion Fund support ranges from just over 12 per cent for Greece to around 20 per cent for Spain.

Details of the breakdown of the Structural and Cohesion funds by member state are given in Table 8.3.

In absolute terms Spain is by far the largest recipient country during the 2000–06 period (as well as before), followed by Germany, Italy, Greece, Portugal and – at some distance – the UK. Per capita allocations, however, are by far the highest in Greece and Portugal (around €220 per person), followed by Spain (around €140 per person) and Ireland (around €100 per person). Per capita allocations in all other member states are substantially lower, ranging from around €20 per person in the Benelux countries to around €50 per person in Italy.

EU regional policy and enlargement

Including the ten new member states – in particular those from Central and Eastern Europe – in the EU regional policy arrangements is often seen as one of the two key budgetary challenges of EU enlargement (besides the CAP).

Whereas the EU had started to support the then Central and East European candidate countries as early as 1989 (start of the PHARE programme), the level of support was significantly stepped up in 2000 when two new programmes were launched. SAPARD (Special Accession Programme for Agriculture and Rural Development) was primarily designed to support the efforts made by the applicant countries to join the CAP. However, it also has an impact on the development of rural regions. ISPA (Instrument for Structural Policies pre-Accession) was modelled along the lines of the Cohesion Fund and finances large environmental and infrastructure projects. Until 2004 all the programmes together provided financial assistance in the range of €3 bn pa to the twelve candidate countries.

The countries that joined the EU in May 2004 became eligible for support under the Structural and Cohesion Funds on that date and are expected to receive a total of €21.7 bn during the remaining 2.5 years until the end of the 2000–06 programming period (in 1999 prices). Around two-thirds of this funding is earmarked for the Structural Funds and the remaining third for the Cohesion Fund (European Commission, 2003).

Given their relatively low level of per capita income most parts of the new member states will become eligible for assistance under Objective 1. The only exceptions are the city regions of Prague and Bratislava, as well as Cyprus. The implementation of the Structural Funds in the new member states will be a major challenge for the beneficiaries themselves, especially in view of the rather complex programming and implementation procedures outlined above.

From a medium-term perspective the main challenge for the EU will be to balance the substantial investment needs of the new member states, the desire of the old member states to preserve, at least for a substantial amount of time, some of the financial support they currently enjoy and the unwillingness of the net contributors to the EU budget to increase their contributions. Solutions to this complex problem have to be found in time for the next regional policy programming period starting in 2007.

Evaluating EU regional policy

EU regional policy does not intend to provide a safety net against asymmetric regional shocks but to improve the competitiveness and hence the long-term growth prospects of the supported regions. In order to achieve this aim, EU regional policy would need to have positive supply-side effects in the supported regions. Identifying such effects is, however, a very difficult task. All EU-supported regional policy programmes are now subject not only to mandatory ex-post evaluations, but often also to ex-ante and interim assessments. However, most of these evaluations suffer from major problems (Bachtler and Michie, 1995). Apart from the usual anti-monde problem of policy evaluation, the availability of regional data in the EU still leaves much to be desired.

Ex-post evaluations of the effects of structural policy based on macro-economic models partly depend on the assumptions on which these models are based. There are therefore large differences in the estimations of additional growth that arises from the structural funds. The HERMIN models focus not only on the demand-side effects of regional policy transfers but also on the supply-side improvements due to increased infrastructure and human capital stocks. HERMIN models for the four cohesion countries as well as eastern Germany predict that annual GDP growth in these countries/regions will be permanently between 1 and 2 per cent higher than without Structural and Cohesion Fund interventions (European Commission, 2000).

The QUEST II model estimates take into account that some of the positive shorter-term growth effects of regional support will be reduced by a deterioration of the trade balance (due to an appreciation of the real exchange rates) and some crowding-out of private investment due to an increase in real interest rates. Regarding the longer-term supply-side effects of regional policy, however, the QUEST II results for the cohesion countries are by and large comparable with the results of the HERMIN models. Estimates for the effect of structural funding for other economic variables such as employment follow broadly the results for GDP growth.

Econometric tests using cross-section or panel-data analyses of the effectiveness of EU structural funding are often more pessimistic than the model-based approaches but their results differ substantially. Canova and Marcet (1995), for example, are very pessimistic regarding the impact of the SFs on convergence in the EU. In contrast, Ederveen et al. (2002) argue that Structural Funds are only effective for countries with the 'right' institutions and Beugelsdijk and Eijffinger (2003) argue that the importance of the Structural Funds for income convergence cannot be neglected, regardless of the quality of national institutions in the recipient countries.

It should also be kept in mind that these studies investigate only the effectiveness of structural funding on economic convergence. Whether the net welfare effect of regional policy remains positive if one takes the financial costs and the opportunity costs of structural support into account remains an open question.

Conclusion

Since the seminal changes to EU regional policy in the late 1980s, the EU's activities in this field have become one of the most important policy fields of the Union. In terms of budgetary importance it is only surpassed by the CAP and the future design of regional policy in the enlarged EU is thus one of the most hotly debated issues in EU politics.

Although the large body of work evaluating the effects of EU regional policy does not arrive at uniform conclusions, on balance the results tend to suggest that EU regional policy has a positive long-term impact on economic growth, at least in the main recipient countries and regions. At the same time, however, many observers of EU regional policy flag that the current system of regional support could be further improved. Suggestions for such improvements for EU regional policy come under two different categories – first, improvements within the present framework and, secondly, more fundamental changes to the way in which regional economic imbalances within the EU should be tackled.

As far as the first category is concerned, a further increase in the level of spatial concentration of support and further simplifications of the procedures would appear desirable, although these demands have been partly accommodated with the changes in 1999. Another area where further improvements should be achieved relates to the coordination between EU regional policy, national regional policy and non-spatial European and national policies.

Looking at the second type of recommendations, it is often argued that member states and regions should take the link between factor returns and productivity more closely into account. To use an example, centralised wage-setting systems that do not take regional productivity differences sufficiently into account are bound to increase regional unemployment problems. Another way to improve intra-European factor allocation would be to encourage factor mobility within the EU, for example by abolishing remaining administrative obstacles to labour mobility.

Especially in view of the economic and budgetary challenges that enlargement will bring about for EU regional policy, it is important to look also at alternative mechanisms to cope with regional heterogeneity within the EU.

References

Alesina A and Rodrik D (1994) 'Distributive Politics and Economic Growth', *Quarterly Journal of Economics*, Vol. 109, May, pp. 465–90.

Bachtler J and Michie R (1993) 'The Restructuring of Regional Policy in the European Community', *Regional Studies*, Vol. 27, pp. 719–25.

Bachtler J and Michie R (1995) 'A New Era in EU Regional Policy Evaluation?: The Appraisal of the Structural Funds', *Regional Studies*, Vol. 29, No. 8, pp. 745–51.

Barro R and Sala-i-Martin X (1995) *Economic Growth*, McGraw-Hill, New York.

Beugelsdijk M and Eijffinger S (2003) *The Effectiveness of Structural Policy in the European Union: An Empirical Analysis for the EU15 During the Period 1995–2001*, CEPR Discussion Paper 3879, London.

Bianchi G (1993) 'The IMPs: A Missed Opportunity?' in R Leonardi (ed.), *The Regions and the European Community*, Frank Cass, London, pp. 47–70.

Canova F and Marcet A (1995) The Poor Stay Poor: Non-convergence across Countries and Regions, CEPR Discussion Paper 1265, London.

CEPR (Centre for Economic Policy Research) (1993) *Monitoring European Integration 4 – Making Sense of Subsidiarity: How Much Centralization for Europe*, CEPR, London.

Ederveen S (2002) *Fertile soil for Structural Funds?: A Panel Data Analysis of the Conditional Effectiveness of European Cohesion Policy*, CPB discussion paper No. 10, The Hague.

European Commission (1993) 'New Location Factors for Mobile Investments', *European Regional Development Studies*, Vol. 6, Office for Official Publications of the European Communities, Luxembourg.

European Commission (1996) *First Report on Economic and Social Cohesion*, Office for Official Publications of the European Communities, Luxembourg.

European Commission (1999) *Reform of the Structural Funds 2000–06: Comparative Analysis*, Brussels.

European Commission (2000) 'The EU Economy 2000 Review', *European Economy*, No. 71, Office for Official Publications of the European Communities, Luxembourg.

European Commission (2001) *Second Report on Economic and Social Cohesion*, Office for Official Publications of the European Communities, Luxembourg.

European Commission (2003) *Second Progress Report on Economic and Social Cohesion*, COM(2003)34 final, Brussels.

Fujita M, Krugman P and Venables A J (1999) *The Spatial Economy: Cities, Regions and International Trade*, MIT Press, Cambridge, Mass.

Kenner J (1994) 'Economic and Social Cohesion: The Rocky Road Ahead', *Legal Issues of European Integration*, No. 1, pp. 1–36.

Lammers K (1992) 'Mehr regionalpolitische Kompetenz für die EG im Europäischen Binnenmarkt?: Akademie für Raumforschung und Landesplanung (Hrsg), Regionale Wirtschaftspolitik auf dem Weg zur europäischen Integration', *Forschungs- und Sitzungsberichte*, No. 187, Hannover, pp. 70–82.

McAleavey P (1993) 'The Politics of European Regional Development Policy: Additionality in the Scottish Minefields', *Regional Politics and Policy*, Vol. 3, No. 2, pp. 88–107.

Martin R (1999) *The Regional Dimension in European Public Policy*, Macmillan, Basingstoke.

North D (1994) 'Institutional Competition', in H Siebert (ed.), *Locational Competition in the World Economy*, Mohr, Tübingen, pp. 27–37.

Roberts P (1993) 'Managing the Strategic Planning and Development of Regions: Lessons from a European Perspective', *Regional Studies*, Vol. 27, No. 8, pp. 759–68.

Temple M (1994) *Regional Economics*, St Martin's Press, New York.

Tsoukalis L (1997) *The New European Community: The Politics and Economics of Integration*, Oxford University Press, Oxford.

Weise C (1995) 'EU-Politik zur Steigerung regionaler Wettbewerbsfähigkeit', *Vierteljahreshefte zur Wirtschaftsforschung*, Vol. 64, No. 2, pp. 266–77.

Further reading

Armstrong H W and Vickerman R W (eds) (1995) *Convergence and Divergence among European Regions*, Pion, London.

Biehl D (1991) 'The Role of Infrastructure in Regional Development', in Vickerman R W (ed.), *Infrastructure and Regional Development*, Pion, London, pp. 9–35.

Crafts N and Toniolo G (eds) (1996) *Economic Growth in Europe since 1945*, CUP and CEPR, Cambridge.

de la Fuente A and Vives X (1995) 'Infrastructure and Education as Instruments of Regional Policy: Evidence from Spain', *Economic Policy*, April, pp. 12–51.

Hansen N (1995) 'Addressing Regional Disparity and Equity Objectives through Regional Policies: A Sceptical Perspective', *Papers in Regional Science*, Vol. 74, No. 2, pp. 89–104.

Krugman P (1991) *Geography and Trade*, LUP, Leuven, and MIT Press, Cambridge, Mass.

Chapter 9

Environmental policy

John Hassan and Stephen Dearden

Introduction

The Treaty of Rome made no provision for a Community environment policy. When it became apparent in the early 1970s, however, that environmental problems might disrupt the Community's economic mission, the desirability of taking action in this field was recognised.

In 1971 the Commission made its first detailed Communication to the Council on the need for a Community policy. The impending oil crisis and pressures from environmentalists led heads of state to agree on the adoption of a policy in 1972. The EU's environmental programmes now cover many fields, ranging from chemicals to climate change, but, briefly, the aims of the policy today are to protect the natural environment so as to contribute towards the realisation of sustainable growth and to bolster the single market. This chapter considers the case for an EU environment policy; it traces the development of Community actions, and illustrates the application of the policy with reference to traditional concerns in the fields of water and air pollution and waste management before, finally, assessing the impact of the policy.

The need for an EU environment policy

Three major factors have influenced the development of the environmental policy of the EU:

1 issues connected to transfrontier pollution;
2 determining the conditions for fair and free trade;
3 developing efficient and sustainable growth.

Transfrontier pollution

That the EU should have an environment policy can be argued on a variety of grounds. Environmental degradation might provoke economic or even ecological disaster. In the 1970s, a decade dominated by the oil shocks of 1973 and 1979, there were fears that resource shortages might destroy the world's economic prospects. Since the 1980s new concerns have developed especially about atmospheric pollution, which results in acidification, ozone depletion and global warming and which leads therefore to climate change, threatening not just economic activity but the very existence of the human species. Such pollution does not respect national frontiers. The EU, with its unique supranational institutions and legal instruments, is well qualified to coordinate Europe-wide actions in the field.

Fair and free trading conditions

To fulfil the objectives of the Treaty of Rome and, in particular to realise a single European market, implies the implementation of common environmental policies by member states. The adoption by member states of different environment standards may lead to a form of social dumping where industries in countries with lax regulations enjoy a competitive advantage by ignoring marginal environmental costs. This leads them to overproduce and sell products at less than their true costs of production to the detriment of their trading partners (see Exhibit 9.1). In these conditions the harmonisation of environmental policies and standards is necessary in order to ensure that neutrality of competition between members of the EU is achieved.

Economic efficiency and sustainability

The problem of selecting appropriate policy instruments to progress the aims of the EU's environment policy is related to the need to achieve efficient and sustainable economic growth. In principle, efficiency is promoted by requiring firms to internalise the external costs created by their polluting actions, so that output is set where price equals total costs. An effective method of achieving this, thereby curbing pollution, is through the use of market instruments, such as emission charges or, arguably, the theoretically even more desirable solution of tradeable instruments (see Exhibit 9.2). However, in some countries, for example where municipal authorities are responsible for water quality management, there is a strong reluctance to replace traditional instruments of control with market-based methods of pollution control. In other cases a country, such as the Netherlands, may wish to retain tough regulatory controls in order to maintain world leadership in pollution abatement technology. There is a great deal of rhetorical support for market instruments in governmental and EU forums. However, as long as the relevant Community legal instruments prescribe only the ends, and not the means, of the environment policy, the pursuit of its objectives will remain contingent upon national factors. The incorporation of market-based methods into the EU environment policy therefore faces considerable obstacles, as the failure to agree on a carbon tax in 1993 illustrates. Consequently, traditional regulatory methods, such as setting quality standards for water and air, are likely to continue to be relied upon for some time. While this pragmatism may not produce economically optimal outcomes, it is much better than no action and can still contribute towards the realisation of the objectives of the EU's environment policy.

Exhibit 9.1 Environmental standards and fair trade

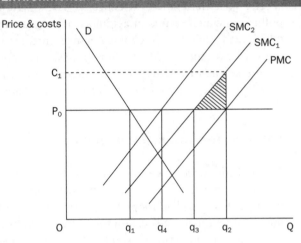

D = demand in the UK

P_1 = ruling market price in both Germany and the UK

PMC = private marginal cost in the UK

SMC = PMC plus the marginal cost of the pollution associated with the production of output

SMC_1 = social marginal cost in the UK

SMC_2 = social marginal cost in the UK if German environmental standards are used

If no account is taken of the cost of pollution, UK companies would produce an output of Oq_2. As demand in the UK is equal to Oq_1, the extra output (i.e. q_2–q_1) would be exported to Germany. At this level of output the UK is not taking into account the pollution costs of producing the output. This imposes a cost (on the UK economy) shown by the shaded area (i.e. the area of social cost above the revenue received from selling output Oq_2 at the price of P_1). The UK could be accused of social dumping because it is not covering the social cost of the production. However, it should be noted that this cost falls on the UK economy. The unfairness on the German economy is that, if the UK covered the social costs of the pollution, it would have an output of Oq_3, which would mean that exports to Germany would fall to q_1–q_3, thereby leaving more of the German market to their own producers.

However, if UK firms had to endure the social marginal costs of Germany when producing this output, production in the UK would fall to $Oq4$. Such an outcome would be inefficient because in this example the UK has lower social costs of pollution than Germany. Nevertheless, if Germany succeeded in having its views on the costs of pollution accepted by the EU, then UK companies would be treated unfairly. This example illustrates how environmental standards can be used to protect domestic markets. Moreover, in cases where the social costs of pollution differ between countries, the analysis indicates that environmental standards should vary according to the SMCs that prevail across countries.

Empirical studies appear to demonstrate that non-action is costly. Environmental regulations may well increase industrial production costs. However, pollution and corrosion cause damage to forests, agricultural land, buildings, equipment and human health and productivity. Public spending on environmental programmes in leading industrial countries in the 1980s was in the region of 0.8 to 2 per cent of GDP. To estimate the benefits of environmental protection policies is more problematic, and the methodologies chosen obviously have a major impact upon the

Exhibit 9.2 Efficient level of pollution

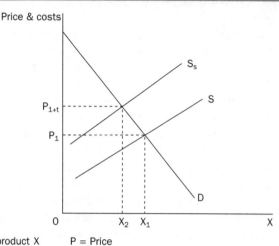

D = Demand for product X   P = Price

S = Supply of product X

Ss = Supply of product X including social costs of pollution

If there are no prohibitions on pollution associated with the production and consumption of X the price and output would be P1 : X1. However, if the costs of pollution are taken into account in the production and consumption, the output should be OX_2. This output can be induced by a variety of means. Regulations could be issued to restrict output to OX_2. Alternatively, a tax could be placed on the good X until the price becomes P + t. A market-based solution would allocate permits to pollute up to the output level OX_2. If these permits were tradeable on markets, producers or consumers could purchase permits to pollute. In these circumstances those companies or consumers who obtain most benefit from the pollution (in terms of their valuation of the good X) would buy most of the permits. By this method the right to pollute would be given to those who put most value on this activity. The other two systems (regulation or taxation) may not achieve such an efficient outcome. However, if the distribution of income is not equal, the right to buy and sell the permits to pollute will reflect income differences as well as the valuation of the use of product X. The use of tradeable permits is often objected to on the grounds that they would reflect income differences more than the valuation that people place on the goods and services that pollute the environment when they are produced and/or consumed. For example, selling the right to pollute by driving cars would favour those who have high incomes. In these circumstances the use of regulation or taxes may offer a better solution.

findings obtained. The potential savings to the national economies vary, according to some studies, from 3.5 to 6 per cent of GDP (European Commission, 1987; OECD, 1984, 1989).

Such findings support the thrust of much contemporary thinking that sustainable economic development and environmental protection are not competing but are, in fact, mutually supporting objectives. Most famously popularised by the Brundtland Report (World Commission, 1987), this approach emphasises the interdependence of ecological and economic imperatives. These principles have been formally adopted by the EU, Article 2 of the Maastricht Treaty of 1991 committing the signatories to develop environmental policies which achieve sustainable growth.

The development of the Community's environment policy

After ministers had agreed to the adoption of an environment policy in 1972 an Environmental and Protection Service was established. This was elevated to full DG status in 1981. Once the decision had been made to add the environment to the Community's agenda it was not unnatural for attention to turn to the water environment where, at Europe's heart, there existed the apparently intractible problem of the grossly polluted River Rhine. The first Environmental Action Programme (EAP) covering 1973–77 stressed the need to reduce water pollution. In 1975 and 1976, as well as legislation specifying quality standards for different categories of water, agreements were also reached on smoke and SO_2 emissions and on waste management. Framework Directives were followed by Daughter Directives, which prescribed detailed rules or standards in more narrowly defined areas.

EAPs set out a broad framework for Community policy. The first made a commitment to the 'polluter pays' principle and stressed the need for preventive rather than remedial actions. Although the second EAP (1977–81) extended and updated the first, actual actions taken during this period were reactive and sought to redress urgent problems in specific sectors.

The limitations of this reactive approach were gradually recognised. It was realised that account should be taken of the interactions between polluting discharges and the environments which receive pollutants, and of the transfer of pollution from one part of the environment to another. In the third EAP (1982–86) environmental protection was viewed as a key factor in many fields, not just as a separate problem. An overall framework for policy development was proposed, which sought to encourage the integration of environmental considerations into the planning activities of other areas, including energy, industry and tourism.

Acknowledging the interdependency of environmental problems, agreement was reached on an Environmental Impact Assessment (EIA) Directive in 1985. It required member states to carry out assessments of the likely environmental effects of major industrial or infrastructure proposals before planning consent is given. Assessment has to be made of the probable polluting effects of planned projects, and of the impacts upon wildlife, natural resources and the cultural and archaeological heritage. Certain projects are exempted, and the EIA Directive does not apply to projects authorised by specific national legislation, for example the Channel Tunnel.

The growing importance of environmental protection to the Community was reflected in the agreement to the SEA of 1986. This measure was of fundamental importance for the development of environment policy. Hitherto Community action was based on a liberal interpretation of the application of the Treaty of Rome's omnibus clause, Article 235, to environmental issues. The SEA not only reiterated the goals of the Community's policy, but also explicitly confirmed for the first time, under Article 130, its competence to act in the field of environmental protection. Moreover, the power of the Council to take decisions by qualified majority voting (QMV) on environmental measures that bear on the single market was established. In addition, it was stated that: 'environmental protection requirements shall be a component of the Community's other policies'. Requiring that all other Community policies should take account of the environmental dimension is a unique clause in

EC law. If fully enforced, it would have far-reaching implications for other policy areas, such as agriculture and transport. The Maastricht Treaty confirmed the commitment to such principles and reiterated the Union's competence in the environmental field.

Meanwhile, the fourth EAP (1987–92) continued established themes, but also reaffirmed the new emphasis upon integration in the Community's policy. As well as urging action in a number of sectoral areas, such as the use of agro-chemicals and the treatment of agricultural wastes, the need for measures to bolster the completion of the SEM was identified. Further, the necessity of improving the implementation of environmental Directives was a central theme of the fourth EAP.

The decision in 1990 to create a European Environment Agency (EEA) was an expression of the moves to promote integration, the preventive principle and better implementation as core themes of the environment policy. The European Parliament (EP) wanted the Agency to have the power to enforce environmental law and to execute EIAs for EU-funded policies. However, wider disputes over the location of several EU institutions delayed the establishment of the EEA until 1994. It has been concerned primarily with monitoring the progress and impact of the environment policy and with improving the standardisation and exchange of environmental information.

The fifth EAP, entitled 'Towards Sustainability', was adopted in 1992 and covers the period 1993–2000. To achieve the reconciliation of economic growth and environmental protection, it identified the need for a proactive approach in a number of areas, including the integration of environmental considerations into other policy fields, the broadening of the range of instruments, and the stricter enforcement of legislation. Reflecting major concerns over issues like global warming and the increased loads placed upon the natural environment, the fifth EAP called for specific action in a number of sectors, notably energy, transport, agriculture and tourism, and also adopted a number of targets for the reduction of polluting emissions by 2000.

In 2002 European Parliament and Council adopted the sixth EAP, covering the period up to 2010 (COM(2001)31). The new programme focuses upon four areas: climate change; nature and biodiversity; environmental health; natural resources; and waste. In regard to climate change the principal objective is to achieve the Kyoto Protocol target of reducing greenhouse gas emissions by 8 per cent by 2008–12. To achieve this the Commission proposes, among other strategies, the introduction of an EU-wide emissions trading scheme. Under biodiversity the Commission emphasises the implementation of the existing legislation, particularly in regard to the air and water Directives. Similarly, for environment and health the Commission will be pursuing the adoption of a Directive on noise pollution, the banning of the use of hazardous pesticides and developing a new system of evaluation and risk management for new chemicals. The Commission is also proposing a 20 per cent reduction in waste by 2010 through strategies including taxation of resource use and the introduction of integrated product policies, which take account of resource use and disposal.

The sixth EAP continues to recognise the importance of the effective implementation and monitoring of existing legislation. However, it also emphasises a broader approach – integrating environmental considerations into other policies, employing market incentives, and encouraging both businesses and consumers to adopt best practice (e.g. encouraging the wide adoption of the Community's Eco-management and Audit Scheme (EMAS) and eco-labelling). This broader 'participatory' approach is seen as central to achieving the Community's commitment to 'sustainable' growth.

The EU's environment policy faces a particular challenge from the accession of the new member states from Central and Eastern Europe. While 'Agenda 2000' lays down the requirement that the accession states adopt the EU's existing legal framework (the 'acquis communitaire'), the Community also recognises the difficulties that this will present. To assist in the transition the Community will be providing €3.5 bn, over the period 2000–07, for environmental infrastructural investment (ISPA), €1.5 bn pa under Phare and €500 m pa for rural schemes, including afforestation. However, it is estimated that this will meet only 4 per cent of the €120 bn investment required to conform with the EU's existing environmental standards. Therefore the Commission has proposed a phased approach (COM(98)294) which identifies priority areas and objectives, especially with regard to water and air pollution.

Examples of EU environmental legislation

We can now turn to examination, in greater detail, of three major areas of EU environmental legislation:

- quality of water;
- atmospheric pollution;
- waste management.

Water Directives

Measures to control water pollution have been so numerous that they have been described as 'the jewel in the crown of the EU's environment policy' (Economist Intelligence Unit, 1989). If oversimplifying, it is convenient to distinguish three groups of water directives: those detailing quality standards applicable to specified categories of water, including bathing, drinking, shellfish waters and inland fisheries; those aiming to control the emission of dangerous substances; and those seeking to secure a greater protection of water resources as a whole.

The implementation of all these Directives has invariably provoked controversy. Since 1993 the Commission has developed proposals for an updating and simplification of the bathing and drinking water Directives, but there is little prospect that this will lead to a dilution of EU water law. More specific daughter Directives, which followed the agreement on the parent Dangerous Substances Directive, have led in some cases to significant reductions in particular sources of pollution, notably mercury emissions. Nevertheless, the original ambition to extend such controls to 109 'black list' substances has now been abandoned, only 17 having been agreed since 1976. The Urban Waste Water Treatment Directive, which greatly reduced the sewage pollution of coastal waters from the late 1990s, and a Nitrate Directive, which targets pollution from agricultural fertilisers, were both agreed in 1991. They are illustrative of the Commission's attempts to achieve a more general protection of the water environment which received fresh impetus with the issue of a Communication in 1996 on the need to develop a more flexible and integrated approach to the EU's water policy.

After consultation the Commission brought forward a comprehensive Water Framework Directive. This Directive (2000/60/EC) replaces seven of the existing water Directives. The Commission intends to set minimum ecological and chemical standards for water quality to be achieved by specific deadlines. The Directive signifies a move away from either source controls, which can allow the unsustainable accumulation of pollutants, or quality controls, which can underestimate the adverse cumulative effect of particular substances. Instead, the Commission introduced a 'combined approach'. Here, after the adoption of all existing basic technology-driven source-based controls, there will be a focus upon the further reduction of those pollutants identified by the EU as presenting the highest risk.

River basin management, regardless of political boundaries, is central to this Directive. A river basin management plan, revised every six years, will specify the approach to be taken to achieve the broad objectives of the protection of drinking and bathing water, and of the local ecology. After a review of the basin's characteristics, including an economic analysis of water use and the impact of existing legislation, any continuing inadequacies can be identified. Considerable emphasis is placed upon the public consultation, which must follow, in identifying cost-effective solutions to continuing problems. Finally, the Directive requires member states, by 2010, to ensure that the prices charged for water and waste treatment accurately reflect their true costs.

A further Directive is intended to address the issue of groundwater pollution. In addition to enforcing compliance with the European standards on the discharge of nitrates, pesticides and biocides, there will be a general prohibition of direct discharge to groundwater. Groundwater extraction will also be limited to that which can be sustained.

Atmospheric pollution

For a number of reasons, EU rules on air quality are less comprehensive and ambitious than those pertaining to water quality. However, from the 1980s those forms of pollution which contribute to acidification, ozone depletion and global warming have warranted more decisive actions. Nevertheless, EU moves frequently consist of endorsing broader international agreements.

Directive 88/609 was the first major attempt to tackle the problem of acid rain. It requires reductions of emissions of SO_2, NO_x and dust from power stations. This step has been followed by several others setting stricter standards for emissions from power stations and motor vehicles.

The Montreal Protocol of 1987 on ozone depletion led to EU regulations being agreed in 1988, 1991 and 1994, which have set progressively tougher targets with a view to achieving the virtual elimination of CFC gases in Western Europe by 2000.

Box 9.1 Greenhouse gas emissions trading system

The concept of tradable allowances is not new and has already been adopted in the case of the CAP (dairy quotas) and fisheries policy (catch quotas).

Under the Directive (COM(2002)680) existing polluters will be allocated an emission allowance by their national authorities. If they are able to reduce their emissions below their existing level, they would be able to sell their excess emission allowance to other polluters through an emissions trading market.

Such a system introduces flexibility into the regulatory process. It provides an incentive to polluters to develop and adopt cleaner technology, while allowing individual companies to exceed their existing emission levels on the condition that they are able to purchase spare allowances. Such a trading system 'internalises' the external cost of pollution. It places a monetary value upon the use of clean air.

The Commission is proposing the gradual introduction of such a system from 2005, starting with the largest sources of carbon dioxide. The later reduction in the allocation of emission allowances to meet the Community's Kyoto commitments is going to present one of the greatest difficulties. Nonetheless, a community-based scheme is essential to avoid distortions to the internal market, which might arise with any national approach.

The EU signed up in 1992 to a convention on climate change at the Rio de Janeiro conference. The chief method of squaring up to global warming has been to seek agreement on reductions of emissions of CO_2, the main greenhouse gas. In 1990 the EU had agreed, under the UN Framework Convention on Climate Change, to a stabilisation of CO_2 emissions by the year 2000 at their then current levels. Under the Kyoto Protocol, agreed in 1997 under this Convention, the EU committed itself to a further 8 per cent reduction in six key greenhouse gas emissions (expressed in 'CO_2 equivalents') by 2008–12. To realise these targets in 2000 the EU launched the European Climate Change Programme (ECCP). The ECCP's initial work focused on the energy, transport and industry sectors. The priorities for action were outlined in the first Action Plan (COM(201)580). These included a proposed Directive promoting the use of biofuels, a voluntary commitment by carmakers to improve fuel economy by 25 per cent and the adoption of an EU-wide emission trading scheme (Box 9.1).

By 2000 the EU's total greenhouse gas emissions stood at 3.5 per cent below their 1990 level. However, most member states are well above their target reduction rate, and without the effective implementation of recent additional measures, both at European and national level, the EU will not meet its commitments.

Waste management

Each year the EU generates 1.3 bn tonnes of waste, 40 m tonnes of it hazardous. This represents 3.5 tonnes per person across the Community and 67 per cent of it is either burnt or dumped in landfill sites. On current trends it is estimated that, by 2020, the EU will be generating 45 per cent more waste than in 1995.

The Framework Directive 75/442 to promote the safe disposal of hazardous substances was one of the earliest pieces of EC environmental legislation. A proliferation of agreements have built upon this Directive, specifying detailed procedures over the disposal of products like polychlorinated biphenyl, waste oils, liquid containers, sewage sludge and other toxic or dangerous substances.

While EU waste management policy has made progress in certain areas, such as the transboundary shipment of hazardous substances, other agreements, for example recycling and the re-utilisation of waste, initially made little impact. Policy statements in this area did little more than piously extol good practice rather than laying down regulatory standards. The need for more determined actions to harmonise the management and disposal of waste was implied by the disappearance of national border controls after 1992. Partly in anticipation of the single market a long-awaited Commission paper, 'A Community Strategy for Waste Management', was approved in 1990. By 1996 parts of the strategy had been realised, including agreements on landfills, incineration, packaging and eco-labelling.

The Sixth EAP prioritises waste reduction and the Community has set a target of a 20 per cent reduction in the 'final disposal' of waste between 2000 and 2010, and 50 per cent by 2050. The strategy is a based upon three elements: waste prevention, recycling and improving final disposal. Waste prevention can be achieved through improving manufacturing methods and reducing packaging. Recovery of materials and reuse has focused upon vehicles, batteries and electrical goods. The Directive on electrical and electronic equipment (COM(2000)347) requires member states to create a free collection system for redundant items and the creation of suitable waste treatment facilities. Five years after the adoption of the Directive (i.e. 2005) the cost of collection and treatment will fall upon producers – the 'polluter pays' principle. The Directive also sets a recovery target of 80 per cent of large household items and 60 per cent on small items to be achieved by 2004. To deter households from disposing of electrical equipment with other household waste, the Directive sets a separate collection target rate of 4 kg (9 lb) per household to be achieved by 2006.

The EU has also recently approved Directives setting emission levels for incinerators (2000/76/EC) and the guidelines for landfill management (99/31/EC). Landfill is seen as the least satisfactory solution to waste disposal and certain types of material (e.g. tyres) can no longer be landfilled.

Assessment

Environment policy was often regarded as one of the EU's major successes. Despite the lack of an explicit legal basis and unanimous voting being required, by 1986 some 100 Community texts in the environment field had been agreed, and the number has continued to grow since then. In addition to this legislative achievement, elaborate systems have been developed to gather and harmonise environmental data and to monitor the numerous initiatives that have been adopted under the environment policy. For some time, however, observers (e.g. Klatte, 1986) have commented upon a marked discrepancy between the weight of environmental legislation and the effect it has exercised upon the natural environment.

Studies published in 1987 reveal ambiguous evidence regarding the policy's environmental impact (European Commission, 1987; Weidner, 1987). In the 1980s declining emissions of smoke and SO_2 could be contrasted with growing emissions of CO_2 and NO_x. There was some evidence of an improvement in inland water quality, to be set against a continued loss of habitats in marine waters, dumping in coastal zones and the gathering of a variety of pollutants in the seas, leading to a complex range of difficulties.

In the 1990s further reviews of the EU's environment policy were published (EEA, 1995a, 1995b, 1996; European Commission, 1992, 1996). Their conclusions were that pressures on the environment showed little sign of abating and that there was a danger of critical loads being exceeded. Some progress towards achieving targeted reductions in polluting emissions by 2000 have been made, including CFCs and SO_2. In regard to river water quality, the latest assessment has identified a significant reduction in phosphorus, ammonia and organic waste, although these remain above the natural level. However, nitrate run-off from agricultural land remains unsatisfactory, suggesting inadequate implementation of the Nitrate Directive. However, disappointing trends in the 1990s were reported for a number of categories, from biodiversity and climate change to industrial accidents and urban noise levels. The fall in CO_2 emissions in the early 1990s was due to unusual factors, such as the collapse of industrial activity in East Germany. By contrast CO_2 and other greenhouse gas emissions rose between 1999 and 2000, leaving CO_2 emissions only 0.5 per cent lower than a decade earlier. The greatest environmental challenges continued to be presented by transport and agricultural activities.

The implementation deficit

In reviewing the environment policy the Commission is wont to present a brave face and express 'cautious optimism' about the future. But it accepts that significant obstacles thwart the realisation of policy objectives and that the impact of the policy has been disappointing. As well as the emergence of disquieting trends as regards the meeting of sectoral targets, the Commission is equally concerned about the political problems which underlie EU policy formation. Where the EU had a 'lead role', by 1996 allegedly 70 per cent of the commitments envisaged by the fifth EAP had been achieved, but realisation had been much more problematic at the member state level. For example, negligible progress had been made in broadening the range of policy instruments.

The fundamental reasons for the patchy impact of the EU environment policy lie with the long-recognised difficulties facing the implementation and enforcement of the policy. Several factors account for the 'implementation deficit'.

Insufficient resources

Given that it would not be legitimate to count Cohesion Funds as instruments of environment policy (Wilkinson, 1994), it may be argued that it is supported by insufficient resources. The proportion of the general budget dispensed through DG XI, the environment directorate, increased from 0.02 per cent in 1978 to only

0.05 per cent in 1994. In 2002 only €181 m (0.19 per cent) of the EU's general budget was allocated to environmental expenditure. With only 550 Brussels-based staff at its disposal the Commission has left the initiation of complaints against contravention of the environmental rules to individual persons or organisations.

Policy conflicts

The pursuit and implementation of environment policy is undermined when its goals are in conflict with other EU policies. The pursuit of economic growth, the CAP and the energy policy, especially in its stress, for example, on the need to expand indigenous energy production, may all potentially lead to a worsening of water or air pollution. Recent attempts to seek an integration of environmental considerations into other policy fields have recognised this weakness, without necessarily resolving it.

Policy instruments

For many years member states seemed to approach their environmental commitments as if they were discretionary rather than legally binding. This was encouraged partly by the non-coercive nature of the policy instruments. EIAs are compulsory for most major projects, but their conclusions may be ignored. The Commission's EAPs were merely 'noted' by the Council of Ministers; they were not formally adopted. The weaknesses of the EAPs were recognised in 1995 and 1996 when the Commission called for an 'acceleration' of the policy, and issued a proposal to supplement the EAPs with new Action Plans. The significance of this initiative would lie with the process leading up to the adoption of the so-called Action Plans, namely that compromises would be made in order to reach agreements on targets, which would then, however, become legally binding, whereas the EAPs set tough targets without legal obligations.

The principal instruments of the environment policy are Directives, and here lies the fundamental difficulty. They are technically binding as to outcome, but the choice of method to achieve the desired result is left to member states (a two-stage process involving legislative 'transposition' at the national level, followed by practical implementation). Delegation of responsibility to member states, and the sometimes ambiguous phraseology employed in the Directives, have permitted considerable scope for distortion, misinterpretation and delay. Klatte (1986) and Haigh (1987) noted how the environmental Directives were often badly implemented, incorrectly or not at all. A classic case of mischievous misinterpretation was the UK's initial designation in 1979 of only 27 bathing beaches under the bathing water Directive, in contrast to France's 3000 designated beaches, and even land-locked Luxembourg recorded 39.

The difficulties over non-compliance have been recognised, and enforcement was an important theme of the fourth and fifth EAPs. Since the late 1980s the Commission has been more ready to instigate legal proceeding against the governments of errant states. Even the threat of legal action can have an effect, encouraging the UK, for instance, to designate a further 326 bathing areas. However, the enforcement procedure available to the Commission has limitations. It is an extremely ponderous process and, moreover, the final decision whether to start proceedings is taken collectively by the Commissioners. It is, therefore, more a political than a legal decision, as is obvious when government ministers indulge in much publicised 'rows' over the environmental Directives that are clearly intended to influence the Commissioners' outlook. Dilatory application of EU environmental law by member states remains a serious weakness of the environment policy to this day.

Conclusion

It would be inappropriate to conclude on too negative a note. Some of the weaknesses arising from policy contradictions or the devolution of responsibility for implementing Directives to member states are not peculiar to environment policy.

Despite the reservations made in this chapter, the policy has undoubtedly had major environmental, industrial and institutional effects. When it involved agreements to non-legally binding objectives or, as has been the tendency recently, takes the form of complex and ambitious goals in relatively elusive areas such as biodiversity, then assessment of the environmental policy's impact may conclude that it has been limited. However, this is not the direction in which the Commission wishes to take the policy. When well-defined standards are established for controlling the discharge of specified pollutants then its effect has been palpable.

Protestations by politicians and interest groups that the Directives are very costly to implement and undermine national sovereignty suggest that the environment policy does force changes in national behaviour. This was reflected by the vain hopes, expressed in industrial and government circles in the UK in 1992–93, that the concept of subsidiarity and proposals to rationalise the water Directives would lead to a lessening of legislative and financial burdens. In fact, it is demonstrable that EU environmental law has led to several sectors undertaking multi-million, if not multi-billion pound investment programmes to improve pollution abatement methods. Examples include the requirement to reduce mercury emissions, the need to control discharges from power stations and motor vehicles, and the obligations under the bathing water and urban waste water Directives to control the effluent pumped from coastal sewage works into the marine environment.

Finally, the environmental policy has developed over time into a powerful and independent force in environmental politics and economics, representing not just a common denominator of national interests, but a factor that influences public opinion and empowers green pressure groups. It has required significant modifications to national practice in order to bring it into line with EU obligations. In the UK the Environmental Protection Act of 1990 provided for an integrated approach to pollution control under a new environmental protection agency and established air quality standards. These innovations were introduced to satisfy requirements which were established by EU environmental law. Such has been the impact of the environmental Directives that a number of scholars now argue that national environmental policies have been 'Europeanised' throughout the EU.

References

Economist Intelligence Unit (1989) *European Trends 1988–89*, London.

EEA (1995a) *Environment in the European Union 1995: Report for the Review of the Fifth Environmental Action Programme*, EEA, Copenhagen.

EEA (1995b) *Europe's Environment: The Dobris Assessment*, EEA, Copenhagen.

EEA (1996) *EEA Annual Report 1995*, EEA, Copenhagen.

European Commission (1987) *The State of the Environment in the European Community 1986*, Brussels.

European Commission (1992) *The Fifth Environmental Action Programme: Towards Sustainability*, Brussels.

European Commission (1996) *Progress Report on the Implementation of the Fifth Environmental Action Programme*, Brussels.

Haigh N (1987) 'Assessing EC Environmental Policy', *European Environment Review*, Vol. 1, No. 2, pp. 38–41.

Klatte E (1986) 'The Past and the Future of European Environmental Policy', *European Environment Review*, Vol. 1, No. 1, pp. 32–7.

OECD (1984) *The Macro-economic Impact of Environmental Expenditure*, OECD, Paris.

OECD (1989) *Environmental Policy Benefits: Monetary Valuation*, OECD, Paris.

Weidner H (1987) *Clean Air Policy in Europe: A Survey of Seventeen Countries*, Internationales Institut für Umwelt und Gesellschaft, Berlin.

Wilkinson D (1994) 'Using the European Union's Structural and Cohesion Funds for the Protection of the Environment', *Rectel*, Vol. 3, No. 2/3, pp. 119–26.

World Commission on Environment and Development (1987) *Our Common Future*, Oxford University Press, Oxford. (Also known as the *Brundtland Report* after the chairperson.)

Further reading

Andersen S and Eliassen K (eds) (1993) *Making Policy in Europe: The Europeification of National Policy Making*, Sage, London.

Guruswamy G, Papps I and Storey D J (1983) 'The Development and Impact of an EEC Directive: The Control of the Discharge of Mercury into the Aquatic Environment', *Journal of Common Market Studies*, Vol. 22, No. 1, pp. 71–100.

Haigh N (1984) *EEC Environmental Policy and Britain*, ENDS, London.

Haigh N (1992) *Manual of Environmental Policy*, Longman, Harlow.

Howarth W (1992) 'New Strategies for Water Directives', *European Environment Law Review*, Vol. 1, No. 4, pp. 117–21.

Jachtenfuchs M (1990) 'The European Community and the Protection of the Ozone Layer', *Journal of Common Market Studies*, Vol. 28, No. 3, pp. 261–77.

Johnson S and Corcelle G (1989) *The Environmental Policies of the European Communities*, Graham & Trotman, London.

Liefferink J D, Lowe P D and Mol A J P (eds) (1993) *European Integration and Environment Policy*, Belhaven Press, London.

Lister C (1996) *European Union Environmental Law: A Guide for Industry*, Wiley and Sons, Chichester.

Semple A (1993) 'The Implication of EC Legislation and Future Water Quality Obligations', *Journal of the Institution of Water Officers*, Vol. 30, No. 2, pp. 14–17.

Sheate W R and MacRory R B (1989) 'Agriculture and the EC Environmental Assessment Directive Lessons for Community Policy Making', *Journal of Common Market Studies*, Vol. 28, No. 1, pp. 68–81.

Stanners D and Bourdeau P (eds) (1994) *Europe's Environment: The Dobris Assessment: An Overview*, EEA, Copenhagen.

Taylor D, Diprose G and Duffy M (1986) 'EC Environmental Policy and the Control of Water Pollution: The Implementation of Directive 76/464 in Perspective', *Journal of Common Market Studies*, Vol. 24, No. 3, pp. 225–46.

Weale A (1992) *The New Politics of Pollution*, Manchester University Press, Manchester.

The *ENDS Report* is published monthly, directed at a business readership, and provides detailed surveys and reports on current developments in environment policy.

European Environment appears every two months and contains articles which provide an accessible analysis of European environmental issues.

Chapter 10

Transport policy

Stephen Dearden

Introduction

The transport industry accounts for 7 per cent of the Community's GNP, provides 7 per cent of employment and receives 40 per cent of member states investment. Goods transport has grown consistently by 2.3 per cent pa for the last twenty years and passenger traffic by 3.1 per cent.

Transport, together with agriculture and external trade, was one of the few areas specified in the Treaty of Rome where the Commission was specifically required to develop a common policy (Articles 3 and 74–84). A Common Transport Policy (CTP) was expected both to contribute to European economic integration and to enhance economic development.

The adoption of a CTP was restricted to road, rail and waterways, but could be extended to marine shipping and aviation if decided by the Council of Ministers (Article 84). The CTP requires common rules for all cross-border traffic (Article 75), forbids discrimination in transport charges (Article 79) and called for reductions in the costs of crossing frontiers (Article 81). However, while prohibiting general subsidies to transport undertakings, the Treaty permits State subsidies for the coordination of transport or for public service obligations (Article 77), or as part of regional assistance (Article 80). Article 78 also states that any measures concerning transport rates and conditions 'shall take account of the economic circumstances of the carriers'.

Thus, from the beginning, transport policy has been an uneasy amalgam of two approaches:

1 The establishment of non-discriminatory competitive conditions in the European transport market.

2 The adoption of an interventionist and regulatory approach, based on the view that efficient transport is central to the functioning of modern economies and to the process of economic integration in the EU.

Given that individual member states gave a different priority to these two approaches, conflict and policy inertia were the inevitable outcome.

The development of transport policy

The first attempt to establish the general principles of a CTP was offered by the Schaus Memorandum (European Commission, 1961) and embodied in an Action Programme which was to be implemented by 1970. Three alternative policy approaches were considered in the Memorandum:

1 A policy focusing on fostering competition.

2 The establishment of a common market in transport.

3 The pursuit of an active interventionist approach.

Although the last of these would seek to ensure that all transport modes faced harmonised conditions of competition, with a fair allocation of infrastructure costs, it was intended that capacity controls should be established to avoid the emergence of unstable market conditions. Regulations should also take into account the wider social and regional objectives of the Community.

The Council of Transport Ministers failed to reach any consensus upon either the Memorandum or the Action Programme. The Commission therefore prepared proposals in four areas. First, the control of road and inland waterway transport capacity with the establishment of common rules for entry into the industry. In particular, the Commission proposed the introduction of Community quotas of authorisation for inter-state road haulage. Secondly, the adoption of a 'forked tariff', setting upper and lower tariff limits to prevent operators exploiting dominant positions, or of creating destabilising cut-throat competition. Thirdly, to harmonise member state technical, tax and subsidy regimes in transport. Finally, to coordinate investment in transport infrastructure and to ensure that each mode of transport contributes fairly to the infrastructure costs that it imposes.

Opposition from member states, however, meant very little progress was made until a Council Decision in December 1967 established a timetable for implementing these proposals. Over the next few years a 'forked-tariff' regime was introduced in road haulage, together with common driving hour regulations, and competition rules and criteria were agreed for controlling rail subsidies. Nevertheless, overall the development of the CTP remained a hesitant affair. The entry of Denmark, Ireland and the UK in 1973 deepened the paralysis as disagreements emerged over adjusting the Community's road haulage quotas to accommodate the new member states, and over attempts to introduce new weight and dimension limits for commercial road vehicles.

The Commission attempted to stimulate development of the CTP by the publication of a policy statement and Action Programme in 1973. This was mainly a restatement of the 1961 Memorandum, with an emphasis on establishing the right to the freedom of Community transport operators to provide services throughout the EU and the creation of a harmonised competitive transport market across the Community. However, it also turned attention away from operational controls through quotas and regulated tariffs towards the planning and financing of an integrated Community transport network. This approach was reflected in the four priority areas selected in the Action Plan:

1 The creation of a Community network transport plan.
2 The development of criteria for the allocation of infrastructure costs between modes of transport.
3 Addressing the role of railways in the Community's transport plan.
4 Planning the development of the inland transport market.

Once more, resistance by the Council ensured that by the end of the 1970s little progress had been made in developing the CTP. Although the number of Community quotas for inter-state road haulage had risen over the years, they still represented only 5 per cent of all road haulage within the Community. Meanwhile difficulties remained in implementing Community regulations on road haulage drivers' hours. Nevertheless, pressure from the new member states, and a ruling by the European Court in 1974, extended the authority of the Treaty to marine and aviation transport.

In a further attempt to rouse the Council of Transport Ministers from its lethargy, the Commission, in October 1980, presented a list of 35 proposals for action over the next three years. The failure of the Council to respond to these proposals led the European Parliament to instigate action against the Council of Ministers in the European Court of Justice (ECJ) under Article 175 of the Treaty. The Parliament accused the Council of failing to establish a CTP as required by Articles 3 and 74 of the Treaty. In May 1985 the ECJ (13/83) ruled that the Council had indeed infringed the Treaty of Rome by 'failing to ensure freedom to provide services of international transport and to lay down the conditions under which non-resident carriers may operate transport services in a member state'.

This judgement, together with Jacques Delors's accession to the presidency of the Commission in 1985 and the commitment to the establishment of the SEM, gave new impetus to the development of a CTP. Not only is the transport industry a significant part of the European economy but its efficiency is essential to the achievement of a successful SEM. Subsequently, in Articles 129b–129d of the Treaty on European Union the Community specifically committed itself to an active role in the development of trans-European transport networks. To achieve this objective it was to foster the harmonisation of technical standards, and contribute, through feasibility studies, loan guarantees and interest rate subsidies, to national programmes of common interest. Transport infrastructure projects were also to be eligible for support from the Cohesion Fund that the Treaty established.

The most recent statement of Community policy, covering the period up to 2010, is the 2001 White Paper (COM(2001)370). This emphasised the economic costs being imposed by increasing congestion across Europe – estimated to be affecting 10 per cent of the road network, 20 per cent of the rail network and delaying 30 per cent of flights – and the contribution that transport is making to environmental pollution – 28 per cent of all carbon dioxide emissions, for example. To meet the EU's international environmental commitments and to reduce the social costs imposed by the transport industry, the Commission is proposing a programme of sixty specific measures, details of which can be found in the rest of this chapter. These are intended to shift traffic from road and air, to rail and the inland waterways and to public transport. It will also seek to foster efficiency gains through creating a competitive, integrated, internal transport market, where pricing accurately reflects the full social costs that are being imposed.

Infrastructure

Transport infrastructure is the fixed capital of any transport system and includes the provision of ports, airports, roads and railway lines. There are two aspects of Community interest with regard to transport infrastructure, namely pricing and the finance and coordination of investment.

Pricing

A correct pricing regime for the use of infrastructure is essential to ensure that users make the economically optimum choice of transport mode. To establish such a pricing regime and to secure a Community transport market that was fair and competitive, it was also necessary to ensure that state aids were clearly identified and subjected to Community controls. To this end, in 1970, a Regulation was introduced establishing a standard system of accounting for expenditure on transport infrastructure and, in 1971, a Memorandum was published containing the Commission's views on a suitable pricing regime. This was the result of six years of study of infrastructure costs and benefits.

Economic theory suggests that charging for the use of infrastructure should reflect the equilibrium outcome in a perfectly competitive market, i.e. price should equal marginal cost. It also suggests that pricing should take account of any additional social costs that the market is failing to identify. These social costs, or externalities, include accidents, air and noise pollution. Thus, in the case of road infrastructure the Commission argued that charges should reflect the marginal social costs that an additional vehicle would impose and they specifically recognised that congestion costs are an important externality. One additional vehicle on a congested road slows all other vehicles, increasing their travel time and therefore imposing a significant social cost. Therefore in cases where congestion exists the Commission argues for a fixed 'congestion tax' (see Exhibit 10.1a).

Infrastructure charging based on these proposals raises a number of serious practical problems. In particular, where economies of scale are being experienced (marginal cost less than average cost), which is usually the case in transport where the capacity of the system has not been reached, then marginal cost pricing will not generate enough revenue to cover total costs (Exhibit 10.1b). For the inland waterways, such a pricing regime would substantially raise freight rates since, historically, this mode of transport has made the smallest contribution to its infrastructure costs. For road transport, where the greatest social costs in terms of congestion and pollution are occurring, existing systems of fuel and motor vehicle taxes are incapable of reflecting the true marginal social costs. Although a 1968 Council Directive had suggested that commercial road vehicles should be taxed on the basis of the marginal costs they imposed on the road network, as determined by their axle weights, this failed to take into account the wider externalities of pollution and congestion. To reflect marginal social costs, more complex systems of road pricing would be required. The practical difficulties of adopting such a system, together with the reluctance of member states to lose control of an important source of tax

Exhibit 10.1 Congestion tax

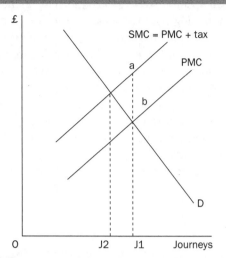

Drivers are faced with private marginal costs (PMCs) – wear and tear, petrol, travel time, etc. – which increase as the volume of traffic rises and congestion slows the journey. Faced with these costs, J1 journeys will be made. However, this represents over-use of this resource since the private costs faced by each driver are failing to reflect the full social costs they are imposing. Each additional vehicle not only experiences a slower journey, but slows all other vehicles on the congested road, imposing social costs. The imposition of a tax (ab) equal to these congestion costs reduces the volume of traffic to the optimum J2.

(a) Transport pricing with congestion costs

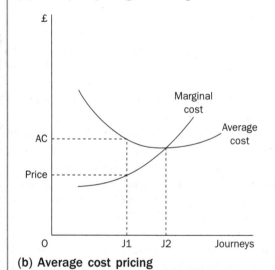

However, charging each user the marginal social cost that they impose can result in insufficient revenue being raised to cover the costs of provision on the infrastructure. If the number of journeys being made (J1) is less than the optimum capacity of a road (J2), marginal cost pricing will not cover the average cost of each journey. Again the Commission recognised this problem and advocated imposition of a 'balancing charge' (AC = Price) to cover any remaining funding deficit.

(b) Average cost pricing

revenue (which a harmonised Community pricing regime would imply), have ensured that, so far, only limited progress has been made in this area.

In 1996 the 'Eurovignette' Directive (European Commission, 1996) had set a non-discriminatory maximum infrastructure vehicle access charge for Heavy Goods Vehicles (HGVs), set on the basis of average infrastructure costs. For ports and airports (European Commission, 1997) access charges were to be based upon the underlying costs with adjustments for 'fair' competition. For rail a 2001 Directive (2001/14/EC) requires marginal social costs to be the basis of charging, while allowing supplementary charges to reflect the scarcity of capacity and the environmental costs of operations. A further non-discriminatory levy can be imposed to cover any financial shortfall.

In 1998 the Commission had reaffirmed its intention to move towards comprehensive marginal cost pricing (European Commission, 1998) and had financed a comprehensive research programme addressing the problems of measurement, the estimation of externalities and the impact upon the modal split of the required relative price changes (see Nash and Sansom, 2001). In the Transport White Paper (COM(2001)370) the Commission has indicated it intends to introduce a Directive establishing a common methodology for determining charging levels across the industry. This will reflect the congestion and environmental costs that are being imposed, while ensuring that all modes of transport and all operators are treated in an equal manner. Surplus payments arising from new pricing structures will be directed to further infrastructure development which reduces the adverse environmental impact of transport, particularly the improvement of the railways.

Finance and investment

It was recognised in the 1961 Memorandum (European Commission, 1961) that the Community had an important interest in the coordination of infrastructure investment since investment decisions by member states were likely to reflect only national priorities. With increased intra-EU traffic it was essential that infrastructure projects were also assessed in their wider Community context and, if necessary, funded by Community resources. The inadequacies of national transport planning were confirmed by preparatory studies by the Commission. Thus in 1965 the Commission proposed a programme of infrastructure work focusing on harmonising rail electrification schemes, identifying a strategic European road network, improving links between seaports and their hinterlands and establishing links between the European waterway systems. In 1966 the Council instigated a system of Community consultation on transport infrastructure projects, but resistance by the member states to the erosion of their autonomy undermined the effectiveness of this procedure.

However, in 1978 the Commission proposed the creation of a Transport Infrastructure Committee (TIC), composed of representatives of the member states, to consider national infrastructure programmes in the context of the development of a Community transport network. By the mid-1980s this had identified a core 24,700-mile trans-European motorway network requiring ECU 120 bn for its completion. Meanwhile, the Commission continued the work begun in 1973 to identify the likely future transport needs of the EU up to the turn of the century. However, the Council continued to resist the development of a more active role for the Community in planning, evaluation and financing of projects of Community interest.

Having identified projects with an important Community benefit, the issue of Community finance was clearly crucial. In 1976 the Commission proposed a Regulation (OJ C 207, 2.9.1976, p. 9) identifying four categories of projects that were to receive financial support:

1 Projects within a member state designed to eliminate bottlenecks in EU traffic.

2 Cross-frontier projects.

3 Projects fulfilling broad Community objectives.

4 Projects which standardise the EU transport network.

These were translated into a more detailed list of short- and long-term objectives including the upgrading of inter-city rail links (e.g. Amsterdam/Brussels/Strasbourg), links with peripheral areas (e.g. Dublin/Cork/Galway, East Anglia, Mezzogiorno), routes overcoming natural obstacles (e.g. Channel Tunnel, Appenine crossings) and bridging 'missing links' between transport networks (e.g. inland waterway link between Belgium and France). Qualifying projects would have been eligible for all forms of EU financial assistance, including EIB, ERDF and, since 1979, New Community Instrument loans.

In response to this Memorandum, the Council, in 1981, asked the Commission to evaluate the Community 'interest' in a limited number of specific projects. Subsequently the Commission presented a list of projects to form an experimental programme selected from among submissions by the member states. The total cost to the EU budget was to be ECU 968 m to be dispersed over the years 1984–86, and was to offer a maximum support of 20 per cent of the cost of each project. Of the total, ECU 250 m was to be spent on rail projects and ECU 550 m on roads.

The European Parliament was critical of this road bias and advocated instead an intermodal approach and greater attention to the needs of the inland waterways, ports and airports. In response, in 1983, the Commission proposed a multi-annual transport infrastructure programme (MTIP) (COM(83)474 final) to continue until the Council finally responded to the 1976 Memorandum. The MTIP would have provided a maximum of 70 per cent support for eligible projects which could have been combined with other sources of Community assistance. The MTIP was not realised, but the concerns of the European Parliament were reflected in the shift of priorities expressed in the 1986 Medium Term Transport Infrastructure policy. Priorities were now to be:

1 Improvements in land–sea corridors.

2 Links to peripheral regions.

3 Construction of a high-speed rail network.

4 Reductions in transit traffic costs, including the development of combined transport (road/rail).

The modernisation of ports and airports was specifically identified as an important part of infrastructure policy, as were the demands created by the accession of Greece, Spain and Portugal to the Community.

The 1986 document also attempted to clarify the complex financial sourcing of infrastructure projects. It proposed concentrating funding under Specific Transport Instruments (STCs). However, the Council resisted the establishment of a specific fund for transport. Nevertheless, in 1990 the Council of Ministers accepted an Action Programme designed to complete the single market (European Commission, 1990). This called for the creation of trans-European networks in telecommunications, energy and transport (3359/90). It also established the concept of a 'Declaration of Community interest', allowing up to 25 per cent of a project's total cost and 50 per cent of the cost of the feasibility studies to be funded by the EU.

Between 1989 and 1992 the EU contributed ECU 702.7 m to a transport infrastructure investment of ECU 11.2 bn by the member states (Vickerman, 1994). Over half of this expenditure was on rail projects. At the same time the ERDF expended

ECU 7 bn on transport developments in the Objective 1 peripheral regions and the EIB made loans of ECU 12 bn (1987–91). The EIB had proposed raising ECU 5 bn from the international financial markets for transport projects in 1993, but this was rejected by member states. More recently, in 1995–2000, €1.8 bn was contributed to transport infrastructure investment under the Trans-European Networks for Transport (TEN-T) budget. A further €4 bn was allocated to cover the years up to 2006. In addition €14 bn was provided to Ireland, Spain, Portugal and Greece from the ERDF and the Cohesion Fund. The European Investment Bank is the other major provider, with loans of €8.5 bn granted in 1996–97. The total value of the EU's various contributions to the total transport investment approved in 1996–97 was approximately 30 per cent. Of this investment 60 per cent went to the railways, where two-thirds was allocated to the high-speed network, and 15 per cent to roads. However, these sums need to be compared with the €400 bn required to fund the fourteen priority projects identified at the 1994 Essen European Council, which form the core of the trans-European network and of which only one-fifth have so far been completed. In addition, it is estimated that the integration of the transport systems of the accession countries will require a further €100 bn of investment.

Finally, mention must be made of Switzerland's position in relation to the development of the EU's transport network, lying as it does across the route from Italy to the northern member states. In 1992 a goods transit agreement had been made between Switzerland and the EU, addressing the problem of the Swiss 28-tonne heavy goods vehicle (HGV) limit. However, in 1994 a plebiscite decided to ban all foreign lorries from Swiss roads within ten years, forcing all international traffic to traverse Switzerland by rail. This required bringing forward the ECU 14 bn Gotthard rail tunnel project and the improvements to the Simplon and Lotschberg links.

The railways

Across Europe the share of freight carried on the railways has been falling. In 1970, 21 per cent of freight in the EU15 was carried by rail and 31 per cent by road, but by 1999 the relative shares had changed to 8 per cent and 44 per cent respectively. Similarly, by 1999 the railways were providing only 6 per cent of passenger transport compared with 10 per cent in 1970.

The railway systems of the EU vary considerably in their extent and importance in national transport (see Table 10.1). Although these characteristics are determined in part by the economic geography of each member state, they also reflect the transport policies pursued by the individual governments. Thus, in both Germany and France there was discrimination against road haulage for freight traffic beyond 150 km. These two countries, together with Italy, also shared a commitment to the development of new high-speed rail lines, of which the French Train à Grande Vitesse (TGV) is the most well known. Over the years 1976–82 German railways had invested ECU 9000 m, French railways ECU 4500 m, and British Rail (BR) ECU 3000 m. In 1985 the German government had approved a ten-year investment programme of ECU 17500 m with a doubling of its high-speed network

Table 10.1 Share of rail transport, 1999

	Route km	Freight '000 m.t.km	Passenger '000 m.p.km
Austria	5643	15.6	2.73
Finland	5836	53.4	0.46
Belgium	3472	7.4	0.82
Denmark	2324	1.9	–
France	31589	53.4	10.4
Germany	37536	71.4	14.5
Ireland	1919	0.5	–
Italy	16108	21.6	5.4
Netherlands	2808	3.5	1.42
Portugal	2813	2.2	0.56
Sweden	10799	18.9	1.46
Spain	12319	11.6	5.06
United Kingdom	16984	18.4	7.5

Notes:
m.t.km = million tonne kilometres
m.p.km = million passenger kilometres
Source: EU Energy and Transport in Figures 2001

to 2000 km by the end of the century. In France, the completion of the South-East TGV to Marseilles and Switzerland was followed, in 1983, by the development of the TGV Atlantique to the South-West at a cost of ECU 1900 m. In Italy, a new line has been constructed from Rome to Florence at a cost of ECU 2270 m.

By contrast, in the UK the only major modernisation of the system, completed in the 1980s, was the electrification of the East Coast Mainline. BR had not only been constrained to relatively low levels of investment but had also been expected to cover a much higher level of its operating costs from its revenues – 76 per cent in 1990, compared with 31 per cent in Italy and 56 per cent in Germany.

State subsidies

Despite this diversity in the railways of the EU they share a common problem in the need for state subsidies to cover continuing financial deficits. The level of state subsidies has varied significantly across the EU, ranging from 54.8 per cent of Belgian railways' value added to only 5.7 per cent in the case of the Netherlands (see Table 10.2). By 1999 these were totalling €32 bn across the Community. This arises in part from the requirements imposed upon the railways to maintain non-commercial services and from state intervention in their pricing structures. A major concern of the CTP, therefore, has been to establish clear rules to regulate the level of such subsidies and to ensure that they do not significantly distort the transport market of the Community.

This began with a Council Decision in 1965, which committed member states to harmonising the rules governing the financial relations between governments and their railway undertakings. This was subsequently translated, in 1969, into two Regulations (1191/69 and 1192/69). These attempted to establish common

Figure 10.1 Europe's railways

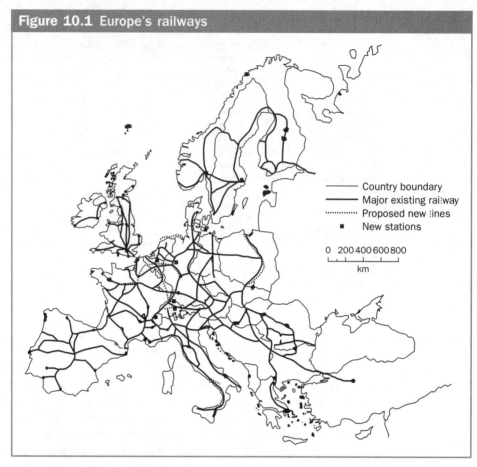

Source: Derived from *Employment in Europe*

Table 10.2 State aid to railways

	Gross value added 1988–90 %
Belgium	54.8
Denmark	14.8
France	25.2
Germany	28.7
Greece	6.4
Ireland	14.6
Italy	6.9
Netherlands	5.7
Portugal	8.4
Spain	26.3
United Kingdom	5.9

Source: European Commission, *Second Survey on State Aids*, 1992

accounting standards for member states' railways, and allowed transport undertakings to apply to their governments for the removal of any public service obligation (PSO) that imposed a financial burden. If a government wished this PSO to be maintained, then the cost was to be borne by the state in accordance with common compensation criteria. Regulation 1107/70 sought to limit state aid beyond these PSO grants to help with coordination, research and development of transport systems, and for the elimination of excess capacity. Unfortunately these Regulations had only a limited impact as member states differed in the compensation offered to the railways for their PSOs, and the Regulations applied only to the mainline network services.

Thus, as early as 1971 the Commission was preparing further legislation to require railway undertakings to be given greater autonomy in their management and finance, with a clear definition of the responsibilities of the undertaking and the state. This proposal was embodied in a Council Decision (74/327/EEC) in 1974, which laid down a five-year legislative programme. At the end of this period the railways were expected to be operating in a commercial manner, except for their PSO activities for which they were to receive specific payments from the state. These subsidies were to be applied according to agreed Community rules. However, these further attempts to restrict the level of member state subsidies continued to be frustrated by the vagueness of existing EU Regulations and the difficulties of assigning railway costs.

In December 1989 the Commission again returned to these problems with a proposal for new PSO rules (European Commission, 1989). Under the resulting 1991 Regulation, the existing systems of PSO grants were required to be replaced by a system of public service contracts agreed between the states and the railways but following a market approach. These grants can be retained for urban, suburban and regional services. The 1989 Commission proposals also raised again the issue of the separation of infrastructure management from service provision, and under Directive 91/440 separate accounts are now required for infrastructure and train operations. This separation was also intended to encourage competition through open access to the rail networks. In the late 1980s both Sweden and Switzerland had separated the control of the infrastructure from that of train operation, while the UK had gone even further and privatised its rail infrastructure, under Railtrack, as well as creating 25 train-operating companies. However, the UK experience has underlined the considerable dangers of fragmenting a railway industry. Although rail infrastructure was effectively brought back into public ownership through the creation of Network Rail and it is intended to reduce the number of train operating franchises, there still remain serious doubts as to the viability of separating train operations from infrastructure management.

In 1995 further Directives were adopted establishing common criteria for licensing railway undertakings (95/18/EC) and the rules to be followed in allocating railway capacity (95/19/EC) – train paths – by the separate railway infrastructure management organisations that had to be created. These managers were also to be responsible for setting non-discriminatory usage fees, which were to reflect market prices.

The need to create an 'arms length' relationship between the states and their railways was reiterated in the 1996 White Paper 'A Strategy for Revitalising the

Community's Railways' (COM(96)421). It also called for the creation of rail freight 'freeways', with every national infrastructure manager being able to offer open access to the whole Community-wide rail network. However, little use was made of this opportunity. Nonetheless, the White Paper laid the foundations for the three infrastructure Directives, which formed the first 'railway package'. Directive 2001/12 (modifying 91/440) required member states to extend access rights to the national elements of the 50,000 km Trans-European Rail Freight Network (TERFN) – which accommodates 75 per cent of all EU rail freight – in March 2003. Directive 2001/13 (amending 95/18) sets out the conditions for the licensing of railway undertakings to gain access to the TERFN, while Directive 2001/14 (replacing 95/19) outlines the principles to be followed in allocating train paths and determining tariff structures. Each national infrastructure manager is now required to publish a network statement identifying the systems limitations, outlining investment plans and indicating tariff structures, access requirements and capacity allocation rules.

The Commission, as has already been described, has attempted to remove distortions in the transport market by establishing clear common criteria for the allocation of infrastructure costs. In the case of the railways, it has been argued that equality of treatment with the public road network would require the state to accept the financial responsibility for the infrastructure, with individual services being charged their marginal cost. This appears to offer an attractive means of alleviating the recurring financial deficits of railway undertakings. However, where marginal cost pricing is inadequate to cover average costs, additional charges must be made. Generally, governments receive more in road taxes than is spent upon road construction and maintenance, but overall railway revenues fail to cover their infrastructure costs. A transfer of responsibility for the infrastructure from the railways to the state would merely result in a reassignment of the underlying deficits. The core problem remains that of the nature of railways with their high fixed costs and economies of scale, which result in falling average costs as the volume of traffic increases. A more fruitful approach to improving the financial performance of the railways is likely to be found through focusing upon matching capacity to demand and to achieving potential productivity gains in their operation, particularly through the greater integration of the Community's national railways.

Integrating railway networks

The Commission has an important role in fostering the integration of the Community's national railway systems. Although the rail systems of the EU share the Berne loading gauge (with the exception of the UK) and the core countries a common track gauge, this differs from that on the periphery in Spain, Portugal, Finland and Ireland. Their power and signalling systems also often differ. Thus the Channel Tunnel requires locomotives that can operate under three different electric power systems, and with the smaller rolling stock compatible with UK railways. There was also a preference for national suppliers for rolling stock and equipment, leading to high-cost products and excess capacity in the industry. However, the manufacture of railway equipment is one industry that has undergone considerable rationalisation under the pressures of the single market. The manufacture of rolling stock, for example, is now dominated by Bombardier of Canada, Siemens of Germany and Alsthom of France.

However, there is also a long history of cooperation between the railways of Europe through a variety of institutions, but especially the Union Internationale des Chemins de Fer (UIC). Its European Infrastructure Plan, adopted in 1973, identified those lines whose development is necessary to the establishment of an integrated trans-European network, based around the core of a Paris–Brussels–Cologne–Amsterdam link. As we have already seen, the Commission has also given priority in its infrastructure proposals to the development of a Community high-speed rail network. In 1990 the Commission submitted a plan (European Commission, 1990), based upon national intentions, for a 35,000 km network to meet the needs of passenger traffic up to the year 2010.

The plan identified 14 key rail links, and one of these, and the most significant from a UK perspective, was the Channel Tunnel. Opened in 1994, at a final cost of ECU 12.5 bn, finance was provided by 210 commercial banks and the EIB, the largest single investor. Half of its capacity was to provide through-rail services, which were expected to carry 10.2 million passengers and 3.3 million tonnes (mt) of freight in its opening year, but only achieved 3 million passengers and 1.3 mt of freight. However, 5 million people and 4 mt of freight were moved on the shuttle service, and by 1997 the direct rail service had captured 60 per cent of the London–Paris passenger market. The UK government's preference for private finance also led to delays in the construction of the London high-speed link, but it is hoped that the link will finally be ready in 2007. However, given this problem, and the competition from air services for those passengers travelling beyond London–Brussels–Paris, the Tunnel is likely to be of greater significance for road vehicles and rail freight than passenger services.

In 1996 the Commission took the initiative to foster greater inter-operability across the trans-European network (Directive 96/48/EC). Technical specifications were to be drawn up by the European Association for Railway Inter-operability (AEIF) and member states were to ensure that any national high-speed developments were to be compatible with these standards. Two further Commission Decisions (2001/260/EC and 2001/290/EC) outlined the basic parameters for a European Rail Traffic Management System (signalling, etc.) and the requirements of a trans-European high-speed rail system. Under Directive 2001/16/EC similar technical harmonisation was sought for existing conventional rail systems.

In 2002 the Commission presented its proposals for a second 'railway package' of measures intended to accelerate the creation of an integrated, open-access and competitive trans-European rail system (European Commission, 2002). The opening up of the rail freight market, which was to have been confined to the TERFN, was now to be extended to the entire railway network and completed by 2006. This in turn requires much greater inter-operability and therefore the need for new Directives to drive forward technical harmonisation. These measures will include a rail safety Directive, which will harmonise the safety regulatory structure across the EU and allow mutual recognition of safety certification for railway operators. A European Railway Agency will be established to provide the necessary technical advice on both safety and inter-operability and to liaise with the national railway authorities.

Despite the new found enthusiasm of the Commission for the development of an integrated trans-European rail network finance remains a central problem. Most countries' railways remain state-owned monopolies, characterised by inefficiencies and substantial accumulated deficits. The German railways alone had accumulated debts of ECU 37.8 bn by 1993. While the involvement of private finance will probably be essential, the Channel Tunnel experience illustrates the difficulties that this will involve. Private capital will require a return of 15 to 25 per cent upon its investment in contrast to the test rate of discount of governments of 8 per cent. Although some TGV routes are estimated to have returned 15 per cent, other projects, such as the Spanish Madrid–Seville AVE line, have been considerably less profitable. There is also concern that the demands of HST development have diverted funds from the needs of other areas of the rail system, some of which may be of greater social significance.

Combined transport

The Channel Tunnel has already proved of importance in the development of combined transport, with 75 per cent of freight trains being inter-modal. Combined transport is the carriage of goods that involves more than one mode of transport. It includes containers and 'piggyback' road/rail systems. Of these, containerisation is the most well established, with Intercontainer, a consortium of 23 railway companies, carrying over a million containers a year. Traffic is concentrated on Marseilles-Fos and Rotterdam and is particularly important for German and French railways. The carriage of road vehicles or swapbodies by rail is less developed, with only half as many consignments carried by this means. Germany has the largest volume of piggyback traffic for internal freight transport, and Italy for international trade.

Combined transport can be cost-effective over longer distances, beyond 500 km, and offers environmental benefits if it can divert freight traffic from road to rail. It is also hoped that it may contribute to improving the financial performance of the railways. For these reasons the Community has been encouraging its development since 1975 when a Directive freed heavy goods vehicles (HGVs) from all restrictions if the trunk haul was by rail. In 1982 these exemptions were extended to road haulage combined with inland waterway carriage, and a scheme was adopted to reduce vehicle excise duties for HGVs for that part of journeys undertaken by rail. The Community also offered financial assistance for the development of combined transport terminals and recommended the adoption of competitive tariff structures that encourage combined transport.

A study by the Kearney Group of consultants for the Commission, completed in 1990, confirmed the economic advantages of combined transport and predicted a tripling of such traffic by 2005. It suggested that further improvements were possible through standardisation of equipment and organisational changes. In October 1990 a working party was formed with the specific remit of identifying those measures necessary for the establishment of a European combined transport network. By 1992 the Commission had outlined a network of rail and waterway routes, with road links for local haulage, that would cost ECU 2 bn to complete. But the plan was merely indicative and, although some EU funding was available for the required infrastructure investment, most of the cost will fall upon the member states, who are likely to give priority to their national requirements.

In 1991 a Directive had further liberalised controls of the road element of combined transport, including allowing non-resident hauliers to carry out the road legs of the journeys, and exempted the road trip elements from any domestic tariff regulations. Directive 92/106/EEC extended the existing concessions for combined transport to all multi-mode unitised freight transport.

Over the period 1997–2001 €35 m was provided under the PACT programme (Pilot Actions for Combined Transport). This supported two types of project – feasibility studies and operational measures – undertaken by firms or public bodies in at least two member states. This was succeeded by the MARCO POLO programme providing €115 m for the years 2003–07 and, unlike PACT, it will support any scheme that will shift freight from road to some other mode of transport. Accession candidate countries are also eligible and the programme will support the start-up of new non-road freight services as well as the provision of strategic facilities. However it will focus on international rather than national projects.

Road haulage

By 1999 road haulage accounted for 75 per cent of the movement of freight within the Community, 40 per cent of which was cross-border, and had been growing at 4 per cent per annum since 1970. It is therefore not surprising that the EU has had a far greater impact upon the operational environment of the road haulage industry than that of the railways. It has consistently pursued its objective of establishing a common competitive market in road transport, and to this end has sought the harmonisation of national regulations and the removal of restrictions. Road haulage has been subject to licensing in all member states at some time, leading to restrictions on entry to the industry or in the business for which road haulage can compete with rail. In the UK these controls had been abandoned by 1968, but by 1985 the UK and Sweden were still the only fully deregulated road haulage markets in Europe. Complementing these domestic restrictions were licensing regimes for controlling road haulage between member states. But these clearly conflicted with the Treaty commitment to establishing the free provision of services (Article 52).

The Commission recognised that transitional arrangements would be necessary, and sought to achieve this by introducing a Community quota of licences for intra-EU haulage. A hesitant start was made in 1968 with an experimental three-year scheme, which was applicable only to cross-border traffic; domestic haulage still required a national licence. These EU permits were shared between member states, and this allocation was to become a source of considerable acrimony. A succession of Regulations extended the scheme, but by 1983 only 5 per cent of all road haulage was under a Community licence. In 1984, the Council decided to increase the EU quotas by 30 per cent from 1985 from their then current 4038, and subsequently by 15 per cent in each of the following four years. The commitment to the SEM increased the pace of deregulation. In 1988 agreement was reached to increase the EU quota by 40 per cent for two years and, more significantly, in 1993 the Council agreed to phase out all permit requirements (Regulation 3118/93/EEC). This was to be completed by 1998 and applied to all of the European Economic Area.

Linked to the issue of intra-EU road haulage have been the restrictions upon cabotage – the carriage of goods for customers at any stage of a journey between member states. This involves the opening up of the road haulage business of every member state to any EU operator. Article 75 of the Treaty requires the Council to determine the conditions under which non-resident operators may provide services within a member state other than their own. Despite an 1985 ECJ ruling, little progress was made on this sensitive issue until 1989 when Regulation 4059/89 created an EU quota of 15,000 cabotage permits. In 1993 the number of permits was increased to 30,000, to rise annually by 30 per cent until July 1998 when all quota restrictions were abolished. However, the evidence suggests that this process of liberalisation has had a limited impact (COM(2000)105). The extent of national transport (goods transport by national carriers within their own states) was 300 times greater than the amount of cabotage.

Similar liberalisation has been taking place in the road passenger industry. The EU has concentrated its attention upon international coach and bus services, leaving national services to be regulated by individual member states. Although there were existing international regulations on which the EU could build, it was a judgement of the ECJ in 1987 that forced the pace of liberalisation. It was not until 1992 that the Council finally agreed a Regulation abolishing licensing (Regulation 2454/92/EEC). They also agreed to allow cabotage on 'closed-door' tours, where the same group of passengers stays with the same coach. A subsequent Regulation (12/98/EC) laid down the conditions under which non-national operators could provide services and required equal treatment with national passenger carriers.

Complementing the liberalisation of the entry of operators into member states' road transport markets has been the deregulation of tariff controls. As has already been described, the issue of tariff controls illustrated the clear conflict of philosophy between those member states advocating the primacy of market forces, and those attempting to avoid instability or the abuse of market power by maintaining regulation. The compromise that finally emerged in 1968 was the 'forked tariff', setting compulsory maximum and minimum rates. This 'forked tariff' was to apply only to international road freight traffic, and the rates were to be set by agreements between the relevant member states. This system was never adopted by Denmark, the UK and Ireland. In 1977 it was watered down by the introduction of an alternative voluntary system of reference tariffs. Again the choice was to be determined by mutual agreement between the member states concerned with a particular traffic. This system clearly failed to establish a uniform Community common market in road freight traffic, and with the movement towards the SEM it was finally agreed that from 1 June 1990 all tariff controls would be abolished (Regulation 4058/89/EEC).

However, a truly fair and competitive transport market would also require a common vehicle taxing regime. In 1992 the national vehicle tax for a 38-tonne lorry varied from ECU 5314 in Germany and ECU 3824 in the UK to ECU 411 in Greece. In 1988 the Commission had proposed harmonisation of HGV taxation on the basis of a common method of infrastructure charging. Vehicles over 12 tonnes were to be taxed in their country of registration but on the basis of their use of the total road network of the Community. Germany sought upward harmonisation to protect its road haulage industry and linked the issue to liberalisation of cabotage, but faced stiff opposition from the Benelux countries who have significantly lower levels of taxation. The final compromise (Directive 93/89/EEC) recognised the burden on a particular country's transport infrastructure by allowing the introduction of a supplementary licence for the use of the motorways and principal roads of Germany, Denmark and the Benelux countries. This resulted in 73 per cent of the proceeds of these 'vignettes' being received by Germany. Member states also agreed upon a maximum annual vehicle tax of ECU 1250, reviewable every two years, and the ultimate harmonisation of fuel excise duty. The Commission has indicated that it intends to return to this issue and propose the introduction of uniform fuel taxation.

Differing vehicle technical specifications were also viewed as an obstacle to the efficient operation of HGVs, and to the development of the European vehicle manufacturing industry. A series of Directives had established common vehicle requirements covering safety features, noise and air pollution standards. Finally, in 1992 the Council of Ministers agreed an EU vehicle 'type approval', allowing lorries constructed to this standard to operate throughout the Community. This replaced the national regulations from 1996.

Attempts to establish common weight limits for HGVs proved more controversial. These differences had arisen from the various national assessments of the trade-off between vehicle-operating efficiency and environmental damage. Member states also varied substantially in the standards applied to road construction and therefore to their vulnerability to particular vehicle weights. Axle weights in particular are crucial in determining the level of road damage that a vehicle can inflict; for example a 10-tonne axle weight does 17 times more damage than a 5-tonne axle. Attempts to arrive at a Community consensus proved extremely difficult.

It took ten years to achieve agreement among the original six members for a maximum axle weight of 11 tonnes and 40 tonnes overall. Unfortunately, this was rejected by the new member states, Denmark, Ireland and the UK. In 1985 a compromise was finally reached, with a derogation for the UK and Ireland to continue with their lower limits of 32 tonnes. Following the Armitage Enquiry, in 1980 the UK government raised the weight limit to 38 tonnes (see Dearden, 1990) and subsequently it fell into line with the Community 44 tonne limit. Existing EU maxima only apply to international transport, and each country may also allow domestic operation of vehicles in excess of these limits.

Fair competition and road safety considerations have also led to a series of social measures controlling the working conditions of drivers. As early as 1969, a Regulation (543/69/EEC) established controls over driving hours. This was to be enforced through personnel log books, but the inadequacy of this method quickly led to a Regulation (1463/70/EEC) requiring the installation by January 1976 of automatic recording equipment (tachographs). The UK rejected this Regulation, but legal proceedings by the Commission forced compliance, and it was applied in the UK from January 1982. However, the EU recognised that the existing Regulations were too restrictive and, in 1985 (3820/85), revisions were made extending driving hours and increasing their flexibility. At the same time there was concern at the failure of all member states to enforce the Regulations fully. It has been estimated, for example, that half of the own-account vehicles in Portugal are regularly overloaded and only 1 per cent have paid their vehicle tax. Consequently in 1989 common enforcement standards were prescribed in a further Directive.

Inland waterways

The inland waterway network is an important mode of transport in continental Europe. It joins the Mediterranean to the North Sea, and extends from the Channel into Central and Eastern Europe. There are 29,500 kilometres of navigable water-way in Europe centred on two systems – the Meuse/Scheldt linking Belgium, France and the Netherlands; and the Rhine/Main/Danube (see Figure 10.2). Of these two, the Rhine is the most significant, carrying 57 per cent of Europe's 121 bn tonne-kilometres of waterborne freight. This represents one-third of all intra-community goods traffic. However, it is an industry that has seen its share of freight traffic fall from 13.7 per cent in 1970 to only 7 per cent in 1998. It has consistently suffered from over-capacity, resulting in low returns to capital, with a consequent failure to invest in modern vessels. This problem has been exacerbated by competition from Eastern European boats operating at artificially low prices.

The Rhine navigation is governed by the long established Mannheim Con-vention (1848) and this has inhibited EU intervention in the inland waterways industry. Nonetheless, the EU has harmonised the technical specification of vessels (82/714/EEC) and established mutual recognition of navigation licences (76/135/EEC). In 1983 the Commission submitted five proposals to the Council, concerning entry to the industry, working conditions, introduction of a voluntary set of reference tariffs, cabotage and access to the Rhine navigation. The sub-sequent Action Programme included the preparation of a compensation scheme for scrapping vessels, combined with a ban on state aids for new vessels and an examination of the problems of infrastructure charging. Since 1993 carriers owned by nationals of any member state have been able to carry goods and passengers across the Community (91/3921/EEC) and from January 2000 the industry has been fully deregulated.

Aviation

Of all the modes of transport, aviation is the most highly regulated. The EU has to develop its policies within the context of well-established international and bilateral agreements. The foundations for the post-war system of international civil aviation

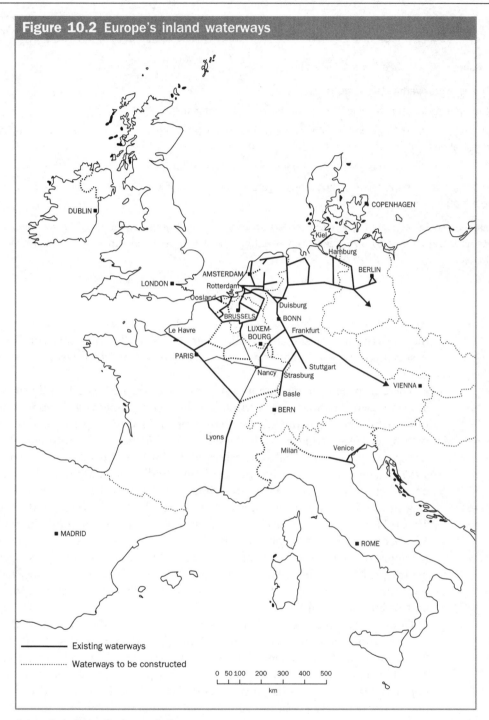

Figure 10.2 Europe's inland waterways

Existing waterways

Waterways to be constructed

0 50 100 200 300 400 500
km

Source: Derived from *Employment in Europe*

Box 10.1 The Chicago Convention

The Convention identified five air freedoms:

1 The right to overfly states' territories.

2 The right to land for technical reasons, for example refuelling.

3 The right to land to disembark passengers and cargo travelling from the country of an airline's registration.

4 The right to pick up passengers and cargo for journeys to the country of an airline's registration.

5 The right to transport goods and passengers between two countries other than the country of registration.

Signatories to the Convention granted the first two rights to all other signatories, but the remaining rights were determined by bilateral agreements (e.g. the 1946 Bermuda Agreement between the UK and US).

---

were laid with the Chicago Convention of 1944 (see Box 10.1). Complementing the Convention was the creation in 1945 of IATA (International Air Transport Association), which organises a series of conferences at which fares are agreed for scheduled services.

The European civil aviation industry was characterised by relatively small, usually state-owned national flag carriers. Scheduled services between states were usually restricted to the flag carriers, who were often entitled to 50 per cent of the traffic, with a revenue-sharing pool. In 1989, of the 750 non-stop short-haul flights in Europe, 71 per cent had only one carrier and a further 24 per cent only two (Pryke, 1991). Fares were agreed by the regulatory bodies of the two states. The high operating costs of many European airlines were sustained by this regime, producing fares 45 to 75 per cent above those in the USA (McGowan and Trengove, 1986). Nonetheless, during the 1980s scheduled domestic air traffic increased by 65 per cent, and intra-European traffic by 31 per cent. Domestic flights accounted for approximately 11 per cent of European airlines' total revenue passenger kilometres (RPKs), and intra-European flights a further 20 per cent. However, only three airlines – Air France, British Airways and Lufthansa – accounted for 46 per cent of Europe's total RPKs.

Despite this highly regulated environment one of the earliest actions in the European aviation industry was an attempt to establish a European Civil Aviation Community. In 1958, Sabena, Lufthansa, Air France, KLM and Alitalia had discussed an agreement to foster cooperation and possibly a merger. The principal objective was to standardise their aircraft fleets, coordinate ground control and pool traffic rights. Negotiations soon moved beyond the companies to involve their respective governments. In 1962 the companies and their governments signed an Air Union pact. Until 1965 inter-governmental negotiations continued between all of the original six member states, but outside the aegis of the Community. Meanwhile, the Commission attacked these activities as incompatible with the Treaty and called for the development of a Community-based air transport policy.

Early attempts at liberalisation

In 1972 the Commission proposed action on air transport covering three main areas – improving regional scheduled services, developing a common approach to negotiations within IATA and to air links with non-Community countries. However, no significant progress was made until 1979 with the Commission's Civil Aviation Memorandum No. 1 (COM(79)311). Although this document suggested that freedom of entry into the industry was only a long-term prospect, it also represented the first clear commitment to the goal of establishing a competitive market environment. This shift had been encouraged by ECJ rulings in 1974 (167/73) and 1978 that the competition requirements of the Treaty (Articles 85, 86 and 90) also applied to air transport. It was also recognised that the move to a competitive environment would require a clear Community policy regulating the level of state aids to their national airlines. However, the endeavours of the Commission to establish a more liberal regime were frustrated by the Council, including its attempts to deregulate regional air services. Meanwhile Lord Bethell's action before the ECJ to force the Commission to intervene against the fare-setting arrangements in the industry failed.

However, the movement towards deregulation that had begun in the USA in the mid-1970s was beginning to influence the tenor of international negotiations. The apparently rigid regulatory regime of the Chicago Convention/IATA had always offered some scope for flexibility. The Convention had always excluded non-scheduled services from its ambit, and hence there was considerable growth of the charter market in Europe, encouraged by those states who wished to develop their tourist industry. By 1992, 60 per cent of European air traffic (passenger kilometres) consisted of charters. Most charter airlines are based in the UK and some are comparable to national airlines. Britannia Airways flew 14.1 bn RPKs in 1991, compared with Aer Lingus 4.1 bn, Alitalia 19.1 bn and SAS 16.5 bn. Also the international regulatory controls had never applied to domestic flights, and offered considerable scope for liberalising bilateral agreements. Thus, in 1984, the UK and the Netherlands opened access on all their bilateral routes to all of their national airlines. Fare controls were removed unless both governments disapproved (double disapproval). Subsequently the UK extended such liberalising agreements to flights to Germany, Belgium and Ireland. This reflected the commitment of the UK to a liberal market environment in air transport, and followed the US government's radical experiment in domestic deregulation begun in 1978. The USA applied its deregulatory zeal not only to its domestic air transport market, but also to its bilateral agreements and its dealings with IATA, assisted by the competitive pressures from Southeast Asian airlines who had remained outside the system. The beneficial results for passengers of the US experience increased the pressure upon the EU to curtail its protectionist regime.

Discussions within the Community moved slowly forward in 1984 with the Civil Aviation Memorandum No. 2 (COM 84)72 final). It introduced the concept of 'zones of flexibility' into fare setting. Governments would determine a reference tariff and a 'zone of reasonableness' in bilateral agreements. Within this zone airlines would be free to set fare levels, subject to country of origin approval or 'double disapproval', i.e. vetoes by both governments. The dominance of national flag carriers remained relatively unchallenged, although 50 : 50 traffic-sharing deals would be allowed to vary to 75 : 25. In return for this limited increase in flexibility the Commission was prepared to exempt fare setting, capacity sharing and revenue pools from the application of the competition rules of the EU for a period of seven years.

This proposal was overtaken by another landmark judgement by the ECJ in the Nouvelles Frontières case of 1985. This involved an attempt by the French regulatory authorities to prevent a travel agent from offering cut-price air tickets. Although the ECJ had already ruled on the applicability of the EU's competition rules, the 1985 judgement opened the way for parties to a dispute to force reference by national courts to the Commission's ruling on any restrictive agreement.

The first aviation package

This judgement forced the hand of the Council, and the result was a package of Regulations and Directives, accepted in 1987, which took the first positive steps towards deregulation. Regulation 3975/87 explicitly confirmed the authority of the Commission to apply the EU's competition rules. However, Regulation 3976/87 allowed the Commission to give block exemptions until 1991 to three categories of airline agreements:

1 Those concerning planning of capacity, revenue sharing and consultation on tariffs.

2 Those concerned with Computer Reservation Systems.

3 Those covering ground handling services.

These exemptions seriously undermined the immediate impact of the Regulation, but, being under the control of the Commission, created leverage in forcing the transition to a more competitive environment. This was indeed what was to occur.

The Council also accepted a Directive (601/87) which significantly reduced the ability of individual member states to control air fares. Although a government might still reject a proposed fare to prevent 'dumping' or predatory pricing, they were unable to reject fares on the grounds that they were lower than those currently offered. The Directive also specifically established the discounting of fares, within a broad range, as an automatic right. These arrangements were to apply for three years, after which further liberalisation was to take place. Similarly, greater access was to be allowed to new airlines, but in stages. Over the next three years member states were to allow traffic shares to move from 50 : 50 to 60 : 40, to accept additional airlines on routes (on a bilateral basis), and to introduce limited fifth freedom rights (cabotage).

The second and third aviation packages

The Second Aviation Package (1991) extended the right of the Commission to give block exemptions to airline agreements until the end of 1992, but it also committed the member states to ending the capacity-sharing arrangements from January 1993.

From that date, scheduled fares were also to be allowed to match non-scheduled fare levels. This process of liberalisation was completed in the Third Aviation Package of three Regulations, which were also to apply from 1993. The Licensing Regulation introduced uniform criteria for the issue of an air transport operator's licence, to be recognised by all member states. The Market Access Regulation opened all EU routes to all licensed operators. Limited cabotage (i.e. the right to operate between two points within any country that is not the airline's home state) continued until April 1997, after which full cabotage became available. Finally, the Fares and Rates Regulation removed all controls on fare levels, subject only to safeguards against excessive tariffs. All remaining restrictions on non-scheduled services were also removed. These three Regulations finally established a single competitive air transport market within the EU. These conditions were extended to Norway and Sweden in an agreement signed in June 1992, and to the European Economic Area.

Industry restructuring

The final deregulation of the air transport market is by no means the end of the story. The problem of distortions arising from state subsidies and from the potential abuse of monopoly power remains. Indeed, European airlines have quickly responded to the changing transport environment by seeking partners. British Airways made no secret of its global ambitions, and had swallowed British Caledonian (in 1988) and Dan Air (in 1992), and taken stakes in TAT and Air Liberté (French regional carriers), Delta Air (a German regional airline renamed Deutsche BA), Iberia (Spain) and Qantas (Australia). Air France took over UTA, Air Inter and, in 2004, KLM, which in turn had invested in Air UK, Transavia (Holland), Air Littoral (France) and Northwest (USA). Meanwhile Lufthansa has a significant minority stake in British Midland.

Already facing the challenge of new low-cost airlines, the collapse in the demand for air travel in 2001, after the destruction of the World Trade Center in New York, resulted in European carriers losing 15 per cent of their revenues and exacerbated their already difficult financial position. For Sabena and SwissAir it proved too much and led to bankruptcy; they were succeeded by Brussels Airlines and Swiss respectively. As well as reducing capacity, some national carriers, such as British Airways, initially attempted to increase profit margins through focusing on the full-price business market. However, low-cost airlines continued to make serious inroads into the existing short-haul European airline market. By 2002 easyJet was carrying 17.3 m passengers a year and had absorbed BA's low-cost airline 'Go', while Ryanair, which had taken over KLM's low-cost brand 'Buzz', was carrying another 17 m. Some flag-carriers have attempted to meet the challenge of the new entrants on these short-haul routes through their own low-cost subsidiaries (e.g. 'bmibaby' (British Midland International) and Germanwings (Lufthansa)), while others have attempted to meet the competition head on through revising their fare structures and aggressive marketing.

Airlines had also followed the US companies in attempting to develop hub-and-spoke route networks. Dominating central hub airports creates the potential for the control of take-off and landing slots. With traffic growing at 7 to 9 per cent pa, more than half of Europe's international airports are facing capacity problems. Flag carriers have traditionally retained their historic 'grandfather rights' to slots at their national airports, inhibiting competition and generating monopoly rents. The Commission has identified this problem and a 1993 Regulation (95/93/EEC) establishes explicit rules for slot allocation. While recognising historic rights, under-utilised slots (those with less that 80 per cent usage) would be surrendered to a 'pool', which would also include newly created slots. Preferential rights to half of these 'pooled' slots would be given to new entrants. These 'pools' would only be created at 'coordinated' airports, to be designated by the national governments. Since this leaves discretion with member states, dominant airlines might choose to utilise their existing slots, even at a loss, to avoid potential competition from new entrants. Therefore this Regulation may have only limited impact. However, the Regulation also requires reciprocity between states in slot access for airlines and provides for intervention by the Commission if the entry of new airlines appears to be being frustrated. Recently the Commission required Lufthansa and SAS to surrender, without compensation, slots at Frankfurt, Copenhagen and Stockholm. Nevertheless, the airlines regard these slots as valuable assets and a grey market has developed between airlines for their sale. The demand that BA surrender 168 slots at Heathrow, valued at £1 m each, to obtain approval for its code-sharing with American Airlines, brought this issue to a head. The Commission intended to review the current situation in 2003.

The Commission has also taken action against Lufthansa and Aer Lingus for their attempts to place restrictions upon 'interlining', where passengers may exchange tickets between airlines serving the same route. Problems may also emerge with the ownership of Computer Reservation Systems (CRSs) by airlines. Such systems (e.g. Galileo), used by travel agents, provide the owning airline not only with the ability to give priority to its own services, but also with information as to the bookings of any other airline using the system. Attempts are being made to establish a Code of Conduct, but the issue of 'dehosting' – forcing companies that own CRSs to display their service information on competing companies' CRSs – is proving a major obstacle. These CRSs are likely to be closely monitored by the Commission, with the threat that the block exemption under the 1987 First Aviation Package (3976/87) could be ended. Similar problems may emerge with the use of code-sharing by airlines for through flights, or with agreements coordinating fares and services, marketing or providing customer or ground services (e.g. Star Alliance (Lufthansa, British Midland, Austrian Airlines, SAS, Singapore Airlines and United Airlines), Oneworld (BA, Iberia, American Airlines) and SkyTeam (Air France, Alitalia)).

Evaluating liberalisation

An attempt had been made by the UK Civil Aviation Authority in 1995 to assess the impact of EU liberalisation (CAA, 1995). It examined 500 intra-EU routes between 1992 and 1994 and found little evidence of increased competition. The number of routes served by more than two airlines only increased from 5 per cent to 7 per cent, while the proportion of monopoly routes increased from 57 per cent to 60 per cent. There also remained a variation in the degree of competition on routes between member states. Whereas the proportion of multicarrier routes for France, Germany, Italy and Spain was between 4 per cent and 8 per cent, that for the UK was 11 per cent. The CAA also examined the trend in Fifth Freedom Rights (Exhibit 10.2) and cabotage. In 1992, 19 Fifth Freedom services were in operation, and by the end of 1994 the number had only grown to 33, dominated by national flag carriers. In the case of cabotage services, restrictions were still in force until 1997. Thus only five such services existed in 1992, doubling to ten by 1994.

The study also identified airport congestion as a major factor in reinforcing the dominance of the market by national airlines through their control of slots. Nonetheless, the CAA recognised that the entry of new carriers since 1994 had begun to reduce the market share of these flag carriers. This trend has continued with the entry of new low-cost airlines (easyJet, Ryanair, Hapag-Lloyd Express, Air Europa) operating out of small regional airports. By 2002 in the UK they had captured 30 per cent of the market and, although across Europe they still only accounted for 5 per cent of European air travel, this was expected to grow within a few years to 12–15 per cent.

There is also concern about the poor international competitiveness of European airlines with the industry continuing to be dominated by American airlines (Table 10.3). A 1992 study had found that European airline productivity was only 72 per cent of that of comparable US airlines, and labour costs of the US 'Big Three' (American, Delta and United) were only two-thirds of those of Alitalia and Lufthansa (McKinsey, 1992). On the highly competitive North Atlantic routes, by 1992 European airlines were offering only 44 per cent of the total capacity, compared with 50 per cent in 1978. With their lower fares, US airlines were also achieving higher payloads, carrying 71 per cent of passengers on US–France routes, and 61 per cent on US–Germany routes. Only on the US–UK route were shares roughly equal.

Unfortunately, external long-haul flights are particularly important for European airlines. In 1999 they accounted for 80 per cent of all the mileage flown by the EU's major airlines, compared with only 35 per cent for US airlines, and the North Atlantic continues to represent a significant part of such traffic, especially for BA, KLM and Lufthansa.

Table 10.3 Major world airlines 2002

Airline	m.r.p.km	Airline	m.r.p.km
American Airlines	195,775	Lufthansa	88,570
United Airlines	176,118	Singapore Airlines	74,171
Delta	164,165	Southwest	73,035
Northwest	115,891	Air Canada	69,404
British Airways	100,787	US Airways	64,404
Air France	98,095	Quantas	63,946
Continental	95,492	KLM	58,595

Note: m.r.p.km = million route passenger kilometres

Source: Eurostat

Air traffic control

The EU member states have an important role in the rationalisation of the highly fragmented system of air traffic control (ATC). In 1991 there were 44 control centres with 31 separate operating systems, three-quarters of which were reported as having significant deficiencies. It has been estimated that inadequacies in Europe's ATC cost €4 bn pa in delays and that Europe's airways could accommodate 30 per cent more traffic with an integrated system. With air traffic expected to grow by 4 per cent pa over the next 15 years there has been growing demand for reform of the EU's ATC.

A European Organisation for the Safety of Air Navigation (Eurocontrol) was established as early as 1960, and in the 1970s it launched an initiative to integrate European ATCs. Since this involved the loss of national sovereignty over member states' air space, little progress was made. Technical incompatibilities between national ATCs also raised serious obstacles to integration. To fill this vacuum the Commission has recently taken the initiative with the adoption of its 'Single European Sky' programme. This involves a package of Regulations to establish a common European upper airspace with redrawn trans-national 'functional blocks', administered by one ATC provider. National authorities would remain responsible, in the short run, for the regulation of separate national ATC providers covering the lower airspace. These would be expected to meet Community-determined standards and be subject to greater transparency in terms of performance and costs. Other associated services would be provided under Community-wide tenders (e.g. meteorological, navigation, communication and information). The opportunity will also be taken to integrate military and civilian uses of the airspace to increase efficiency. Finally, ATC equipment specifications will be harmonised to ensure inter-operability. The Commission intends these changes to be achieved by the end of 2004.

External relations

The Commission has also sought a role in the external relations of the EU industry with the rest of the world. Although as early as 1969 the Council of Ministers had adopted a proposal that member states should notify and consult the EU in the negotiations of their bilateral agreements with third countries, nothing happened. In 1990 the Commission reminded member states of this requirement and proposed that under Article 113 of the Treaty of Rome – the authority to negotiate matters related to the Community's common commercial policies – it should assume responsibility for external negotiations. It believed it was supported in this by the decision of the ECJ that its competition rules applied to air services between member states and third countries. It returned to this proposal in 1992, in response to the completion of the single internal aviation market, with the adoption of the Third Aviation Package, and the US–Netherlands bilateral Air Service Agreement. This agreement embodied an 'open skies' formula, allowing any US carrier access to any Dutch city for reciprocal access. In practice, it offered far more to the American airlines, giving access to a central European hub, and placed pressure on other European states for similar advantageous agreements. This 'divide and rule' strategy had been successfully employed by the USA for a number of years.

The 1992 Commission proposal did not seek Community involvement in all external negotiations, but sought to identify those cases where it would give better economic results. It was particularly concerned to achieve more balance in the negotiations with the USA and Japan. Negotiations were to be guided by an ad hoc Aviation Committee composed of two representatives from each member state. The benefits obtained from such negotiations were to be allocated at the discretion of a Management Committee for Air Transport, with decisions by QMV. Despite these attempts to reconcile member states' conflicting commercial interests with their varying aviation policies and established rights under their bilateral agreements, the Council of Ministers strongly rejected any such role for the community.

However, in November 2002 the ECJ made a landmark judgment, upholding a Commission complaint that bilateral agreements between eight member states and the USA broke Community law. These bilateral deals, such as Bermuda II between the UK and the USA, through restricting landing rights to the national flag carriers of the two states involved, were found to be discriminating against the airlines of other Community member states. As such bilateral agreements can no longer offer any exclusive advantages to a country's own national airlines, the member states finally accepted the Commission's claim that it should have a role in negotiating on behalf of the EU as a whole, where it will have greater collective economic and political leverage. As a final compromise the Commission was given a mandate to negotiate an 'open skies' collective agreement with the USA, while the individual member states retained the right to negotiate the key aspects of bilateral agreements with all other countries, subject only to consultation with the Commission.

At the same time the ECJ also ruled that restrictions on the ownership or control of national airlines were incompatible with EU legislation. This is likely to open up the Community's airline industry, currently dominated by twelve major national carriers, to a long overdue restructuring. However, the Commission will have the difficult task of ensuring that a balance is maintained between the achievement of economies of scale in operation through mergers and the potential abuse of monopoly power. The existence of competition from charter airlines, from new low-cost airlines such as easyJet and Ryanair, and from the high-speed rail network, has already provided a stimulus to efficiency. But the major obstacle to realisation of a competitive common air transport market in the EU remains the existence of state subsidies. Since 1990, Sabena, Air France and Iberia alone have received more than $3 bn in state aid.

Maritime transport

The EU accounts for approximately 20 per cent of world trade, 85 per cent of which is seaborne. The EU15 merchant fleet of the Community represents 35 per cent of the world total, earning $9 bn per annum. Nonetheless, like aviation, maritime transport was initially excluded from consideration under the CTP. This arose from the 'continental' orientation of the original six member states, between whom sea transport was of little importance, and from the complexities of attempting to apply the Treaty within the context of a substantial number of existing international agreements.

In 1970 the Bodson report had first called for the development of a coherent Community approach to shipping under the powers of Article 84(2) of the Treaty of Rome. It identified a number of issues which needed to be addressed, i.e. agreements with non-EU states on cargo reservations and action on discrimination, a common approach to international negotiations and harmonisation of state aid and crew conditions. Although supported by the Parliament, action under Article 84(2) required unanimity, and French opposition ensured that no progress was made until the 1974 ECJ judgement (ECR 631). This arose from an action against France for maintaining rules that discriminated against non-French seamen and found that the competition rules of the EU also applied to air and sea transport. This judgement coincided with increasing concern in the UK, the Netherlands and Germany about unfair competition from COMECON fleets, and from the French about the dangers of oil spillages. Thus from 1974 the Commission was to focus upon four issues:

1 Relations with the COMECON countries.

2 Organisation of liner shipping, and in particular the United Nations Conference on Trade and Development (UNCTAD) code of conduct.

3 The application of the EU's competition rules.

4 Marine pollution and safety at sea.

By 1976 the COMECON fleet accounted for 64 per cent of bilateral trade with the UK, 75 per cent with Germany and 95 per cent with the Netherlands. In the international market it was also capturing an increasing share, with 25 per cent of North Atlantic trade. In 1978 the EU asked member states to monitor the freight liner trade (regular scheduled shipping services) with East Africa, Central America and the Far East, where competition with COMECON shipping was thought to be most acute. Member states could then apply to the Council for permission to instigate counter measures against countries where they believed unfair competitive practices were taking place.

More controversial was the debate within the EU on the ratification of the UNCTAD Convention on a Code of Conduct for Liner Conferences signed in 1974. This had arisen from political pressure by the developing countries for a greater share of the shipping between themselves and the industrialised world. Liner Conferences are composed of the shipping companies involved in a particular trade, and determine shipping rates and conditions of services. They usually cover between 50 and 70 per cent of total cargo shipments on any route. The crucial feature of the Code was the adoption of a 40/40/20 rule for participation in a trade. The national shipping companies of the two countries in the trade would each be reserved 40 per cent of the traffic, with 20 per cent open to 'cross-traders'. The USA was opposed to a further reinforcement of these shipping cartels. In the EU, Denmark and the UK, with their established fleets, also opposed ratification, while France, Belgium and Germany supported the Code. Disagreement focused upon two issues – the share to be allocated to non-EU OECD countries and the treatment of non-EU non-OECD carriers. The final compromise Regulation

(954/79/EEC) that allowed ratification confined the 40/40/20 rule to those Conferences involving developing countries. Elsewhere, commercial criteria were to apply in determining the shares of cargo traffic. The Code finally came into force in 1983. Some of the concerns about the consequences for EU shipping's share of liner trade may have proved well founded. The EU's share of world liner capacity fell from 45 per cent in 1983 to 38 per cent in 1992, while that of Far Eastern companies (excluding Japan) grew from 25 per cent to 34 per cent.

Although, contrary to expectations, the ratification of the Code did not require adaptation of the EU's competition rules in relation to Liner Conference agreements, the Commission remained concerned that they were compromising the Treaty. First submitted in 1981, a proposed Regulation sought to empower the Commission to enforce Article 85, against restrictive agreements, and Article 86, against abuse of dominant positions, with regard to sea transport. Block exemptions were to be given to the Liner Conference agreements, subject to certain conditions, since these were seen as contributing to a stable market environment. These conditions included non-discrimination in rates and conditions of carriage in services from different EU ports or users and consultations with customers. It was not until 1986 that this extension of the powers of the Commission was agreed under Regulation 4056/86/EEC.

The Commission remains concerned that Liner Conferences compromise the competition rules of the Community. In particular, it has focused on the issue of whether the fixing of multimodal rates (inclusive rates for both the shipping and road/rail components of a freight movement) under a Conference agreement is outside the block exemption that has been given. In 1995 a Committee of enquiry was appointed, the Multimodal Group under Sir Brian Carsberg, to establish whether the establishment of uniform rates by Conferences for multi-modal transport was justified on efficiency grounds. Its report supported the critical position of the Commission (Multimodal Group, 1996). The Commission had already ruled in 1994 that the Trans-Atlantic Agreement violated the block exemption requirements, not only for setting associated inland transport rates, but also for establishing a capacity management programme and constraining individual service contracts by shippers. The shipping lines involved have challenged this ruling before the ECJ and judgement is still awaited. So far the ECJ has only given a judgement in the CEWAL case, where it supported the Commission's position that the liner conference covering services between Northern Europe and Zaire was an abuse of their dominant market position.

Regulation 4056/86/EEC was one of a package of four Regulations accepted by the Council to realise its commitment to establishing free and fair competitive conditions in shipping. A second Regulation (4055/86/EEC) prevented discrimination by a member state against the shipping companies of any other EU members in any of its trades. Existing unilateral cargo reservations were to be phased out by 1993. Similarly, cargo sharing agreements with third countries are now allowed only in exceptional circumstances. Attempts by third countries to impose such agreements can be met by countermeasures by the Community under the third Regulation 4058/86/EEC. Finally, Regulation 4057/86/EEC empowers the EU to impose compensatory duties on non-EU ship owners found to be engaging in unfair pricing practices. This Regulation was of particular relevance to the problem of competition from Central and Eastern European fleets.

These four Regulations created the foundations for a Common Shipping policy, and committed the EU to concerted action to combat protectionism by non-EU countries. It represented a significant transfer of power from individual member states to the Community. The EU, by combining the individual influence of the member states, will have a much greater impact upon the international negotiations that will determine the shape of this industry. Some rationalisation of the EU shipping industry is inevitable in the longer term. The EU still boasts twelve major shipping lines, compared with Japan's three and the US's two. But consolidation is more likely to occur through joint enterprises and the development of 'consortia', pooling shipping, than through mergers.

The Commission also attempted to address the problem of the major shift of registrations from EU national registers to the 'flags of convenience' such as Panama and Liberia (see Table 10.4). The extent of 'flagging out' by EU shipping companies varies from 34 per cent in Italy to 100 per cent in Belgium, with the UK at 66 per cent and Greece, with the largest fleet in the EU, at 69 per cent. This has a major impact upon operating costs. It is estimated that a 1500 gross ton container vessel with a crew from less-developed countries costs $350,000 per annum, while a Dutch crew costs $1,286,000. This has not only distorted competition within the Community but has undermined the international competitive position of all Community shipping. It is also seen as compromising attempts to establish common and acceptable standards of operation.

In 1989 the Commission had proposed the creation of an EU shipping registry (EUROS) under an EU flag (COM(89)266). It would be open to any shipping company controlled by EU nationals, regardless of the company's domicile. Vessels had to be under 20 years old, be on an EU national register and employ EU nationals as officers and half the crew. It would have offered registered vessels cabotage rights within any member state, tax rebates on seafarers' earnings and state aids. A number of problems emerged with this proposal and it has yet to be adopted. In the event of accidents the law of the country of registration applies and as yet no similar body of EU law is available. The proposal would also exclude from the register ships controlled by non-EU nationals administered from within the Community. This is particularly a problem for the UK, with the large number

Table 10.4 Major national fleets, 2000

	National Flag m.d.t.	Foreign Flag m.d.t.	World %
Denmark	6.66	8.67	2.1
Finland	2.53	2.95	0.8
France	2.53	2.95	0.8
Germany	7.51	21.73	4.1
Greece	40.78	21.73	18.4
Italy	8.44	4.39	1.8
Netherlands	2.79	2.16	0.7
Sweden	1.54	13.02	2.0
Spain	1.58	2.03	2.0
UK	6.23	11.97	2.5

Source: EU Energy and Transport in Figures 2001

of foreign shipping companies operating from London. However, most significantly it appears to offer little assistance in addressing the central problem of international competitiveness. Subsidies to EU shipping companies to encourage investment in new vessels are likely to be temporary and limited, while attempts to increase international competitiveness through a reduction in the tax burden on ship-owners and seafarers, through the replacement of national taxes by a single EU tax linked to a vessel's age and tonnage, are frustrated by the limited competence of the Community in determining levels of direct taxation. Nonetheless, in the recent Transport White Paper (COM/2001/370) the Commission has indicated that it intends to propose a Directive to introduce tonnage-based taxation, to promote reflagging to Community registers and to revise the guidelines on state subsidies. It was resistance to the transfer of control of shipping industry subsidies from the national governments to the Community that resulted in a compromise that member states should have the option of whether or not their national shipping companies should join EUROS.

Despite these limitations EUROS is seen as offering a potential contribution to meeting the concerns of some member states about operating standards and the threat of marine pollution. Concern had focused on this issue, in 1978, after the Amoco Cadiz oil spillage on the Brittany coast. In response to a Council request, the Commission proposed a programme of action for the control of oil pollution, and also for Directives requiring member states to ratify a series of outstanding international agreements. These included the 1974 International Convention for the Safety of Life at Sea (Solas), the 1973 International Convention for the Prevention of Pollution from Ships (Marpol) and the ILO Convention 147 concerning minimum standards on merchant ships. Although the Council authorised a series of technical studies, it declined to impose ratification upon all member states; instead it merely agreed a Recommendation.

However, the Council did agree Directives on pilotage in the English Channel and North Sea and for compulsory notification of potential marine hazards from oil tankers using Community ports. This failed to satisfy the European Parliament, which prepared its own critical report on what it regarded as the Council's inadequate response. Again it was the grounding of an oil tanker in 1993, this time the Braer off the Shetland Islands, that galvanised the Commission and member states into action. Following a special Council meeting a commitment was made to the harmonisation of the implementation of existing international rules and their uniform enforcement to all vessels, regardless of their flags, using EU waters (COM(93)66). The latest Communication from the Commission, *Towards a New Maritime Strategy* (COM(96)81), reaffirms these commitments, calls for non-binding International Maritime Organisation resolutions to be embodied in Community law, for port controls to be strengthened and for common minimum standards to be established for all Community shipping registers. A requirement for compulsory third party insurance for all shipping using Community ports is also to be examined.

The conflict between the need to restore the international competitiveness of the EU's maritime industry and the desire to raise and harmonise operating conditions within the Community remains a central policy dilemma. Although the Commission has had very limited success in addressing the problem of European shipping's deteriorating international competitiveness, it has laid the foundations for fair competition within the Community. This culminated in 1992 with the agreement by the Council of Transport Ministers to maritime cabotage rights across the Community as part of the SEM (3577/92/EEC). Short-sea shipping is also seen as having a major contribution to make to shifting dependence away from road transport and overcoming transport bottlenecks, such as the Alps, Pyrenees and German–Polish border. For this reason certain shipping links will be included in the trans-European network plan.

Conclusion

The Common Transport Policy differs fundamentally from the common policies for agriculture and external trade. In contrast to external trade policy, it has both an external and internal dimension and, unlike agriculture, there has been no inclination to develop a highly interventionist regulatory regime. Indeed, the history of transport policy has been one of the gradual erosion of the influence of those member states attempting to sustain, at Community level, their national interventionist traditions. However, the differing views of the nature of a CTP, and the political debate about the appropriate boundaries for 'subsidiarity', ensured an impasse in its evolution for the first two decades of the Community. As in other areas of policy, it was the commitment to the establishment of the SEM that broke the logjam of policy development.

The success of the transport dimension of the SEM initiative has had a major impact upon the internal transport market of the EU, laying the foundations for fair and competitive market conditions. This enhanced internal competition may also produce the efficiency gains necessary to restore the international competitiveness of the European airline and maritime industries. It has also reinforced the claims of the Commission to represent the Community in external negotiations on international bodies such as the International Maritime Organisation (IMO) and the International Civil Aviation Organisation (ICAO). Internally, the problem of funding major transport infrastructure investment remains, together with the failure to establish a clear system of infrastructure pricing that can take account of the social and environmental costs imposed by each mode of transport. Until this is achieved, significant distortions will remain, causing substantial economic costs. However, since no member state has found this an easy issue to address at the national level, it would be harsh to condemn the Community for the lack of progress that it has made.

References

AEA (1990) *Association of European Airlines Yearbook*, Brussels.

Civil Aviation Authority (1995) *The Single European Aviation Market: Progress So Far*, CAP654, London.

Dearden S (1990) 'Road Freight Transport, Social Cost and Market Efficiency', *Royal Bank of Scotland Review*, No. 168, December.

European Commission (1961) *Memorandum on the General Lines of a Common Transport Policy*, Brussels.

European Commission (1989) *Communication on a Community Railway Policy*, COM(89)238, Brussels.

European Commission (1990) *Towards Trans-European Networks: For a Community Action Programme*, COM(90)585, Brussels.

European Commission (1996) *Proposal for a Council Directive on the Charging of Heavy Goods Vehicles for the Use of Certain Infrastructures*, COM(96) 331, Brussels.

European Commission (1997) *Proposal for a Council Directive on Airport Charges*, COM(97)154, Brussels.

European Commission (1998) *Fair Payment for Infrastructure Use: A Phased Approach to a Common Transport Infrastructure Charging Structure in the EU*, COM(98)466, Brussels.

European Commission (2002) *Towards an Integrated European Railway Area*, COM(2002)18, Brussels.

McGowan F and Trengove C (1986) *European Aviation: A Common Market?*, Institute of Fiscal Studies, London.

McKinsey Global Institute (1992) *Service Sector Productivity*, Washington.

Multimodal Group (1996) *Interim Report of the Multimodal Group*, European Commission, DG IV, Brussels.

Nash C and Sansom T (2001) 'Pricing European Transport Systems: Recent Developments and Evidence from Case Studies', *Journal of Transport Economics and Policy*, Vol. 35, Part 3, pp. 363–80.

Pryke R (1991) 'American Deregulation and European Liberalisation' in D Banister and K Button (eds), *Transport in a Free Market*, Macmillan, London.

Vickerman R W (1994) 'Transport Infrastructure and Region Building in the European Community', *Journal of Common Market Studies*, Vol. 32, No. 1, pp. 1–24.

Further reading

Abbati C (1986) *Transport and European Integration: European Perspectives*, European Commission, Brussels.

Bayliss B and Millington A (1995) 'Deregulation and Logistics Systems in a Single European Market', *Journal of Transport Economics and Policy*, Vol. 29, No. 3, pp. 305–16.

Button K and Swann D (1989) 'European Community Airlines: Deregulation and its Problems', *Journal of Common Market Studies*, Vol. 17, No. 4, pp. 259–82.

Gwilliam K (1997) 'EU Competition Policy and Liner Shipping Conferences', *Journal of Transport Economics and Policy*, Vol. 31, No. 3, pp. 317–24.

Holder S (1999) 'Recent Developments in Rail Infrastructure Charging', *Journal of Transport Economics and Policy*, Vol. 33, Part 1, pp. 111–18.

Papaioannou R and Stasinopoulos D (1991) 'The Road Transport Policy of the European Community', *Journal of Transport Economics and Policy*, Vol. 25, No. 2, pp. 201–08.

Ross J F (1994) 'High-Speed Rail: Catalyst for European Integration?', *Journal of Common Market Studies*, Vol. 32, No. 2, June, pp. 191–214.

Stasinopoulos D (1993) 'The Third Phase of Liberalisation in Community Aviation and the Need for Supplementary Measures', *Journal of Transport Economics and Policy*, Vol. 27, No. 3, pp. 323–8.

Chapter 11

The Common Agricultural Policy

Tidings P. Ndhlovu

Introduction

Since its inception in 1962, the Common Agricultural Policy (CAP) has had to wrestle with two contradictory positions. On the one hand the urgent need to address food shortages following the Second World War and ensure self-sufficiency necessitated a reinforcement of interventionist and protectionist policies, which had existed at the national level. Thus, market regulation to stabilise prices, export subsidies and financial support were all put in place. In recent years (Agenda, 2000) this complex agricultural support system has also involved the roles of a sustainable and integrated European Union (EU) Rural Development Policy: improvement of living and working conditions, preserving the rural way of life, food safety and production of high quality food that takes account of environmental needs. On the other hand, price support measures and compensatory payments have been depicted as trade-distorting and, therefore, in urgent need of reform to enable free market forces to operate smoothly. Indeed, it could also be argued that the replacement of national policies by a CAP in the early years (1957–67) was in line with 'the common market principle of competition on equal terms' (Hitiris, 2001, p. 47). It is to this end that Agenda 2000 sought to replace price support with direct payments as a first step to reducing the distortions of the CAP.

Tensions between Europe and the USA over the latter's export credits and pricing practices have not helped matters. Nevertheless, proponents of the free market philosophy contend that the changing conditions in the global agricultural economy demand that subsidies be abolished and domestic support reduced in order to facilitate greater market access and export competition, in line with WTO (World Trade Organisation, formerly GATT, General Agreement on Tariffs and Trade) commitments.

For its part, the EU Commission has often attempted to straddle the two contradictory positions, seeking a 'middle' or 'third' way enabling subsidies and financial support to be retained, while seeking to sever the link between production and subsidies. According to this line of thought, not only will the EU retain its social responsibilities, but farmers can also make production choices in response to consumer tastes and preferences. The latter, in turn, results in a more competitive EU agricultural market. Freedom of choice is thus accompanied by the EU guaranteeing higher and more stable farm incomes, with a fairer distribution of income support. This will no doubt meet the challenges arising from the process of enlargement.

This chapter seeks to establish the relative significance of political and economic factors in the development and subsequent reform of the CAP. In so doing it addresses two key questions. Is the drive towards liberalisation a direct result of pressures from within or outside the EU? To what extent will the EU's proposals for the reform of the CAP help to defend its position in the WTO? The chapter begins by examining the background to and instruments of the CAP and moves on to explore the factors which necessitated reform, culminating in the adoption of a compromise package of reforms on 26 June 2003 by the 15 EU farm ministers. Particular attention is paid to the way in which the EU addressed problems associated with reform. These reforms undoubtedly had a major bearing on the Doha round of trade talks in Cancun in September 2003 vis-à-vis the WTO commitments. What cannot escape the casual observer is the tension between interventionist and free market advocates during the discussions of CAP reform. Indeed, the French government could only be persuaded not to veto the deal after the EU agreed to maintain the partial link between production and subsidies for many products.

The Common Agricultural Policy: background and price support system

In the aftermath of the disruptions to agriculture caused by the Second World War the original six member states set about reviving the fortunes of the sector. After all it had been, and continued to be, the largest employer; there were many rural communities, and the recent experience of the 1930s – at the national level, at least – suggested that interventionist and protectionist policies were the surest way of achieving self-sufficiency and erasing the memories of rationing.

It was also recognised that agricultural markets were inherently unstable. Left to their own devices free markets were unlikely to cope with fluctuations in prices resulting from changes in weather conditions which, in turn, led to excess supply in one (good) year and scarcity in another (bad) year. Moreover, the sluggish way in which output adjusted to current market prices also contributed to price volatility. In addition, the continued preponderance of small (arguably inefficient) farms, well after the abolition of the strip system of the feudal era in the eighteenth and nineteenth centuries, did not help matters. Previous tenants had simply become the owners of the strips, slowing down the introduction of more advanced technology and thus the rate of increase of supply.

Insofar as demand for agricultural products is relatively income inelastic, it is understandable that the original six member states should seek not only to raise farm incomes, but also stabilise them. Paradoxically, the intense efforts to resuscitate the agricultural sector enabled the farm lobby to assume a political importance, making it increasingly crucial to winning general elections. It was this farm lobby, with its growing political influence, that was to add its weight to the pursuance of interventionist and protectionist measures. Competition from North America and Australasia only reinforced the perceived need for such measures to meet the challenge.

Negotiations of the CAP were conducted under these circumstances. Indeed, the requirement by the Treaty of Rome in 1957 for a common external tariff for imported goods, and abolition of internal tariffs within the common market, chimed out a pleasant tune to agricultural interests. Clearly this was the way to promote price stability and transfer income to farming communities. The cost of managing storage and disposal of output, over and above what was demanded by commercial consumers, could then be borne by central budgets and ultimately the taxpayer. The buoyant mood was, by 1957, further fuelled by Europe's recovery from the war and Germany's return to prosperity.

In the early years (1957–67), the main concern of the original six member states was to establish an agricultural policy that would eventually replace national agricultural policies (Article 38 of the Treaty of Rome). The fact that agriculture appears early in the Treaty indicates its importance regarding the promotion of European integration. However, this did not obviate contradictions in policy. Although Article 38 did refer to free competition, it is equally clear from Article 42 that the European Council could, and did, allow for non-competitive market organization in agriculture, as well as state aid.

A number of objectives of the CAP, which was originally introduced in 1962, were enshrined in Article 39 (1) of the Treaty of Rome:

- to increase agricultural productivity by promoting technical progress and by ensuring the rational development of agricultural production and the optimum utilisation of the factors of production, in particular labour;
- to ensure a fair standard of living for the agricultural community, in particular, by increasing the individual earnings of persons engaged in agriculture;
- to stabilise markets;
- to assure the availability of supplies;
- to ensure that supplies reach consumers at reasonable prices.

Until the mid-1980s, the first two objectives were regarded as crucial in ensuring that there were increases in employment and economic growth, that balance of payments problems were tackled and that farmers and farm workers were rescued from grinding (rural) poverty. Securing the supply of food to consumers at reasonable prices would also ensure that there was no return to the chronic food shortages of the Second World War.

The achievement of these objectives was predicated on a number of principles. Here, the role of agriculture in promoting integration figured prominently. More precisely, the establishment of 'a single agricultural market' (Article 39 (1) of the Treaty of Rome) – i.e. free movement of agricultural goods within the Community – was seen as the basis of European integration. This entailed the removal of 'every distortion on competition, harmonising legislation and operating a common intervention system' (ibid.). The latter required centralisation of the administration, policies and market organisation in order to establish common prices. Furthermore, Community preferences – i.e. restrictions of cheaper agricultural goods from outside the Community – were regarded as necessary for stabilising volatile agricultural markets and ensuring the survival of the agricultural support system, without ignoring the EU's social responsibilities. Finally, joint financial responsibility was not only a recognition of the similarities of interest in agriculture, including the acceptance by member states that they share in the cost of maintaining the CAP, but also pointed to the continued need for financial support for the sector as a whole.

Indeed, the precise aim of the European Agricultural Guidance and Guarantee Fund (EAGGF), which was set up by Regulation No. 25 of 1962 (amended by regulation No. 728/70 and established in 1972), was to finance agricultural market organisation and facilitate an integrated agricultural market. It also provided funds for modernisation of farms, training and aid to remote and mountainous agricultural areas. The Guidance Section has, at various times, played an important role in funding export subsidies and, latterly, supporting rural development measures, i.e. structural reform. For its part, the Price Guarantee Section seeks to buttress the price support system with an annual price review setting targets and intervention prices designed to bring about stability in agricultural markets.

Exhibit 11.1 is a simple illustration of how the price support system operates.

Exhibit 11.1 EU's price mechanism (CAP): agricultural support system

The EU demand for agricultural products, dd, is shown to be downward-sloping, while the supply of EU farmers, ss, is upward-sloping, implying that the costs of production are increasing. The macroeconomic equilibrium can then be described by the intersection of demand and supply curves. We also represent the supplies entering the EU market by SS (world). Clearly the EU supply curve, ss, is above the world market price, OP_1. Put another way, the EU farmers' cost of production is above the world price, meaning that EU farmers are less efficient than their international competitors.

For simplicity, we also assume that SS is perfectly (infinitely) elastic. By this it is meant that the price remains at OP_1 whether the EU imports more or less. This, of course, is patently unrealistic, considering the sheer size of the EU market. Nevertheless, if, in these circumstances, imports were freely available at price OP_1, the EU market would be flooded

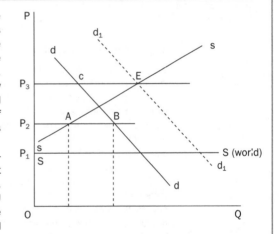

with cheap food, spelling disaster for most EU farmers whose cost of production was above the free market price.

What then is the solution to this conundrum? The answer lies in the role played by intervention prices and variable import levies, without which the price support system would collapse like a pack of cards. To illustrate this point, let us start in Exhibit 11.1 by applying a variable import levy of P_1P_2 per unit. At this point imports will be equivalent to AB, while domestic supply stands at P_2A. Now let us suppose we fix the variable import levy at the higher level of P_1P_3. The resulting higher intervention price of OP_3 will be a strong incentive to increase domestic supply to P_3E, while domestic demand will now stand at only P_3C. To the extent that the EAGGF helped to finance modernisation of farms, the resulting technological advances have led to an increase in productivity and contributed to even more production. There is, thus, an excess supply of CE which, if we allowed market forces to operate, would eventually reduce the price back to equilibrium.

How then can we prevent the weakening of the intervention price, OP_3? The answer is simple: the National Intervention Agencies will buy CE (the accumulating beef or butter mountains, wine lakes, etc.) at the intervention price. If, as mentioned earlier, exporters have to sell the excess outside the EU at a loss (P_1P_3 per unit), they will only do so if they are guaranteed some compensation in the form of an export refund or restitution. Meanwhile the effect of intervention buying, to make up for the low income elasticity of demand for food, is the rightward shift of the demand curve dd to d_1d_1. Here, consumers buy P_3C at the intervention price, OP_3, while the authorities buy the excess CE. As a result, price OP_3 is maintained.

By 1968, the CAP was up and running and most of the national price policies had been superseded by the CAP (Sinnott and Winston, 2000, p. 360). It is to this end that a number of instruments were introduced to manipulate prices, i.e. to fix administrative prices which were above market clearing rates. Exhibit 11.2 illustrates the instruments that underlie the price support mechanism.

Exhibit 11.2 The CAP pricing system – Instruments

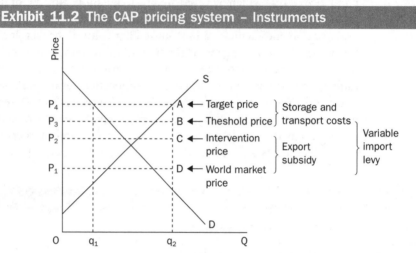

Source: Diagram adapted from McDonald and Dearden, 1999, p. 283

First, the target price (or guide price for beef, veal and wine, and norm price for tobacco), P_4, is an annual estimation by the Council of what level the product is likely to achieve on the market. To this price transport costs to dealers and storers are added, so the price will vary from month to month as storage costs are taken into account. Unsurprisingly, the Council takes a very optimistic view of this guide or ideal price, such that it has historically been set at a level much higher than the prevailing world market price, P_1. Clearly this is a political rather than a producer price, designed to help EU farmers 'maintain or appropriately increase their standard of living' (Pelkmans, 2001, p. 208).

Secondly, the threshold price, P_3, is the acceptable price at which imports can enter the EU market (it is also 'known as the *reference price* for fruits, vegetables, wine and fishery products, and as the *sluice-price* for pork, eggs and poultry meat' (Hitiris, 2003, p. 166). It takes into account the transport and distribution costs incurred within the EU (El-Agraa, 2001, p. 244). While this created a theoretical possibility of entry into the EU market, the EU was quick to erect barriers against international competitors. Up until July 1995, a variable import tariff or import levy system did precisely this. The EU virtually ruled out all competition by imports below the threshold price, thus preventing the EU market from being flooded with cheap imports. With import demand having become inelastic in regard to changes in world market prices, the bigger the fall in the prevailing world market price, the larger will be the variable import levy required to maintain the threshold price, hence insulating the EU from the vagaries of the market place.

Little wonder the critics argue that, without these trade-distorting effects, together with the price support system, free market prices would not have been so depressed. The replacement of the variable import levy system with fixed tariffs in August 1995 has done nothing to allay these fears. In fact, it is clear from Exhibit 11.1 that excess supply, q_1–q_2, results from the target price, P_4, being set above the threshold price, P_3.

Finally, the EU seeks to remove the resulting surplus by setting a (theoretical) minimum price which is 'about 7 or 8 per cent below the target price' (El-Agraa, 2001, p. 244). This intervention price (or basic price for pig meat), P_2, is set in euros at the annual price-fixing review. It is not only guaranteed to all producers, but also forms the basis for an EU-wide pricing policy. If the price falls below this minimum guaranteed price, the National Intervention Agencies, acting on behalf of the EU, step in to support the price by buying produce at the intervention price. This produce, we must add, has to meet certain minimum quality standards.

Disposal of surpluses is achieved in a variety of ways: it can be sold to the needy as food aid, or even destroyed if needs be; it can be stored until prices rise to the intervention level, with storage costs funded by the EAGGF; or it can be dumped onto the world market at below the intervention price, thus further depressing the world market price. In these circumstances there has to be an export subsidy or export restitution if it is going to be worthwhile for EU exporters to dispose of their surplus at the prevailing world market price. In other words, a refund, which is periodically set by the Commission, has to take account of the difference between the intervention price and the price exporters can command on the non-EU market. It is perhaps not surprising that international competitors have identified these export subsidies as yet another example of trade distortion.

Undoubtedly, the guaranteed price and rapid technical change have provided the main incentive for increasing domestic production even beyond the level of self-sufficiency. The rate of growth of supply has consistently exceeded that of consumer demand. And this excess supply has been characterised by the wine lakes, butter mountains, etc. As surpluses have grown over the years, National Intervention Agencies have been called upon more and more to maintain the intervention price. Not surprisingly, the cost of maintaining the CAP has correspondingly increased.

Why were reforms necessary?

Clearly the introduction and establishment of the CAP not only addressed the problem of shortages, but also had unintended side-effects. While the CAP enabled agricultural goods to be freely traded within the EU, it was not until 1992 that, for example, 'veterinary and phytosanitary controls at the national level . . . were at long last removed . . . by means of (minimum) harmonization of the required domestic controls and mutual recognition of inspections and certificates' (Pelkmans, 2001, p. 214). A number of studies have also concluded, among other things, that trade diversion, when couched in terms of trade flows, has been greater than trade creation as a result of the CAP. Moreover, guaranteed prices to farmers encouraged overproduction, while the cost of maintaining the CAP was escalating.

This is the background against which critics of the CAP have called for fundamental reforms. Subsidisation of the EU's agricultural production under the CAP, so the argument goes, has distortionary effects on world agricultural markets. While the EU has trumpeted the recent reforms of the CAP as enabling farmers to respond to market demand, Franz Fischler, the EU Commissioner for Agriculture, Rural Development and Fisheries, has correspondingly laid the blame for distortionary policies squarely on the shoulders of the United States.

What then triggered these reforms? Exploration of the reasons underpinning these reforms will assist in understanding the shape they have taken.

First, the incentives related to the price mechanism not only contributed to self-sufficiency, but guaranteed prices also led to structural excess-supply, while export subsidies increased the cost of farm support. In other words, the achievement of market stabilisation was accompanied by supply outstripping demand, particularly in the 1980s when the EU 'was up to 120 per cent self-sufficient in some areas' (Church and Phinnemore, 1994, p. 103; see also Swann, 1995, p. 253; Pelkmans,

2001, p. 215). While agricultural production rose by 2 per cent pa for the period 1973–88, consumption within the EU rose by only 0.5 per cent per annum (Phinnemore, 1994).

Moreover, export subsidies, and increasing expenditure on storage and disposal designed to maintain the intervention price, contributed to the growing cost of the support system. As production increased in response to the price incentives, imports into the EU correspondingly fell and less revenue accrued from import levies. Thus, there were insufficient funds for the EAGGF, necessitating increases in financial (guaranteed) support from the EU budget. As the proportion of revenues to finance the Guidance Section of the EAGGF continued to fall from about 5 per cent of the total EU budget in 1991 to approximately 2.4 per cent in 1998, a large proportion of the resources were devoted to the Guarantee Section, which accounted for around 53 per cent and 48 per cent of the total EU budget in 1991 and 1998, respectively. Indeed, the budgetary cost of the CAP had grown from ECU 4.7 bn in 1976 to ECU 32.9 bn in 1991, rising to ECU 90 bn in 1998. While the CAP is allegedly responsible for 85 per cent of the world's agricultural subsidies, the annual cost of the policy was estimated at about ECU 50 bn in 2000 (Fitzgerald and Gardiner, 2003, p. 1).

Colman (2001, pp. 102–3) notes that budgetary costs are, in effect, transfers. In other words, taxes are levied on certain groups and it is these revenues that are then transferred to other groups in society. This is the context in which the UK became a net contributor to the cost of the CAP. Little wonder that the British Prime Minister, Margaret Thatcher, was at the forefront of budgetary reform of the CAP. In the end, the 1984 Fontainebleau European Council agreement accorded the UK a rebate. But this abatement mechanism, insofar as it meant that the cost of the rebate was borne by other member states, only served to sour the atmosphere and further isolate the UK.

Secondly, enlargement of the EU exacerbated the spiralling costs. For example, the UK, which was a major importer of food, and Denmark and Ireland, both dependent on agricultural exports, had become members of the EU in 1975. They were soon followed by Greece in 1981, and Spain and Portugal in 1986. Far from enlargement being seen as opening the EU markets to agricultural imports from other countries, it was often regarded as another example of trade diversion. According to Colman, this process 'switched a significant proportion of their [new member states] agricultural imports from non-member to member states' (2001, p. 104).

Thirdly, the advent of 'technological progress and capital investment . . . [which was] fostered by the CAP . . . [while] regional specialization in the internal market [was] far less' (Pelkmans, 2001, p. 215), resulted in productivity in agriculture between 1961 and 1990 increasing by more than 5 per cent per annum, compared with approximately 3 per cent in the EU's industries (Hitiris, 2003, p. 169). The adoption of capital-intensive farming systems was financed, not by the farmer, but by the EU via the CAP. It is also noteworthy that, while 'the restructuring of the agricultural sector towards larger farms and a faster pace of mechanization' (ibid.) was taking place in countries such as the UK, the picture was different for those countries, notably Greece, Italy and Portugal, whose average holdings were small in comparison. Clearly, there was uneven development, with large variations in labour productivity among the EU member states.

The initial response of the EU was to increase spending on products (e.g. cereals, milk, beef) from the poorer, larger farming communities such as Spain and Portugal. However, to balance the benefits, more money was also spent on products (e.g. fruit, vegetables and wine) from the more prosperous member states, thus further contributing to overspending on agricultural policy.

Fourthly, the incentives and subsidies of the CAP not only encouraged over-production and the adoption of capital-intensive farming methods in the northern EU countries, but also had damaging effects on the environment. Indeed, those areas that did not adopt farming methods involving increased use of chemical and energy inputs were more likely to experience problems of 'agricultural decline and depopulation' (Colman, 2001, p. 107). Not surprisingly, environmental pressure groups began to voice their concerns and correspondingly called for reforms.

Fifthly, there have been questions raised about the objective of securing supplies at reasonable prices. It is understandable that banishing the spectre of food shortages and rationing reminiscent of the Second World War should be uppermost in the minds of the EU leaders. However, critics have argued that the very CAP instruments that set prices above world market levels make these guaranteed prices 'unreasonable' (Pelkmans, 2001, p. 216; Swann, 1995, p. 254). If it is accepted that the poorer members of society spend a larger amount of their income on food, then it could be concluded that they may indeed bear around 60 per cent of the cost of maintaining the CAP (Colman, 2001, p. 103).

Sixthly, one of the objectives of the CAP was to address distributional issues. Apart from the problems of finding an acceptable measure for 'fair' incomes for farmers, there were also problems of comprehensiveness (e.g. does 'real farming income' take account of the whole farming community, including part-time farmers?) and comparison (are we comparing like with like when inflation rates differ from one member state to another, and some member states have comprehensive social security systems while others have rudimentary ones, if at all?). Notwithstanding these problems, Pelkmans concludes that there are strong indications 'that the much-discussed income gap between agricultural and non-agricultural personal incomes has disappeared for the sector as a whole' (2001, p. 215).

This does not, however, mask the inequalities within the agricultural sector itself. With price tied to output, approximately 80 per cent of the CAP support went to around 20 per cent of the large, efficient farmers. In recent years, even with the proposals for partial decoupling subsidies and production, about 70 per cent of support goes to 20 per cent of farmers, of which the 'chief beneficiaries . . . are the French farmers, who receive over $10 billion a year, nearly 20 per cent of the total CAP budget' (Fitzgerald and Gardiner, 2003, p. 1).

Seventhly, the EU's unit of account (UA) had been designed to ensure that there would be common prices, with exchange rates remaining unchanged. This system of green rates in the CAP meant that prices within the EU were fixed in the European currency unit (ECU), while payments to farmers/exporters were in national currencies. In the interest of stabilising farm prices in response to fluctuating exchange rates, some flexibility in changing green rates was permitted. All this might have worked well if it were not for the devaluation of the French franc by as much as 11.11 per cent in August 1969, meaning that the increase in prices for French farmers would encourage more and more production, leading to even larger food surpluses. The contrary case was when the German mark was revalued, resulting in a fall in the farm price. There were some attempts to resolve these problems: 'It was therefore decided that France should grant subsidies to imports from member states and levy compensatory duties on French exports in order not to distort the free movement of agricultural produce . . . Germany was . . . empowered to apply levies on imports and subsidies on exports – the reverse of the French case' (Swann, 1995, p. 255).

Finally, the aforementioned domestic pressures for reform were also accompanied by external ones. The fact that the EU had become the largest global food importer, while also being the second largest food exporter, caused problems for its international competitors. Indeed, the USA and the 'Cairns Group' of agricultural exporters (including Australia and New Zealand) were, and still are, concerned with the EU subsidies, which they argue distort trade and reduce market access. While the earlier rounds of the GATT negotiations made no mention of agriculture, it was clear from the September 1986 Uruguay Round that, without a commitment by the EU to dismantle its agricultural protectionism and desist from surplus dumping, no meaningful agreements could be reached at these Rounds and the subsequent WTO talks.

Clearly, internal and external pressures played a crucial role in the introduction of reform. The annual cost of maintaining the support system, together with the growing cost of accommodating new, relatively underdeveloped agricultural economies, became burdensome. Moreover, the complex bureaucratic structures of managing the CAP hardly helped matters. The success towards achieving certain objectives, such as self-sufficiency, has also been accompanied by failure in achieving others, such as 'fairer' distribution. While intensive farming practices, encouraged by incentives and subsidies, had led to overproduction, these labour-saving techniques had also resulted in environmental damage. In addition, external pressures for liberalisation have increased over the years.

While confidence in Keynesianism has been questioned in certain quarters, it must also be borne in mind that the CAP has had a differential impact on member states, thus ensuring that there have also been differing responses to reform. On the one hand, beneficiaries of the CAP, such as France, Greece and Ireland, regard existing Keynesian tools, such as guaranteed prices and subsidies, as crucial to the health of their economies. On the other hand, there are those member states, such as the UK, who contribute more to the CAP than they receive from it. Not surprisingly, these countries have pushed hardest for reform, the argument being that changes will enable farmers to respond to market demand. The tension between these two positions runs throughout the whole reform process.

Pre-1992 reforms

Typically, the debate on the subsequent reforms, whether addressing questions of costs and (income) distribution, or the more fundamental issues of whether the CAP should continue in its present form, has polarised opinion along free market (neoclassical) and interventionist (Keynesian) lines. There has also been a division on how to view the lurking primacy of international treaties over national and/or regional policies. It is in this light that the Commission has tried to make compromises in order to reach an accommodation. It is to the nature of these reforms attention is now directed.

The 1970s and early 1980s witnessed a series of tentative measures designed to modernise and restructure agriculture in the face of fierce opposition from the powerful farming lobby. There was the imposition of quotas on milk output in 1984, while restrictions on the quantity entitled to support were put in place. During the 1980s, there were even environmental reforms that involved paying farmers to switch to environmentally friendly agricultural production, particular attention being paid to planning and more stringent rules and regulations were also introduced. Clearly,

> From an economic point of view, such payments represent financial recognition by the state for the positive externalities such as beautiful landscape and valued wildlife, which farming had so far been expected to provide 'free'. On the other hand negative externalities such as water pollution, soil erosion and hedgerow removal were tackled by means of regulations and prohibitions, rather than the more recent 'polluter pays' principle which requires costs being imposed on farmers or farming methods responsible, e.g. via a fertilizer tax (Thomson, 2002, p. 69).

Initially, hesitant steps prepared the ground for the EU to finally grasp the nettle. The 1988 Agreement imposed cut-backs on expenditure and/or limits on farm price support which were (in future) to be part and parcel of 'budgetary discipline'. Moreover, enforcement of rigorous quality controls was regarded as a way of denying support to output that had not reached the designated standards.

Crucially, (automatic) stabilisers were seen as central to production controls. The EU could only guarantee support to quantities up to a predetermined ceiling or upper limit, beyond which there would be automatic reductions in price support. So far as the neoclassical (free market) position was concerned, Hitiris argues, 'the "budget stabilizers" were potentially promising in terms of allocation effects but they were not extensive, nor were they fully implemented' (Hitiris, 2003, p. 176).

The 1988 Agreement lay at the heart of a range of measures which were introduced at this time. Crucially, the Commission sought to tackle the perennial problem of how to cut rewards to farmers for increased production. One way of doing this, so the argument went, was to cut support prices in real terms, which would benefit consumers in terms of cheaper food. The only flaw in this argument was its underestimation of the political difficulties associated with the implementation of these cuts, with the Council, under severe pressure from the organised and vocal farming lobby, dragging its feet. An alternative strategy was the introduction, in 1988, of co-responsibility levies which had, from 1977, applied to milk. Producers would contribute to the storage and disposal of excess production without, however, fundamentally changing the support system. In addition, if export restitution (refund) was to be subject to competitive tender, then it followed that the subsidy required could be minimised.

Meanwhile, 'set-aside measures would also be provided for and the Community would contribute to the cost thereof' (Swann, 1995, p. 261). In other words, direct payments would be given to those farmers who were willing to take large areas out of production. There was also an attempt to limit Monetary Compensatory Amounts

(MCAs). Put in another way, 'when the green rate deviated from the official rate, ...taxes on, and subsidies to, intra-EC traded products were used to maintain uniform agricultural prices' (El-Agraa, 2001, p. 247). However, the system was complicated by, among other things, the tendency of stronger EU currencies to use MCAs to cushion their economies from rising farm prices, leading to the charge that MCAs were nothing more than a way of 'topping up' farmers' incomes, while affecting the EU's aggregate level of output. These difficulties were not made any easier by appreciating and depreciating currencies, culminating in the crisis in the Exchange Rate Mechanism (ERM) which had been partly designed to coordinate adjustment of national currencies. The ongoing process of enlargement also served to add more currencies to an already complex system (For a more detailed analysis of MCAs, see e.g. El-Agraa, 2001, pp. 246–8; Swann, 1995, pp. 254–6). Suffice it to say that the introduction of the euro by all (rather than some) member states is expected to render the MCA system obsolete.

Finally, and despite toying with a number of ideas such as an 'objective method of price fixing', direct income aid and bias in favour of farmers in poorer areas/regions, the EU was unable to successfully address distributional issues. Apart from the measurement problems (with different levels of inflation, how could we adequately measure changes in real income?), any incentive under existing arrangements, such as direct income, was likely to encourage more production, particularly if payments were made on the basis of past output levels without taking account of social need. And as long as there was no harmonisation of social security systems, it was difficult to see how meaningful comparisons could be made of minimum income between EU member states. Moreover, not all farmers in 'less favoured' (poorer) regions could be classified as poor, nor could 'the degree of commercialisation of agriculture, the level of agricultural productivity, and farm size' (Sinnott and Winston, 2000, p. 361) be regarded as similar. This reason, allied to political pressure, has forced the EU to treat each member state differently. For example, CAP support to 'northern products' (livestock, cereals) has been less than that given to 'southern products' (fruit, vegetables, wine) (ibid.).

The MacSharry reforms

Clearly then the reform process did not go as smoothly as first envisaged, and internal and external pressures were building up for further change. By 1991 CAP surpluses and intervention stocks were rising again, despite measures to cut them back. There were growing concerns about food safety and quality, culminating in the salmonella scare in eggs, so-called mad cow disease (BSE) and debates on the (de)merits of genetically modified crops compared with organic ones, both on safety and taste criteria. In addition, trading partners expressed their concerns about the EU's 'unfair' subsidisation of its agricultural products. They even went so far as to lay the blame for the failure of the Uruguay Round of GATT talks on the EU. Very little progress had been made on eliminating or phasing out the so-called trade-distorting subsidies, import barriers and CAP support. The EU was also 'being encouraged to open up its markets to agricultural imports from the countries of

Central and Eastern Europe in an attempt to assist them in developing their fledgling market economies' (Church and Phinnemore, 1994, pp. 103–4).

After much haggling – with shifting positions being influenced by the significance of agriculture in each of the countries of the EU, USA and Cairns group, the degree of agricultural support, how vocal the farming lobbies were and even the brinkmanship of the negotiating teams – the 'Peace Clause' ensured that the EU and USA would not take 'unilateral trade action against each other's farm policies until . . . [2003]' (Colman, 2001, p. 107). According to Colman,

> This Accord, which formed the basis of the final GATT Agreement, paved the way for the European Council of Ministers to approve the MacSharry reforms of the CAP in 1992, before the Uruguay GATT Round was concluded [in December 1993], in a way which reduced the impression that the EU had been forced into reform by external pressure' (Colman, 2001, p. 107).

Whether the EU acted prematurely in order to save face, or responded to both internal and external pressures, is a moot point. What is not in dispute is that Ray MacSharry (the European Commissioner for Agriculture), under the Portuguese Presidency of the EU and mindful of the disagreements within the Community, set about gaining support for his reform proposals during negotiations which took place between July 1991 and May 1992. It was suggested that target prices of, say, cereals should be drastically cut cumulatively over the three years from 1993/4, bringing them closer to world market prices. Meanwhile, farmers would be compensated for the resulting fall in income via a system of acreage payments. Allied to this proposal was the suggestion that compensation should be 'modulated', i.e. small farmers should receive full compensation, but increases in acreage would result in scaled-down compensation, with larger farmers receiving no compensation. In addition there would be a set-aside scheme, meaning that there would be a shift from export subsidies to direct income compensation. The system was also complemented by a number of 'accompanying measures'. Farmers would be paid for switching from intensive farming methods to environmentally friendlier ones. For example, a subsidy scheme would enable farmers to convert agricultural land into woodland (afforestation). Finally, an EU-financed early retirement scheme – first suggested in the 1970s, but scuppered by high and rising unemployment – was resurrected. The land of the early retirees (at 55 years of age) could either be taken out of production or amalgamated with other farms.

The final Agreement, which excluded 'modulation', was reached in June 1992. Opposition to scaled down compensation had been led by the UK, with negotiators contending that this would discriminate against large farmers. The agreement was undermined almost as soon as the ink dried. There were violent demonstrations against the perceived threat to guaranteed markets and prices, particularly by the powerful farming lobby in France. But they need not have worried. While the intention of the MacSharry reforms was to reduce surpluses and the cost of exports, a number of commodity regimes, notably sugar, were not covered by the agreement. Moreover, high import tariffs continued to protect the EU agricultural sector, while rewards granted to farmers for leaving land fallow (the set-aside scheme) and the 'accompanying measures' were not only voluntary, but also served to increase the cost of maintaining the CAP.

The Agenda 2000 agreement

Perhaps we should not have expected fundamental changes to the CAP, since the EU never promised to end support, but instead sought to cut prices for *some* commodities as well as addressing the thorny issues of social welfare and sustainable agriculture, i.e. integrating economic, social and environmental objectives. Clearly, state intervention, social and environmental protection could not be ruled out of the question if economic and social progress were to go hand in hand with environmental considerations.

It is in this light that the EU approached the next stage of the reform process. There were increasing problems of financing the CAP, which could only be exacerbated by pressures to expand the EU to include Central and Eastern European countries. In addition there had been growing external (GATT) pressures on the EU to reduce subsidies for its agricultural products as well as a need to face up to the challenges of further trade liberalisation.

This is the background against which Agenda 2000, agreed during the Berlin European Council in March 1999, sought to reform the 'first pillar' of the CAP (the original support system, i.e. market price support, operating mainly through import tariffs, export subsidies, intervention agencies and direct payments to farmers), while also putting more emphasis on the 'second pillar' of the CAP (rural development and environmental measures under the auspices of the Rural Development Regulation, RDR). Each of these reforms is examined below. Despite Agenda 2000 being declared 'the biggest ever negotiated [agreement] for the EU's Common Agricultural Policy' (*Financial Times*, Hitiris, 2001, pp. 51–2), the reform of the 'first pillar' seemed to tread the same path as the MacSharry reforms. Cuts in the prices of certain commodities were designed to encourage competitiveness and reduce 'distortions', but these price cuts were to be offset by compensatory direct payments. This became known as the 'deepening' of the shift from price support to direct aid payments. Just as in the MacSharry reforms, cereal prices and also, this time, milk and beef prices, would be brought closer to world market levels, while income levels would be safeguarded by significant increases in compensatory payments.

It was envisaged that there would be 15 per cent cuts in the intervention price of skimmed milk powder and butter over the three years from 2005/6, while phasing in direct payments. The same cuts were applied to cereals, but were implemented in two stages, with increased compensation. Just as in the MacSharry reforms, the set-aside scheme was to remain, even in its voluntary form, including the 'accompanying measures'. Further, in the face of the BSE crisis, there was to be a 20 per cent reduction in the intervention price of beef, phased over three years, also carrying some compensation. Reduction in support for oilseeds was to be accompanied by increasing compensation to reach the same level as cereals by 2002/3. Other commodities which came under consideration were wine, olive oil and tobacco.

The inclusion of the 'second pillar' of the CAP implied a recognition by the EU that greater emphasis had to be placed on environmental protection and public goods output. First, member states were required to implement necessary environmental measures by January 2000. In order to address the problem of 'free-riding', these measures were to be accompanied by simpler, more stringent, transparent and accessible rules for direct payments.

It also became incumbent upon member states to produce seven-year (2000–06) Rural Development Plans (RDPs). In so doing, member states were given discretion over policy, but within general rules (i.e. within the context of an integrated EU rural development policy). For example, 'modulation' was taken to mean that a certain percentage of compensatory direct payments (up to 20 per cent of the CAP funds going to rural development) was to be matched by national funds, and they could be diverted to environmental schemes or other EU-approved schemes such as early retirement and afforestation.

Clearly, Agenda 2000 had now introduced decentralised decision-making between the Commission and member states, but within the ambit of the EU, which would continue to set the ground rules to ensure consistency and comprehensiveness of policy. Indeed this is the principle of subsidiarity which is discernible in the Maastricht Treaty and the Treaty on European Union (Cameron and Ndhlovu, 2001). In other words, member states would increasingly be expected to finance a greater proportion of the cost of farm support, while the EU's involvement (funding) would become less over time.

Overall, the intention of reforms of the 'first pillar' of the CAP was to reduce price support measures, while cushioning the impact with compensatory direct payments. The inclusion of the 'second pillar' of the CAP meant that a proportion of the direct payments would be matched by an increasing ratio of national funds, so that funding of rural development and environmental measures would increasingly become the responsibility of national governments. At face value, this situation was likely to enable the EU to reduce the potential problems related to the negotiations of further enlargement. However, since the Berlin European Council had decreed a spending ceiling on any new members, the EU could either reduce payments to existing member states (in order to spread resources equally to a growing number of applicant countries), or continue with the current payments to existing member states, but offering fewer payments to new members. To the extent that a single agricultural market was uppermost in the minds of Council members, price support had to be applied equally to current and applicant countries. This left the reform of the direct payments system as the only alternative.

In the face of political pressure, proposals 'by member states to cut direct payments to farmers, which account for about 60 per cent of the annual CAP budget rising to 68 per cent in 2006, were . . . abandoned' (Hitiris, 2001, p. 52; see also 2003, p. 179). According to Pelkmans (2001, p. 221), the removal of 'digressivity' of compensatory direct payments (that is, the abandonment of progressive reduction of direct payments over time) has undermined 'market incentives'.

With new member countries set to join the EU in 2004, and given current spending limits, applicant countries could only be offered '25 per cent of EU15 payments in 2004, 30 per cent in 2005 and 35 per cent in 2006, rising to 100 per cent in 2013' (Ackrill, 2003, p. 15; see also European Commission, 2003). Little wonder that the prospective new member states made vocal representations for equal treatment, even during this transition period of ten years. In the end compromise solutions were thrashed out. New member states could raise the level of their direct payments by dipping into, first, the Rural Development Funds and, later (from 2007), topping up their income from national government funds. Some new member countries (Cyprus and Slovenia), whose economies were already being generously funded by the EU, would also benefit from special arrangements. Moreover, increases in the volume of production would be permitted, but only in exchange for reductions in compensatory direct payments (Ackrill, 2003, p. 15). It goes without saying that reaching the 2013 target of equal (100 per cent) payments is likely to be impossible without more fundamental reforms of the CAP. Further, because of the differential impact of these policies on member states, those members (France, Spain, Ireland, Austria and Belgium) who benefit from CAP are likely to be less enthusiastic about further change, even clamouring for increases in the current direct payment levels, while the main net contributors to the EU budget (the UK, Germany, the Netherlands, Sweden) are opposed to new members being given equal treatment, and even advocate the reduction of their direct payment levels (Ackrill, 2003, p. 16). These disagreements became more acute as the deadline for the expiry of the Peace Clause (Article 13 of the WTO Agriculture Agreement) approached. At the end of 2003, any member of the WTO could (theoretically) challenge the EU to reduce (or eliminate) its subsidies for its farmers, in line with GATT rules.

Mid-term review of Agenda 2000

Agenda 2000 had anticipated some of the problems which were lurking on the horizon. Indeed it was agreed that there should be a mid-term review of some of the CAP sectors, starting from 2002 and running into 2003. In the face of the impending threat to subsidies, the Commission (July 2002) sought to address this problem in advance of the WTO Doha Trade Round ministerial meeting in Cancun, Mexico, in September 2003. With the Peace Clause coming to an end in 2003 and the November 2001 Doha Declaration anticipating an agreement among WTO members before 1 January 2005, the onus was on the Brussels European Council in October 2002 to come up with a negotiating stance for the Cancun meeting.

This was not made any easier, as mentioned earlier, by the disagreements between those member states favouring reform and those opposed to it. Lurking in the background was the perennial problem of the cost of maintaining the CAP which, by 2003, stood at some €44.5 bn (nearly half the EU budget). Moreover, the Sugar Protocol, because of its economic and political significance in the EU and world commodity markets, was excluded from the reform process, even though it still faces threats to its existence (Dickson and Ndhlovu, 2002, p. 1; Rice, 2003). Reforms to the dairy regime were fairly limited, at least up to 2005/6. The Commission proposed cereal price cuts of 5 per cent.

While a stronger emphasis was put on environmental protection, rural development, food safety and animal welfare standards, there were still polarised positions on how to proceed with compensatory direct payments. Tentative gestures to address subsidies were made via limited cuts in price support. The reform process did not specifically address market access, although there was a pledge at the Copenhagen European Council on 13 December 2002 to admit ten new Central and Eastern

European countries into the EU (on 1 May 2004). Rumblings continued about how to divide the cake (the level of spending remaining the same) among a growing number of countries. Dr Franz Fischler, Member of the European Commission responsible for Agriculture, Rural Development and Fisheries, was still concerned that CAP support remained tied to how much each farmer produced, thereby implying that 80 per cent of the CAP budget went to the largest and richest farmers. He wanted to break the link between what farmers receive and what they produce, in line with WTO rules on subsidies. This breaking of the link between payments and production is described as 'decoupling'.

After consultation, the Commission proposals, which were adopted on 22 January 2003, included 'decoupling' subsidies and production. While spending on farm support would be reduced, farmers would get a one-off payment rather than subsidies. This payment would be based on the 'historical option', a calculation based on how much farmers received in the period 2001–02. Not only was this supposed to break the link between subsidies and production, as well as stopping payments to farmers for doing nothing, but it was also intended to encourage farmers to find more competitive markets. Under the new regime, farmers would also 'grow to contract'. In other words, they could even grow crops with a lower yield using less pesticides; payments would be linked to rural development, animal welfare and environmental and food safety standards.

On 25 March 2003 the Commission published two new impact analyses which sought to show that 'decoupling' would lead to more environmentally friendly farming methods, as well as significant increases in the income of EU farmers. Despite this, it was not until 13 June 2003 that a compromise text was put in front of the Council, while Agriculture Commissioner Franz Fischler anticipated that 'the EU was well on the way to adopting a balanced and comprehensive reform of the CAP next week' (Europa, 2003). Even then, long and fraught meetings followed this optimistic prediction.

It was left to Pascal Lamy, the EU Trade Commissioner, to field questions on the likely impact of the proposed reforms on the rest of the world, particularly less developed countries (LDCs). In an interview with Jeremy Paxman for BBC's Newsnight Programme (17 June 2003), Mr Lamy contended that what was not at issue was whether the proposals on the table were more generous or not; instead the focus should be on whether the reforms would have a 'trade-enhancement impact'. Paxman asked Mr Lamy whether he would be

> at the very least embarrassed, if not ashamed, to be going into these [WTO] negotiations [in Cancun, in September 2003] with many arrangements left in place which subsidise European farmers when we have insisted, along with much of the rest of the West, that farmers in the developing world should remove their intervention (BBC Newsnight).

In response to this apparent conundrum, Mr Lamy presented the EU case in 'more development or trade-friendly' terms. He persuasively argued that

> the problem is not whether we subsidise agriculture – we do subsidise education, we do subsidise transport, because we care about education, we care about transport. We care about agriculture and we know that in the world, as it is, European farmers, given their size, given the conditions under which they have to produce, cannot compete with an average US or Australian farm of 400 hectares (BBC Newsnight).

He went on to elaborate this argument and to pledge continual support for agriculture and reiterated that, not only was there no question about the EU proposals being 'development or trade-friendly', but that the whole purpose was to

> find modalities of our support of agriculture which are not negative . . . for developing countries . . . this is what we are doing now. How could we be the biggest importers on this planet of food from developing countries if our system was not open to developing countries? Look at the numbers, the numbers are there, we want to push them further, but the numbers are there (BBC Newsnight).

One would like to think that Mr Lamy had succinctly encapsulated the position of the EU. However, it took three weeks of furious negotiations for the EU's farm ministers to reach an agreement on CAP reform in the early hours of 26 June 2003. Beneficiaries of the CAP, led by the French President, Jacques Chirac (arguably the most effective agricultural minister when he previously held that post), had taken a tough stance against the reforms. Concessions to the French-led resistance finally enabled the deal to be struck, leaving Portugal as the lone objector. Significantly, securing French support for the deal involved the abandonment of the Commission's cherished proposal of cutting cereal prices by 5 per cent. In other words, 'the Commission agreed to ditch proposed cuts in the intervention price (a minimum price guarantee for farmers) for cereals – a move with big implications, since the cereals sector is the largest single absorber of CAP funds' (*The Economist*, 28 June 2003, p. 45). The new CAP regime, however, would proceed with cuts in intervention prices for butter, powdered milk and beef.

As mentioned earlier, the CAP budget was to remain unchanged (see also Fitzgerald and Gardiner, 2003, p. 1). The contention is that,

> as France and Germany agreed in a bilateral stitch-up last autumn [2002], there will be no change in the size of the CAP budget, which at some €50 billion a year will continue to take up nearly half of all EU spending (*The Economist*, 28 June 2003, p. 16).

Furthermore, France managed to extract more concessions that enabled the government to delay

> applying the new terms of the CAP for two years, until 2007, even though other countries can bring in the rules in 2005, if they wish (precisely how this can be made compatible with the free movement of farm products inside the European single market remains fuzzy) (ibid.).

Finally, 'decoupling', as suggested by the Commission, was only going to be applicable from 2005, although many countries, along with France, could put it off until 2007. Indeed, the separation of subsidies from production was only going to be partial for many agricultural products:

> For beef there will be only partial decoupling, covering 70 per cent of the aid, and countries will be able to choose from a complex set of options. Decoupling is also only partial in cereals and mutton. Some sectors, such as olive oil and sugar, which both absorb billions of euros in production-linked subsidies, are completely untouched, though the Commission will suggest further reforms next year [2004] (*The Economist*, 28 June 2003, p. 45; see also Rice, 2003, pp. 1–5).

Despite the retention of some form of subsidies, Dr Fischler, Europe's Farm Commissioner, hailed the reforms of the CAP as marking the beginning of a new era. European agricultural policy will change fundamentally. In future our products will be more competitive, and our agricultural policy will be greener, more trade-friendly and more consumer-oriented' (Europa Press Conference, 26 June 2003; see also European Commission, 2003).

Many officials trumpeted the agreement, particularly 'decoupling', as one that ensured that 'butter mountains' and 'wine lakes' would be a thing of the past, 'while giving EU farmers the freedom to produce what the market wants' (Europa Press Release, 26 June 2003), at the same time protecting the countryside. While the British delegation at the Council meeting in Luxembourg would have preferred further and more radical reforms, it regarded the introduction of partial decoupling as a step in the right direction towards trade liberalisation, particularly since it ensured that France reluctantly came on board (*The Economist*, 28 June 2003, p. 45).

For its part, the French farm ministry regarded the reform of the CAP as preserving 'the essential principles of the Common Agricultural Policy' (Fitzgerald and Gardiner, 2003, p. 1). This implied that the retention of some form of export subsidies is what persuaded the French to reluctantly accept the compromise deal. And with an eye to the Doha Round of talks in Cancun, Mexico, Pascal Lamy, the EU Trade Commissioner, saw the agreement (however one interprets it) as giving the EU delegation 'negotiating capital in the WTO round . . . and I have plenty of ideas how I can use this negotiating capital' (Rice, 2003, p. 1). With good reason, one

> diplomat from the Cairns Group of countries, which has been pushing the EU to reform the CAP, declared himself 'suspicious' of the concept of partial decoupling. His initial reaction was that the deal, particularly over livestock, 'reduced the impact of decoupling a lot and preserved the incentives to over-produce' (*The Economist*, 28 June 2003, p. 45).

For its part, the USA, which can hardly be described as being on the side of the angels – the US farm bill rose by 70 per cent in 2003 and subsidies 'will cost American taxpayers $180 billion' over 10 years – pressed for a reduction of 'farm tariffs from 62 to 15 per cent. The proposal [if adopted] will also reduce trade-distorting subsidies by over $100 million by establishing a cap of no more than 5 per cent of total agricultural production' (Fitzgerald and Gardiner, 2003, p. 1).

The reformed CAP and the Doha Development Agenda

This is the background against which the ministerial meeting to assess the Doha round of trade talks took place in Cancun, Mexico, on 10–14 September 2003. The Doha Development Agenda had been initiated in Doha, Qatar, in 2001 with the precise aim of liberalising agricultural markets and giving Less Developed Countries (LDCs) greater market access. After a number of false starts it had latterly been envisaged that agreement on the specific ways (modalities) for meeting the Doha Mandate (of reducing subsidies and import tariffs in agriculture) would be reached by May 2003. All along the stumbling block to progress, or so it seemed, had been the inability of the EU to agree on further reforms of the CAP.

Once this hurdle had been overcome (in June 2003), the US Trade Represent-ative Robert Zoellick, while expressing disappointment that the CAP reforms had not gone far enough, welcomed the development for kick-starting the stalled WTO talks (US Mission, 2003b). Agricultural Secretary Ann M. Veneman who, with Mr Zoellick, led the US delegation, added that the USA was also committed to 'greater fairness in agricultural trade. Further we will strive to bring develop-ing countries more fully into the global community' (Press release, US Mission, 2003a).

But there was a sting in the tail; the US were anxious that their proposed cuts in subsidies and import tariffs be accompanied by similar moves from the LDCs. To temper the high and rising expectations Mr Zoellick said that 'It's very important to realize that Cancun represents the midpoint, and that the goal is to ensure that we will have the opportunity to negotiate high-ambition results as the trade talks continue' (ibid., p. 1).

For the EU delegation Dr Fischler contended that the reform of the CAP was not only compatible with WTO commitments, but also showed that the EU had made the most movement while others dragged their feet. He also argued that the claims concerning Fortress Europe were fictitious since the EU was the largest importer of agricultural exports from LDCs and had accorded them preferential treatment. In addition, the EU promoted the 'Singapore issues', so-called because they were first mooted in Singapore in 1996. In other words, the EU favoured discussion of these 'issues' (investment, competition, transparency in government procurement and trade facilitation) to be done as a package rather than being 'unbundled' or discussed separately. And if this was acceptable, then this would have implications for some LDCs' preferences via the CAP (EuropaWorld, 2003).

For their part the LDCs sought the elimination of export subsidies, particularly in agriculture, and more access for their agricultural products to the markets of the developed countries. On the eve of the Cancun talks, the G21 (variously described as the G23, G29, G20 and, latterly, G19 depending on the fluid membership of this Group), led by Brazil, China and India, was formed. Its main aims were to have a coordinated position in the talks, ensure that its concerns were given priority in the discussions and to urge the EU to make more concessions than had so far been offered.

When the talks opened, each delegation among the 146 WTO members (soon joined by Nepal and Cambodia to bring the number to 148) held doggedly to their entrenched positions. After much toing and froing, the talks began to slowly grind to a halt. Even the eleventh hour intervention by Commissioner Lamy on 'unbundling' the 'Singapore issues' could not save the Fifth WTO Ministerial Con-ference, particularly since Japan and Korea insisted that these 'issues' be considered as a package, while most LDCs took the opposite view. Without any prospect of consensus, Luis Ernesto Derbez, Mexican Foreign Secretary and chairman of the meeting, decided to halt the talks on Sunday 14 September 2003.

This was followed by recriminations for the collapse of the WTO talks. US Trade Representative Robert Zoellick believed that the USA could not 'do it by ourselves' (US Mission, 2003c). He blamed 'some developing countries' for the 'flow of rhetoric' which led to the breakdown of the talks. In a moment of pique, he threatened to abandon multilateral talks concerning the Doha Round in favour of 'regional and bilateral trade deals' (Watkins, 2003). In the light of the forthcoming 2004 presidential elections, one could not hold much hope for a lot of movement from the US delegation.

Developing and least developed countries blamed, in particular, the EU (and, to some extent, the USA) for the collapse of the Cancun talks. They argued that the draft Declaration had not addressed the thorny issue of agriculture in any meaningful way. Moreover, the introduction of the 'Singapore issues' to the Doha agenda had soured the atmosphere.

The EU maintained the original position of having been committed to the talks, while there was allegedly posturing on the part of others. Commissioner Lamy argued that: 'We [the EU] fed the beast meat on Doha, meat in Cancun and meat in between. It didn't work. We have not seen much coming from other people's pockets, apart from the US on agriculture' (Denny, 2003). Despite having initially 'declared he would leave his last-minute concessions from Cancun on the table when negotiations restart' (Elliott and Denny, 2003), he subsequently withdrew the offer (Denny, 2003). Divisions also began to appear in the EU camp, with the UK reportedly blaming Commissioner Lamy for delaying making concessions on the Singapore Agenda until it was too late to save the WTO talks (Elliott, 2003a; Watkins, 2003). For his part Lamy dismissed these allegations, while also suggesting that failure to reach agreement at Cancun might set the deadline for the Doha Development Agenda (December 2004) back two or more years (Denny, 2003; Elliott and Denny, 2003).

It is worth noting that all the parties in the Doha Round of talks, while anxious to restart these negotiations, aside from minor adjustments, maintained their original positions. Tempers had cooled down enough for the USA to abandon its threat to walk away, but they still expected the LDCs to show 'more commitment' regarding deep cuts in subsidies and lowering of import tariffs. Deputy US Trade Representative Linnet Deily told delegates at the WTO General Council meeting in Geneva, on 15 December 2003, that every effort was required 'to rebuild trust and confidence' (US Mission, 2003d).

By contrast, LDCs were unhappy that the proposals on import duties in agriculture seemed to imply they should make relatively more substantial cuts than their EU and US counterparts. In a meeting held in Accra, Ghana, on 28–29 November 2003, African delegates still maintained that only the re-evaluation of proposals on subsidies and import tariffs, together with the 'unbundling' of the 'Singapore issues', were the basis for relaunching the Doha Development Agenda (Post-Cancun Expert Group, 2003). It was also agreed that 'development issues' should be included at the Geneva WTO General Council Meeting while more emphasis should be put on 'procedural and substantive matters, which need to be considered in order to move the negotiations forward' (ibid.).

However, internal and external pressures (e.g. the presidential elections in India in April 2004) made resolution of these issues more difficult to attain. Led by India, some LDCs also sought increases in subsidies of some products to compensate for reductions in subsidies of other products. The Brazilian Foreign Minister even went as far as suggesting that the G21 should form a free trade area in order 'to fully exploit the potential among us, which does not depend on the concessions of the rich countries' (*Bridges Weekly Trade News Digest*, 17 December 2003).

The EU position remained more or less the same, with the exception that the Commission promised to be more flexible on the question of 'unbundling' the

'Singapore issues', while also abandoning its previous stance that no meaningful talks could take place without major changes to the WTO decision-making process. Instead what was now being proposed was 'a modest but feasible package of reforms focusing on the preparation and management of WTO Ministerial meetings, better participation of smaller members and other means to improve the efficiency and inclusiveness of WTO negotiations' (European Commission, 2003b, pp. 2–3, 5).

In the light of problems encountered at Cancun, emphasis now shifted from proposals to make substantial cuts in the 'amber box' (domestic policies involving incentives that trigger over-production, and direct payments that also encourage production, thus regarded as having a 'distortionary effect') to the acceptance of more cuts in the 'blue box' (which the EU had regarded as 'less distortionary' because it referred to those measures, other than the 'amber box' ones, that limited production, such as area payments) (ibid.). Nonetheless there was still the impression that the EU was doing its fair share, while others did very little, if anything. What was required was reciprocity. Dr Fischler caught the mood in the EU by contending that, 'Europe would be penalised for constantly reforming, for making its support more and more trade-friendly, while others would be rewarded for going in the opposite direction' (ibid.).

In response to requests from West African governments to keep the question of increasing market access of their cotton producers to Western markets separate from the general discussions on agriculture, the Commission argued that the solution 'should contain three key elements: an explicit commitment to grant duty and quota-free access for least developed imports, as the EU already provides through the "Everything but Arms' initiative"' (ibid., p. 4, see also Dickson and Ndhlovu, 2002, pp. 143–4, 147; Elliott, 2003c; European Commission, 2003a).

Despite the EU being 'convulsed by a row between free traders and protectionists' (Elliott, 2003c), the deadline of 1 January 2005 for completing the Doha Round soon concentrated the minds of the 147 WTO members, starting with the Geneva Council meeting on 15 December 2003 and culminating with the revised draft deal on 1 August 2004. A 20 per cent cut in the subsidies given to US, EU and Japanese farmers was proposed, as was a five per cent cap on subsidies to limit production, together with the elimination of future export subsidies. Apart from least-developed countries, LDCs (less developed countries) were to reciprocate by lowering tariff barriers on manufactured products from MDCs (WTO, 2 August 2004).

Conclusion

Ever since the Second World War the organised and powerful farming lobby has occupied a central position in the development of the EU agricultural sector. With the achievement of the original objective of self-sufficiency, pressures for reforming the CAP began to build up, both inside and outside the EU. Despite the rising costs of maintaining the CAP, and associated problems with income distribution, the farming lobby continued to resist pressures for change. There were perfectly plausible reasons for resisting reforms of the CAP, and the farming lobby had allies in the

Commission, the Council and among EU citizens. Keynesian interventionist or protectionist theoretical analysis could be looked upon as the rationalisation for policies that not only considered the economic, but also the social and the political.

By contrast, the CAP reform was driven by the need to eliminate distortions in the market, increase choice and put the consumer at the centre of developments. Again theoretical justifications can be derived from free market or neo-classical analysis. Tensions within the Commission have resulted from trying to straddle these positions. Consequently, the CAP reforms have often involved tinkering at the margins. To the extent that reforms do not occur in isolation from the world agricultural market, external pressures have also played a part in shaping them. Indeed, the tensions between free market and protectionist views have been played out on the world stage. The implications and/or direction for the CAP have been uncertain, particularly since geo-political factors have also played a crucial role in the development of the CAP. Further attempts to fundamentally change the CAP will depend on economic, social and political forces, both inside and outside the EU.

References

Ackrill R (2003) 'EU enlargement', *Developments in Economics: An Annual Review*, Vol. 19.

Bridges Weekly Trade News Digest (2003) 'G-20, EC Agree to Intensify Doha Round Talks', Vol. 7, No. 43, 17 December (**www.ictsd.org**).

Cameron J and Ndhlovu T P (2001) 'The Comparative Economics of EU "Subsidiarity": Lessons from Developing/Regional Economic Debates', *International Journal of Urban and Regional Research*, Vol. 25, No. 2, June.

Church H and Phinnemore D (1994) *European Union and European Community: A Handbook and Commentary on the Post-Maastricht Treaties*, Harvester Wheatsheaf, London.

Colman D (2001) 'The Common Agricultural Policy', in M Artis and F Nixon (eds), *The Economics of the European Union: Policy and Analysis*, Oxford University Press, Oxford.

Denny C (2003) 'Lamy hits back at critics: EU negotiator refuses to shoulder blame for Cancun', The *Guardian*, 29 October.

Dickson A and Ndhlovu T P (2002) 'The Sugar Protocol', in S J H Dearden (ed.), *The European Union and the Commonwealth Caribbean*, Ashgate, Aldershot.

The Economist (2003), 'Cap it all', p. 16; 'More fudge than breakthrough', p. 45, 28 June.

El-Agraa A M (2001) 'The Common Agricultural Policy', in A M El-Agraa (ed.), *The European Union: Economics and Policies*, Financial Times/Prentice Hall, Harlow.

Elliott L (2003a) 'DTI leak blames Lamy for Cancun failure: Report says tactical error left WTO talks without a deal', The *Guardian*, 22 October.

Elliott L (2003b) 'WTO admits hope of reviving Cancun talks is fading', The *Guardian*, 10 December.

Elliott L (2003c) 'WTO admits statement scuppered relaunch of Cancun trade talks: Negotiators still struggle to find compromise', The *Guardian*, 16 December.

Elliott L and Denny C (2003) 'Breakdown means no end in sight to Doha round', The *Guardian*, 16 December.

Europa (2003) **www.europa.eu.int/comm/press_room/presspacks/cap**, press statement, 13/26 June.

EuropaWorld (2003) 'WTO Farm Talks/Cancun: EU's Fischler Calls for Renewed Effort to Bridge Differences', **www.europaworld.org/week138/wtofarm/803.htm**, 1 August.

European Commission (2003a) *EU Agriculture and the WTO: Doha Development Agenda, Cancun – September 2003*, European Commission, Agriculture and Rural Development, July.

European Commission (2003b) Press release of delegation to Australia and New Zealand, 27 November.

Fitzgerald S J and Gardiner N (2003) 'The WTO Cancun Meeting: Why the US should Question Europe's Orwellian Farm Reforms', *The Heritage Foundation*, 25 July (**www.heritage.org**).

Hitiris T (2001) 'The UK and the European Union', in M Sawyer (ed.), *The UK Economy: A Manual of Applied Economics*, Oxford University Press, Oxford.

Hitiris T (2003) *European Union Economics*, Prentice Hall/Financial Times, Harlow.

Pelkmans J (2001) *European Integration: Methods and Economic Analysis*, Financial Times/ Prentice Hall, Harlow.

Post-Cancun Expert Group Meeting for African Trade Negotiators and Officials (2003) 'Fulfilling the Doha Development Agenda: A Road Map for Future Negotiations', **www.uneca.org**.

Rice T (2003) 'CAP Reform Agreement and Implications for Developing Countries', **www.Actionaid.org/resources/pdfs/cap.pdf**, 1 July.

Sinnott R and Winston N (2000) 'Neo-functionalism and the Legitimacy of Integration: The Case of the CAP and Support for European Integration among Farmers, 1962–98', *Journal of European Integration*, Vol. 22, pp. 355–79.

Swann D (1995) *The Economics of the Common Market: Integration in the European Union*, Penguin Books, London.

Thomson K J (2002) 'Agriculture and agricultural policy', *Developments in Economics: An Annual Review*, Vol 18.

US Mission to the European Union (2003a) 'Zoelleck, Veneman to lead US delegation to Cancun meeting', press release, 5 September (see **www.useu.be/**).

US Mission to the European Union (2003b) 'Zeolleck urges WTO negotiators to focus on more market access', transcript of press conference, 9 September (see **www.useu.be/**).

US Mission to the European Union (2003c) 'The Public Affairs Office 2003 Dossier', 14 September (see **www.useu.be/**).

US Mission to the European Union (2003d) 'The Public Affairs Office 2003 Dossier', 15 December (see **www.useu.be/**).

Watkins K (2003) 'Cancun was where the WTO found glasnost – and a chance for renewal', The *Guardian*, 22 September.

WTO (2004) 'Doha Development Agenda – text of the "July package" – the General Cancun decision', WT/4/579, 2 August (**www.wto.org/english/traptop-e/draft_text_gc_dg_31july04_e.htm**).

Further reading

Colman D (2001) 'The Common Agricultural Policy', in M Artis and F Nixon (eds), *The Economics of the European Union: Policy and Analysis*, Oxford University Press, Oxford.

Hitiris T (2003) *European Union Economics*, Prentice Hall/Financial Times, Harlow.

Koester U and El-Agraa A M (2004) 'The Common Agricultural Policy', in A M El-Agraa (ed.), *The European Union: Economics and Policies*, Financial Times/Prentice Hall, Harlow.

Part 3

THE EXTERNAL POLICIES OF THE EUROPEAN UNION

Chapter 12

External trade policy

Olga Kuznetsova

Introduction

Together with monetary and development policies, external trade policy forms the mainstay of the European Union's relations with the rest of the world. It is based on developing and applying common commercial principles in regard to changes in tariff rates, the conclusion of tariff and trade agreements, the achievement of uniformity in measures of liberalisation, export policy and proceedings to protect trade. The purpose of the external trade policy is to promote the economic and political interests of the EU in such areas as trade in goods and services, intellectual property, investment and competition. According to Article 131 of the Nice Treaty, the trade policy of the EU should 'contribute, in the common interest, to the harmonious development of world trade, the progressive abolition of restrictions

Box 12.1 The Nice Treaty Article 133

1 The common commercial policy shall be based on uniform principles, particularly in regard to changes in tariff rates, the conclusion of tariff and trade agreements, the achievement of uniformity in measures of liberalisation, export policy and measures to protect trade such as those to be taken in the event of dumping or subsidies.

2 The Commission shall submit proposals to the Council for implementing the common commercial policy.

3 Where agreements with one or more States or international organisations need to be negotiated, the Commission shall make recommendations to the Council, which shall authorise the Commission to open the necessary negotiations. The Commission shall conduct these negotiations in consultation with a special committee appointed by the Council to assist the Commission in this task and within the framework of such directives as the Council may issue to it.

4 In exercising the powers conferred upon it by this Article, the Council shall act by a qualified majority.

5 The Council, acting unanimously on a proposal from the Commission and after consulting the European Parliament, may extend the application of paragraphs 1 to 4 to international negotiations and agreements on services and intellectual property insofar as they are not covered by these paragraphs.

on international trade and the lowering of customs barriers' for the sake of the promotion of a balanced and sustainable development of economic activities; a high level of employment and social protection; the raising of the standard of living and improvement of the quality of the environment throughout the Community.

The EU as a trade power

International trade has become a major factor of economic growth and prosperity across the globe. In the thirty years since 1970 the value of global trade in goods and services has increased from just US\$ 1.5 trillion (thousand billion) at current prices to nearly US\$ 8 trillion. In relative terms international trade of goods and services has increased from 13 per cent of the world GDP to about 25 per cent (Stern, 2002, p. 7).

The EU is the largest trading power in the world even with intra-EU trade excluded. In the late 1990s its share of world exports was 20 per cent (USA 16 per cent, Japan 10 per cent) and the share of world imports was 17 per cent (USA 20 per cent, Japan 7.6 per cent). Because during this period its exports were growing faster than imports, the EU has achieved an impressive external trade surplus, which measured €50.3 bn in 1997 compared to €5.1 bn in 1994. These figures look even more impressive if we remember that extra-EU trade represents less than 40 per cent of the overall EU trade turnover. (See Table 12.1.)

There has been a strong growth in EU goods exchanged with virtually all countries and regions, but the USA, Switzerland and Japan remain the main trading partners. Other important partners are Russia, Poland, Norway, Turkey, Hong Kong, China and South Korea. As a group, the industrialised countries account for more than half of the total extra-EU trade. The balance of trade differs from country to country but certain trends can be noted. In the last few years the EU has had a trade surplus with non-EU Europe, the USA and Canada. The positive balance with Central and Eastern European countries has been growing especially fast. By contrast, there is a negative trade balance with China and Japan, and large increases in imports from South-East Asia suggest that countries from this region may join the club of net exporters to the EU quite soon. The EU also runs a deficit in trade with Africa.

Table 12.1 EU trade in goods 2002

	The major import partners				The major export partners		
Rank	Partners	€ (million)	%	Rank	Partners	€ (million)	%
	World*	989,328	100.0		World*	994,781	100.0
1	USA	175,461	17.7	1	USA	242,147	24.4
2	China	81,870	8.3	2	Switzerland	70,744	7.1
3	Japan	68,553	6.9	3	Japan	42,688	4.3
4	Switzerland	58,738	5.9	4	Poland	37,375	3.8
5	Russia	47,728	4.8	5	China	34,232	3.4

Source: European Communities, 2004

Table 12.2 EU trade by sectors 2002

	The major imports by sectors			The major exports by sectors	
Rank	Sectors	%	Rank	Sectors	%
	TOTAL of which	100.0		TOTAL of which	100.0
1	Manufactured products	55.0	1	Manufactured products	65.5
2	Services	24.2	2	Services	25.2
3	Energy	11.0	3	Agricultural products	1.9
4	Agricultural products	6.5	4	Energy	4.9
5	Other primary products	3.3	5	Other primary products	1.5

Source: European Communities, 2004

As would be expected the EU countries have recorded their largest deficit in terms of the trade in primary products (oil, gas, raw material other than fuel, food and tobacco), accounting for almost a third of total EU imports. At the same time the EU surplus in manufactured products has been growing, in particular the surplus in machinery, transport equipment and chemicals. (See Table 12.2.)

The objectives and mechanisms of EU trade policy

The EU seeks to protect the interests of EU firms whenever they act as exporters or importers of products, services and intellectual property. Consequently EU trade policy pursues two sets of objectives: the defence of the internal EU market from trading practices that damage the interests of the EU firms and assistance to EU exporters to fight unfair restrictions on their operations.

In the EU the decision-making process on trade issues is based on a division of authority: some powers are delegated to the Commission while others are retained by the Council. The Commission acts as a defender of general European interests. It has the sole right to propose the opening of trade negotiations, but the Council of Ministers decides whether to pursue them and on what conditions, and then approves the results of the negotiations. Since 1970 decisions on trade require a qualified (two-thirds) majority within the Council. In practice major policy decisions often need unanimity since a member state has the right of veto if it believes that fundamental national interests are endangered.

The European Parliament and the European Court of Justice are the other two entities that can influence the decision-making process. The decisions of the Court of Justice may be particularly important since it has the power of interpretation in the course of judicial review that may significantly alter the scope of the regulations devised by the Commission and the Council. The result of this multi-centre system is that both large and small companies alike may successfully lobby by approaching politicians at either national (governments) or international (Commission) levels.

Since the 1980s the Commission has made great strides in taking over a major role in formulating EU trade policy from national governments (Bilal, 1998). The

Community, represented by the Commission and the Council of Ministers, has sole competence for common commercial policy and enjoys the right to conclude bilateral agreements and participate in international negotiations in its own right. The consolidation of authority strengthened the Community's position and influence in the process of bilateral trade negotiations with other countries and multilateral negotiations within the World Trade Organization (WTO). It is important to stress, however, that member states remain responsible for most of the actual implementation of EU trade policy.

To achieve its trade policy objectives, the EU combines multilateral, regional, and bilateral approaches. The EU is a leading force in WTO but at the same time it relies on an extensive network of preferential trade agreements. As a result the EU market for non-agricultural products has largely become open, except for textiles and clothing products where the EU has only lifted restrictions on 20 per cent of the products restricted in 1990, leaving the elimination of the remaining 80 per cent of restricted imports 'back-loaded' until the end of 2004.

It has become a feature of EU trade policy to show strong commitment to enhancing the participation of developing countries in the WTO. This has taken the form of the 'Everything-but-Arms' (EBA) initiative for 49 Least Developed Countries (LDCs), preferences offered to the African, Caribbean and Pacific (ACP) countries, and donations for trade-related technical assistance. EBA has been presented as a major policy undertaking by the EU within the framework of the Doha Development Agenda of the WTO, reflecting the conviction of the EU that integration into global markets offers the LDCs a potential for more rapid growth and poverty reduction. But market barriers to some key developing country exports have made it harder for them to take full advantage of this opportunity. The EU's EBA initiative has granted comprehensive tariff and quota free access to LDCs since coming into effect in March 2001. It covers all products originating in LDCs, except for arms and ammunition. Only sugar, bananas and rice, which are the three most sensitive agricultural products, have remained under a special regulatory regime. Privileges under the EBA are conferred on an indefinite basis subject to some broad safeguards.

Commercial defence measures

The European integration process started in the form of a customs union. Since then a common external tariff (CET) has been one of the essential features of the EU. It involves applying uniform customs duties to products imported from third countries, irrespective of the member state of destination. Originally, the CET was the arithmetic mean of the tariffs applied in 1957 by member states. It has since been amended several times, either independently or in the course of tariff negotiations. In 2002 the simple average applied tariff on non-agricultural products was 4.1 per cent. The simple average tariff on agricultural products was 16.1 per cent, with above average tariffs on products subject to the Common Agricultural Policy (CAP). The common external tariff is a major protection for internal EU producers vis-à-vis those from a third country. It is the responsibility of the Commission to ensure that this protection remains effective in the face of such practices as price dumping or subsidised pricing.

Anti-dumping measures

After the United States, the EU is the second most frequent user of anti-dumping measures, but some 40 per cent of the anti-dumping investigations initiated by the EU are terminated without measures being taken (WTO, 2002). Anti-dumping rules apply to all products and to all countries that are not members of the EU. In reality, products imported from China and India are those most frequently affected.

The regulation lays down two conditions for the application of anti-dumping duties: the existence of dumping and proof of injury to the Community industry as a result of this dumping. Charging low prices for exported goods should not be penalised if lower prices reflect lower costs or greater productivity. Dumping occurs when the price of the exported product is below its normal value, which is established on the basis of the comparable price for a like product that is normally applied within the exporting country. However, where the exporter does not produce or sell a like product in the exporting country, the normal value may be established on the basis of prices of other sellers or producers. For example, Russian exports of steel, fertiliser and aluminium are subject to anti-dumping sanctions following the ruling that these products were sold at unfairly low prices because of state-controlled prices for such inputs as electricity, gas and coal.

The determination of injury (or the threat of injury) caused to an industry established in the Community is based on the analysis of such evidence as the volume of the dumped imports, the price of dumped imports and the consequent impact on the Community industry concerned, particularly in relation to production and utilisation of capacity, stocks, sales, market share, price changes, profits, return on investments, cash flow and employment.

Anti-dumping procedures may be initiated by the Commission following a written complaint by any person or upon the provision of evidence of dumping and of resultant injury by a member state. The Commission may find the complaint unsubstantiated or the dumping and injury to be negligible and terminate the proceedings. Alternatively it may take measures aimed at stopping the dumping and compensating the injured party. Such measures usually take the form of imposing provisional or definitive anti-dumping duties, which must not exceed the actual damage caused by dumping. The Regulation imposing the duty specifies the amount of duty applied to each supplier or, if that is impracticable, to the supplying country concerned. Provisional and definitive duties may not be applied retrospectively. The duties expire five years after their date of imposition or five years after the conclusion of the review of the measures concerned.

Data are available for cases initiated between 1989 and 1994. Overall, there were 98 anti-dumping cases (excluding cases against countries of the former Soviet Union and Yugoslavia) involving 47 products. Of these, 31 cases resulted in no further action due to lack of dumping, lack of injury or 'other reasons'. Dumping cases mostly involved such products as minerals, organic chemicals, electrical machinery and equipment. Brenton (2001) estimates that the anti-dumping measures increase the cost for exporters by 25 per cent, compared with the average tariff for industrial products entering the EU during this period of around 5 to 6 per cent. This is bound to have serious consequences for exporters implicated in dumping.

Anti-subsidy measures

The EU considers any direct or indirect subsidy that gives an external exporter a competitive advantage over local producers as unfair. If as a result EU producers suffer financial damage the EU may impose countervailing duties for the purpose of offsetting the effect of the subsidy. The definition of subsidy applied by the Commission includes a direct transfer of funds by the government but also indirect transfers such as loan guarantees and tax credits.

The amount of countervailable subsidies is calculated in terms of the benefit conferred on the recipient. This is determined per unit of the subsidised product exported to the EU. Some elements may be deducted from the subsidy, such as any fees or costs incurred in order to qualify for the subsidy or export taxes intended to offset the subsidy. Where a subsidy is not granted by reference to the quantities, the amount of the subsidy is determined by spreading the value of the subsidy over the total level of production, sales or exports of the product.

State subsidies are a fact of life inside the EU itself where state aid amounted to 1 per cent of the EU's GNP in 1999. The Commission regards state aid as compromising the principles of free trade and it encourages member states to reduce their aid. It is also very strict in enforcing rules on state aid to individual enterprises. This provides the Commission with moral grounds to react vigorously against unfair competition from subsidised third-country firms. However, there is one area in which state support is likely to continue to play a great role – agricultural production under the CAP. In fact, support for farmers has increased continually in the EU, putting in question the EU's commitment to 'fair' trade.

Fighting unfair restrictions

The access of EU goods and services to markets around the world 'for the benefit of consumers and business world-wide' remains a primary objective for the EU. The EU's market access strategy focuses on the elimination of important market access barriers, by using to the full the various multilateral and bilateral instruments and opportunities at its disposal: the WTO dispute settlement procedure, consultation and bilateral agreements with WTO members and others, and the new WTO negotiating round (EU, 2002).

Protection against trade barriers

Member states may request the EU to respond to any trade barriers put in place by a third country. The term 'trade barrier' refers to any trade practice prohibited by WTO. The complaints may be lodged either on behalf of an industry or of one or more EU firms that have suffered as a result of trade barriers, or by a member state denouncing an obstacle to trade. If the Commission is satisfied that the complaint is valid it may choose to apply one of the following measures:

- suspension or withdrawal of any concession resulting from commercial policy negotiations;

- the raising of existing customs duties or the introduction of any other charge on imports;

- the introduction of quantitative restrictions or any other measures modifying import or export conditions or otherwise affecting trade with the third country concerned.

Two of the main instruments of the EU's market access strategy are the market access database and the Trade Barriers Regulation (TBR). In the first case the Commission has compiled a sectoral and trade barriers database that provides for information about the general features of the trade policies of 58 countries, as well as the trade barriers affecting EU exports of goods, services and investment. The applied tariffs section includes customs tariffs and internal taxes applied by over 100 countries. There is also the exporter's guide section, covering over 25 countries, and the market access database that contains information on the commitments of WTO members. The purpose of making this database available is both to help exporters to cut the cost of red tape and to disclose instances of discriminatory practices that require the intervention of the EU.

When such instances are identified the EU may make a decision to deal with them through diplomatic contacts or raise the issue with WTO. In the latter case the Commission initiates a Trade Barriers Regulation procedure. One example of a successful use of TBR was the case concerning the US Anti-dumping Act of 1916. European Confederation of Iron and Steel Industries (EUROFER) members faced the threat of huge fines and/or imprisonment if found guilty by the US courts under the 1916 Act. On behalf of EUROFER the Commission invoked action in the WTO, where a WTO Panel and the Appellate Body found the US in violation of several provisions of the WTO Anti-dumping Agreement, GATT 1994 and the WTO Agreement. Although this had taken about three years, the members of EUROFER felt that it was necessary and the result justified the effort. The Commission believes that rule-making in the WTO is crucial for securing market access, thus the EC has been very active in tabling for discussion new rules on foreign direct investment, competition, red tape, etc., that are intended to provide a more transparent trading environment.

Technical barriers to trade

Technical barriers to trade (TBTs) create obstacles to exporters through increasing the costs of operation through the requirement that certain imported products must comply with local regulations regarding health, safety, environment and consumer protection. It is customary in most countries that particular products may only be authorised for sale after they have passed necessary certification procedures.

Exporters, however, are likely to face the additional costs of multiple testing and certification because of slow progress in the harmonisation of technical standards across the globe. The consequences for the producers of high-tech goods and pharmaceuticals, the two areas in which EU firms are particularly active, can be very severe as the need to adapt the product to a whole spectrum of requirements may cause the fragmentation of the production system. The EU has responded by promoting the principle of the mutual recognition of standards. Mutual Recognition Agreements (MRAs) do not aim at harmonising technical requirements and securing the common assessment procedures; instead, under these agreements, certification by the exporting state is given the same status as testing by the importing country. As a result, exporters do not have to meet the additional cost of conforming to standards and procedures of the importer country. MRAs were recently concluded with Japan and Switzerland, and are already in force with Australia, Canada, Israel, New Zealand and the USA.

Another line of action pursued by the EU is support for the introduction of a coherent global set of common standards through the harmonisation or mutual recognition of national standards and procedures. Accordingly, the EU is prominent in the WTO TBT Committee, the Global Harmonisation Task Force for medical devices, the Trade Facilitation Action Plan under Asia–Europe Meeting (ASEM) and technical assistance for the Mercosur Technical Committee for Standardisation (Mercosur is a free trade process comprising Brazil, Argentina, Paraguay and Uruguay).

It is important to note that in turn the EU is accused by some trade partners of applying TBT. Recently the EU and the member states have put in place new regulations in relation to the safety of products and in particular to the disposal of waste, that are widely perceived as a significant barrier to trade. One example is the ban, in March 2002, on imports of Chinese food, valued at $330 m pa, on the grounds that shrimp, rabbit meat and honey from China were found to contain trace elements of an antibiotic called chloramphenicol, which some studies have linked to cancer. This ruling proved to be controversial as Chinese exporters questioned the claim that it was entirely motivated by public health considerations. They pointed to the fact that Dutch veal farmers were allowed to continue to use chloramphenicol in products exported from the EU, while German sausage makers won an exemption allowing them to use intestines from China as sausage casings (Wall Street Journal, 2002).

Conclusion

The EU's trade policy has gone through a number of stages. Initially it was designed to protect domestic producers from foreign competition. Beginning in the 1970s a whole array of tariff and non-tariff barriers were erected, including national import quotas, complex rules of origin and 'voluntary' export restraints. There had been little foreign trade liberalisation prior to 1990, but a noticeable change in policy occurred in the mid-1990s: the EU started to progressively dismantle trade barriers. This change in policy reflected growing awareness of the experience of many countries in previous years, which showed a strong positive relationship between openness to trade and economic expansion. Research was able to demonstrate that reducing barriers to trade was conducive to faster income growth. For example, Frankel and Romer (1999) found that an increase of one percentage point in the ratio of trade to GDP raised income by at least 0.5 per cent. Another factor was a spread of concern within the EU that excessive protection was damaging the competitiveness of European firms in the long run. Finally, the EU was convinced that the objectives of trade policy that it had set for itself could be more effectively promoted through international cooperation, most notably the WTO process, rather than through unilateral action.

Since the process of trade liberalisation began, the EU has granted preferential access to most of its trading partners for some or all categories of imports. Nine countries – Australia, Canada, Taiwan, Hong Kong, China, Japan, Republic of Korea, New Zealand, Singapore and the USA – enjoy Most-Favored-Nation (MFN) treatment in all product categories. These countries accounted for 45.2 per cent of the EU's total merchandise imports in 2001. The most beneficial treatment is granted to LDCs, ACP countries and countries under the Generalised System of Preferences (GSP). In the WTO the EU demonstrates support to an open, rules-based multilateral trading system. The process of international trade liberalisation, however, has not been free of tension. Trade in textiles and food products continues to face barriers erected when the EU was in its infancy. There are powerful pressure groups concerned that cheap competition will be ruinous for domestic producers and suppliers. Also there is criticism on the part of the LDCs that new EU technical regulations regarding waste disposal and environmental protection are just trade barriers in disguise. Some of the EU initiatives look very impressive on paper, but their real consequences for parties involved are small. For example, the EBA initiative has received a lot of publicity as a major goodwill gesture on the part of the EU, making a significant contribution to the prosperity of the LDCs, but LDCs' exports account for only 1 per cent of European imports currently, and 99 per cent of these imports are already exempt from customs duties. Clearly international trade remains an area of tension and further efforts will be required to secure progress.

References

Bilal S (1998) 'Political Economy Considerations on the Supply of Trade Protection in Regional Integration Agreements', *Journal of Common Market Studies*, Vol. 36, No. 1, pp. 1–32.

Brenton P (2001) 'Anti-dumping Policies in the EU and Trade Diversion, *European Journal of Political Economy*, Vol. 17, pp. 593–607.

EU (2002) *Trade Policy Review Body: **European Union**. Report by the Government*, WTO Secretariat, Geneva.

Frankel J and Romer P (1999) 'Does Trade Cause Growth?', *American Economic Review*, Vol. 89, No. 3, pp. 379–99.

Stern N (2002) 'Making Trade Work for Poor People', Speech delivered at National Council of Applied Economic Research, New Delhi.

Wall Street Journal (2002), 29 March, New York, NY.

WTO (2002) *EU Trade Policy Review*, WTO Secretariat, Geneva.

Further reading

Bhagwati J (2003) *Free Trade Today*, Princeton University Press, Princeton.

Brenton P and Manzocchi S (eds) (2002) *Enlargement, Trade and Investment: The Impact of Barriers to Trade in Europe*, Edward Elgar, Cheltenham.

Brenton P, Sheehy J and Vancauteren M (2001) 'Technical Barriers to Trade in the European Union: Importance for Accession Countries', *Journal of Common Market Studies*, Vol. 39, No. 2, pp. 265–84.

Dillon S (2002) *International Trade and Economic Law and the European Union*, Hart, Oxford.

Farrell M (1999) *EU and WTO Regulatory Frameworks: Complementarity or Competition?* Kogan Page, London.

Finger M, Ng F and Wangchuk S (2001) *Anti-dumping as Safeguard Policy*, Policy Research Working Paper 2730, The World Bank, Washington, DC.

Heidensohn K (1995) *Europe and World Trade*, Pinter, London.

Hocking B and McGuire S (eds) (1999) *Trade Politics: International, Domestic and Regional Perspectives*, Routledge, London/New York.

Hoekman B and Kostecki M (2001) *The Political Economy of the World Trading System: The WTO and Beyond*, Oxford University Press, Oxford.

Lane J V (ed.) 2002 *European Union–U.S. Trade Conflicts and Economic Relationship*, New York, Novinka Books.

MacGregor L, Prosser T and Villiers C (eds) (2000) *Regulation and Markets Beyond 2000*, Ashgate, Aldershot.

Moor L (1999) *Britain's Trade and Economic Structure: The Impact of the European Union*, Routledge, London.

Sapir A (2001) 'Domino effects in Western European regional trade, 1960–1992', *European Journal of Political Economy*, Vol. 17, pp. 377–88.

Stephen R (2000) *Vehicle of Influence: Building a European Car Market*, University of Michigan Press, Ann Arbor.

Chapter 13

The European Union and Central and Eastern Europe

Andrei Kuznetsov

Introduction

Relations between the EU and the countries of Central and Eastern Europe (CEECs) have seen unprecedented changes in the last decade. For most of the second half of the 20th century Eastern and Western Europe were isolated from each other economically, following the political divide of the continent into two camps, 'communist' and 'capitalist'. The collapse of Soviet-style communism in the late 1980s presented the EU with unique opportunities and challenges. For the first time in the history of the EU there was a chance to create a united Europe spreading from the Atlantic Ocean to Russian borders. However, EU enlargement was not a straightforward task considering the number of candidates, the area (an increase of 34 per cent) and population (an increase of 105 million). Probably even more important has been the scope of economic, political and social differences. At the beginning of 2002, after a decade of economic reforms, a per capita GDP in the CEE applicant countries was still less than 40 per cent of the EU average. CEE applicant countries had to achieve considerable advances in many areas in order to make themselves eligible for EU membership. In turn, the EU was also facing a demanding task. On the one hand, the EU sought to encourage reforms in CEE and make them irreversible. On the other hand, the responsibility of the EU was to protect the interests of its members in the face of a dramatic change in the political and economic situation on the European continent. This chapter examines the key economic factors that influenced the process of EU Eastern enlargement.

The legacy of communism

In the 1990s the CEECs had to succeed in moving from a Soviet-style economic mechanism, based on central planning and public ownership, to a capitalist economy dominated by private property and a market-based allocation of resources. This task was very difficult on its own and was made even worse by the protracted economic crisis experienced by the European socialist countries. Its visible features were declining rates of economic growth, wasteful use of resources including labour and capital, a widening technological gap with advanced countries, persistent shortages on the supply side and serious financial imbalances.

The old central planning system has been analysed by Kornai (1986) using the concept of the 'soft budget constraint'. According to Kornai, the planning system sought to maximise desired output and financial considerations were secondary to this. Efficiency in allocating resources could, therefore, not be achieved by financial criteria such as profit as few prices were determined by market conditions, and differences between costs and the value of sales were covered by taxes and subsidies. There was also little effective competition between enterprises, and costs and revenues were determined in an arbitrary way by administrative discretion. Consequently, enterprises had little incentive to use resources efficiently, as they faced few financial pressures, i.e. they operated with soft budget constraints. Indeed, the incentive was for the enterprise to acquire the maximum amount of resources possible in order to produce as much output as possible. This resulted in low productivity and a tendency to make poor quality goods. A secondary effect was that enterprise managers had little experience in setting prices, marketing and selling products, and financial control procedures.

These inherent problems were exacerbated by the 'closed' nature of socialist economies. Producers were isolated from external competition and could not fully participate in the international division of labour. Nor could they benefit from direct foreign investments, joint-ventures and technology transfer. Trade and other economic transactions with the West were also hindered by the inconvertibility of currencies. Most exchange rates were administratively determined and had little relationship to the true value of the currency. Eastern European countries also found difficulties in exporting to the West because of the trade restrictions imposed on them, and problems in penetrating Western markets because of the poor quality of their manufactured goods. The countries of Eastern Europe, therefore, have a legacy of poor integration into the markets of the West.

While the exact size of macroeconomic imbalances inherited by democratic regimes in Eastern Europe is debatable, it is clear that they were serious enough to provoke, at a certain point, an economic crisis. Hidden inflation in Poland, which existed in the form of a price gap between an official and a 'black' market, had already become hyper-inflation under the last communist government, while in Romania stagnation and decay became evident in the early 1980s. However, the squeeze in the economies of Central and Eastern Europe in the 1990s would not have been so pronounced had there not been some important external shocks.

The ruinous impact of the decline in trade between the European socialist countries must be placed first in the list of such shocks. Intra-COMECON trade was responsible for 40–50 per cent of their industrial exports. As COMECON collapsed at the beginning of the 1990s, East European producers, due to the poor competitiveness of their goods and also because of trade barriers imposed by the EU, failed to increase their share of Western markets quickly enough to compensate for the shrinkage in their traditional markets. Another consequence of the collapse of COMECON was the erosion of the financial position of the ex-socialist countries, which for years had benefited from implicit trade subsidies from the Soviet Union. Partly for political reasons and partly owing to the inefficiency of the price mechanism, the Soviet Union sold its energy and non-food raw materials to Eastern

Europe at prices below prevailing world market prices and bought manufactured goods from Eastern Europe at prices above world prices. Experts estimate the value of this transfer to be in billions of US dollars (Marrese and Vanous, 1988). Finally, the Gulf War of early 1991 not only disrupted trade with some Arab countries but also inflated world oil prices, thus aggravating the economic situation in Central and Eastern European countries, all of which depended heavily on imported oil.

The agenda for reforms

The task of marketisation has proved to be extremely challenging owing to the precarious state of the European ex-socialist economies and the difference between the two economic models. Problems ranged from technical deficiencies, such as the lack of functioning capital markets and the credit systems required for efficient capital formation and resource allocation, to the more general issue of changing prevailing behavioural patterns at all levels of society. They also involved finding the shortest way towards creating jobs with high value-added and wealth-generating capacities, improving labour productivity and providing sustained technological innovation in order to increase national competitiveness in the face of the growing importance of international markets. What made a systematic change of European Soviet-style economies particularly challenging was the fact that reformers could not rely on any of the elements of the existing economic mechanism as being adequate to meet the standards of a market-based system. The task facing reformers was to redesign this mechanism, but at the same time avoiding a complete economic breakdown following from the progressive disintegration of their economic and political systems. There appears to have been no great difference in opinions in the former socialist countries, as well as in the West, as to the nature of the essential stages of transition towards a market-type economy.

The first necessary stage is 'economic stabilisation', which implies the initial adaptation of the existing economic mechanism (prices, credit, money supply, wages) to the standards of the capitalist system. Macro-economic stabilisation is essential in order to eliminate the most dangerous financial imbalances inherited from central planning (monetary overhang and fiscal deficit) and to kick-start the price mechanism which, under the market economy, facilitates the allocation of resources.

The second element or stage is a radical 'institutional reform' aimed essentially at the restoration of private property and competition. Privatisation in the broadest sense is meant to eliminate the indeterminacy of capital ownership in former socialist states, one of the main reasons for inefficient employment of capital assets in the period of the command economy. Privatisation is also expected to induce changes in entrepreneurial behaviour and to make enterprises profit-motivated (under central planning they were output maximisers). Micro-economic reform is also necessary to create a market relationship between the owner of the capital and the manager of the firm, which is more conducive to better performance by enterprises. This presupposes the adoption of new laws (e.g. bankruptcy legislation), but no less important is the creation of an appropriate institutional environment, including investment banks, capital exchanges, auditing and consulting firms and other types of business services. These services were non-existent under socialism. Another important issue is to put an end to the monopolistic position of producers in the market by the direct break-up of large enterprises and through new business formation.

The third element, closely linked to the second, is 'capacity restructuring', the shift of capital and labour from primary and machine-building industries to those producing consumer goods and high-tech products, and from industrial production to services. Moreover, integration of the ex-socialist economies in the international market is normally regarded as an important component of such a restructuring.

Early difficulties

The immediate consequences of marketisation have proved to be quite disappointing. From the outset a temporary deterioration of performance was regarded as an inevitable cost of transition. Indeed, marketisation in Central and Eastern Europe may be accurately described as a transition from one system of development with a related set of priorities and ruling principles, institutions and regulatory mechanisms to a completely different, if not an opposite, system with its own priorities, institutions and regulatory mechanisms. Such a profound qualitative change could not but provoke some drastic adjustments. However, the actual scale and persistence of the crisis vastly exceeded expectations, as falling national output, growing inflation and unemployment, and financial imbalances have proved to be general attributes of the initial stage of transition.

These new challenges, including devastating hyperinflation, growing shortages and a deteriorating foreign debt position, required immediate action. This took the form of monetary and fiscal restrictions, price liberalisation, devaluation of domestic currencies and wage guidelines. Because of the speed and radicalism of reforms this approach was dubbed 'shock therapy.' It had already been used in some developing countries. What made the difference was the swiftness with which these measures were applied and the fact that they were introduced for the first time in a non-capitalist economy characterised by the absence of a comprehensive banking system, labour and capital markets and developed taxation. Unlike most developing countries, in CEECs stabilisation initially enjoyed an enormous credit of public confidence, permitting reformers to realise some very daring projects. This 'social pact' was based on the assumption that reforms would produce a swift result in the form of amelioration of the living conditions of the majority of the population. 'Shock therapy' was effective in eliminating pervasive shortages of consumer goods, but the extent of poverty has not diminished, and may have grown, while a relatively small group of people with very high incomes has been emerging.

Countries that pursued a coherent 'shock therapy,' in particular Poland, Hungary and the Czech Republic, have emerged as more successful in restoring economic growth. Since 1994 they have been showing healthy growth rates. Nonetheless, nowhere in the CEECs was the course of economic austerity implemented consistently enough to claim that 'shock therapy' was fully applied. The actual practice of reforms has been very individual and, due mainly to social pressures, characterised by opportunism and manoeuvring not provided for in the theoretical schemes. This suggests that there are no generally valid recipes for success without reference to country-specific conditions. The more it became clear that the transformation was going to split nations into losers and winners, the more important became the social and political dimensions of reforms. Governments were tempted to postpone unpopular decisions, introducing last-minute changes in already accepted policies, or, in contrast, to rush into measures favourable to particular interest groups. This often distorted the contemplated effects of reforms and made the process of transformation more uncertain in terms of results.

It is important to realise the relative nature of recovery even in the most successful of transitional economies. Almost ten years after the market reforms were started the most successful of transition countries like Poland, Slovenia, the Czech Republic, Slovakia and Romania are only edging back to their 1989 level of GDP.

The challenges of marketisation

There are three major adjustment problems that have emerged with the onset of the reform programmes, namely inflation, unemployment and deindustrialisation.

Inflation

Price liberalisation at an early stage of reform caused dangerous levels of inflation in many countries. The problem with price liberalisation is that, in order not to allow a switch to market prices to be translated into sustained hyper-inflation, it is necessary to enact very firm anti-inflationary measures that carry the risk of inducing recession. Stabilisation reforms succeeded mainly in establishing more realistic prices and exchange rates, eliminating queuing and improving the quality of goods and services as a result of increasing foreign competition. Nonetheless, inflation was not curbed. A sharp price rise during the initial stage of stabilisation had been expected. However, many countries found themselves stuck in this stage for much longer than had been foreseen. Persistent double- to triple-digit inflation became a fact of life in most CEECs in the early 1990s and, with the exception of the Czech Republic, continued into the late 1990s. In 1996 in Bulgaria inflation was still in excess of 150 per cent. Even in Hungary and Poland, which belong to the leading group of transitional economies, the rate of inflation is four to five times above the average for the OECD countries.

Unemployment

Unemployment rates have risen dramatically during the transition, creating an uneasy situation in societies previously enjoying full employment. Registered unemployment leapt from almost zero to over 7 million in 1995 of which 40 per cent were out of work for more than 12 months (Eatwell et al., 1995, p. 40). The economic and political cost of unemployment is enormous, making it a serious obstacle to restructuring the transition economies, since a substantial part of the population may lose hope of finding a job and become an under-class. This divides the society and creates social and political tension. Such 'transitional unemployment' has all the characteristics of a stagnant pool and, once in the pool, it is very difficult to get out of it (Boeri, 1997). CEE governments are aware of the political discontent caused by growing unemployment and limited social security provisions were introduced. However, only steady economic growth will provide a long-term solution.

Deindustrialisation

Tight monetary, credit, fiscal and wage policies forced a collapse in demand which led to major problems for nationalised industries in transitional countries. In Poland, Bulgaria, Romania and the former Czechoslovakia real wages dropped by 25–30 per cent and have stayed low ever since, sometimes below pre-reform levels. A rapidly shrinking economy drove up unemployment, undermining demand even further. At the same time national markets were opened to previously unavailable foreign products. Local producers found themselves competing with leading international brands at the moment when they were least fit to do so. They were further disadvantaged by governmental policies that discriminated against state-owned enterprises (SOEs). Public enterprises found themselves deprived of traditional state subsidies, while clear provisions as to how the state sector was to be financed were generally absent. It was assumed that the enterprises would try to adjust to hard budget constraints by cutting costs. But macro-economic measures alone were not sufficient to bring about desirable responses. Many SOEs had a potential for market success but could not realise it following the 'hands-off' attitude taken by CEE governments in the early transition period, when assistance and protection were particularly important (Amsden et al., 1994). As a result, even the most promising companies could not build upon their strengths and were overwhelmed by exposure to free-market forces to which they had no time and resources to adjust. In 1990–93 the average annual fall in industrial output for CEECs was close to 20 per cent, before eventually stabilising at levels far below those achieved in the 1980s.

Recovery of industrial production, the most important component of GDP, has been uneven, reflecting a generally poor investment situation. Securing investment growth has become a crucial issue. But the situation is not straightforward. Foreign investors show considerable interest in the region, but they tend to focus their activities on a very limited number of favoured destinations like Hungary and the Czech Republic. Most CEECs have to find ways to raise resources locally, which appears to be a serious deterrent to recovery given the collapse of living standards and the inadequate development of the banking system.

Problems with privatisation

The privatisation of public property is universally regarded as another major issue in the post-communist transition process. In East Germany the public sector included 8,000 firms, in Poland about 7,500, in former Czechoslovakia 4,800, in Romania

4,000, in Hungary 2,500 and in Bulgaria 5,000. The public sector accounted in each case for not less than 80 per cent of national value added. By comparison, in the UK the much-heralded privatisation programme of the first Thatcher government involved only about 20 firms, accounting for a mere 5 per cent of value added.

What made privatisation such a challenge was the role public enterprises played in national economies. High concentration of production and employment in big enterprises was a general feature of socialism. In 1990, the share of industrial enterprises employing more than 500 people was 43 per cent in Czechoslovakia, 86.9 per cent in Poland, 74.5 per cent in Romania and 72.1 per cent in Bulgaria. Also the enterprises were more narrowly specialised than is usual in the West, often with only one national producer of a particular product. The large scale of many state-owned companies aside, it was typical of state enterprises to be overmanned and to have a vast array of supporting services such as kindergartens, medical centres and holiday homes. It was obvious that they could not survive unchanged under any other conditions than those of a centrally planned economy. The economic recession has made things worse as enterprises have lost markets, reduced production, accumulated debt and discontinued their normal investment. As a result many enterprises seemed to be unsaleable unless prior streamlining and financial restructuring was undertaken. However, the dominating belief has been that if large enterprises remained in state ownership they would not adapt to market conditions.

There are two principal ways of handling these problems. One reflects the perception that the duty of the government is to speed up the process, while a market mechanism is to be entrusted with the task of restructuring national property. Alternatively, restructuring could precede or accompany the privatisation of state companies in order to increase their value and attractiveness as an asset.

The Czech Republic has chosen the first approach. There the voucher scheme has proved the most intriguing part of a large-scale privatisation programme. Each adult citizen was entitled, almost for free, to a voucher booklet allowing him or her to bid for the shares of privatised entities at public auctions. Over eight million people became owners of vouchers. In the first round of auctions, in 1992, corporate assets with a 'net book value' of about $9.3 bn were distributed to millions of new shareholders (*Transition*, 1992). The implications of the scheme raised general scepticism outside the Czech Republic. Voucher privatisation is being blamed for lack of corporate restructuring and the sluggish growth of industrial output. Probably the main problem with this approach is that it does not provide any visible evidence that the change in ownership has promoted profit maximisation and business efficiency. As a rule no new capital or expertise has been introduced into troubled companies. Furthermore, the individuals receiving a share in privatised enterprises, if ownership is broadly spread, do not have any influence over the specific competitiveness of the companies they have come to own. The acquisition of assets involved a considerable element of chance, with some new owners discovering that their property was uncompetitive and unprofitable. In other cases enterprises, which were competitive in their operations, have fallen into the hands of incompetent individuals who lack the necessary entrepreneurial skills. As a result, business conditions in the country on the whole have remained uncertain.

The idea of prior restructuring of most enterprises is implicit in the privatisation programmes of Poland, Hungary and Bulgaria. However, financial and organisational restructuring takes time and money, and extends the period of transition during which public bodies continue to interfere with economic processes. To many this seems unacceptable. Only Germany provides an example of privatisation based on prior comprehensive micro-economic restructuring. In July 1990, 10,500 East German enterprises, employing four million people, were put in the care of a government agency called the Treuhandanstalt. The Treuhandanstalt was entrusted with a mandate to maximise the returns on the sales of state assets while ensuring optimum employment. Its stated policy was to privatise quickly. However, if a company could not be sold the Treuhandanstalt's policy was to attempt to restructure it to salvage at least the core business or any other viable part. By June 1992 some 4,803 companies had been privatised, 1,209 closed down and 5,435 were still owned by the Treuhandanstalt (East European Markets, 1992).

Few Central and Eastern European governments are able to spare the resources and expertise that the Treuhandanstalt was able to lavish on state property. The apparent dilemma of privatisation programmes is that case-by-case privatisation by a central agency cannot accomplish much, given the resources available to be applied to this end. However, speedy mass privatisation may prove to be a shaky alternative unless supported by far-reaching institutional reform. The major flaw of any mass privatisation, as demonstrated by Czech and Russian experience, is that it fails to impose corporate governance on privatised companies. Hence the importance of regulations and institutions reinforcing the ability of asset owners to exercise control over their assets and persons entrusted with the task of managing them. So far mass privatisation of large enterprises changed little in managers' behaviour inasmuch as it did not expose them to new centres of control or provide them with the means to restructure.

The EU and reconstruction of Eastern Europe

As mentioned above, international factors have had a major impact on the dynamics of post-communist transition. The communist governments of Eastern and Central Europe received loans from the West in the 1970s totalling $49.8 bn. These resources were generally misallocated and did not generate a flow of income in hard currency sufficient to repay them. By the time CEECs started market reforms they had an enormous cumulative debt of $103.1 bn, putting a great strain on their economies, with Poland and Yugoslavia being in particular difficulties.

Unfolding marketisation boosted demand for foreign capital. Transitional countries sought financial credits to support structural adjustments and foreign direct investments to start up privatisation and modernisation of nationalised industries, and to make up for the chronic undercapitalisation typical of centrally planned economies.

The G24 countries and international institutions have made commitments to the Eastern and Central European countries amounting to $100 bn including food and medical aid, economic restructuring and technical assistance, export credit and investment guarantees, debt relief and balance-of-payments support (*Transition*,

1992). However, only a meagre share of what the West promised has actually been delivered. A fraction of these funds was in grant form; the rest were loans and credit guarantees.

Economic difficulties in CEECs gave Western governments, international organisations and multinational corporations considerable leverage over Eastern and Central European governments. The EU insisted on measures leading to accelerated opening of the markets of the ex-socialist countries to Western products. The argument was that an end must be put to a situation in which Central and Eastern European countries were protected from competitive pressure of international trade which, in market economies, provided a strong incentive to improve efficiency. Transitional economies were called on to lift or restrict foreign trade control and facilitate access to foreign exchange resources for the residents by introducing internal convertibility of the national currency.

As a result, at the initial stage of transition the post-communist economies made a great stride towards openness when the slump in industrial production was at its deepest. Furthermore, although exports to the West increased they could not compensate for the collapse of intra-COMECON trade because Western governments were not ready to open Western markets to Eastern European goods. When Poland volunteered to drop all import restrictions the EU did not reciprocate. Soon Poland had one of the lowest tariff regimes in the world, but half of Poland's exports to the EU confronted some kind of restraint. In order to facilitate relations with the Community, Poland, Hungary and Czechoslovakia initiated the creation of a free-trade area in Central Europe under the Central European Free Trade Agreement (CEFTA) signed in December 1992 and joined by Slovenia in 1995. They obtained associated status with the EU, amounting largely to a promise of a ten-year transition to free trade. In the meantime the steel lobby ensured that the EU set an extremely low ceiling on East European imports – 1 per cent of total EU raw steel capacity. The EU also refused to relax restrictions on imports of food, textiles, clothing and chemicals. Together with iron and steel, these are the most competitive Eastern European industries (they account for 33–46 per cent of exports to the EU from the former Czech Republic, Slovakia, Poland and Hungary).

The EU was concerned that cheap imports from CEECs, where labour costs were low, would adversely affect the employment situation and regional development in Western Europe. In particular competition from Eastern Europe was feared in the markets for low value-added manufactured goods. Such industries are often located in the poorer regions of the EU, therefore trade liberalisation could well worsen the regional problems of the Community. These concerns, as well as problems with agricultural products, were limiting the access of the CEECs' economies to the markets of the EU. In reality, as regards the four CEFTA countries, the trade balance has been positive for the EU ever since 1991. Even the traditional deficit in agricultural products turned into a surplus in 1993. But restrictions were slow to disappear. As far as agriculture was concerned, the EU market in the 1990s remained almost as closed to exports from the East as in the previous decade. This provided grounds for the claim that the total employment effect of the first tentative steps towards trade liberalisation vis-à-vis Eastern Europe was positive for the EU.

Extending EU membership

Expansion of the EU internal market to nearly 500 million consumers offers major growth opportunities for all member states. The influential Centre for Economic Policy Research (CEPR) estimated that accession of countries of Central and Eastern Europe would – even in a conservative scenario – bring an economic gain for the EU15 of €10 bn and, for the new members, €23 bn.

The EU member states took a decisive step toward eastward enlargement at the Copenhagen European Council in 1993, agreeing that 'the associated countries in Central and Eastern Europe that so desire shall become members of the European Union'. Thus, enlargement was no longer a question of 'if' but 'when'. The Council established three criteria that future members had to meet:

■ stability of institutions guaranteeing democracy, the rule of law, human rights and respect for and protection of minorities;

■ the existence of a functioning market economy as well as the capacity to cope with competitive pressure and market forces within the EU;

■ the ability to take on the obligations of membership including adherence to the aims of political, economic and monetary union.

In March 1998 the EU formally launched the accession process, covering ten Central European countries and Cyprus. Six countries (Cyprus, the Czech Republic, Estonia, Hungary, Poland and Slovenia) were selected by the European Commission as having met the criteria sufficiently to be invited to open accession negotiations (Table 13.1). The objective was that the first group of new members should join the EU in time for the elections to the European Parliament scheduled for June 2004. To meet the entry criteria CEE governments have made some prodigious and often costly efforts. They had to rigorously implement certain restrictive policies, taking

Table 13.1 EU and CEE countries: key indicators

Indicators	1993 %	1996 %	1999 %	2001* %	2002* %
GDP (annual growth)					
EU	−0.3	1.7	2.6	1.7	1.3
CEE	−0.3	3.9	2.0	3.0	3.2
Inflation (consumer prices)					
EU	3.8	2.5	1.4	2.7	1.6
CEE	79.9	41.8	12.8	9.3	7.3
Unemployment					
EU	10.7	10.8	9.2	7.7	7.2
CEE	10.4	9.4	10.8	12.5	13.1

Notes: * forecast

Sources: Adapted from *IMF World Economic Outlook*, December 2001; *Eurostat*, August 2002, Enlargement Directorate General, European Commission

the risk of becoming unpopular with the public by putting pressure on the standard of living. The emphasis on deregulation forced many national firms to close down or shed labour.

The EU closely monitors developments in the applicant countries. Since November 1998 the Commission submits regular reports to the Council on the further progress achieved by each country. The reports serve as a basis for the Council to take decisions on the conduct of negotiations. They show that all CEE applicant countries have fulfilled the political criteria for accession and good progress has been made by some countries with the economic criteria, in particular Hungary, Latvia and Bulgaria, but in others, such as Poland and the Czech Republic, the pace of change was slow. Nonetheless, in October 2002 the Commission recommended that the negotiations on accession to the European Union by the Czech Republic, Estonia, Hungary, Latvia, Lithuania, Poland, the Slovak Republic and Slovenia should be concluded by the end of the year. This indicated that the Commission had come to the conclusion that these countries would be ready for membership from the beginning of 2004 (see Box 13.1). As for Bulgaria and Romania, the Commission expressed hope that these two countries would achieve their objective to join in 2007.

While keeping a watchful eye on developments in the East, the EU also showed an awareness of the need for a substantial reform of EU policies as a necessary precondition for enlargement. This was mostly caused by existing member states' concerns about the redistribution of funds arising from the growth of financial claims as a result of EU expansion. A much-cited example is that of Poland, which, were it currently eligible for funds under the CAP, would cost the EU 40 per cent of the CAP's total annual budget. But this is as much a comment on problems with the CAP in its present form as it is a testimony to the troubled state of Polish agriculture. It implies that the CAP, and the Structural Funds in particular, should be revised before the completion of the enlargement. However, these reforms have been slow to materialise, reflecting the conflicting interests of existing member states. In order to pacify concerns regarding the budgetary consequences of enlargement, and the impact of enlargement on the labour market and migratory flows, the EU has now agreed to the imposition of certain restrictions. Thus, transfers to the Central and East European countries should not exceed 10 per cent of the EU budget for the period up to 2006, and a flexible transition period of up to seven years has been agreed for limiting the inflow of workers from new member states.

Integration of new members from the East has put relations between EU15 member states through yet another test. For Germany and France, relations with Eastern European countries have high priority, while for countries such as the UK these relations are not on the top of the list of priorities. EU enlargement will require changes in the way decisions are taken within the organisation in such a way that majority voting will increasingly replace the principle of consensus. Some member states are worried that enlargement may reduce them to second-class members. It is also clear that with the accession of new members the degree of homogeneity within the EU is going to decline and a net transfer of resources in favour of newcomers will occur, in particular through structural funds and agricultural subsidies.

Box 13.1 Towards the enlarged union

The next EU enlargement will further strengthen the unity of the European continent and help create an area of lasting peace and prosperity.

The historical and political arguments in favour of enlargement are compelling. It will also produce substantial economic benefits.

Stable democracies have emerged in Central and Eastern Europe. The credit for this success belongs mainly to the people of those countries themselves. The political stability in the Central and East European candidate countries is rooted in common European values: democracy, the rule of law, respect for human rights and the protection of minorities.

Candidate countries already conduct between a half and two-thirds of their trade with the EU. The rapid growth in trade has helped to develop new markets and investment. Full integration with accession, together with the adoption of common rules and standards across the world's largest single market, will further enhance the opportunities to achieve socially and environmentally sustainable growth.

On the basis of political and economic stability, the enlarged EU will be better equipped to confront global challenges. An enlarged EU will add weight to its external relations, in particular to the development of a common foreign and security policy.

The Commission's assessment of candidate countries in this year's Regular Reports carries three important messages:

- The EU's pre-accession strategy has proved a success. The transformation process in the candidate countries has been considerably accelerated by the prospect of enlargement.

- The accession negotiations, which have been based on the principles of own merits, differentiation and catching up, can be concluded with most candidates by the end of 2002. Preparations for enlargement will continue.

- Enlargement is an inclusive process which is not yet completed with the first accessions. The EU continues to give its full support to current candidates that will not be in a position to participate in the next wave of enlargement.

The EU is determined to conclude the negotiations with Cyprus, Malta, Hungary, Poland, the Slovak Republic, Lithuania, Latvia, Estonia, the Czech Republic and Slovenia by the end of 2002, if those countries are ready. The objective remains that these countries should participate in the elections for the European Parliament in 2004 as full members.

(European Commission Strategy Paper, 9 October 2002, extracts.)

In the long run the EU has much to gain from aiding the reconstruction process in Central and Eastern Europe. According to the analysis presented at the Round Table of Industrialists, May 2001, gains will be driven by four factors:

- a strong boost to foreign direct investment, which has already grown significantly and is speeding up the transformation of the economies of the ten Central and East European candidates. Accession will give a further stimulus to capital flows by encouraging business confidence in a predictable political and regulatory framework delivering common standards and a level playing-field across 27 (or eventually more) economies. The result will be rising training and skills standards, as well as productivity improvements, technology transfers, modernised plant and equipment, and better environment and social standards;

- more confidence in the political and economic futures of the new member states. The process of legal and administrative reform leading to stable laws, regulations and standards will be better implemented, enabling businesses to make longer-term decisions on strategy and investment;

- keener international competitiveness in both new and old member states;

- increased cross-border trade between new and old member states.

The CEECs have the potential for rapid growth as they progress towards the market economy. The demand for goods, services, capital and 'know-how' increases and is likely to be substantial. The EU is well placed to benefit from this growth in demand. The consumer market is also potentially very large, especially for consumer durables such as cars. Central and Eastern Europe may also provide a useful production base for many European firms seeking to supply this growing market, and for exports to Western Europe. Already many European car firms have reached agreements to produce cars in Central and Eastern Europe to supply the growing demand there and, if trade liberalisation is successful, to export to Western Europe.

Direct help by Western companies in the form of selling equipment and providing 'know-how' has been a quick way of helping in the reconstruction process. Most Central and Eastern European countries welcome joint-venture enterprises. Some encourage direct investment in the form of purchasing existing enterprises or establishing new enterprises. The privatisation programme provided a quick method for Western companies to gain production plants in Central and Eastern Europe. Such companies could then easily transfer technology and processes; this would greatly assist the transition process.

However, the troublesome heritage of centrally planned economies indicates that many long-term problems need to be solved before Central and Eastern Europe becomes an attractive area for many Western firms to operate in. The inflow of private capital has been below expectations and far below levels that policy makers consider desirable. Hungary, Poland and the Czech Republic have been the three destinations most favoured by Western investors. Still ownership of productive assets by foreigners in Hungary remains notably below the 20–25 per cent target set by the government. Private investors are mainly discouraged by the high political and policy risks. In turn, the barriers to the export of products to the EU were important deterrents to some foreign investors, including firms from North America and the Far East, who would like to exploit the location and cost advantages of ex-socialist countries to compete in Western European markets.

Analysis shows that the volume of financial claims by Eastern European members on EU funds will be moderate compared with the immense boost to their economies which the provision of these resources is likely to give. This is possible because the size of the EU economy is so much greater than that of CEECs. The combined GDP of the ten applicants is barely 4 per cent of the Union's present total. The anticipated transfer of EU funds will be below 0.5 per cent of EU GDP but for the recipient countries it will still represent a very substantial contribution. Poland alone, for example, is expected to receive a net transfer equal to 7 per cent of its GDP (Gabrisch, 1997). The potential impact of such a transfer becomes clear if one recalls the outcome of the Marshall Plan that amounted to just about 2 per cent of the recipient countries' GNP. At the same time accession to the EU may prove to be a painful experience for the applicants.

The EU and Russia

Russia is a huge country rich in resources with outstanding industrial capacity. The population is large and well educated, and the country has a great tradition of scientific research and academic training. Yet the transition to a market economy has been extremely painful and slow. First attempts to modernise the Russian economy along the lines of marketisation can be traced back to 1985, when President Gorbachev inaugurated a programme of economic 'acceleration'. Under President Yeltsin some radical steps were taken towards dismantling the command economy and central planning, which opened the way, in 1992, to a quick shift to a market-regulated system. It so happened that it also inaugurated a period of dramatic decline in the Russian economy and the quality of life of the population. By the end of 1996 the Russian economy, in terms of GDP, was only 61 per cent of its size when capitalist reforms began, shrinking to what it used to be in 1979. In 1997 industrial production was only 45–50 per cent of the pre-1992 level and continued to decline. Some 31.5 million Russians (21 per cent of the total population) had incomes below the official poverty line, while another 31 million were making just enough money to meet this minimal standard. Life expectancy was the lowest it had been for 20 years.

Whatever the explanations for this failure, the precarious state of the Russian economy is a serious obstacle in the way of integrating this country into the European economy. Not surprisingly, Brussels showed little enthusiasm when the Russian Prime Minister Vladimir Chernomyrdin made a statement in July 1997 that Russia would like to join the EU. A number of unresolved political issues, the confused legal environment and growing protectionism leave a considerable gap between Russia and the economies of the EU member states.

A lot of contacts have, however, developed at the level of private companies. Russia is much more open than it used to be. Foreign trade and foreign capital have been growing in importance. Some $5.9 bn of foreign investments has been attracted to Russia. This may be impressive on its own but it places Russia in only fourth place among former socialist countries after much smaller economies such as Hungary ($13 bn), Poland ($10.1 bn) and the Czech Republic ($6.1 bn). The paradox of the situation is the fact that national capital has fled the country on an unprecedented scale, vouching for the total lack of confidence by Russians in governmental policies. Capital flight from Russia's private sector was $24 bn in 2000, $16 bn in 2001 and $10 bn in 2002 (Johnson's Russia List, 2003). The only significant sector of the Russian economy generating profits is the natural resources industry, which accounted for 46 per cent of exports in 1996 (Business Central Europe, 1997). Understandably, natural gas, oil and metal extraction are the key targets of foreign investors in Russia. The Russian government has so far failed to induce foreign capital to participate more actively in restructuring and modernising Russia's industrial structures. This contributes to the general wariness by the

Russian public about Western intentions vis-à-vis the regeneration of Russia through aid and investment.

Developing the relationship with Russia will be very difficult for the EU. Russia poses a greater problem than the CEE countries simply because of its great size. Russia has also preserved a high level of economic integration with other former Soviet republics. Bringing Russia into a closer relationship with the EU would mean that areas with very different economic, political and cultural characteristics would be drawn towards the EU. Only in the long run, when these countries have reconstructed their economic and political systems, would it be possible for them to establish close economic links with the EU. Given the nature of the economic and political crises that faces the former Soviet Union, this is likely to require a substantial reform of all aspects of their societies.

Conclusion

The CEECs are undergoing a painful process of transition towards market-based economies. Most of them wish to join the EU and the first wave has occurred in 2004. However, this enlargement will pose many economic and political challenges for the EU and the new member states. Most of the CEECs not in the first wave appear to be determined to join the EU. Therefore, there is a good prospect that the EU will soon encompass all or most of the CEECs. Such a change in the member state characteristics is bound to have significant implications for the future development of the EU. The relationship between the EU and Russia is also likely to develop, but it is very difficult to predict its direction and significance.

References

Amsden A, Kochanowicz J and Taylor L (1994) *The Market Meets Its Match: Restructuring the Economics of Eastern Europe*, Harvard University Press, Cambridge, Mass.

Boeri T (1997) 'Heterogeneous Workers, Economic Transformation and the Stagnancy of Transitional Unemployment', *European Economic Review*, Vol. 41, Nos 3–5, pp. 905–14.

Business Central Europe (1997) 'The Annual 1996/7', *European Economy*.

East European Markets (1992) Vol. 12, issue 13, p. 15.

Eatwell J, Ellman M, Nuti M and Shapiro J (1995) *Transformation and Integration: Shaping the Future of Central and Eastern Europe*, Institute for Public Research, London.

Gabrisch H (1997) 'Effects of EU Enlargement on New Members', *Europe–Asia Studies*, Vol. 49, No. 4, pp. 567–90.

Johnson's Russia List (2003) JRL 7139, **www.ccli.org/russia/johnson/7139-20.cfm**.

Kornai J (1986) 'The Soft Budget Constraint', *Kyklos*, Vol. 39, pp. 27–39.

Marrese M and Vanous J (1988) *Soviet Subsidisation of Trade with Eastern Europe: A Soviet Perspective*, University of California, Berkeley.

OECD (1997) *Transition Brief*, No. 6, Winter, Paris.

Transition (1992) The Newsletter about Reforming Economies, Vol. 3, No. 7.

Further reading

Bieler A (2002) 'The Struggle Over EU Enlargement: A Historical Materialist Analysis of European Integration, *Journal of European Public Policy*, Vol. 9, No. 4, pp. 575–97.

Dobrinsky R and Landesmann M (eds) (1995) *Transforming Economies and European Integration*, Edward Elgar, Aldershot.

Fernandez J (2002) 'The Common Agricultural Policy and EU enlargement: Implications for Agricultural Production in the Central and East European Countries', *Eastern European Economics*, Vol. 40, No. 3, pp. 28–50.

Gabrisch H and Pohl R (1999) *EU Enlargement and its Macroeconomic Effects in Eastern Europe: Currencies, Prices, Investment and Competitiveness*, Palgrave Macmillan, New York.

Hedlund S (1999) *Russia's Market Economy: A Bad Case of Predatory Capitalism*, UCL Press, London.

Inotai A (1996) 'From Association Agreements to Full Membership?: The Dynamics of Relations between the Central and East European Countries and the European Union, *Russian And East European Finance And Trade*, Vol. 32, No. 6, pp. 6–29.

Kornai J (1997) *Struggle and Hope: Essays on Stabilization and Reform in a Post-Socialist Economy*, Edward Elgar Publishing, Cheltenham.

Nello S S (2002) 'Preparing for Enlargement in the European Union: The Tensions between Economic and Political Integration, *International Political Science Review*, Vol. 23, No. 3, pp. 2913–17.

Nowicka M (2000) 'Social and Economic Aspects of the European Union Enlargement to the East: Assessment of Potential Costs and Benefits', *Yearbook of Polish European Studies*, No. 4, Warsaw. Available at **www.ce.uw.edu.pl/ce/wydawnictwo/yearbook_no4/Nowicka.pdf.**

OECD (2001) *Migration Policies and EU Enlargement: The Case of Central and Eastern Europe*, Paris.

Rosati D (1992) 'The CMEA Demise, Trade Restructuring and Trade Destruction in Central and Eastern Europe', *Oxford Review of Economic Policy*, Vol. 8, No. 1, pp. 58–81.

Stiglitz J (2002) *Globalization and Its Discontents*, W.W. Norton, New York.

Chapter 14

The European Union and the Developing World

Stephen Dearden

Introduction

The economic relationship between the EU and the developing world has been heavily influenced by the colonial histories of many of its member states. From the inception of the Community, France sought the inclusion of its overseas territories in the customs union and special arrangements for Morocco and Tunisia. Italy sought similar concessions for Libya. Thus, under Articles 131–136 of the Treaty of Rome there was provision for 'association' status for non-European countries who had a 'special relation' with Community members.

Although the Yaoundé Conventions, offering trade concessions and aid to some developing countries, began in 1964, it was not until the Maastricht Treaty on European Union (TEU) in 1993 that development cooperation became a shared European responsibility. Here under Article 130u the EU was to foster 'the sustainable economic and social development of developing countries . . . and their gradual integration into the world economy'. To achieve this, Article 130u states that development policy should be 'complementary to the policies pursued by the member states', while Article 130v requires the EU to take account of its development objectives in all its policies. This new explicit competence for the Community now gives the Commission the right to initiate new policies and programmes, and the responsibility to elaborate strategy. It also allows the Council of Ministers to make binding decisions by qualified majority voting rather than unanimity.

However, some forty years after decolonisation, does dependence still characterise the economic relationship of the least developed countries (LDCs) to the EU? Do these countries remain exporters of primary products and importers of European manufactures? For trade remains central to the long-term sustained economic development of the LDCs, and is a barometer of the degree of their past success in achieving the necessary structural transformation of their economies.

Trade preferences

The pyramid of preferences

The pattern of trade preferences faced by exporters to the EU is a complex one and is illustrated in Figure 14.1. Recent changes have undermined the distinction between the various levels of the pyramid of preferences but six broad categories of trade preferences can be identified:

1 *Tariff-free trade*: member states and the European Economic Area.

2 *Reciprocal free trade*: Baltic States, Israel

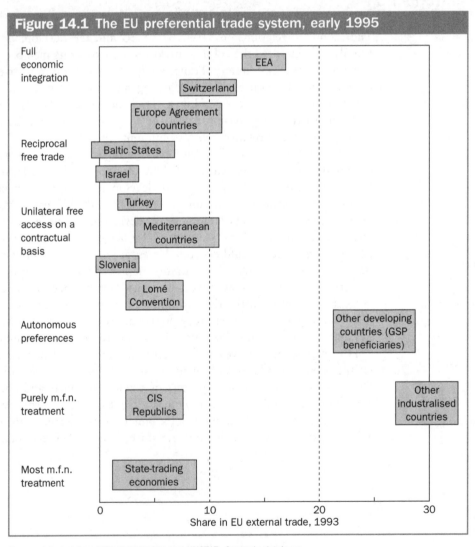

Figure 14.1 The EU preferential trade system, early 1995

Source: Adapted from WTO Secretariat; and UNSTAT, Contrade database

3 *Non-reciprocal free access*: Mediterranean countries and Lomé ACP (African, Caribbean and Pacific) states. Duty-free access for manufactured goods and most non-CAP agricultural products. Under Cotonou the middle-income ACPs will move to a reciprocal free trade regime.

4 *General System of Preferences*: non-ACP LDCs. Offers similar preferences to Lomé but on a narrower range of products.

5 *Most favoured nation*: CIS republics and remaining industrialised countries.

6 *State trading economies*: for example Vietnam, North Korea.

The Lomé Conventions

The first Lomé Convention was signed in 1975, and replaced the Yaoundé Conventions, which had mainly benefited the ex-French colonies. Lomé was a response to the UK's entry and the problem of preserving British Commonwealth LDC trade preferences. Although it excluded many of the Asian Commonwealth countries, the number of associated states benefiting from Lomé finally totalled 70 – the ACP group (Africa, Caribbean and Pacific). Each Convention lasted for five years and had both an aid and trade component. Lomé IV offered duty-free access for ACP exports of primary products and manufactures and most non-CAP agricultural products. Special arrangements existed for bananas, rum, beef and sugar, offering access for quotas from certain ACPs at higher guaranteed EU prices. Approximately 97 per cent of ACP exports entered the EU duty-free, but 63 per cent of ACP exports would have entered the EU duty-free even without the Lomé Conventions. The greatest benefit to the ACPs from Lomé arose with products that would have otherwise faced substantial tariffs, and therefore commanded artificially high prices within the European market. Unfortunately these comprised the smallest category of ACP exports to the EU and were being eroded. It has been estimated that only 7 per cent of ACP exports received this significant preferential margin in 1989 (McQueen and Stevens, 1989). In return for these tariff preferences the Community only required that the ACP states did not discriminate in their own markets between EU member states.

The Mediterranean countries

In 2000, the EU accounted for 48 per cent of the exports of its Mediterranean Partner Countries (MPC) and supplied 47 per cent of their imports (Table 14.1). Between 1995 and 2001 EU imports from the MPC grew by 110 per cent (compared with 87 per cent for all EU imports) and EU exports by 49 per cent (70 per cent for all EU exports). Turkey is the most important trading partner in the group, with a balanced trade worth €20 bn in 2001. The next two significant partners are Algeria (exports to EU €15.8 bn, imports €7.4 bn) and Israel (exports to the EU €9.4 bn, imports €14 bn).

Unlike relations with the ACPs through Lomé, those with the MPCs lack any coherence or institutional framework, being embodied in a succession of individual

Table 14.1 Mediterranean exports to the EU (1995)

	% of total exports
Algeria	66
Cyprus	35
Egypt	49
Israel/Palestinian Authority	31
Jordan	6
Lebanon	21
Malta	71
Morocco	63
Syria	57
Tunisia	78
Turkey	51

Source: Direction of Trade Statistics Yearbook, IMF, 1995

Association Agreements. They began in 1962 with Greece, followed by Turkey (1963), Morocco (1969), Tunisia (1969), Israel (1970) and Spain (1970). The last two were particularly controversial and led to the offer to extend similar trade agreements to other MPCs, including Egypt, Jordan and Syria.

However, as these agreements varied from country to country and required continual renegotiation, in 1972 the EU proposed the development of a General Mediterranean Policy (GMP). It was intended to create a free-trade area in industrial goods, except for 'sensitive products', and to give preferential access to 80 per cent of the MPCs' agricultural exports. Preferences were not as generous as under Lomé for 'non-traditional' fruit and vegetables, to protect EU suppliers. Reciprocity of the trade concessions had to be abandoned in the face of US opposition. The final outcome was little different from the preceding piecemeal agreements. The first unlimited duration agreement under the GMP was concluded with Israel in 1975.

In November 1995, at Barcelona, the EU launched the Euro-Mediterranean Partnership. This aims to create a free-trade area and requires the MPCs to give tariff and quota free access to EU exports of manufactured goods. At the same time the MPCs are expected to remove duties on goods originating from other MPCs. The Commission ultimately expects the MPCs to adopt the EU's competition and origin rules. At the same time the EU increased its financial assistance to the MPC and has allocated €5.3 bn from the general budget for the period 2000 to 2006.

The General System of Preferences

For those LDCs excluded from the Lomé Conventions, the General System of Preferences (GSP) is of significance. Originally conceived as a worldwide scheme, it was intended to offer duty-free access to developed country markets for LDC manufactured exports. The EU's GSP was instituted in 1971 and each scheme was intended to run for five years, but the Community's overriding commitment to the ACPs compromised the emergence of any comprehensive concession to the LDCs.

Over its history the EU's GSP had become increasingly discriminatory, both by product and by country of origin. Thus, from 1986 the GSP was withdrawn from those countries' products where income per capita was greater than $2000, and where the country's share of EU imports of those products exceeded 20 per cent; for textiles the share limit is 10 per cent.

Brazil, Hong Kong, China, South Korea and Singapore have all experienced the withdrawal of some GSP concessions, and some authors have concluded that GSP benefits were withdrawn from most LDCs' manufactured products that have penetrated EU markets to any significant degree. In addition, some 140 sensitive products, including textiles and clothing, were subject to tariff quotas or volume limits under the GSP. Once exports reached their tariff quota further sales were subject to the higher 'most favoured nation' (MFN) tariff arrangements. These tariff quotas or volume limits were often applied by individual EU member states.

In January 1995 a new ten-year GSP was adopted by the EU. In order to maintain the LDCs' preference margins, the GSP concessions are to be expressed as a percentage of the MFN tariff. This is to be 85 per cent of the MFN for 'very sensitive' products, 70 per cent for 'sensitive' products (e.g. footwear, electronics and motor vehicles), and 35 per cent for 'semi-sensitive' products, with other imports entering duty-free (European Commission, 1994). A safeguard clause remains, allowing the reintroduction of duties should imports threaten to cause serious difficulties to an EU producer. There is also a 'graduation mechanism', providing for the exclusion of specific country-sector combinations from the GSP, depending upon the exporting country's overall level of industrial development and degree of 'export specialisation' as defined by the EU.

The single market

The movement towards the Single European Market (SEM) was an important development in EU–LDC relations. Although not an aspect that had been addressed by the Commission, a number of authors attempted to evaluate its impact and it is best considered in terms of trade creation and trade diversion.

The Cecchini report (1988) suggested a 4.5–7 per cent enhancement of the growth rate as a result of economic integration and this in turn was expected to increase demand for LDC exports. Matthews and McAleese (1990), assuming an extra 5 per cent growth of GDP for the EU, calculated that this would increase LDC exports by 6 per cent ($5.5 bn), although 75 per cent of this increase would be oil. For other products, especially manufactures, the efficiency gains of the EU's own producers arising from the SEM (e.g. economies of scale) would lead to enhanced competition for LDC exports. The extent of this effect would vary from product to product, and was expected to be most severe for LDCs where EU producers experienced the greatest efficiency gains. Davenport (1990) believed that on plausible assumptions trade creation for LDCs' manufactured goods would be approximately offset by trade diversion.

For the LDCs the existing national preferential arrangements for their exports were often inconsistent with the 1992 programme and many member state quotas,

Voluntary Export Restraints (VERs), etc., needed to be replaced by EU arrangements. Under Article 115 of the Treaty of Rome member states had been allowed to suspend imports of goods from other member states where third countries were attempting to circumvent quotas through trans-shipment. Although this Article was restated in the Maastricht Treaty, with the ending of border controls it has not been employed since 1993. However, VERs were of more significance in limiting the volume of LDC exports and these survived 1992 on a Community basis. For although the Commission generally believes that many industries should be able to withstand import competition after the restructuring following from economic integration, footwear, consumer electronics and ceramic tableware all continued to face quotas. Thus, VERs were required from South Korea and Taiwan for both footwear, where they supplied one-third of all EU imports in 1987, and consumer electronics.

The most significant VER affecting LDCs was the Multi-Fibre Arrangement (MFA). Although MFA IV introduced a new mechanism whereby unused individual member state quotas could be transferred to other member states, in practice the total EU quota limit on LDC exports remained under-utilised. The elimination of individual member state VER quotas, as required by the SEM, offered potential benefits to LDC exporters. However, the future of MFA IV was bound up with the Uruguay Round negotiations of the General Agreement on Tariffs and Trade (GATT).

The move to a single market also precipitated a major confrontation with the World Trade Organisation (WTO), the successor to GATT, over the Banana Protocol (see Box 14.1). This threw into doubt the whole future of trade concessions under Lomé.

Technical standards

The SEM also required the adoption of common technical standards. The mutual recognition of certification implies that any LDC export need only satisfy the conditions for any one member state, but certification may in some cases only be required for non-EU producers, which may create opportunities for discrimination. The close involvement of EU industries in setting Community technical standards may also offer further opportunities for deterring non-EU competition.

EU standards have existed for some time in relation to the health of plant and animal product imports. Since 1993 all inspections are carried out at the first port of entry, or in the exporting country, and Community-wide clearance is given. This may result in tighter standards being applied to achieve uniformity, with adverse consequences for particular LDC exports, for example planting materials and cut flowers. A Directive for meat products requires Community licensing of both slaughterhouses and processing plants for all non-EU suppliers, presenting problems for some African exporters. Another Directive setting standards of water quality may pose a threat to South-East Asian shellfish exports.

Some aspects of EU–LDC trade relations were unaffected by the 1992 programme. For example, the national export credit agencies continued to operate independently. By contrast, 'tied aid' is required to be directed towards any EU

Box 14.1 The Banana Protocol

Over the ten years to 1992 the EC12 imports of bananas from the ACP countries doubled to 0.7 million tonnes, worth €413 m. The ACP's share of total banana imports had peaked at 25 per cent in 1986, but declined to 15.4 per cent by 1992. These are an extremely important source of export earnings and employment for a number of ACP island economies. For St Lucia, St Vincent and Dominica, for example, they represent over half of export earnings and employ one-third of the labour force of the Windward Islands. However, they are in competition in EU markets with exports of 'dollar' bananas from Central and South America, where large plantations have a cost advantage. These 'dollar' bananas dominated the German market, which accounted for one-third of all EU imports. Special arrangements had therefore been made to preserve their traditional markets in the UK, France and Italy. But these arrangements were incompatible with the abolition of Article 115 restrictions on intra-Community trade. The Commission had proposed imposing an import quota on non-ACP bananas (COM(92)359). However, the GATT negotiations were seeking the abolition of non-tariff barriers to the trade in agricultural products. Thus, the new regime commencing in July 1993 established a tariff quota of 2 million tonnes for non-ACP banana imports. Up to this limit a duty of €100 per tonne was imposed, increasing to €850 per tonne on any additional imports – an effective tariff of 170 per cent. ACP banana imports continued to be duty-free, but the CAP was extended to include support for EU banana production.

However, it was challenged before the WTO by the US and four major multi-national banana producers. In 1997 the Disputes Panel issued its Interim Report, ruling against the size of ACP quotas and the guarantee of 30 per cent of the EU market. However, unlike GATT decisions the EU was obliged to accept these rulings and, after the threat of a trade war with the the US, adopted a new banana regime from July 2001. This re-allocated quota shares to Latin American producers and committed the EU to a tariff-only regime by 2006. The EU has allocated €450 m over ten years to the twelve ACP banana producers to assist in the structural adjustment that will be necessary as they lose their preferential access to the European market.

exporter rather than exclusively to those of the member state granting the assistance. Of the $13.63 bn of bilateral aid of eight EU states in 1987, 57 per cent was partially or entirely 'tied'. This widening of the LDC recipient's choice of suppliers should significantly increase the real value of the aid, as enhanced competition should reduce prices.

The pattern of trade

In 2000 the EU imported goods to the value of €43.8 bn from the ACPs, €48.6 bn from Latin America, €64.6 bn from the Mediterranean and €178.4 bn from Asia (Table 14.2). In that same year exports to Asia were valued at €106 bn and to the ACP group only €39.7 bn.

In real terms LDC exports to the EU have increased dramatically since the EU's inception. In the 1970s the LDCs' export performance was particularly impressive, growing faster than either developed countries' exports to the EU or intra-EU trade. However, in the 1980s the position reversed equally dramatically, with only

Table 14.2 LDC–EU trade

	EU imports, € bn						
	1976	*1980*	*1985*	*1990*	*1995*	*2000*	*2003*
ACP	10.5	19.4	26.8	21.9	28	43.8	43.3
Asia	6.7	16	26	50.9	80.7	178.4	178.0
Latin America	8.3	13.7	25.8	25.7	30.4	48.6	47.8
Mediterranean	9.6	16.4	32.3	29.8	32.1	64.6	66.7
All LDCs	70.7	114.3	128.9	143.8			
Total EU Imports	157.7	269.9	399.7	461.5	545.3	1026.8	988.9

	EU exports, € bn						
	1976	*1980*	*1985*	*1990*	*1995*	*2000*	*2003*
ACP	9.6	15.7	17.4	16.6	27.3	39.7	40.4
Asia	7.5	13.1	29.4	41	80.3	106.6	86
Latin America	7.7	12	13.5	15.6	32.4	54.4	43.2
Mediterranean	13.3	19.8	29.8	28.5	50.6	86.6	81.2
All LDCs	550.9	83.4	121.7	134.2			
Total EU Exports	141.3	221.1	380.8	415.3	573.3	937.9	976.7

Source: Adapted from Eurostat

Table 14.3 LDC share of EU imports (%)

	1976	*1980*	*1985*	*1990*	*1992*	*1994*	*2003*
ACP	6.7	7.2	6.7	4.7	3.7	2.8	3.3
ACP non-oil	6.1	5.3	4.8	3.5	2.9		
Asia	4.2	5.9	6.5	11	13.6	13.1	15.3
Latin America	5.3	5.1	6.5	4.6	5.1	5.4	4.1
Mediterranean	6.1	6.1	8.1	6.5	6.2	6.1	7.3
All LDCs	44.8	42.4	34.7	31.2	29.2	34.2	

Source: Adapted from Eurostat

the LDCs experiencing a reduction in the value of their exports. In 1976 the LDCs accounted for 45 per cent of the EU's imports, but by 1990 their share had fallen to 31 per cent (Table 14.3). This deterioration in export performance can be accounted for by two factors: the switch in oil imports away from LDCs and the fall in primary commodity prices.

However, of greater long-term concern is the trend in manufactured exports. Although primary products dominate LDC exports, accounting for two-thirds of the total, it is the trend in manufactured products that would be expected to reflect the process of sustained economic development in LDCs. Unfortunately, this growth has been confined to a very small number of LDCs. While the share of the ACP countries in manufactured exports to the EU fell from 6.6 per cent in 1962 to 1.5 per cent in 1987, that of the six Asian newly industrialised countries (NICs) – Taiwan, Malaysia, Thailand, Singapore, Hong Kong and South Korea – demonstrated significant growth. In 1962 the Asian NICs accounted for only

1.7 per cent of EU manufactured imports, 16 per cent of the LDC total. In 1980 this share had reached 8.6 per cent of total EU manufactured imports and 60 per cent of the import of manufactures from the LDCs. By 1995 their share of LDC manufactured imports had risen even further, to 83 per cent. Worldwide, the NICs' share of the trade in manufactured goods was 21 per cent, which is comparable to the EU's 26 per cent and Japan's 24 per cent.

The NICs have continued to increase their penetration of the EU market, with their exports increasing 198 per cent between 1990 and 2000. By contrast Latin American exports only increased by 80 per cent and those from the Mediterranean by 126 per cent. But the most dramatic feature of recent years has been the rise of China. Over the last ten years its exports to the EU have increased by 516 per cent, and now represent 7 per cent of all EU imports. On current trends China will soon be a more important supplier to the EU than Japan.

The ACPs

Turning specifically to the ACP group among the LDCs, trends in their share of EU imports suggests that there has been little apparent benefit from the preferences given under Lomé. In 1976 the EU imported €10.5 bn of goods from the ACP countries, giving them a market share of 6.7 per cent. By 2000 their share of EU imports had fallen to 4.2 per cent and were worth €44 bn, roughly equal to the EU's imports from Norway. The ACPs have also failed to diversify with five commodities – oil, diamonds, gold, wood and ore – accounting for half their total exports to the EU (Table 14.4). Although manufacture exports doubled between 1976 and 1992 they still accounted for only 29 per cent of total ACP exports in 1992. This performance is also significantly poorer than that achieved by the non-ACP LDCs. Whereas these increased their processed goods exports by an average of 13 per cent per annum over the period 1976 to 1993 the ACP group only managed an increase of 4.4 per cent.

ACP exports are also dominated by a small number of countries. Ten countries account for three-quarters of all ACP exports to the EU. Of these South Africa is by far the most important and the only significant supplier of manufactured goods. It accounted for one-third of all ACP exports to the EU in 2000 (Table 14.5).

Table 14.4 ACP and LDC exports to EU

	EU imports 1993 (%)		Annual growth (1976–93)	
	Other LDCs	*ACP*	*Other LDCs*	*ACP*
Processed food	41.4	8.3	9.0	9.0
Chemicals	10.8	0.3	17.3	3.3
Textiles	45.1	2.3	11.3	9.4
Metal products	15.8	1.8	8.5	−3.8
Other manufactures	17.3	0.5	16.8	28.6
Total processed	21.7	1.1	13.0	4.4

Source: Adapted from Eurostat

Table 14.5 % ACP exports to EU (1992)

	ACP exports to EU (%)
Nigeria	22
Côte d'Ivoire	9
Cameroon	6
Gabon	6
Mauritius	5
Angola	5
Zaire	4
Congo	4

	EU as % total export earnings
Cameroon	74
Central African Republic	82
Equatorial Guinea	99
Mauritius	80
Niger	80
Sierra Leone	73
Uganda	75
St Lucia	72

Source: Adapted from Eurostat

However, South Africa is not eligible for the non-reciprocal trade preferences that are currently extended to the rest of the ACP group. The next largest ACP trading partner is Nigeria whose exports are dominated by oil. The largest importer of ACP products in the EU is the UK, which accounts for 20 per cent of the total.

Although Lomé appears of limited value from the perspective of the overall performance of the ACPs, it may have been significant in fostering and protecting exports of particular products. However, this is difficult to demonstrate, as can be seen from Table 14.6. Here, a comparison of ACP and total LDC shares in the growth of tropical products suggests a very mixed pattern. In the case of coffee, tobacco and palm oil, where there are significant ACP preferences, these countries had gained market share relative to other LDCs. But similar gains had occurred with tea, where there was no ACP preference. Nonetheless, the ACP countries dominate in the supply of certain tropical products to the EU, including pineapples, cocoa beans, palm nuts, raw sugar and wood.

For some non-traditional non-primary products, McQueen and Stevens (1989) have suggested that the foundations had been laid for significant export growth. Although the absolute value of these exports is small, totalling only 6.9 per cent of non-fuel ACP exports to the EU in 1987, they had shown sustained growth. These products are based upon processing raw materials that increase the value added of previously exported primary commodities. They include wood and leather products, cotton yarns, fabrics, clothing and canned tuna. In some cases, such as man-made yarns and veneers, this export growth had been associated with substantial ACP preferences over other LDC exporters, but this advantage failed to produce gains in market shares in other products, for example tinned pineapples and wooden furniture.

Table 14.6 The European Union and the Third World

	EU import ECU m. 1986–87	Import Share 1986–87		Average growth		ACP tariff preference margin
		LDC	ACP	1978–89 LDC	1986–87 ACP	
Bananas, fresh	1266.1	100.0	23.4	1.6	3.4	20
Pineapples	121.9	99.1	92.6	9.0	8.8	9
Coffee beans	5364.0	99.2	41.4	3.4	4.7	4.5
Tea	489.0	88.5	44.9	0.2	3.4	0
Cocoa beans	1506.2	100.0	85.0	4.5	3.7	3
Tobacco	1745.2	50.4	15.9	0.4	7.0	7.5
Palm nuts/kernels	17.8	97.4	92.3	−3.4	−2.9	0
Palmoil	392.3	99.8	24.1	4.9	6.3	5.5
Oilcake, meal	112.8	99.8	8.6	14.1	−3.1	0
Raw sugar	674.2	99.6	81.7	−0.0	1.2	L
Crude rubber	768.0	99.6	15.8	27.4	6.9	0
Sisal etc.	29.6	99.5	39.4	−1.0	−7.6	0
Wood, rough	744.7	81.3	78.4	−2.9	−2.1	0
Weighted averages*						
all products	–	75.7	34.0	4.0	3.9	–
crude products	–	91.2	44.7	3.8	4.3	–

Notes:
* Averages are weighted by 1986–87 total EU imports
L: Levy on non-ACP imports. The major ACP sugar producers have specific quantities of imports guaranteed at Community sugar prices
Source: Adapted from Comext

Similarly, studies of export diversification in individual ACP countries (McQueen (1990) of Mauritius; Riddell (1990) of Zimbabwe; Stevens (1990) of Jamaica, Kenya and Ethiopia) suggest some contribution from Lomé preferences, but again there is no evidence that it was the decisive factor.

Causes of failure

In certain commodities, the ACP countries in particular, and the LDCs in general, have achieved an increased market share in EU imports. However, over the two decades of Lomé the ACP group had seen their share of EU imports halve, while studies of the impact of the GSP upon non-ACP LDCs (Davenport, 1986; Langhammer and Sapir, 1987) suggested that it has been of very limited value in stimulating exports. Several factors might account for this. First, it had been suggested that it reflected a deterioration in LDCs' internal supply conditions and therefore their international competitiveness. Overvalued exchange rates, rising wage costs or capital shortages that lower productivity could all have undermined competitiveness. Similarly, poor infrastructure, an inadequate financial services sector or poor human capital may have been additional contributory factors. However, this does not explain the contrasting experience of LDC exports to the USA and EU. Whereas the value of EU imports had risen by only \$4.1 bn over the period 1979–89, US imports from LDCs increased by \$36.9 bn.

Secondly, it is argued that technological change is undermining the comparative advantage of LDCs. Automation and the microchip revolution are challenging the advantage LDCs have held in low labour costs for product assembly. Without this advantage production plants will tend to be located near their main markets, where design, marketing and production can be more easily integrated and production made more responsive to changing market conditions. The new automated methods of production, essential to the new sophisticated products, also require the specialist support industries only found in the developed world. Although this may be a long-term phenomenon that may challenge the competitive position of LDCs in the export of manufactures, it is unlikely to explain the short-term deterioration in their export performance, and again is unable to explain their differential experience in the US and EU.

Finally, many commentators have suggested that trade preferences were of limited value to many LDCs. Small preference margins, quantitative limits and problems associated with 'rules of origin' are all regarded as serious limitations. Rules of origin specify the minimum level of domestic value added for a product to qualify as originating from a given LDC, and therefore to receive the appropriate trade concessions. It has been argued that these rules have failed to take into account the changes in the international division of labour, with the growth of outward processing and off-shore assembly. The Lomé Convention restricted non-ACP inputs to 10 per cent of the good's domestic value added for it to qualify for duty-free access. These restrictions are particularly onerous for the Caribbean and Pacific ACPs who look to the USA and Japan for industrial partners (McQueen and Stevens, 1989).

More importantly, Lomé and the GSP had been compromised by other protectionist measures. Isolating the trends in the degree of protectionism by the EU presents a number of serious difficulties. These arise from the significance of non-tariff barriers to LDC exports, which take many forms, were often cumulative for particular products and for which information was difficult to obtain. They were also applied both at the national and the EU level.

Tariffs faced by the LDCs rarely appear to have presented any serious obstacles to most of their exports since the Tokyo Round of tariff reductions (1973–79). For example, the non-agricultural 'most favoured nation' average tariff is only 4.7 per cent. However, certain products did face significant duties – textiles 10–20 per cent, clothing 16 per cent and agricultural products under the CAP regime often exceeding 100 per cent.

In terms of the non-tariff instruments eight categories can be isolated: state aids to industries; public procurement restrictions; technical regulations; minimum import prices (under CAP); voluntary export restraints (VERs); quotas; anti-dumping duties; and surveillance. Public procurement restrictions, industry subsidies and technical regulations also distorted intra-EU trade and hence were a focus for harmonisation and EU control. Industry subsidies in particular have often inhibited LDC export growth, given their use in labour intensive industries where LDCs might be expected to demonstrate a comparative advantage. However, perhaps the most important barriers are the five remaining non-tariff 'trade instruments'.

Turning first to quotas, it was only in 1982 that member states began to publish a general list of quotas. Assessment of their impact was difficult given the level of aggregation, both by product and geographically, i.e. some member states applied quotas to individual countries, others to 'zones' of 30–50 countries. Although some quotas were not necessarily enforced, they remained available. Given these considerable qualifications there is still no evidence to suggest that the application of quotas had increased in later years, although France and Italy employed significantly more than other members of the EU.

However, the volume limits on LDC exports were more likely to arise under the more extensive VERs. There are two broad categories to consider – the Multi-Fibre Arrangement (MFA) and non-MFA VERs. The MFAs, first established in 1974, run for four years and currently involve VERs negotiated with 25 countries. The ACP countries are exempt from the MFA and therefore gain a significant advantage over other LDCs. Although negotiated at EU level they were subsequently expressed as national quotas. Successive MFAs became increasingly restrictive until the mid-1980s, with both more LDCs and more products being subject to quotas. By 1986, 60 per cent of LDC textile exports and 78 per cent of clothing exports were facing non-tariff barriers in developed country markets. A review of non-MFA VERs is more problematic but Pelkman (1987) concluded that they became popular in the late 1970s and were even more extensively employed in the early 1980s.

Short of VERs the EU may undertake surveillance of particular imports, i.e. the accelerated gathering of statistical information on imports from particular countries. This is not as innocuous a process as it might at first appear. It may require prior import documentation, which may be refused, or be used to inhibit LDC exports by threatening the imposition of other safeguards should they exceed informally notified growth rate limits. Surveillance is central to triggering the MFA's 'safeguard options' and it occurred with all 159 'sensitive' products in Benelux, France, Italy and the UK, but only to a very limited extent in Germany and Greece and not at all in Denmark. Pelkman suggests that the extent of surveillance increased over the period 1975–85, but since the early 1980s the Commission has attempted to reduce the number of approvals, requiring member states to make a more substantial case.

In contrast to the ad hoc approach taken to quotas and VERs, the EU has subscribed to the Anti-Dumping Code of GATT since 1980. Dumping is identified where the prices charged in export markets diverge from those charged for the product in the country's home market, i.e. it is a form of international price discrimination. Where there is evidence of dumping, and of a resultant 'material injury', an anti-dumping duty can be imposed. Although the EU subscribed to the GATT Code, the determination of 'normal prices' and the 'injury test' have led to accusations of hidden protectionism. The mere threat of investigation is often sufficient to ensure small LDC producers accept 'price undertakings', i.e. raise their export prices. In the period 1980–84 the EU initiated 218 anti-dumping investigations, with LDCs' exports being involved in 25 per cent of this total. Of these 54 cases, 25 resulted in 'price undertakings' being given and 15 in anti-dumping duties being imposed. From 1989 to 1993 the percentage of EU imports subject to anti-dumping duties fell from 2.2 per cent to 1.3 per cent (OECD 1996), but the prohibition of VERs under the Uruguay Round of GATT may lead to their more frequent use.

Finally, it must not be forgotten that the CAP continues to represent a serious obstacle to the development of LDC agricultural exports – not only to the EU itself, but also through the competition on world markets presented by subsidised EU exports of surplus produce. The major losers from the CAP among the LDCs include: Argentina and Brazil, efficient producers of cereals, meat and sugar; Turkey, fruit and vegetables; and the Philippines and West Indies, sugar. Nonetheless the LDCs' share of EU imports of fruit and vegetables has risen from 47 per cent to 63 per cent since 1976, although most of this increase has come from Asian and Latin American suppliers.

Future prospects

The future prospects for LDC trade with the EU will be determined by developments within the EU, its external policies and the world trade environment. In particular, the impact of tax harmonisation and the outcome of the Uruguay Round of GATT will be examined.

Tax harmonisation

As part of the single market programme, harmonisation of national tax regimes may occur. It has been proposed that all member states should set their VAT and excise duties within common bands, with excise duties limited to alcohol, tobacco and petroleum products. If adopted, this will have important implications for LDC exports of coffee, cocoa and tobacco. Currently coffee is subject to excise duties in many member states, for example Germany 41 per cent, Denmark 15 per cent. Abolition of these duties would raise the value of EU imports by €466 m (3 per cent), the main beneficiaries being Brazil, Colombia and Côte d'Ivoire. Similarly, the abolition of excise duties on cocoa and the imposition of a 5 per cent VAT rate would increase LDC exports by €50 m. By contrast, an upward harmonisation of excise duties on tobacco within the EU would produce a 40 per cent price rise, with a consequent 10–15 per cent fall in LDC exports, worth €50–80 m. Here the major losers will be Brazil, Zimbabwe, India and Malawi.

The Uruguay Round

The latest Round of the GATT was completed in 1994 and included the creation of the World Trade Organisation (WTO). It will affect LDC trade relations with the EU in a number of ways.

The trend towards increasing agriculture protectionism was challenged in the Uruguay Round by the thirteen-nation Cairns Group, which included both developed (Australia, Canada and New Zealand) and developing countries (Brazil, Chile, Philippines, Malaysia). This group pressed for the inclusion of agricultural products in the negotiations, a position supported by the USA but opposed by the EU. Through the reduction in agricultural protectionism the Cairns Group sought the eventual elimination of EU agricultural subsidies and the movement towards free trade, benefiting not only efficient LDC and developed country agricultural exporters, but also EU consumers. The reduction in agricultural subsidies was one of the major areas of contention between the USA and the EU in the GATT negotiations. The final agreement required the substitution of tariffs for the existing complex system of quotas, VERs, controls and variable levies. The average tariff reduction was 36 per cent over six years. However, as this was calculated on the basis of the large difference between Community and world prices in the years 1986–88, when tariffs were at a maximum, the real reduction was considerably smaller. In addition, the EU cut its agricultural export subsidies by 36 per cent over the six years from 1994. The overall effect was to raise world food prices to the disadvantage of those LDCs who are net importers. It also eroded the market advantage enjoyed by those LDCs who had privileged access to the EU, and reduced EU prices. Overall, the ACPs were expected to see a deterioration in their trade balance of $226 million in temperate and $177 million in tropical agricultural products (Davenport et al., 1995).

The preference erosion that occurred under the agricultural changes also applied to manufactures. For LDCs as a whole manufactures have become of increasing importance. In 1970 manufactures represented only one-third of their export earnings, but by 1992 this had risen to 75 per cent. By 1979 EU tariffs on manufactured imports were already low, with MFN tariffs at an average of 6.3 per cent. The LDCs enjoyed a further 2 per cent reduction under the GSP, and ACP manufactures entered duty-free. The Uruguay Round agreed a further reduction in MFN tariffs to 3.9 per cent, eroding the GSP and ACP preferences. But these average tariffs disguise the discrimination against particular products. Clothing, leather, rubber, shoes and transport equipment all experienced small cuts on high tariffs. Unfortunately, these products are of particular importance to some LDCs. But overall these changes were expected to cost the ACP countries only $317 million in lost exports.

Of more significance was the agreement to bring textiles back under the auspices of GATT. The MFA was phased out over ten years, with tariffs replacing quotas, but these will remain relatively high at 12 per cent. An overall increase in textile and clothing exports to the EU of 20 per cent over the period was expected. Efficient producers such as China, India and Pakistan were likely to gain at the expense of established exporters such as Jamaica and Mauritius. Other VERs either had to conform with GATT rules or be phased out within four years.

The overall effect of the Uruguay Round on LDC world exports was mixed. The ODI (1995) has estimated that by 2005 Africa's exports would be reduced by 0.72 per cent on their 1992 figure, Latin America's increased 0.62 per cent and Asia's increased by 2.05 per cent. For the ACPs as a group, they were expected to see their exports fall by 1.7 per cent. Indeed, the general benefits from the new GATT agreement were to be received principally by the developed world. The OECD estimates that, of the $250 bn increase in world trade over a decade, three-quarters would accrue to the developed countries. The Asian NICs were expected to gain $7.1 bn–$8.3 bn from farm liberalisation, $1.8 bn from textile trade and $1.1 bn from services. India was expected to gain $4.6 bn and South America $8.0 bn, but Africa as a whole was expected to lose $2.6 bn.

In terms of the ACPs' trade with the EU alone, export revenues were expected to fall by €256 m (1.3 per cent of export earnings). The biggest losers were anticipated to include Ethiopia, Fiji, Trinidad and Tobago, Guyana, Mauritius, Senegal, Jamaica, Tanzania and Malawi.

Aid

Aid disbursements from the EU are provided from two sources – the European Development Funds (EDF), associated with the Lomé and Cotonou Conventions, and the general EU budget. The EDF was the major source of EU development assistance in 1990 (Table 14.7) but by 2000 expenditure from the EU's general budget for 'external actions' was more than three times greater. Over these ten years there was also a significant shift in the focus of EU assistance towards Central and Eastern Europe. The EDFs cover a period of five years and, although administered by the Commission, have separate member state contributory arrangements from those for the EU's general budget. There is also a separate EDF Committee to supervise it.

From 1984 to 1993 the aid disbursed by the EU increased at an average annual rate of 20 per cent. By 1994 aid totalled €4.1 bn making the EU the second largest multilateral donor after the World Bank. However, this represented only 17 per cent of the total official aid given by member states and was smaller than the bilateral aid budgets of France or Germany. In 2002 EU Official Development Assistance (ODA) had grown to €6.5 bn, of which 23 per cent was provided by the EDF. It is now the fourth largest aid donor, in its own right, after Japan, the US and Germany.

Table 14.7 Allocation of EU aid, € bn (% General budget)

	1990	%	2000	%	2002	%
European Development Fund	1256		1548		1852	
General EU Budget	953		5049		6051	
of which:						
Eastern Europe and Central Asia			1212	(24)	1101	(18)
Food aid	485	(51)	437	(9)	417	(7)
Asia and Latin America	245	(26)	858	(17)	635	(10)
Mediterranean	103	(11)	909	(18)	765	(13)
Humanitarian aid	20	(2)	54	(10)	474	(8)
NGOs	85	(9)	131	(3)	152	(2)
Total EU aid	2209		6597		7904	

Source: Adapted from *Aid Review*, 1992–93 and 1994–95, Eurostat and Annual report on development policy and external assistance 2002

Lomé

The Lomé and Cotonou Conventions are the basis of aid provision to the ACP countries. There is no requirement that the funds must be disbursed within the period of any given Lomé convention. Thus by May 1989 74 per cent of Lomé III funds had been committed, but only 11 per cent disbursed.

The aid is administered principally through the European Development Fund (EDF) which had been established under the Treaty of Rome. Lomé III, which commenced in 1986, was associated with the sixth European Development Fund (EDF6), disbursing €7.4 bn. In addition, the European Investment Bank (EIB) made available €1.1 bn to the ACPs. Some 80 per cent of EDF6 funds were allocated to agreed programmes of conventional aid projects in each ACP, while 20 per cent funded specific purposes such as STABEX and emergency aid (non-programmable). STABEX began with Lomé I and provides partial compensation to the ACPs for falls in agricultural export earnings, either from a decline in commodity prices or from a fall in output; 48 'soft' commodities were covered. Similar earnings support was offered to states dependent upon mineral exports under SYSMIN, created under Lomé II. There is also provision under Article 188 of the Treaty for assistance with the financing of imports during structural adjustment.

Programmable aid was divided, at the commencement of a Convention, into shares for each region and state. Each ACP government then negotiated a National Indicative Programme (NIP), setting out, in broad terms, the framework within which the aid will be spent. Within this framework specific projects were then planned.

Lomé IV

Although the economic situation of many ACP countries has deteriorated throughout the period of the Conventions, this deterioration became more marked during the period of Lomé III. Falling commodity prices, rising world interest rates and substantial borrowings resulted in a serious debt problem for many LDCs, especially the African States; for example, ACP African countries' debt had risen from $56 bn in 1980 to $128 bn in 1987.

Two major issue began to be addressed during Lomé III, and became a major focus of debate in the negotiations for Lomé IV: trade versus aid, and structural adjustment in the ACPs.

With regard to trade the northern member states of the EU sought a further extension of trade preferences on temperate agricultural goods to ACPs rather than further increases in the volume of EU aid. However, they have faced opposition from the southern member states, whose produce would face the enhanced competition.

The second major focus of debate within the EU had been the degree to which aid should be directed towards countries undertaking 'structural adjustment' policies, i.e. economic reforms involving cuts in government expenditure, removal of price controls, devaluation and privatisation. Initially, under the Conventions, the ACPs were left with substantial freedom in deciding their aid priorities, but with Lomé III an attempt was made to influence ACP development strategies by stating

EU preferences, for example development of the food sectors, including drought and desertification control. Thus three-quarters of funds allocated under the NIPs were focused upon rural development, and the EU succeeded in establishing a 'policy dialogue' with each ACP government, asking them to indicate the range of policy measures they would take to support these priorities.

Nonetheless, in the negotiations over Lomé IV, some member states, especially the UK and the Netherlands, wished the ACPs to focus even more clearly upon structural adjustment policies by reallocating a greater proportion of EU aid funds away from conventional projects. The EU influence over the ACPs is clearly greater the larger the proportion of Lomé funds that have not been pre-allocated to countries under their NIPs. A further constraint on the ACPs arises with the issue of coordination of Lomé aid with IMF/World Bank funding, which is itself conditional on a commitment to structural adjustment. Again, the greater the proportion of Lomé aid dispersed under 'special structural adjustment' funds the greater the potential for such coordination.

A structural fund had been established in 1988, under Lomé III, of €500 m to provide balance of payments support for the poorest African States, in response to the STABEX fund becoming overdrawn. The eligibility criterion to draw from this fund was that each LDC must have introduced appropriate economic policies, and agreements with the IMF/World Bank were taken as evidence of this. Thus, ACPs that have obtained a World Bank structural or sectoral adjustment loan (SAL/SECAL) may then apply for EU funding for a general import support programme. About half of the ACPs have sought adjustment credits from the World Bank. In the absence of World Bank support the EU will make its own assessment as to a specific sectoral import support programme. However, fundamental disagreement with the IMF/World Bank may create difficulties for ACPs then applying to the EU.

Lomé IV was finally signed in December 1989 and, unlike previous Conventions, ran for ten years until the year 2000. The financial resources allocated to the

Table 14.8 Volume of aid for the first five years of Lomé IV in comparison with Lomé III

	Lomé III Value (million ECU[1])	%	Lomé IV Value (million ECU)	%
Aid	4790	64.54	6845[2]	63.38
Risk capital	635	8.58	825	7.64
Stabex	925	12.50	1500	13.89
Sysmin	415	5.61	480	4.44
Structural adjustment support (SAS)	–	–	1150	10.65
Soft loans	635	8.58	–	–
Total EDF	7400	100	10800	100
EIB	1100		1200	
Total resources	8500		2000	

[1] 1 ECU = approximately £0.7 or 69 French francs (February 1990)
[2] Part of it can be used for SAS

Source: European Commission

first five years of the Convention totalled €12 bn, a 20 per cent increase in real terms over Lomé III (Table 14.8). Of this total, €10.8 bn will be disbursed through EDF7 and the remaining €1.2 bn through the EIB. Recognising the increasing financial difficulties of the ACP countries, more of the assistance will be in the form of grants rather than loans, and EIB loans were at lower interest rates (3–6 per cent) than under Lomé III. Of the EDF funds, €1.25 bn was set aside for assisting regional cooperation among the ACPs themselves and €1.15 bn has been allocated specifically to structural adjustment support (SAS). The Commission had proposed an SAS fund of €2 bn and, in view of the smaller sums allocated, anticipated that only 30 to 35 ACP countries would benefit. These were most likely to be those already receiving IMF/World Bank approval. Thus, Lomé IV SAS could be regarded as merely complementary to IMF/World Bank funding.

In terms of trade concessions there was a reduction in restrictions on 40 agricultural products; the value of these concessions varies considerably. In the case of rum, all restrictions were abolished after 1995, but with other products concessions had been limited. For example, the ACPs sought an increase of 30,000 tonnes in the EU imports of rice and received an increase of only one-tenth of that. Critics suggest that it failed to provide the ACPs with the transparent trading regime for agricultural products that they needed. However, these agreements must be seen within the context of the wider GATT negotiations under the Uruguay Round, which to a considerable extent have superseded it.

STABEX and SYSMIN were both expanded and revised under Lomé IV. STABEX funding was increased by 62 per cent to €1.5 bn in the face of falling commodity prices, and the threshold for assistance was lowered from a product contributing 6 per cent of an ACP country's total export earnings to a contribution of 5 per cent. STABEX transfers were also no longer repayable, but the EU had greater control of the use of the funds, directing them particularly towards greater diversification.

SYSMIN was increased to €480 m with a change from loans to grants. It also now covered uranium and gold, as well as copper, cobalt, phosphates, manganese, bauxite and alumina, tin and iron ore. Any ACP where 20 per cent of export earnings was derived from these minerals could now seek assistance.

Finally, Lomé IV offered a crucial concession on the issue of rules of origin. If at least 45 per cent of the value added of a product could be shown to have been created within an ACP, it could be imported into the EU duty free (compared with 60 per cent under Lomé III) as long as no market disturbance was entailed.

Lomé IV also emphasised the role of private sector development within ACPs. This was to be encouraged with the provision of risk capital through the EIB, technical assistance and investment protection, environmental assessment of development projects, encouragement of 'micro projects' with non-governmental organisations and the encouragement of active population policies.

The mid-term review

The mid-term review of Lomé IV began in May 1994 and had been intended only to consider the levels of aid to be given for the remaining five years, under EDF8. However, the international environment had changed significantly with the end of the Cold War and the EU was dissatisfied with the lack of results from their long-term aid programme. Increasing emphasis was being placed upon the adoption of structural adjustment policies by the LDCs, i.e. devaluation, privatisation, free markets, tight monetary and fiscal policies, by all international aid donors. The EU sought to enhance its influence over the ACP governments to achieve these structural changes.

Administrative failings

In addition to these general criticisms the actual operation of the Lomé Conventions had been subject to complaint. In particular, attention was drawn to the slowness of its disbursement of allocated funds. At the end of the third year of Lomé IV (EDF7) only 15.5 per cent of funds had been paid, while in 1994 EDF5 had finally closed, having disbursed only 87 per cent of its monies. STABEX was criticised for its lack of clear rules and failure to monitor the use of funds. In 1993 it had disbursed no funds at all and in 1994 met only half of requests. SYSMIN was regarded as even more unsatisfactory; under Lomé III it had disbursed only 35 per cent of its funds.

The evaluation of EU project aid had also been regarded as inadequate, while the Commission itself recognises that one-third of projects were likely to have offered poor value for money. This relatively poor record had given weight to the argument that greater emphasis should be placed upon macro structural adjustment funding. Thus, project aid had recently taken a smaller share of EU aid, declining from 66 per cent to 42 per cent over the last ten years.

Concern has also been expressed about the role of the EU Humanitarian Office (ECHO), which was created in 1992 to coordinate emergency aid. EU emergency aid has been growing rapidly and there is the possibility that funds will be diverted from long-term development assistance. This problem is exacerbated by the separation of the ECHO from the other EU Development Directorates and its poor coordination with them. Seen as bureaucratic and inefficient, it disperses most of its funds indirectly though international non-governmental (NGOs) and UN agencies.

The provisions

Despite an original Commission proposal of €16.5 bn for EDF8 and an increase in the number of EU aid donors from 12 to 15, the total value of Lomé IV aid for its final five years was pegged in real terms to €14.96 bn (see Table 14.9), including €292 m of unutilised funds from previous EDFs. France became the largest contributor followed by Germany. The UK remains the third largest contributor but was the only EU member to cut its payments (see Table 14.10).

There was a 16 per cent reduction in tariffs on a number of products, including cereals, pork and rice, but sensitive products such as olives, wine and lemons were not included. The tariff-quota on sheep, poultry, milk products and pears was

Table 14.9 Financial Protocol, 1995–2002

	€ million		2002 payments
EDF VIII	12967	EPF IX	1852
of which:			
Risk capital	1000		188
STABEX	1800		1.6
SYSMIN	575		87.2
Structural adjustment	1400		284
Emergency aid	260		17
Interest rate subsidies	370		18
Regional cooperation	1300		
Programmed	6262		959
European Investment Bank	1658		

Source: *The Courier*, No. 155, European Commission, January 1996; Annual report on development and external assistance 2003

Table 14.10 Major contributors to the EDF

	€ million	
	EDF VII	*EDF VIII*
Belgium	433	503
Denmark	227	275
Germany	2840	3000
Spain	645	750
France	2666	3120
Italy	1418	1610
Netherlands	609	670
UK	1791	1630
Austria		340
Finland		190
Sweden		350
EIB	1200	1658
Total	12140	14965

Source: *The Courier*, No. 153, European Commission, September 1995

doubled. More importantly, the rules of origin were relaxed. The limit on the non-ACP value of inputs for the product to still enjoy duty-free access to the EU was raised from 10 to 15 per cent of domestic value added. A further concession was given allowing inputs from neighbouring non-ACP LDCs to be regarded as a part of the domestic value added.

To address the problem of slow disbursement and unallocated funds, and to enhance the influence of the EU in ensuring the commitment of ACP countries to structural adjustment programmes, aid was now to be phased. Only 70 per cent of a country's NIP aid is allocated for the first three years, the remaining 30 per cent being conditional upon satisfactory performance. Satisfactory performance now included the issue of human rights and Article 366 of the Convention would allow the EU to suspend aid if an ACP infringes these rights.

Cotonou

The successor Cotonou Agreement was signed in June 2000 and will run for 20 years, with provision for revision every five years, coinciding with a new EDF. The number of members of the ACP group has now increased to 79, although South Africa continues to be excluded from the current trade preferences. Although presented as a radical departure from the arrangements of the Lomé Conventions, the Cotonou Agreement shares many features with its predecessors, especially Lomé IV (see Salama and Dearden, 2001).

The major change in the new Convention is in regard to the trading preferences offered by the EU to middle-income LDCs. The current non-reciprocal preferences will continue to be offered until 2008, but over the intervening years the middle-income LDCs will be required to negotiate WTO-compatible reciprocal Economic Partnership Agreements (EPAs). The EU is anticipating that these will be established on a regional basis. From 2008 the new EPAs will be phased in over a 12-year period. Those ACPs who feel unable to agree an EPA with the EU may be offered the less generous General System of Preferences, which itself is due for review in 2004. The remaining sugar and beef Protocols will be subject to review in the light of the EPAs. The 39 low-income ACPs will continue to enjoy their current concessions under the 'Everything-but-Arms' non-reciprocal trade initiative, concessions which are being offered to all 48 low-income LDCs. This will remove tariffs and quotas for virtually all products and will be in place by 2005. However, as a consequence of this new EU concession to all low-income LDCs the ACPs will see their relative advantage eroded. The existing 15 per cent limit on non-ACP/EU value added (rules-of-origin) continues to apply.

With regard to the aid component, the total value of resources to be made available over the period 2000–07 is €25 bn. Of this EDF9 will provide €13.5 bn and the remaining undispersed balances of the €9.9 bn from previous EDFs. In addition, the European Investment Bank will be providing €1.7 bn of funds. The aid instruments have been radically simplified into two 'envelopes' – grants (€11.3 bn) and the risk/loan Investment Facility (€2.2 bn). The creation of a single grant envelope eliminates the previous distinction between programmable and non-programmable aid. Thus, the separate STABEX and SYSMIN funds disappear. Further, the grant facility represents a move away from individual project finance towards more general sectoral and general budget support. Of the grant element €1.3 bn is specifically allocated to funding regional programmes. The EU regards itself as having a particular contribution to make to the fostering of regional integration and the regional aid programme will complement the move to regional EPAs.

For each ACP there will be a Country Support Strategy, based upon an indicative resource allocation covering five years. In turn this is translated into rolling annual National Indicative Programmes (NIPs). There will also be a 'performance assessment' every two and a half years (mid-term and end-of-term review). Rolling programming will be carried out at the level of the local EU Delegations, as part of the trend towards decentralisation of aid administration. This is intended to enhance the dialogue between the EU and the ACP recipient. A similar approach to monitoring is being taken to the regional programmes.

Development of the private sector was seen as crucial to the long-term development of the ACPs. Cotonou therefore places an emphasis upon promoting the public–private sector dialogue, building the capacity of private sector organisations and providing financial support. The €2.2 bn Investment Facility is a revolving fund, reinvesting its returns, to be administered by the EIB. It will provide equity investment, credit guarantees and concessional loans, and will focus upon assisting small local businesses, local financial institutions and enterprises being privatised.

Cotonou completes the process begun under Lomé IV in that the funds allocated to individual ACPs are now subject to rolling review and can no longer be regarded as an entitlement. A country's aid will be allocated on the basis of both need and performance. The criteria for assessing 'need' include per capita income, economic and social development indicators, level of indebtedness and dependence on export earnings. The 'performance' assessment will include progress in the implementation of institutional reform, efficiency in the use of resources, poverty reduction, sustainable development and macroeconomic and sectoral policy performance. Clearly this assessment process is vulnerable to arbitrary application. Although it is intended that the performance assessment should be the product of 'dialogue' between the EU and the ACP government, the role of the Commission in developing transparent and consistent criteria will be crucial.

Of even greater political sensitivity was the increasing emphasis being placed upon human rights, democracy and the rule of law. The EU insisted that these be included as 'essential' elements of the Cotonou Agreement, breaches leading to the possible imposition of sanctions, including the suspension of aid. The EU had also wished to include good governance, but after ACP resistance this was included as a 'fundamental' element, breaches of which will follow its own distinct procedure, although even here aid may be suspended in serious cases as a measure of last resort. The problem of corrupt and inefficient government was also addressed through the increased emphasis upon the role of 'civil society' – i.e. the private sector, local NGOs, trade unions, farmers' organisations, etc. Similarly there is recognition of the potential to develop the role of local government. These 'non-state actors' are seen as having a central role in the rolling review process. To assist both good governance and the capacity building of these non-state actors, substantial funding is to be allocated to 'institution building'. Institution building, gender and the environment are all identified in Cotonou as 'thematic' or cross-cutting issues to be addressed across all development initiatives.

Private investment

The long-term success of LDCs' economic development depends crucially upon investment. Although this may be funded by aid, as both grants and loans, increasing emphasis is being placed upon the role of the private sector. This can be seen in the €2.2 bn allocated to the Investment Facility under Cotonou, providing risk capital and loans to foster the development of the private sector. Private investment is regarded as offering greater efficiency. It is more likely to identify commercially viable projects, implement them efficiently and provide essential complementary factors, for example managerial skills, marketing and distribution.

In the 1950s the USA had already begun to shift its focus of investment away from LDCs towards other developed countries. This trend was followed in the 1970s by the UK and in the 1980s by Japan. By this date most EU countries had already re-orientated their investment, for example France and West Germany were only directing 10–20 per cent of their overseas investment to the LDCs. In 1983 direct investment in the LDCs had fallen dramatically to only $9 bn from $14 bn. However, during the 1990s there was a rapid recovery, with a fivefold increase between 1990 and 1995, averaging $25 bn per annum. The share of the LDCs in world foreign direct investment (FDI) had increased from 15 per cent in 1990 to 32.5 per cent in 1992. Part of this was attributed, by the IMF, to debt equity-swaps in Latin America, whose share in FDI had risen to 11.2 per cent. Japanese investment in Asia had increased substantially, raising their share of FDI to 18.6 per cent, with China an important recipient. This pattern is reflected in the shares of world FDI inflows over the years 1995–99 (Table 14.11), which are dominated by the EU (37 per cent), the USA (25 per cent) and Asia (16 per cent). By contrast Africa received an inflow of only €7 bn per annum (1.4 per cent). Nonetheless even in 1993 net private flows to the ACPs were 16 per cent of the total flow of funds to these countries.

Six of the EU's member states account for the bulk of the Community's foreign investment (France, Germany, Italy, the Netherlands, Spain and the UK). In the mid-1980s their annual investment in the LDCs was averaging $4.5 bn; by 1989 this had increased to $10 bn. However, this investment had been concentrated in the NICs (35 per cent in 1988/9) and Latin America (38 per cent). In 1990 this outflow fell significantly. Although this may be explained as a response to the Kuwait crisis and the onset of recession in Europe, it is also possible that the advent of the single market had an adverse impact.

Developments in Central and Eastern Europe have also generated substantial demands for investment funds. The Community responded by initiating the foundation of the European Bank for Reconstruction and Development, with a capital of

Table 14.11 Distribution of FDI inflows by region and country, 1982–92 (in percentages)

Country/Region	1982–87	1988	1989	1990	1991	1992
Western Europe of which:	31.5	37.9	44.9	52.5	49.8	52.0
EU	28.2	35.9	41.3	48.0	44.4	49.7
US	41.3	39.2	36.5	27.0	19.8	7.0
Japan	0.2	0.1	0.1	0.0	0.2	0.1
LDCs of which:	21.8	17.5	14.0	15.0	24.1	32.5
Africa	2.8	1.7	2.5	1.0	1.7	1.9
Latin America and Caribbean	8.9	5.7	3.2	4.2	9.3	11.2
East, South and South-East Asia	9.3	9.4	7.9	9.3	12.5	18.6
Total of above	94.8	94.7	95.5	94.5	93.9	91.6
Other countries	5.2	5.3	4.5	5.5	6.1	8.4
All countries (US$ billion)	67.5	159.1	196.1	207.9	162.1	158.4

Source: UN CTAD (1994), World Investment Report 1994, Transnational Corporations, Employment and Workplace

€10 bn, one of whose principal aims was to act as a catalyst for private sector investment in Central and Eastern Europe. By contrast the poorer LDCs might appear a less attractive destination for corporate investment.

Over the period 1995–99 the EU provided an average of €17.3 bn per annum of FDI to South America, €6.3 bn to Central America, €7.8 bn to Asia and €3.2 bn to Africa. In 1999, of the EU's stock of foreign investment of €1187 bn only 2.8 per cent was in the ACP countries, 3.9 per cent in the first wave NICs (Hong Kong, South Korea, Singapore and Taiwan) and 9.3 per cent in Latin America.

Immigration

Finally, mention might be made of the impact upon immigration control policy of the creation of the SEM and the Treaty on European Union (TEU). So far our discussion has focused solely on the movement of goods and capital. However, for some LDCs, especially those of North Africa, the EU has been a significant destination for emigration. Faced with rapidly increasing populations, but limited employment creation, emigration has made some contribution to reducing these pressures, while remittances have been an important source of income. The creation of the single internal market entails free movement of labour and removal or minimising of border controls. In turn this implies the need for the development of a common immigration control policy.

In 2000 of the one million increase in the EU population 680,000 arose from international migration. Sixty per cent of the net migration into the Community was accounted for by Italy, Germany and the UK. But despite the increasing average age of Europe's population there has been increasing political pressure to curb illegal immigration and the abuse of the asylum system. The TEU singled out immigration control as an area for a 'twin-track' approach of both inter-governmental agreements and Community law (see Baldwin-Edwards, 1991; Geddes, 1995). It adopted cooperation provisions for the harmonisation of asylum policies and immigration controls, and amended the Treaty of Rome to allow the Community to establish common visa requirements. The draft Regulation on visa requirements, based upon the policies agreed by the Schengen group of EU countries, requires visas for most visitors from LDCs. However, the Dublin Agreement, addressing asylum applications, has been found to be inadequate and will be amended. More radically there has been pressure from a number of member states, especially the UK and the southern EU member states, who are often the first point of entry, to link aid to LDCs to cooperation in stemming the flow of illegal immigrants and in repatriation.

Conclusion

In 1989 EU external assistance was €2.3 bn; by 2002 it had grown to €6.6 bn. However, as significant has been the change in its orientation. In 1989, 94 per cent of aid was directed at the ACP countries and Latin America. By 2002 Central and

Eastern Europe, Central Asia and the Mediterranean countries were taking almost half of EU assistance. This change resulted from two factors – first, the increasing concern over political instability in North Africa and Central and Eastern Europe, with the concomitant threat of mass immigration and, secondly, the decision in 1992 that member states should contribute increasing amounts to the general EU budget for external assistance to non-ACP countries. This allowed funding of an aid policy aimed at meeting Europe's new political concerns but also placed traditional ACP aid through the EDF under pressure.

At the same time the EU is seeking greater effectiveness in its aid programme. The desire of the EU to have greater leverage over the LDC governments' use of funds has led to the end of the 'entitlement' culture of Lomé and the adoption of rolling programming, subject to constant review. Although the new Cotonou Agreement continues to emphasise partnership and dialogue, the focus is now upon performance, with increasing attention to the political objectives of human rights and democracy, as well as the goals of good governance and the rule of law. Where central government weaknesses are seen as major obstacles, an enhanced role for 'civil society' and the private sector is seen as the way forward. This model is informing the approach of the EU to all its relations with developing countries.

Commitments have been made, by the EU, to coordination and complementarity between the aid programmes of the Community and member states, and coherence between its development and other policies. However, there remains a long way to go. There is a fundamental political conflict between those member states who advocate a distinct development policy, with the need for a clear poverty reduction objective, and those who see development as merely one aspect of the Community's wider external relations agenda. This is reflected in the continuing debate as to the separation between DG Development, responsible for the ACP states, and DG External Relations, responsible for all other LDC aid programmes. Similarly the integration of the EDFs into the general budget of the EU continues to be debated (budgetisation), complicated by the differing basis for member states' contributions.

At the same time member states are demanding fundamental reforms of the Commission's aid administration. In response the implementation of the aid programme has been centralised in EuropeAid and a process of decentralisation of decision-making and staff to the EU's country delegations has begun. A greater emphasis is also being placed upon quality control, although critics remain concerned that the Commission places too much emphasis upon the rate of disbursement of funds, rather than upon the effectiveness of the aid programmes.

But many issues remain unresolved. For the ACPs the negotiations have yet to commence for the new EPAs and a question mark hangs over the future coherence of the ACPs as a group in the face of pressures from the EU for regionalisation of its relationships. The approach of the EU to assessing 'need' in the LDCs remains unclear, as does its attitude to perceived violations of human rights, democracy, rule-of-law and good governance objectives. Meanwhile, the Millennium trade round of the WTO may change the context of the debate.

With the end of the Cold War the EU has adopted a far more critical approach to its aid programme. Its attention has shifted to the process of enlargement and the demands of the 'near abroad'. While paying lip service to the objective of global poverty reduction, wider political considerations, both internal and external, will continue to have a profound influence in shaping EU development policy. Only in trade may the LDCs gain from the opening up of the EU market under WTO pressure, especially for the agricultural products currently protected by the CAP. But to take advantage of these opportunities will require the structural transformation in their economies that is at the heart of the development problem.

References

Baldwin-Edwards M (1991) 'Immigration after 1992', *Policy and Politics*, Vol. 19, No. 3, pp. 199–211.

Cecchini P (1988) *The European Challenge: 1992, The Benefits of a Single Market*, Wildwood House, Aldershot.

Davenport M (1986) *Trade Policy, Protectionism and the Third World*, Croom Helm, London.

Davenport M (1990) 'The External Policy of the Community and its Effects on the Manufactured Goods of the Developing Countries', *Journal of Common Market Studies*, Vol. 29, No. 2, pp. 181–200.

Davenport M, Hewitt A and Koning A (1995) *Europe's Preferred Partners?: The Lomé Countries in World Trade*, ODI Special Report, London.

European Commission (1992) *Proposal for a Council Regulation (EEC) on the Common Organisation of the Market in Bananas*, COM (92)359, Brussels.

European Commission (1994) *Council Resolution for Applying a Three-year Scheme of Generalised Tariff Preferences (1995–97)*, COM (94)337 final, Brussels.

European Commission (1996) *Relations between the European Union and the ACP Countries on the Eve of the 21st Century*, COM (96)570 final, Brussels.

Geddes A (1995) 'Immigration and Ethnic Minorities and the EU's "Democratic Deficit"', *Journal of Common Market Studies*, Vol. 33, No. 2, pp. 197–217.

Langhammer R and Sapir A (1987) *The Economic Impact of Generalized Tariff Preferences*, Thames Essays 49, Gower, London.

Matthews A and McAleese D (1990) 'LDC Primary Exports to the EC, Prospects post 1992', *Journal of Common Market Studies*, Vol. 29, No. 2, pp. 157–79.

McQueen M (1990) *ACP Export Diversification: The Case of Mauritius*, ODI Working Paper 41, London.

McQueen M and Stevens C (1989) 'Trade Preferences and Lomé IV; Non-traditional ACP Exports to the EC', *Development Policy Review*, September.

OECD (1996) *Indicators of Tariff and Non-Tariff Trade Barriers*, OECD Publications, Paris.

ODI (1995) *Developing Countries in the WTO*, Overseas Development Institute Briefing Paper No. 3, London, May.

Pelkman J (1987) 'The European Community's Trade Policy towards Developing Countries', in C Stevens (ed.), *Europe and the International Division of Labour*, Hodder & Stoughton, London.

Riddell R (1990) *ACP Export Diversification: The Case of Zimbabwe*, ODI Working Paper No. 38, London, June.

Salama C and Dearden S (2001) *The Cotonou Agreement 2001*, European Development Policy Study Group (EDPSG) Discussion Paper 20.

Stevens C (1990) *ACP Export Diversification: Jamaica, Kenya and Ethiopia*, ODI Working Paper 40, London, September.

Further reading

Davenport M and Page S (1989) *Regional Trading Agreements: The Impact of the Implementation of the Single European Market on Developing Countries*, ODI Report, London, October.

Dearden S (2002) *The European Union and the Commonwealth Caribbean*, Ashgate, Aldershot.

ODI (1989) *The Developing Countries and 1992*, Overseas Development Institute Briefing Paper, London, November.

ODI (1997) *Foreign Direct Investment Flows to Low-income Countries: A Review of the Evidence*, Overseas Development Institute Briefing Paper, London, September.

Salama C (2002) *The Euro–Mediterranean Partnership: Political and Economic Aspects*, EDPSG Discussion Paper 23.

Zimmermann K L (1994) 'Some General Lessons for Europe's Migration Problem', in H Giersch (ed.) *Economic Aspects of International Migration*, Springer-Verlag, Berlin.

Zimmermann K L (1995) 'Tackling the European Migration Problem', *Journal of Economic Perspectives*, Vol. 9, No. 2, pp. 45–62.

See also the following websites:

European Forum on International Cooperation: **www.euforic.org**
European Development Policy Study Group: **www.edpsg.org**
Overseas Development Institute: **www.odi.org.uk**

Chapter 15

Economic relations with the Triad and emerging economies

Frank McDonald

Introduction

For many years the EU tended to regard commercial relationships with European countries as its top priority. This was reflected in the efforts that went into enlarging the EU, establishing trading agreements with nearly all European countries, and the emphasis placed on integrating the countries of Central and Eastern Europe into the EU's sphere of economic and political influence. The current enlargement of the EU, with the prospect that most European countries will either be members of the EU or strongly linked to its economic institutional framework, has led to external economic relationships becoming increasingly focused on non-European issues. Trade relationships with the USA and Japan have had a strong influence on external economic relations for many years because of trade disputes and the desire to provide means for dialogue on areas of common interest with these large and important economies. As these countries, together with the EU, form the basis of the Triad, trading and investment issues within the Triad have had a prominent place in the EU's external economic relations policies. However, emerging economies such as China, India and the newly industrialised countries (NICs) in Asia are becoming significant trading partners of the EU and this has increasingly led to a perceived need in the EU to develop improved economic relations with these countries.

The spread of trade liberalisation from its predominant focus on trade in goods to trade in services and to matters connected with the protection of intellectual property and foreign investment rules has increased the importance of economic relations in these matters and has led to the development of ways to improve dialogue with major trading partners on these issues. The introduction of the euro led to the rise of a new world currency that has had important implications for economic relations with the USA.

This chapter investigates economic relationships with the Triad and with emerging economies and also considers the development of dialogue on trade in services and investment rules within the Triad and with the emerging economies. Finally, the impact of the euro on economic relations with the USA is considered.

The Triad

The trade and business relationship between the USA, Japan and Europe is often referred to as the Triad – a term popularised by management theorists (Ohmae, 1985). The countries of the Triad are the powerhouses of the world economy. The economic relationships between the members of the Triad have a strong impact on the transmission of booms and slumps across the world economy. The mechanisms that link these economies in the economic cycle are not clearly understood, but trading and investment links play a key role in the process. Equally important, or perhaps more important, are the links created by international financial markets. The centres of these international financial markets are in the USA (New York and Chicago), Japan (Tokyo) and Europe (London and Frankfurt). Changes in stock, futures and exchange rate markets in one of these centres are quickly picked up by the other centres, and funds flow freely between these markets in response to the changes. This process is of great importance in the transmission of cyclical changes in economic activity. The fairly minor effects of the financial crisis of 1998 among the Asian NICs on member state economies indicate that the strength of the linkages between the EU, the USA and the Asian economies is not symmetrical. The strongest links are between the USA and the EU, and between the USA and Japan. The links between the EU and Japan are not as well developed as those with the USA, and the links to the Asian NICs are at an early stage of development. The linkages between these economies are further examined in Box 15.1.

Another reason for the importance of the Triad is that most of the large multinational corporations have their base in one of the countries of the Triad. Many of these companies are also world leaders in their fields. There is little doubt that, of the members of the Triad, the USA is the most important economy. The USA has the largest economy in terms of absolute and per capita GDP, the dollar is the most important currency in international trade and the USA is also the home base of many of the largest multinational companies in the world. About 30 per cent of the top 100 multinationals (as measured by size of foreign assets) are American and 18 per cent are Japanese. However, European countries have the largest number of such multinationals, with 38 per cent.

The establishment of EMU will affect relationships with Japan and the USA; the emergence of the euro as a world currency will have implications for international money markets. Currently the international money markets are dominated by the dollar, but the euro is increasingly becoming an important world currency. It is hard to see the dollar losing its dominant position in the near future. However, the development of the euro in international financial markets will affect the role of the dollar in the medium to long term. This will have important implications for relationships within the Triad.

American influence, therefore, arises not only from the size of the US economy and the important role that the dollar plays in world trade, but also from its relatively good economic performance in the 1990s and early 2000s. The political and military power of the USA further adds to American dominance in most matters connected with international relations.

The development of economic integration in Europe and the creation of the North American Free Trade Area (NAFTA) between the USA, Canada and Mexico

Box 15.1 Economic linkages in the Triad

US Exports and Imports ($ bn) 2003

	Exports	Imports
Western Europe	164.8	266.2
Japan	52.1	118.0
NICs	71.3	92.5
China	28.4	152.4
Canada	169.7	224.1
Mexico	97.4	138.1

Source: **www.census.gov**

The size of trade flows indicates that flows of exports and imports between Europe and the USA are more important than the flows between Japan and the USA. Trade flows between the USA and the newly industrialised countries (NICs) of Asia are less than those with Japan and are considerably lower than those with Europe. China provides a large share of US imports but is not a large market for US exports. The importance of China and the NICs is mainly connected with their role as providers of imports to the US markets. Interestingly, the most significant trading partners of the USA are Canada and Mexico. Mexico is a more important trading partner of the USA than is Japan. This highlights the growing importance of NAFTA for the US economy.

Overall about half of world trade in goods and services is between the members of the Triad and about 90 per cent of foreign direct investment outflows come from multinational corporations based in the Triad. Of the top 500 companies (as measured by turnover) about 70 per cent have their headquarters in the Triad. US multinationals account for about 50 per cent of the Triad-based top 500 companies with Japan having approximately 20 per cent (Rugman, 1999).

Clearly, the Triad is dominated by the USA, but Europe is more important than Japan in terms of both trade flows and direct foreign investment flows. China and the NICs are important as sources of imports for the USA, but Canada and Mexico are more important than Europe as trading partners for the USA.

hold the prospect that the Triad may evolve into three trading groups, based on NAFTA, a 'Fortress Europe' and Japan (possibly with close links to the Asian NICs). Another possibility is the development of Asia–Pacific Economic Cooperation (APEC) as a free-trade area that would include the East Asian economies, the USA and Canada (Funabashi, 1995). The Triad could develop into a complex set of relationships between regional trading blocs (see Box 15.2).

Conflict and cooperation with the Triad

Conflict between members of the Triad would raise serious difficulties for the world economy. Theory suggests that in such circumstances cooperation can result in mutually beneficial outcomes, whereas conflict can lead to all parties suffering losses. However, these theories also suggest that cooperation between such parties can be very difficult to achieve and maintain.

Box 15.2 The Triad and regional trade blocs

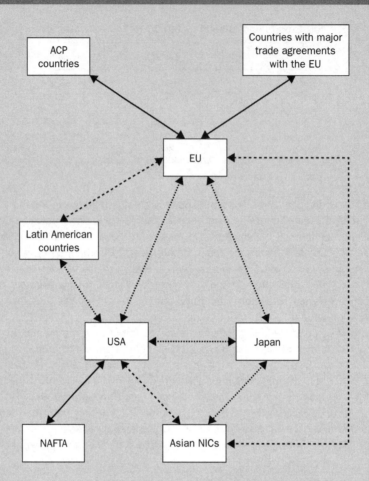

Asian NICs = Asean countries, China, South Korea, Taiwan and Hong Kong

Countries with major trade agreements with the EU: Turkey, most CEECs that are not members of the EU, Maghreb countries (Algeria, Morocco and Tunisia) and Mashreq countries (Egypt, Jordan, Syria and the Lebanon)

Key:

◄──► = institutional links with strong trading and business component

◄┄┄► = substantial trading links

◄-·-► = less substantial trading links

The links between the main members of the Triad and regional trade blocs mean that the bulk of world trade is connected with the economic relationships of the Triad.

Box 15.3 Cooperation and conflict

Suppose that the EU and Japan are considering whether or not to grant trade concessions by easing or eliminating barriers to trade imposed on foreign firms.

		EU	
		A	B
Japan	A	2.2	0.3
	B	3.0	1.1

A = policy of granting trade concessions
B = policy of not granting trade concessions

If both parties adopt A, the outcome is a pay-off of 2 each. If they both choose B, the outcome is a pay-off of 1 each. If the EU chooses A, and Japan B, the pay-off becomes 0 for the EU and 3 for Japan (vice versa if the EU chooses B and Japan adopts A). This is the classic 'prisoner's dilemma' game, where the outcome for a player depends on the choice of policy of the other player. Obviously, the best aggregate outcome is for both to choose trade concessions and adopt policy A. However, if one player chooses B and the other player chooses A, the pay-off is 3 for the player who opts for B and 0 for the player who chooses A. There is therefore an incentive for both players to choose policy B, as by doing this the minimum pay-off is 1 and the maximum is 3, as opposed to a minimum pay-off of 0 and a maximum of 2 if policy A is adopted. In these circumstances a non-cooperative, or conflict, outcome prevails, even though the cooperative outcome yields the greater aggregated benefits.

The issue of cooperation versus conflict can be analysed using game theory. This theory is useful for analysing international relations as it provides a relatively straightforward method of investigating cooperative and non-cooperative behaviour between nations (see Nicholson, 1989). A simple example of the use of game theory to illustrate international trade liberalisation is given in Box 15.3.

The simple nature of these games tends to conceal some of the problems of using such models directly to explain real world behaviour. First, traditional economic theory suggests that unilateral trade concessions are better than no trade concessions. This follows from the gains to consumers of reducing trade barriers that lead to lower prices and higher output. In these circumstances it is not clear why the policy of not reducing trade barriers confers benefits to either party in the game. In the real world, however, trade concessions are often denied unless there is a reciprocal granting of concessions. In trade liberalisation in services and foreign investments, reciprocity is normally an important consideration. Even in the granting of trade concessions on goods, agreement on trade liberalisation packages is often dependent on reciprocal agreements to reduce barriers. The rationale for these actions may be based on placing consumer interests on a lower level than producer interests. It is also possible to provide a theoretical justification for this behaviour, as some of the new theories of international trade suggest that unilateral trade concessions are not necessarily beneficial. In a world of increasing returns to scale and imperfectly competitive market structures, there can be a sound economic case for providing strategic protection to allow domestic industries to reap advantage from economies of scale and to benefit from the learning effects of expanding domestic production. However, the advocates of these new theories maintain that it is probably not possible to pursue such policies efficiently and that the objective of free trade is on balance the best policy (Krugman and Obstfeld, 2003). Nevertheless, to engage in unilateral free trade while your trading partners are implementing strategic protection policies is likely to harm your economy. This suggests that the implementing of free-trade policies is best achieved by negotiations on some kind of reciprocal basis.

Secondly, there is the assumption that the games are played in isolation from each other, which implies that the players do not learn. If the non-cooperative solution emerges from several games, it might be expected that the players would learn how to make arrangements to allow for cooperative outcomes to be achieved. This can be analysed using the theory of supergames, where the same game is repeated a large number of times. The problems of playing supergames in international trade relations are discussed by Keohane (see Guerrier and Padoan, 1988). In such games problems arise with free-riding, when some players in the game reap benefits from cooperative solutions without themselves granting concessions. This results in a sub-optimal outcome in the sense that the maximum possible benefits to the system as a whole are not reaped. It might be argued that Japan has done this by benefiting from trade concessions that have opened up US and EU markets to foreign competition, without granting significant liberalisation of the controls on entry to Japanese markets. The solution to this problem revolves around various forms of reciprocity. In this respect the insistence by the EU and the USA on using the principle of reciprocity may be wise.

This does not mean that the way in which the EU is using this principle is useful in achieving a cooperative outcome. Indeed, Ishikawa (1990) maintained that the EU adopted too rigid a concept of reciprocity in dealing with Japan and the USA. The main problem was the attempt by the EU to obtain 'mirror image' treatment. This involves the granting of very similar concessions by all parties, and presents problems in areas such as financial services where laws and regulations govern access to the market. In the past the EU has insisted that, in order for Japanese or US firms to gain equal access to the European financial services market, EU firms must face the same conditions in the Japanese or the US market. This was asking Japan and the USA to adopt in their home markets the emerging EU rules and regulations governing access to a single European financial services market. This hard form of reciprocity is unlikely to succeed. The principle of equivalent but not identical access would seem to be useful to achieve a cooperative solution to this problem.

These problems increase the need for the EU, Japan and the USA to find ways of playing these supergames in a manner that permits cooperative solutions to be found. This requires mechanisms to control free-riding by utilising loose forms of reciprocity. Systems to reduce cheating and non-fulfillment of agreements are also needed. Keohane regards international institutional innovations as having an important role in this process. Institutions can monitor and publish data to identify, and therefore deter, cheating and free-riding behaviour. These institutional forums can also be used to forge issue linkages. This involves linking separate issues to reach agreement, so that, for example, the EU could grant US firms access to the European financial services market in return for US concessions on agricultural problems. Hence institutional forums and agencies could play a key role in allowing cooperative outcomes to emerge. The Uruguay Agreement led to the creation of the WTO (Bourgeois, 1995), which is seeking to promote a more open trading environment and to liberalise trade, particularly in the area of services – General Agreement on Trade in Services (GATS). However, the WTO has a large number of members and unanimous agreement is required to achieve settlements on trade liberalisation. The failure of the WTO to make progress in the Doha round of liberalisation has highlighted the problems of reaching agreement in large-scale multilateral negotiations. In these circumstances bilateral negotiations between the EU and the USA and Japan, or Triad-based talks, may help to forge agreements that could form the basis for WTO agreements.

The existing institutional frameworks could hamper such developments. International agencies such as the IMF, G8 and the OECD have representation from member states rather than from the EU. Only in the WTO does the EU represent all member states. With the growing importance of EU–Japanese–US relations, it might help to achieve cooperation if the EU rather than member states were the prime negotiator. The creation of the SEM added impetus to the role of the EU in these agencies. The establishment of EMU in the EU has further increased the role of the EU in the main international monetary agencies. In the future not only trade issues but international monetary issues are likely to be within the competence of the EU, rather than handled by member states. In these circumstances good relations between the members of the Triad could become very important. This implies a need to change international institutional arrangements to allow the EU a greater role.

Trading relations with the USA

The USA adopted a benign attitude towards the EEC in the 1950s and 1960s. The demise of the Bretton Woods system and the increasing industrial power of the EEC led to a change in US attitudes towards the Community. The prime dispute has been over the CAP (see Chapter 11). The periodic crisis in the world steel industry led to some bitter trade disputes. Both parties were heavily involved in helping their steel industries, the USA by the use of import quotas and the EU by a host of policies implemented under the ECSC. This led to both sides accusing each other of unfair trading practices, and to the implementation of a series of trade restrictions (Featherstone and Ginsberg, 1996). In 2003 the USA introduced tariffs to protect US steel producers leading to a protest to the WTO by the EU, Japan and other steel producing nations. The WTO decided that the US tariffs were contrary to WTO rules and they were eventually removed in 2004.

The US insistence on trying to apply US law to foreign individuals and companies outside the USA has also caused friction with the EU. This is the so-called extraterritoriality problem. An early example of this problem was the US embargo in 1982 on the use by European firms of US goods, patents and licences to build the Siberian pipeline. This was a pipeline to carry natural gas from Siberia to Western

Europe. The USA regarded the pipeline as a threat to the independence of Western Europe, and the US government tried to take unilateral action to control the activities of European firms engaged in work for the pipeline. This action was deeply resented in Western Europe, and eventually the embargo was withdrawn.

The passing of the Omnibus Trade Act in 1988 led to a further deterioration in relationships. The Super 301 provisions of this Act required the US government to identify countries using unfair trading practices, and to take unilateral action to induce such countries to stop these practices. The EU maintained that such trading conflicts should be resolved by WTO rather than by unilateral action. No actions were taken against the EU under the provisions of Super 301, but the threat of action soured relationships between the USA and the EU.

In the 1990s the LIBERTAD (Helms-Burton) Act and the Iran and Libya Sanctions Act (ILSA – commonly referred to as the 'D'Amato Act) provoked further tension by raising questions about the use of extraterritoriality powers by the US government. These Acts related to US foreign policy objectives to isolate Cuba (Helms-Burton), Iran and Libya. The USA threatened to exercise federal laws regarding investments in Cuba and trade with Iran and Libya on foreign-owned subsidiaries in the USA and on executives of foreign companies who entered the USA. In October 1996 the EU began a disputes procedure with the USA over the Helms-Burton Act and lodged strong opposition with the US government over the ILSA. An agreement was reached in April 1997 that allowed the USA to preserve the letter of these Acts but guaranteed that they would not be enforced against EU companies (European Commission, 1997b).

The trade disputes between the EU and the USA have been increasing. Both parties have issued complaints about the other's trading behaviour. The EU complained about US policies for public procurement contracts, as a host of federal, state and even local government rules and regulations control public procurement in the USA. Federal and state governments also operate 'Buy American' policies on many public procurement contracts. The EU is also concerned with the system of setting and maintaining technical standards in the USA. These standards are issued by a multitude of federal and state authorities, and often pay little regard to international systems of setting standards. This makes it difficult for EU firms to collect information to comply with US standards. Meanwhile, the EU is moving to a system of common European standards that will make it relatively easy for US firms to gather information on European standards.

The USA has complaints about EU trading practices. The public procurement directives to open up public tendering within the EU discriminate against non-EU firms. A directive issued in 1989 called for most European television broadcasting to be domestically produced. The Uruguay Round was agreed only after this dispute over broadcasting was dropped from the negotiations. The Broadcasting Directive was clearly aimed at reducing US television programmes on European networks. There have also been complaints from the USA about the large subsidies from European governments for the European Airbus. As the USA is the only alternative source of such civil aircraft, this is regarded as a protectionist policy against the USA. The CAP provides a perennial source of US complaints about EU trading practices.

Disputes over regulations in health and safety and environmental standards have also soured EU–US relationships. The USA has complained about EU regulations on beef hormones, the EU ban on the use of leg-hold traps in the fur trade and eco-labelling. The EU has argued that US regulations in areas such as fuel economy standards, drugs inspections and an embargo on tuna caught without due considerations for possible harm to dolphins were types of NTBs that were being used to protect US companies from legitimate competition. It has been argued that differences in regulations are not being used primarily to protect domestic industries, but rather they reflect cultural attitudes, for example the ban on leg-hold traps (Vogel, 1997). Vogel argues that, because the EU and the USA exercise a large influence in the development of regulations that are used to govern world trade, it is important that they find ways to cooperate in the setting and development of regulations. However, if cultural differences are the root of the diversity of regulatory systems, it will be difficult to reach agreement. Furthermore, Japan and the NICs are likely to be unhappy about accepting an EU–US arrangement for establishing trading rules. In these circumstances the prospects for WTO rules are bleak. The scene seems to be set for the continuance of disputes between the USA and the EU over regulations that affect trade.

Trading relations with Japan

The post-war incorporation of Japan into the world trading system has been a difficult process. Although Japan applied for membership of GATT in 1952, it was not granted membership until 1955. Even then many West European countries refused to grant Japan MFN treatment, because of claims that Japan engaged in unfair export practices and that the Japanese domestic market was effectively closed to Western exports. Many Western European countries continued to apply quantitative restrictions on some Japanese exports. It was not until the mid-1960s that Japan was granted MFN treatment and admission to the OECD. Consequently, by the time the EU developed a common commercial policy the attitude of Western European countries towards Japan was one of distrust and suspicion.

It is difficult to find rational reasons for this attitude. There was a legacy of bad relations because of the export policies of Japan in the 1920s and 1930s. In this period the Japanese had practiced large-scale dumping of imitation Western products and had frequently ignored trademarks and patents. In the 1950s Second World War experiences resulted in opposition from the UK and the Netherlands to granting Japan full rights in the world trading system, but these explanations seem inadequate to explain the hostile attitude of Western Europe towards Japan in the immediate post-war period. The cultural differences between Japan and Europe, and a marked lack of interest about Japan, may have contributed to this hostility. In this period Europe was preoccupied with the growth of the Cold War, and the early moves towards European unity. When Europe finally began to take an interest in Japan, the dramatic growth of the Japanese export-led industries led to what might be regarded as a kind of paranoia. There developed a school of thought that regarded Japan as a country engaged in economic warfare to destroy Western industries. The persistent and growing trade surplus of Japan only added to this paranoia, particularly as Japanese exports in the 1960s and 1970s tended to be concentrated in sensitive sectors, such as shipbuilding, steel and textiles. During the 1970s and 1980s the growth of Japanese exports of cars and consumer electronics made further inroads into highly sensitive sectors. In the late 1980s Japan became a leading exporter of computers and other IT equipment. The increasing dominance of Japanese exports in these sensitive areas has led to a continuing hostility towards Japan. This rather sad history of trading relations between Europe and Japan has had a powerful influence on EU attitudes.

The EU has a variety of complaints about Japan's protection of its domestic market, in particular impenetrable technical rules and regulations, exclusion from public procurement contracts and heavily bureaucratic import documentation procedures. Ishikawa (1990) argues that these problems are also experienced by Japanese firms seeking to export to the EU. Nevertheless, the EU maintains that market access into Japan is hampered by complex regulations that are considerably more of a barrier to entry than the rules that govern entry into the SEM. The Commission has threatened to refer conflict over quotas on fish imports and the taxation systems for alcoholic beverages that discriminated against foreign-produced products to the disputes procedures of the WTO.

The export of services to Japan is hampered by legal barriers, and the Japanese marketing and distribution system is complex and involves close collaboration between Japanese producers and wholesalers and retailers. This makes it difficult for EU companies to sell consumer goods in Japan, unless they have Japanese subsidiaries. The marketing and distribution costs that EU companies face in Japan are therefore likely to be higher than for Japanese firms selling in the EU. Japanese companies have close collaboration with each other under the auspices of the Japanese Ministry of International Trade and Industry (MITI). Much of the collaboration that is encouraged by MITI would be illegal if carried out in the EU. The EU therefore maintains that this is tantamount to an unfair trading practice.

The Japanese government instituted a Deregulation Programme 1995–98, and in 1997 an Action Plan for Economic Structural Reform. The Commission submitted a list of 200 proposals to the Japanese government that suggested how the Deregulation Programme and Action Plan might improve market access for European companies. Attempts are also being made to complete an agreement with the Japanese government over mutual recognition of testing and certification procedures for EU–Japanese trade. The Commission hopes to obtain a similar agreement to those it has already reached with the USA, Canada and Australia. Talks are also being held to open up the Japanese market for services and for FDI inflows.

The Commission collaborated with MITI on an Export Promotion Programme (EXPROM) to help European companies to enter the Japanese market. The Gateway to Japanese Export Promotion Campaign is geared towards SMEs and is seeking to help European companies to take advantage of the liberalisation programme that is slowly opening up Japanese markets to foreign competition. Ten sectors have been identified as offering good potential for European companies: medical equipment; packaging machinery; internal moving equipment; food; waste management technologies; alcoholic beverages; marine equipment; and IT equipment and software. However, reducing the cost of exporting by removing NTBs is not sufficient to promote an increase in trade. A reduction in NTBs in Japan will stimulate an increase in exports to Japan only if companies can reap profits from exporting. This depends on the revenue and especially the cost conditions that companies face (see Exhibit 15.1).

Exhibit 15.1 The profitability of exporting

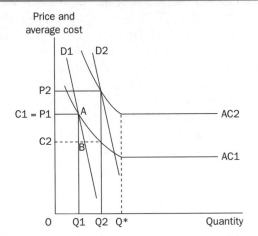

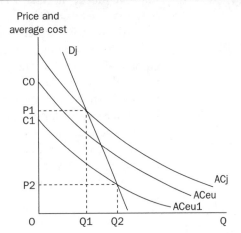

(a)
Q* = minimum efficiency scale
D1 = demand in the EU
D2 = demand in the EU plus demand in Japan
AC1 = average cost (including normal profit)
AC2 = average cost including the cost of exporting
Cost of exporting = transport costs, transaction costs
of fulfilling regulations, and exchange rate risk

(b)
ACj = average cost in Japan
ACeu = average cost in EU plus the cost of exporting to
Japan
ACeu1 = average cost in EU plus new lower cost of
exporting to Japan
Dj = demand in Japan

If the market is competitive, P will equal AC. If there were no exports a price of P1 and output of Q1 would emerge and normal profits would be reaped. However, at P1 : Q1 minimum efficiency scale is not reached. If the company took advantage of the possibility to export Q1–Q2 to Japan at a price of P2, the costs of exporting would be covered and normal profits would be reaped from the output that is exported. As output rises from OQ1 to OQ2 the average costs of producing output for the EU market falls from OC1 to OC2. This leads to an increase in profits (on EU output) shown by the area C2C1AB.

If the costs of exporting fall because of reductions in the transaction cost of complying with Japanese regulations, AC2 would move downwards, thereby increasing the volume of exports and further increasing the profits available from output for the EU market. However, when output reaches Q* (i.e. minimum efficiency scale) no additional profits from EU output are available because in the example illustrated above the cost of producing output becomes constant after minimum efficiency scale output is reached. The incentive to export would then arise from the contribution to normal profit from exported output.

The costs of exporting mean that European companies cannot enter the Japanese market at low levels of output because the costs of supplying the Japanese market (a cost close to CO) are greater than the price received (i.e. P1). However, if the cost of exporting fell such that the average cost became ACeu1, European companies could enter the market as the price is now higher than the cost of low levels of output (i.e. cost close to C1). It would now be possible for European companies to enter the Japanese market at low levels of output and gradually expand exports to the Japanese market, thereby moving down their AC. In these circumstances European companies would end up with the entire Japanese market with price of P2 and output of Q2. In this case, reducing the cost of exporting would allow European companies to exploit their comparative advantage.

The above examples illustrate that the incentive to take advantage of improved market access to Japan depends to a larger extent on the profitability of exporting, which is strongly influenced by production costs (level of output relative to minimum efficiency scale) and the costs of exporting.

The efforts by the EU, backed by even greater pressure from the USA, to improve market access to Japan seem to have lessened some of the problems with the Japanese trade surplus. The perceived success of the market access strategy and the growing contact between the Commission and the Japanese government seem to have led to an improvement in EU–Japanese relationships from the rather frosty climate of the 1980s. The Japanese economy encountered a series of economic and financial crises in the 1990s that led to a long-term decline in Japanese growth and a consequent decline in Japanese influence in EU markets. The persistent problem in EU–Japanese relations in this period has been connected to attempts to kick start the Japanese economy so that it can once again be a fully functioning part of the engine of growth and development in the Triad. Increasingly, the EU has regarded trading relations with the NICs and particularly China as more problematic than relationships with Japan.

Trading relations with the NICs and China

Relationships between the EU and the Asian NICs and China are not as developed as those with the USA and Japan. However, as the Asian NICs and China have increased their share of the EU market, the Community has extended its relationships with these countries in efforts to find solutions to trading problems. In the early 1990s there were several visits by senior members of the Commission to the NICs in attempts to develop dialogue on trading matters. These efforts culminated in 1996 in the first meeting in Bangkok of the Asia–Europe Meeting (ASEM). The second meeting of ASEM was held in London in 1998. Economic and business issues form an important part of the work of ASEM as it provides an umbrella organisation for a number of specialised economic forums – Asia–Europe Business Forum, Investment Promotion Action Plan and co-operation between customs authorities to develop better procedures for dealing with export and import documentation. The establishment of ASEM provides an institutional structure that allows the EU and the Asian NICs to discuss problems related to trading and business links. Therefore, the EU has a number of institutional frameworks that allow for discussions on trading problems with the Asian NICs.

In the main the EU takes the view that the NICs and China should be encouraged to liberalise their trading systems to grant companies in the EU easier access to their markets. Thus, the Commission has complained about the close relationship between South Korean manufacturers and their subcontractors and distributors – the so-called 'chabeol' system. There has also been concern over the difficulties of tendering for public procurement contracts. The EU claims that these systems act like a series of NTBs, and that they are a significant barrier to entering the markets of South Korea. These complaints from the EU and the USA are very similar to those made about the difficulties of entering the Japanese market because of the system of 'keiretsu' (the collaborative relationships that exist between Japanese assemblers, suppliers and distributors, based on close financial links and technical collaboration). These problems have led the EU to embark on a process of seeking to promote 'fairer' market entry conditions and trading arrangements with South Korea and the other Asian NICs.

The Commission has imposed a number of anti-dumping measures on mainly Asian NICs, for example electronic weighing scales from Singapore, South Korea, Malaysia and Thailand. Very few non-Asian countries have been subject to anti-dumping duties. China has been the target of the largest number of anti-dumping and surveillance measures since 1999 (**www.europa.eu.int/comm/trade/index**).

The EU initially adopted a hostile approach to the rise of new low-cost Asian competitors in Community markets. The arrival of these new competitors has stimulated growing interest by the EU in the trading activities of the NICs and China and the EU is taking a very similar approach to the NICs to that taken to Japan. The main complaints against the NICs are very similar to those levelled against the Japanese. In essence, these complaints are often based on accusations that these economies do not operate on European norms for the conduct of business. The issue of the transfer of jobs to China because of large-scale foreign direct investment in manufacturing plant is not as pronounced in the EU as it is in the USA. This is probably because the main destination of manufacturing plant foreign direct investment from the EU has been to the Central and Eastern European countries. However, European investment in China and increasingly in India is beginning to focus attention on issues of job transfer to these countries. It is likely, therefore, that this issue will assume increasing importance in relationships between the EU, China and India.

Cooperation with major trading partners

The linkages that exist between the members of the Triad mean that macroeconomic changes in one of the members of the Triad are likely to spill over to the other members. This leads to a coordination problem (see Chapter 2). The persistent recession in Japan in the 1990s and early 2000s illustrated the nature of the spill-over effect. The Japanese economy experienced low growth in the late 1990s and the government was unable or unwilling to take appropriate macroeconomic policy measures to stimulate growth in Japan. This led to low growth of imports and contributed to the fall in the value of the yen. The latter effect led to a rise in Japanese exports and, in combination with the low growth of imports, contributed to the continuance of trade surpluses with the USA and the EU despite improved access to the Japanese market. This example illustrates that Japanese macroeconomic conditions have implications for trading conditions in the USA and the EU, and also for those countries closely connected with the Triad.

The asymmetric nature of the linkages in the Triad (i.e. US dominance) means that the spill-over effects do not have equal effect. Recession or booms in the USA tend to have more impact on trading conditions in the Triad than do such factors in the EU and Japan. The financial crisis in some of the Asian NICs in 1998 demonstrated the asymmetric nature of spill-over effects within the Triad and those countries that are closely associated with it. The crisis led to a marked fall in the price of financial assets and large-scale depreciation of the currencies of many

Asian NICs, although it did not have very significant effects on the EU and the USA. The largest effects were experienced by Japan, but they were not sufficient to have any marked effect on economic conditions in Japan. The distribution of the effects of the crisis depends on the amount of trade and investments that companies had with the Asian NICs. The impact of a revival in the Japanese economy on the Asian NICs would be pronounced and has been considered as the most useful contribution that could be made to help the Asian NICs to recover (*Financial Times*, 1998).

The institutional frameworks that exist among the members of the Triad and associated countries do not provide a suitable means of discussing problems that arise from macroeconomic factors (see Box 15.4). The IMF, BIS and G8 discuss these issues, but they are not specifically Triad-based forums. Moreover, they do not provide the sort of practical arrangements that exist within the NTA, ASEM or APEC where forums have established structures to discuss issues related to trade, market access and FDI flows. However, macroeconomic problems are normally discussed in these forums only at formal and largely ceremonial meetings of the heads of government.

Box 15.4 Major institutional frameworks within the Triad

EU–USA Transatlantic Agenda

The New Transatlantic Agenda (NTA) was established in 1995 when agreement was reached to develop the 1990 Transatlantic Declaration into a more work-like body. The NTA has four main objectives:

- Promotion of peace, stability and democracy.

- Cooperation on global challenges – environmental issues and organised crime.

- Promotion of economic relations and expansion of world trade.

- Building bridges between business, civic and academic communities.

The last two objectives have significant implications for trading and business links between the EU and the USA. Cooperation between the EU and the USA within the NTA was important in securing a WTO agreement to remove progressively all barriers to trade in the IT and telecommunications sectors. The Transatlantic Business Dialogue component of the NTA enabled an agreement to be reached to develop a system of mutual recognition of testing and certification procedures in EU–US trade. This is seen as an important step towards the objective of the NTA of establishing a transatlantic marketplace – a type of single market for EU–US trade. The NTA has also provided a variety of forums where problems related to liberalisation of trade in services and the establishment of rules on foreign investment can be discussed. This has led to several proposals being made to governments and to the WTO on the best methods for promoting trade and of overcoming problems related to trading activities.

Asia–Europe Meeting (ASEM)

ASEM was inaugurated in 1996 at a meeting in Bangkok. This forum includes all of the Asian NICs and Japan. It provides a forum for sharing information and for discussion of economic relationships,

Box 15.4 (*continued*)

development issues, environmental concerns and educational and cultural matters. The second ASEM meeting was held in London in 1998. Much of the work of ASEM has involved establishing bodies to gather and disseminate information on economic, business, environmental and cultural conditions and problems in the ASEM countries. The economic and business forums, especially the Asia–Europe Business Forum (AEBF), have identified a number of problems associated with trading and are working on ways to reduce the obstacles to trade that arise from tariffs and NTBs. However, ASEM does not have the same kind of practical agenda as the NTA. Moreover, the large differences in the cultures and economic development of the members of ASEM mean that it is very difficult for clear policy proposals to emerge from ASEM-based forums. However, ASEM may represent the beginnings of an institutional framework that could develop into a practical system of resolving problems connected to EU–Asian trade.

EU–Japan framework

A Joint Declaration signed in 1991 established the basis for an annual meeting between the Presidents of the European Council and the Commission with the Japanese Prime Minister as well as a variety of bodies to discuss particular areas of interest in EU–Japanese relationships. The EU–Japan framework covers political dialogue, economic and trade matters, and global challenges (pollution and organised crime). The framework allowed the Commission to make a number of suggestions to the Japanese government on how the deregulation of the economy could be framed in ways that would facilitate attempts by EU companies to enter Japanese markets. The framework has also helped the Commission to collaborate with MITI to promote Japan as a market for EU-based companies. As well as these market access issues, the framework has also facilitated the development of cooperation schemes in the areas of R&D and environmental protection issues.

Asia–Pacific Economic Cooperation (APEC)

APEC was established in 1989 to promote economic integration of the countries of the Pacific Rim. In 1993 at an APEC meeting in Seattle, agreement was reached on a Declaration on APEC Trade and Investment Framework. This was followed at a meeting in Jakarta in 1994 to a commitment to create a 'free and open trade and investment area' – a type of free-trade area. The creation of this area requires the removal of tariffs and NTBs that affect trade in goods and services and that limit FDI flows. The area is planned to be completed by 2010 for the developed members of APEC and 2020 for the less developed members. A large number of groups and committees have been formed to determine the conditions that are necessary for such an area. However, very few concrete steps have been taken to remove barriers to free movement among the APEC countries. There are also very different attitudes concerning the benefits of free movement and regarding the best way to establish such an area among the members of APEC. Nevertheless, APEC provides many specialist forums that facilitate the sharing of information and the pursuit of solutions for trading problems.

Members of APEC – Australia, Brunei Darussalam, Canada, Chile, China, Hong Kong, Indonesia, Japan, South Korea, Malaysia, New Zealand, Papua New Guinea, Philippines, Singapore, Taiwan, Thailand and the USA.

Information on the current activities of these bodies can be found on **www.europa.eu.int/comm/enterprise/enterprise_policy/index.htm#external-relations** for information on mutual recognition agreements and **www.europa.eu.int/comm/trade/index_en.htm** for information on political and trade relations.

US and Japanese information on their EU relationships can be found on US State Department (**www.state.gov**) and Jetro (**www.jetro.go.jp**) websites.

The impact of European Monetary Union

The establishment of European Monetary Union (EMU) is likely to have two main effects on relations in the Triad:

1 The introduction of a new currency that may become important for the finance of international transactions.

2 A change in the balance of power and influence in the international monetary system.

The first effect will alter the significance of the dollar as a means of financing international economic activities. This will have important implications for the development of financial and currency markets. The second effect could lead to significant changes to the main characteristics of the international monetary system.

Financing international business activities

International business transactions benefit from the use of a currency that is widely used in world markets. Such currencies perform three functions:

1 A means of invoicing and payments for international business activities.

2 A vehicle currency in the exchange markets.

3 The provision of financial assets to facilitate international capital activities.

The attraction of using a major world currency to finance international business activities follows from the lower transaction costs made possible by using such currencies. Buying and selling currencies to finance business activities involves transaction costs. If a large number of currencies are used, the transaction costs can be large. Furthermore, a measure of risk is involved when different currencies are used because of fluctuations in exchange rates and lack of detailed knowledge on the conditions prevailing in the currencies' home countries.

To fulfil the conditions for reducing transaction costs a currency most have both a wide and a deep market. A wide market means that a large number of different financial instruments exist that are denominated in terms of the currency, for example the currency itself, bonds, equities, derivatives and swap instruments. A deep market has a large number of traders in the primary and secondary markets (primary markets issue financial instruments; secondary markets provide a means whereby these instruments can be traded). In deep markets the competitive environment is likely to be keen, hence the transaction costs of buying and selling financial instruments will be low relative to these costs in thin markets. The markets for dollars and dollar-denominated financial assets are wider and deeper than those for other currencies. Furthermore, the US economy is large, and information on conditions in the US economy and political system is easily available. The size of the US economy means that it is unlikely that dollars (held outside the US) could not ultimately be used to buy American assets, goods and services. In smaller economies the ability to convert the currency into assets, goods and services is limited due to the size of these economies. In these circumstances, holding large amounts of a country's currency poses a risk that holdings cannot be converted easily into tangible assets. Good access to information on the state of the US economy means that there is a low risk of large-scale unexpected changes in the value of the dollar. This gives the dollar advantages over most other currencies in terms of the transaction costs of using the currency to finance international business activities.

The deutschmark (DM) used to be used as a world currency and the yen is still used in this role, but to a much lesser extent than the dollar because the German and Japanese economies are smaller than the US and have less well-developed markets for their currency. The DM tended to be used in European countries and the yen in Asia. However, even in these regions the dollar was the most important world currency.

Much of international trade is invoiced and paid for in dollars, for example all trade in crude oil, most primary commodities and a substantial part of the ordinary trade of countries. The use of the dollar reduces the costs of invoicing and paying in a multitude of currencies, and its significance is shown by the proportion of world exports invoiced in dollars – about 40 per cent in 1999.

The dollar is also used as a vehicle currency in the exchange markets. Instead, therefore, of exchanging Australian dollars for Swedish kroner, Indian rupees and Russian roubles, Australian dollars can be exchanged for US dollars, and the US dollars are then exchanged for the required currencies. The depth of the dollar markets means that there are lower transaction costs by using the US dollar when converting into these minor currencies rather than using direct conversion from Australian dollars.

Dollar-denominated assets are the most important means by which capital is recycled (across frontiers) from savers to borrowers, and dominate capital markets. For example, about 40 per cent of international bonds are valued in dollars, compared with 15 per cent in yen and about 10 per cent in DM (BIS, 1997). Most financial instruments that are traded internationally (e.g. equities, derivatives, swaps) are also denominated in dollars. Governments hold the majority of their foreign currency reserves in dollars. The dollar is, therefore, the most important currency in international capital markets and in government reserves. This leads to a significant demand for dollars held outside the US and benefits to the US economy because of seigniorage effects.

Seigniorage effects arise because holding dollars (in currency form) does not yield a rate of interest. However, to obtain dollars it is necessary to exchange some kind of asset in return for the dollars – normally a financial asset that yields a rate of interest. The dollars that are obtained are a promise by the Federal Reserve Bank of America to pay an equivalent sum as stated on the dollar bill. This equivalent sum is paid in dollars – a dollar bill for $10 can be converted into another dollar bill valued at $10. Hence the Federal Reserve Bank of America obtains interest-yielding assets in return for dollars that are non-interest bearing assets. This means that the Federal Bank receives an interest-free loan when it issues dollars. In periods of high inflation these seigniorage effects can be quite large because the holders of dollars have acquired a non-interest bearing asset in return for an interest-bearing asset and, furthermore, the real value of their dollars is declining because of inflation. The benefits related to seigniorage are assumed to be fairly small (in a period of low inflation) but the large amount of dollars held outside the USA indicates that their accumulation is not insignificant (European Commission, 1990).

Effects of the introduction of the euro

The introduction of the euro led to a shift from the dollar in the invoicing and payment of international trade, as a vehicle currency and in international capital markets. There was also a shift from the dollar in government holdings of foreign reserves.

Most intra-EU trade (except for crude oil and basic commodities) and some of the countries that conduct the bulk of their trade with the EU are moving to the euro for invoicing and payment. This is leading to a slight decline in the demand for dollars.

The introduction of the euro eliminated the use of the dollar as a vehicle currency for third-party exchanges involving members of the monetary union. The euro may also be used as a vehicle currency for those countries that have significant trade with the EU (e.g. the CEECs). In the long run it is possible that the euro would be used as a vehicle currency throughout the world. This is likely to happen if the euro develops deep and wide markets that lead to low transaction costs compared with the dollar. Such developments could only happen over a fairly long period as the euro financial markets will have to develop. However, it is possible that the euro could become a serious competitor to the dollar in this area.

The denomination of government and private bonds in euros created a very large euro bond market. In the period 1999–2002 the issue of euro-denominated bonds was significantly greater than dollar-denominated bonds (Bergsten, 2004). This market could develop low transaction costs relative to the dollar markets and thereby lead to substantial movements from dollar assets to euro assets. Euro equity markets could also develop as serious competitors to the dollar-dominated equity markets. Much will depend on how these euro markets develop. If regulatory systems are light but effective, and if the euro financial markets are stable, competitive and efficient, they could become lower-cost sources of international finance than the dollar markets. However, dollar financial markets have pronounced first-mover advantages and they are well developed in all of the major financial centres of the world. Furthermore, the US has well-developed regulatory frameworks that govern financial reporting requirements and the control of trade in financial assets. The euro market will have to be developed in a system where there are many different regulatory frameworks, and where international trade in financial assets is often governed by US rules. These benefits will make it difficult for the euro to replace the dollar quickly.

Governments shifted some of their foreign reserves from dollars and yen to the euro. Those countries that held DM (and other currencies that disappeared with European Monetary Union) converted them to euro holdings, so the euro became a reserve currency very early in its history. Countries that have significant trade with the EU may also wish to hold a part of their reserves in euros. However, the euro bloc countries had to increase their holdings of dollars and yen because they could not convert their foreign currency reserves into euros because the euro is not a foreign currency for them. These factors led to only a very small shift from the dollar as the major reserve currency in the world. However, if the euro develops as a stronger currency than the dollar, because the ECB consistently delivers a better inflation record than the Federal Reserve Bank of America, the euro could develop into a major reserve currency.

The current dominance of the dollar and the need for euro markets to be firmly established and developed are limiting the shift from the dollar to the euro. The dollar has been in gentle decline as a world currency since the late 1970s as the DM and the yen became more important for international financial transactions. In these circumstances it is likely that the introduction of the euro will not have any significant effect on the use of the dollar in the short term. In the medium to long term the euro may slightly accelerate the decline in the use of the dollar. In this scenario the dollar would remain the dominant world currency for the foreseeable future (European Commission, 1990). The main effect of the introduction of the euro in this case might be to undermine the use of the yen as a world currency, because the EU has a larger economy than Japan, and the financial markets for the euro will be larger and perhaps have lower transaction costs. However, if the euro develops quickly into a stable and strong currency with well-developed financial markets, the international monetary system could experience considerable turbulence as the euro displaces the dollar and perhaps also the yen.

If the introduction of the euro leads to a small and gradual decrease in the use of the dollar it is probable that euro–dollar–yen exchange rates will not be significantly affected by the shift to the euro. Moreover, the loss of seigniorage revenues will be low and should not cause undue problems for the USA. However, a large and rapid shift towards the use of the euro could have significant effects on the dollar exchange rate and on seigniorage revenues. In these circumstances euro–dollar–yen exchange rates could be very volatile, and cooperation between members of the Triad may become difficult to maintain. Given the importance of the Triad for the stability and growth of world trade, such an outcome would be harmful to the well-being of the world economy.

The early indications are that the introduction of the euro has led to a small decline in the role of the dollar as a world currency but that the underdeveloped nature of euro-denominated capital and financial markets, the poor growth of eurozone economies and inertia have meant that the dollar continues to be the major world currency. However, this may change if the US economy and the dollar were to encounter a period of economic weakness that coincided with improved performance in economic conditions, and capital and financial markets in the eurozone (Bergsten, 2004).

New international monetary system

It is possible that EMU will stimulate a greater degree of cooperation in international monetary and economic affairs. In particular, monetary union could lead to a tri-polar (USA, Japan and EU) system of cooperation that could be more effective than the current G7 system in terms of creating the conditions that would allow for a more stable international monetary order (Alogoskoufis and Portes, 1990; Boles et al., 2002). Gains of approximately 0.5 to 1.5 per cent of the GDP of the members of the G7 have been estimated to be possible from effective coordination among the countries of G7 (Currie et al., 1989). However, effective coordination may depend upon a hegemonic power controlling the process. This view, based on the importance of the hegemony of the USA in the post-war period, casts doubt on the possibility of a multi-polar system being able to generate stable coordination systems (Keohane, 1983). It is therefore possible that monetary union could further undermine the hegemony of the USA and thereby promote greater instability in international monetary markets. In this scenario, EMU would lead to costs in terms of greater instability in exchange rate markets and problems in finding cooperative solutions to macroeconomic problems within the Triad.

The euro may fluctuate between being a strong and stable currency, or a weak and unstable currency. The euro–dollar–yen exchange rate will reflect the conditions between the USA, Japan and the EU eurozone. These conditions may be different from those that prevail in the current dollar–yen relationship of the member states. This could lead to euro–dollar–yen exchange rates that are significantly different from the rate that prevailed in the dollar–yen exchange rates of member states before EMU. It is possible that some member states could be faced with significant changes to their exchange rate against the dollar–yen. This will have important implications for companies based in countries that have large levels of extra-EU transactions. Moreover, the emergence of a weak dollar relative to the euro has largely unknown implications for the health of the eurozone economy and for the world economy (Gros, 2002).

If the international monetary system becomes unstable as a result of a rapid and large decline in the use of the dollar, there may be significant implications for relationships within the Triad. A large shift out of dollars would lead to changes to euro–dollar–yen exchange rate parities. This would generate changes in nominal and probably real exchange rates, with a consequent effect on the competitiveness of companies. Large-scale changes would also affect seigniorage revenues and the size and importance of financial markets in different parts of the Triad. A series of adjustment problems would arise from such large-scale shifts out of the dollar. Even if the changes are slow and minor it is likely that there will be problems in adjusting to the new environment (Bergsten, 2004).

The loss of hegemonic power by the USA may make it more difficult to achieve macroeconomic cooperation. In a hegemonic system power can be exercised on weaker partners to adjust their behaviour. This process has been identified as important in the early post-war experience in establishing the Bretton Woods exchange rate system and in the early moves to liberalise trade by the GATT (Eichengreen, 1989). The decline of US hegemony has probably contributed to the difficulty of finding solutions to international problems because the USA lacks sufficient power to force settlements to disputes. However, the continuing power of the dollar gave the USA considerable influence in world financial matters. This power has been declining, but, because there was no serious competitor to the dollar, the USA has retained considerable influence on international financial matters. The introduction of the euro may accelerate the decline of the dollar and lead to a new non-hegemonic international monetary system. In these circumstances new and effective institutional frameworks that can help to find solutions to international monetary problems may become necessary to avoid instability in exchange markets and recurrent financial crises.

Prospects for future relations

Relations in trade and business matters within the Triad have been characterised by disputes and conflict. Creation of the SEM and EMU make it important for all parties to improve this situation. The EU has been developing institutional frameworks as a means to finding solutions to these problems. The Community is placing a higher priority on relations with the USA, Japan and the NICs and China than it has in the past. The work of the WTO also holds out the prospect for a more open and liberal trading regime, or at least for the development of institutional systems that can effectively find solutions to trading problems. However, the extension of trade to cover services and FDI flows is likely to increase the number and complexity of disputes. The role of bilateral arrangements between the EU and the major parties of the Triad may play an important part in the development of the world trading system.

All parties in the Triad have much to gain from creating a more liberal trading environment. The EU is the largest trader in the world and, together with the USA and Japan, it exercises enormous influence on the development of world trade. A more restrictive trading environment would be harmful to long-term EU interests. One of the main benefits of creating the SEM was to increase competition in order to induce lower prices and higher outputs (see Chapter 1). In principle, opening the European market to US, Japanese and NIC and Chinese competition should add to these benefits. Some European companies would suffer from increased competition from Triad countries, but this would also be true of increased competition from other member states. For a company operating within the EU it would not matter whether the increased competition came from a Japanese or a German source. The increase in competition would be painful for the company, and beneficial for the consumer. Companies that could not adjust to the new competitive environment would have to exit the market, leaving the more effective companies to operate in that market. This gives rise to structural and regional problems as the system adjusts to the new competitive environment. The EU has already accepted the need for such adjustment by agreeing to the creation of the SEM and has to accept more structural change resulting from EMU. Indeed, these structural changes are deemed beneficial for the economy and citizens of the EU. It is therefore difficult to see why opening up the EU economy to foreign competition, which would have much the same effects, should be deemed harmful to the EU.

If a very pessimistic view is taken of the ability of European companies to compete with the best American, Japanese and NIC companies, it might be beneficial to provide some temporary protection for European companies to allow them time to undertake the necessary adjustment and to ease balance of payments problems. There may also be some strategic reasons to protect high-technology industries from being overwhelmed by US and Japanese companies. Similarly, the transfer of jobs by foreign direct investment to China and India may lead to calls for temporary protection to allow adjustment to the new conditions. The danger with this approach is that 'temporary protection' is often extended to permanent protection and this is not normally conducive to an efficient and dynamic economy. Generally, the EU operates on the basis that competition is beneficial to the long-term interests of all EU citizens, so that to restrict such competition to European sources does not seem to have much of an economic rationale.

The EU has much to gain from adopting an open approach to the rest of the world, and to the USA, Japan and the Asian NICs in particular. In a few politically sensitive and strategically important areas it might be necessary for the EU to adopt a protectionist stance, but generally the EU is likely to adopt a fairly pro-competitive approach. However, as was indicated above, there are a host of unresolved problems between the EU and the USA, Japan and the NICs and China.

EMU brings a new set of problems to relations with the USA and Japan. The euro is likely to develop into a major new world currency and this will have significant implications for the role of the dollar, and to a lesser extent the yen. This makes it more urgent to develop effective institutional arrangements for the world international monetary system. If this does not occur, there could be an increase in instability in the exchange rates of the major currencies of the world. Provided that the euro is developed within the context of a new and effective arrangement with the USA and Japan, the prospects for a mutually beneficial outcome may be good. However, the likely displacement of the dollar in some parts of the international monetary system, and the emergence of a new large financial market based on the euro, may alter the balance of power and influence in the international monetary system. This could have significant implications for the development of good relationships between the USA and the EU, and could have some impact on relationships with Japan.

The prospects for the EU to establish good relations with the USA, Japan and the NICs and China depend to a large extent on the ability of governments to build effective institutional frameworks. However, problems with trade surpluses and large-scale adjustment costs to new trading patterns that emerge within the Triad could undermine the ability of even the must robust of institutional frameworks. Good relationships between the members of the Triad depend to a large extent on stable and healthy growth which increases income levels that are able to compensate for the adjustment costs that accompany growing trade and investment flows within the Triad. Institutional frameworks that can cope with pressures arising from macro-economic policy inconsistencies and monetary/exchange rate instability will be important to good relationships among the members of the Triad. The establishment of EMU may alter the balance of power in the Triad in these matters. Furthermore, the possibility of a substantial shift from the dollar to the euro in international financial markets may lead to instability in exchange markets that will require strong institutional frameworks to help to achieve cooperation among the members of the Triad. If such institutional frameworks are not developed, significant problems with macroeconomic policy inconsistencies may arise that could undermine the tendency for the Triad to open up their markets progressively and to develop trading and business links.

References

Alogoskoufis G and Portes R (1990) 'International costs and benefits from EMU', *European Economy*, The Economics of EMU, special issue, Office for Official Publications of the European Communities, Luxembourg.

Bergsten, F (2004) 'The Euro versus the Dollar: Will there be a Struggle for Dominance?' Lecture by Fred Bergsten, **www.iie.com**.

BIS (1997) *Annual Report*, Bank for International Settlements, Basle.

Boles K, Healey N and McDonald F (2002) 'The Euro: A Future International Currency?', in *European Integration in the 21st Century*, M Farrell, S Fella and M Newman (eds), Sage, London.

Bourgeois J (1995) *The Uruguay Round Results*, European Interuniversity Press, Brussels.

Currie D, Holtham G and Hughes-Hallett A (1989) 'The Theory and Practice of International Policy co-ordination: Does Co-ordination Pay?', in R C Bryant and D A Currie (eds), *Macroeconomic Policies in an Interdependent World*, IMF and Brookings Institution, Press, Washington DC.

Eichengreen B (1989) 'Hegemonic Stability Theories of the International Monetary System', in R Cooper, B Eichengreen, C Randall Henning, G Holtunan and R D Putuam (eds), *Can Nations Agree?: Issues in International Economic Cooperation*, Committee to Protect Journalists, New York.

European Commission (1990) 'One Market, One Money', *European Economy*, No. 44, Office for Official Publications of the European Communities, Luxembourg.

European Commission (1996) *Investing in Asia's Dynamism*, Office for Official Publications of the European Communities, Luxembourg.

European Commission (1997) *US Extraterritorial Legislation*, Facts Brief from DGI, Brussels.

Featherstone K and Ginsberg R (1996) *The United States and the European Union in the 1990s*, Macmillan, London.

Financial Times (1998) Special Issues on Asia in Crisis, 12 to 16 January.

Funabashi Y (1995) *Asia Pacific Fusion*, Institute of International Economics, Washington DC.

Gros D (2002) 'The Dollar and the European Economy', in F Bergsten and J Williamson (eds) *Dollar Overvaluation and the World Economy: Special Report 16*, Institute for International Economics, Washington DC (available on **www.iie.com**).

Guerrier P and Padoan P C (1988) *The Political Economy of International Co-operation*, Croom Helm, London.

Ishikawa K (1990) *Japan and the Challenge of Europe 1992*, RIIA/Pinter, London.

Keohane R (1983) *After Hegemony*, Princeton University Press, Princeton.

Krugman P and Obstfeld M (2003) *International Economics, Theory and Policy*, HarperCollins, New York.

Nicholson M (1989) *Formal Theories in International Relations*, Cambridge University Press, Cambridge.

Ohmae K (1985) *Triad Power*, The Free Press, New York.

Rugman A (1999) *The End of Globalization*, Random House, London.

Vogel D (1997) *Barriers or Benefits?: Regulation in Transatlantic Trade*, Brookings Institution Press, Washington DC.

Index